INTRODUCTION TO MASS COMMUNICATIONS

Seventh Edition

Warren K. Agee
University of Georgia

Phillip H. Ault
South Bend Tribune

Edwin Emery
University of Minnesota

1817

HARPER & ROW, PUBLISHERS, New York
Cambridge, Philadelphia, San Francisco, London, Mexico City, São Paulo, Sydney

Sponsoring Editor: Phillip Leininger
Supervisor of Editing: Karla Billups Philip
Designer: T. R. Funderburk
Production Manager: Marion A. Palen
Photo Researcher: Mira Schachne
Compositor: Lexigraphics

Cover montage: Gerald McConnell

INTRODUCTION TO MASS COMMUNICATIONS, Seventh Edition

Library of Congress Cataloging in Publication Data

Agee, Warren Kendall.
Introduction to mass communications.

Bibliography: p.
Includes index.
1. Mass media. I. Ault, Phillip H., 1914–
II. Emery, Edwin. III. Title.
P90.A35 1982 302.2'3 81-6791
ISBN 0-06-040175-3 AACR2

CONTENTS

FOREWORD

With this seventh edition of *Introduction to Mass Communications* the authors enter their third decade of writing about the world of the mass media in the United States for readers here and abroad. The first edition in 1960 helped shape the introductory mass communications course in scores of colleges and universities. Throughout successive editions, our purpose has held true: to give readers a full description of the mass communications industries, to introduce them to all the areas of professional work in journalism and mass communications, and to demonstrate the importance of the communicator in modern society. For those who are considering careers in mass communications, this book offers detailed analyses of the communications agencies that seek their talents.

International communications have grown increasingly more important among nations now interacting so strongly upon each other; hence a new chapter detailing the characteristics and problems of this exciting field of development and confrontation has been prepared for this edition.

Also added are a new chapter exploring the effects of communication upon our thinking, attitudes, and behavior, replacing materials now dealt with elsewhere in the book; a chapter on recording, expanded from a previous chapter combining radio and recording; and a chapter on legal decisions affecting the media that have drawn substantial public, legal, and media debate during the past decade. Discussion of media ethics and social responsibilities has been greatly enlarged. The advertising, television, and book publishing chapters have been expanded considerably, and all chapters have been updated. In a major reorganizational move, discussions of first the print media and then the electronic and film media have been gathered in their single places, respectively; and, as a logical culmination, an account of the criticisms and challenges facing the media concludes the book.

In Part One, "The Role of Mass Communications," the opening chapter briefly and simply describes the communication process and outlines the scope of the mass media. Chapter 2 shows how researchers are trying to provide a better picture of the place and influence of the mass media in the lives of all citizens.

Part Two, "The Print Media," examines newspapers, press associations and syndicates, magazines, and book publishing in both historical and contemporary aspects. The opening chapter describes the basic theories of the press developed during the past five centuries and reviews the unending battle to win and preserve the rights to print, to criticize, and to report the news. The next chapter offers a comprehensive synthesis of the history of the print media in terms of journalistic trends and the contributions of the men and women who helped to shape the American print media. Included are sections dealing with the New Journalism and the black press. The evolving worlds of newspapers, press associations, magazines, and book publishing are then explored in turn, with special emphasis on changing technological, management, and marketing functions.

Part Three, "The Electronic and Film Media," provides a similar historical and contemporary examination of radio, recording, television, photographic communication, and the film. The opening chapter traces in detail the relatively brief histories of radio, television, and film. The multifaceted world of television, including cable, satellite transmission, videocassettes and videodiscs, and public television, are thoroughly explored in one chapter.

Part Four, "The Persuasive Professions," describes advertising and public relations from historical and contemporary perspectives. The expanded advertising chapter contains a new section on regulation as well as a review of the criticisms of advertising previously included in the chapter dealing with social issues. J. Carroll Bateman, an internationally known public relations practitioner, has revised the chapter on public relations, which he wrote for the fifth edition. In 1979 Bateman was elected president of the International Public Relations Association. He retired from his longtime position with the Insurance Information Institute, New York, in 1980, and began teaching at the University of Tennessee College of Communications.

Part Five, "Research and Education," provides updated accounts of developments in those two important fields. The research chapter is a natural followup to Chapter 2.

Leading off Part Six, "Criticisms and Challenges," is a chapter describing the credibility duel between the media and government, and the media and the public, that reached its zenith during Richard Nixon's second term as president. The civil riots and the political demonstrations, which set the stage for this dramatic confrontation, are discussed, as well as the Pentagon Papers case and other developments. The story of Watergate and the media is related in detail.

First Amendment confrontations and other legal issues affecting the media, which crested during the 1970s, are discussed under section headings of the right to print, to criticize, and to report, the same method of examining this subject matter as in Chapter 3. Major cases involving confidentiality of reporter sources, police raids on newsrooms, law enforcement access to telephone records of news organizations, and closed pretrial hearings and courtroom trials are reviewed. Among other issues discussed are freedom of information, privacy, libel and slander, open meetings and open records legislation, cameras in the courtroom, free press and fair trial, and citizens' efforts to gain access to the media.

A discussion of how the moral law affects media decisions opens the chapter, "The Media's Social Responsibilities." The section on violence has been expanded to include an examination of terrorism in relation to the media. The equally controversial subjects of obscenity, sex, and good taste in the media are discussed at length. The efforts of minorities and women to gain equal employment opportunities and rewards also are examined. A new section dealing with codes of ethics opens a section that describes the numerous ways in which the media, affiliated organizations, and foundations are seeking to improve professional and industry performance.

Chapter 22, "Who Owns the Media?," handles media economics and the still-growing phenomena of newspaper group and cross-media ownerships. The limits on broadcast ownership and efforts of minorities to gain access to and ownership of broadcast properties are reviewed.

Appropriately closing this examination of criticisms and challenges confronting the media is a new chapter, "International Media and Organization Roles." The roles that the mass media and the major organizations concerned with mass communications are playing in world society, and some of the vexing problems involved, are discussed in this chapter. These topics include the beginnings of international mass communication, national media systems, foreign correspondents, print and electronic development including the rapid growth of telecommunications and other technology, international and national government and private sector organizations, advertising, public relations, research, education, and the demands of Third World countries for a New World Order of Communications.

A selected, annotated bibliography is offered to readers who wish to explore further some of the many facets of mass communications.

A revised *Instructor's Manual* containing study questions and projects, lesson plans, and examination questions is available. The manual incorporates a number of successful approaches to the study provided by instructors who have taught the introductory course during the last two decades and whose adoption of the book has made it the most widely used textbook in its field.

For the first time, a new book of more than 100 readings selected by the authors, *Perspectives on Mass Communications*, is available from the publishers of this book. Unlike other introductory readers in the field, *Perspectives* contains not only articles analyzing and criticizing the media and the professions and industries, but also articles illuminating the techniques and strategies of professional work (such as "how-to-do-it" accounts) and biographical sketches and photographs of major personages. The book is designed to shed more light on the issues, functions, and people presented in condensed form in *Introduction to Mass Communications*.

Acknowledgments

The seventh edition of *Introduction to Mass Communications* represents a pooling of the professional media experience and scholarly interest of its authors, who wish to thank the more than 100 professors whose suggestions and criticisms, elicited by questionnaire, have helped shape these seven editions.

The authors also wish to thank especially a number of other persons for their aid and interest in the project. They include J. Carroll Bateman, who wrote the chapter on public relations; R. Smith Schuneman of the University of Minnesota, who wrote the photographic communication chapter in an earlier edition; Barbara McKenzie of the University of Georgia, who wrote the film chapter in a previous edition; and Jack Haskins of the University of Tennessee, who wrote the research chapter in the first edition.

Leslie G. Moeller of the State University of Iowa reviewed the manuscript for the first edition and made many valuable suggestions and criticisms; Joseph A. Del Porto of Bowling Green State University read galley proofs and made helpful comments. John T. McNelly of the University of Wisconsin and Hugh E. Curtis of Drake University supplied criticisms in the preparation of the second edition.

Among professionals in the mass media with whom the authors have consulted (including their titles at the time) were James A. Byron, general manager and news director, WBAP and KXAS-TV, Fort Worth; Jack Douglas, general manager of WSBT and WSBT-TV, South Bend, Indiana; Andrew Stewart, president, Denhard & Stewart, Inc., advertising agency, New York; David F. Barbour, copy chief, Batten, Barton, Durstine & Osborn, Inc., Pittsburgh office; Chandler Grannis, editor-at-large, *Publishers' Weekly*; Earl J. Johnson, vice president, United Press International; William C. Payette, president, United Feature Syndicate, Inc., New York;

K. P. Wood, vice president, American Telephone & Telegraph Company; William Oman, vice president, Dodd, Mead & Company, Inc.; and Phillip Leininger, editor, Harper & Row, Inc.

Professors of journalism and mass communications who proved helpful in contributing to or reviewing chapters of the book during the past two decades included Milton Gross, University of Missouri; Max Wales and Warren C. Price, University of Oregon; R. C. Norris, Texas Christian University; Baskett Mosse, Northwestern University; William A. Mindak, Tulane University; Sam Kuczun, University of Colorado; Harold W. Wilson, Everette E. Dennis, and James W. Brown, University of Minnesota; John R. Wilhelm, Ohio University; Michael C. Emery, California State University, Northridge; Emma Auer, Florida State University; Emery L. Sasser, University of South Florida; Frank Pierce, University of Florida; Mel Adams and Lee F. Young, University of Kansas; James E. Dykes, Troy State University; John Merrill, Louisiana State University; Leo Jeffres, Cleveland State University; and James L. Aldridge, William S. Baxter, Beverly Bethune, Scott M. Cutlip, A. Edward Foote, Al Hester, Worth McDougald, Ronald Lane, Frazier Moore, Charles Martin, J. Thomas Russell, and Leila Wenthe, University of Georgia.

The authors express a special note of thanks to their wives, Edda Agee, Linken Ault, and Mary Emery, who have considerately shared much of their husbands' time with this enterprise throughout the past 22 years.

The authors wish to thank all these persons, as well as others who have expressed their interest in the book since it first helped establish the introductory mass communications course in American colleges and universities more than 20 years ago. Thanks also are extended to the United States International Communication Agency (formerly USIA), which has placed successive editions of the book in its reading libraries throughout the world and for which translations have been published in Korean, French, Spanish, and Portuguese, joining the editions published in India, Taiwan, and the Philippines. We hope that the many changes incorporated in this seventh edition will meet with the approval of all who read it.

Warren K. Agee
Phillip H. Ault
Edwin Emery

Part One

THE ROLE OF MASS COMMUNICATIONS

Chapter 1

THE MASS COMMUNICATION PROCESS

THE IMPACT OF MASS COMMUNICATIONS

Although few of us fully realize the extent of our involvement, citizens of today's world are engulfed in an outpouring of mass communications. Never before has such a torrent of spoken and written information, persuasion, thought stimulation, and entertainment been directed at the mind and emotions—and the abundance will multiply. Spectacular developments in the physical methods of communication speed the process, such as the use of satellites 22,300 miles in space to distribute words, pictures, and sounds around the earth. Intensified psychological perceptions and demographic statistics developed through recent research help to shape the material being addressed to our eyes and ears, and often to focus it upon closely defined targets.

The impact of mass communications upon our decisions and our style of life is enormous. Because of this, a heavy burden rests upon those who work in the mass media to use the power they have intelligently and responsibly. Their messages may stir the intellect and arouse the emotions of those to whom they are addressed; the forces that thoughtless words or destructive motives may unleash have the potential for causing grave harm.

Those who receive the products of the media will be more socially aware citizens if they understand how the media function and, armed with that knowledge, exercise selectivity in judging the mass of material thrust upon them. Indeed, even those who work professionally in one communications medium are consumers of the other media. Witness the newspaper reporter who listens to the car radio on the way home after work and watches a movie on television in the evening. It is the purpose of this book to explain the theory, the operation, the historical background, and the philosophical framework of mass communications both for those who will be professional practitioners in the field and for those who will be consumers of their work.

People who choose careers in the media should pursue them with ardor balanced by judgment; a desire for truth, tempered by compassion; and a realization that the words they write or speak, when cast widespread by the media, may affect personal lives, the fates of institutions, and even governments, far more than they realize. This responsibility is stimulating and challenging. Work in the media is at times exciting, frequently fun, and almost always satisfying for the person who undertakes it well prepared, with flexibility and ingenuity to handle the unexpected.

WHAT COMMUNICATION MEANS

The need to communicate with fellow human beings is as fundamental as the physical requirements of food and shelter. This urge for communication is a primal one and, in our contemporary civilization, a necessity for survival.

Simply defined, *communication* is the act of transmitting information, ideas, and attitudes from one person to another.

Upon this foundation society has built intricate, many-faceted machinery for delivering its messages. The unfolding achievements of science are making this communication machinery more and more fantastic in its ability to conquer the physical barriers of our world. Our minds and our electronic devices are reaching into areas not considered even remotely possible by our grandparents.

Astronauts hurtling through space send back radio and color television reports of what they experience. Cameras mounted on space vehicles give us closeup televised photographs of the moon and the planets Mars and Saturn, and of men walking on the moon itself. Television programs are transmitted from one side of the world to another by bouncing their signals off a satellite in orbit. Each year brings additional wonders in the craft of communicating our messages.

Yet these costly structures lose meaning unless their users have something significant to say. The study of communication thus involves two aspects—a broad comprehension of the mechanical means and the underlying theories of communication and, more importantly, an understanding of how we use these tools in our daily round of informing, influencing, inspiring, convincing, frightening, and entertaining one another.

Each of us communicates with another person by directing a message to one or more of the person's senses—sight, sound, touch, taste, or smell. This is known as *interpersonal communication,* in contrast with *intrapersonal communication,* in which one "talks to oneself." Both forms are subjects of much research study. When we smile, we communicate a desire for friendliness; the tone in which we say "good morning" can indicate feelings all the way from surliness to warm pleasure; and the words we choose in speaking or writing convey a message we want to "put across" to the other person. The more effectively we select and deliver these words, the better our communication.

Contemporary society is far too complex to function only through direct communication between one individual and another. Our important messages, to be effective, must reach many people at one time. A consumer who is angry at high meat prices may talk to a half-dozen neighbors about organizing a boycott, but if the editor of the local newspaper publishes a letter from the consumer, the idea is communicated to hundreds of others in a fraction of the time it would take to visit them individually. The politician running for the Senate spends much time visiting factories and meetings, shaking hands with the citizens in the hope of winning their votes. The candidate knows, however, that only a small percentage of the voters can be reached this way, so time is bought on television and radio to deliver the message to thousands of voters simultaneously. This is *mass communication*—the process of delivering information, ideas, and attitudes to a sizable and diversified audience through use of media developed for that purpose.

The art of mass communication is much more difficult than that of face-to-face discussion. The communicator who is addressing thousands of different personalities at the same time cannot adjust an appeal to meet their individual reactions. An approach that convinces one part of the audience may alienate another part. The successful mass communicator is one who finds the right method of expression to establish empathy with the largest possible number of individuals in the audience. In some instances, such as network television shows, the audience for a message numbers in the millions. In the case of weekly newspapers, it may be only a few thousand. The need to catch and hold the individual's attention remains the same.

The politician reaches many more individuals with a single television speech than through handshaking tours, but that person's use of mass communication may be a failure if the same feeling of sincerity and ability that is conveyed through a handshake and smile cannot be projected over the air.

Thus, the mass communicator's task breaks down into two parts, knowing *what* to communicate and *how* to deliver the message to make the greatest possible impact on an audience. A message of poor content, poorly told to millions of people, may have less total effective impact than a well-presented message placed before a small audience.

Every day each of us receives thousands of impressions. Many of these pass unnoticed or are quickly forgotten. The effectiveness of the impression is influenced in part by our individual circumstances. A news story from Washington about plans by Congress to increase unemployment benefits raises hopes in the mind of the person who fears being laid off a job; the same dispatch may disturb the struggling entrepreneur who sees in it the possibility of higher taxes. The communicator's message has differing effects upon these two members of the audience; it may have none at all upon another consumer who is somehow distracted while scanning the newspaper or listening to a newscast.

Obviously, the mass communicator cannot know the mental outlook and physical circumstances of everyone to whom the message goes. There are many principles and techniques that can be used, however, to ensure that the message has an effective impact upon the greatest possible number of individuals in the largest possible audience. Some of these are learned by mastering the basic techniques of journalistic communication (writing, editing, newscasting, graphic presentation); others are learned by studying the mass communication process and by examining the character of the mass media.

THE COMMUNICATION PROCESS

Researchers call our attention to four aspects of the communication process: the *communicator,* the *message,* the *channel,* and the *audience.* (In research language, the communicator is also known as the *encoder;* the message—whether words, pictures, or signs—becomes *symbols;* the channel, in the case of mass communications, is one of the mass *media;* the person in the audience is known as the *decoder.*) A properly trained communicator understands the social importance of his or her role and also knows what to transmit as the message. The communicator understands the characteristics of the channels (media) to be used and studies the varying interest and understanding levels of groups of people who make up the total audience. The message is molded to the requirements of each channel used and to the capabilities and interests of the audiences being sought.

The communicator also knows about the limitations and problems communications researchers have studied. One of these is *channel noise,* a term used to describe anything that interferes with the fidelity of the physical transmission of the message (such as static on radio or type too small to be read easily); but broadly speaking, channel noise may be thought of as including all distractions between source and audience (Figure 1.1). The professional communicator helps overcome its effects by attention-getting devices and by careful use of the principle of *redundancy* (repetition of the main idea of the message to ensure that it gets through, even if part of the message is lost).

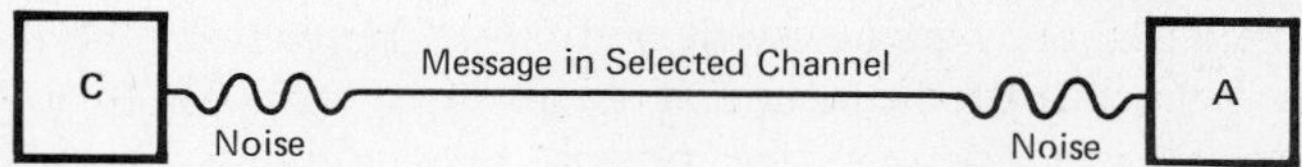

Figure 1.1 The communication process: Communicator (C) places a message in selected channel to reach audience (A) but is subject to "noise" interferences.

A second kind of interference, called *semantic noise,* occurs when a message is misunderstood even though it is received exactly as it was transmitted (Figure 1.2). The communicator, for example, might use words or names that are unfamiliar to an audience member (material outside that person's *frame of reference*). Or the words used may have one meaning for the communicator and another for the listener or reader (the common or dictionary meaning is called *denotative,* the emotional or evaluative meaning is called *connotative*—a word like "socialist" has widely differing connotations). Semantic noise can be reduced if the communicator will take pains to define terms and adjust vocabulary to the interests and needs of the audience. Sometimes, difficult or strange words are understood because the reader grasps the *context* in which they appear, but it is also possible for a poorly defined word to be misunderstood this way. And if the material presented is too complex, the reader either will be forced to *regress* and restudy the message or, more likely, will turn to some other more rewarding and pleasant material.

Even if all these obstacles are surmounted, the communicator still has other problems in message reception. The receiver interprets the message in terms of a frame of reference, we have said. Each person has a *stored experience,* consisting in part of individual, ego-related beliefs and values and in part of the beliefs and values of the groups to which he or she belongs (family, job, social, and other groups). A message that challenges these beliefs and values may be rejected, distorted, or misinterpreted. Conversely, one whose beliefs on a given subject are under pressure may go out of the way to seek messages bolstering his or her viewpoint. In cases where beliefs are firmly fixed, the communicator finds it is often more effective to try to redirect existing attitudes slightly than to meet them head on. Another audience problem is called *dissonance*. This occurs when an

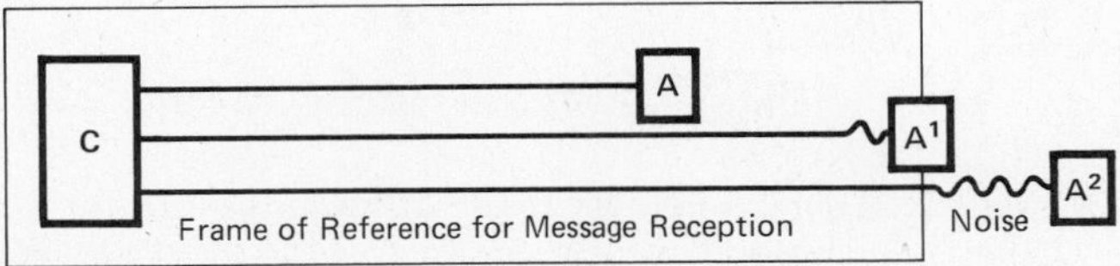

Figure 1.2 Communicator and audience member A have the same frame of reference; A^1 is only partially receptive; A^2 is unable to understand.

action is taken that is inconsistent with what a person knows or has previously believed, or the action is taken after two or more attractive alternatives are considered. The person is uncomfortable until some dissonance-reduction is achieved by seeking out messages that help adjust beliefs to action (a familiar example is the person who, having bought one make of car from among several attractive ones, continues to read advertisements for the car purchased; if makes have been switched, even more reassurance is required).

The communicator is aided by what are called *feedback effects* (Figure 1.3). These are reactions that take place along the communication process and that are transmitted backward: by the communicator (reporter) to the original news source; by another media worker (editor) to the reporter; by members of the audience to the editor, the reporter, or the news source; and by different persons in the audience to each other. Obviously, there is much more discernible feedback in person-to-person communication than in mass media communication, and thus a better opportunity to deliver a convincing message face to face. But the communicator who has knowledge of feedback reactions in mass communication and who solicits them may enhance acceptance of the messages.

Nonverbal communication is an important aspect of the communication process. Popularly known as "silent language" or, in some of its aspects, "body language," nonverbal communication may include such attributes as facial expression, eye movement, posture, dress, cosmetics, voice qualities, laughing, and yawning. For example, a TV newscaster may, consciously or unconsciously, alter the meaning of the spoken message through a lifted eyebrow or a shrug of the shoulders. A weak voice may convey uncertainty or an arms-folded stance defiance. A politician's rolled-up sleeves and tieless shirt may produce votes from laborers.

All this is summed up in Professor Harold D. Lasswell's question: "Who, says what, in which channel, to whom, with what effect?" Chapter 2, on communication effects theories, and Chapter 17, on mass communications

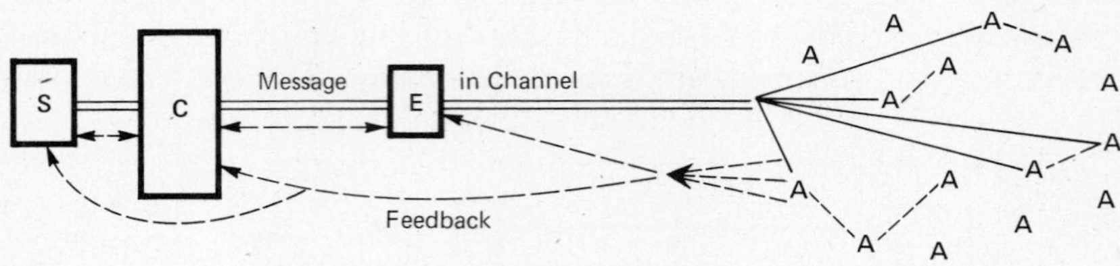

Figure 1.3 Mass communication for a given message at one moment in time is illustrated here: Source (S) has the message reported by communicator (C) in channel controlled by editor (E); some audience members (A) receive the message directly, others indirectly, but some are inattentive; feedback interactions may occur along the communication route.

research, examine the different types of studies carried on by the mass media and by individual scholars to aid in more effective communication. Essential steps for a would-be communicator, however, are to gain an understanding of the role of the communicator in our contemporary society and to examine the mass media through which audiences are reached. To take the communicator through these steps is the purpose of this book.

WHAT ARE THE MASS MEDIA?

A message can be communicated to a mass audience by many means: hardly an American lives through a day without feeling the impact of at least one of the mass media. The oldest media are those of the printed word and picture: the weekly and daily newspapers, magazines, books, pamphlets, direct mail circulars, and billboards. These carry their messages through the sense of sight. Radio is the mass communications medium aimed at the sense of sound, whereas television and motion pictures appeal both to the visual and auditory senses.

The reader turns to a newspaper for news and opinion, entertainment, and the advertising it publishes. In the weekly, the focus is on the reader's own community; in the daily, upon the nation and the world as well. Magazines provide background information, entertainment, opinion, and advertising; books offer a deeper and more detailed examination of subjects, as well as entertainment; pamphlets, direct mail pieces, and billboards bring the views of commercial and civic organizations to the reader. Films may inform and persuade as well as entertain. Television and radio offer entertainment, news and opinion, and advertising messages, and can bring direct coverage of public events to the listener.

Important agencies of communication are adjuncts of the mass media. These are 1) the press associations, which collect and distribute news and pictures to the newspapers, television and radio stations, and news magazines; 2) the syndicates, which offer background news and pictures, commentary, and entertainment features to newspapers, television and radio, and magazines; 3) the advertising agencies, which serve their business clients on the one hand and the mass media on the other; 4) the advertising departments of companies and institutions, which serve in merchandising roles, and the public relations departments, which serve in information roles; 5) the public relations counseling firms and publicity organizations, which offer information in behalf of their clients; and 6) research individuals and groups, who help gauge the impact of the message and guide mass communicators to more effective paths.

Who are the communicators who work for and with these mass media? The list is extensive. They include reporters, writers, editors, photographers, cinematographers, announcers, and commentators for newpapers, magazines, television and radio, press associations, and syndicates; book and publication editors and creative personnel in the graphic arts industry; advertising personnel of all types; public relations practitioners and information writers; business management personnel for the mass media; radio-television script and continuity writers; film producers and writers; trade and business publication writers and editors; industrial publication editors; technical writers in such fields as science, agriculture, and home economics; specialists in mass communications research; and teachers of journalism and mass communications. Actors in television and motion pictures also are communicators in a special sense, for they add emotional impact to the written script.

THE COMMUNICATOR'S TASK

Recording history as it happens is an exciting assignment. In this day of almost instantaneous mass communications, members of the mass media are doing even more than recording history; they are helping to shape it. The responsibility is stimulating. Mass communications work demands from its practitioners broad knowledge, sound judgment, quick decisions, and the realization that the words they write or speak may influence the lives of many millions of people.

This sense of influence and responsibility extends from those dealing with breaking news to many others in mass communications work. Perhaps all this sounds overwhelming, and in some ways it is. But an intelligent, college-educated person who approaches the job with a proper sense of ethical responsibility and adequate knowledge of the basic techniques will find the work satisfying, mentally and financially, and at times truly exciting.

There is the excitement of creative accomplishment: writing a series of stories exploring the successes and failures of a ghetto youth club project; helping to entertain a nation with a television program; writing a story for *Esquire* interpreting the personality of a noted musician; helping to solve a marketing problem for a great industry through an advertising campaign; coming up with the magic of a slogan like "We try harder"; or shooting a photo series that catches the hopes and feelings of the participants in an Upward Bound program.

There is the additional sense of participation felt by those handling the flow of the day's news. Reporting and commenting take many forms, such as a television reporter's on-the-scene description of a forest fire as massive flames illuminate the sky; a newspaper writer's word-for-word account as the jury delivers the verdict in a murder trial; a radio reporter's summary of the world's main news developments packed tightly into a five-minute period; or an editorial writer's analysis of the forces shaping a foreign policy decision by the president of the United States. Or the form may be a conference by the little-publicized persons behind the news, the editors. They must decide which stories in the day's flow of events deserve the most prominent place in print or on the air. Or it may be a political news writer patiently checking the advance text of a prominent political leader's speech against its actual delivery to see whether an unscheduled piece of major news has been inserted. That is exactly the way President Lyndon Johnson unexpectedly informed the world that he would not run for reelection in 1968 at the height of the Vietnam conflict.

Mass communications work is not always exciting. To pretend that it is would be misleading and unrealistic. As in any business, there are hours of routine, often repetitious work. A solid, disciplined routine and a well-defined set of operating principles underlie everything. What makes news work so intriguing, however, is that exciting events may break loose at the most unexpected moment. Then, in an instant, the reporter's or editor's training, experience, and judgment are called into action. The instantaneous quality of radio and television has added even greater challenges for all those seeking to provide a fair and objective presentation of news.

Throughout the mass media, the challenge of social responsibility is felt by those at work. Frequently their judgment is tested under pressure in matters of taste, social restraint, and fairness, with few absolute rules to guide them. The jobs they perform make possible the general diffusion of knowledge about life in today's world and, further, influence many aspects of our social, political, and economic patterns. By the way they select and present information, they help in sometimes small, sometimes unintentional, ways to shape our society.

Our mass media illuminate the social fabric of the nation. They are essential to the continued development of the economic fabric in a modern industrial state. And they continue to fulfill their historic role in protecting and improving the political fabric of a democracy. Among the many opportunities enjoyed by the communicator, none is more important than the opportunity to help shape public opinion.

Chapter 2

COMMUNICATION EFFECTS: THEORIES AND RESEARCH TRENDS

THE CONVENTIONAL WISDOM

Every writer on the topic of communication effects must recall the panic that seized part of the eastern seaboard on October 30, 1938. That night, Orson Welles and the CBS radio theater group broadcast a terrifying and realistic report of an invasion from Mars taking place near Princeton, New Jersey. Conventional radio news bulletin devices convinced thousands of citizens that giant mechanical monsters were roaming the countryside, and people fled without waiting to hear that the report was only an adaptation of H. G. Wells' novel, *War of the Worlds*.

Wilbur Schramm, a distinguished communication research scholar, cites the Orson Welles hoax as an obvious communication effect, saying that many people were emotionally aroused, and that some of them abruptly changed their behavior in a way that could never have been predicted before the broadcast. Indeed, the incident ranks high among classic examples of a mass medium's producing effects on its audience.

How effective are the mass media in shaping thought (the cognitive aspect of mass communication)? In changing attitudes (the affective aspect of mass communication)? Or in moving people to action (the behavioral aspect of mass communication)? Scholars have been asking these questions for decades. Historians and journalists have found many convincing examples of media effects involving the cognitive aspects of mass communication: attention, awareness, information. These indicate that people do learn from mass communication, and sometimes then change their attitudes and opinions.

Social scientists, however, in their research of the 1940s and 1950s, chose to emphasize the affective and behavioral aspects of mass communication. Focusing their attention on voting behavior and using precise measurement and analysis techniques, they found only minimal direct effects of mass communication on attitudes and behavior. When they later concentrated on cognitive aspects they found new paths, which will be detailed in this chapter. By 1980 communication researchers generally agreed that the mass media have effects and are used by many people in ways important to them.

Other examples of the conventional wisdom are:

• Both participants in the 1960 debate between presidential candidates John F. Kennedy and Richard M. Nixon agreed with the experts that the positive image of Kennedy, perceived by a majority of the great television audience, gave him the necessary edge for election. Jimmy Carter enjoyed a positive reaction during his 1976 debate with Gerald Ford, which buttressed his campaign. But in 1980, Carter was perceived negatively in contrast to Ronald Reagan and pollsters said his popularity slumped immediately after the debate. These three events illustrate the effect of mass media upon voting behavior.

• Historians of the American Revolution, reviewing their literature during the bicentennial year, generally agreed that the colonial weekly newspapers and pamphlets such as Tom Paine's *Common Sense* played a crucial role in first informing colonists about events and ideas and then persuading them to support the Declaration of Independence. This is an example of political communication, since the radicals espousing independence had a carefully planned propaganda effort.

• Press historians point out that public consciousness of Lincoln's "Gettysburg Address" or William Jennings Bryan's "Cross of Gold" oration could have been developed only by the print media during the nineteenth century. Many Americans learned Lincoln's lines by heart. Bryan was nominated for the presidency three times.

• One can argue that the mass media are capable of creating a presidential candidate if the public fails to find other candidates attractive. In 1940, Americans learned about Wendell Willkie, a relatively unknown businessman, through the print media and radio. A "We Want Willkie" chant swept other hopefuls aside in the Republican nominating convention. In 1976, "Jimmy Who?" caught the public fancy and catapulted Carter to the lead in the Democratic party primaries, with voters in some states becoming aware of him solely through television and radio newscasts, newspapers, and news magazines.

• A classic story of mass media effects is, of course, that of Watergate. In this instance, the effects of mass media brought about the forced resignation of a president in the face of changing opinions of him among members of the Congress and the general public. The media effort in the Watergate story was primarily an informational one. When convincing evidence accumulated, it had a persuasive effect that brought about changed attitudes and behavior. That, in brief, is what journalism has been all about over the centuries.

EARLY THEORIES OF POWERFUL EFFECTS

Walter Lippmann spent his life as an editor of magazines and newspapers, an author, and a highly influential political columnist. He also was a member of the academic and intellectual communities centered at Harvard University, and in the liberal political and media clusters of New York and Washington. With this background, he wrote a brief book in 1921, *Public Opinion*, which served as a challenge to the development of scholarly research and writing in the fields of public opinion and mass communications.

The first chapter of *Public Opinion*, "The World Outside and the Pictures in Our Heads," was rich in provocative thought. "The world we have to deal with politically," he said, "is out of reach, out of sight, out of mind. It has to be explored, reported, and imagined." Each person gradually makes for "himself a trustworthy picture inside his head of the world beyond his reach." The pictures in the minds of citizens collectively constitute public opinion, Lippmann continued. Fragmented, distorted, and subject to preconceptions and prejudices, the pictures inside people's minds often mislead them in their dealings with the outside world. Part of Lippmann's analysis is how the pictures in our heads affect the "trickle of messages from the outside," which includes mass communications.

Harold D. Lasswell, a professor of law at Yale University, contributed much to the study of propaganda during World War II. From his writings came the concepts popularly called the "silver bullet" and "hypodermic model" theories of mass communications effects. These assume that communication is something someone does to someone else; the communicator, not the consumer or receiver, is the causative person. This was a natural avenue for Lasswell to take, steeped as the academic world was in wartime studies of the influence of propaganda and its use in political and social spheres. His query, "Who, says what, in which channel, to whom, with what effect?," structured the thinking and research of communication scholars and students for two decades. The fields of research became, in the order of the phrases in the question, communicator or systems analysis, content analysis, media analysis, audience analysis, and effect analysis. Though Lasswell was a valuable guide in many of these fields, he misdirected effect research by focusing so heavily on the affective role of mass communications.

Lasswell also described the function of communication as "1) the surveillance of the environment; 2) the correlation of the parts of society in responding to the environment; 3) the transmission of the social heritage from one generation to the next." In simpler terms, these are 1) collecting and distributing information and news; 2) interpreting that information and writing editorials suggesting reaction to it; 3) educational activity. Entertainment and marketplace roles are also added to the functions of mass communications.

SCIENTIFIC STUDIES: MINIMAL EFFECTS

With the image of powerful mass media created by the "hypodermic model" it was natural for large-scale research projects to be launched. One was the Yale Communication Research Program, directed by psychologist Carl I. Hovland for the U.S. Army in wartime and later for Yale University. Another was an intensive field study of voting behavior in Erie County, Ohio, conducted by sociologist Paul Lazarsfeld and his colleagues at Columbia University.

The Yale University studies were at first designed to analyze differences in communication techniques and the effectiveness of various types of messages and communicators. Using carefully designed experiments in laboratories, schools, and military units, the researchers examined one variable after another in different combinations and situations, with attitude change as the dependent variable. Out of these years of experiment came what Wilbur Schramm calls a wealth of information about variables in communication and descriptions of then-new research designs. Hovland obtained greater effects in his laboratory studies than Lazarsfeld and others found in field studies, a result that Hovland defended as scientifically valid. Even so, there was little resemblance between the results of Hovland's experiments and the concept of the "hypodermic model."

Lazarsfeld, Bernard Berelson, and others in the Columbia University voting study found no evidence of the "hypodermic needle" in their 1940 study of Erie County voting behavior. Lazarsfeld reported in *The People's Choice* that the media have relatively few direct effects on voting during an election campaign. Rather, the Columbia researchers said, the media serve to reinforce preconceived beliefs. Whatever influence the media do have on voting change they attributed to the "two-step flow." Opinion leaders obtain information and opinions from the media and pass along their ideas to other members of their voting groups. Magazines could thus become important sources of voter information through the "two-step flow" concept. Later research determined that this model was too simplified. Many researchers concluded that the more personal a medium is, the more likely it is to be persuasive. Face-to-face communication is most effective, followed by television, film, radio, and print.

Lazarsfeld and Robert K. Merton published a paper in 1948, as part of the book, *The Communication of Ideas,* which argued that the primary social effect of the mass media is to maintain the status quo, exercising a status-conferral power. They have a "narcotizing dysfunction" of absorbing their audiences' time without energizing them. According to Lazarsfeld and Merton, the media have the ability to "canalize" behavior, directing persons who already accept one idea or product to accept a similar one.

In 1960, Joseph T. Klapper, a disciple of Lazarsfeld and a professor at Columbia University, summed up the "minimal effects" research in his book, *The Effects of Mass Communication*. "Mass communication *ordinarily* does not serve as a necessary and sufficient cause of audience effects," he wrote, "but rather functions among and through a nexus of mediating factors and influences." He qualified that statement, however, with the following remarks: "It must be remembered that though mass communication seems usually to be a *contributory* cause of effects, it is often a major or necessary cause and in some instances a sufficient cause. The fact that its effect is often mediated, or that it often works among other influences, must not blind us to the fact that mass communication possesses qualities which distinguish it from other influences, and that by virtue of these qualities, it is likely to have characteristic effects."

To many observers, the impact, influence, and effect of the mass media on audiences seemed obvious. Granting that the effects of mass communications may have been judged to be too powerful, particularly in the ability to persuade, observers insisted that the generalizations of some social scientists, who said that the media had "nil effects," were equally misleading. Those who believed the mass media could affect audiences noted the conflict in findings by researchers using laboratory methods and those working in the field. They noted that generalizations were being based on a limited number of controlled experiments and studies. The time was ripe for what historians call a revisionist school of thought, to bring the balance of judgment back toward the middle.

CONSISTENCY THEORIES: SELECTIVE PERCEPTION

A series of consistency theories, developed during the 1950s, hypothesized that people want their beliefs and judgments about things to be consistent with one another. Professor Leon Festinger's cognitive dissonance theory is the most well known of these theories. In order to reduce dissonance created by inconsistencies in belief, judgments, and action, people expose themselves to information that is consistent with their ideas and actions, and they shut out other communication.

As Professors Maxwell E. McCombs and Lee B. Becker stated in *Using Mass Communication Theory,* "a key part of each individual's experience that influences his or her perceptions is the set of previously acquired attitudes and opinions. Stereotypes straddle the boundary between cognitions, our mental pictures of the world about us, and affective attitudes, our feelings and evaluations of persons, issues, and situations in the world around us."

In *selective perception,* items in the news that are regarded favorably are more likely to be recalled by a viewer than items that are regarded unfavorably. Further, the viewer will, if possible, shape his or her interpretation of a news event to be congruent with the viewer's existing attitude. In a study of reactions to the surgeon general's warning about the hazards of smoking, Festinger found that the more cigarettes an audience member smoked each day, the less convinced the smoker was that an actual link had been established between smoking and lung cancer.

Two areas similar to selective perception are *selective exposure* and *selective retention*. Some persons habitually listen to news on Channel 4 rather than on Channel 5, or read *Time* rather than *Newsweek*. Some persons consistently avoid materials they know to be distasteful, or that would create dissonance. Researchers find that selective retention plays a role in the effectiveness of efforts to change attitudes through informational campaigns. People remember what they want to remember.

Professor L. John Martin points out that the consistency theories switched the Lasswellian paradigm around. Rather than "Who says what to whom?," the question for researchers now seemed to be, "Who needs to receive the message from whom?" "The emphasis was on the seeking and avoiding of information rather than on the transmission of instruction or urging of opinion change," Martin says. "Furthermore, a distinction began to be made between informational communication and persuasive communication," in discussions of the effects of mass communications.

MEDIA SYSTEMS AND AGENDA-SETTING

Lasswell's concept of a surveillance function of the media, and early studies of what became known as gate-keeping by editors who were charged with selecting or rejecting items to fit a daily newspaper's available space, pointed to new avenues of research. As sociologists Melvin L. DeFleur and Sandra Ball-Rokeach have written, "The ultimate basis of media influence lies in the nature of the three-way relationship between the larger social system, the media's role in that system, and audience relationships to the media." One avenue was *systems analysis,* the other the *agenda-setting* function of the press.

Some researchers have examined mass media as a part of the larger social system. Sociology professors George Donohue, Phillip Tichenor, and Clarice Olien have done extensive research and writing to demonstrate that "mass media represent subsystems which cut across other subsystems and transmit information among and between them." This means that the mass media have the ability to penetrate other aspects of society with their messages. It also means that control of the media subsystems, and of gate-keeping activities within them, is crucial.

Information control has been practiced for centuries with the realization that knowledge is vital to social power. Those who control the flow of communication have the ability to exercise power over other people. Gate-keeping, the three sociologists point out, should be viewed as more than the simple exercise of choice among available news stories. The editor accepting or rejecting a story is part of a subsystem that has input into many decisions regarding information control. These include message selection, shaping, display, timing, withholding, and/or repetition. Thus the study of mass media as social subsystems plays a part in the overall study of mass communications effects, including agenda-setting.

Agenda-setting became a leading area of mass communications research in the 1970s. The basic idea of agenda-setting—the ability of the media to influence the salience of events in the public mind—was a part of Walter Lippmann's description of "the pictures in our heads." In 1963, political scientist Bernard C. Cohen declared in his book, *The Press and Foreign Policy,* that "the press may not be successful much of the time in telling people what to think, but it is stunningly successful in telling its readers what to think *about*." Theodore White wrote in 1972: "The power of the press is a primordial one. It sets the agenda of public discussion . . . . No major act of the American Congress, no foreign adventure, no act of diplomacy, no great social reform can succeed in the United States unless the press prepares the public mind. And when the press seizes a great issue to thrust onto the agenda of talk, it moves action on its own. . . ."

Two professors of mass communication, Maxwell E. McCombs and Donald L. Shaw, offered in 1972 their scientific concept of the agenda-setting function, that media emphasis on an event influences the audience to also view the event as important. This impact of the mass media—the ability to effect cognitive change among individuals, to structure their thinking—is characterized by McCombs and Shaw as perhaps the most important effect of mass communication, "its ability to mentally order and organize our world for us."

McCombs and Shaw made the first empirical attempt at verification of the agenda-setting function of the mass media in a study of voters in the 1968 election. Among undecided voters, there were substantial correlations between the issues emphasized in the news media and what those voters regarded as the key issues of the election. The voter agenda was ascertained independently of what the media were reporting, the results indicating that indeed the press had set the agenda for its audience. Since the mass media provide many of the facts that make up the cognitive world of each individual, it could be possible that the press merely relays information, as a transmission belt. But agenda-setting studies have developed evidence that the press selects certain issues to play up at times when they are not significant in the public mind; they then become part of the accepted agenda. By 1980, the concept of agenda-setting was well established, although its status as a detailed theory remains to be determined.

McLUHAN'S "HOT" AND "COOL" MEDIA

A theory that the medium is the key element in the mass communications process evoked widespread attention and controversy during the 1960s. This was mostly due to the colorful writing and lecturing of its originator, Marshall McLuhan, a professor of English and director of the Center for Culture and Technology at the University of Toronto. His books, *The Gutenberg Galaxy* (1962), *Understanding Media* (1964), and *The Medium Is the Massage* (1967), coupled with extensive lecture and television appearances, projected McLuhan as the prophet of a new age of electronics in which the medium, in his opinion, is more important than the message and conventional values less relevant than "depth involvement."

In his work McLuhan carried forward explorations of various earlier observers. Among them was the late Harold Innis, whose *Empire and Communications* (1950), and *The Bias of Communication* (1951), analyzed the relationship of media to power structures, beginning with those of ancient times.

McLuhan declared that each new medium alters our psychic environment, imposing on us a particular pattern of perceiving and thinking that controls us to an extent we scarcely suspect. For example, the written language, mass-produced by print, was the main cultural transmission belt for many generations. Knowledge and ideas were necessarily processed into the linear, one-step-at-a-time form required by the medium. People were thus pushed into sequential habits of thinking that are quite unlike the complexity and richness and all-at-onceness of face-to-face communication, and without the resonance of the human voice.

Today, however, the electronic media have restored the resonance (radio) and reintroduced the complexity and all-at-onceness (film, television), and have done it on a scale that gives the world potentially a tribal unity. McLuhan viewed modern men and women as in a state of shock, unable to adjust to the rapidly changing state of communication and clinging to linear habits in an all-at-once world. Given to puns and a measure of flippancy, McLuhan insisted not only that "the medium is the *message*" (that is, more important in itself than what is transmitted) but also that "the medium is the *massage*" (that is, it "roughs up and massages" our senses, altering the environment of the preelectronic world).

Two key terms in McLuhanese are "hot" and "cool." The cooler the medium, the more information must be supplied by the audience, and that is why wide-screen movies are "hot" and a fuzzy television picture is "cool." The more information the audience supplies, the more involved it becomes, and television has given its audience a sense of "depth involvement" more far-reaching than any previous medium, McLuhan believed. "When you go to the movies," he states, "you are the camera, but when you watch TV, you are the screen. The image is not projected from you, but charges at you. The movies were an extrovert orgy, but television is a depth experience."

Critics charge that his theories are confusing, illogical, mystical, and lacking in documentation. They deplore his "pop-art intellectualism," his puns, and his seeming call for a return to the jungle, for the abandonment of print-based civilization as we have known it. McLuhan retorted that he was merely an investigator and explorer of ideas trying to persuade us to think about the changes in our environment caused by successive mass media, and that he saw no need to offer logical explanations.

By the 1980s, excitement generated by McLuhan's far-reaching theories had died down, but his ideas were still being reviewed in classrooms and in scholarly circles in many countries. McLuhan died in 1980.

USES AND GRATIFICATIONS RESEARCH

Psychologist Elihu Katz of Israel has led the argument that there should be less attention paid to what the media do to people and more attention on what people do with the media. The *uses and gratifications* concept is associated with Katz's writing and research. But Katz points out that studies of the gratifications that the media provide their audiences with were well represented in the Lazarsfeld–Stanton collections of the 1940s and other early research.

Katz summarizes recent direct empirical investigations of audience uses and gratifications as "being concerned with the social and psychological origins of needs, which generate expectations of the mass media or other sources, which lead to differential patterns of media exposure, resulting in need gratifications and other consequences, perhaps mostly unintended ones."

Uses and gratifications research might have important, practical policy effects in daily mass media operations, Professor Everette Dennis points out in his book, *The Media Society*. Audience gratifications research could be used to change those media policies that do not help to satisfy media-related needs, wants, and expectations of the audience. Dennis points out that research in the area is somewhat fragmentary, and that it "flies in the face of the more humanistic popular culture critics of the media."

Study of communication as a consequence is more rewarding than study of communication as a cause, says Professor Alex S. Edelstein, an international communications scholar. Researchers should study the process of change in time and space, the consequences of that change in uses of communicated messages, and the effects of the change on the personal life of the subject. In research based upon the uses and gratifications concept, Edelstein studied audiences in both the United States and Yugoslavia and concluded that they evaluated sources of information not in terms of the sources' credibility but in terms of content, breadth of perception, and availability. Newspapers ranked ahead in content, television in breadth of perception, and radio in availability. The consumer determines which medium to use, the decision depending on which medium gratifies his or her needs.

THE POWERFUL MEDIA REVISITED

In a research paper published in 1973, German communication researcher Elisabeth Noelle-Neumann reviewed the state of mass communication effects research, found the "minimal effects" literature badly wanting, and called for a "return to the concept of a powerful media." Noelle-Neumann, insisting that "the decisive factors of mass media are not brought to bear in the traditional laboratory experiment designs," was joined in this attack on the minimal effects concept by sociologists DeFleur and Ball-Rokeach. By 1980, support was growing rapidly.

One assault was upon the selective perception theory, which limits the possibility of media effects. Noelle-Neumann said that "real life" is different from laboratory-controlled studies; the media are so ubiquitous that it is difficult for a person to escape a message; repetitive messages have reinforced impact; and, news stories are so much the same that there are few options for selective perception. Noelle-Neumann's longterm studies demonstrated that the effects of mass media increase in proportion to the degree to which selective perception is made difficult. The larger the marketplace for ideas is, the more attitudes can be influenced or molded by the mass media.

In another revisit of the powerful media concept, mass communication researcher John P. Robinson, in a study conducted under the auspices of the University of Michigan Survey Research Center, found that the media can affect voting behavior after all. Data from studies of the presidential elections of 1968 and 1972 showed that "a newspaper's perceived support of one candidate rather than another was associated with about a 6 percent edge in the vote for the endorsed candidate over his opponent." The study in 1972 revealed that independent voters who had been exposed to a newspaper endorsing Democratic candidate George McGovern were twice as likely to vote for McGovern as independent voters exposed to a newspaper supporting President Richard Nixon for reelection. Robinson pointed out that the numbers of voters affected were small, and the effects of newspaper endorsements peripheral. But in a closely contested election, a change in attitude and behavior by a small group of voters could be decisive.

As Everette Dennis summarizes, "One thing seems certain: the press is neither the all-powerful giant imagined by the propaganda researchers nor the peripheral influence seen by the political researchers." Instead, mass communications effects research has found exciting areas to explore and new assessments to make. Professors Peter Clarke and F. Gerald Kline, moving away from the narrow focus of the attitude-change literature, suggest that "what people learn from communication activity is a more rewarding topic for media effects research than attitude formation or change." Those carrying forward research in agenda-setting, uses and gratifications, media systems, and information-seeking join in this spreading of media research interests, which will provide a better picture of the place and influence of the mass media in the lives of all citizens.

Part Two

THE PRINT MEDIA

Chapter 3

HISTORIC PRESS FREEDOMS

SOCIETY'S CRUCIAL FREEDOMS

The history of journalism and of the development of the mass media begins with the story of the long struggle of people for personal liberty and political freedom, upon which the freedom to write and speak depends. Without that freedom, the magic of print and electronic technologies is of no value to free minds. One basic tenet of Anglo-American society has been freedom to print without prior restraint. How fragile such concepts are became apparent during the 1970s when, for the first time in the history of the American republic, the government succeeded in imposing a temporary prior restraint upon publication of a news story—once in the influential New York *Times,* and again in the obscure *Progressive* magazine. Both stories were eventually published, but the future of press freedom was left undetermined, as it has always been in the historic duel between the people's press and the people's governors.

Five centuries ago, the printing press began to revolutionize people's ability to communicate information and ideas. But almost from the moment Johann Gutenberg introduced movable type to the Western world around 1440 in Germany, barriers were erected against its use to influence public opinion through the free flow of news and opinion. In the English-speaking world printers and writers struggled until 1700 to win the mere right to print. They fought for another century to protect that liberty and to win a second basic right: the right to criticize. Addition of a third right—the right to report—came equally slowly and with less success.

Today's journalist knows that there remains a constant challenge to the freedoms to print, to criticize, and to report and that therefore the people's right to know is in constant danger. This is true in the democratic Western world, where freedom of the press is a recognized tenet, as well as in the larger portion of the world where it is denied. And it is true of the twentieth-century additions to the printing press: film, radio, television, and cable.

Freedom of the press is intertwined with other basic freedoms. These are freedom of speech, freedom of assembly, and freedom of petition. Upon these freedoms rest freedom of religious expression, freedom of political thought and action, and freedom of intellectual growth and communication of information and ideas. A society possessing and using these freedoms will advance and change as it exercises democratic processes. Very naturally, then, these freedoms will come under attack from those opposed to any change that might diminish their own power or position in society—today as in past eras. The press, occupying a key role in the battle for these basic freedoms, is a particular target. To the closed mind, the press has been a dangerous weapon to be kept as far as possible under the control of adherents of the status quo; to the inquiring mind, it has been a means of arousing interest and emotion among the public in order to effect change.

The social and political environments of the past five centuries have produced two basic theories of the press. The older we call the *authoritarian theory*. The controlled society of the Renaissance era, into which the printing press was introduced, functioned from the top down; a small and presumably wise ruling class decided what all of society should know and believe. This authoritarian concept of the relationship between citizens and the state could brook no challenge from those who thought the rulers were reflecting error, not truth. Publishing therefore existed under a license from those in power to selected printers who supported the rulers and the existing social and political structure. The authoritarian press theory still exists today in those parts of the world where similar controlled societies are dominated by small ruling classes. A variant of this theory, called the *Soviet Communist theory* of the press by the authors of *Four Theories of the Press* (Fred S. Siebert, Theodore Peterson, and Wilbur Schramm; University of Illinois Press, 1956), arose with the twentieth-century dictatorship. Whether fascist or communist, it exalts the state at the expense of individuals and its government-owned and party-directed press is dedicated to furthering the dictatorship and its social system.

As the Western world advanced through the Renaissance and Reformation into the democratic modern era, the second basic theory of the press developed. This we call the *libertarian theory*. Its roots extend back into the seventeenth century, but it did not become dominant in the English-speaking world until the nineteenth century. In libertarian theory, the press is not an instrument of government, nor does it speak for an elite ruling class. The mass of people are presumed able to discern between truth and falsehood themselves, and having been exposed to a press operating as a free marketplace of ideas and information, will themselves help determine public policy. It is essential that minorities as well as majorities, the politically weak as well as the politically strong, have free access to public expression in the press of a libertarian society.

In the battle against authoritarianism, the printer gradually became an ally of thinkers and writers who struggled for religious, political, and intellectual freedom and of the rising commercially based middle class that demanded economic freedom and political power in its contest with feudalism. Slowly the journalist developed dual functions: the opinion function and the news function. The journalist's media were the printed broadside and the pamphlet before the development of regularly issued newspapers in an established format. These appeared on the European continent before 1600, in England after 1622, and in the American colonies after 1704. In the eighteenth century they were joined by the early magazines. By our standards early newspapers were poorly printed, haphazard in content, and limited in circulation. But their influence can be measured by the amount of effort expended by those in authority to erect barriers against them and the stimuli to thought and action they contained. The traditions of freedom their printers and editors won by breaking down the barriers in the seventeenth and eighteenth centuries are the heritage of the modern newspapers and magazines developed in the nineteenth and twentieth centuries and of the film and electronic media of our times.

It was John Milton in his *Areopagitica* of 1644 who argued against repression of freedom of expression by advocating reliance upon truth: "Let her and Falsehood grapple: who ever knew Truth put to the worse in a free and open encounter?" Those who are afraid of truth will of course seek to prevent its entrance into a free marketplace of thought, but those who believe in the public liberty should realize that its existence depends upon liberty of the press. Thomas Jefferson put it well in a letter to his friend, Carrington, in 1787:

> I am persuaded that the good sense of the people will always be found to be the best army. They may be led astray for a moment, but will soon correct themselves. The people are the only censors of their governors; and even their errors will tend to keep these to the true principles of their institution. To punish these errors too severely would be to suppress the only safeguard of the public liberty. The way to prevent these irregular interpositions of the people, is to give them full information of their affairs through the channel of the public papers, and to contrive that those papers should penetrate the whole mass of the people. The basis of our government being the opinion of the people, the very first object should be to keep that right; and were it left to me to decide whether we should have a government without newspapers, or newspapers without a government, I should not hesitate a moment to prefer the latter.

Jefferson qualified his final statement, however, by adding: "But I should mean that every man should receive those papers, and be capable of reading them." Jefferson used the word "reading" because the problem of literacy still was a major one in his day; he also meant "understanding" in the sense of intellectual literacy. In these words of Milton and Jefferson are found the libertarian arguments for freedom of printing and other forms of communication, for freedom to criticize, and for freedom to report. They also argue for public support of the kind of mass media that carry out their responsibilities to provide the free flow of news and opinion and to speak for the people as "censors of their governors." The ability of journalists to discharge their responsibilities to society is conditioned, as Jefferson warned, by the level of public education and understanding; there is a public responsibility implied in this philosophic statement of the role of press liberty in supporting all of society's crucial freedoms.

There is also a public responsibility, and a journalistic one, to maintain the libertarian theory that everyone can be freely heard in the press, through a variant concept called the *social responsibility theory* of the press. Today it is no longer economically feasible for one to start printing or airing one's views. Concentration of much of the mass media in the hands of a relatively few owners imposes an obligation on them to be socially responsible, to see that all sides of social and political issues are fairly and fully presented so that the public may decide. The social responsibility theory contends that should the mass media fail in this respect, it may be necessary for some other agency of the public to enforce the marketplace of ideas concept.

THE RIGHT TO PRINT

William Caxton set up the first press in England in 1476. It was more than two centuries later, in 1694, before the freedom to print without prior restraint became a recognized liberty of the English people and their printer-journalists.

Prior restraint means licensing or censorship before a printer has a chance to roll the press. Unauthorized printing in itself becomes a crime. Under our modern concept anyone is free to have his or her say, although subject to punishment if what is printed offends society (obscenity, sedition) or harms another individual (libel). Authoritarian government does not care to grant this much freedom; it wishes to control communication from the start and to select the communicators.

Caxton printed the first books in the English language and otherwise aided in bringing the culture of the Continent to England. He enjoyed royal support and needed subsidizing by the ruling class, since his market was limited by illiteracy. He and his successors improved the quality and volume of printing during the next half-century, which saw the rise of the Tudor dynasty. Henry VIII, in his efforts to grasp absolute power, issued a proclamation in 1534 requiring printers to have royal permission before setting up their shops. This was a licensing measure, imposing prior restraint. Except for short periods, the theory of prior restraint remained in effect in England until 1694.

Henry VIII took other measures to control the press, including banning foreign books, issuing lists of forbidden books, and punishing ballad printers who offended Henry and his powerful Privy Council. But neither he nor Queen Elizabeth I was able to frighten all the printers and writers into compliance. After 1557 the Stationers Company, an organization of the licensed publishers and dealers, was given power to regulate printing and to search out bootleg jobs that had not been registered with it. Severe penalties for unauthorized printing were imposed in 1566 and 1586, in the latter year by the authority of the infamous Court of the Star Chamber. But despite arrests and smashing of presses of unlucky printers, some defiance always remained.

The struggle between the rising commercial class and the crown, which broke into revolution in 1640 and brought the establishment of the Commonwealth in 1649 by Oliver Cromwell, gave printers some temporary freedom. James I and succeeding Stuart kings found that Puritan

The shop of William Caxton, who set up the first printing press in England in 1476. Caxton learned printing on the Continent, where it had been a craft since the middle of the fifteenth century. The press was established "at the Sign of the Red Pale" in the abbey at Westminster. Nearly two centuries elapsed, however, before England had a genuine newspaper. (Culver)

opposition was increasingly difficult to contain, and the journalists were more alert to their opportunities. Public interest in the Thirty Years' War in Europe and in other political and economic affairs inevitably brought increased publication. Nathaniel Butter, Thomas Archer, and Nicholas Bourne produced the first regularly issued news book in 1621, on a weekly basis. Containing translated news from European news sheets, it was called a coranto. Diurnals, or reports of domestic events, appeared first as handwritten newsletters and later, after the Long Parliament raised the crown's ban on printing in 1641, in print.

But freedom was short-lived. By 1644 Milton was protesting against new licensing laws. After the execution of Charles I in 1649, Cromwell and his Puritan regime permitted only a few administration publications, censored by none other than Milton. The return of the Stuarts under Charles II in 1660 merely brought a switch in the licenser and censor to the royal party and more strict repression of unauthorized printing. Noteworthy, however, was the founding of the court newspaper, the London *Gazette,* in 1665. It remains today the oldest English newspaper.

The decline of the Stuarts, preceding the Revolution of 1688 that brought William and Mary to the throne, restored freedom to printers. Parliament allowed the licensing act to lapse in 1679. It was revived temporarily but finally died in 1694. Though severe seditious libel laws remained, and taxes on print paper and advertising were to be instituted beginning in 1712, the theory of prior restraint was dead. Newspapers by the score appeared in London, among them the first daily, the *Daily Courant,* in 1702. The early eighteenth century saw a flowering of newspapers and popular "essay" papers, edited by such figures as Daniel Defoe, Richard Steele and Joseph Addison, and Samuel Johnson.

Licensing and the theory of prior restraint did not die immediately in the American colonies. The Puritans imported the first press to New England in 1638 to print materials for their schools and Harvard College. Commercial presses followed, and some news broadsides and pamphlets appeared. In 1690 a refugee editor from London, Benjamin Harris, issued the first number of a Boston newspaper, *Publick Occurrences*, but his frank reporting nettled the colonial governor and council, which promptly ruled him out for not having a license. When the postmaster, John Campbell, brought out the first regular weekly paper, the Boston *News-Letter*, in 1704, he voluntarily trotted to the authorities for advance censorship and put "Published by Authority" at the top of his columns. It was not until 1721, when James Franklin began publishing his famed *New-England Courant*, that a colonial editor printed in defiance of authority.

Freedom to print became an accepted principle in America; nine colonies had already provided such constitutional protection by 1787, when the Constitutional Convention met in Philadelphia. Many felt it was a state matter, but when the Bill of Rights was added to the Constitution, the First Amendment included freedom of the press among the basic liberties that Congress could not violate. Under British common law and American judicial interpretation, prior restraint violates press freedom. Suppression of publications in anticipation of wrongful printing, or licensing measures to control those who would publish, cannot be authorized by Congress. In 1931 the Supreme Court for the first time applied the press guarantees of the First Amendment to the states, through the due process clause of the Fourteenth Amendment. The ruling came in the case of *Near* v. *Minnesota,* on an appeal against suppression of a Minneapolis news sheet under the Minnesota "gag law" of 1925 permitting suppression of malicious and scandalous publications. The court held the Minnesota law unconstitutional because it permitted prior restraint and said that those damaged by the newspaper had proper recourse through libel action.

There was a flaw, however, in the court's protection of the press. Was the prohibition of prior restraint absolute? When the New York *Times* in 1971 began publication of a summary of the secret Pentagon Papers laying bare United States decisions to escalate the Vietnam War, the government won a temporary restraining order prohibiting more stories. Shaken, the newspaper attorneys retreated, arguing only that the government had failed to show a danger to national security. The Supreme Court agreed, six to three, but legal scholars warned that the ban on prior restraint could not be considered absolute. In 1979 the government used the provisions of the Atomic Energy Act to restrain for six months publication of a story in the *Progressive* magazine of Wisconsin, which recounted presumed secrets of the hydrogen bomb. Chapter 20 will examine the reasons for these setbacks.

The Post Office, with its power to exclude publications from the mails under certain conditions, has given publishers many censorship troubles. Matters came to a head in 1946 after it sought to withdraw use of the second-class mailing rate from *Esquire* magazine on the grounds that the rate was a privilege intended only for those making a "special contribution to the public welfare." *Esquire,* faced with an additional half-million dollars a year in postal bills, appealed to the Supreme Court, which ruled in its favor. The court commented: "But to withdraw the second-class rate from this publication today because its content seemed to one official not good for the public would sanction withdrawal of the second-class rate tomorrow from another periodical whose social or economic views seemed harmful to another official." The decision put the Post Office back to judging specific issues on the basis of obscenity or illegal news of lotteries.

The motion picture industry instituted its own regulatory code in 1922, as a form of self-censorship, through the Motion Picture Association of America. Even before that date, state and city censorship boards were exercising precensorship functions by viewing and ordering the clipping of films in advance of movie showings, or banning them, a practice that still continues despite court challenges. Extralegal pressures have been brought by such unofficial groups as the former Legion of Decency. The same informal pressures have affected book publication and book purchases by public libraries and school systems. In addition, book publishers run the risk of having specific volumes barred from the mails as obscene. (Supreme Court decisions on obscenity are reviewed in Chapter 21.)

Radio and television, like the printed media, are not subject to precensorship. But more charges of censorship are raised in their cases, with the objection being to self-censorship or control of content in anticipation of adverse reaction. The broadcast media are more sensitive on this score because their managers realize that violations of what is considered to be "good taste" might cause difficulties for an individual station with the Federal Communications Commission under broadcasting licensing provisions.

If history has proved licensing to be a dangerous practice inimical to press freedom, why did the American public agree to licensing of radio and television stations? The answer is that by common consent we have recognized that broadcast channels are in the public domain. Congress in 1912 first legislated that the Department of Commerce should issue licenses to private broadcasters and assign them wavelengths so that they would not interfere with government wavelengths. During World War I all wireless operations were put under government control, but by 1919 private broadcasters were again experimenting. The numbers of stations increased rapidly and chaos developed on the airwaves. The radio industry, the National Association of Broadcasters, the American Newspaper Publishers Association, and other groups petitioned the government for relief.

This came from Congress through the Radio Act of 1927, which established a five-member commission to regulate all forms of radio communication. The government retained control of all channels, granting three-year licenses to broadcasters "in the public interest, convenience, or necessity" to provide "fair, efficient, and equitable service" throughout the country. Federal authority was broadened in 1934, with establishment of the seven-member Federal Communications Commission to exercise jurisdiction over all telecommunications. The responsibility of the license holder to operate a station in the public interest was more clearly spelled out. The commission was given the power to refuse renewal of a license in cases of flagrant disregard of broadcasting responsibility, but the FCC rarely has used this power. The law forbids any attempt at censorship by the commission; no station can be directed to put a particular program on or off the air. But the FCC undeniably is able to exercise indirect pressure upon license holders, who are understandably wary of its ultimate powers. FCC insistence upon stations' building some record for broadcasting in the public interest has led to attention to news and public affairs programs; on the other hand, the licensing problem has led to broadcasters' dragging their feet in airing controversial issues.

American radio and television are as free as American newspapers and magazines to provide whatever news their news editors see fit. Radio and television also have widely broadcast the opinion programs of individual commentators. But they were long reluctant to broadcast opinion as that of the station itself. The FCC in 1941 issued a ruling that "the broadcaster cannot be advocate"; then in 1949 the commission decided that stations could "editorialize with fairness" and urged them to do so. Many broadcasters felt they did not have the trained staffs to do effective editorializing or did not wish to identify the station management as an advocate in controversial situations, but three decades later, more than half the stations were broadcasting editorial opinions.

THE RIGHT TO CRITICIZE

Winning the liberty to print without prior restraint did not free the press from the heavy hand of government. In eighteenth-century England, and in the American colonies, the laws of seditious libel ran counter to the philosophical theory that the press should act as "censor of the government." To the authoritarian mind, the mere act of criticism of officials was in itself a crime, and "the greater the truth, the greater the libel" was an established tenet. This meant that publishing a story about a corrupt official was all the more seditious if the official indeed was corrupt.

The journalist's problem was to establish the principle of truth as a defense against charges of sedition or criminal libel. Mere fact of publication then would not be sufficient to determine guilt, and the accused printer or editor would be able to present the case in open court, preferably before a jury. Once the principle of truth as a defense could be won, governments would be less likely to press sedition charges, and laws defining what constitutes sedition could be revised.

The landmark case in what is now the United States was that of John Peter Zenger, who was tried in New York colony in 1735 for seditious libel. Zenger was an immigrant printer who lent the columns of his weekly paper, the *Journal,* to the cause of a political faction opposed to the royal governor. Some of the leading citizens of the colony were aligned with Zenger in the struggle against the governor, whom they accused of various arbitrary actions in the *Journal's* columns. Zenger was jailed and brought to trial in a hostile court. At this juncture a remarkable 80-year-old lawyer from Philadelphia, Andrew Hamilton, entered the case as Zenger's attorney.

The crown prosecutor reviewed the laws of seditious libel and argued that since Zenger had admitted publishing the newspaper issues in question, the trial was as good as over. His aged opponent skillfully jousted with the presiding justice and the prosecutor and insisted that truth should be permitted to be offered as a defense, with the jury to decide upon the truth of Zenger's publications. These arguments were denied by the court, but Hamilton ignored the ruling and delivered a stirring oration to the jury. He ended with a plea for the jury to take matters into its own hands: "The question before the court . . . is not just the cause of the poor printer. . . . No! It may in its consequence affect every freeman . . . on the main of America. It is the best cause; it is the cause of Liberty . . . the liberty both of exposing and opposing arbitrary power . . . by speaking and writing Truth."

Zenger was acquitted, and the court did not challenge the jury's verdict, even though it ignored existing law. A similar court victory on the issue of admission of truth as evidence was not won in England itself until the 1770s. The threat of trials for seditious libel remained until the end of the century, although in the colonies no further court trials of editors were held. Some editors were harassed by governors and their privy councils, but in general the colonial press was free to criticize the English authorities and to promote the cause of American independence (the reverse was not true, however, and Tory editors were suppressed by colonial radicals). By the early 1770s such papers as the Boston *Gazette* were openly seditious in their attacks upon constituted authority, but they continued to appear and to fan the fires of revolution.

Once the revolution was won, there was sharp cleavage along political and economic lines in the new nation. The newspapers continued to take pronounced partisan stands. The two political factions, the Federalists headed by Alexander Hamilton and the Republicans headed by Thomas Jefferson, split on many domestic issues and particularly over the country's emotional reaction to the French Revolution. Most of the weeklies and the few dailies that had started after 1783 were published in seaboard towns for the commercial classes and tended to be Federalist in sympathy. Hamilton sponsored some party organs in addition: John Fenno's *Gazette of the United States,* Noah Webster's *American Minerva,* and William Coleman's New York *Evening Post*. Topping the Federalist editors in partisan criticism was William Cobbett with his *Porcupine's Gazette*.

Jefferson countered with Philip Freneau's *National Gazette* and also had other Republican supporters, including William Duane and Benjamin Franklin Bache at the *Aurora*. The impulsive Bache, grandson of Benjamin Franklin, more than matched Cobbett in vituperative criticism. When it appeared that war with France was imminent in 1798, the Federalists decided to crack down on their tormentors.

The Alien and Sedition Acts they passed in 1798 were aimed at deportation of undesirable aliens and at curbing criticism of the government. Undesirable aliens in Federalist eyes were those who supported Vice-President Jefferson; some were deported and others were harassed. The Sedition Act by its terms restricted prosecutions to those who "write, utter, or publish . . . false, scandalous and malicious writing" against the federal government, its officials and legislators, or its laws (including the Sedition Act itself). It provided for admission of truth as a defense. In theory, only false criticism was to be punished; but in practice, Federalist politicians and judges set out to punish anti-Federalist editors. One, for example, was jailed and fined for printing a letter to the editor that accused President John Adams of "ridiculous pomp, foolish adulation, and selfish avarice."

Vice-President Jefferson, fearful for his own safety, retired to Monticello, where he and his supporters drafted the Virginia and Kentucky Resolutions, advocating the theory of nullification by the states of unconstitutional acts of the Congress. But the issue did not need to be joined; Federal excesses in administering the Alien and Sedition Acts contributed to a popular revulsion and to Jefferson's election as president in 1800. The dangerous Alien and Sedition Acts expired the same year. Jefferson insisted that his administration permit partisan journalism "to demonstrate the falsehood of the pretext that freedom of the press is incompatible with orderly government." He urged that individuals protect themselves against journalistic excesses by filing civil suits for libel. The calm course Jefferson took was vindicated when his party retained control of the government for a generation. Party newspapers, with one-sided news and fiercely partisan opinion, continued to flourish, but after the great crisis of 1798 no federal administration attempted to repress criticism. Soon after 1800 the libertarian theory of the press had eclipsed the authoritarian theory by common consent.

During wartime, national safety requirements and emotional feelings bring some restriction of criticism. The Civil War saw suppression of a few newspapers in the North, but considering the violence of many editors' criticisms, retaliation by Lincoln and his generals was almost negligible. During World War I, the Espionage Act of 1917 widened the authority of the Post Office to bar periodicals from the mails, and the Sedition Act of 1918 made it a crime to write or publish "any disloyal, profane, scurrilous or abusive language" about the federal government. The axe fell heavily upon German-language newspapers, in many cases, unfairly. It also fell upon Socialist magazines and newspapers, because they opposed the war, and upon pacifist publications. Max Eastman's brilliant magazine, *The Masses*, was barred from the mails, as were two leading Socialist dailies, the New York *Call* and the Milwaukee *Leader*. Socialist party leader Eugene Debs went to prison for criticizing America's allies as "out for plunder." Clearly the theory of liberty to criticize was disregarded in these violations of minority opinion rights. During World War II only a few pro-Nazi and Fascist publications were banned—and they had few friends to plead their cause.

The right to criticize needs constant protection, as was demonstrated when Louisiana political boss Huey Long attempted to punish newspaper opponents through taxation. Long and his political machine imposed a special tax on the advertising income of larger Lousiana dailies, virtually all of which were opposed to him. The Supreme Court held the punitive tax unconsititutional in 1936. In the early 1950s courageous newspapers and magazines that spoke out against Senator Joseph McCarthy of Wisconsin and what became known as McCarthyism were harassed and denounced. But neither McCarthy nor his followers could bring about actual legislation restricting criticism, much as they might have liked to do so.

Contempt-of-court citations bring about another kind of clash over the right to criticize. A series of Supreme Court decisions in the 1940s widened the freedom of newspapers to comment upon pending court cases and actions of judges. This was done by applying the "clear and present danger" theory to a judge's contention that administration of justice was being impeded by newspaper comment. But judges have great power in contempt-of-court matters, and editors remain wary of criticizing their acts without pressing need to do so.

THE RIGHT TO REPORT

The right to report is not nearly as much a right safeguarded by law and legal precedent as the right to print and the right to criticize. Rather, it is based on a philosophical argument. What would be gained through the right to print and to criticize if no news were forthcoming? What good would a free press be for the reader if editors and reporters had no way to find out what government was doing? Denial of the right of access to news is a denial of the people's right to know, the journalist maintains.

Yet, no person can be compelled to talk to a reporter; no government official need grant an interview or hold a press conference; courts and legislatures admit the press through historical tradition and have the power to eject the press (unless specific statutes have been passed requiring open legislative sessions). There is another side to the coin: No newspaper can be compelled to print any material it does not wish to use, including paid advertising.

While the laws of seditious libel were in vogue, no right to report was recognized. The mere reporting of a government official's action, or of a debate in Parliament, was likely to be construed as seditious (unfavorable) by some person in authority. William Bradford in Pennsylvania, James Franklin in Massachusetts, and other colonial editors were hauled before authorities for reporting a disputed action of government. In England, reporting of the proceedings of Parliament was banned until 1771, when the satirical writings of Dr. Samuel Johnson and the open defiance of newspaper publisher John Wilkes crumpled the opposition.

The House of Representatives of the American Congress opened its doors to reporters in 1789, two days after it was organized as a legislative body. The Senate, however, excluded reporters until 1795. Congress came to depend upon journalists, particularly the editors of the Jeffersonian party organ, the *National Intelligencer,* to publish a record of debates and proceedings. Not until 1834 did the government publish its own records.

Today there is little likelihood that Washington correspondents will be denied access to the congressional press galleries, except when the legislators are meeting in emergency executive session (a rare event). But reporters are admitted to sessions of legislative committees only with the consent of the committee chairperson and members. Some 40 percent of congressional committee sessions are closed to the press. The situation in state capitals is similar. Television and radio reporters and photographers have won access to legislative sessions only by persistent effort, and their ability to use all their equipment is often circumscribed.

Reporters similarly are admitted to court sessions only by the agreement of the presiding judge. They may be excluded, with other members of the public, if the court deems it necessary. Juvenile courts, for example, operate without reportorial coverage in most cases. Ordinarily reporters are free to attend court sessions, since public trials are the rule, but they have no automatic right of attendance. Photographers and television-radio reporters have had only limited success in covering trials with cameras or microphones, due to restrictions applied to them by Section 35 of the Canons of Judicial Ethics of the American Bar Association. A long campaign by the National Press Photographers Association, the Radio Television News Directors Association, and the American Society of Newspaper Editors to persuade the bar association to revise its Canon 35 failed when that group reaffirmed its stand in 1963. In 1972 the association replaced Canon 35 with Canon 3A7, equally as restrictive, and the impasse continued (see Chapter 20).

An important doctrine that has emerged is the doctrine of qualified privilege. This doctrine protects a news medium from the threat of libel suits when reporting the actions of a legislative body or a court, provided its report is accurate and fair. This doctrine carries with it the implication that the media have an obligation to report legislative and judicial sessions so that the public may know what government and courts are doing. Defamatory statements affecting the reputations of individuals made in legislative sessions and courts may therefore be reported without fear of damage suits.

The right to report is denied more often at the grass roots level of government than at the national level, insofar as legislative bodies are concerned. Boards of education, water commissions, city councils, county boards, and other similar groups often seek to meet in private and conduct the public's business in virtual secrecy. Newspeople wage an unending battle against this practice, without much avail, unless the public demands to know. Some editors and publishers accept the practice and forfeit their right to report the news firsthand, thereby forfeiting their most important right as journalists. Passage of "open meetings" laws in an increasing number of states during the 1950s, at the insistence of various news groups, somewhat improved the access to news at the local level. These laws provide that actions taken in closed sessions are invalid; but they do not force a reluctant legislative group to open the doors wide. By 1975 virtually all states had some form of open meeting law as well as laws guaranteeing the opening of public records to reporters needing access to them.

Perhaps the most publicized denial of access to news has been in the national executive departments. This increasing trend—stemming from the necessity for secrecy in limited areas of the national defense establishment and atomic energy research—has alarmed responsible journalists. The American Society of Newspaper Editors and the Society of Professional Journalists, Sigma Delta Chi, have well-organized campaigns demanding free access to news so that people may know the facts necessary to make intelligent decisions.

Appointment in 1955 of a House subcommittee headed by Representative John Moss of California to study the information policies of the government brought some relief. The Moss committee acted as the champion of the people's right to know and the reporter's right of access to news. By publicizing executive department refusals to make information available on public matters, the Moss committee forced some reforms, including passage of the Freedom of Information Act of 1966, giving the citizen legal recourse against arbitrary withholding of information by a federal agency. The law was strengthened in 1974 (see Chapter 20), but tenacious officials in some government agencies still used every tactic to prevent disclosure of information they thought the public should not know. But reporters determined to find out the facts can usually obtain them despite the opposition of such reluctant public officials.

Chapter 4

GROWTH OF THE PRINT MEDIA

THE BASIC EDITORIAL FUNCTIONS

Newspapers, despite their impact on society, have a relatively brief historical tradition. Two hundred eighty years ago, there was but one struggling weekly in the colonial outpost of Europe that was to become the United States. It was only 150 years ago, in the 1830s and 1840s, that the "penny press" dailies ushered in America's first era of popular journalism, made famous by James Gordon Bennett and his New York *Herald,* Horace Greeley and his New York *Tribune,* and Henry J. Raymond and his New York *Times.* Bennett taught others how to search out and report the news; Greeley fashioned an editorial page; Raymond put his emphasis on news interpretation. With their contemporaries and successors, they laid the foundations for present-day American journalism.

The basic journalistic principles thus espoused were further advanced before the nineteenth century had ended by such noted publishers as Joseph Pulitzer, Edward Wyllis Scripps, and Adolph S. Ochs. These publishers had two goals. The primary goal was an ever-increasing concentration of effort on impartial gathering and reporting of the news and its comprehensive display. The other was demonstration of responsible opinion leadership, provided both through an intelligently written editorial page and integrity and zealousness in telling the news.

As even the colonial editor knew, however, there is a third editorial function of the press and that is to entertain the reader, as well as to provide information and instruction. What is called "human interest" news—stories with appeal based on writing skill rather than necessarily upon news value—has always been in great reader demand. Sensational news—stories involving the human passions, crime and violence, and spicy accounts of the doings of the famous—is likewise age-old in its appeal. The newspaper has also always contained a budget of nonnews material: short stories and other literary content (more prevalent a century ago than today), comics and Sunday feature sections (favorites since the 1890s), advice to the lovelorn (highly popular for early eighteenth-century readers), and a host of varying entertainment items.

The responsibility of the mass media has been to strike a balance among the functions of informing, instructing, and entertaining. The newspaper, as it reached out for mass circulation, sought to fulfill the first two functions in more popularized ways: a more readable writing style, skillful use of human interest elements in news, better makeup and headline display, effective pictures, and use of color. Such popularizing, in the interests of appealing to the entertainment desire, need not detract from the newspapers' social usefulness. There is no reason why the "hard news" of political and economic importance should not be presented as interestingly as possible and in company with other less important, but more attractive, ingredients. But there is a line to be drawn. Overemphasis on sensationalism at the expense of news and a lavish dressing up of purely entertainment features are merely cheapening, not popularizing.

How well American newspapers have responded to these basic principles over the decades is a matter of judgment. One thing is certain: they responded differently, for there is no such thing as a typical newspaper to analyze any more than there is a typical magazine, television or radio station, or book publishing house. What can be measured is the response made by the leaders in different historical periods, as they reshaped their journalistic products to fit the demands of their times and the desires of their audiences. As the sociologist Robert E. Park put it:

> The newspaper has a history; but it has, likewise, a natural history. The press, as it exists, is not, as our moralists sometimes seem to assume, the willful product of any little group of living men. On the contrary, it is the outcome of a historic process in which many individuals participated without foreseeing what the ultimate product of their labors was to be. The newspaper, like the modern city, is not wholly a rational product. ... it has continued to grow and change in its own incalculable ways.

THE COLONIAL PRESS

Early Concepts of News

Reporting, as defined today, means gathering information of interest to other people and presenting it to them accurately in a way that makes them understand and remember it. This definition is broad enough to fit all media of information, and comprehensive enough to provide a measuring stick for present and past performance.

The first newspaper publishers were primarily printers, not editors. The majority had a sense of what interested people, but only a few had real reportorial instincts. Only a few, too, were good enough writers to tell their stories in an interesting way. Since their access to news was severely limited, and inadequate transportation and communication facilities made the collecting of news a very haphazard business, they scarcely could be expected to be either complete or accurate in their reports. But even so, very few made any move to go out and find the news; they ran what came over their doorsteps or what could be gleaned from other newspapers and periodicals, particularly those coming from London. None had local news reporters as we know them today. Nevertheless, what meager news and entertainment they offered were eagerly devoured by their readers, who had little other choice.

James and Benjamin Franklin were early publisher-printers who were also journalists. James, in his *New-England Courant,* gave Boston readers of the 1720s the first readable and exciting American newspaper. He printed news, despite the opposition of Puritan political and religious authorities, and covered local issues in a dramatic and crusading fashion. He and his contributors, including his younger brother Ben, wrote well; and the paper, modeled on the successful "essay" papers of Joseph Addison and Richard Steele in England, had high literary qualities. Personality sketches, feature stories, and human interest material lightened the pages. Benjamin Franklin carried on the traditions in his *Pennsylvania Gazette,* editing his meager scraps of news more cleverly than his rivals and offering more substance.

During the Revolutionary War period, publishers such as Benjamin Franklin and Isaiah Thomas of the *Massachusetts Spy* were alert to forward the patriot cause, but even a well-to-do publisher such as Thomas did not attempt to have his own correspondent with Washington's army. The paper nearest to the scene of an event covered it; other papers copied the report or relied upon official announcements, messages sent to their local authorities from military and governmental headquarters, and reports of travelers.

The Political Pamphleteers

Throughout the eighteenth century, the political pamphleteer was more important than the editor-printer. Three examples from the years preceding the American Revolution are John Dickinson, Samuel Adams, and Thomas Paine—all well known in the pages of American history, and all of whom used the newspaper of their day as a vehicle to reach the public.

John Dickinson of Pennsylvania, an articulate spokesman of the colonial Whigs, wrote his "Letters from a Farmer in Pennsylvania" for the

THE [No 58

New-England Courant.

From MONDAY September 3. to MONDAY September 10. 1722.

Quod eſt in corde ſobrii, eſt in ore ebrii.

To the Author of the New-England Courant.

SIR, [No XII

IT is no unprofitable tho' unpleaſant Purſuit, diligently to inſpect and conſider the Manners & Converſation of Men, who, inſenſible of the greateſt Enjoyments of humane Life, abandon themſelves to Vice from a falſe Notion of *Pleaſure* and *good Fellowſhip*. A true and natural Repreſentation of any Enormity, is often the beſt Argument againſt it and Means of removing it, when the moſt ſevere Reprehenſions alone, are found ineffectual.

I WOULD in this Letter improve the little Obſervation I have made on the Vice of *Drunkeneſs*, the better to reclaim the *good Fellows* who uſually pay the Devotions of the Evening to *Bacchus*.

I DOUBT not but *moderate Drinking* has been improv'd for the Diffuſion of Knowledge among the ingenious Part of Mankind, who want the Talent of a ready Utterance, in order to diſcover the Conceptions of their Minds in an entertaining and intelligible Manner. 'Tis true, drinking does not *improve* our Faculties, but it enables us to *uſe* them; and therefore I conclude, that much Study and Experience, and a little Liquor, are of abſolute Neceſſity for ſome Tempers, in order to make them accompliſh'd Orators. *Dic. Ponder* diſcovers an excellent Judgment when he is inſpir'd with a Glaſs or two of *Claret*, but he paſſes for a Fool among thoſe of ſmall Obſervation, who never ſaw him the better for Drink. And here it will not be improper to obſerve, That the moderate Uſe of Liquor, and a well plac'd and well regulated Anger, often produce this ſame Effect; and ſome who cannot ordinarily talk but in broken Sentences and falſe Grammar, do in the Heat of Paſſion expreſs themſelves with as much Eloquence as Warmth. Hence it it is that my own Sex are generally the moſt eloquent, becauſe the moſt paſſionate. "It has been ſaid in the Praiſe of ſome Men, "(ſays an ingenious Author,) that they could talk "whole Hours together upon any thing; but it "muſt be owned to the Honour of the other Sex, "that there are many among them who can talk "whole Hours together upon Nothing. I have "known a Woman branch out into a long extempore Diſſertation on the Edging of a Petticoat, and "chide her Servant for breaking a China Cup, in all "the Figures of Rhetorick."

BUT after all it muſt be conſider'd, that no Pleaſure can give Satiſfaction or prove advantageous to a *reaſonable Mind*, which is not attended with the *Reſtraints of Reaſon*. Enjoyment is not to be found by Exceſs in any ſenſual Gratification; but on the contrary, the immoderate Cravings of the Voluptuary, are always ſucceeded with Loathing and a palled Appetite. What Pleaſure can the Drunkard have in the Reflection, that, while in his Cups, he retain'd only the Shape of a Man, and acted the Part of a Beaſt; or that from reaſonable Diſcourſe a few Minutes before, he deſcended to Impertinence and Nonſenſe?

I CANNOT pretend to account for the different Effects of Liquor on Perſons of different Diſpoſitions, who are guilty of Exceſs in the Uſe of it. 'Tis ſtrange to ſee Men of a regular Converſation become rakiſh and profane when intoxicated with Drink, and yet more ſurprizing to obſerve, that ſome who appear to be the moſt profligate Wretches when ſober, become mighty religious in their Cups, and will then, and at no other Time addreſs their Maker, but when they are deſtitute of Reaſon, and actually affronting him. Some ſhrink in the Wetting, and others ſwell to ſuch an unuſual Bulk in their Imaginations, that they can in an Inſtant underſtand all Arts and Sciences, by the liberal Education of a little vivifying *Punch*, or a ſufficient Quantity of other exhilerating Liquor.

AND as the Effects of Liquor are various, ſo are the Characters given to its Devourers. It argues ſome Shame in the Drunkards themſelves, in that they have invented numberleſs Words and Phraſes to cover their Folly, whoſe proper Sgnifications are harmleſs, or have no Signification at all. They are ſeldom known to be *drunk*, tho they are very often *boozey, cogey, tipſey, fox'd, merry, mellow, fuddl'd, groatable, Confoundedly cut, See two Moons*, are *Among the Philiſtines, In a very good Humour, See the Sun*, or, *The Sun has ſhone upon them*; they *Clip the King's Engliſh*, are *Almoſt froze, Feavouriſh, In their Altitudes, Pretty well enter'd*, &c. In ſhort, every Day produces ſome new Word or Phraſe which might be added to the Vocabulary of the *Tiplers*: But I have choſe to mention theſe few, becauſe if at any Time a Man of Sobriety and Temperance happens to *cut himſelf confoundedly*, or is *almoſt froze*, or *feavouriſh*, or accidentally *ſees the Sun*, &c. he may eſcape the Imputation of being *drunk*, when his Miſfortune comes to be related.

I am SIR,
Your Humble Servant,

SILENCE DOGOOD.

FOREIGN AFFAIRS.

Berlin, May 8. Twelve Pruſſian Batallions are ſent to Mecklenburg, but for what Reaſon is not known. 'Tis ſaid, the Emperor, ſuſpecting the Deſigns of the Czar, will ſecure all the Domains of the Duke of Mecklenburg. His Pruſſian Majeſty, to promote the intended Union of the Reformed and Lutherans in his Dominions, has charged the Miniſters of thoſe two Communions, not to make the leaſt mention in the Pulpits of the religious Differences about ſome abſtruſer Points, particularly the Doctrine of Predeſtination, and to forbear all contumelious Expreſſions againſt one another.

Hamburg, May 8. The Imperial Court has order'd the Circles of Lower Saxony, to keep in Rea-

The front page of the *New-England Courant*, the American colonies' first good newspaper. An essay on drunkenness by Benjamin Franklin, under the pseudonym "Silence Dogood," occupies most of the page.

Pennsylvania Chronicle of 1767–1768. Dickinson was opposed to revolution and was actually a spokesman for the business class and its Whig philosophy rather than for the agrarian class. But he and the colonial Whigs could not afford to let the British Whigs impose commercial restrictions that were harmful to American interests. The mercantile system, which prevented development of colonial industry and trade, and taxation measures imposed by a Parliament in which the colonial Whigs were not directly represented, were threats Dickinson could not ignore. His forceful arguments for home rule helped swing Americans of his economic group to the revolutionary cause after it became apparent that compromise was no longer possible.

Samuel Adams, the great propagandist of the revolution, belonged to the Radical party. Only briefly an editor himself, he worked with the group of Boston patriots assembled in the office of the Boston *Gazette* that included the publishers, Benjamin Edes and John Gill, and the engraver, Paul Revere. Sam Adams was called the "master of the puppets" and the "assassin of reputations" by his enemies, and undoubtedly he was both. He wrote tirelessly for the columns of the *Gazette,* twisting every possible incident or administrative action of the British into an argument for revolution. When the news was dull and the fires of dissatisfaction needed fanning, he turned minor scrapes into events of seemingly major import. When a crisis arose, such as the passage of the Stamp Act or the imposition of the tax on tea, Adams worked with others to fire up resistance throughout the colonies. His Committees of Correspondence, organized in 1772, kept the word moving among patriot editors. When British rifles fired in Boston to restrain a street crowd, the *Gazette* called the affair the Boston Massacre. But a year later the *Gazette* was reporting on a memorial service held for the massacre victims, consisting of a propagandistic display in the windows of Paul Revere's house. Such touches as this were the work of Sam Adams, who knew how to stir the popular emotions.

Tom Paine, the political philosopher, arrived in the colonies from England in time to make two great pamphleteering contributions to the patriot cause. His *Common Sense,* which sold 120,000 copies in three months in the spring of 1776, was a hard-headed, down-to-earth argument for independence that the common citizen could understand. That December, when Washington's discouraged army was camped on the Delaware River across from Trenton, Paine was drafted to write the first of his *Crisis* papers for a Philadelphia weekly:

> These are the times that try men s souls. The summer soldier and the sunshine patriot will, in this crisis, shrink from the service of their country; but he that stands it NOW, deserves the love and thanks of man and woman. Tyranny, like hell, is not easily conquered; yet we have this consolation with us, that the harder the conflict the more glorious the triumph. What we obtain too cheap, we esteem too lightly; it is dearness only that gives every thing its value. Heaven knows how to put a proper price upon its goods; and it would be strange indeed if so celestial an article as FREEDOM should not be highly rated.

Paine's words lived to be broadcast to occupied Europe during World War II; at the time, they helped to spur the first American victory of the war.

PRESS OF THE NEW REPUBLIC

In the early years of the new nation, two types of newspapers were developing. One was the mercantile paper, published in the seaboard towns primarily for the trading and shipping classes interested in commercial and political news. Its well-filled advertising columns reflected the essentially business interest of its limited clientele of subscribers—2000 was a good number. The other type was the political paper, partisan in its appeal and relying for reader support on acceptance of its views, rather than upon the quality and completeness of its news. Most editors of the period put views first and news second; the political paper deliberately shaped the news to fit its views. In the struggle over the adoption of the Constitution and the establishment of the new federal government, these party papers played a key role.

The *Federalist Papers,* written for the newspapers of New York state and reprinted throughout the country, were largely the work of Alexander Hamilton, brilliant leader of the pro-Constitution party that took its name from the series of 85 articles. Written for mass consumption, they still rank as one of the best expositions of political doctrine ever conceived. When Hamilton's party assumed control of the new federal government, Hamilton directed the editorial opinion of the Federalist party papers he helped to establish. He dictated his ideas to his editors, who, with their Jeffersonian opponents, developed a briefer, one-argument form of editorial writing.

Ranged on the anti-Federalist side with Thomas Jefferson were his personally sponsored poet-editor, Philip Freneau of the *National Gazette,* and other masters of partisanship like Benjamin Franklin Bache of the *Aurora.* Editors on both sides attacked each other with biting sarcasm and bitter invective. Their political sponsors were also viciously treated; the climax came when Bache accused Washington of being a "front man" for the Federalists and said, "If ever a nation was debauched by a man, the American nation has been debauched by Washington." William Cobbett, the most fiery of the Federalist editors, retaliated in his *Porcupine's Gazette* with a classic character sketch of Bache in which the kindest word was "liar."

The American press survived the excesses of the 1790s and the dangerous effort at repression of press freedom through the Alien and Sedition Acts. But the traditions of partisan journalism lived on in the political party press of the nineteenth century. This was particularly true of the frontier papers that supported Andrew Jackson and the Democratic party. The *Argus of Western America* of Frankfort, Kentucky, was one of these grubby but virile sheets that helped to spark the Jacksonian revolution. Amos Kendall and Francis P. Blair, two of its editors, graduated to Jackson's "kitchen cabinet," where Kendall served as postmaster general and journalistic adviser to the president, and Blair as editor of the hard-hitting administration paper, the Washington *Globe.* The tradition of an administration organ in Washington had begun with the *National Intelligencer* of Jefferson's day, but none was edited with more single-minded driving purpose than Blair's *Globe.* "Give it to Bla-ar," Jackson would say, and Blair would pass the word along to the party faithful. The Whigs had their strong editors too, such as Thurlow Weed of the Albany *Evening Journal.* The attitude of the political paper was well expressed by the pro-Jackson New York *Evening Post,* which advised its readers to buy a Whig paper if they wanted the other side of the argument of the moment.

The political papers were much more important in the story of the development of the opinion function. The mercantile papers, however, played a role in the development of the news function concept. Even though their primary interest was in shipping news and digests of foreign news taken from European newspapers arriving in American ports, the leading mercantile papers took pride in excelling in their specialties. And as the struggle between the Federalists and the Republicans for control of the national government intensified, news of Hamilton's fiscal policies and Jefferson's moves became important to the business community. Competition was tough, too; in 1800 there were six dailies in Philadelphia (twice as many as in 1980), and five in New York. The weekly publishers had been forced into the daily field to meet the demands of patrons of the coffee houses, where the London papers were filed as soon as ships arrived with the latest issues and where news was freely exchanged.

So the individual papers began to go out after the news. Correspondents covered sessions of Congress in Washington as early as 1808 and were well established by the late 1820s. Seaport dailies hired boats to meet the incoming ships out in the harbor so their editors would have a head start on digesting the foreign news. The leading New York mercantile papers, the *Courier and Enquirer* and the *Journal of Commerce,* set up rival pony express services between Washington and New York to get presidential messages and congressional news faster.

What the mercantile papers did not do, however, was widen the appeal of their news columns to satisfy the demands of a new reading audience that was emerging from what is now called the Jacksonian revolution. More widespread education, extension of the right to vote, increased interest in politics by a growing working class, and other socioeconomic factors were operating to pave the way for a more popular and responsive journalism that was destined to overwhelm the older types of newspapers.

THE PENNY PRESS

Between 1833 and 1837, the publishers of a new "penny press" proved that a low-priced paper, edited to interest ordinary people, could win what amounted to a mass circulation for the times and thereby attract an advertising volume that would make it independent. These were papers for the common citizen and were not tied to the interests of the business community, like the mercantile press, or dependent for financial support upon political party allegiance. It did not necessarily follow that all the penny papers would be superior in their handling of the news and opinion functions. But the door was open for some to make important journalistic advances.

The first offerings of a penny paper tended to be highly sensational; human interest stories overshadowed important news, and crime and sex stories were written in full detail. But as the penny paper attracted readers from various social and economic brackets, its sensationalism was modified. The ordinary reader came to want a better product, too. A popularized style of writing and presentation of news remained, but the penny paper became a respectable publication that offered significant information and editorial leadership. Once the first of the successful penny papers had shown the way, later ventures could enter the competition at the higher level of journalistic responsibility the pioneering papers had reached.

This was the pattern of American newspapers in the years following the founding of the New York *Sun* in 1833. The *Sun,* published by Benjamin Day, entered the lists against 11 other dailies. It was tiny in comparison; but it was bright and readable, and it preferred human interest features to important but dull political speech reports. It had a police reporter writing squibs of crime news in the style already proved successful by London papers. And, most important, it sold for a penny, whereas its competitors sold for 6 cents. By 1837 the *Sun* was printing 30,000 copies a day, which was more than the total of all 11 New York daily newspapers combined when the *Sun* first appeared. In those same four years, James Gordon Bennett brought out his New York *Herald* (1835) and a trio of New York printers who were imitating Day's success founded the Philadelphia *Public Ledger* (1836) and the Baltimore *Sun* (1837). The four penny sheets all became famed newspapers.

Bennett and News Enterprise

James Gordon Bennett serves as the symbol of the penny press news enterprises. He had been a Washington correspondent, reporter, and editor for other dailies before he launched the *Herald* in 1835. Disillusioned by a previous venture with a political paper, he kept the *Herald* relatively free of political ties. He more than matched the *Sun* with sensational coverage of crime and court news, on the one hand, and challenged the more sober journals with detailed coverage of Wall Street affairs, political campaigns, and foreign news, on the other. As profits from his wide circulation and extensive advertising piled up, he spent money on news coverage. He matched his rivals in establishing pony express services to carry the news from Washington and other points. One *Herald* courier service reached all the way from Newfoundland, carrying European news by pony rider, boat, and train to the first telegraph point. Bennett was among the first to use each of the new means of communication as they burst upon the scene in the 1830s and 1840s, hiring locomotives to race presidential messages from Washington and utilizing the telegraph as soon as Samuel F. B. Morse's invention proved itself in 1844 and wires were strung from city to city. He personally toured the country with presidential candidates and sailed to London on the newest steamship to arrange for better coverage of foreign news. By the 1850s he had made the *Herald* the leading newsgathering paper and the richest in advertising.

Bennett's competitors were not left in the dust. The New York *Sun,* Philadelphia *Public Ledger*, and Baltimore *Sun* were all in the race for news. So were such older New York papers as the *Courier and Enquirer, Journal of Commerce,* and *Evening Post.* So were two new competitors, Horace Greeley's New York *Tribune,* founded in 1841, and Henry J. Raymond's New York *Times,* founded in 1851. Greeley shunned the sensationalism that had helped the *Sun* and *Herald* to their initial circulation successes and concentrated instead on building up an editorial page and offering news interpretation, but he also covered the running news. His managing editor, Charles A. Dana, directed a reportorial staff of high quality, although perhaps not as slambang as the *Herald's* group. By the time Raymond entered the New York field with the *Times,* the lines of staff organization were fairly well defined. The owner might still be editor-in-chief, but he had a news executive and a business manager operating the day-to-day business. Raymond concentrated on foreign coverage and editorial policy, seeking to give his reports more depth and meaning in the pattern of the *Times* of London.

The coming of the telegraph speeded the gathering of news, but it also increased the cost. In 1848 six New York morning papers formed the Associated Press of New York, forerunner of the modern press association of the same name. They did so to share the costs of telegraphing digests of foreign news from Boston and of routine news from Washington. Soon other papers asked to share in this common news report, and the New York papers began selling it. Papers in the interior of the country could now, with the telegraph, get the news as rapidly as their eastern metropolitan competitors. The excitement of the Mexican War and of the political crises leading up to the Civil War spurred attention to the need for better mass communications.

The Civil War called for great efforts in news enterprise. The *Herald* sent its own small army of correspondents into the field; other leading papers followed suit. Printing advances of the previous two decades—the flat-bed cylinder press, the type-revolving press, and stereotyping—were needed to handle increased circulations. Sunday editions of daily papers came into being. The illustrated periodicals, *Harper's Weekly* and *Frank Leslie's Illustrated Newspaper,* led the way in using woodcut illustrations and maps, and newspapers followed suit as best they could. By the time the guns ceased firing, the traditions of news enterprise and emphasis upon the news function had been well established.

Greeley and the Editorial Page

Horace Greeley is recognized as one of the most influential editors in the history of American journalism. His New York *Tribune,* which he founded in 1841, was the first American newspaper to develop an editorial page that was the product of the thinking of a group of individuals. Not that it was the well-tailored, coherently organized page many newspapers publish today. Orderly departmentalization had not yet come to newspapers in Greeley's day, and in any event methodicalness and consistency were not part of the Greeley temperament. But what the *Tribune* printed represented a dramatic change from the tradition of the pamphleteer.

Greeley was deeply conscious of his responsibility to the reader. He knew the *Tribune* had to be enterprising in reporting the news if it was to compete successfully for readers. But he felt it his responsibility to be just as enterprising in seeking to influence public opinion by devoting much space to serious discussion, editorial argument, and interpretation of events. The *Tribune* examined issues and debated ideas; it did not follow a set party line or insist that there was only one solution to a problem. True, it advocated some of its opinions as vehemently as did the pamphleteer, but in total it illuminated the social and economic issues of the day, from differing viewpoints, far more than any other paper had.

Unlike Bennett's *Herald,* which minimized the opinion function while concentrating on news enterprise, Greeley's *Tribune* made the opinion function the key to its popular acceptance. And popular it was. His weekly edition, in which the best of the daily news and opinion was reprinted for mail circulation (a practice of some bigger papers of the period), had the largest circulation of any contemporary publication. It was called the "Bible of the Middle West," where many of the 200,000 copies went. "Uncle Horace," as Greeley was called, was as well known as any American of his time—only Lincoln, of the men of the period, has had more books written about him. Greeley lived through a period of momentous events and of great social change and, like Lincoln, was able to give expression to the aspirations and hopes of less articulate citizens.

To many, the activities of Greeley and the *Tribune* must have appeared strangely inconsistent. The editor was greatly concerned with the impact of the industrial revolution on society and the social ills unrestricted capitalism produced. He was willing to examine and debate any seemingly reasonable experiment in social reform or economic theory, in the hope that it would give workers and farmers a more equitable share in the accumulating wealth. So the *Tribune,* ostensibly a Whig newspaper, advocated a form of collective living called "associationism" and ran many columns of material written by the Socialist Albert Brisbane and the Communist Karl Marx. Few of Greeley's readers were won over to socialism, but they enjoyed the debate. Greeley's fight for free land in the West, to which people in the slums could emigrate, was more popular—but that stand was inconsistent with Whig political principles. Eventually his stand on the slavery issue led him into the Republican party, and he ended his career by running unsuccessfully for the presidency in 1872 as the candidate of the Liberal Republicans and the Democrats, against General Ulysses S. Grant, candidate of the Whig-minded Republicans.

The Personal Editors

Greeley belonged to the group of editors of the middle nineteenth century called the "personal editors," men who were as well known to their readers as were their newspapers, in contrast to the much more anonymous editors of modern corporate journalism. Some of Greeley's farmer readers were surprised to keep getting the *Tribune* after his death; they assumed the paper would quit publishing, so much did he seem to be the newspaper itself.

William Cullen Bryant, who joined the New York *Evening Post* staff in 1825 and remained to edit it for a half-century, also fell into this category of the personal editor. His journalism was much more reserved than Greeley's and his thinking more logical, but through Bryant's personal editorial opinion, the *Post* exercised considerable influence. He supported Jacksonian democracy and, like Greeley, he showed sympathy for the worker. During the Civil War, he was one of the most effective interpreters of Lincoln's policies. Henry J. Raymond, founder of the New York *Times,* played a personal role outside the newspaper office as a leader in the Republican party, although he tried to make the *Times'* editorial columns calmly interpretive in character.

There were editors outside New York City who made their influence felt during the Civil War period. One was Samuel Bowles III, publisher of the Springfield *Republican* in Massachusetts, a daily of just 6,000 circulation. Bowles' editorial ability was so great that his weekly edition of 12,000 copies rivaled Greeley's 200,000 circulation in reputation and did much to unify the North and Middle West in the pre-Civil War years. Another was Joseph Medill, builder of the Chicago *Tribune,* who was one of Lincoln's firmest supporters. The abolitionist editors, William Lloyd Garrison of the *Liberator* and the martyred Elijah Lovejoy, should be noted too, although they were agitator-pamphleteers.

In the post-Civil War years, the name of Edwin Lawrence Godkin stands out. Godkin founded the *Nation* magazine in 1865 and succeeded Bryant as the driving force of the New York *Evening Post* in 1881. Born in Britain, Godkin decided the United States needed a high-grade weekly journal of opinion and literary criticism similar to those in England. His distinctive style of writing and skill in ironic analysis made the *Nation* a favorite of other intellectuals. William James, the philosopher, said of him: "To my generation his was certainly the towering influence in all thought concerning public affairs, and indirectly his influence has assuredly been more pervasive than that of any other writer of the generation, for he influenced other writers who never quoted him, and determined the whole current of discussion." This was high accomplishment and praise for the editor of a weekly magazine with a circulation of no more than 10,000.

THE NEW JOURNALISM

Between 1865 and 1900, the dynamic capitalism of an expanding America, utilizing vast natural resources and the new machines of the industrial revolution, transformed the national economy. Industrialization, mechanization, and urbanization brought extensive social, cultural, and political changes: the rise of the city, improved transportation and communication, educational advances, political unrest, and the rise of an extensive labor movement. The mass media could not fail to go through great changes along with the society they served. In the world of newspapers, the era is known as that of the "new journalism," a designation used by people who lived through that time to describe the activities of the master editor of the period, Joseph Pulitzer.

In the 35 years between the end of the Civil War and the turn of the century, the population of the country doubled, the national wealth quadrupled, and manufacturing production increased sevenfold. It was the period of the coming of the age of steel, the harnessing of electricity for light and power, and the mechanizing of production processes. National growth and increased wealth meant cultural progress in literature, science, and the social sciences; a great stirring in scholarship and a rapid increase in the number and size of universities; and sharp increases in public school attendance and adult interest in popularized knowledge. Growing social and economic interdependence could be measured by two statistics for the year 1900: a third of the population was urban and 62 percent of the labor force was engaged in nonagricultural work.

Communication facilities expanded in this period of the nationalization of the United States. Telegraph lines and railroad tracks reached near-saturation points; the telephone, coming into use in the 1870s, provided direct communication through intercity lines that covered the country by 1900. The federal postal service greatly extended free carrier service in the cities and instituted free rural delivery in 1897. The low postal rate for newspapers and magazines in 1885 opened the way for cheap delivery of publications. By 1900 there were 3,500 magazines with a combined circulation of 65 million an issue. Weekly newspapers tripled in number between 1870 and 1900, reaching a total of more than 12,000. During the same 30 years, the number of daily newspapers quadrupled and their total circulation increased almost sixfold; the figures for 1900 were 1,967 general circulation dailies selling nearly 15 million copies each day. It was this tremendous increase in the circulation of the printed mass media that was the impetus for inventions such as the rotary press, the typesetting machine, photoengraving, and color printing, which transformed the newspaper into its modern form.

Obviously a new journalism would emerge for this new society. Again, as in the penny press period, there was a new audience: more people were interested in reading; the labor class increased rapidly; and there was a heavy concentration of immigrants in the rapidly growing eastern cities (New York City residents, who increased 50 percent between 1880 and 1890, were 80 percent foreign-born or of foreign parentage). Such readers, stirred by political and social unrest in a period when reform movements sought to readjust the economic balance to bring relief to the worker and farmer, looked for aggressive editorial leadership and opinion-forming crusading in their newspapers and magazines. But they also wanted impartial and thorough coverage of the news. The newspaper that appealed to them was also low-priced, easily read, popularized in content, and bright in appearance. Particularly in the big cities, the entertainment ingredient had to be high, and for the really new readers a new cycle of sensationalism was the major attraction.

Pulitzer and the News

Joseph Pulitzer serves as the symbol of the new journalism era. An immigrant himself, he served his apprenticeship as a reporter before founding the St. Louis *Post-Dispatch* in 1878. In the next five years, Pulitzer built it into the city's leading paper by giving his readers what they wanted. He developed a liberal, aggressive editorial page and gave both the editorial and news columns a fierce crusading spirit. He insisted on accuracy, digging for facts, thoroughness of local news coverage, and good writing. One of his famous commands to his staff was: "Accuracy! Accuracy!! Accuracy!!!" Another was: "Terseness! Intelligent, not stupid, condensation." Still another showed his concern for the lighter side of the news: he reminded reporters to look for both the significant news and the "original, distinctive, dramatic, romantic, thrilling, unique, curious, quaint, humorous, odd, apt to be talked about" news.

In 1883 Pulitzer left the *Post-Dispatch* as his monument in St. Louis and invaded New York City by buying the run down *World.* Within four years the paper had reached a record-breaking 250,000 circulation, had eclipsed the *Herald* as the leader in advertising volume, and had become the country's most talked-about newspaper.

Pulitzer's success lay in the fact that he had not forgotten the basic news function while he was wooing new readers with entertaining and sensational material. He gave his audience its money's worth in the quality and extent of significant news coverage and presented it in an enlivened style.

He poured money into the building of a competent staff of reporters and editors and he kept pace with mechanical innovations that permitted them to fashion a better product. He combined a popular editorial aggressiveness and crusading spirit with great promotional skill to make the mass of readers feel the *World* was their friend. To attract them to its solid news stories and editorial column, the *World* offered big headlines, human interest stories, illustrations, and other sensationalized approaches. With the advent of color printing in the early 1890s, the *World* added popular Sunday supplements and the comic strip.

Some of Pulitzer's competitors did not sense the total character of his journalistic product and mistakenly assumed that sensationalism alone had made the *World* successful. One of these was William Randolph Hearst, who took over the San Francisco *Examiner* in 1887 and then invaded New York in 1895 by buying the *Journal.* The circulation war between Pulitzer's *World* and Hearst's *Journal* brought the cycle of sensationalism to a new height. Critics who eyed one of the comic strip characters of the times, the "Yellow Kid," dubbed the papers "yellow journals." The yellow journal prided itself on being the crusading friend of the "common man," but it underestimated the public's interest in significant news and overestimated its capacity for absorbing gaudy, oversensationalized news. The result was a degrading of the news function that reached its climax during the period of the Spanish-American War. After a few years the *World* and other serious-minded papers withdrew from the competition, leaving the techniques of yellow journalism to Hearst and his imitators. Although the yellow journals cannot be held solely responsible for causing the war, their news policies certainly contributed to the war fever of 1898.

There were other notable leaders in the new journalism era. The master teacher of the art of human interest writing was Charles A. Dana's New York *Sun,* which developed many a great reporter and editor. Dana, however, resisted change, and the *Sun* set its face against the general trend of the times. Edward Wyllis Scripps began developing his group of papers, headed by the Cleveland *Press.* They were low-priced, small in size, well-written and tightly edited, and hard-hitting in both news and editorial columns. Melville Stone's Chicago *Daily News* and William Rockhill Nelson's Kansas City *Star* were two more distinctive new papers fashioned in the new journalism pattern. In the South, Henry W. Grady became known as a master news executive for his work with the Atlanta *Constitution,* and because of his own reporting skill.

THE PEOPLE'S CHAMPIONS: PULITZER, HEARST, SCRIPPS

The rise of the architects of the new journalism in the 1870s and 1880s brought a heightening of attention to the exercise of the opinion function. Joseph Pulitzer, the leading exponent of the new journalism, has been named by his colleagues of this century as the leading American editor of modern times. A memo written by Pulitzer to an editor of his St. Louis *Post-Dispatch* summarizes his idealistic goal for the editorial page:

> . . . every issue of the paper presents an opportunity and a duty to say something courageous and true; to rise above the mediocre and conventional; to say something that will command the respect of the intelligent, the educated, the independent part of the community; to rise above fear of partisanship and fear of popular prejudice.

No finer statement of the responsibility imposed upon those who exercise the newspaper's opinion function has ever been written. Those who can even occasionally meet such a challenge win the respect of both colleagues and readers.

Pulitzer and his contemporaries developed a growing independence of editorial opinion from partisan pressures. They did not hesitate to support political candidates, but they did not do this automatically as part of a political machine, as did the political press. Most of the leaders were champions of the "common man"—people's champions, doing battle against the trusts and monopolies that characterized big business, the crooked politicians who were "the shame of the cities," the moneylenders and the speculators, and the opponents of reform. The majority supported the political leaders of the Democratic party—Grover Cleveland, William Jennings Bryan, Woodrow Wilson—but they also gave aid to such progressive Republicans as Theodore Roosevelt and Robert M. La Follette. Pulitzer himself believed that the Democratic party best carried out the principles he espoused, but he bolted from the radical Bryan candidacy and gave aid and comfort to such New York Republicans as Charles Evans Hughes in the battles with Tammany Hall. His great editor, Frank I. Cobb, who carried on the traditions of the New York *World* after Pulitzer's death in 1911, was a close adviser to Woodrow Wilson and his solid champion. Cobb, however, insisted that it was part of his job to criticize the administration as well as to defend it. This is part of what is meant by "independence of editorial opinion from partisan pressures."

A distinctive feature of the new journalism paper was its eagerness to crusade in behalf of community welfare. Pulitzer developed the coordinated crusade, using both the news and editorial columns, at the *Post-Dispatch,* and that paper remained famous for its tenacious attacks on wrongdoers in public or business life. These words written by Pulitzer in 1907, which became the *Post-Dispatch* editorial platform, sum up the crusading spirit:

> I know that my retirement will make no difference in its cardinal principles; that it will always fight for progress and reform, never tolerate injustice or corruption, always fight demagogues of all parties, never belong to any party, always oppose privileged classes and public plunderers, never lack sympathy with the poor, always remain devoted to the public welfare, never be satisfied with merely printing news,

Three leaders of the "new journalism" who crusaded for reforms on behalf all people. *Top to bottom:* Edward W. Scripps, on his yacht; Joseph Pulitzer, as depicted by John Singer Sargent, American portrait and mural painter; and William Randolph Hearst, at the height of his career.

always be drastically independent, never be afraid to attack wrong, whether by predatory plutocracy or predatory poverty.

William Randolph Hearst, in his New York *Journal* and other newspapers, likewise was a crusading champion of the people. His editorial platform at the turn of the century called for nationalization of the coal mines, railroads, and telegraph lines; public ownership of public franchises; the "destruction of the criminal trust"; a graduated income tax; election of United States senators by popular vote rather than by state legislatures that could be influenced by big business; and extensive new financial support for the public schools. To this he added an active support of labor unions that made them regard his papers as their champions.

One would suppose the liberals of the time would have clasped Hearst to their bosoms. But they did not. They distrusted Hearst's own political ambitions, which extended to the White House; they disliked the bitterness of his editorial attacks upon his opponents. Repelled by the sensationalism and near-cynicism of his news policies, they rejected his editorial page as shallow and insincere. But undoubtedly Hearst had great influence on the ordinary reader of the pre-World War I generation. By the 1920s, however, the Hearst papers were much less progressive in outlook, and by the 1930s their position was almost reversed from the one they had held in 1900. Always strongly nationalistic, in contrast to Pulitzer's support of international cooperation, the Hearst papers became bitterly isolationist by the time of World War I, and remained so even past their founder's death in 1951.

Edward Wyllis Scripps was the third of the great people's champions of the new journalism era. Scripps set his circulation sights on the working people of the smaller but growing industrial cities of the country as he developed his chain of newspapers from his headquarters at the Cleveland *Press.* His social goal was to improve the position of the mass of people through better education, labor union organization and collective bargaining, and a resulting reasonable redistribution of wealth. In this way, he reasoned, a peaceful and productive society could emerge in an industrialized America.

Scripps viewed himself as the only real friend of the "poor and ill-informed." He said his newspapers were the only schoolroom the working person had; the public school system did not serve him or her adequately, and other newspapers were either capitalistic in outlook or too intellectual in their appeal. He pictured himself as a "damned old crank" who was instinctively rebellious against the status quo in any field of human activity. He made a point of running small, tightly edited papers that could assert their independence of the business community and resist any attempted influence by advertisers. But he was businessman enough to make a profit on his journalistic ventures, and his employees found him to be cautious in wage policies. Politically, the Scripps papers were strongly liberal; they supported the third-party candidacies of Theodore Roosevelt in 1912 and Robert M. La Follette in 1924, Woodrow Wilson's New Freedom, the right of workers to organize, and public ownership. This liberal pattern continued after Scripps' death in 1926 and until the late 1930s when, under the influence of the late Roy W. Howard, the Scripps-Howard papers became substantially more conservative.

THE OPINION MAGAZINES

Important among the people's champions of the reform era at the beginning of the twentieth century were the magazines. Dismayed by the bitterness of some of their attacks, Theodore Roosevelt called their work "muckraking," comparing the more sensational writers to the Man with the Muckrake in *Pilgrim's Progress,* who did not look up to see the celestial crown but continued to rake the filth. The magazine men and women, however, considered the appellation a badge of honor.

Magazines had been published since colonial times. Surviving in 1900 were such leaders as the *North American Review,* which began its long career in 1815; *Harper's Monthly,* which appeared in 1850; and the *Atlantic Monthly,* which began in 1857. These literary periodicals were joined by the *Century* in 1881 and *Scribner's* in 1886.

More influential in public affairs were *Harper's Weekly,* edited by George William Curtis and famous for the political cartoons of Thomas Nast; Godkin's *Nation;* the *Independent,* founded in 1848; and the following new arrivals of the 1880s and 1890s: Albert Shaw's *Review of Reviews,* Lyman Abbott's *Outlook,* the *Literary Digest,* and the *Forum.* Three new magazines of the same period that depended upon humor, cartoon, and satire were *Puck, Judge,* and *Life* (the original *Life* featuring the famed Gibson girl drawings).

Entered in the mass circulation field during the 1880s and 1890s were Cyrus H. K. Curtis' *Ladies' Home Journal* and *Saturday Evening Post,* Robert J. Collier's *Collier's,* Frank Munsey's *Munsey's,* S. S. McClure's *McClure's,* and *Cosmopolitan,* which became a Hearst property. Low-priced and popular in appeal, they carried both fiction and nonfiction.

This was an impressive battery of magazines to turn loose during the reform era of the Theodore Roosevelt administrations (all of the public affairs and mass circulation magazines except *Munsey's* and the *Saturday Evening Post* joined in the chase). *McClure's* touched off the major muckraking movement in late 1902 when it offered almost simultaneously Ida M. Tarbell's "History of the Standard Oil Company" and Lincoln Steffens' "Shame of the Cities" series. *Cosmopolitan* countered with "Treason in the Senate," an attack on conservative supporters of "the interests" written by David Graham Phillips, a Pulitzer editorial writer. Samuel Hopkins Adams and Mark Sullivan exposed the patent medicines in *Collier's.*

The elite of the writers moved to John S. Phillips' *American Magazine* in 1906, after a break with McClure. In the crowd were Ida Tarbell, Steffens, Ray Stannard Baker, Finley Peter Dunne ("Mr. Dooley"), and a progressive named William Allen White, who achieved primary fame as the highly personal editor of the Emporia *Gazette* in Kansas. They continued to lead the muckraking movement until it dwindled away by the time of World War I.

Coming on the scene in 1914 was the *New Republic,* featuring the writing of Herbert Croly and Walter Lippmann. Shocking American complacency in the 1920s was H. L. Mencken's *American Mercury.* Of all the magazines listed in this account, only the *Nation* and *New Republic* survived as magazines of dissent, joined at their right by the *National Review. Harper's* and *Atlantic* were the only survivors among the public affairs and literary periodicals; joining them in the quality magazine field that plays a role in opinion formation were the *New Yorker* and *Saturday Review.* Among all the more general magazines mentioned, only the *Ladies' Home Journal* and *Cosmopolitan* are still published. Showing interest in public affairs is a current leader in the general magazine field, *Reader's Digest.* The news magazines—*Time, Newsweek,* and *U.S. News & World Report*—also exercise the opinion function.

TWENTIETH-CENTURY NEWS TRENDS

Impartial gathering and reporting of the news were generally recognized to be the basic obligation of newspapers by the early 1900s. Some did the job in a much more comprehensive and intelligent fashion than others. But the editor who put views ahead of news, and who tied his newspaper to a political machine, had pretty well gone out of style. Slanting of news to fit the prejudices or political preferences of a publisher was also recognized as a detriment, although some newspapers continued the practice. The Canons of Journalism adopted by the American Society of Newspaper Editors in 1923 contain these two paragraphs, which summarize the aspirations of modern journalistic leaders:

> The right of a newspaper to attract and hold readers is restricted by nothing but considerations of public welfare. The use a newspaper makes of the share of public attention it gains serves to determine its sense of responsibility, which it shares with every member of its staff. A journalist who uses his power for any selfish or otherwise unworthy purpose is faithless to a high trust.
>
> Partisanship, in editorial comment which knowingly departs from the truth, does violence to the best spirit of American journalism; in the news columns it is subversive of a fundamental principle of the profession.

No matter how impartial and well intentioned a newspaper's editors might be, they had to expend an increasing effort on comprehensive coverage and display of the news, and its intelligent interpretation, if they were to meet their full responsibilities. Great events of this century made the business of reporting the news far more complex, decade by decade. In the first decade, the story was one of economic and political reform in the United States. In the second decade, it was World War I. In the third decade, it was the world's effort at postwar readjustment. The fourth decade brought the Great Depression and a collapse of world order. The fifth brought World War II, the atomic era, and the cold war; the sixth and seventh the climactic crises of Korea and Vietnam. The eighth decade brought Watergate and continuing international crises.

The mass media made a reasonable effort to fulfill their increased responsibilities for interpreting the news of events that all but overwhelmed the world. Professional standards had to be raised to meet the challenge. Better-trained and more knowledgeable men and women came to occupy key reportorial assignments and news desk posts. The range of subject matter with which a Washington correspondent had to be familiar in the 1920s was narrow indeed compared to the complexities of Washington news in the 1970s. And since all news tended to become local in its impact with the narrowing of geographic barriers in the atomic age, every general assignment reporter had to know far more about such areas as international affairs, science, and economic trends than did his or her predecessors. The modern press associations, particularly, were put under heavy pressures. Newspapers were stimulated by the appearance of new competitors: radio, television, and the news magazine. Radio and television challenged the newspaper both in providing spot news coverage and in news analysis. The news magazines competed with the newspapers by giving the reader background information and point-of-view interpretation. Together, the print and electronic media offered a persistent reader-listener-viewer a sizable amount of information about the swirl of events that virtually engulfed even the most conscientious citizen.

The New York *Times*

The editors of the New York *Times* built what is generally conceded to be the greatest single news machine of this century, publishing what was called by its admiring competitors a "newspaper of record." The story of the growth of the *Times* since Adolph S. Ochs rescued it from bankruptcy in 1896 illustrates the trend in acceptance of the news function responsibility, even though it is the story of an atypical journalistic leader. For what the *Times* did in its methodical completeness was done at least in part, and in some respects as successfully, by other responsible newspapers.

Ochs told his readers in 1896: "It will be my aim . . . to give the news impartially, without fear or favor. . . ." He also promised them all the news, in concise and attractive form, and a paper that would be "a forum for the consideration of all questions of public importance, and to that end . . .

invite intelligent discussion from all shades of opinion." He made no attempt to match the sensationalism of the yellow journals of the time, and he shunned many of the popularized entertainment features of most newspapers, including the comic strip. His Sunday magazine featured articles of current news significance and became, with its 1.4 million circulation of today, an important fixture in the magazine world. His book review section became the best known in the country. His coverage of financial and business news soon matched that of any older competitor. His editorial page, if quieter and more cautious than that of Pulitzer, was intelligently directed.

What made the *Times* great, however, was not so much these accomplishments as its persistence in gathering and printing the news in all its varied aspects. One of the great managing editors, Carr V. Van Anda, was given control of the *Times* newsroom in 1904 with the understanding that he should do whatever it took to do a comprehensive job with the news. Ochs was willing to spend money to get the news; Van Anda was willing to do the spending, and he knew how to get the news. World War I gave Van Anda an opportunity to show his ability. Using the cables and wireless almost with abandon, the *Times* added the reports of its own correspondents to those of the press associations and syndicates. It reported in detail not only on military operations, but on political and economic developments in the European capitals. War pictures were carried in a rotogravure section added in 1914. Most importantly, the paper began to publish the texts of documents and speeches. The Treaty of Versailles filled eight pages—more than any other American paper was willing to give that important document. This policy, combined with the publication of the annual *New York Times Index*, made the *Times* the leading newspaper for librarians, scholars, government officials, and other newspaper editors.

If there was any complaint to be registered against the *Times* of the Van Anda period, it was that the paper presented a voluminous amount of news without sufficient interpretation or screening for the average reader. The objective fashion of reporting was considered the best, if impartiality was to be achieved, as late as the 1920s. But Van Anda did a goodly share of interpreting the news, and the editors who followed him did more. The Washington and foreign staffs built by the paper ranked with the best, and during the following decades they came to offer interpretive analysis along with factual reporting.

The *Daily News*

One more wave of sensationalism, however, was to precede the "era of interpretation." The 1920s were known as the Jazz Age, and the papers that catered to a new group of readers won the dubious honor of being identified as Jazz Journalism. Their sensationalism was accompanied by the two identifying techniques of the period: the tabloid format and great emphasis on photography.

Leading the sensationalist tabloids was the New York *Illustrated Daily News,* founded in 1919 by Joseph Medill Patterson, cousin of Robert R. McCormick and partner with him in the publishing of the Chicago *Tribune.* Patterson, unlike his ultraconservative Chicago cousin, was unconventional in his socioeconomic beliefs—socialistic, his wealthy friends said. He wanted to reach and influence the lowest literate class of Americans and was attracted to the tabloid format by the success Lord Northcliffe was enjoying with it in England. The *Daily News* appeared with a photograph spread across its front half-page and was well stuffed with pictures, human interest stories, and entertaining features. By 1924 it had the largest circulation of any newspaper in the country, a position it continued to hold by a wide margin until surpassed by the *Wall Street Journal* in 1980.

The tabloid format, it should be noted, did not have to be equated with sensationalism. It was used by other papers that were similar to the dailies of conventional size in all respects but that of the half-fold style.

Interpretive Reporting

This type of more skillful, yet impartial, handling of the news was not unknown before the 1930s. But by then the socioeconomic revolution known politically as the New Deal, coupled with the impact of international crises, forced editors to emphasize "why" along with "who did what." Old-style objectivity, which called for the reporter to stick to a factual account of what had been said or done, did not give the reader the full meaning of the news. The new concept of objectivity was based on the premise that the reader needed to have a given event placed in its proper perspective if truth was to be served. Also discarded were older assumptions that subjects such as science and economics could not be made interesting to a mass readership. Reporter-specialists who could talk both to their subjects and to a popular reading audience emerged to cover politics, foreign affairs, business, science, labor, agriculture, and urban affairs.

E. W. Scripps' Science Service began blazing one trail in 1921, along with such reporters as William L. Laurence of the New York *Times* and Howard W. Blakeslee of the Associated Press. In labor news, two pioneers were Louis Stark of the *Times* and Edwin A. Lahey of the Chicago *Daily News.* The 1960s saw the rise of urban and architectural specialists such as Ada Louise Huxtable of the New York *Times* and Wolf Von Eckardt of the Washington *Post.* Examples of successful interpretive writers in Washington are Jack Nelson, Los Angeles *Times* bureau chief; David Broder, Washington *Post* political columnist; Elizabeth Drew, the *New Yorker's* political correspondent; and syndicated columnist Mary McGrory.

ANOTHER NEW JOURNALISM

In the late 1960s the literature of the mass media began to herald a New Journalism that borrowed the title of the innovations of the 1880s. Its reportorial and writing techniques were variously described as tell-it-as-you-see-it, impressionistic, saturation, humanistic, investigative—and even interpretive. Its second and more controversial characteristic was described as advocacy, activist, or participatory. The latter trend merely reflected the widespread frustration of the era and the demand that the conservative establishment give heed and power to others—youth, minorities, women. The mass media should be used, the argument ran, to further such reforms.

Perhaps the leading spirit of this new journalism was Tom Wolfe, although he viewed his efforts as a revolt against old-fashioned book writing rather than news writing. Other major figures were Truman Capote, Norman Mailer, Gay Talese, and Jimmy Breslin. Their work appeared in *Esquire,* the *New Yorker, Harper's,* and the fast-rising *New York.* Those magazines, the old New York *Herald Tribune,* and such underground papers as the *Village Voice* served as vehicles for the new style of reporting, perhaps best described as "saturation." Capote's *In Cold Blood,* although a novel, demonstrated intense journalistic research; Mailer's description of the antiwar demonstrators' march on the Pentagon was powerfully impressionistic; Talese utilized incredible detail in his account of life at the New York *Times* in *The Kingdom and the Power;* Breslin made his readers feel the crunch of police clubs on their skulls as he wrote of the 1968 Democratic convention riots in Chicago.

Out of that 1968 crisis came the best-known example of advocacy journalism. The *Chicago Journalism Review* was founded in October 1968 in the wake of disillusionment among young Chicago newspeople over management and public reaction to the role of the press in the riots. Edited by Ron Dorfman, the monthly aggressively criticized the city's press and offered a forum for general media criticism and self-improvement until its demise in 1975. Across the country similar publications appeared, among them the late New York review, [*MORE*]. In many city rooms "reporter power" movements developed among young staff members who sought to make their professional contributions more meaningful and also challenged the established system of command. Among the advocacy journalists were Gloria Steinem, Jack Anderson, Seymour Hersh, and Sander Vanocur.

First of the underground papers spawned by the sexual revolution and the credibility gap was the *Village Voice,* founded in 1955 and boasting such contributors as Norman Mailer, Jules Feiffer, and Jack Newfield. Art Kunkin's *Los Angeles Free Press* proved more radical and antiestablishment. Best known of the campus-based papers was the *Berkeley Barb,* founded by Max Scherr as spokesman for the free speech movement and a passionate opponent of the older educational order. San Francisco's

SM14170 OCTOBER 25th, 1975/ISSUE NO. 198 85¢UK30p

ROLLING STONE®

THE INSIDE STORY

By HOWARD KOHN AND DAVID WEIR

PATTY HEARST and Emily Harris waited on a grimy Los Angeles street, fighting their emotions as they listened to a radio rebroadcasting the sounds of their friends dying. On a nearby corner Bill Harris dickered over the price of a battered old car.

Only blocks away, rifle cartridges were exploding in the dying flames of a charred bungalow. The ashes were still too hot to retrieve the bodies of the six SLA members who had died hours before on the afternoon of May 17th, 1974.

Bill Harris shifted impatiently as the car's owner patted a dented fender. "I want five bills for this mother."

The SLA survivors had only $400. Reluctantly Harris offered $350. The man quickly pocketed the money.

Minutes later Bill picked up Patty and Emily and steered onto a freeway north to San Francisco. They drove all night—the Harrises in the front seat of the noisy car and Patty in back, hidden under a blanket. They were too tense to sleep, each grappling with the aftershock of the fiery deaths.

They exited twice at brightly lit service station clusters that flank Interstate 5, checking out each before picking what looked like the safest attendant. They made no other stops and reached San Francisco in the predawn darkness.

The three fugitives drove to a black ghetto with rows of ramshackle Victorians—and sought out a friend. Bill and Emily's knocks brought the man sleepy-eyed to the door.

"You're alive!" Then he panicked. "You can't stay here. The whole state is gonna be crawling with pigs looking for you." He gave them five dollars and shut the door. "Don't come back."

The Harrises returned to the car and twisted the ignition key. Patty poked her head out from under the blanket. "What's the matter? Why won't it start?"

The fugitives had no choice—to continue fiddling with the dead battery might attract attention—so they abandoned the car. Walking the streets, however, was a worse alternative.

"C'mon Tania," said Emily. "You better bring the blanket." Bill and Emily both carried duffel bags. Inside were weapons, disguises and tattered books.

A few blocks away, under a faded Victorian, they spotted a crawl space, a gloomy cave for rats and runaway dogs. As Patty and the Harrises huddled in the dirt under the old house, the noise of a late-night party began in the living room above. Patty gripped her homemade machine gun. "The pigs must have found the car!"

"Shhh," came a whispered response. "Shut up, goddamnit. Please shut up!"

[Continued on page 41]

14023

A series of exclusive stories helped the *Rolling Stone*, a San Francisco underground newspaper, rise to prominence in the mid 1970s. (Reprinted by permission of the publisher.)

Rolling Stone became highly successful in the mid 1970s. Among other underground papers that enjoyed at least brief fame were Chicago's *Seed*, Boston's *Avatar*, and New York's *East Village Other*.

Combining radical dissent and underground qualities were such pungent political journals as *I. F. Stone's Weekly* (1953–1971), the *Guardian* of New York, the *Texas Observer*, and Bruce Brugmann's *San Francisco Bay Guardian*, a crusading opponent of that city's orthodox press.

THE BLACK PRESS

Only recently have the American mass media exhibited an understanding interest in the black 10 percent of citizens; even so, the capacity to be sensitive to blacks as readers or viewers has been severely limited. There has always been a clear need for a black press.

More than 3000 such newspapers—owned and edited by blacks for black readers—have appeared since the first, *Freedom's Journal,* in 1827. But the black community has had few socioeconomic resources to support a press. Historically, the average life span of a black newspaper has been nine years. Henry G. La Brie III, a research specialist on the black press, found that 213 black newspapers were being published in 1974, of which only 11 had founding dates before 1900, as compared to 90 founded since 1960. Total circulation was 4.3 million; only five were dailies; and only 38 had their own printing equipment. In 1979 he found only 165 black papers surviving, with a total circulation of 2.9 million. But collectively this struggling press had made its impact on the country.

"We wish to plead our own cause. Too long have others spoken for us," said the editors of *Freedom's Journal,* John B. Russwurm and Samuel Cornish, in 1827. The first black journalist to do that effectively was Frederick Douglass, the remarkable ex-slave who founded *The North Star* in 1847 and became the symbol of hope for blacks of his generation and of today. Douglass helped rally public opinion against slavery and through his writing and speaking helped white men and women to see the degradation of slavery through black eyes. Published in Rochester, New York, *The North Star* reached a circulation of 3000 in the United States and Europe, particularly among influential readers. Renamed *Frederick Douglass' Paper* in 1851, it survived until the Civil War. Douglass then edited magazines for 15 years. He wrote three autobiographies, tracing the career of an ex-slave who became a skillful editor, polished orator, and inspiring leader.

Ranking in fame with Douglass is W. E. B. Du Bois, who founded *The Crisis* in 1910 as the militant protest voice of the National Association for the Advancement of Colored People. "Mentally the Negro is inferior to the white," said the 1911 *Britannica;* to Du Bois, this belief was the crisis that had to be eliminated before discrimination in education, housing, and social status could be overcome.

Just as the standard daily press grew in numbers, circulation, and stature during the new journalism era between 1880 and World War I, so did the black press. Important papers today founded in that period include the largest, New York's *Amsterdam News* (1909); the leading papers in the two most important publishing groups, Baltimore's *Afro-American* (1892) and the Chicago *Defender* (1905); and the Pittsburgh *Courier* (1910), Philadelphia *Tribune* (1884), and Norfolk's *Journal and Guide* (1909). Among the major figures in black publishing up until 1910 were Robert S.

Rhodesian pact could mean war

(See page 4)

Chicago Defender

CHICAGO'S DAILY PICTURE NEWSPAPER

WEATHER

Today will be mostly cloudy, cold, high in the 20s.

VOL. LXXIII - NO. 201 — THURSDAY, FEBRUARY 16, 1978 — 20¢ Outside of Chicago — 15¢

Postal workers at O'Hare in uproar

By PHYLISS HUDSON

A union representative speaking for minority employees at the post office's O'Hare facility charged that black workers were discriminated against by the distribution of administrative leave.

During last month's blizzard,the post office put its administrative leave policy into effect. Employees who made an "honest effort" but could not get to work because of adverse weather conditions were a full day pay.

At the O'Hare facility, officials decided to give administrative leave to workers who live in the suburbs. According to Grady Davis, a representative of the employees, the majority of the black workers live in the city and most of the whites live in the suburbs.

"The administrative leave should be based on your effort to get to work," said Davis, who is also on the executive board of the American Postal Workers Union, "and not on where you live."

Davis said the facility employes about 500 workers, of which 300 are black. He stated many employees were forced to use their vacation time for the days they were unable to get to work. The representative said the workers were "upset" when their checks came up short.

Tom Messick, of the post office, said employees who live near public transportation, such as the CTA, were expected to come to work. "Public transportation doesn't really serve the suburbs," he stated. "Those people who live in the suburbs have a harder time getting to work."

Messick denied charges that the administrative policy was discriminatory and said black employees who live in the suburbs were given the same treatment as the whites.

Davis, who lives on the South side and has worked at the O'Hare facility for 14 years, said he was held up on the Dan Ryan Expressway for three hours on Jan. 26. "I made every effort I could to get to work but I have no control over the weather," he explained. "Other black employees who live in the city had similiar problems."

(Continued on page 3)

Make temporary repairs...

Taking advantage of a lull between snows, a crew from the Department of Streets and Sanitation does "cold patching" of a few of the many potholes in the Chicago streets. An official of the department explained that only after the last of the snows (whenever that is) and after the spring thaw, can the permanent street repairs be done.

Burglar slain over snowblower

A 24-year-old burglar was shot to death early Wednesday, after he apparently tried to heist a snowblower from the garage of a Southside meat packer.

The deceased, Andrew Sanders of 7840 S. Cregier, was pronounced dead at Jackson Park Hospital from a gunshot wound in the neck. Police said that Sanders had an accomplice who is still at large, after he vanished into the pre-dawn darkness.

According to reports, there are no charges presently against the meat packer 52-year-old who lives on S. Cornell.

The man told investigators he was preparing to leave for work when he heard the frantic barking of his dog from the backyard, so he armed himself and went to investigate.

Approaching the back door, he reportedly saw one of the burglars, who spotted him, and warned his accomplice, Sanders, as he fled.

Sanders however was less fortunate and was felled by a bullet as he attempted to run from the scene.

Police said that nothing was taken from the garage, and they were unsure what the burglars were after until the homeowner showed them the snowblower, just visible to the left inside the garage door.

A typical front page of the Chicago *Defender*, one of America's leading black newspapers.

Abbott of the Chicago *Defender*, John H. Murphy, Sr., of the *Afro-American*, Robert L. Vann of the Pittsburgh *Courier*, T. Thomas Fortune of the New York *Age*, and William Monroe Trotter of the Boston *Guardian*.

In 1970, Abbott's nephew, John H. Sengstacke, was elected to the board of the American Society of Newspaper Editors, the first black to be thus honored. Sengstacke was head of the Chicago *Defender* group, which included the Pittsburgh *Courier* and the *Michigan Chronicle* of Detroit. John H. Murphy III headed the *Afro-American* papers.

Out of 45 efforts to publish dailies in the United States for blacks, as recorded by Professor Armistead Scott Pride of Lincoln University, only the Chicago *Defender* and the Atlanta *Daily World* have published for long periods, the latter since 1932. Its founder, William A. Scott, was murdered in 1934; his successor, Cornelius A. Scott, produced an essentially conservative newspaper. Most of the leading black papers have been moderate in tone, heavily local in news coverage, strong in sports and social news, and occasionally crusading.

Largest in audited circulation in 1980 was the *Amsterdam News* with 51,000 copies. Second was the Los Angeles *Sentinel,* founded in 1934 and edited by Ruth Washington as a mildly sensationalist and liberal paper. By far the largest in unaudited circulation was *Muhammad Speaks,* voice of the Nation of Islam, reportedly rolling 625,000 copies weekly out of its ultramodern Chicago plant. The *Central News-Wave* group of free circulation weeklies in Los Angeles totaled 233,000 for seven editions. The *Black Panther,* voice of the radical left, once claimed 100,000 copies in circulation. The *Defender* group had circulation claims exceeding 100,000; the *Afro-American* group, some 600,000. Historically, black newspaper circulations peaked during the World War II period, when the Pittsburgh *Courier* achieved a national circulation of 286,000. As the regular press covered stories involving racial issues better, black newspaper readership declined, and community-based weeklies replaced the nationally circulating papers.

If there was a single major voice in black journalism in the 1970s, it was *Ebony,* the monthly picture magazine founded by John H. Johnson in 1945 in full imitation of *Life.* By 1980 it had a circulation of 1.2 million copies. Johnson also published *Jet, Tan,* and *Black World,* the latter an outlet for black authors. *Essence,* a New York-based women's magazine founded in 1970, had zoomed past 600,000 circulation by 1980. *Encore,* a biweekly news magazine, had a circulation of 150,000.

THE NEWS MAGAZINES

The news magazines offered a relatively small segment of the population another means of keeping abreast of events. *Time,* the largest in circulation, had 4.2 million subscribers by 1980; *Newsweek* had nearly 3 million; and *U.S. News & World Report,* 2 million. Although some issues go to subscribers who use them to bulwark inadequate news coverage by small local newspapers, many go to relatively well-informed citizens who read one or more daily newspapers, listen to television and radio news, subscribe to public affairs magazines, read books, and take one to three news magazines.

Henry R. Luce's formula for *Time* was to organize and departmentalize the news of the week in a style "written as if by one man for one man," whom *Time* described as too busy to spend all the time necessary to peruse the other media. Coverage of national affairs, foreign affairs, science, religion, education, business, and other areas was to be written for this busy person, not for experts in each of the fields. The magazine developed a large research and library staff, as well as its own good-sized newsgathering organization, to supplement press association services. Begun in 1923, *Time* helped to drive the older *Literary Digest* out of business with this approach. *Newsweek* appeared in 1933, with an almost identical format. *U.S. News & World Report,* which grew out of a combination of two of David Lawrence's publications in Washington, hit its stride in the late 1940s. Two picture news magazines, Luce's *Life* (1936) and Gardner Cowles' *Look* (1937), offered additional news coverage and interpretive articles.

It should be noted that the news magazines offered their readers both news and opinion. *Time* made no attempt to distinguish between the two functions, intermingling opinion and editorial hypotheses with straight news. Its use of narrative and human interest techniques, and overuse of adjectives, added to its editorial bias. *Time* said it wanted to be "fair," not objective or even impartial. The trouble was, some readers mistook *Time's* "fairness" (opinion-giving) for factual reporting. *Newsweek* injected less opinion into its columns and offered separate editorial opinions written by commentators.

THE PRESS ASSOCIATIONS

The major job of newsgathering beyond the local level is done not by the mass media themselves, but by the two big associations, Associated Press and United Press International. Newspapers, of course, cover their own local communities (although sometimes they even use press association reports about events taking place in their own cities). Some newspapers maintain area or state coverage through strings of correspondents who filter in news to a state desk; this practice varies from one part of the country to another, and many a large paper depends upon the press associations for news of events as close as 50 miles from the city room. Only a small percentage of American dailies have their own Washington coverage, and the bulk of this is directed toward stories of regional or local interest, rather than the major news stories of the day. And only a handful of newspapers have their own correspondents abroad. The situation is much the same in television and radio, where the press associations supply virtually all the news for smaller stations, all but local news for many larger stations, and even the bulk of the news for the network affiliated stations.

The news magazines, too, use the press association reports for the basis of their work.

Cooperative newsgathering in this country began, as we have seen, in 1848 with the Associated Press of New York. The telegraph enabled the New York papers that controlled this early AP to sell its news to a gradually expanding group of papers. The opening of the Atlantic cable in 1866 gave the agency better access to European news, which it obtained under exchange agreements with Reuters of Great Britain, Havas of France, and other press services. Regional AP groups formed, the most powerful of which was the Western Associated Press. The dailies outside New York City resented the tight-fisted control of the AP by the New York morning dailies that had founded it; the new evening dailies of the Midwest felt they were being ignored in the supplying of news on the two differing time cycles for morning and evening publication.

A bitter battle broke out among the newspapers in the 1880s. Control of the AP fell to the Western members, headed by Melville E. Stone, founder of the Chicago *Daily News.* Stone drafted exclusive news exchange contracts with the European agencies, cutting off the New York papers from their traditional supply of foreign news, and broke his rivals by 1897. An adverse court ruling in Illinois threatened the membership status of the AP at this same moment, so its headquarters were returned to New York in 1900.

The basis of the AP was its cooperative exchange of news. The members found it necessary to finance a larger and larger staff, however, and that staff took over direction of the flow of news and eventually much of the newsgathering. Its organizational structure was not entirely democratic; the older and larger newspapers kept control of the board of directors by giving themselves extra voting rights during the 1900 reorganization. Until an adverse Supreme Court decision in 1945, an AP member could prevent the entry of a direct competitor into the group by exercising a protest right that could be overridden only by a four-fifths vote of the entire membership.

Newspapers that could not gain entry to the AP, or that disliked its control by the older morning papers of the East, needed press association service from another source. Edward Wyllis Scripps, possessing both a string of evening dailies and an individualistic temperament that made him dislike monopoly, founded the United Press Associations in 1907 from earlier regional agencies. William Randolph Hearst, whose newly founded papers were denied AP memberships, started the International News Service in 1909. Other agencies came and went, but the AP, UP, and INS survived until 1958, when the Hearst interests liquidated a losing business by merging the INS into the UP to form United Press International.

The strong men in the AP over the years were Stone, the first general manager, and Kent Cooper, general manager from 1925 to 1948. Builders of the UP were Roy W. Howard, who later became a partner in the Scripps-Howard newspaper group, and presidents Karl A. Bickel and Hugh Baillie. More recently, Wes Gallagher became president and general manager of AP, followed by Keith Fuller, while Roderick W. Beaton became president of UPI.

Unlike the AP plan of organization, the UP and INS had a service to sell to clients. Howard set out to do this job for the young and struggling UP by building up a foreign service, first in Latin America and then in Europe. He embarrassed his agency by sending a premature flash announcing the end of World War I, but both Howard and the UP survived the incident. The enthusiasm and aggressiveness of the "shoestring" UP operation brought it into competitive position with the AP by the 1930s. In 1934 Kent Cooper brought an end to the restrictive news exchange agreements between the AP and foreign news agencies, and the AP joined in the foreign service race more determinedly. The AP also capitulated in supplying news to radio stations five years after UP and INS entered that field in 1935, and made the radio and television stations associate members, without voting rights. The INS, smallest of the three agencies, did not attempt to supply news at the state level except in a few states; it concentrated instead on outreporting and outwriting the other two on major news breaks and features. The UP-INS merger put United Press International in a position of competitive equality with its older rival in gathering and distributing the news, but by 1980, UPI was suffering substantial financial losses in its effort to ensure that there would be an intense rivalry between two well-managed worldwide press associations.

SOME CURRENT NEWSPAPER LEADERS

Opinions differ about the quality of individual newspapers; any "list of ten" compiled by one authority would differ to some degree from the listing made by a second competent observer. But newspeople generally agree that a top-flight newspaper must offer both impartial and comprehensive coverage of the news as a first prerequisite for national recognition. The second prerequisite for recognition by the craft is a superior demonstration of responsibility in providing community opinion leadership and of integrity and zealousness in protecting basic human liberties. The second prerequisite is much harder to judge than the first.

The United States, unlike many other countries, has no truly national newspapers. It has two dailies without "home communities," however, that have won widespread respect and that circulate nationally with their regionally edited editions. These are the *Christian Science Monitor* and the *Wall Street Journal* (neither of which carries a nameplate that seems to indicate the general-interest character of the paper). The *Monitor,* founded in 1908 by the Church of Christ, Scientist, built a high reputation for its Washington and foreign correspondence and its interpretive articles. Edited by Erwin D. Canham from 1945 to 1970, it serves 175,000 readers in this country and abroad from its offices in Boston. The *Wall Street Journal's* staff, led by Bernard Kilgore from 1941 to his death in 1967, has seen its readership rise from 30,000 to more than 1.6 million to make the paper the nation's largest. It is produced in 12 regional plants, using satellite or microwave transmissions of ready-to-print pages from its New York office. It won its position on the basis of its excellent writing, coverage of important news, and specialized business reporting.

The New York *Times,* generally recognized as the country's leading daily and newspaper of record, also has a sizable national circulation, particularly for its Sunday edition. It clearly has been the leader over a period of time in developing its own Washington and foreign staffs, whose stories are also sold to other papers. Publisher-owner Arthur Hays Sulzberger ably carried on the duties of his father-in-law, Adolph S. Ochs, after Ochs' death in 1935 and maintained a remarkable news institution to which many staff members—editors and reporters—contributed leadership. His son, Arthur Ochs Sulzberger, succeeded to power in the late 1960s and favored the judgments of reporter-columnist James Reston and news executive A. M. Rosenthal, who directed the paper's Pentagon Papers publication. In the late 1970s the *Times* added popularized sections—Weekend, Living, Sports Monday, Business Day—to its solid fare in order to maintain its readership appeal.

Across the continent, the Los Angeles *Times* surged forward in the 1960s to reach the top levels of American newspaper journalism. Young publisher Otis Chandler and a competent staff turned the paper to a more progressive editorial outlook than it had exhibited in earlier years, plunged vigorously into civic affairs, and vastly improved the news content. Chandler joined with the Washington *Post's* owners in establishing a spectacularly successful news syndicate covering the nation's capital and worldwide news centers. The *Times'* editorial page showed intellectual depth and enjoyed the cartooning skill of Paul Conrad. By 1980 the paper had passed 1 million in circulation and reflected reportorial skill and influence in national and state affairs.

Rising to prominence since the 1930s has been the Washington *Post.* Financier Eugene Meyer and his son-in-law, Philip L. Graham, the paper's publishers, had as their major aim the molding of a vigorous, intelligent, and informative editorial page for capital readers. This they accomplished, with the help of an able staff who could tap Washington news sources for background and interpretation, and the provocative cartoons of Herbert L. Block. Meyer's daughter, Katharine Graham, maintained the *Post's* quality after the deaths of her father and husband in the 1960s, and pushed the *Post* to levels of news excellence that ranked it with the New York *Times* and the Los Angeles *Times.* The *Post's* major role in Washington reporting (see Chapter 19) won it wide public attention and the admiration of others in the media.

The St. Louis *Post-Dispatch,* published by a third generation of the Pulitzer family, continued to offer American journalism an excellent example of the exercise of the opinion function—excelling the standard set by Joseph Pulitzer's New York *World,* which ceased publishing in 1931. A talented *Post-Dispatch* editorial page staff, writing superbly and with a depth of understanding on a wide variety of subjects, made the editorial columns outstanding. The paper continued to win recognition for its crusading zeal and its outstanding Washington bureau.

Known as "Milwaukee's Dutch Uncle," the staff-owned Milwaukee *Journal* has demonstrated editorial page excellence since the days of founder Lucius W. Nieman. The *Journal* has paid close attention to city and state affairs and has cultivated both good writing and a wide grasp of political and human affairs on the part of its good-sized group of editorial writers. The same characteristics have been exhibited by the Louisville *Courier-Journal,* owned and edited by Barry Bingham, Sr., and his son, Barry Bingham, Jr. Both these papers enjoy local and regional news reporting of excellent depth.

Moving up in rankings by media peers are the Miami *Herald* and the Boston *Globe.* The *Herald,* emerging as the most dynamic paper in the South, was started on its way by Lee Hills, later executive editor of all Knight newspaper group dailies, who built its Latin American area coverage. Boston's century-old *Globe,* guided by sons of earlier executives, publisher William Taylor and editor Thomas Winship, won attention for investigative reporting, political writing, and community leadership during the 1970s, in a long school desegregation controversy.

A change of style and outlook from the ultraconservative stance given it by owner Robert R. McCormick and maintained through the 1960s brought the Chicago *Tribune* an enhanced national reputation and improved circulation in Chicago. Editor Clayton Kirkpatrick played a guiding role in reducing controversial activities and in encouraging revitalized reporting that won three Pulitzer prizes for local investigative work and one in international reporting before 1980.

Among other papers of high quality, those respected for their news skills include Long Island's *Newsday,* the Baltimore *Sun,* Philadelphia *Inquirer,* and Toledo *Blade* in the East; the Chicago *Sun-Times,* Minneapolis *Star* and *Tribune,* and Kansas City *Star* in the Midwest; the Atlanta *Constitution,* Charlotte *Observer,* and Memphis *Commercial Appeal* in the South; and the Denver *Post* in the West. Another dozen could be named with almost equal justice to such a list of current leaders in exercising the news function.

Although all these newspapers have capable editorial pages, some have won particular attention. When one turns to newspapers that have won top recognition for their editorial leadership and for their aggressiveness in defense of basic liberal principles of a progressive democracy, the names of four are readily apparent: the Washington *Post,* the St. Louis *Post-Dispatch,* the Milwaukee *Journal,* and the Louisville *Courier-Journal.* Examples of effective conservative opinion are found in the editorial columns of the Los Angeles *Times,* the *Christian Science Monitor,* the Chicago *Tribune,* and the *Wall Street Journal.*

As Gerald Johnson once said, "The greatest newspaper is as difficult to identify as the greatest man—it all depends upon what you require." Certainly an intelligent, honest, and public-spirited editorial page is as much an essential of an effective newspaper as is comprehensive and honest reporting and display of the news.

Chapter 5

NEWSPAPERS

THE CHANGING NEWSPAPER

Huge saucers ten feet wide started to appear atop newspaper buildings across the United States as the 1980s began. Plucking news stories and photographs out of space, these satellite receiving antennas symbolize the fundamental and fascinating changes through which the newspaper industry has been passing.

Newspapers once received their news from the press associations by Morse telegraph wire in dots and dashes, copied by hand at 30 words a minute. Now dispatches flash on video screens in electronic newsrooms after being bounced off a communications satellite 22,300 miles above the earth. Some dispatches arrive at 10,000 words a minute.

This new form of news transmission, freed from costly, trouble-plagued wires and teletype machines, is a small but dramatic portion of the upheaval that has shaken newspapers during the past quarter-century in methods, appearance, attitudes, personnel, and news goals and styles. As the age of electronics develops, even the most astute publishers and editors are uncertain about future changes in methods of production and distribution. The challenges ahead will test the best minds in a business long known for attracting tough, resilient people.

Editors have been jarred into acceptance of fresh approaches to coverage that reach beyond the rigid traditionalism of crime, tragedy, and politics as primary sources of news. Now, most editors recognize that readers also want articles that help them to deal with the complexities of contemporary life and to understand the "why" of the news. Interpretations of what news includes are changing along with the ways of producing it.

Despite the changes in techniques, however, the fundamental role of newspapers remains unaltered. They continue to be the written record of contemporary civilization. They report in detail events great and small, from the Carter-Reagan-Anderson presidential campaign to the automobile collision down the street. Despite the handicap of short-range perspective forced on them by the demands of daily, indeed hourly, deadlines, they seek increasingly to evaluate the news as well as report it. The word "perspective" is heard and pondered more among today's editors than it was among those of the past. To achieve balance and significance tests the technical skill and intellectual capacity of editors and writers because they operate under severe time pressures in a society whose standards are in flux. Few absolutes guide their decisions. They work not in the luxury of contemplation, but under the tyranny of the clock.

For the majority of the population, newspapers probably still are the basic news medium. They have been outdistanced by television in speed and visual punch, but they still provide greater depth and variety of reporting than television can, and with more lasting impact. Wise editors recognize the changes television has brought about and seek to focus their efforts on the function they can perform most valuably. Without newspapers, the American public simply could not be well informed.

In this chapter we shall look at newspapers in operation. We shall observe the roles individuals play in producing them; examine the changes in technology that have swept from the mechanical departments into the newsrooms, intertwining departments that in the old days were often run as antagonistic empires; and discuss the problems that must be solved before the first copies of the latest edition are delivered.

Approximately 62 million copies of daily newspapers are sold each day. The term *newspaper* covers a surprisingly broad range of publications. It includes publications ranging from the small weekly in which every task is done by a handful of people to the huge metropolitan daily with a staff of thousands and a daily circulation of nearly 1 million copies.

No matter what their circumstances, all newspapers are alike in the sense that they are made of type, ink, and newsprint. They exist to inform and influence the communities in which they are published, and the men and women who produce them share a common urge to get the news and advertising into print. Into the pages of every newspaper goes an essential but intangible extra ingredient, the minds and spirits of those who make it.

Newspaper work is an adventure, so full of fresh experiences that men and women who have been in it for years still come to work with a subconscious wonder about what unexpected developments the day will bring. It is based upon a firmly disciplined routine, because "getting the paper out'' on time is paramount, and this can be done only if a definite work pattern exists in all departments.

The exciting things that can happen within that framework are innumerable. For those in the news department, there is the stimulation of being on the inside of big developments, of watching history being made, and of meeting intriguing people. For those who work in advertising and circulation, there is satisfaction in conceiving and executing ideas that bring in money and influencing people through skill with words. Working on a newspaper is an open invitation to create ideas and put them to work. The newspaper people who succeed best are those who handle the necessary routine meticulously and bring to their jobs an extra spark of creative thinking. Those for whom the atmosphere and work lose their excitement frequently move on to other media or occupations.

As one of the mass communications media, the contemporary newspaper has three fundamental functions and several secondary ones. The fundamental ones are these: 1) to inform readers objectively about what is happening in the community, country, and world; 2) to comment on the news in order to bring these developments into focus; and 3) to provide the means whereby persons with goods and services to sell can advertise their wares. The newspaper's secondary roles are these: 1) to campaign for desirable civic projects and to help eliminate undesirable conditions; 2) to give readers a portion of entertainment through such devices as comic strips, cartoons, and special features; 3) to serve readers as a friendly counselor, information bureau, and champion of their rights.

When a newspaper performs all or most of these tasks well, it becomes an integral part of community life. Television ''sells'' its news by developing on-the-air personalities whose mannerisms and aura often have more impact on the viewer than the content of the news they are delivering. Newspapers lack that personality advantage; a familiar byline on a story carries the impress of authoritative knowledge to the steady reader but cannot match the congenial smile or the cynically lifted eyebrow of the TV news commentator. Therefore the newspaper must build a personality of a different sort based upon its complete contents and tailored to its audience. It may be brisk, breezy, and compact like the New York *Daily News,* whose readers often digest its contents while standing in a subway train; gray and consciously stodgy in appearance, and full of long foreign and national stories like the New York *Times,* which aims to create an image of significance and permanence; or, in the case of a smaller city newspaper, where many residents know each other, filled with local stories on minor police actions, meetings of organizations, Eagle Scout awards, and local civic disputes, along with an adequate number of major national and foreign stories. The job of the editor is to give a particular audience what it wants and needs.

The printed word has a lasting power and precision beyond that of the spoken word or the visual image, although it has less ability to startle and shock. Readers can refer to it again and again. Stories may be clipped and saved by readers for many years and be readily examined in the newspaper's files decades later. This fact increases the reporter's feeling of writing history. It contributes to the newspaper's position as a stabilizing, continuing force in the community.

In the self-examination by the newspaper industry brought about by the challenge of television, editors as a group came to realize that too often the history they were recording was only the surface manifestation of the day's events—there was too much emphasis on who said this or did that, and not enough attention to why this had happened. This has led to an upsurge in investigative reporting, frequently by teams of reporters, in which the newspapers try to report frankly how our complex society is actually working. Reporters are given time to probe into such situations as conditions inside mental hospitals and nursing homes, the devious and sometimes illegal deals between political leaders and contractors, and the manner in which charitable institutions actually spend the money they receive from kind-hearted donors. The possibilities are almost endless, if an editor is sufficiently curious and has a staff large and aggressive enough to carry out instructions for this type of story.

How far should reporters go in practicing deception to obtain stories? That question is sharply debated among editors as investigative reporting flourishes. Some contend that having a reporter pose as a nurse or mechanic to gain access to a story is unethical. They point out that editors are angry when policemen pose as reporters. How then, they ask, can reporters pose as ambulance drivers to expose collusion between the police and private ambulance firms? Other editors dismiss this concern as unnecessarily self-righteous, arguing that when the public good is served by such reportorial deception, that takes precedence. More intense examination of reportorial ethics goes on today than ever before.

For decades, the front pages of most newspapers were eight single columns of news stories, mostly with one-column headlines, broken by an occasional picture or two-column type box, and an eight-column banner headline across the top. The page had a vertical stripe effect. Many newspapers today use horizontal makeup. Stories are wrapped across the page under multiple-column headlines, often with type set in two-column width. A rapidly growing number of newspapers are using six wider columns on each page, rather than the traditional eight narrow columns. Graphics experts are experimenting with other combinations of type and pictures, not only on front pages but throughout the paper, seeking ways to make the pages more eye-catching without complicating production methods so much that the deadlines can't be met.

GENERAL ORGANIZATION OF NEWSPAPERS

Newspapers in the United States can be divided into three categories: weeklies and semiweeklies, serving small areas with limited circulation;

small and medium-sized dailies, which comprise the great bulk of our daily press; and metropolitan newspapers whose circulation areas have populations of 1 million or more.

No matter what their size, newspapers have a common organization. Each has five major departments: *editorial,* which gathers and prepares the news, entertainment, and opinion materials, both written and illustrated; *advertising,* which solicits and prepares the commercial messages addressed to readers; *production,* which turns the editorial materials and advertisements into type and prints the newspapers; *circulation,* which sells and delivers the newspapers to the readers; and *business,* which oversees the entire operation.

The goal of a newspaper story is to present a report of an action in easily understood language that can be comprehended by a mass audience of different educational levels. Simplicity of writing is emphasized. If newspapers are to fill their role of communicating to the mass of the population, they cannot indulge in writing styles and terminology so involved that many readers cannot comprehend them. The best newspaper reporters are those who can accurately present complex situations in terms that are easily understood by the majority of their readers. Newspapers today put more emphasis on depth and less on excitement than in the past, a change that has opened new fields for the thoughtful, competent writer.

Newspaper advertising is divided into two types, *display* and *classified.* The former ranges from inconspicuous one-inch notices to multiple-page advertisements in which merchants and manufacturers proclaim their goods and services. Classified advertisements are the small-print, generally brief announcements packed closely together near the back of the paper; they deal with such diverse topics as help wanted, apartments for rent, used furniture and automobiles for sale, and personal notices. On almost all newspapers except the very smallest, display and classified advertising are handled by different staffs. Most newspapers receive about three-fourths of their income from advertising and one-fourth from circulation.

The staff setup of all newspapers is also basically the same, although naturally the larger the newspaper, the more complex its staff alignments. The top person is the publisher, who also may be the principal owner of the newspaper. On some papers the publisher's decisions on all matters are absolute; on others, the publisher must follow policies set by group management or by the board of directors. The publisher's task is to set the newspaper's basic editorial and commercial policies and to see that they are carried out efficiently by the various department heads. On quite a few newspapers, especially smaller ones, the publisher is also the editor.

Usually a business manager or general manager under the publisher administers the company's business operations, which range all the way from obtaining newsprint to the purchasing of tickets as the newspaper's contribution to a community concert series. The heads of the advertising, circulation, and production departments answer to the publisher through the business manager, if there is one. But the editorial department, traditionally jealous of its independence to print the news without in theory being subject to commercial pressures, demands and generally gets a line of command direct to the publisher. The titles of executive editor and managing editor are most commonly used to designate heads of the news operations. The associate editor usually directs the newspaper's editorial, or opinion making, function.

THE EVOLVING NEWSPAPER PATTERN

The American newspaper industry is the third largest industry in the nation. It consists of approximately 1,750 daily newspapers and 7,600 weekly newspapers, a total that fluctuates slightly from year to year. Despite concern about slow circulation growth, the newspaper is in a healthy and expanding condition. A slightly smaller number of daily newspapers are being published than at the end of World War II.

Fewer than a third of the daily newspapers in the United States have a circulation above 20,000. About 125 of these exceed the 100,000 mark. Thus, while the greatest public attention is focused on huge metropolitan newspapers such as the New York *Times* and Chicago *Tribune,* their place in the total industry is relatively small.

If there is an average American daily (and the individualistic patterns of publishing make the description of a typical newspaper almost impossible), it has a circulation of not more than 15,000 copies and serves a city of about 30,000 in population and its surrounding trade area. A typical weekly has a circulation of about 2,000 to 4,000 copies in a small town and its surrounding countryside. Neither has direct newspaper competition in its own community.

Traditionally, evening papers have dominated the daily field. They still do, by a ratio of approximately four to one over morning papers. However, a steady but not spectacular shift to morning publication is going on, especially in the larger cities, and as a whole, morning papers show more circulation gains than evening papers. Some newspapers are 24-hour publications with both morning and evening editions. Family reading habits have changed; many women now are away from home at jobs during the day and television watching dominates the evening. Thus many families apparently prefer to have their newspaper arrive before breakfast. Dozens of evening newspapers have switched their small Saturday editions from afternoon to morning delivery. Most of the best-known American newspapers are morning publications.

The most striking manifestation of the changing American newspaper pattern has been in the great cities. One famous newspaper after another has been forced to quit publication, leading poorly informed observers to the false conclusion that the American newspaper industry was declining.

What actually has happened is that newspapers have been heavily affected by changing patterns of American life. Earlier in the century metropolitan populations lived close to the center of the city, so the newspaper's newsgathering, circulation, and advertising efforts were concentrated near that center. As population spread to the suburbs, the problems of distribution grew, especially for evening papers through heavy traffic. Suburbanites developed loyalties to their outlying communities, which had their own governments, places of employment, and branches of downtown stores. Many people no longer commuted downtown. Higher purchasing power was concentrated around the fringes of the city, not in the core area.

Quickly, suburban daily newspapers in the largest metropolitan areas were created to serve this new audience. Some were long-time weeklies that went daily. Others were entirely new. Their growth has been one of the major publishing success stories of the last quarter-century. Between 1950 and 1968, the number of metropolitan newspapers in New York was reduced from eight to three; in Los Angeles, from five to two; and in Boston, from seven to four. The local newspaper's greatest advantage over larger "invaders" from out of town, and over local television and radio news broadcasts, is its more detailed presentation of hometown news. Many readers regard this as the most important ingredient in their newspaper.

What Do Readers Want?

Industry leaders awakened during the 1970s to the disturbing fact that fewer Americans were purchasing newspapers than in the past. Between 1969 and 1975, total daily newspaper circulation declined from 62,059,589 to 60,655,431. Population rose during those years; obviously newspapers were not keeping pace with national growth. Why? The problem was intense for newspapers in large cities, with mobile population.

Editors and publishers subjected their newspapers to searching examination. They sought through polls, seminars, in-depth interviewing and other forms of public contact to discover what contemporary Americans wanted in their newspapers and how to satisfy those desires. Editors were shocked to learn that large segments of the American population, especially young adults and low-income minority groups, felt little or no need for newspapers in their daily lives. Many claimed they received all the news they wanted from television. The "turned off" readers called newspapers dull. The age group from 21 to 35 was especially weak in newspaper readership and became a target for reawakened editors.

In order to reach new readers, the newspapers made changes in their format and content: magazine-like graphics to brighten pages and tell stories in visual form; more stories about daily living problems and styles; greater emphasis on personalities in the news; adoption of concise news summaries, often on the front page, to meet the challenge of television's brief news coverage, for persons who thought they didn't have time to read; more investigative reporting. In sum, they created briefer, brighter, and more searching newspapers.

Convinced by research that a newspaper's readership consists of an accumulation of small audiences with special interests, rather than a homogeneous mass population, some publishers redesigned their papers to attract these groups. Their idea was that while all readers share an interest in general news developments, each audience segment desires something more from the newspaper. Demographic information gathered through market research identified groups by income, age, residential area, and type of background. To please them, these newspapers now produce enlarged special sections, usually weekly, focused on a field of interest such as entertainment, sports, contemporary living styles, and finance. Sections covering specific topics—sports cars or camping, for example—are included at intervals. Some papers produce sections of localized news for specific neighborhoods. Using computerized circulation lists, newspapers have experimented with delivering special sections only to those readers who desire them. Intensive research on methods of improving content and circulation is conducted by the National Readership Council, supported by leading industry associations.

Critics have argued that at times newspapers have gone too far in this change of direction, becoming soft in content and neglecting the hard news that traditionally is the primary function of a daily newspaper. They have urged, instead, greater attention to accuracy and thoroughness of basic news coverage. By the early 1980s, American newspapers as a whole had become more attractive and more relevant to changing social patterns. Their circulation was rebounding, too; not yet up to the pace of population growth, but advancing. As the 1980s began, the national daily total had risen to 62,223,040. Editors were doing a better job of producing newspapers with appeal to all ages and interest groups, but still had much to learn about what the American public wants.

Further changes, perhaps even more spectacular, face newspapers as they encounter the challenge of news delivered textually on the home TV screen (teletext), as discussed in Chapter 12. Some planners believe that news and advertising in this form will replace the printed newspaper entirely, when this service becomes technically feasible on a general basis. Other industry leaders disagree strenuously. They contend that readers still will wish to hold the copy in their hands. They envision news delivered textually on the home TV screen by cable as a supplement to, rather than replacement for, the newspaper as we know it. Even if they are proven correct, availability of up-to-date teletext in the home at all hours will cause further changes in newspaper content to meet this competition. Some newspapers have leased cable TV channels and offered classified advertisements on them as a supplement to the classified sections of their newspapers. They consider this to be a new source of income, as well as a way to preempt the market before a nonnewspaper competitor enters the field of cable TV classified advertising. Experiments in offering retail advertising on cable TV, tied in with newspaper display advertisements, have been made.

During the next few years, the relationship between newspapers and cable-delivered textual news will be determined. Since only about one-fifth of the homes with TVs have cable connections, the changeover, in whatever form it takes, will be gradual. Some alert newspaper organizations began in 1980 to supply segments of cable TV news experimentally to home sets, drawing it from their own pool of news material. Since local newspapers have the largest newsgathering facilities in every community, it seemed logical that they should find ways to use the electronic methods of delivery, rather than surrender the role to a newly developed competitor.

Other newspapers offered their news, as well as background information stored in their computers, to home subscribers who possessed computer terminals. For a fee, the resident could have the terminal connected to the data retrieval network by ordinary telephone line and receive a wide range of information.

OPPORTUNITIES IN NEWSPAPER WORK

Not so many years ago, the newsroom was a white, male haven. The occasional woman who crashed the reporting staff was assigned to emotional feature stories and was dubbed a "sob sister." The only other women on the editorial department payroll worked in the women's department, generally known as "society" or more casually as "sock," where they wrote wedding stories and club reports. The chances of a black or other minority member getting a job on the news staff of a newspaper were minimal.

Newsrooms were not much different in this respect from many other business operations during the pre-World War II era. A change in attitude became apparent after the war, influenced by the social upheaval accompanying that conflict. A few black reporters began to appear on metropolitan news staffs. Young women hired as city room office "boys" during the wartime manpower shortage in some cases were able through aggressiveness and demonstrated ability to take over reporter jobs.

Change came slowly, nevertheless. Only in the late 1960s and early 1970s did women and minority members, especially blacks, begin to get equal treatment in hiring. Now, in most newspaper organizations they are given equal consideration to white male candidates as job openings arise. Long-overdue changes in social attitudes plus the competent performance of those hired have brought this about, and newspapers are much better for it. Reporting has a broader outlook and reflects a background more in line with the makeup of contemporary society.

The complaint remains that few women and black staff members hold high editorial posts on newspapers, that they still are regarded as second-line staff members. Although they are still largely not found in decision-making editorial positions, the situation is changing rapidly. Time will bring about the cure. In most cases they have been held back not by prejudice, but by seniority and the well-earned claim of longer-experienced staff members to climb up the ladder as openings occur. Today women hold city editorships and managing editorships in growing numbers. Some are publishers. The *Christian Science Monitor* named a woman its chief editorial writer, for example, and the New York *Times* has a female associate editor.

Relatively few blacks have been graduated from journalism schools or come out of college with other suitable degrees and shown an interest in journalism. As a result, competition to hire able young black reporters is intense. Because of this demand, qualified black news men and women tend to gravitate to higher-paying metropolitan newspapers faster than their white counterparts.

Many news jobs open up on American newspapers each year; since some 9,300 publications are in operation, counting the combined total of daily and weekly papers, the turnover in personnel is extensive. Because interest in journalism as a career has been increasing among college

The editing nerve center of a daily newspaper with a circulation of 125,000. The city editor is in the foreground with his back to the camera. The copy desk is to the far left, the news editor is in the checked shirt, and the men to the city editor's right are the Sunday edition editor and state edition editor. Each desk has a video display terminal. The "Lazy Susan" in the center revolves to distribute material among the editors. (Photo courtesy of the South Bend *Tribune*.)

students, competition for these jobs is lively. Some college education, preferably a degree, is increasingly being regarded as a prerequisite for a job in a newsroom. When hiring beginners, many editors place the ability to spell and write grammatical English, plus indications that the applicant has a liberal stock of general knowledge and a variety of interests, above the applicant's supply of technical newspaper knowledge.

A growing number of daily newspapers have summer intern programs for college undergraduates with journalistic ambitions to fill the gaps in their staffs caused by vacations. Frequently, a successful summer internship leads to a permanent job upon graduation. Internships are filled quickly, so those desiring them should make initial contacts with possible summer employers early, perhaps during Christmas vacation.

Weeklies and small dailies are the most common places for students to get their start. They will have personal involvement in more aspects of newspaper work on a small paper than on a large one; the experience acquired on a small paper, and the confidence gained, are important assets when the reporter or advertising representative seeks to step up to a larger newspaper.

News and Editorial

There are two main divisions of newsroom work—*reporting,* which includes gathering and writing news and feature stories and the taking of news and feature photographs; and *desk work,* which is the selection and preparation for printing of the written material and photographs submitted by the reporters, photographers, and the wire and syndicate services. Those who do the desk work are the editors.

This distinction between the newsgatherers and the news processors is quite sharp on large daily newspapers. Some editors will go a year or more without writing a single news story, and metropolitan reporters have nothing to do with the selection of a headline or page placement of the stories they write. On smaller papers, the distinction is less pronounced, and in many cases an editorial staffer spends part of the day as a reporter, photographer, and writer and the other part in selecting and processing the news for publication.

Some men and women find their greatest satisfaction in being reporters all their lives—probing for information, being close to events as they happen, and mingling with the people who make the news. Theirs is the most exciting part of newspaper work when big stories are breaking, and they are the people the public knows. Few outsiders have any knowledge of the inside office workers who really put the paper together. Many of the finest reporters in the country abhor the idea of being bound to a desk all day, shuffling paper and fighting the mechanical demands of type and newsprint.

The fact remains, however, that a reporter rarely is promoted directly to a high editorial place on a large or medium-sized daily. The top jobs go to those who have had desk experience. They are the organizers, the planners, the people who think automatically of whether a head will "count" and whether all the essential stories for an edition are moved out to the composing room before deadline so the papers will come off the press on time. They also have demonstrated a keen sense of news value and judgment. By the same token, few desk workers are truly successful unless they have had a thorough grounding in reporting in order to know the problems a reporter faces on a story and to supply useful suggestions.

A beginner may be a city hall beat reporter for a small daily, or the telegraph editor, handling the wire and writing headlines. Sticking to the first choice could lead eventually to a metropolitan reporting staff; to the latter, to a large paper's copy desk. Or, in either capacity, the newcomer may remain with the small daily and soon rise to editorial management status.

On most daily newspapers there are specialized editing-reporting jobs, in which the editorial worker gathers news and also helps to prepare it for print. The sports page, the business page, and the entertainment page fall into this category. Some people prefer to become specialists and do their reporting in one area. The life style page may offer many opportunities for stimulating writing. Sports is also a magnet for prospective young reporters. Business news has become a specialty on many papers, with staffs of as many as six or eight persons assigned to that area. Some metropolitan papers offer opportunities for critical reviewers of films, television, theater, and books. Varied opportunities for specialization may arise in one of the broader general news areas: politics, science, labor, religion, education, urban and racial problems, space and aviation, social work, and public health.

A very important area of work is the editorial page. Editorial page staffs run to eight or ten members on metropolitan papers that pride themselves on the quality of their opinion offerings. Some members specialize as writers of editorials on international affairs; others specialize in economics and business, or perhaps local subjects. The editorial page director coordinates their work and consults with the publisher on major policy decisions. At the smaller daily level, there may be only one editorial writer, plus a managing editor who also may attempt to comment on the day's news part of the time. Weekly newspaper editors sometimes write regular editorial columns; others prefer to write what they call "personal columns," in a more informal style.

Opportunities to advance on an editorial staff come in many forms. Much depends upon the staff member's temperament, and a bit of luck. As a rule, the management chooses for promotion to the top positions, when an important vacancy occurs, a man or woman with all-around experience and a record of dependability, good judgment under pressure, and creative thinking.

Photography

The newspaper photographer fills a large and growing role on the staff of every daily newspaper, large or small, as the field of photojournalism expands. On a newspaper, the photographer's primary task is to record in a single picture or a sequence, rapidly and accurately, the news and feature developments of the day that lend themselves to pictorial treatment. The photographer may take pictures for the news, sports, life style and entertainment pages, as well as for the promotion and advertising departments, so versatility is important. On large staffs employing 20 or more photographers and technicians, individuals may develop specialties and work primarily in these fields. Reporters on small newspapers frequently take the pictures themselves.

Planning photographic coverage on good newspaper staffs is as meticulous as the arrangement of coverage by reporters. Large newspapers have photo editors who specialize in this work. Memorable news photos usually are the result of having a photographer assigned to the right place at the proper time, plus the photographer's instinct for the climactic moment in a news situation and technical ability to take an effective picture when that moment comes.

Newspaper photography has advanced far from the days when an aggressive copyboy of limited education could be taught the rudiments of a camera and turned loose as an ambulance-chasing photographer. Today many news photographers have college educations or have attended professional photography schools. They look upon photojournalism as a satisfying career and know that their income will increase with their skill. News photography is not a field for a shy person. The photographer must be ready at times to fight for the picture. However, the widely held concept of the photographer as a rough, brash person shoving heedlessly into the middle of things is inaccurate and misleading.

Newspaper photographers receive the same salaries as reporters under Newspaper Guild pay scales. They frequently supplement their salary with overtime assignments and with after-hour jobs such as photographing weddings. Freelance photographers, not on the newspaper payroll, are paid for newsworthy pictures that they submit for publication.

The movement of experienced photographers among media compares to that of writers and editors. A photojournalist may remain on newspapers permanently, move to the photographic staff of a television station or a magazine, or choose to enter the commercial or industrial photographic field (see Chapter 13).

Advertising, Circulation, Management

Although news reporting is the most glamorous and best-publicized part of newspaper work, many other opportunities are available for young people in advertising sales and copywriting, circulation, promotion and public relations, personnel, research, production, and general business management.

The advertising department is one of the most attractive for salesminded persons. A good newspaper space salesperson must be much more than a glib talker. The advertising representative must be able to supply the potential advertiser with abundant and accurate figures about the paper's circulation pattern and totals, the advertising rates, and the kind of merchandising support the advertiser will receive. Knowledge of at least the rudiments of layout and artwork is important. In addition, the representative should be enthusiastic and able to give the merchant ideas about how best to use an advertising budget. Selling newspaper advertising requires the art of persuasion, a briefcase well loaded with facts and ideas (about competing media as well), and a strong personal belief that newspaper space will move merchandise off the merchant's shelves.

Advertising work for weeklies and small dailies is an excellent training ground. Some recent college graduates become advertising managers of weeklies, handling all types of business for their papers from classified ads to major local accounts. The same sort of opportunities for diversified experience come on small dailies, although as they increase in circulation the dailies tend to specialize their advertising staff functions. On smaller papers, the advertising representative is likely to be copywriter as well; on larger dailies, there are positions for copywriting specialists and artists.

Many advertising careers begin in the classified department of larger newspapers, where the newcomer deals with many small accounts in a variety of fields. A certain amount of classified advertising comes in voluntarily, but most of it must be solicited. Classified is sold on a day-to-day basis with deadlines only a few hours before publication. As on a reporter's beat, sales representatives have territories and detailed lists of accounts to cover.

Classified advertising is closer to the people than any other type. A three-line ad offering a desirable item for sale at a reduced price may cause the private advertiser's phone to ring dozens of times within a few hours after the paper appears. The advertiser is delighted and impressed by the paper's readership. Conversely, the failure of an advertisement to get results may lead the advertiser to grumble, "That paper is no good!" A good classified copywriter seeks to learn the tricks of concise, alluring wording. Readership tests show that classified sections are among the best-read in a newspaper.

The young sales representative is often promoted from classified into the local display department, and later perhaps into the smaller and more select national (or general) department. While classified ad department members scramble to meet daily quotas of lines for the next day's paper, national advertising department members work with manufacturers and distributors of brand-name products, often weeks in advance of publication. Schedules are sold in multiple insertions, sometimes in color. A newspaper's national sales staff works in conjunction with its national newspaper representative organization, which solicits advertising for it in other cities.

The circulation department offers some opportunities for college-trained individuals with organizing ability, promotional ideas, and a liking for detail. A supervisor who has a knack for working with carriers, much like a high school coach, is in demand. Although the top circulation jobs on large newspapers carry high salaries, the number of jobs available in this department for college-trained persons is somewhat less than in editorial and advertising.

On larger dailies, well-paying and interesting jobs exist in such supplementary departments as promotion and public relations, research, personnel, and administration. Some newspapers put out their own institutional publications for employees.

In the production department, which puts the words into type and prints the newspaper, the work is mechanical in nature, requiring technical skill. The work attracts few college-educated persons. Most employees in the department work their way up through apprenticeship programs to journeyman status, and perhaps into supervisory positions. Graduate engineers and those with advanced training in electronics are becoming more frequent in production work. The revolution in printing methods, which we shall discuss shortly, recently has drawn women into the nation's composing rooms, long almost exclusively a man's world.

Cost control is extremely important in newspaper production, just as in any manufacturing process. Elaborate accounting sheets are kept showing the cost of setting a column of type, making up a page, printing a thousand papers, increasing the size of an edition by two pages, working a press crew overtime because of a missed deadline, and other expenses. All these costs are weighed carefully in setting the newspaper's advertising rates. The publisher who pegs space rates too low will attract additional advertising but will lose money by doing so.

Many editorial people on large newspaper staffs, it might be added, know little and care less about such production and cost problems. They regard the business aspects of publishing as something remote and of scant concern to them. This is unfortunate, especially if they have thoughts of striking off on their own some day on the small weekly they dream about.

Salaries

Newspaper salaries, although not at the top of the list, compare favorably as a whole with those in other businesses and professions that require a good education and creative thinking. They have improved sharply during the past 30 years. The activities of the Newspaper Guild have been an important factor in this improvement. Organized in 1933 during the Depression when editorial salaries in particular were low, the guild has campaigned as an organized labor union for higher wages and more favorable working conditions. It has called strikes against newspapers to enforce its demands. A rise in newspaper salaries was inevitable, even without the existence of the guild, or the industry could not have held its workers as economic conditions improved. But the activities of the guild speeded the process.

Today the guild has 32,000 members, mainly on larger papers. Its contracts with management cover salaries, vacations, severance pay, and working conditions. The salary levels are minimums, covering all people in the categories specified. Some guild contracts cover just editorial departments; others, all nonprinting employees. The basic contract provides a graduated pay scale, with annual steps from the starting minimum through five or seven years to a top minimum. Salary advancement faster than, and beyond the top of, guild scales is by individual negotiation with management. Salaries on newspapers without guild contracts usually are in line with guild papers of similar circulation.

Like pay in other industries, newspaper salaries rose rapidly during the recent years of inflation, especially on papers whose contracts included cost-of-living increases. In a handful of metropolitan cities—Washington, for example—reporters' top minimum salaries were well above the $500-a-week point in the early 1980s. Many veteran staff members are above guild minimum levels.

Such salaries are paid only in a few cities where living costs are exceptionally high; newspaper people do not expect that kind of money in smaller cities, where living is more reasonable. Beginning salaries in a number of cities exceeded $200 a week in the early 1980s. Broadly speaking, average newspaper staff members can expect to start at salaries comparable to beginning teachers with the same amount of education, perhaps somewhat higher, but as their years of experience increase, their salary advantage over teachers becomes greater. Most newspaper people cannot expect to earn as much as successful doctors and attorneys.

Newspaper salaries in general are comparable to those paid in broadcasting, but lower than those on large magazines and in public relations. This fact often attracts the young graduate directly into the public relations field. Many newspaper editors contend, however, that a few years of the discipline and challenging experiences of news reporting generally will make the person more effective in other fields later.

The guild salaries are for 37- to 40-hour weeks, for average people. Superior people get above-minimum salaries. But as in all professions, they must expect to work more than a mere 40-hour week to get extra pay. Any newspaper person can add income by becoming a specialist, or doing outside writing and speaking so long as this work does not conflict with the person's basic employment. Another route to the top pay levels is through skilled desk work, where a pronounced shortage of qualified personnel has existed in recent years, particularly since the introduction of video display terminals.

Although many men and women spend their entire careers in the newspaper business, others move on from it into related fields. Newspapers are a training ground for workers in all mass communications media.

THE PRINTING REVOLUTION

The word "revolution" should be used cautiously. By proper definition, it means a complete or drastic change. Thus it is precisely the word to describe the upheaval in the methods of printing newspapers that has taken place during the past dozen or so years, and is continuing. The changes that have already occurred, and further ones now being developed, soon will make the typical newspaper plant of 25 years ago look like a prehistoric metal graveyard. Or as *Gannetteer,* the publication of the Gannett Group, said of its last Linotype machines, "like pterodactyls looking for a tarpit."

By 1900 most of the basic daily newspaper letterpress printing processes that largely have been tossed onto the dumpheap had been developed—the Linotype machine that set lines of hot metal type at the command of an operator's fingers on the keyboard, the makeup of hot metal type into page forms, and the stereotype plates that were locked on the presses. During the next 50 years the United States saw the development of the automobile, the invention of the airplane, radio, and television—yet the techniques for printing the newspapers that reported these events remained static: noisy, slow, and prone to error.

Then, with a slow rumbling, the revolution began. It first involved long rolls of specially treated paper tape, about half an inch wide. Instead of fingering a Linotype keyboard and releasing one matrix at a time, an operator punched the words on a keyboard that perforated the roll of tape. A different combination of holes in the tape represented each letter, figure, and punctuation mark. This was known as TTS, *teletypesetting.* These tapes were fed through the Linotype or Intertype machines, automatically releasing the matrices at high speed. One operator could monitor two or three machines simultaneously. TTS speeded up the traditional *hot metal* method of creating type but was only a forerunner of greater changes. The real upheaval came when that electronic marvel, the computer, was created, and ways were found to harness it for setting type.

Preparing Type for Newspapers

The goal of electronic typesetting is to reduce keyboarding to an absolute minimum. That is, to eliminate the wasteful duplication of physical effort traditionally involved in transforming a news story from a sheet of copy paper in a reporter's typewriter into corrected type, ready for printing.

Under the old method, the reporter wrote a story and submitted it to the city desk. The city editor marked it up with a copy pencil, then a copy desk editor gave it a further dress-up and wrote a headline for it. Next the Linotype operator typed out the corrected story on his keyboard, changing it into lines of metal type. A proof of the type was pulled and read by a proofreader; errors marked by the proofreader were corrected by having the Linotype operator set replacement lines for the erroneous ones. Sometimes the operator created new errors while correcting the original ones. A printer pulled out the bad lines from a galley of type and put the corrected ones in their place. All too often the printer carelessly placed the new lines in the wrong spot in the galley, creating a fresh error that appeared in print as mixed-up lines. Finally, another printer placed the galley of type in the page form where an editor had dummied it to appear.

Contrast that system with the electronic method that has emerged in newsrooms throughout the country. Competing electronic systems have been developed, so that variations are found in different modernized newspapers, but all are designed to achieve the same goal. And that is to have a story that has been typed by a reporter go directly into a computer storage bank, from which it is called out by an editor onto a screen by the push of a button, for review and correction; by another push of a button, the computer feeds the story into the phototypesetter, from which it emerges as errorless type on a long sheet of paper with headline attached. It is ready to be pasted onto a page-size sheet of light cardboard; this in

A copyeditor studies a news story she has "called" from the newsroom computer onto her video display terminal for editing. (Photo courtesy of South Bend *Tribune*, South Bend, Indiana.)

turn will be processed into a printing plate for the press. Only one typing effort by the reporter is required. The savings in time and labor, and the reduction in the possibilities of error, are huge.

The key piece of machinery that makes this possible, in addition to the computer itself, is a cathode ray device called the *video display terminal,* or VDT. This is a special electric typewriter keyboard, supplemented with command keys, with a small television screen on top. As the reporter types the story, it appears line for line on the video screen. By pushing certain command keys the writer can move the words around on the screen to make inserts, spelling corrections, and deletions, until the story is considered finished and ready to submit to the editors.

In the old days on a big newspaper the reporter called out "Copy!" and a boy rushed the typewritten page to the city desk. Or, if time wasn't pressing, the reporter carried it to the editor's incoming basket. On the VDT, the reporter pushes a command button and the story is placed in computer storage. A brief memo of its content goes to the city editor. With the video screen cleared, the reporter can write another story. Portable terminals enable a reporter covering a football game or in a distant bureau, for example, to transmit the story directly into the home office computer storage.

The editor, when ready for the story, strikes the proper symbol key on the VDT and the words appear on the screen. The editor too can make changes on the keyboard; the story then can be passed to a VDT screen on the desk of a copyeditor, who makes a final check for errors, writes a headline, and indicates the size and column width of the headline by striking the proper symbol keys. Finally, the copyeditor touches the key "Set" and the computer dispatches the story to the phototypesetting machine. Incoming press association stories also may flow directly into the computer's memory bank, for similar handling.

The phototypesetting machine is the compact electronic replacement for the old Linotype. It contains a whirling disk of type letters in different faces, or a cathode ray tube device. At the flowing electrical impulse commands of the computer, the phototypesetter records the indicated letters in sequence on fast film; this film produces a positive print of the words on a sheet of coated paper that emerges from the darkroom through a slot, ready for pasteup. This is called *cold type.*

Another electronic typesetting machine, often used in conjunction with the VDT, is the *optical character reader,* or OCR. The reporter types a story on a special electric typewriter using hard white paper. The writer and the editor mark corrections on the story pages with a light blue felt-tipped pen to which the electronic eye is "blind" and strike out unwanted words with a heavy black pen. An operator types in the corrected words in certain positions under the original typed line. The copy sheet is placed face down into the OCR, or scanner, which resembles an office copying machine. A small electronic "reader" inside scans the copy line for line, inserting the corrections as marked, at tremendous speed. The output can be fed directly into a phototypesetting machine or into the computer storage bank for later callup, or produced as punched tape that can be placed physically into the phototypesetter at a desired time. A "souped-up" Linotype machine in the old days did well to produce ten lines a minute. A phototypesetter can produce as much as 500 lines a minute.

Because of the delicate machinery involved, the changeover to electronic equipment has been full of "bugs." Nor has it been easy for oldtimers in the newsrooms. Accustomed to pounding out stories on favorite typewriter "mills" whose idiosyncrasies they knew, some found it difficult to remember the modes and technical instructions involved in operating the VDT. They discovered, too, that the computer can talk back. It is programmed to query steps the operators take and buttons they push that seem inconsistent to its mechanical "brain."

One tale illustrative of the frustrations involved, told around the Gannett organization, involves an operator who typed something into the computer. The machine answered on the terminal screen, "Are you sure?" The irritated reporter typed out, "Hell, no." He didn't know that the first two letters of his mild expletive, *he,* were the same letters as the command, "Help." Whereupon the computer printed out for him a list of all the commands for the entire system.

Other news staff members adapted quickly to the electronic systems as faster, cleaner and, indeed, more fun. After a while, even the reluctant ones admitted that they wouldn't want to go back to the old ways.

An important result of the typesetting revolution has been to break down the ancient barriers between the composing and news rooms. Control of typesetting has been largely moved "up front" into the hands of the editors, away from the composing room. The further the revolution proceeds, the smaller the role of the composing room becomes. The traditional proofreader may disappear, except for small special tasks.

On the near horizon, but still in the experimental stage, is a video terminal arrangement by which an editor can make up an entire news page on a large desk-instrument screen, placing premeasured stories, pictures, and advertisements in the desired positions. Then by punching a button the editor orders the entire page to be photoset swiftly, ready to be transformed into a printing plate for the press. This process is called full *pagination.* When fully operative, it will put control of page production primarily in the news department's hands. By facsimile transmission and satellite, full pages are moved electronically to subsidiary printing plants miles away, even across the country, or abroad.

Because of the heavy investment involved, labor contracts, and disputes as to which commercial systems are best, adoption of all this new machinery has been uneven. A substantial majority of American daily newspapers adopted the new methods by the early 1980s, and the remainder are changing over as rapidly as their circumstances permit.

Printing the Paper

Traditional printing methods in the pressroom are undergoing a radical change, too, if one that is not quite so spectacular. The heavy lead stereotype plate formed from a made-up page of metal type and locked onto a press cylinder is rapidly becoming a museum piece.

Two systems are replacing it. One is *offset printing,* the use of which began on weekly newspapers and spread rapidly to small and then larger daily newspapers. By the early 1980s, three-fourths of American daily newspapers were being printed by offset, although the largest ones were hesitant to switch to this method, because of the millions of dollars involved in replacing their letterpresses.

Offset printing is based on lithography, an older process in which printing was done from a smooth flat surface of stone. In surface printing, the image is placed on the stone by a greasy substance that has an affinity for ink. The nonprinting surface is covered with a thin film of water that repels the ink. Thus only the image is printed on paper when pressure is applied. The image is transferred from the printing plate cylinder to a rubber blanket attached to a second cylinder. It is then transferred to the paper, which is carried by a third impression cylinder (Figure 5.1). Development of offset presses capable of printing on a continuous web of paper was a major step in adapting this process to newspaper printing. Newspapers printed by offset are noted for their excellent photographic reproduction and strong, solid black tones.

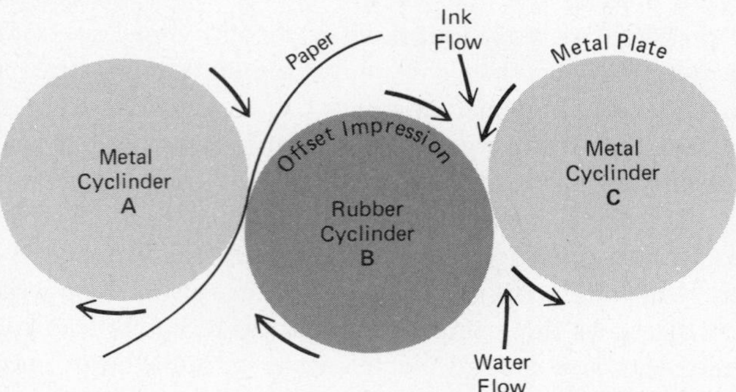

Figure 5.1 How offset printing works. The impression on the plate affixed to cylinder C is "offset" onto rubber cylinder B, then printed on paper passing between cylinder B and cylinder A. Because of the lack of wear on a metal plate, thousands of additional pages may be printed, and more clearly, with this method.

Newspapers unwilling to discard their traditional presses, beause of cost or other factors, have turned to the lightweight printing plate, weighing a few ounces, as a replacement for the bulky stereotype plates. Several commercial variations of this concept exist. The underlying principle is the same. A thin photosensitive polymer substance is spread onto a page-size aluminum plate. The image of the pasted-up news page in negative form is exposed photographically onto the polymer and the nonprinting surface material washed away. Laser beam techniques also have been developed to transfer the page impression onto a thin plate. The plate is mounted on a lightweight, curved "saddle" and locked onto the press cylinder.

Still in the future, but expected to emerge from the laboratories into daily newspaper pressrooms during the 1980s, is an even more radical system called *plateless printing,* which will eliminate the printing plates. The printed word will be applied to rolls of newsprint by computer-controlled ink jet technology. Some of the country's most imaginative scientists and engineers are working to make this ultimate step in the printing revolution a reality.

THE WEEKLY NEWSPAPER

A Midwestern weekly newspaper editor recently told a story about the pharmacist in his small county seat city who gave the wrong dosage for a prescription. The boy to whom the medicine was given died, and charges of negligence were brought against the druggist. His attorney obtained a change of venue to have the case tried in another county, so the trial publicity would not be seen in detail locally and damage the druggist's reputation. This offended the editor's principles of reporting the news, so although the extra expense strained his limited budget, he sent a reporter to the other county and covered the trial in detail. The druggist lived across the street from the editor. They saw each other every day. The druggist escaped without imprisonment, but because of the editor's action he still refused to speak to him more than two years after the trial.

This incident illustrates an essential point about weekly journalism—its intimacy. The people about whom the editor writes are neighbors, social acquaintances, fellow members of churches and clubs. They pressure the publisher and editor of the weekly newspaper to conform, to shush up unpleasant news. Although less subject to time pressures than editors on daily newspapers, weekly editors have special problems. A large daily would not publish reviews of high school plays; the weekly is expected to do so, and if the review speaks ill of the performance, the editor can expect phone calls and visits from the actors' parents, accusing the newspaper of painting a false picture of the town's teenagers.

In thousands of American towns, the weekly newspaper is at the core of community life. It is the chief source of information about the activities of individuals and organizations, and the merchants look to its advertising columns as a weekly tool for selling goods. In the files of a small-town weekly are recorded the vital statistics of the town's life—the births and deaths, marriages, social events, and tragedies, and the ludicrous moments that give life zest. Even when it is overshadowed by a big-city daily a few miles away, the weekly newspaper often has a secure place in the heart of its community and can continue to thrive. The chief stock in trade it has to offer is names—subscribers reading about their neighbors and about themselves. The larger the newspaper, the less impact the names in news stories have on readers, because they do not know all the people mentioned. This personal link is an advantage the community weekly newspaper has over its larger, more sophisticated city cousin.

The weekly newspaper illustrates editing and publishing in its simplest form, although anyone who believes that putting out a weekly is easy has been badly misled. All the jobs involved in any newspaper must be done: getting news and editing it, selling advertising, handling circulation, and seeing to it that the paper is printed on time. On a large daily many people handle each of these operations, but on a weekly everything is done by a handful of workers. The 40-hour week is only a dream to the editors and publishers of weekly newspapers. After the day's work at the office is finished, the weekly editor covers civic meetings, attends social functions in the hope of getting news, and listens to the complaints of fellow townspeople. Weekly newspaper publishing is a risky enterprise for a person who thinks only in editorial terms; unless the publisher quickly learns the business tricks of obtaining revenue from advertising and circulation, the paper won't live long. Nor does the free time between editions exist in the way envisaged by a metropolitan newspaper worker who dreams of settling down in a small town to the easy life of a weekly editor. The minute one week's edition is out, the editor starts churning out copy for the following week and the publisher starts a new round of advertising solicitation. When the two jobs are handled by one person, as often is the case, he or she rarely has a free day, even on weekends.

The development of offset printing has changed life on weekly newspapers. In earlier days, most were printed in the newspapers' own small hot metal shops, on aged equipment and a flat-bed press of nineteenth-century vintage. The resulting newspaper was poorly printed, often with miserable reproduction of photographs. Today, most weeklies are produced by offset, either in their own plants if the paper is large enough to justify the investment, or in a central plant along with several other weeklies.

Most weekly newspapers carry a Thursday publication date, for a sound commercial reason. It is the day on which local merchants want to reach readers with news of their weekend sales. The grocery stores in particular key their merchandise pattern to their Thursday newspaper advertisements, offering special items on sale through Saturday or Sunday. Some weeklies appear on Wednesday, if many of their merchants desire a longer sales span.

A look at the operation of a typical up-to-date weekly newspaper in a small city gives us a picture of what this kind of newspaper life is like. The paper has been in continuous publication, with some changes of name, since 1879. It is published in a city of slightly less than 5000 population whose economy is based on farming and small manufacturing. The newspaper's circulation is 2700, most of it within the radius of a few miles of its downtown office. Usually its edition is 16 pages, dropping occasionally to 12 or rising to 22. Six persons compose its staff: a general manager who handles business affairs, sells and lays out advertisements, and takes news pictures and prints them in the darkroom; an advertising manager; a general worker and runner who makes the trips to the printing plant; a bookkeeper; an all-around staff member who handles subscriptions, helps out at the front counter, writes the society news and a chitchat column, and lays out advertisements; and the editor. The manager specialized in graphics at a two-year college. The editor is a recent journalism school graduate.

Virtually every story and picture is of local origin, except for a weekly handout column from the district congressman and a few public interest publicity releases for organizations such as the National Safety Council. No press association or other national news is included. Stories and pictures of weddings and engagements take extensive space; so does high school sports material.

The editorial and advertising staffs must keep a daily flow of material moving to the printing plant. The advertising deadline is Friday noon for the issue that carries a dateline of the following Thursday, although an occasional small ad is slipped in Monday morning. The deadline for news is noon Tuesday. With their final copy in hand, the manager and editor drive 27 miles to the small daily publishing plant that prints their paper, where the final type is set early Tuesday afternoon and the news pages made up.

Wednesday at the daily newspaper plant is a busy one. It prints three weekly newspapers that morning—one at 9 A.M., "ours" at 10 A.M., and a third at 11 A.M.; then it clears the presses for its own daily edition.

The paper we are examining distributes some of its copies to subscribers by mail, but sells 1200 copies directly to cash customers at stores and at its home office, where people are waiting when papers arrive from the printer's at noon Wednesday. These cash customers are too anxious to receive the paper to await its delivery by mail the next day.

Three out-of-town daily newspapers, one a major daily from a city 30 miles away, are sold in the town, yet the weekly manager does not consider them direct competition, even though they carry some news from the town.

The range of editorial excellence among weekly newspapers is wide. Splendidly edited weeklies are to be found throughout the United States, along with others that barely qualify for the label "newspaper." Weeklies are rarely of the crusading type, again with outstanding exceptions. Most weekly editors see their role as that of printing constructive, orthodox news without dealing in what often is called sensationalism. In some cases the newspaper's profit margin is so thin that the publisher cannot risk irritating an important advertiser by printing something the person dislikes. Frequently a weekly newspaper, such as the one we have examined, has no editorial page at all. Without resorting to big-city street sensationalism, many weekly editors could serve their communities better if they dealt more bluntly with local problems, despite the pressures not to do so. The American weekly press as a whole is conformist and conservative.

The next step above the weekly newspaper is the semiweekly, published twice a week, frequently on Monday and Thursday, or sometimes with a Sunday edition. Relatively few semiweekly and triweekly publications exist, because usually a weekly that seeks to expand into broader fields makes the jump directly to daily operation.

Free Circulation Weeklies

In recent years, especially in suburban areas, some weeklies have changed to a free distribution basis. They give their paper away instead of selling it, delivering it to every home addressed to Occupant. Those who use this practice prefer to call it "controlled circulation"; their opponents use the derogatory term "throw-away." Some such publications are "shoppers," containing only enough editorial filler to close up the chinks around the ads.

To counteract the attractiveness to advertisers of these free weeklies, about half the daily newspapers use some form of unpaid supplemental coverage to increase penetration of the market. Usually this is a weekly shopper of their own in which advertisements are picked up from the daily editions, or "blanket coverage" in which occasional daily editions are delivered without charge to nonsubscriber homes.

The publisher who gives away a newspaper accepts three financial disadvantages to gain one important advantage. The newsprint bill rises and income from circulation disappears, and if copies are distributed by mail, postal costs rise too. But by convincing advertisers that the town is blanketed with copies of the paper the publisher can obtain a higher advertising rate and more linage. As advertising income rises, so does net profit. Such free distribution methods usually work best in those areas where there is a large concentration of homes.

THE SMALL AND MEDIUM-SIZED DAILY NEWSPAPER

The great difference in operation between weekly and small daily newspapers is the addition of the element of timeliness. The principle of "today's news today" dominates minds of all daily newspaper staff members. Because the process of assembling and printing the newspaper is done six or seven times a week, thinking must be accelerated.

Working on a daily does not necessarily make a reporter or an advertising solicitor a better worker, but the worker must be fast. Deadlines take on a fresh, compelling meaning. On a daily, if the copy deadline is 12:40 P.M., any stories sent to the composing room after that minute may cause a late press start. That in turn can mean missed bus connections and lost street sales for the circulation department.

A substantial overlap exists between the weekly and small daily fields, in the sense that weekly cities sometimes are larger than small daily cities, and some weeklies have more circulation and advertising than small dailies. Yet, given a choice of jobs at identical pay, the majority of staff members probably would choose the daily. They find more stimulation in the faster pace and in having a greater kinship with world affairs through the presence of wire service news in the office.

What, then, causes some towns to have daily newspapers and other larger ones to have weeklies? Essentially it is a matter of geography, supplemented at times by the commercial audacity of the publisher. When a good-sized town is close to a large city, competition from the big neighboring paper may make successful operation of a small daily financially impossible. Yet there is room for a weekly newspaper to present community news and advertising. A small daily in a relatively isolated region may operate at a profit, whereas the same paper would fail if published in the shadow of a large city.

The primary problem a daily newspaper publisher faces is that the cost of producing the paper is the same every day, regardless of how much or how little advertising each issue carries. A bulky paper produced one or two days a week cannot carry all the burden if the other issues have little advertising content. Most newspapers try to average better than a 50:50 ratio between the amount of editorial and advertising content, with the greater weight going to advertising—up to 65 percent or more on some days.

A small daily is excellent training ground for all journalists; many who later attain fame have started on such publications. On the smallest dailies, those in the 5000 circulation range, staff members "double in brass" by doing a little bit of everything. The key newsroom figure on the very small daily is the managing editor.

Usually the managing editor of even such a small daily has a college education and perhaps five years of newspaper experience. The work of managing editor, city editor, and copy desk person is now performed by a single person responsible for producing a newspaper that fluctuates in size from 8 to 16, or occasionally 20, pages a day. Typically, the staff under the managing editor includes one or two persons with some college education and some local workers who have been hired at some time to help out, shown sufficient talent to filler lesser jobs, and become permanent fixtures.

The advertising staff of a very small daily often consists of a business-advertising manager who handles most of the big accounts, another display advertising salesperson, a clerk-secretary, and a classified advertising manager. The circulation manager frequently is a young local person who has come up from the ranks of carriers. There must be a bookkeeper, too, and a clerk-proofreader—a very small group, altogether, to produce a newspaper day after day. This is daily journalism at its simplest level.

An important aspect of newspaper work a young journalist learns on a small daily is meeting deadlines. With mechanical facilities limited, the flow of copy must be scheduled closely, giving the beginner a sense of urgency. The editorial newcomer learns to make do with the available time and equipment, to cover local stories, to observe the workings of a press association wire, to write headlines. Mistakes in stories are brought home to the writer quickly because of close business and social ties with the news sources. Also, the person breaking into the business has an opportunity to practice photography and to get a taste of photojournalism under realistic operating conditions. If a beginner has that extra spark of creative writing and imagination so sought after by newspapers of all sizes, it will shine forth more quickly on a small daily than almost anywhere else in journalism.

Small-Daily Editorial Problems

Perhaps you wonder how a five-person editorial staff can produce enough copy day after day to fill the newspaper. Where does this small staff in a little city find sufficient news and get it all written fast enough to make the daily deadline? The answer is, help from other sources of copy. Part of the allotted editorial space is filled with feature material purchased from newspaper syndicates, and part is filled with wire service stories selected from the global news reports delivered by the AP or UPI. Photographs help, too, plus adding to reader interest. Some are local photographs taken by staff members or supplied by commercial photographers; others are purchased from the news picture services. A three-column picture 6 inches deep occupies 18 column inches, almost the equivalent of a full column of type.

Taking a 500-word story from the press association teleprinter and sending it to the composing room is quicker and easier than writing a local story of the same length. Even the smallest daily needs to give its readers highlights of major world developments, but overdependence on wire service copy diminishes the local newspaper's value to its readers. They would prefer to read well-developed local enterprise stories and interviews than second-rate telegraph stories. The diligent small-city managing editor, knowing this well, is torn between providing readers with as much of the latter material as the small staff can obtain, and meeting the demands from the mechanical department to get the pages filled by deadline so the press can start on time.

As the circulation of a newspaper increases, so does the staff. With somewhat larger staffs, the tasks performed by the managing editor of the small daily are divided among several persons, and the functional organization that reaches its peak on the staff of a metropolitan newspaper begins to emerge.

The managing editor's primary role is to oversee all the operations. Under that person is a city editor, who directs the work of the local reporters and photographers, and a telegraph editor, who selects and edits stories from the wire. As the staff grows, a copy desk is set up to handle the editing of copy and the writing of headlines. With specialists at work, the result is a better-edited newspaper.

Impact of the Medium-Sized Daily

The medium-sized daily—say one approaching the 50,000 circulation point that is sometimes used arbitrarily to mark the start of the big-city group—often reaches far beyond the city limits because its copies are distributed by truck, bus, mail, and even airplane to surrounding rural areas. A motorist driving along a country road can often judge the impact of the newspaper published in a nearby city by the number of brightly painted tubes nailed on posts outside farmhouses to receive delivery of the daily editions.

Papers of this size are financially strong enough to have editorial staffs of considerable scope, usually with persons of outstanding ability (Figure 5.2). Some may eventually move on to metropolitan papers; others are content to spend their working lives in the congenial atmosphere of a medium-sized paper in a community sufficiently large to have an urban flavor, yet small enough for comfortable living.

At first glance, the medium-sized daily operating under the shadow of a metropolitan giant would appear at a severe disadvantage. Usually it cannot offer the bulk that American readers too often associate with a desirable product. In fact, frequently the result is just the opposite. The medium-sized daily prospers because it provides the reader with as much, or nearly as much, press association and feature material as desired, and in addition provides detailed news of the local community. Density of population in these fringe areas is sufficient to provide a strong circulation potential. The presence of branch outlets of major downtown stores offers large advertising sources. Most department stores with suburban branches place advertising in the community dailies—advertising revenue that might previously have gone to the metropolitan papers. Metropolitan newspapers in some cities, notably Chicago, have sought to counteract this trend by operating community dailies of their own that concentrate on local news as supplements to their downtown general publications.

The standards of medium-sized dailies in content, policies, and personnel frequently are high. Their salaries, although not equal to the metropoli-

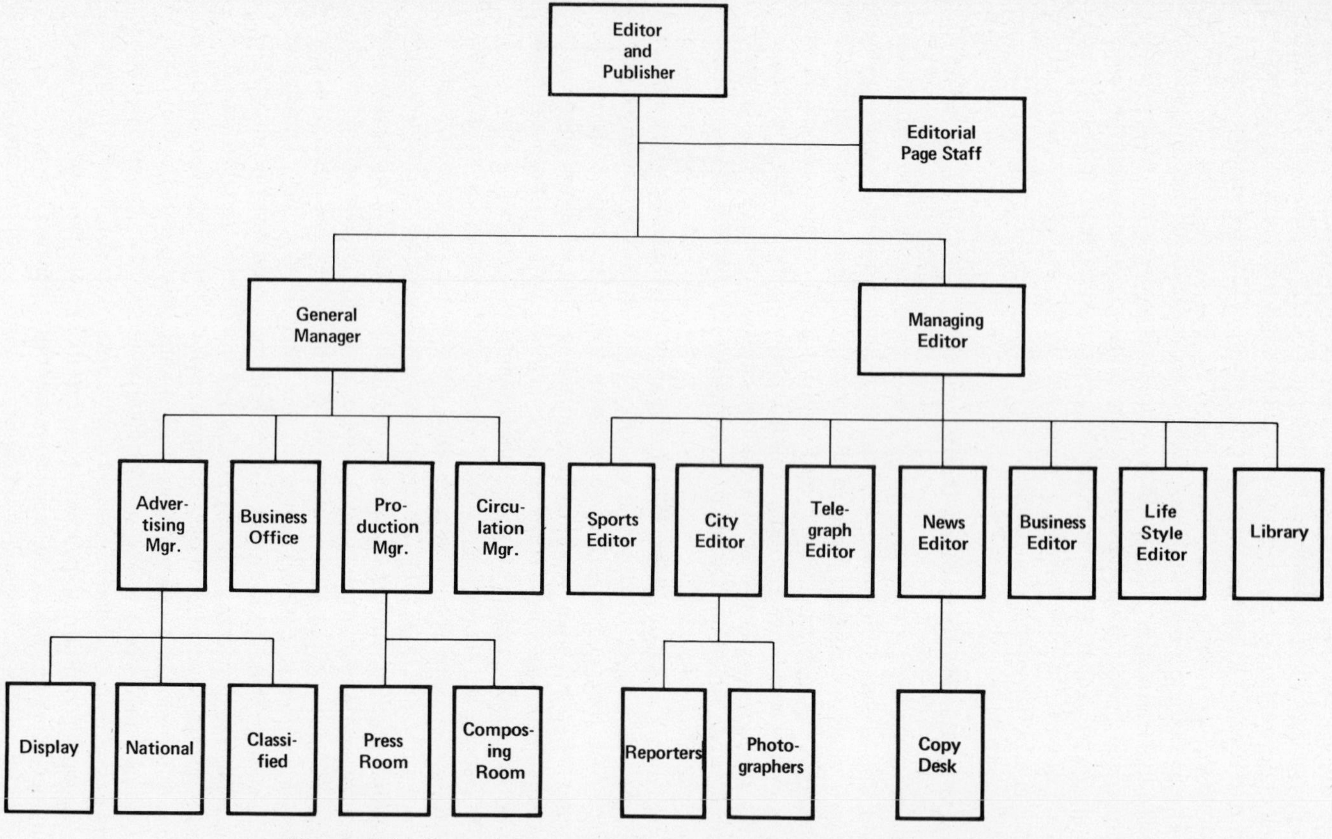

Figure 5.2 Typical organization of a medium-sized daily newspaper.

tan levels, are generally higher than living costs. For a young reporter whose ultimate goal is metropolitan journalism, a period of work on a well-regarded medium-sized daily is an excellent recommendation.

Editors of suburban community dailies keep a keen eye on the news "play" by their metropolitan rivals. They can give their readers later news than the afternoon big-city newspapers can, because the latter are handicapped in distributing their editions through heavy city traffic. By establishing a later deadline, the fringe daily can take advantage of quick delivery within its own community.

Selling the Papers

When it comes to selling the product it has produced, the daily newspaper is unique. It may have millions of dollars of equipment and a staff of experienced professional men and women to create it—yet leave the delivery of its newspapers and much of the selling effort to boys and girls, many of them not yet in their teens.

Management experts consider this a crazy system, yet it works. Under this carrier system, a large majority of the daily papers sold in the United States reach their purchasers. Circulation managers have put computers to work in their offices to handle billing, maintain circulation lists, and speed up truck loading, but so far they have not found an electronic replacement for the carrier who brings the newspaper to the subscriber's door. Use of older people, often retirees, as carriers instead of boys and girls is a recent trend in numerous cities.

Only in very large cities with heavy commuter traffic on public transportation do street sales of papers have the importance they once did. The home delivery carrier collects weekly or monthly for the daily service. Copies of an edition sold on the street, including through vending machines, are called single-copy sales.

Most methods of selling a newspaper are based upon the principle of having the publishing company sell copies to a distributor or delivery agent at a wholesale price several cents below the announced price per copy. The agent, including the home delivery carrier, sells the papers to the public at the published price; the difference between wholesale and retail prices provides the agent's profits.

Single-copy street sales are affected by the weather, traffic, shopping conditions, holidays, and the nature of the main headline. These factors do not influence home delivery sale. Thus home delivery gives a newspaper assured income and a firm circulation figure to quote to advertisers.

Decades ago, in the fight to win circulation and outdo their rivals, some newspapers resorted to making exaggerated claims about their sales. Since advertising rates are based on circulation figures and on the cost of reaching each thousand readers, this led to many discrepancies and a chaotic situation in which honest publishers were placed at an unfair disadvantage by the unscrupulous operators. To correct this situation, the Audit Bureau of Circulations (ABC) was formed in 1914.

Newspapers that belong to the ABC, as most dailies do, submit detailed reports of their circulation every six months and open their books to a detailed examination by ABC auditors every year. Rigid rules are enforced. The organization puts limits on methods of solicitation, the number of low-cost subscriptions, bulk sales, and other devices used by publishers to inflate circulation figures. Types of circulation that fail to meet ABC standards are disallowed, and others of a somewhat transitory nature are appropriately indicated on the statements published by the ABC about each paper.

No newspaper can afford to have its advertisers see that its daily sales are slipping. If that happens, the advertiser demands lower rates and the financial woes multiply. In the recent history of American newspapers there are many proofs of the fact that once a newspaper goes into a prolonged circulation decline, its prospects for survival are slim.

One widely used method of handling home delivery is known as the little merchant system. A carrier boy or girl has a route of several city blocks and is responsible for delivery of papers over that route, as well as for collecting the subscribers' fees. The more new subscribers or "starts" the carrier obtains, the more the carrier's monthly income will be. In effect, the carrier is an independent small merchant. The circulation departments conduct prize contests to stimulate production of new orders, giving rewards such as bicycles, sporting equipment, and trips to amusement centers to carriers who reach specified quotas. The underlying premise in this circulation system is incentive; the paper tries to make it worthwhile for the carrier to give up free hours, or to rise very early each morning, in order to deliver papers.

Changes in our life style are causing problems that earlier generations of carriers did not face. Thousands of families in large cities live in high-rise apartment buildings that have strict security systems. The carrier has difficulty entering the building to deliver and collect; newspapers left outside apartment doors are stolen. With an increasing number of women working at jobs outside their homes, no one is at home when the carrier makes a daytime collection round. Many newspapers encourage their subscribers to prepay for the service direct to the newspaper, to reduce the extent of the collection problem.

There are preprints, a swiftly growing phenomenon. These are advertising sections printed in advance, separately from the basic newspaper, often by a commercial printer outside the newspaper plant. Properly labeled and dated, these are inserted into the newspaper. By the early 1980s "on-line" stuffing machines that insert the preprint sections into the regular papers as fast as they roll off the press were being used mostly by smaller dailies, which do not need the high press speeds large city newspapers require. Frequently insertion of the preprint sections is done by the carrier, who usually receives extra payment for the task.

Given proper adult supervision, the carrier system works for newspapers because the product is partly presold. An appetite for news exists, and in most communities the newspaper is a household word. The youthful appeal of the carrier is often the decisive sales factor. Some critics, however, contend that overheavy reliance on juvenile sales representatives has held newspapers back from reaching their full sales potential. Recognizing this, the American Newspaper Publishers Association engaged Massachusetts Institute of Technology management experts to study the newspaper distribution system in search of new ways to do the job. Among the facts uncovered was that it costs more than ten cents to get a copy of a daily newspaper into a reader's hand from the time it rolls off the press. The subscription price of a home delivered copy often is little more than ten cents. This means that all other costs of writing and printing the paper, plus any profit, must come primarily from advertising sales.

THE METROPOLITAN PRESS

The newspaper as a mass communications medium reaches its highest development in our metropolitan centers. Here the publishers and editors think of readers in terms of millions. If we calculate three readers to each copy of a paper printed, which is a common rule of thumb, a big-city newspaper with a Sunday circulation of a million copies is read by 3 million persons. The impact of a single news story published in such an edition is easy to perceive.

Many newspaper workers in editorial, advertising, and circulation departments look upon a metropolitan newspaper job as the goal of their careers, the sign of professional success. Ironically, quite a few big-city newspaper people in quiet talk sessions between editions speak longingly of escaping the scramble of metropolitan journalism for what they conceive of as a calmer, more orderly and satisfying life on smaller papers. Given an opportunity to break away from metropolitan work, however, many of this wistful brigade either refuse to do so or drift back to the so-called big time. The tempo, adventure, and prestige are alluring.

As stated earlier, metropolitan newspapers are the one group of the American press that has suffered severe attrition in the last quarter-century. Many of those whose names had been household words for decades have ceased publication, amid sentimental scenes of desolation and farewell in newsrooms that have seen the handling of so many dramatic stories in American history. No matter how understandable the underlying social and economic reasons for these deaths, the passing of individual newspapers grieves both readers and staff members. A newspaper is such an ingrained part of public life that its sudden disappearance leaves a painful sense of loss.

Undoubtedly, the best-known newspaper in the country is the morning and Sunday New York *Times*. The *Times*, edited as the country's newspaper of record, publishes lengthy texts of official documents and exhaustive reports on national and international developments. Its circulation—more than 800,000 daily and 1.4 million Sunday—is nationwide. It appeals to readers who want an abundance of government and cultural news. The *Times* is not written for a general mass audience, however, and many Americans find it less interesting than their own more personalized local newspapers. Like all newspapers, the *Times* commits its share of errors and shadings of news coverage. Such missteps are not surprising in a publication of its size, but they underline the point that no newspaper is totally accurate, no matter how great its reputation. Primarily because of its work on the Watergate story, the Washington *Post* also has become a household word nationally.

Few if any stories in a metropolitan paper are read by all who purchase the paper. Every reader chooses selectively, picking a limited number of items from the huge tray of reading delicacies on the basis of personal needs, interests, and whims. Even so, every story in a metropolitan paper, no matter how insignificantly displayed, is seen by thousands of readers.

Thus the reporter's writing on a large newspaper is absorbed by a large number of persons. Yet the very size of the metropolitan region makes it impossible for the reporter to have direct contact with the audience. Except for personal acquaintances and the handful of readers who are either irate or thoughtful enough to report their reactions to an individual story, the metropolitan reporter has little opportunity to determine how stories are received. This is one of the most striking differences between big-city and small-town newspaper work.

The young person looking toward metropolitan papers as a place to work discovers two major differences from smaller cities: greater speed and greater specialization.

Most small dailies have one basic edition a day. Some may supplement this with a street-sale edition in which the front page is remade with larger, flashier headlines and late news bulletins for sale to casual purchasers. Or they may have an early, less complete edition for distribution in rural areas. In contrast, some metropolitan newspapers publish at least five editions within a period of eight hours. Afternoon newspapers are especially burdened with numerous editions because of the fast-changing nature of news during the daytime hours and distribution problems. This requires high-speed work. The edition schedule is an almost sacred document, whose stated deadlines govern the work of several hundred employees. If the press run of a big newspaper starts 15 minutes late, a bluntly spoken postmortem often results in the publisher's office.

During the final minutes before the deadline, each newspaper department is atingle with concentrated work. When the deadline has passed, and each department in the complicated process knows that it no longer can call back anything it has done or push anything more into the paper, there comes a period of relaxation and waiting for the fresh edition copies to be brought from the pressroom. Then the buildup process for the next edition begins.

A typical metropolitan deadline sheet has minute-by-minute rules telling when the final story must cross the city desk and the copy desk and move to the composing room; when the last photograph must leave the editorial art department; when the final page must move out of the composing room; and what minute the press must start. A smooth flow of pages through the assembly line is essential. In a huge newspaper plant the production of a daily newspaper is a coordinated effort rarely exceeded in manufacturing, especially when we remember that the primary product fed into this conveyor belt system, news, is an intangible raw material difficult to find and hard to define.

The new reporter who obtains a metropolitan job right out of school usually considers himself or herself extremely lucky, as having gotten a big jump on classmates who go to work on weeklies or small dailies. Unfortunately, this is not necessarily the case. The big-city novice finds stimulation in associating with skilled veterans and watching exciting stories move through the production line. But too often the novice is shunted into a minor reporting job, like covering the overnight police beat, and is unable to get the all-around experience classmates are absorbing on smaller papers. Years may pass before the newcomer gets an opportunity to work on the copy desk. Seniority plays an important part in assignments on metropolitan staffs, and unless the young reporter is fortunate or shows exceptional talent for writing, advancement is slow.

Many editors and personnel managers of metropolitan papers advise beginners to work on small papers from three to five years before trying the metropolitan field. Often a young person coming to a metropolitan staff with a few years of small-town or small-city work will advance faster than one of similar age who has spent those same years on the big-city paper. The all-around experience of a smaller paper prepares the young reporter to fill many different jobs as they become available.

How a Metropolitan News Staff Functions

The key figure in the local newsgathering activities is the city editor, who has one or more assistants. Possibly a hundred reporters, even more in a few cases, are deployed at the most productive news sources, held in reserve as general assignment reporters, or organized into investigative teams. The reporters placed on specific beats, such as the police department or city hall, are responsible for gathering all news that occurs in their territory and submitting it to the city desk. When time permits, they write the stories themselves. But the urgency of deadlines often makes this impossible, so they telephone their facts to a rewrite specialist. These writers are old hands, hardened under pressure, swift in their writing and quick at organizing a mass of facts into a story that reads smoothly and concisely.

When the story has been written, it is submitted to the city desk. There the city editor or an assistant reads it to catch errors, makes sure that it is easily understood, and finds "angles" that need further development. Writers and editors concentrate on finding a good "lead" for the story, an opening paragraph that summarizes the situation or entices the reader further into the article.

Much reporting is done by telephone. The reporter assigned to a story calls as many sources as possible to cross-check the facts for accuracy and to obtain the best-rounded story possible. Some metropolitan beat reporters, especially those covering the police department, may not write a story a week, even though they have worked on dozens by telephone.

While the city staff is gathering the local news, other groups are putting together other parts of the paper. News from the rest of the country and abroad arrives from the press associations and special correspondents. This is edited and coordinated on the telegraph desk.

City news and telegraph stories pass across the news desk, where they are weighed for importance and general interest. The news editor assigns them appropriate headline sizes and marks them into position on dummy sheets; it is these sheets that tell the printers how to assemble the mass of stories into the proper pages. The stories then pass to the copy desk for final editing. The appearance of video display terminals in a rapidly growing number of newsrooms has changed the familiar physical routine of most copy desk work, but the principle is the same whether copyeditors are working with stories typed in the traditional manner or displayed on video screens. The language experts, supervised by the copy desk chief, give the stories a final polishing and write the headlines. From the copy desk the stories are released to the composing room.

The sports department, the life style department, the financial editors, and other special groups are at work filling the pages allotted to them in a similar manner.

The person in charge of the entire news department is the managing editor, just as on the very small daily. Instead of doing the detailed work in person, the editor supervises the dozens of staff members who do it. The managing editor's post on a metropolitan newspaper is one of the most demanding and responsible jobs in all journalism.

SUNDAY PAPERS —WORLD'S LARGEST

By far the bulkiest newspapers published anywhere are the Sunday editions of American metropolitan newspapers. These mammoth publications wrapped in sections of color comics often contain more than 300 pages, nearly four pounds of reading matter covering everything from the current world crisis to interior decorating advice, theatrical notices, baseball scores, and weekly television logs.

In the United States there are about 20 such Sunday newspapers with 500,000 or more circulation, and several with more than 1 million. Even these mammoth figures are greatly exceeded by the circulation of several Sunday papers printed in London and distributed throughout the British Isles. They do not, however, have the advertising bulk of their American counterparts.

The Sunday paper is designed for family reading and is distinguished from the daily editions by two elements: a large feature package and bulk retail advertising. As a medium for late spot news, the Sunday paper is less important than the daily editions because less news occurs on Saturday (which it is covering) than on weekdays. Much of the material in the news sections is of a feature or background nature, stories for which no space exists in the smaller daily editions. Most newspapers print part of their Sunday editions well in advance because of the difficulty of printing such huge issues on the available press equipment on the publication date.

The Sunday editions of most newspapers have substantially higher circulation than the daily editions and sell at a price often more than double that of the daily paper. Publishing a Sunday paper is an expensive operation because of the heavy costs involved in buying the color comics and nationally syndicated magazine inserts and in preparing the abundance of locally created feature material, such as the weekly TV log, and the local magazine section that is edited by the staff. Newsprint costs on bulky papers are enormous. Smaller newspapers find Sunday publishing unprofitable in many instances, especially since they must compete against widely distributed metropolitan editions. As a result, the Sunday field is dominated by big-city newspapers that can afford to enter it: for most of them, it is very lucrative and provides a substantial share of annual profits.

Department stores have found Sunday editions to be one of their most effective selling tools. The paper is read at home in leisurely surroundings, and almost every member of the family peruses at least one part of the edition as it is scattered around the living room floor. So the stores put a heavy share of their advertising budget into the Sunday edition, often taking many pages in the same issue to publicize their wares.

Chapter 6

PRESS ASSOCIATIONS AND SYNDICATES

THE ROLE OF PRESS ASSOCIATIONS

For decades the chatter of press association teleprinters has been a symbol of news excitement. The dispatches typed out by their automatic keys on continuous rolls of paper represent the world of action, under datelines of Washington, London, Moscow, state capitals, and a thousand other cities.

In the electronic revolution now sweeping the printed media, the traditional teletype has begun to disappear, just as the Morse telegraph key did. Some large newspapers do not have a teleprinter left in their newsrooms; dispatches are transmitted directly from a press association office computer into their computers, for editing on a video display terminal, at an increased tempo.

Supplying the news dispatches that come in such abundance are the Associated Press and United Press International, the fiercely competitive American entries among the five major international newsgathering agencies. Without the service of at least one press association, a daily newspaper or broadcasting station would find distribution of a well-balanced news report to its audience virtually impossible.

The press associations take over where the local and area news coverage of the city desk ends. Even the largest dailies and the broadcasting networks with extensive staffs of their own correspondents in Washington and abroad are heavily dependent upon the press associations for domestic and foreign dispatches.

Intense hour-to-hour rivalry between AP and UPI exists in their effort to deliver simply written dispatches that are comprehensive, accurate, objective, and perceptive—and to get them there first. When they are reporting United States news to media abroad, or engaging in international newsgathering, they run into equally intense competition from Reuters, the British news agency; Agence France-Presse; and, to a lesser degree, TASS of the Soviet Union.

This competitive urge is one of the attractions of press association work, especially for younger reporters and editors; it adds a zest to newsgathering that has disappeared to some degree from the local news staffs in many cities where only one newspaper now exists. Commercially, to be faster and better than one's rival has great importance, because the AP and UPI are in constant battle to take away customers from each other. (The AP calls them *members;* the UPI refers to them as *clients.*)

Although the services they deliver to newspapers, television, and radio stations here and abroad are similar, the two United States press associations are organized quite differently. The Associated Press, which is much older, is a cooperative newsgathering association. Each American newspaper that purchases its services becomes a member of the cooperative and has a voice in setting the association's newsgathering and financial policies; also, it is obligated to turn over its local news coverage to the cooperative. Television and radio stations taking AP service become associate members without voting rights; the total now exceeds that of newspaper members (Figure 6.1). The Associated Press was founded in 1848 by six New York publishers, primarily to cooperate in the gathering of news from ships arriving in eastern harbors from Europe. It has been in continuous existence ever since, having gone through several major reorganizations including one in 1900 that established it in its present form.

United Press International is a privately owned company, dealing on a contract basis with newspapers, television and radio stations, and other organizations that have need for a news report. Its individual clients influence the shape of the UPI news report through their suggestions and criticism, solicited by UPI management, or through their ultimate power to cancel the service. UPI has advisory boards of newspaper and broadcast clients to help management set goals and policies. The United Press was founded in 1907 by E. W. Scripps, the owner of a large group of newspapers, with the purpose of supplying news to papers that could not obtain Associated Press membership under then-existing rules. In 1958 the United Press absorbed the International News Service, which had operated as a relatively weak third American competitor in the field since William Randolph Hearst founded it in 1909. The combined service became known as United Press International.

The new UPI was able to compete fully with the AP in gathering news and pictures worldwide, but it had only the smaller share of financial support from United States daily newspapers. Deficits incurred in that area wiped out profits from service to broadcast, picture, and overseas clients,

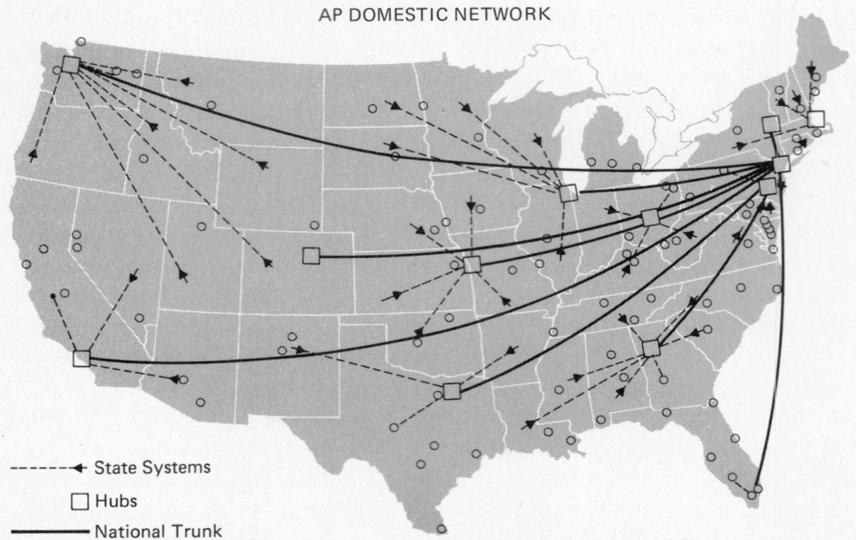

Figure 6.1 The communications network of the Associated Press in the United States. "Hubs" are regional bureau offices. The AP also has an extensive worldwide communications network. (Courtesty of the Associated Press.)

building up to a $7 million loss in 1980 that brought the Scripps Company owners to a search for other investors.

The Associated Press is the largest of the international news agencies. It collects and sells news in more than 100 countries to some 7500 newspapers and broadcast stations, including 1180 newspapers and 3500 stations in the United States (Figure 6.1). More than 2000 staff members work in 175 news bureaus. United Press International also operates in more than 100 countries, serving 7100 publications and stations, including 800 newspapers and 3700 stations in the United States. More than 1800 staff members work in 177 news bureaus.

Reuters, the third international agency, became a cooperative trust in 1941, owned by the British press. Founded in 1851, it grew with the British empire, laying cable systems centered on London. Reuters serves some 6500 clients worldwide, and reports a staff of 500 fulltime and about 4000 special correspondents. Agence France-Presse, successor to Havas (founded in 1835), became press-owned in 1957 and claims 2500 clients in 50 countries, served by 75 bureaus and 2000 staff members and correspondents. TASS has operated since 1918 as a Soviet Union government agency; it claims 5500 subscribers and has correspondents in all major countries and an extensive internal news network.

Regardless of whether a daily newspaper is called a member or a client, the net result is much the same. It receives the UPI or AP news report for a specified number of hours each day, for which it pays a fee based upon its circulation and the amount of news received. Most small dailies, and even some very large ones, operate successfully with only one of the two major wire services. Of the 1750 American daily newspapers, fewer than 20 percent now subscribe to both services. When both provide stories on the same news events, as they do scores of times daily, the telegraph editor of the two-service newspaper selects the dispatch that arrives first, if an urgent news break is involved, or the one that seems more complete, concise, and interesting. Sometimes the two dispatches are combined to provide a more well-rounded and complete story.

The rival agencies keep close watch on selected lists of these two-service papers to determine the play their respective stories receive. Bad play on a big story—or worse, being badly beaten by the rival agency on a news break—brings sharp backstage criticism from the New York home office to the head of the offending bureau.

NEWS IN SATELLITE DISHES

In the late 1970s, UPI and AP each had more than 400,000 miles of leased telephone wires in the United States for transmission of news and pictures. Both used underwater cables, radio teleprinters, and international satellite channels to reach clients abroad. Each had teletype circuits covering more than 20,000 miles in Europe, where their news reports were translated and fed into national wires. Both had automated their transmission facilities, using video display terminals and computers to perfect information storage and retrieval systems.

Soaring costs of leasing telephone wires for their domestic services led AP and UPI to cooperate with a committee from the American Newspaper Publishers Association (ANPA) to work out a plan to transmit news and pictures to newspaper and broadcast station users via satellite. In April, 1980, the first earth satellite station in an Associated Press nationwide network was dedicated at the Seattle *Times.* A retired AP Morse telegraph operator attached a gold-painted bolt to the receiving antenna, a 10-foot-wide "dish" on the roof. AP expected to have 900 dishes in place by the end of 1981. UPI opened a similar system in 1981. Both were transmitting on data and audio channels, with UPI adding pictures. The signals were beamed by Western Union to its Westar III, located in stationary orbit 22,300 miles from the earth and in view from any city in the United States, making possible line-of-sight microwave transmission to the dishes of the press association members and clients at a rate of 1200 words per minute. Dish installation costs ran from $3500 to $8400 and transmission costs were well below landline charges. AP expected to save $3.5 million in leased-line costs by the end of 1982. AP leases its dishes while UPI expects its clients to buy their own.

With use of this 10-foot-wide "dish" adjoining its plant, the Orlando (Florida) *Sentinel Star* receives instant transmissions of Associated Press copy from the Westar III satellite 22,300 miles in space. (Photo by Dave Cotton; courtesy of Orlando *Sentinel Star*.)

The press association satellite dishes could also be used to distribute syndicated material, and to receive photos in a matter of seconds. ANPA began investigating transmission of advertising by satellite. *Time* magazine, using Westar to transmit four-color pages and black-and-white photos and text to its regional printing plants in the United States, broke new ground in 1980 by using Intelsat IV to beam the same material to its Hong Kong printing plant, saving 24 hours for Asian subscribers. Its Netherlands printing plant did the same for Europe and Africa.

HOW PRESS ASSOCIATIONS FUNCTION

Each press association divides its flow of news into P.M. and A.M. reports, or cycles, the former for afternoon newspapers and the latter for morning papers. These reports always begin with a "budget," or checklist, of the most important stories that are to be transmitted. The budget is a summary of the basic stories then available, or known to be forthcoming during the next few hours, plus sports and feature highlights. Usually it contains 10 or 12 items. The news editor is thus able to plan makeup to ensure space for stories that the paper most likely will want to run. Since the large majority of American newspapers are published in the afternoon, and most news occurs during daytime hours, the P.M. reports are generally handled with a greater sense of urgency.

Basic stories on major news situations are transmitted early in each cycle. If later developments occur on a story, a new lead is moved on the wire. This reports the latest news on the situation and ends with a transitional paragraph that blends into the earlier dispatch at a specified place. On big, fast-breaking stories a press association may carry half a dozen leads in a cycle; these are edited so compactly that the dispatch which ultimately appears in a client newspaper reads with smooth continuity, even though it may contain segments of several leads.

Such methods are necessary because press association clients are constantly going to press and must print what is available on a given situation at press time. To use a phrase popular with United Press International, somewhere there is a deadline every minute. This is a major difference between press association and ordinary newspaper writing: the press association correspondent must keep feeding the latest developments in a spot story onto the news wires immediately, even when their meaning and ramifications are not fully disclosed; the newspaper staff correspondent (called a "special" by the wire services) usually has more time before deadline to digest and consolidate the information. Press association writers and editors usually work under time pressure. When we consider this, the amount of background and interpretation an experienced press association writer can weave into a fast-breaking story is remarkable.

Press associations have main trunk distribution circuits running across the country, serving the major metropolitan newspapers. Regional and state circuits from regional centers serve the smaller papers in different areas of the country. The editors who control the flow of news onto these secondary wires must see that the newspapers on each receive a balanced menu of regional news along with the most important national and foreign dispatches. Thus an Associated Press member in Arizona will receive some stories of interest only to readers in the Southwest that will not be delivered to another member in Florida. These members, however, will receive identical dispatches on the day's major news from Washington and London. Proper channeling of the daily news report, so that each newspaper gets the largest possible number of stories pertinent to its needs, is a basic problem for press associations.

The press associations use video display terminals, on which reporters write their dispatches. Their stories go into computer storage from which they are called by editors on control desks. Once edited, the stories are ready for transmission to newspaper and broadcasting clients. They may be delivered as teleprinter-roll hard copy, as punched teletypesetter tape for newspapers still using hot metal typesetting machinery, as hard copy on special white paper that can be inserted into an OCR electronic scanner, or

Close-up view of a press association dispatch called up for editing on a newspaper copy desk video display terminal. (Courtesy of the South Bend *Tribune*.)

directly as electronic signals into the newspaper's computer. Although newspapers with the direct computer intake system no longer require teletype machines, they have a special supplementary high-speed printer that provides a copy for reference when desired.

When the teletype circuit operated at 66 words a minute, press associations faced the problem of having large stacks of copy on hand awaiting transmission. Newspapers received stories under this traditional method in the sequence determined by the editors who were newswire gate-keepers. Satellite transmission changed this. So did computer-to-computer transmission. In that system, a brief abstract of each story is sent to the newspapers. With all the accumulated day's news stored in the newspaper computer within a short time, instead of having to await its arrival piece by piece, the newspaper's telegraph editor can select and edit the stories desired for publication, then release them from the newspaper's computer to be put into type. Spot-breaking stories are transmitted on a priority basis from computer to computer as they develop.

A still further modification called "demand" service is offered by UPI. This provides the telegraph editor of the individual newspaper with abstracts of all stories available in the UPI news report but does not transmit the stories automatically to the newspaper. Instead, the telegraph editor orders transmission from the press association computer of only the stories desired. The editor of another newspaper might order quite a different set of stories. The purpose of demand service is to cut down the huge wasted effort of transmitting stories that a paper does not use and must throw away.

SPECIAL WRITING TECHNIQUES

It is evident that a news story that goes through all these stages of editing from reporter to client editor's desk requires special writing techniques. It may be published 500 words long in one newspaper and only 100 words in another. Thus the writer must keep the fundamental information near the top of the story so the dispatch can be trimmed easily without having key facts omitted.

A press association reporter must write concisely, in simple sentences. Because the dispatches will be printed in newspapers of differing political persuasions, the writer must be carefully objective, especially in handling complicated, controversial stories. The primary goal of press association writing is clear and swift communication of events and ideas. The staff writer's basic stock in trade is straight news, well written. More distinctive forms of self-expression increasingly find their way onto the wires; usually, however, those who wish to concentrate on this type of writing choose other, less restrictive outlets.

Television and radio's instant news coverage of events in progress has had a heavy impact on the press associations. Like newspapers, broadcast news staffs have changed their operating methods, increasing the stress on interpretive and analytical material. Until approximately the mid 1950s, press association reports primarily were happening-oriented, concentrating on reporting events as they took place. Today, they are more situation-oriented. Recognizing that the newspapers they serve no longer can be first with big news stories, the associations supplement spot news with background and interpretive dispatches that help the reader understand the why of the situation.

Although the press associations permit their established writers more freedom in interpreting news situations than in the past, they are on guard against political or social slanting of dispatches. The more complicated the world becomes, the more difficult it is for press associations to find a proper balance between quick-breaking facts and interpretation that gives them perspective without distortion. This calls for highly skilled reporting and editing.

OTHER PRESS ASSOCIATION ACTIVITIES

Both United Press International and the Associated Press were founded to provide news for American newspapers. That remains their basic function, but they have branched out to additional services. Each supplies specially written news reports to thousands of radio and television stations in the

United States, and news to newspapers and broadcasting stations in many foreign countries. A constant flow of news originating in the United States is being sent abroad while foreign news is arriving in New York by a complex network of circuits (Figure 6.2). In Europe, the American associations distribute their dispatches on leased circuits for translation into the local language in each country. Translation into Spanish for Latin American countries is largely done in the New York offices. Bulletins on important news breaks can be flashed within a minute on a Rome-London-New York-San Francisco-Tokyo transmission network, spreading the word around the world almost instantly. Pictures are transmitted throughout the world by radio facilities and satellites.

The foreign bureaus of the American press associations usually are headed by an American, but they also employ local nationals in substantial numbers as reporters, editors, and translators. The number of foreign correspondent jobs available to Americans in the press associations is thus smaller than many people may believe. In normal times approximately 450 American citizens serve overseas as media correspondents, the majority of them for the press associations. It is apparent that the commonly held desire of young writers to become foreign correspondents is not easily fulfilled.

The American press associations have become important transmission belts for presenting a picture of life in America to foreigners. The hunger in many countries for news about the United States reflects this country's major role in world affairs. The Associated Press and United Press International carry a heavy responsibility in their selection and writing of news for the overseas audience, so that a well-balanced picture is presented. This does not imply censorship, the hiding of unpleasant news, or peddling of propaganda, but a judicious budget of stories to provide a multifaceted view of American life. In contrast, the only foreign press association with important news outlets in the United States is Reuters, the British agency. The Reuters news report, which is edited principally in London, is purchased by some metropolitan American newspapers and TV-radio network news departments as a supplementary service.

Special news service for television and radio stations is a major part of the agencies' operations. This is transmitted on different teletype circuits from the newspaper service and is rewritten from the stories in the basic report to please the ear rather than the eye. The style is more conversational, with simpler sentence structure and less detail. Distribution of a

---

Figure 6.2 The worldwide communications network of United Press International. Leased cables, satellites, and radio circuits speed the flow of news. The UPI also has an extensive communications network in the United States. (Courtesy of United Press International.)

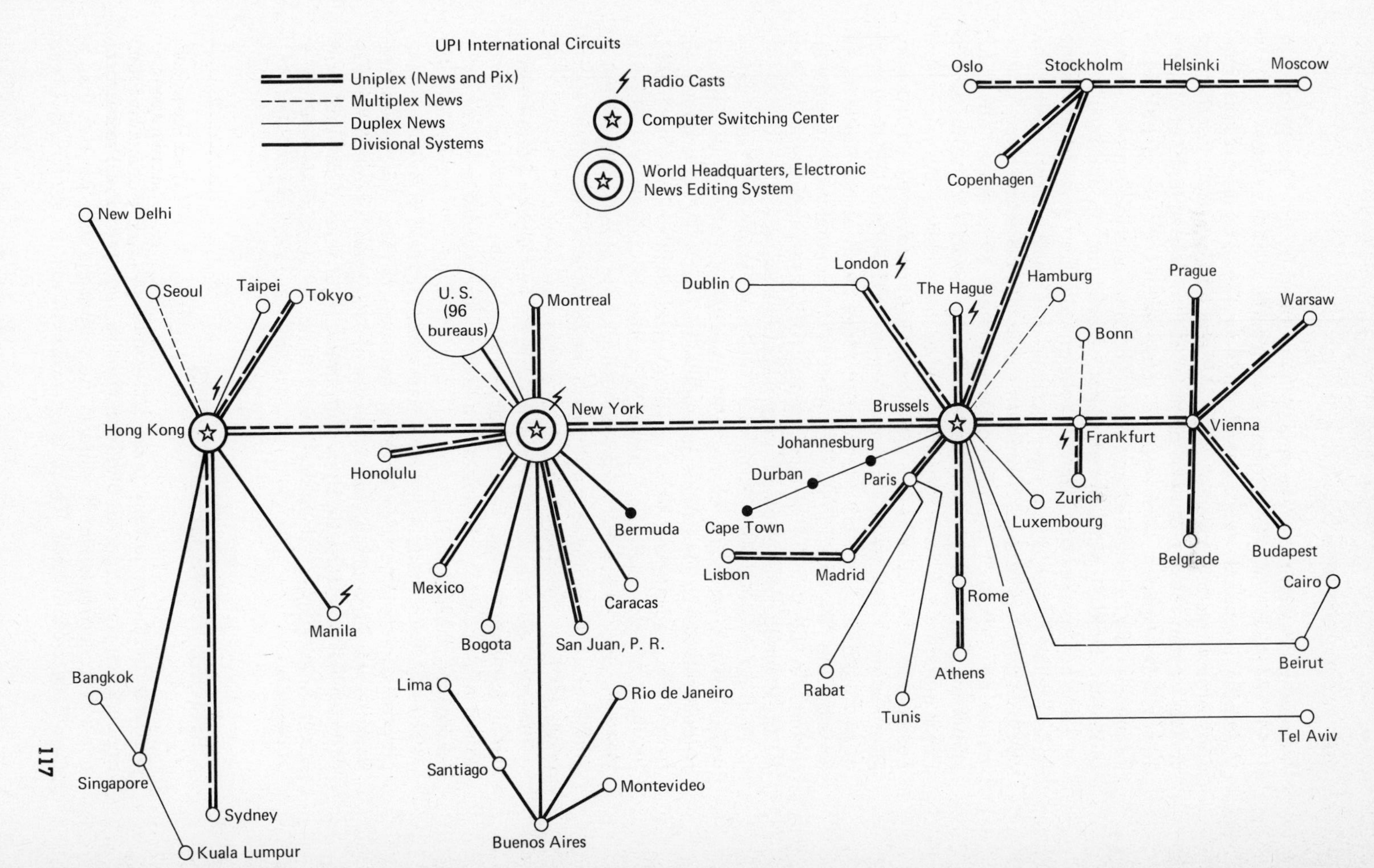

UPI International Circuits
Uniplex (News and Pix)
Multiplex News
Duplex News
Divisional Systems
Radio Casts
Computer Switching Center
World Headquarters, Electronic News Editing System
Oslo
Stockholm
Helsinki
Moscow
Copenhagen
New Delhi
Seoul
Taipei
Tokyo
U. S. (96 bureaus)
Montreal
Dublin
London
The Hague
Hamburg
Prague
Warsaw
Bonn
Hong Kong
New York
Brussels
Frankfurt
Vienna
Honolulu
Johannesburg
Durban
Paris
Zurich
Luxembourg
Bermuda
Cape Town
Lisbon
Madrid
Belgrade
Budapest
Cairo
Mexico
Caracas
Rome
Manila
Bogota
San Juan, P. R.
Beirut
Athens
Bangkok
Lima
Rio de Janeiro
Rabat
Tunis
Tel Aviv
Santiago
Singapore
Montevideo
Sydney
Buenos Aires
Kuala Lumpur

specially processed radio report was inaugurated by the United Press in 1935. The Associated Press followed reluctantly five years later.

Another important service provided to newspapers by the press associations is news picture coverage. Both AP and UPI operate coast-to-coast circuits for transmission of news photographs, a growing number of them in color. Newspapers connected to these circuits receive photographs instantaneously as they are transmitted. The news agencies supply pictures to foreign clients by satellite, radio photo, leased circuits, and mail.

Some newspapers purchasing the nationwide direct service receive the news photos in their offices over facsimile machines, which translate the electrical impulses of the transmission circuit into black and white photographs by means of a scanning device; these pictures are ready for immediate printing in the newspapers. During the 1970s, the Associated Press introduced a new system of photo transmission by wire called Laserphoto, which uses a laser beam to provide improved clarity in the dry glossy prints it delivers to the member papers. Both AP and UPI have staffs of photographers who are assigned to stories much as are reporters. In addition, the Associated Press distributes many pictures taken by photographers on the staffs of member papers. UPI also supplements its staff picture coverage with photos from newspaper sources.

Both press associations deliver an audio news service for radio station voice pickups on news events. UPI operates a daily motion picture newsfilm service to TV stations, an audio-visual cable TV news service, an Ocean Press radio news report to passenger vessels at sea, and, until 1981, operated a voice-over-photo news TV service by satellite. AP offerings include a color slide service for television stations, a mailed tape service, and a book division that produces a news annual and other special volumes.

On still another front, the Associated Press and United Press International, the latter through its subsidiary United Feature Syndicate, provide comic strips, political columns, and a host of other syndicated material for newspaper publication.

Thus the two organizations have journeyed far afield from their original purpose of providing dispatches for newspapers. The daily newspaper report, however, continues to be the core of each agency's operations. The UPI and AP now serve not one but three of our mass communications media—newspapers, television, and radio, plus special services to magazines.

CRITICAL VIEWS OF AGENCIES

Students of the American press sometimes are critical of the heavy dependence of newspapers and broadcasting stations on the press associations; this criticism is aimed more at the role of the wire services than at their daily performance. There is an undercurrent of uneasiness among these critics because approximately 1750 daily newspapers and nearly 9000 broadcast stations look to these two organizations for the great bulk of their nonlocal news. Anyone who listens to a succession of radio newscasts and hears the identical words from the radio news wires spoken repeatedly on different wavelengths realizes the dependence of radio stations in particular on the press associations. In fact, an overwhelming percentage of the American people are largely dependent on the two organizations, through their various newspaper and TV-radio ramifications, as well as their use by the weekly news magazines, for knowledge of what is happening in the world. In the eyes of the critics this constitutes a danger involving conformity of reporting and thought, and some question the qualifications of wire service editors to select the news that is transmitted.

The argument is more philosophic than practical. The economics of newspaper publishing makes it impossible for even the largest, wealthiest newspapers to have staff reporters stationed around the world in sufficient numbers to give them exclusive reports. Therefore some form of cooperative newsgathering is necessary.

The editors of client and member newspapers, and wire service executives themselves, subject the press association news report to constant scrutiny for accuracy and completeness. When instances of insufficient or inaccurate coverage come to light, steps are taken quickly to remedy the weakness. The competitive factor is a very wholesome one. The Associated Press Managing Editors Association has committees making continuous studies of AP operations. The UPI Advisory Council also makes studies.

The press associations are scolded at times by critics because they use the reporting services of part-time local "string" correspondents in some parts of the world. When a major story breaks in a remote area, they must use the sometimes inadequate services of these part-timers until an American-trained correspondent can reach the scene. Governments of developing countries complain that the Western news services give a distorted colonialist view of their countries. At New Delhi in 1976 some of them formed a Non-Aligned News Pool in competition. While admitting basis for their complaint, the Western press saw this as an attempt to distribute government-manipulated and censored news (see Chapter 23).

Another criticism of the press associations is shared by the newspapers themselves: an alleged preoccupation with crisis reporting, or trying to find conflict and excitement in every situation, to the point of distorting the news. In particular, this charge has been made against the methods of handling political and legislative news. It is stated that too much emphasis is placed on the routine partisan postures of the two major political parties in the United States. This allegation results from the striving of each association to find sharp "angles" that induce telegraph editors to print its stories instead of its competitor's. Recently, however, both wire services have been broadening their coverage by offering more thoughtful, interpretive articles in such fields as religion, race, education, labor, and social problems. They are much less open to charges of crisis overemphasis than they were a decade ago. The news services are also criticized for not carrying enough foreign news, to which they reply that their newspapers will print only a limited amount of such news, and there is no use in taking wire transmission time to give them what they will not use.

Actually, the conformity in presentation of national and foreign news by newspapers is less than might be expected. Checks of representative groups of newspapers receiving the same wire service show a surprisingly wide variation in the stories chosen from the telegraphed news report by editors for publication in their newspapers. Stories selected for prominent front page play by some editors may be dismissed by others with brief mention on inside pages, or omitted entirely. This is not surprising when we realize that the press association wire delivers far more dispatches than most newspapers can use, and the pressures of local news vary from city to city. So do the news judgments of the individual editors.

Another way in which editors broaden their national and foreign news coverage is the purchase of a supplementary news service, such as those offered by the New York *Times* and the Los Angeles *Times*-Washington *Post* Service. These services supply to their clients by wire a daily news report that includes dispatches on major Washington and foreign events, plus background dispatches under many datelines. They leave the hourly spot coverage to the press associations, but seek to round out the picture with news material that is exclusive in each client's territory.

JOB OPPORTUNITIES IN PRESS ASSOCIATIONS

The press associations are among the finest training grounds in the entire field of mass communications for young people interested in a career of working with news. The work is challenging. It puts a premium on speed, conciseness, and judgment. These organizations have a tradition of hiring young writers of limited professional experience and training them. Since the turnover in press association personnel is relatively high, there are quite a few job openings each year. A large increase in the number of women on press association staffs has occurred in recent years. The same is true of members of racial minorities.

A beginner in press association work usually is given routine stories to rewrite from the local newspapers, items to check by phone, and similar simple duties. The writer must learn to look outward from the local community, to weigh each story for its interest to readers in other cities. Quite soon, the relative newcomer may be named night manager of a small bureau, an opportunity to exercise a limited amount of administrative responsibility. Because of the nature of press association work, staff members do more editing and less original reporting than newspaper staffs do.

Those who stay with the press associations for a number of years, as many do, usually become managers of small or medium-sized bureaus or are transferred into such large offices as Chicago, Washington, or the New York general headquarters. Members of the foreign staffs normally are given experience in New York or Washington before being sent abroad.

Salaries for press association work are approximately in line with those on large daily newspapers. Although quite a few newspeople spend virtually their entire careers in the press associations, there is a fairly heavy turnover in personnel. Some wire service staff members grow tired of the time pressures and the writing restrictions. They believe that although advancement is relatively fast when they are starting, it slows down as they mature.

They may find better salary opportunities in special reporting jobs and editorships on newspapers or in public relations, radio, television, and other related fields of mass communications. Many of the country's best-known reporters, writers, television commentators, and editors worked for the press associations in their younger years, almost unanimously they are grateful for the experience, especially for the writing discipline it taught them.

NEWSPAPER FEATURE SYNDICATES

The other major source of editorial material used by daily newspapers, and one that tends to bring uniformity to the American press, is the feature syndicate. Syndicates sell to the newspapers a multitude of material for the entertainment and education of their readers, edited and ready for publication upon delivery. Comic strips and other features are provided in proof form for newspaper reproduction; text features are available in proof or duplicated form, prepunched TTS tape, on "scanner-ready" paper for newspapers using electronic typesetting machinery, or by transmission directly into the purchaser's computer system.

An editor may load the newspaper with as much syndicated material as conscience and budget will allow. The larger the feature "package" in a paper, the less space is available to be filled with locally created news and press association dispatches. A publication too full of such "canned" features gets a reputation of being more an entertainment medium than a newspaper and of being deficient in editorial enterprise. Readership polls show, however, that a very strong desire exists among readers for certain syndicated features.

The newspaper editor tries to strike a suitable balance. There is no firm rule of thumb about this; one good newspaper of substantial circulation and a reasonably large editorial "hole" (the space left in a newspaper after the advertisements have been inserted) will publish 16 comic strips daily while a comparable one runs only 10 or 12. The same is true of political columns and other material offered by the syndicates.

Examination of a typical well-edited newspaper with 50,000 daily circulation shows this material purchased ready-made from national feature syndicates: 12 comic strips, 12 cartoon panels, 5 political columns, medical column, personal advice column, crossword puzzle, astrological forecast, political cartoon, 2 entertainment columns, and juvenile information feature.

Some features, especially comic strips, have run in newspapers so many years that they have become household words, a commonplace in contemporary American life. Millions of readers every day look to see how Dick Tracy is getting along in his pursuit of a clever criminal, how Mary Worth's soap opera plots are unfolding, and how Dagwood, the ordinary family man, is dealing with his domestic problems. The political opinions of conservative columnists William Safire, James J. Kilpatrick, and George Will compete in luncheon discussions with those of liberals Tom Wicker, Jack Anderson, and Carl Rowan. The humorous satirical comment of Art Buchwald and the free-swinging advice columns of "Dear Abby" (Abigail Van Buren) and Ann Landers serve many as light predinner fare. An increase in subtlety and sophistication have been noted in such strips as "Peanuts" and "The Wizard of Id." Efforts to inject political and social relevance into the comic world, of which Garry Trudeau's "Doonesbury" is a striking example, have had moderate success. Classic editorial page cartoonists such as Herbert L. Block (Herblock), Paul Conrad, and Bill Mauldin have been challenged by stylized and more conservative artists such as Jeff MacNelly, Tony Auth, and Patrick Oliphant.

Approximately one dozen major syndicates provide the bulk of the features appearing in American newspapers, although there are more than 100 smaller companies, some of which operate in specialized fields such as boating and book serializations. The major syndicates have from 25 to more than 100 features on the lists they offer for sale to editors. An editor who has trouble saying no to the sales talk of the syndicate representative soon finds the paper overloaded with material for which the total weekly fee can run uncomfortably high. But an editor who can't say no is a contradiction in terms. On comics especially, many editors make a habit of dropping one feature whenever they buy a new one. Papers make occasional readership surveys to determine which comics and daily features are most popular. So attached do readers become to individual comic strips that the dropping of one sometimes provokes a torrent of complaints; consequently, fewer changes are made than many editors desire.

Features are sold to newspapers for prices scaled to the paper's circulation. Although some are sold for specific contract periods, many are on a "till forbid" (t.f.) basis, meaning that the feature runs until the editor sends in a cancellation, usually on 30- to 90-day notice.

Competition among the syndicates to sell their features is intense. There are more than 250 daily comic strips on the market, many of which are also issued in color for Sunday comic sections; about 40 health columns, 75 religious features, and a dozen competing columns on stamp collecting. Although many well-established features go on year after year, a new group of comic strips, panels, and text columns is brought onto the market annually. Features that lose popular appeal are dropped by the syndicates.

As a rule an editor organizing a comic page tries to offer readers a mixture of adventure continuity, serial stories similar to TV soap opera drama, children's interest, a strip slanted to teenagers, and gag-a-day strips without continuity except in the characters themselves. Until a few years ago, most comic strips ran five columns wide; now almost all are in four columns. Closely connected with the comic strip is the cartoon panel, usually two columns wide, in which some familiar characters, such as Dennis the Menace, are involved in daily humorous misadventure; there is no continuity of action in these panels, which resemble those published in magazines. The creators of popular strips such as "Peanuts" earn large additional income through merchandising tie-ins featuring their cartoon characters.

The feature syndicates do not offer very great potential for the young person seeking a job. Their editorial and sales staffs are small and mostly drawn from professional journalists with several years of editorial or business experience. Most of the artists and writers whose material is distributed by these organizations do their work outside the syndicate offices and send or bring it in for editing and approval. Usually they work on a percentage arrangement with the syndicate, receiving a portion of the fees paid by the newspapers. Syndicate editing requires knowledge of the public taste, as well as the space problems, buying habits, and idiosyncracies of the various newspaper editors who are the customers for the syndicate products.

Chapter 7

MAGAZINES

THE ROLE OF MAGAZINES

Much communication of ideas, information, and attitudes among American people is carried on through magazines. Thousands of periodicals fall within this category. They range from the slick-paper, four-color monthly with circulation in the millions down to the small, special interest quarterly that, though virtually unknown to the general public, may have very strong influence within its field.

The magazine exists to inform, entertain, and influence its readers editorially and put before them advertising messages of national or regional scope. Magazines never appear more frequently than once a week; thus their writers and editors have more time to dig into issues and situations than do those on daily newspapers, and consequently they have a better opportunity to bring events into focus and interpret their meaning.

So many different types of magazines exist that making broad statements about their functions and goals may lead to inconsistencies. Some are published solely for their entertainment value and are loaded with material of little consequence. Others deal entirely with a serious investigation of contemporary problems, and many combine entertainment and service material with reporting and interpretation.

The magazine, with its more durable cover and bound pages, has a semipermanence the newspaper lacks. Magazines such as *National Geographic* often are kept around a home for years, or passed from reader to reader, like books.

There is another basic difference between newspapers and magazines. A newspaper must appeal to an entire community and have a little of everything for almost everybody. With a few exceptions, like the *Wall Street Journal,* a newspaper cannot be aimed at a single special interest group and survive. Yet hundreds of successful magazines are designed for reading by such interest groups as gasoline station operators, dentists, poultry farmers, and model railroad fans. Therein lies the richness of diversity that makes the magazine field so attractive to many editorial workers. The possibilities for the specialist editor and writer are greater than on newspapers, although the number of editorial jobs on magazines is fewer.

TYPES OF MAGAZINES

Generalizations about the content, style, and appearance of American magazines are dangerous because so many variations exist among the approximately 9500 periodicals now being published. That is the number given in Ayer's *Directory,* as distinguished from listings of newspapers with general circulations. Not all appear in magazine format, however; quite a few are tabloid or regular newspaper size. No more than 600 can be classified as general interest magazines. In contrast, there are 2500 specialized business and trade publications issued quarterly or more frequently, 1300 in the field of religion, and about 700 agricultural periodicals, to list three major subfields. Not included in these figures are some 9000 industrial, or company, publications designed for employees, customers, stockholders, dealers, and others. Many of these are issued in magazine format.

Although all magazines share certain basic problems of production and distribution, their editorial content and advertising are of many hues. Even trying to group them into categories becomes difficult because inevitably there is overlapping, and a few magazines almost defy classification. Most magazines fall into the following general categories.

General Family Interest

Two mass circulation magazines that sell 18 million or more copies each issue lead this group. One is *Reader's Digest,* begun in 1922 by DeWitt and Lila Wallace as a pocket-size compilation of nonfiction articles. Now the centerpiece of a giant publishing enterprise, it is a well-staffed mass circulation monthly blending informative, inspirational, and entertaining nonfiction. The other, *TV Guide,* appears weekly in regional editions; after a quarter-century of publication by the Annenberg family's firm, it has emerged dominant in its specialized function. Its annual gross revenue of one-half billion dollars and circulation above 19.5 million exceed that of any other publication.

Television's diversion of advertising revenues from general family interest periodicals spelled the doom of such formerly great magazines combining nonfiction and fiction as *Collier's* and the *American,* which ceased publication in 1956, and the *Saturday Evening Post,* abandoned as a weekly in 1969 (a monthly "nostalgia" edition still appears on newsstands). In the 1970s, for lack of advertising, the enormously successful picture magazines *Life* and *Look* also disappeared. *Life* reappeared as a monthly with 1.3 million circulation by 1980.

Into the void came *National Geographic,* established in 1888 as a travelog journal that blossomed out as a slickly edited, superbly illustrated monthly with a current circulation of 10.2 million. It absorbed some of the displaced photojournalism specialists. Others from *Life* and *Look* found their way to the Smithsonian Institution, whose *Smithsonian* magazine, founded in 1970, zoomed to 1.8 million circulation in a decade. *Ebony,* founded in 1945 by John H. Johnson as a black picture magazine, had a comfortable 1.2 million circulation in 1980. *Redbook,* with 4.3 million circulation, caters to young adults.

News Magazines

Close behind in general family appeal are weekly publications designed to summarize the news and provide added depth and interpretation that newspapers cannot give. They publish articles on news situations, examine headline personalities, and discuss trends in such diverse fields as religion, labor, sports, art, and the environment.

The present leaders (discussed in Chapter 4) are *Time,* with 4.3 million circulation; *Newsweek,* near 3 million; and *U.S. News & World Report,* a more specialized journal with about 2 million readers. *Jet* has 700,000 circulation among black readers.

Sophisticated Writing Quality

Possibly the most distinctive of American magazines has been the *New Yorker,* founded in 1925 by Harold Ross and carried on after 1951 by William Shawn. E. B. White long conducted its "Talk of the Town"; it has had writers of the quality of James Thurber, Wolcott Gibbs, A. J. Liebling, and Frank Sullivan; artists such as Helen Hokinson, Peter Arno, Otto Soglow, and Charles Addams. It also gives its one-half million readers—along with the cartoons, whimsy, and fiction—penetrating "Profiles" and lengthy, incisive commentaries on public affairs.

Esquire, founded in 1933 by Arnold Gingrich, ran the top bylines of American writing: Wolfe, Hemingway, Faulkner, Steinbeck, Capote, Mailer, Talese. It had 1 million readers but faltered and was sold to Clay

Felker, who in turn sold it to Phillip Moffitt. It retained 650,000 circulation in 1980. Felker also lost control of his successful *New York* and of *Village Voice,* havens for 1960s-style new journalists. Soon after Felker founded *New West* in Los Angeles, his backers sold to Rupert Murdoch. *New York,* founded in 1968, had such talented writers as Tom Wolfe, Jimmy Breslin, Judith Crist, and Gloria Steinem. (Steinem's 1972 creation, *Ms.*, began in *New York*'s offices and became the leading magazine of the feminist movement, with one-half million circulation.)

Quality and Opinion Magazines

Still enjoying about 300,000 circulation each are the quality literary magazines *Harper's* and *The Atlantic,* both more than 125 years old. Both of these publications recently have veered toward nonfiction and public affairs. *Saturday Review,* a fixture in literary circles for 35 years under former editor Norman Cousins, returned to its original strong emphasis on the arts in 1980.

Among the combative magazines of opinion, the widest circulating, at 220,000, is the crusading San Francisco-based monthly, *Mother Jones.* At the 100,000 level are the liberal *New Republic* and William Buckley's conservative *National Review.* More pungent are the *Nation,* well over a century old; Erwin Knoll's *Progressive;* and *Ramparts.* Among other magazines dealing with a variety of ideas and struggling for financial support are *Commentary, America, Commonweal, Society, Nutrition Action, Foreign Policy, Journal of Current Social Issues, Working Papers, Kenyon Review, Virginia Quarterly, Washington Monthly, Dissent, Sojourners, Reason, Inquiry,* and *Katallagete.*

When 16 prominent writers were asked recently to name the publications on which they depended most for their insights, an *Esquire* article reported that the *New Republic* drew the most votes (four). Obtaining three endorsements each were the *Nation, Washington Monthly, New Yorker, New York Review of Books,* and the *Wall Street Journal.* Cited twice were *Commentary, Economist, Catholic Worker, Seven Days, Psychology Today, International Journal of Psycho-Analysis, Public Interest, Village Voice,* and *National Review.*

Women's Interest

Half of the top 15 magazines in circulation in 1980 fall within the category of periodicals intended for the woman reader. The *Ladies' Home Journal, McCall's,* and *Good Housekeeping,* with circulations from five to six million, are three long-time leaders in their field. These traditional women's interest magazines contain articles on food, beauty hints, fashion, homemaking advice, inspirational advice, and personal problems. They also publish some fiction. Others in this category of traditional women's interest magazines include *Woman's Day, Family Circle,* and *Better Homes and Gardens.*

There are many other women's interest magazines ranging from 500,000 to 1.7 million in circulation: *Vogue* and *Harper's Bazaar* for fashion; *Glamour* and *Mademoiselle* for the young adult; *Seventeen* for the teenager; *Essence* for the black woman. Joining *Ms.* as feminist movement publications are *Working Woman* and *WomenSports.*

The sensationalized *National Enquirer* and the *Star* are aimed at women buyers. Although printed in newspaper format, these publications, in their feature content, more nearly resemble magazines. Sold mostly at supermarket checkout counters, the weekly publications are noted for their "hoked-up" headlines; medical, science, and parascience stories; revelations about celebrities, usually TV stars; and first-person testimonials of an inspirational character. Circulation of the *National Enquirer* exceeds 6 million; the publisher's goal is 20 million.

Men's Interest

Two magazines intended for men fall within the top 15 in circulation: *Playboy* and *Penthouse. Playboy,* established by Hugh Hefner in 1953, approached 7 million circulation, then declined below 5.6 million by 1980. *Penthouse* reached 4.6 million circulation in 1980. *Oui* sold almost 700,000 copies and *Hustler* passed the million mark among the rash of "skin" magazines on the sales rack.

In the men's interest category, but increasingly attractive to women, are several magazines of 1 to 2 million circulation: *Sports Illustrated, Outdoor Life, Field and Stream, Popular Science, Popular Mechanics,* and *Mechanix Illustrated* in the how-to field; and *True* and *Argosy* for adventure.

Special Interest Magazines

The hundreds of periodicals intended for special audiences form a very large segment of the magazine industry. Some are little known to the general public because they are infrequently displayed on the newsstands; others fall in major circulation categories.

The latter type includes the "shelter" magazines about family living, headed by *Better Homes and Gardens* and *Sunset;* farm magazines such as *Farm Journal* and *Successful Farming,* such science-interest publications as *Scientific American* and *Science Digest;* youth-oriented magazines such as *Boys' Life, Scouting, Junior Scholastic, American Girl,* and the area-associated *Parents' Magazine;* travel guides such as *Travel & Leisure;* and such diverse publications as *Psychology Today, Popular Photography,* and *Outside* (recreation).

The movie and TV fan magazines form still another special interest area.

THE TOP MAGAZINE MONEY MAKERS

These ten magazines led all others in the United States in total advertising and circulation revenues during the 12-month period ending June 30, 1979. The list is based on a detailed analysis by *Folio: The Magazine for Magazine Management*, the first comprehensive magazine industry revenue study ever undertaken.

TV Guide	$552.3 million
Time	$348.9 million
Reader's Digest	$239.6 million
Newsweek	$236.5 million
Playboy	$176.1 million
People Weekly	$169.8 million
Sports Illustrated	$168.7 million
Family Circle	$150.8 million
Woman's Day	$142.7 million
Better Homes and Gardens	$139.9 million

Others include trade and technical journals, professional and scientific publications, and publications intended for readers with hobbies such as model railroading or stamp collecting. Religious magazine publishing is an influential and important field. There are denominational and nondenominational publications, the largest of which—*Presbyterian Life, Catholic Digest,* and the *Christian Herald*—circulate to hundreds of thousands of readers. The *National Jewish Monthly* serves 200,000 families.

Catering to the life style habits of young adults, city and state magazines such as *Los Angeles* and *Texas Monthly* showed remarkable gains during the late 1970s and early 1980s. America's growing interest in science, sparked by spectacular television color forays into the human body and outer space, was reflected in the start of several new science magazines, including Time Inc.'s *Discover* and Carl Sagan's *Cosmos.*

Sunday Supplement Magazines

Distributed as part of the Sunday newspapers in many large American cities are some large-circulation magazines. Faring badly in the competition for advertising revenues with television, the nationally edited group lost the *American Weekly* and *This Week,* but retained *Parade* with 21.5 million copies and *Family Weekly* with 12 million. A black-oriented supplement, *Dawn,* was a 1970s success distributed with black newspapers. Founded in 1965, another black supplement, *Tuesday,* was distributed with conventional dailies. Best known of the Sunday magazines produced by individual papers is that of the New York *Times.*

The Business Press

The fastest growing area in magazine publishing has been that occupied by the 2500 periodicals known as the business press. One small segment includes the general business or business news magazines, headed by *Business Week, Forbes,* and *Fortune,* all above 650,000 in circulation. The rest are identified by the American Business Press, the industry trade association to which most of the larger business publishing houses belong, as "specialized business publications serving specific industrial business, service, or professional business audiences." Nearly half of these business magazines are industrial, followed, in order, by merchandising, medical, export and import and international, financial, educational, and government.

Largest of the United States publishing houses in the business field is McGraw-Hill, with 27 magazines and a large number of newsletters, 800 fulltime editors and reporters, a worldwide business news service, and such well-known periodicals as *Business Week* and *Aviation Week.* Other large group publishers include Cahners Publishing, Chilton (owned by the American Broadcasting Companies), Penton/IPC, and Technical Publishing (a subsidiary of Dun & Bradstreet). Some well-known titles are Chilton's *Iron Age,* Fairchild's *Women's Wear Daily,* and PennWell's *Oil and Gas Journal.* All told, the specialized business press has a total circulation of about 70 million and puts out about one million pages per year.

Company Publications

These are magazines published by corporations for distribution to their employees and customers, usually without charge. Their purpose is to present the company's policy and products in a favorable light and to promote a better sense of teamwork and belonging among employees. They are known also as industrial magazines; the term "house organ," was once widely used for these publications.

This field of industrial publishing has made large advances as corporations have become more conscious of their public relations. Many of these company publications are edited by people who are widely experienced in general magazine work and who have been given ample funds to produce magazines of sophisticated appearance and high-grade editorial content. More and more companies are realizing that they must hire professional people and set their standards to compare with general magazines on a broad basis. As one leading industrial editor, a veteran of general magazine staffs, expressed it: "No longer can the mail clerk or the personnel manager be regarded as an authority in the field of industrial editing. The emphasis definitely is on editing—and on journalism." Some journalism graduates move directly into industrial editing. In many such publications, articles of general interest, unrelated to the company's products, are included, and company propaganda is kept at a very subdued level. Some large corporations, in fact, publish a number of magazines intended for customers, stockholders, and employees. For example, the International Harvester Company and the Ford Motor Company publish some two dozen employee magazines each at different plants. Some of the more elaborate company publications, intended to reach the public as well as employees, have circulations above 1 million.

Company publications are of many sizes and shapes, and it is difficult to say at any given time how many of them qualify as magazines. Many appear in newspaper format. One recent estimate put the combined circulation of major company periodicals above 100 million. American business and industry invest more than $550 million a year in these 9,000 publications with some 15,000 editors and staff members.

HOW MAGAZINES ARE MARKETED

The magazine industry rests on twin foundations, circulation and advertising. For decades publishers sold each copy to the reader for far less money than it cost to produce it, making their profit through the sale of national and regional advertising. During recent years, however, the rising costs of paper, printing, payrolls, and home and newsstand deliveries greatly increased subscription and single-copy prices. Consequently, as reported in 1980 by *Folio,* a trade magazine for magazine publishers, readers paid $3.32 billion during a preceding measured year (46 percent of total revenues) as compared with $3.95 billion spent by advertisers (54 percent). Thus, as readers now provide nearly half of gross income, the publishers' onetime reliance upon advertising revenue to pay most of the costs of producing and distributing magazines has diminished considerably. *Folio* termed this development the most important change in magazine economics in recent years.

Folio examined more than 12,000 magazines and 6,000 publishing companies, and thoroughly analyzed the 400 largest magazines (by gross sales), representing 94 percent of the entire industry. It found that total gross sales for these 400 amounted to $7.27 billion, with subscribers spending $1.74 billion and single-copy purchasers $1.58 billion, the latter increasingly at checkout counters and family reading centers in supermarkets throughout the country.

Total magazine industry circulation fell just short of 350 million copies per issue, or approximately 7.7 billion copies annually. Of the 350 million copies, 197 million were sold by subscription, while the remainder was divided between newsstand (99 million) and free and controlled circulation. *TV Guide* alone accounted for more than one billion copies sold during the year.

In all, more than 469,000 industry-wide advertising pages were published by the top 400 magazines studied.

With consumer and advertiser interest in magazines high, and the population growing, between 200 and 350 new magazines are announced each year, according to *Folio.* Observers say the odds are ten to one that a magazine will fail, with much depending upon skilled management and the extent of capitalization. ("It depends upon who's starting it," one magazine investor said. "If a *Time* has a child, the odds are much shorter, maybe two to one.") *Look, Viva, New Dawn, Sassy,* and *New Times* are among recent casualties.

The range of subject matter is broad. Here is just a sample of the titles of magazines started in a recent year: *Equus, Harvey for Loving People, Next, Prime Time, New Shelter, Chips, Panorama, Self, Savvy, Games, Geo, Venture, Inside Sports, The Runner, New Woman, American Photographer, Media People, Museums New York, Muse, Quest, Omni, Travel Illustrated, Inc., Women Who Work,* and *Wet.*

Since hundreds of magazines, as well as other media, compete for advertising dollars, successful publishers must convince advertisers that the purchase of space in their pages is a good investment. This proof is based mostly on circulation figures. Magazines must show either very large mass distribution figures among a general readership or a firmly established circulation among the special interest groups to which their publications appeal editorially.

These economic principles have a powerful influence on the shape of the entire magazine industry. A magazine must be designed for appeal to a well-defined segment of the population, such as outboard boating enthusiasts or members of a fraternal order, or it must possess such broad interest that it will attract huge numbers of general readers.

Approximately 50 magazines have circulations of more than 1 million. The rising population in the United States makes the big publishers hopeful of even greater circulation figures in the next decade. The death of a half-dozen mass circulation magazines created the false impression that hard times had hit the magazine field. Circulation figures and other evidence, such as record revenues, show that this is not the case. Individual magazines have suffered because of changing public tastes and marketing conditions, including increased postal rates and the loss of much advertising to television, but the magazine field as a whole is healthy.

Hundreds of small magazines operate profitably year after year by concentrating on their special fields. Since advertising rates are based mostly on circulation, many advertisers cannot afford to buy space in magazines with circulations in the millions, on which the rate for a single black-and-white advertising page ranges from $25,000 to $50,000 and for color from $35,000 to $70,000. Instead, they spend their money in publications they can afford and that offer them an audience especially receptive to their products. To counteract this, some large magazines offer advertising space on regional or fractional split-run bases, and this practice accounts for some 20 percent of total magazine advertising revenues.

One of the largest magazine publishers today, in terms of total income, is Time Inc. Started in the early 1920s, when *Time* made its appearance with a new style of news magazine, this corporation grew spectacularly. Its picture weekly, *Life,* held top place among all magazines in gross advertising revenue from the 1950s to its collapse in 1972. *Time* held that position until surpassed by *TV Guide.* Time Inc. also publishes *Fortune,* devoted to the business world; *Sports Illustrated*; and three new ventures, *Money, Discover,* and *People Weekly* (2.3 million circulation).

The Hearst magazine group is affiliated with that newspaper publishing family's empire. The group includes such large and profitable properties as *Good Housekeeping, Cosmopolitan, Harper's Bazaar, Popular Mechanics, Sports Afield,* and *House Beautiful.* Its group of more than a dozen publications also lists magazines in the motoring, medical, and leisure fields.

Other major groups include the McGraw-Hill trade publications, headed by *Business Week;* the McCall Corporation, with *McCall's* and *Redbook;* Meredith Publishing Company, with *Better Homes and Gardens* and *Successful Farming;* the Johnson Publishing Company, with *Ebony, Jet,* and *Tan;* and the Condé Nast publications, *Glamour, Vogue, Mademoiselle,* and *House and Garden.*

Magazines are sold by two principal methods, single-copy sales on newsstands and mail delivery copies to subscribers. (Some trade publications are distributed free of charge to controlled lists in order to give advertisers a large audience for products.) Circulation is one of the most costly and complex problems a magazine publisher faces. Copies of each issue must be distributed nationwide and must be on sale by fixed dates each week or month. Copies unsold when the publication date for the next issue comes around must be discarded at heavy loss. Newsstand sales of magazines are handled through news wholesalers. Intricate arrangements and deals are made to ensure good display at outlets, since many sales are made on impulse as the buyer walks past the colorful array on the racks. This makes attractive cover design and provocative, attention-getting titles and sales catchlines on the covers extremely important.

Unlike newspapers, a large majority of magazines do not own their own printing facilities. The editors and advertising staffs prepare each issue in the office and then send the material to a commercial printer who holds a contract to produce the magazine. In fact, a few large printing houses with high-speed color presses do the printing for most of the major national magazines. This freedom from the heavy initial investment in printing equipment enables new publishers to start magazines with limited capital;

however, unless the new venture embodies an attractive basic idea or angle, and is well edited, the printing and circulation bills can soon eat up the adventurous newcomer's capital.

EDITORIAL CONTENT AND OPERATION

The editorial content of American magazines is predominantly nonfiction. About three-fourths of the material printed in consumer periodicals is factual, and the percentage is even higher in the trade and professional journals. Many magazines carry no fiction at all.

Editorial operation of magazines varies greatly, depending upon the size, type, and frequency of the publication. Generally, editorial staffs are relatively small. A magazine selling 4 million copies can be prepared editorially by a smaller staff than the one needed to put out a newspaper that sells a half-million copies. This is possible because much of the material published in some magazines is written by freelance writers, either on speculation or on order from the editors. These writers are paid fees for their work and do not function as members of the staff.

The magazine editor's job is to decide what kinds of material to publish, arrange to obtain it, and then present it in a manner pleasing to the reader's eye. Most editors work from a formula; that is, each issue contains specified types of material in predetermined amounts, arranged to give a desired effect. Articles and stories are selected for publication not only on their merit but for the way they fit the formula.

The editor has a staff of assistants to screen freelance material, work with writers, think of ideas, and edit the material chosen for publication. An art director arranges attractive layouts and chooses the covers. A cartoon editor selects such drawings if the periodical carries them. On many magazines a substantial portion of each issue is written by staff members.

The skillful, imaginative use of photojournalism has contributed heavily to the acceptance gained by many magazines in recent years. Combining technical efficiency with an appreciation of the aesthetic and the dramatic, the photojournalist is an able communicator with a camera. Most magazines have their own staffs of professional photojournalists, but freelance photographers, often working through agents, provide many striking pictures. Rates range in excess of $300 per day for black-and-white pictures, $400 for color, and $500 for cover shots. Picture editors make assignments and select the photos wanted for publication.

A key part of most magazine operations is the editorial conference, a session in which the editors discuss the forthcoming issue, make decisions on the material to be used, examine proposed layouts, and agree upon projects for future issues. Magazine projects generally are planned months in advance of publication. On some staffs one editor handles the nonfiction ideas and articles and another editor handles the fiction.

The news magazines operate somewhat differently. All their content is written by staff members, who are responsible for designated categories of material and for specific assignments, somewhat like a newspaper. Bureaus around the country and staff members abroad usually submit material ordered from the home office; the material is then rewritten and condensed to fit the available space. Magazines also lean heavily on press association material. News magazines operate on a rigid schedule in order to put the latest information on the newsstands throughout the United States.

Most magazines have at their command large amounts of freelance material submitted by writers who hope to "strike it lucky" and sell their work for a substantial sum. As most editors will testify, a relatively small amount of the unsolicited material unloaded on their desks by the mail carrier each day ever reaches print. Not that it necessarily is badly written or devoid of fresh ideas, but much of it does not fit the magazine's formula. The problem for the freelance writer is to have the right manuscript in the right editorial office at the right moment—not an easy task. Professional writers usually submit their articles in outline form or as just a brief proposal.

Since editors have found that they cannot depend upon unsolicited freelance material to fit their individual needs, they go in search of what they want. They assign article ideas to writers they know, and then work with them until the manuscripts have the desired flavor and approach. Or the idea might be assigned to a member of the staff and developed in the same manner.

Very few writers in the United States, perhaps only 250 or 300, make a living as full-time freelance magazine writers, but thousands try to join them. Although an established writer may be paid from $1000 up per article, the uncertainties of the craft are many and the number of big money markets is relatively small. Most of these full-time magazine writers work on assignment, being commissioned by editors who know and like their work to prepare articles on ideas proposed by the editors or ideas approved by them. In many cases freelance writers use agents to sell their output to editors on a commission basis. Almost all fiction in big magazines is sold by agents, and many professional article writers use their services. The agent functions to a degree as an adjunct of the editorial staff by channeling worthwhile stories to appropriate magazines. The better-known agents are quite selective about the authors they will handle, and having a well-known agent is a helpful endorsement for a writer.

Much of the contributed material published in magazines is written by writers who do freelance work on a part-time basis as a sideline to their regular occupation. Newspaper reporters, other mass media people, teachers, attorneys and other professionals, and homemakers with a flair for writing try their hands at freelancing with varying degrees of success.

There are hundreds of places where magazine material can be sold.

Competition to place articles and fiction in the mass circulation magazines is intense, and the material purchased must be excellently written and extensively researched. Preparation of a major magazine article requires so much skill and time that the work for the major general magazines is done largely by the small group of full-time professionals and staff members. However, the part-time freelancer can hit even the biggest magazines with short material, such as anecdotes, personal experiences, and humor. With a little luck and a lot of perseverance, a writer can sell numerous articles to smaller magazines and specialized periodicals. However, the pay in these smaller markets is not high; it ranges from $50 for a 2500-word article or short story up to about $500. Rates of payment for the confession-type magazines are 3 to 5 cents a word. At the upper end of the scale, where the competition is intense, the mass circulation magazines pay from $1000 to $3000 or higher for an article. The rates are flexible because the editors will pay extra if they consider that the material is exactly right for them or if the writer has a well-known name worth publicizing on the cover. One of the best ways for the newcomer to break into the market is to submit short-item filler materials, for which many magazines pay $10 or more.

JOB OPPORTUNITIES IN THE MAGAZINE INDUSTRY

The magazine industry provides interesting, stimulating, and generally well-paid jobs for thousands of men and women. On some periodicals, the editorial staff members do extensive writing, handling special departments and articles; on others, the editors are engaged mostly in selection and editing of submitted material.

Historically, magazines have offered greater opportunities for the woman editorial worker than newspapers have. The percentage of staff positions held by women is greater and the opportunity for advancement to high editorial positions has been much brighter. Women associate editors, managing editors, and editors-in-chief are not uncommon.

Although there is no certain formula for either the man or woman college graduate to use in seeking a magazine job, the surest way to draw attention is to sell the magazine some articles or stories. The very fact that the editor buys the material indicates that he or she approves of the writer's work. Personal contacts developed in this editor-writer relationship sometimes lead to staff positions. In some of the large magazines, young graduates get their start in the research department and other jobs around the fringe of the editorial staff.

Large magazines draw many of their staff members from the trade magazines and company publications, much as metropolitan newspapers hire reporters who have had training on smaller dailies. The mechanical techniques of magazine editing and design are complex and can best be learned by experience on smaller publications.

Industrial magazines are among the finest training grounds for magazine workers. This is a rapidly expanding field, as more and more corporations realize the value of issuing a periodical for customers, employees, salespeople, stockholders, and other groups the management wishes to impress. These are divided into internal publications, for distribution within a company, and external ones, which go to nonemployee readers. Many are combinations of these approaches. The type of distribution influences the kind of material published and to some extent the size of the staff. The best available estimate puts the number of editorial employees on company publications at around 15,000. Although many of these publications are prepared by a single editor with clerical help, the more elaborate ones have a staff of six or eight editors. They use the same techniques of design, multicolored artwork, and editorial presentation as those employed by the better-known consumer magazines.

External publications usually are published by manufacturers who hope for repeat sales of products of relatively high price. Automobile manufacturers are among the most lavish publishers in this field; magazines such as *Ford Times* are widely circulated to maintain contact with users and to promote sales and service.

Many fraternal and nonprofit organizations also publish magazines in order to maintain the bond with their members or supporters. Such periodicals as *American Legion* and the *Rotarian* publish a rather broad range of general articles that their editors consider of interest to their readers, and interweave promotional and fraternal material about the sponsoring organization.

Work on specialized magazines, both of the industrial magazine and trade varieties, sometimes requires technical knowledge in such fields as engineering, electronics, and chemistry. It is natural for a young person seeking a job to enter whatever trade field seems particularly interesting. No matter what technical knowledge may be necessary, however, the fundamental requirement in all magazine work is a sound knowledge of the English language. With this foundation and a willingness to work hard at learning the rudiments of a specialized field, the aspiring trade journal or industrial editor can progress steadily. A knack for simplifying technical material for the general reader is a desirable asset. College courses in economics are valuable in almost any kind of magazine work because so much of the material printed in magazines deals in some way with the operations of American business. Many schools offer industrial and technical courses to help students prepare for industrial journalism.

Pay scales on magazines are generally attractive and rise to high figures for a small number of people in the top editorial positions of the mass circulation magazines. The chief editor of a major consumer magazine receives a salary of at least $35,000 per year, up to more than $100,000 if the editor is a veteran with a proven "touch" or directs the work of a magazine group.

These salaries carry with them a substantial amount of job uncertainty. If a magazine begins to lose circulation or advertising, frequently one of the first corrective moves is to change editors, even though the fault may not lie in the editorial department at all. When a magazine is struggling to work out a new formula to regain readership, it may try several editors before finding one who can do the job. The pay offered to college graduates as beginners is in line with that offered by other media.

Salaries in the trade and industrial magazine fields are somewhat lower but still good, and the job security is better. A survey by the International Association of Business Communicators disclosed that in 1979 salaries of its members averaged $20,476. The average corporate salary was in the $22,000 range, while that for communicators employed by hospitals, educational, and financial institutions was in the mid-$16,000 range. More than nine out of ten of the almost 2,800 respondents wrote for or edited publications as part or all of their duties.

Editorial and business offices of most large national magazines are in New York and other eastern cities. Trade publication headquarters are situated throughout the United States, depending in part upon the market being served. There are numerous editorial links between magazine and book publishing, and the movies as well, since much magazine material eventually finds its way into book form and even into films, one example being the article, "Urban Cowboy." This leads to some movement of editorial workers from magazines to book publishing firms and occasionally back in the other direction. Many writers and editors also move into magazine work from positions on newspapers.

Chapter 8

BOOK PUBLISHING

THE ROLE OF BOOKS

Books are a medium of mass communications that deeply affects the lives of all of us. They convey much of the heritage of the past, help us understand ourselves and the world we live in, and enable us to plan for the future. Books are a significant tool of our educational process. And they provide entertainment for people of every age.

The nation's educational, business, and social life could not survive long without books. Judges and attorneys must examine law tomes continually; doctors constantly refer to the repositories of medical wisdom and experience; governmental officials must be aware of all the ramifications of new legislation. Teachers and pupils find in textbooks the vast knowledge of history, philosophy, the sciences, literature, and the social sciences accumulated through the ages. People in every walk of life read to keep abreast of a fast-changing world; to find inspiration, relaxation, and pleasure; and to gain knowledge. Books explain and interpret nearly every aspect of life.

The literary record has been one of the principal hallmarks by which each succeeding world civilization has been measured; the works of Plato and Aristotle, for example, both reflected and refined the quality of early Greek life. Social historians long have examined the creative literature as well as the factual records of a civilization in their efforts to reconstruct the life of the people of a particular time and place. In the United States today the finest published fiction has a reverberating impact upon our society; the ideas and techniques employed by fiction writers have an enormous effect on theater, movie, and television scripts. Many outstanding productions result from the book publisher's enterprise in encouraging and promoting both new and established authors. Creative writing enhances most of the art forms by which our civilization will one day be judged.

Whether they are paperbacks or hardcover volumes printed on high-quality paper, books provide a permanence characteristic of no other communications medium. The newspaper reporter and the radio-television commentator write and speak to an ephemeral audience. Videotapes, audiotapes, records, motion pictures, and filmed products such as microform and microfiche may deteriorate through the years. Magazines, especially those printed on high-quality paper and bound into volumes, may have extremely long lives. If cared for properly, however, books, such as the superb copies of the Bible produced by Gutenberg in the fifteenth century, live virtually always.

For the mass communicator, books perform several important functions. They not only serve as wellsprings of knowledge, but through translation and reprinting, and through conversion into movies, television productions, and live performances, they may convey vital ideas to millions of people throughout the world. And in the publishing trade itself the mass communicator may find a rewarding outlet in writing, editing, and promoting the distribution of books.

In writing books, journalists such as David Halberstam, Tom Wolfe, Jimmy Breslin, Gay Talese, Bob Woodward, and Carl Bernstein, to name only a few, have vastly increased the audience for their reporting efforts, and each has made the impact on the world of ideas that almost invariably accompanies the creation of a widely read book.

Some paperbacks are rushed into print, such as *The Pentagon Papers,* the biography of the late Yankee baseball catcher Thurman Munson, and the books dealing with the revolution in Iran. Even so, because of the relative slowness of writing, editing, and publishing a manuscript, books lack the immediacy that other media have in conveying messages to the public. What may be lost in timeliness, however, is often more than compensated for by the extreme care that is possible for editors and writers to take in checking facts, attaining perspective, and rewriting copy for maximum effectiveness. This sustained, systematic exposition of a story or an idea (with the reader's concomitant opportunity to reread, underscore, and study at leisure) is afforded only by books.

THE CHANGING BOOK PUBLISHING INDUSTRY

By dollar volume, book publishing is a dwarf among American industrial giants; it makes up only a tiny fraction of the nation's economy. Approximately one of every three of the 1,750 publishing houses, employing about

65,000 persons, is situated in New York City, but in recent years many new firms have been established in the West and South. In all, the industry grosses nearly $6.5 billion in sales each year.

The major divisions of the industry are: *trade books,* marketed to the general consumer and sold mainly through bookstores and to libraries; *religious books,* including Bibles and hymnals; *mass-market paperbacks,* sold mainly through newsstands and chain retail stores; *professional books,* such as medical, technical, scientific, and business works; *mail-order publications,* created to be marketed by direct mail to the consumer, frequently as part of a continuing series related to a particular topic; *book clubs,* actually a marketing channel for books published by other publishers; *university presses,* nonprofit adjuncts of universities, museums, and research institutions, mainly concentrating on scholarly or regional topics; *elementary and secondary textbooks* (called el-hi textbooks), hard- or soft-cover texts and manuals, maps and other items for classroom use, mainly sold in bulk to school districts; *college textbooks,* hard- or soft-cover volumes and audiovisual materials, the texts sometimes similar to trade books; *standardized tests,* for schools, colleges and universities, and industry; and *subscription reference books,* mainly sets of encyclopedias sold through the mail or door-to-door; also dictionaries, atlases, and similar works.

As Figure 8.1 shows, trade books currently lead the field with gross sales in excess of $1 billion annually, followed closely by the college and el-hi markets, both with sales totaling more than $930 million, and professional books grossing more than $885 million.

Books are marketed through six main channels: retail stores; college stores; directly to consumers through mail order, book clubs, and door-to-door sales to individuals; libraries; schools and institutions; and in miscellaneous fashion to industry, government, foundations, and research institutions. In addition, more than $500 million in books are sold annually to more than 140 other countries, with Canada accounting for about 40 percent of the international total.

Although book publishers constitute one of the few consumer industries that sell many of their products directly to users, most sales are made through wholesalers and jobbers, who stock the goods of many houses and sell them locally, regionally, and sometimes nationally to retailers, and through independent distributors, known as IDs, who provide retail outlets with mass-market paperbacks and magazines.

A phenomenon of recent years has been the rise of big bookstore chains, such as B. Dalton Booksellers and Waldenbooks. In 1972, the four largest chains accounted for about 11½ percent of all trade book sales in the country, but by 1980 the two largest chains alone sold about a third of all trade books and mass-market paperbacks. There are now more than 450 B. Dalton stores in operation and the company expects to have more than 800 by 1983. Walden has well over 400 branches. These stores,

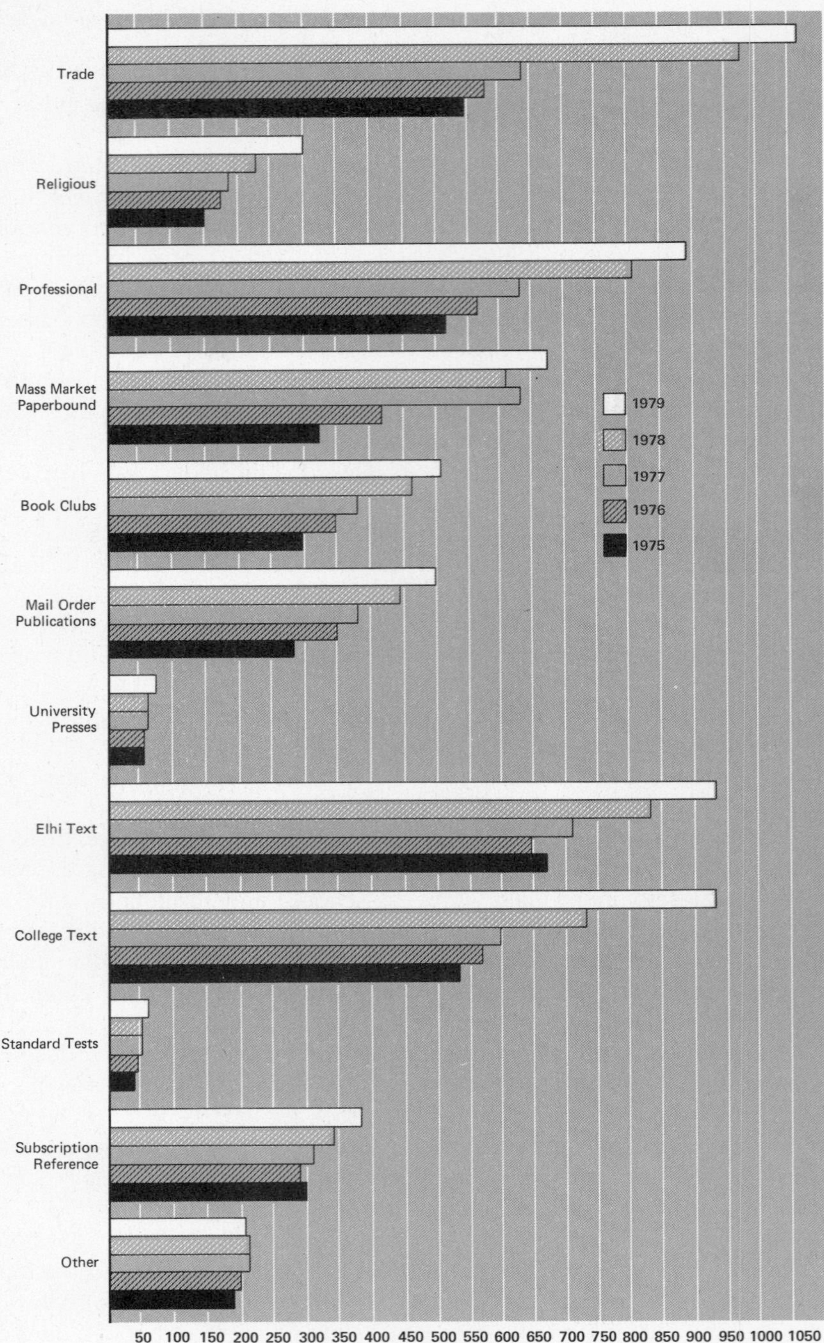

Figure 8.1 The 1975 to 1979 book publishing industry sales by division. (Data courtesy of the Association of American Publishers.)

often located in shopping centers and malls, employ supermarket strategies for sales, including strict computerized inventory control and ordering systems.

The R. R. Bowker Company recently listed more than 12,000 book outlets of all kinds in the United States. They included 6700 that handle new books; 900 department stores; 2900 college bookstores; 7300 that handle paperbacks; 1700 that carry law, medical, technical, and scientific titles; 4000 religious-book sellers; 3000 that handle juvenile books; 1300 rare-book dealers; and 1000 dealers who carry secondhand books.

Few publishing companies print their own books. Instead they rely on the more than 900 printing establishments in this country. In 1970, there were only two-thirds as many printing establishments in existence. The gross receipts of these companies exceeded $2.3 billion in 1980. Books, particularly paperbacks, are increasingly being printed from plastic plates on high-speed rotary presses.

New technology also is being used in book publishing houses in order to reduce costs and improve customer service. Computer-formating devices are widely used by publishing firms to prepare manuscripts prior to typesetting, providing, among other things, easier access to the product for storage and retrieval purposes. Several large publishing houses are experimenting with video editing systems as well. In addition, leading mass-market paperback publishers are printing Universal Product Code (UPC) bars on their title pages; when processed by electronic scanners, UPC speeds order fulfillment and the handling of returns. Publishers are anticipating the day when the International Standard Book Numbers (ISBN) on the spines or back covers of books, will be scanned by optical character recognition (OCR) equipment to help publishers and booksellers record and control inventory.

A seemingly relentless trend toward concentrating the ownership of individual publishing houses into ever-larger corporate organizations began in the 1960s. Primarily because of near-confiscatory personal inheritance taxes and the need to ensure continued fiscal stability, many privately owned companies have been converted into publicly held corporations. They, in turn, often have become absorbed into huge conglomerate organizations. As part of this trend, paperback publishing houses have merged with hard-cover houses, and now nearly all the leading publishers of both kinds of books are owned by conglomerates. A new and more complex corporate and financial environment has replaced the former leisurely and often inefficient atmosphere and practices of the major firms, and publishing decisions are based almost entirely upon bottom-line financial considerations.

In the mass-market paperback field in particular, management people of a new breed now build images, plan marketing, and set production and performance standards, their work closely akin to that of advertising people, TV producers, talk show hosts, and Hollywood producers and packagers. Ever-larger sums, running into millions of dollars, are being paid for the paperback reprint rights to a single bestseller; for example, in 1979, Crown sold Bantam the paperback rights to a single novel, Judith Krantz's *Princess Daisy,* for $3,208,875. Literary agents have become power brokers in the industry, and publishing decisions increasingly are being made with movie and television subsidiary earnings in mind as well as the author's ability to "hype" a book on television talk shows throughout the country.

Contending that many authors of artistically worthy works that lack immediate commercial appeal are being excluded from publication and that the conglomerates also threaten the life of the remaining independently owned companies through unfair business practices, the Authors Guild, representing more than 5000 professional writers, has unsuccessfully sought relief from the Federal Trade Commission, Department of Justice, and the Judiciary Committees of both houses of Congress. The Association of American Publishers, representing more than 300 member companies accounting for about 85 percent of all books published in the United States, has called these charges extreme and distorted. Instead, say industry spokespersons, the publishing industry is in fact "amazingly diverse, flexible, and open," with good books never in more plentiful supply and authors never more numerous or better rewarded. Mergers, they assert, are an absolute necessity to keep publishing financially sound.

STEPS IN BOOK PUBLICATION

All books begin with an idea, germinated by the author or by an editor employed by a publishing house. If the author has the idea, he or she generally prepares a précis and perhaps several sample chapters and submits them to a literary agent or publisher. If it is the editor's idea, the editor seeks out the writer who can best develop the book based upon the concept. Publishing houses vary in the number and level of responsibility of the editors they employ. In general, however, a senior editor works closely with an author in the preparation of a manuscript, and also may shepherd the work through various business and production stages. The editor must keep abreast of matters of public taste and interest and be able to anticipate or intuit the types of books that will find markets in the years ahead. Reference, technical, and textbook editors, who deal with specialized subject matter, often employ professional readers; trade book editors, especially those dealing with fiction, are less likely to employ outside advice.

A common fallacy held by each summer's crop of job applicants in book publishing is that a publisher or an editor is simply a person of taste who sits waiting for hungry authors to arrive with best-selling manuscripts. Book publishing is like an iceberg. The part that shows, mainly books that are reviewed in mass media journals and magazines, often touted on TV talk

A textbook editor prepares an outline for a new book.

shows and sold in the general bookstores, constitutes only about 8 percent of the overall dollar volume in books. For every editor who breaks bread with Phillip Roth or Gay Talese, there are hundreds who edit reference books or work with college and school textbook authors. For most publishing houses, the unsolicited manuscript rarely is publishable, as many disillusioned beginning writers can testify.

Manuscripts that are accepted for publication are turned over to copyeditors, who may do considerable rewriting as well as search for grammatical, spelling, and punctuation errors; corroborate facts; correct discrepancies in style; and perhaps help cut the copy to a predetermined length. The copyeditor must also coordinate entries in the bibliography with the citations in footnotes (if the book has them); ensure that chapter headings correspond with contents; relate pictures, tables, charts, and the like with the text; query the author if necessary; read the galley proofs, including indexes; check corrections made by the author in the proofs; and in general ascertain that the text is as accurate as possible.

The production department, which may consist of from three persons to two dozen or more, normally serves as the book publisher's liaison with the printer. Highly specialized employees oversee the production process. They design the book; obtain art work if necessary; estimate length; select the type and paper; order the typesetting, printing, and binding; and supervise preparation of the cover and the jacket. Every book presents an individual problem and every stage of production must be worked out carefully in advance, the schedule often requiring a full 12 months to complete.

Long before the book has been produced, plans are made for its marketing. The marketing department, increasingly more important in this competitive industry, helps to determine the direction and the form of advertising and promotion, and monitors the information to be sent to the salespeople. The sales representatives visit bookstore buyers throughout the country, and are called together regularly for conferences involving the entire list of books being prepared for sale. In accordance with the advertising and promotion budget established for the book, based on anticipated sales, media are selected and advertisements and dealer aids such as posters, circulars, and mail enclosures are prepared.

The publicity department writes and mails news releases, arranges author interviews on television and radio and other personal appearances, sends copies of the book to reviewers, announces the publication of the book in trade magazines, arranges for exhibits at conventions attended by booksellers, and works on other ways to promote sales. The primary responsibility of the publicity department is to establish a climate of acceptance for the new book by employing every possible means at hand.

General sales representatives call on major bookstores, visiting the largest store perhaps 15 to 20 times a year. These persons normally work on salary or commission or a combination of the two, and sometimes carry the lines of two or more publishing houses. In addition, some sales personnel call on booksellers on behalf of jobbers and other wholesalers.

College textbook sales representatives, on the other hand, perform a distinctly different function. Calling on the nation's college and university professors, they make certain that their clients are acquainted with or receive examination copies of textbooks appropriate to the courses they teach. Textbook salespeople seldom if ever sell directly to bookstores. They must hope that the professors they visit, who usually have freedom of textbook selection, will give them their share of business via their college bookstores. Sales representatives also act as manuscript scouts since most college textbooks are, of course, written by college professors.

Hundreds of el-hi school textbook agents work through state, county, and city adoption systems. Most school textbooks and audiovisual materials are prepared by the staff at a publishing house, working in collaboration with professional teachers.

Many other aspects of the production and sale of books are not covered in this sketch of publishing. It is an intricate, fast-paced business, and it takes many years of practical experience to learn the ground rules.

HOW THE MASS COMMUNICATOR FITS IN

The kinship of book publishing activities to those of other mass media should be apparent. Writing and editing must be done, as well as copyediting and proofreading; illustrating and designing; printing; marketing, advertising, and publicizing; distributing and selling. The editor must have shrewd insight into what interests the public, and why. The book editor identifies with the tastes and needs of various segments of the book-buying population, just as the newspaper city editor maintains a sense of rapport with the newspaper's readers.

Book publishing is a step removed from the operations of some of the other media, which have a mass audience to deal with continually; books are often read by highly selective groups. Yet, work in many other fields of mass communications can provide an ideal background for the responsibilities of book publishing.

Writers for newpapers, magazines, and radio-television, for example, inevitably gain insights into human life that can be drawn upon to advantage at the book editor's desk. With their attention to craft, they can quickly spot good or poor writing in a manuscript. Their experience in rewriting the work of others can help strengthen weak spots in a manuscript. As journalists, they have learned to respect facts and to insist upon documentation. Familiar with the principles of style and grammar, they can effectively supervise the work of copyeditors and proofreaders. Experience gained from having worked with printers and other craftspeople will help in keeping job costs at a minimum. As media reporters or editors, they have drawn paychecks from profit-making organizations; their appreciation of sound business methods will help them deal with authors who may be unfamiliar with the ordinary business world.

The knowledge of graphics that mass communicators obtain in school or on the job will be of use in ordering printing for a book and supervising the production of its cover and jacket. Advertising staff people can draw upon this same knowledge of typography, as well as other journalistic skills, in preparing direct mail folders, posters, and advertisements for print media. They will find that the same principles of copy, layout, illustration color, and selection of paper and ink apply in the preparation of advertisements for new books.

Skills gained in journalism or public relations courses, or in previous practice, should enable book publishing employees to plan and carry out effective promotional campaigns, including writing news releases and other materials and maintaining contacts with the media.

JOB OPPORTUNITIES IN BOOK PUBLISHING

Even the publisher's son or daughter must learn the business from the bottom upward. Traveling to the cultural oases of the nation, to wherever books are sold, is the normal beginning pursuit for those who seek careers in book publishing. The theory (and it has been proved a thousand times) is: You can't become a good acquisitions editor sitting in a New York or Boston office; you can learn the facts of bookselling life only by experience with a constantly changing market, finding out which books will sell and which will not, and learning why in both cases. After three or four years, the sales representative may wish to swap suitcase for swivel chair, better qualified than before to serve as an acquisitions editor or in some other capacity in the main office. Many men and women, however, enjoy lifelong careers as sales representatives.

Most salespeople are personable, college-educated lovers of books whose starting salaries generally range between $12,000 and $14,000 annually. All their expenses are paid while they are on the road. Experienced representatives may earn $30,000 or more each year. Moving into the office, they most likely will put their road experience to work in the editorial, sales, advertising, marketing, or production departments. Eventually, they may become department heads, later perhaps officers or directors of the company, with salaries in the $60,000 to $70,000 range. Hard-headed business acumen is essential for such advancement.

Those people who choose to begin in the editorial offices of book publishing houses are often assigned the task of reading and making initial judgments about the merits of unsolicited manuscripts that arrive with great frequency. As their judgment is corroborated by senior editors, they are assigned greater responsibilities. Some become copy and proof editors and research facts in encyclopedias and other reference works. Editorial assistants usually start at about $12,400 a year; senior editors earn $30,000 to $40,000 a year.

While some people ascend the publishing ladder as editors, others move into marketing and publicity jobs. They write news and feature copy, help plan marketing campaigns, prepare advertising materials, compose jacket blurbs, arrange radio and television personal appearances and lecture tours, and otherwise exercise ingenuity in promoting the sale of books. For these services they may be paid from $12,000 to as high as $30,000 annually. Hundreds of persons freelance as copyeditors and proofreaders at home, earning between $6 and $10 per hour.

The book manufacturer and the publisher employ production managers, whose responsibility it is to see that all elements of a book are in the right place at the right time; they are the liaison between the manufacturer and the publisher. In addition to the production staff, both publishers and manufacturers employ estimators, designers (both freelance and staff), schedulers, and general management people, most of whom have had technical school training or printing plant experience.

Qualifications

A good education, intelligence, a love of books, and an ability to keep abreast of the latest developments in many phases of life, particularly in the area of one's specialization, are prime characteristics of a good editor. One need not be a creative writer. Persons with highly individual ideas and taste are unwilling to remain anonymous and to play second fiddle to authors with quixotic personalities. The good editor has the capacity to deal in a calm, unruffled fashion with everyone, including the occasional prima donna whose genius or near-genius may spell the difference between profit and loss in a publishing year. A sound grasp of the fundamentals of business practice is essential in today's financially oriented publishing business. Companies are looking for bright young people who know how to use computer terminals, analyze profit-and-loss statements, and make decisions based on hard evidence.

Whether one wishes to become a general editor, a copy editor, a sales representative, an advertising specialist, or a marketing and promotion person, the college graduate who aspires to a career in book publishing will profit by an education, as well as experience, in mass communications. He or she should seek to acquire a sound background in a major discipline—in literature, history, languages, the natural and social sciences, or philosophy—in fact, in any of the areas of knowledge that comprise a liberal arts education. The aim is to learn to think, find information, and acquire judgment. Professional education will not be overlooked, for the insights, skills, and fundamental knowledge gained in the classrooms and laboratories of a school of mass communications should prove of inestimable value throughout one's career.

Part Three

THE ELECTRONIC AND FILM MEDIA

Chapter 9

GROWTH OF RADIO, TELEVISION, AND FILM

NEWS TAKES TO THE AIR

Public interest in news made it natural for people to use any new medium of communication—the telegraph, the telephone, the underseas cable, the wireless, the motion picture film, radio broadcasting, telecasting, and the communications satellite—to hurry the news to waiting eyes and ears, or to bring news events directly to distant audiences.

The telegraph, the telephone, the cable, and the wireless were nineteenth-century inventions that could speed the transmission of messages to waiting newspaper editors and printing presses. The motion picture film became a competitor that could bring to audiences in theaters a visual portrayal of such an exciting event as the Corbett-Fitzsimmons heavyweight prize fight of 1897—the first news event shown on film. Soon excerpts of films of news events were put together into newsreels, which were a part of the standard fare of the movie palace of the 1920s. But the time lag before a newsreel could be shown kept it from being more than an incidental competitor for the newspaper. Interpretive films like Time Inc.'s *The March of Time* of the 1930s and the development in that decade of the techniques of the documentary film—*The Plow That Broke the Plain* and *The River* were notable examples—foreshadowed the impact that film would have on other news media once it had the means to reach the public directly, which television later provided. In the meantime, news took to the air through the magic of radio.

The first news broadcast in the United States is generally credited to Dr.

Lee De Forest, who in 1906 invented the vacuum tube that made voice broadcasting possible, the next step beyond Marconi's wireless telegraphy of the 1890s. On November 7, 1916, the New York *American* ran a wire to De Forest's experimental station at High Bridge, New York, so that the "father of radio" could broadcast to a few amateur radio enthusiasts the returns from the Wilson-Hughes presidential election. Like the *American* and other newspapers misled by the early returns from that closely contested election, De Forest signed off with the statement that "Charles Evans Hughes will be the next president of the United States."

The inventive and engineering resources of wireless and radio were subsequently needed for military purposes during World War I, and private broadcasting was banned until 1919. Even then, few people saw the possibilities of mass radio listening. One person who did was David Sarnoff, the son of a Russian immigrant family who got his start as a Marconi wireless operator. When three big companies of the communications and electric manufacturing industries—Westinghouse, General Electric, and American Telephone & Telegraph (AT&T)—pooled their patent rights interests in 1919 and formed the Radio Corporation of America (RCA), Sarnoff became RCA's sparkplug and eventually headed both RCA and its subsidiary, the National Broadcasting Company. His active career extended to 1970.

It was a Westinghouse engineer, Dr. Frank Conrad, who offered the first proof of Sarnoff's contention that people would listen to radio. His broadcasts of music in Pittsburgh in 1919 stimulated sales of crystal sets and led Westinghouse to open KDKA on November 2, 1920, as the first fully licensed commercial broadcasting station. The featured program consisted of returns from the Harding-Cox presidential election, one whose outcome was more easily predictable. The station got its vote results from the obliging Pittsburgh *Post*.

Other newspapers were more directly involved in broadcasting. One, the Detroit *News*, broadcast news regularly beginning on August 31, 1920, over an experimental station that was to become a regular commercial station in 1921, WWJ. Others quick to establish stations were the Kansas City *Star*, Milwaukee *Journal*, Chicago *Tribune*, Los Angeles *Times*, Louisville *Courier-Journal*, Atlanta *Journal*, Fort Worth *Star-Telegram*, Dallas *News*, and Chicago *Daily News*. By 1927 there were 48 radio stations owned by newspapers, and 97 papers presented news over the air. The publishers thought radio newscasts stimulated sales of newspapers—and subsequent events proved them correct.

But despite these evidences of concern for news, radio's pioneers were more intent on capturing the public's interest by entertaining it than by informing it. Dramatic news events and on-the-spot sports coverage combined both objectives. News summaries themselves remained infrequent in the 1920s because they excited little advertiser interest, because radio itself did not collect news, and because news merely read from the newspaper sounded awkward and dull on the air. Meanwhile, in 1921, KDKA broadcast accounts of prize fights and major league baseball games. The next year, AT&T's New York station, WEAF (now WNBC), used phone lines to bring to its listeners the Chicago-Princeton football game from Stagg Field. By 1924 an estimated 10 million Americans heard presidential election returns; there were 3 million sets that year, and the number of stations had grown from 30 in 1921, to 530. Twenty-one stations from New York to California joined in a March, 1925, hookup to broadcast President Calvin Coolidge's inauguration.

The development of networks was vital for radio's progress. In early 1924 the Eveready Battery Company bought time on 12 stations for its Eveready Hour performers—the first use of national radio advertising. By 1925, AT&T had organized a chain headed by WEAF with 26 outlets, reaching as far west as Kansas City. RCA, Westinghouse, and General Electric had a competitive chain led by WJZ, New York, and WGY, Schenectady. In 1926 the big companies reached an agreement under which AT&T would retire from the broadcasting business and in return would control all forms of network relays. RCA, Westinghouse, and General Electric bought WEAF for $1 million. They then formed the National Broadcasting Company as an RCA subsidiary. The station chain organized by AT&T and headed by WEAF became the NBC Red network at the start of 1927, while the chain headed by WJZ became the NBC Blue network. Regular coast-to-coast network operations began that year. Sarnoff emerged in full control of RCA and NBC in 1930 when Westinghouse and General Electric withdrew under pressure of an antitrust suit.

Only 7 percent of the 733 stations operating in early 1927 were affiliated with NBC. Some rivals organized a network service with the support of the Columbia Phonograph Record Company in 1927; financially reorganized the next year under the control of William S. Paley, it became the Columbia Broadcasting System. CBS bought WABC (now WCBS) in New York as its key station and by 1929 was showing a profit. In 1934 it had 97 station affiliates, compared with 65 for NBC Red and 62 for NBC Blue.

Passage of the Radio Act of 1927 strengthened the two big networks, since the number of stations on the air was reduced by the new Federal Radio Commission to avoid interference in receiving programs, and a group of about 50 powerful "clear channel" stations was authorized. By 1938 all but two of the clear channel stations were either network-owned or affiliated. And although only 40 percent of the 660 stations then in operation were network-affiliated, they included virtually all those licensed for nighttime broadcasting. The two independent clear channel stations, the Chicago *Tribune*'s WGN, and WOR, New York, formed the loosely organized Mutual Broadcasting System in 1934 but found competition difficult. Mutual's complaints to the Federal Communications Commission (the regulatory body was renamed in the Communications Act of 1934) brought about the sale by NBC in 1943 of its weaker Blue network to Edward J. Noble, who renamed it the American Broadcasting Company in 1945.

The growth of the networks after 1927, and their success in winning advertising revenues, made radio a more disturbing challenger to the newspaper industry. Radio's increasing interest in broadcasting news and public affairs also provided competition. In 1928, Republican Herbert Hoover and Democrat Alfred E. Smith took to the air, spending $1 million on campaign talks over NBC and CBS networks that reached many of the nation's 8 million receiving sets. That year the press associations—Associated Press, United Press, and International News Service—supplied complete election returns to the 677 radio stations. Radio's success in covering that bitter presidential election whetted listeners' appetites for more news broadcasts. In December, KFAB in Lincoln, Nebraska, responded by hiring the city editor of the Lincoln *Star* to produce two broadcasts daily of what it called a radio newspaper. Other stations developed similar programs, and as the Great Depression deepened after October 1929, the public became even more interested in news. By 1930, KMPC in Beverly Hills, California, had put ten reporters on the Los Angeles news runs.

A bitter war then broke out between radio and newspapers over the broadcasting of news. Newspaper advertising revenues were sharply contracting as the nation moved toward the 1933 depression crisis. Radio, however, as a new medium was winning an increasing, if yet small, advertising investment. Why let radio attract with news broadcasts listeners who would become the audience for advertisers' commercials, asked some publishers. This argument gave more weight to public interest in news than it deserved, considering the demonstrated interest in listening to such entertainers as Amos 'n Andy, Jack Benny, Walter Winchell, the Boswell sisters, Rudy Vallee, Kate Smith, and the stars of the radio dramas. But after both 1932 politicial conventions were aired on coast-to-coast networks, and after the Associated Press furnished 1932 election returns to the networks to forestall the sale of United Press returns, the American Newspaper Publishers Association cracked down. The press associations should stop providing news to radio; broadcasting of news should be confined to brief bulletins that would stimulate newspaper reading; radio program logs should be treated as paid advertising. There were dissenters to this approach, but after a majority of AP members voted in 1933 for such restrictions, all three press associations stopped selling news to radio stations. Radio now had to gather its own.

The Columbia Broadcasting System set up the leading network news service with former newspaperman Paul White as director. He opened bureaus in leading United States cities and in London, and developed a string of correspondents. Hans Von Kaltenborn and Boake Carter, already CBS commentators, did daily news broadcasts. Kaltenborn, a former Brooklyn *Eagle* managing editor, had started broadcasting in 1922 and

Left, Edward R. Murrow, highly regarded radio and television news commentator. He later directed the U. S. Information Agency.
Right, Hans Von Kaltenborn, first American radio commentator. His translations of Hitler's fiery speeches and his analyses of war-torn Europe were heard by millions of people.

had joined CBS in 1930 to become the first of a long line of radio commentators. NBC organized a less extensive news service. Local stations got their news from the early editions of newspapers, despite AP court suits to stop the practice.

A compromise was soon proposed. This was the Press-Radio Bureau, which would present two five-minute newscasts daily on the networks from news supplied by the press associations. Bulletin coverage of extraordinary events also would be provided. In return, the networks would stop gathering news. The bureau began operating in March 1934, but was doomed to quick failure. Stations wanting more news bought it from five new agencies that jumped into the field, led by Transradio Press Service. A year later UP and INS obtained releases from the Press-Radio Bureau agreement and began selling full news reports to stations. UP began a wire report written especially for radio delivery, which AP matched when it began to sell radio news in 1940. The Press-Radio Bureau stopped functioning in 1940; Transradio closed in 1951.

Radio, meantime, was developing a blend of entertainment and news. The trial of Bruno Hauptmann in 1934 for the kidnap-murder of the Lindbergh baby attracted more than 300 reporters, including many with microphones. Listeners were bombarded by more than 2000 Press-Radio Bureau bulletins. President Roosevelt's famed "fireside chats" and the presidential nominating conventions and campaigns were major events. In December 1936, the entire world listened by shortwave broadcast as Edward VIII explained why he was giving up the British throne for "the woman I love." Kaltenborn hid a CBS portable transmitter in a haystack between the loyalist and rebel lines in Spain to give his American audience an audio account of the Spanish Civil War. Kaltenborn, Boake Carter, Lowell Thomas, Edwin C. Hill, and Gabriel Heatter were the public's favorite news commentators. Ted Husing and Clem McCarthy were the leading sports announcers. America's top radio entertainment favorites in 1938 were Edgar Bergen and his dummy Charlie McCarthy, Jack Benny, Guy Lombardo and his orchestra, Kate Smith, the Lux Radio Theatre and "One Man's Family" dramatic shows, Burns and Allen, Eddie Cantor, Don Ameche, Nelson Eddy, Bing Crosby, and announcer Don Wilson. But before the end of the year it was Kaltenborn who stole the laurels as the world stopped all else to listen to news of the Munich crisis, which brought Europe to the brink of war.

RADIO COMES OF AGE

Radio fully met the challenge of diplomatic crisis and world war that began with Adolf Hitler's annexation of Austria and ultimatum to Czechoslovakia in 1938. Beginning with a patched-together but striking coverage of the Munich crisis, the radio networks expanded their news reporting and technical facilities tremendously during World War II. At the station level, newscasts took a place of prime importance.

Network news staffs had continued to develop on a modest scale after the 1933 cutoff of press association news. NBC's Abe Schechter placed staff members in London and Paris, in Geneva for the disarmament conference, and in Shanghai for the Japanese invasion of China. G. W. Johnstone of Mutual was financially handicapped but had reporters in the major news centers. CBS news director Paul White had developed the largest organization for both United States and foreign coverage, but its staff was stretched thin.

In 1937, CBS sent a then-unknown Edward R. Murrow to Europe as news chief. For an assistant, he hired William L. Shirer, who had been working for the just-closed Universal Service, a Hearst-owned press association. Like the others, they did human interest stories and cultural programs for shortwave broadcasts that were rebroadcast by United States stations. Then came Hitler's invasion of Austria and the *Anschluss*. Murrow hurried to Vienna. On March 12, 1938, the first multiple pickup news broadcast in history went on the air. Shirer spoke from London, Murrow from Vienna, and newspapermen CBS had hired gave their impressions from Berlin, Paris, and Rome. The pattern was set for radio's coverage of the fateful 20 days in September, beginning with Hitler's demand that the Czechs cede him the Sudetenland and ending with the Munich Pact. Key staff members such as Murrow (who went on to become television's best-known commentator and director of the United States Information Agency) and Shirer (author of *Berlin Diary* and *Rise and Fall of the Third Reich*) bore the brunt of the effort, reinforced by the best of the United States newspaper and press association correspondents.

American radio listeners heard news broadcasts from 14 European cities during the Munich crisis period. Beginning with the plea for support made by President Eduard Beneš of Czechoslovakia on September 10, 1938, and Adolf Hitler's challenge to the world two days later from Nuremberg, listeners heard the voices of Chamberlain, Goebbels, Mussolini, Litvinoff, and Pope Pius XI. Such broadcasts were not new, but the intensity of coverage was. CBS devoted 471 broadcasts to the crisis, nearly 48 hours of air time; of these, 135 were bulletin interruptions, including 98 from European staff members. NBC's two networks aired 443 programs during 59 hours of air time. On climactic days, these efforts kept the air alive with direct broadcasts, news summaries, and commentaries by the news analysts.

In his "Studio Nine" in New York City, Kaltenborn spent the 20 days catnapping on a cot, analyzing the news reports, and backstopping the CBS European correspondents with hours of analysis and commentary. It was Kaltenborn who provided the translations of Hitler's fiery oratory at the Nazi rallies, and who later predicted what diplomatic steps would follow. He made 85 broadcasts, many of them lengthy commentaries, during the three weeks. A few times he carried on two-way conversations with Murrow, Shirer, and other European correspondents. The CBS "European News Roundup," usually a 30-minute show from three or four points, was matched by NBC after two weeks. Heading NBC's European effort was Max Jordan, who had a 46-minute beat on the text of the Munich Pact, which he broadcast from Hitler's radio station. He relied especially on M. W. Fodor of the Chicago *Daily News* and Walter Kerr of the New York *Herald Tribune* in Prague, Alistair Cooke in London, and leading press association reporters. Mutual had only John Steele in London and Louis Huot in Paris, and used their occasional broadcasts, cabled news, and shortwave pickups to augment the regular press association news flow.

American listeners felt the brutal impact of Hitler's demands when Jordan and Shirer spoke from microphones inside the Berlin Sportpalast, against a background of hysterical oratory and frenzied Nazi crowd reaction. They were grave when they heard Murrow describe war preparations in London, relieved when Kaltenborn predicted that Chamberlain, Daladier, Mussolini, and Hitler would find a peaceful solution at Munich. Although they devoured columns of type, it was radio that brought them a sense of personal participation in what they realized was the world's crisis, not merely Europe's.

By the summer of 1939 Murrow had a four-man staff: himself, Shirer, Thomas Grandin, and Eric Sevareid, a young newsman who also was to become a leading television commentator for CBS. When German troops marched into Poland, Americans tuned in their radios to hear Prime Minister Chamberlain announce that Great Britain was at war. Bill Henry of CBS and Arthur Mann of Mutual became the first front-line radio reporters. Radio news staffs expanded, and eyewitness broadcasts made history. James Bowen of NBC described the scuttling of the German battleship *Graf Spee* off Buenos Aires. Shirer of CBS and William C. Kerker of NBC reported the surrender of the French to a strutting Hitler in the railroad car at Compiègne. Radio brought news of Dunkirk, of the fall of Paris, Winston Churchill's stirring oratory. And in August 1940, Murrow's "This Is London" broadcasts made the Battle of Britain come home to his American audience. His graphic descriptions of bomb-torn and burning London, delivered in a quiet but compelling manner, did much to awaken a still neutral United States to the nature of the world's danger.

The first news of Pearl Harbor reached Americans by radio bulletins that shattered the Sunday quiet of December 7, 1941. A record audience listened the next day to President Roosevelt's war message to Congress. Radio newsmen, using mobile units and tape recordings, joined the coverage of American forces in the Pacific and Europe. There were many memorable broadcasts: Cecil Brown of CBS reporting the fall of Singapore; Murrow riding a plane in the great Berlin air raid of 1943 and describing it the next night; George Hicks of ABC recording a D-Day broadcast from a landing barge under German fire. Network reporters made broadcasts and recordings, filed cables, and competed on equal terms with press association and newspaper correspondents.

The demand for news seemed inexhaustible. In 1937, NBC had devoted 2.8 percent of its total program hours to news; in 1944 the figure had risen to 26.4 percent. CBS in 1945 spent 26.9 percent of its network time on news and sports. Variety shows still ranked highest in audience size—those of Jack Benny, Fibber McGee and Molly, Bob Hope, Edgar Bergen and Charlie McCarthy, and Fred Allen. Dramatic shows and popular music were next. But four of the leading programs in listenership in 1944 and 1945 were new shows: CBS commentator Lowell Thomas; the "March of Time"; Mutual's emotional Gabriel Heatter with his human interest commentaries; and the irrepressible Walter Winchell. As the war drew to a close, radio expressed the sorrow of the people by devoting three days of programming to solemn music and tributes to the late President Roosevelt.

Three of America's most popular broadcast comedians. *Top to bottom:* Bob Hope, Jack Benny, and George Burns. (Photos courtesy of the National Broadcasting Company.)

RADIO'S POSTWAR EXPANSION

The war years were exceedingly prosperous ones for radio. Total annual revenue more than doubled between 1937 and 1945, and income on revenues increased from 20 percent to 33 percent. When the FCC returned to peacetime licensing procedures in October 1945, there were 909 licensed commercial standard (AM) radio stations. Sixteen months later there were approximately 600 new stations either on the air or under construction, and the FCC had 700 more applications pending. These were mainly for smaller stations; the number of communities with radio stations nearly doubled in those 16 months. By 1950 there were 2086 AM radio stations on the air and 80 million receiving sets.

Frequency modulation (FM) broadcasting, done experimentally beginning in 1936, was represented by 30 stations on the air in 1942, when wartime necessity brought a freeze in new construction and licensing. In the postwar years, many AM stations took out FM licenses, and the number of FM stations on the air in 1950 reached 743, a figure that proved to be a high for the ensuing decade. Few of the FM stations were operating independently and giving audiences the selective programming that later was to characterize FM broadcasting.

Radio newspeople, somewhat to their surprise, found listener interest in news sustained during the postwar years. Sponsors, who by 1944 had pushed news and commentaries into third place behind dramatic and variety shows in sponsored evening network time, kept up their interest in news at both network and local levels. The established stations had in many cases developed their own newsrooms during the war, with personnel to prepare both general news summaries and local and regional news shows. The newly licensed stations, often without network affiliation, found news one area in which they could compete. Indicative of the trend was the founding in 1946 of an association of radio news directors, now known as the Radio Television News Directors Association.

Among the network commentators, Edward R. Murrow began his "Hear It Now" program for CBS, where he was joined by his wartime associate Eric Sevareid. H. V. Kaltenborn, who left CBS in 1940, became NBC's leading commentator. Radio listeners who sat glued to their sets all night in 1948, wondering whether President Harry Truman had upset Thomas E. Dewey in the presidential voting, found Kaltenborn one of the first to realize that Truman's popular vote lead would hold up in electoral college totals. ABC had Raymond Gram Swing, one of the finest of the war era commentators. It also obtained Elmer Davis, who had replaced Kaltenborn at CBS before becoming director of the Office of War Information. Davis won high praise for his postwar reporting, his dry humor and telling barbs, and his ability to get at the heart of complex and confusing issues. NBC scored with public affairs programs from the United Nations during 1946 and 1947. The networks and some local stations also offered documentary programs that analyzed important social issues in a semidramatic format.

But television was casting its shadow over radio. Television's breakthrough year was 1948, the one in which the value of time sales for the national radio networks reached an all-time high. Competition among the four networks already was intense, and the vogue for program popularity ratings as a means of snaring sponsors led to such devices as the "giveaway" program featured by 1948 radio. The smaller stations found plenty of local advertising revenues in newly exploited markets, fortunately, and after 1947 radio had more revenue from local advertisers than from network advertisers. The networks were already shifting their attention to television, and station owners were seeking television licenses until the FCC instituted a four-year freeze so that comprehensive plans for television broadcasting could be worked out. In the meantime, CBS forecast the fate of network radio when it made its famed 1948 talent raid on NBC to capture such stars as Amos 'n Andy, Jack Benny, Burns and Allen, Edgar Bergen, and Bing Crosby for future television shows. While network radio dwindled in favor of music, news, and sports programming, radio continued to expand as an industry. By 1981 there were about 8925 radio stations—4575 AM and 4350 FM—and an estimated 456 million radio sets.

TELEVISION ARRIVES

Experimental television broadcasting in the United States began in the 1920s. The scientific advances that preceded actual broadcasting stretched back over a century in the fields of electricity, photography, wire transmission, and radio. Early television experimenters used a mechanical scanning disk that failed to scan a picture rapidly enough. The turning point came in 1923 with Dr. Vladimir Zworykin's invention of the *iconoscope,* an all-electric television tube. Zworykin, then a Westinghouse scientist, soon joined RCA, where he developed the kinescope, or picture tube. Other leading contributors were Philo Farnsworth, developer of the electronic camera, and Allen B. Dumont, developer of receiving tubes and the first home television receivers.

There were experiments in wire transmission of pictures during the 1920s that were to lead to the founding of AP Wirephoto in 1935. One of the researchers, H. E. Ives of AT&T, sent a closed-circuit television picture from Washington to New York in 1927. The next year General Electric's WGY began experimental telecasting. In 1930, NBC began operating W2XBS in New York; in 1939 it became the first station to offer regular telecasting schedules. Large numbers of people first saw television that year at the New York World's Fair. Commercial broadcasting was authorized by the FCC in 1941, but the wartime freeze left only six pioneer stations on the air. Among them were the first commercially licensed stations, NBC's WNBT in New York, and WCBS-TV in the same city. The two big radio networks thus had their entries into television broadcasting.

Because of postwar equipment shortages and industry uncertainties, it was 1948 before television could achieve a significant place among the media. In the meantime, RCA's image-orthicon camera tube had appeared to enhance the possibilities of live pickups, and AT&T was busily extending the coaxial cables that preceded the microwave relay for transcontinental broadcasting. During 1948 the number of stations on the air increased from 17 to 41, and the number of sets in use neared a half-million. Cities with television increased from 8 to 23, and the arrival of the coaxial cable and network programming stirred a city's excitement much like the arrival of the telegraph a century before. Cities along the Atlantic coast from Boston to Richmond saw and heard the 1948 political conventions and the Metropolitan Opera. Television's first great star, Milton Berle, stepped before the cameras for NBC in 1948; as did Ed Sullivan, for CBS.

Then, in the fall of 1948, came the FCC's freeze on additional station authorizations, which lasted until June 1952. During that time the FCC worked out a comprehensive policy for telecasting designed to give all areas of the country equitable service. In the interval only 108 stations were eligible for broadcasting. A few failed, but many became firmly established. The number of sets in use rose to 15 million. The transcontinental microwave relay was completed in 1951, and on September 4 the first coast-to-coast audience saw the Japanese peace treaty conference in San Francisco. NBC also offered the first telecast of a World Series and the first regular coast-to-coast sponsored program, the "NBC Comedy Hour."

The FCC's 1952 plan called for more than 2000 channel assignments to nearly 1300 communities. To do this, the FCC extended telecasting from the established very high frequency channels (numbered 2 through 13) to 70 more ultrahigh frequency channels (numbered 14 through 83). There were more than twice as many UHF as VHF assignments, and in addition 242 channels were reserved for educational television stations. But different equipment was needed to tune a set to UHF and VHF stations, and the established pattern of set-making and broadcasting was VHF. The FCC did not require set makers to include both UHF and VHF tuning until 1964; in the meantime, UHF languished. In a 1953 decision, the FCC ended a long controversy over color telecasting in favor of the RCA compatible system permitting reception in either black-and-white or color.

Television's great "gold rush" came during 1952 and 1953, with the end of the freeze. Among the networks, NBC and CBS were well along in their transition from emphasis on radio to emphasis on television. ABC merged with Paramount Theatres in 1953 and took a third-ranking position in television. Mutual did not attempt to enter television; a Dumont network gave up the attempt to compete nationally in 1955. That year there were 439 stations on the air and 33 million receivers. By 1960 there were 533 stations and 55 million receivers. In 1981 there were 764 commercial stations on the air (242 of them UHF), plus 268 educational stations. There were 125 million sets covering 98 percent of the homes in the United States. Television surpassed radio and magazines by 1955 in total advertising revenues and a year later passed newspapers as the number one national advertising medium, although newspapers continued to lead in total advertising thanks to their top-heavy position in the field of local advertising.

TELEVISION AND THE NEWS

Television's first efforts at news shows too often consisted of newsreels supplied by the United Press and Acme Newspictures and still pictures shown while the on-camera announcer read the script. But television newspeople, equipped with mobile units and magnetic tape, gradually overcame the problems of developing news shows with live film and sound. During the first decade of telecasting, they did far better with on-the-spot broadcasts of major news events, public affairs programming, and documentaries.

In 1951 Edward R. Murrow turned from "Hear It Now" to "See It Now" for CBS. NBC's early morning "Today" show with Dave Garroway, a mixture of news and entertainment, opened in January 1952. That year network viewers saw an atomic blast at Yucca Flats, the political conventions, and a heavyweight championship prize fight. An estimated 60 million Americans saw President Eisenhower inaugurated in 1953. Television audiences next followed live broadcasts of the McCarthy-Army hearings, which resulted in the Senate's censure of the Wisconsin senator, and watched a parade of gangsters before Senator Kefauver's crime subcommittee. Crucial United Nations sessions went on camera. At least 85 million Americans saw one of the "Great Debates" between John F. Kennedy and Richard M. Nixon in 1960, with the presidency at stake. President Kennedy opened some of his news conferences to live telecasting in 1961, and used television extensively at the height of the Cuban crisis in October 1962. An estimated 135 million people saw some part of television's coverage of John Glenn's orbital space flight in 1962.

If proof were needed of television's ability to report great events, it came on November 22, 1963, when President Kennedy was assassinated in Dallas, Texas. Within minutes the networks began a four-day vigil ending with the burial at Arlington. Many heard the first bulletins on radio, then rushed to watch the unfolding drama and hear news summaries on television. A survey of audiences in New York City showed that TV viewing rose from 25 percent to 70 percent on Friday after the assassination reports became known. Viewers saw the new president, Jacqueline

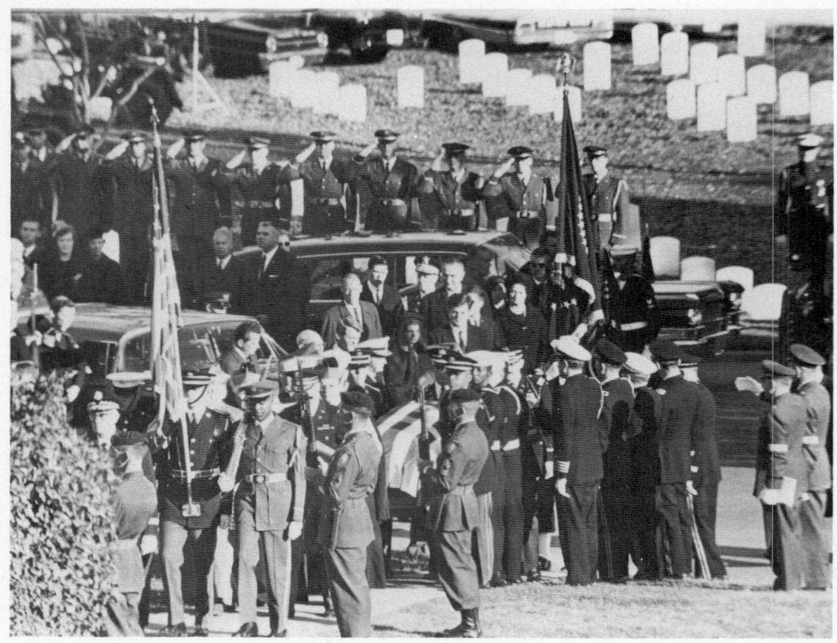

President John F. Kennedy is laid to rest in Arlington National Cemetery. The funeral climaxed three days of mourning during which the nation was bound together by television as never before. (UPI)

Kennedy, and the casket returning to Washington. They went with the cameras into the White House, saw the Sunday ceremonies at the Capitol. Sunday viewers on NBC (the only network "live" at the precise moment) saw Jack Ruby lunge forward in a Dallas police station to shoot fatally the alleged assassin, Lee Harvey Oswald, and heard reporter Tom Pettit describe the incredible event. Viewership in New York homes jumped to 80 percent as all the networks ran and reran their film. On Monday the funeral of President Kennedy drew a 93 percent viewership figure, the highest known level in television history. The nation agreed that both television and radio had reported the four days magnificently.

With full involvement of American troops in Vietnam after 1965, the ugliness of the indecisive war there was brought into American living rooms by television news crews. Public reaction against the war led to President Lyndon Johnson's decision to retire from the 1968 election race—an announcement made live to a Sunday evening television audience. There were even greater public shocks in 1968: the assassinations of the Reverend Martin Luther King and Senator Robert F. Kennedy, and the turmoil and rioting accompanying the Democratic convention in Chicago. In each event television played a major news coverage role.

In July 1969, however, television played a happier role when it brought

Three famed network personalities. *Top to bottom:* Walter Cronkite, CBS; Tom Brokaw, NBC; and Barbara Walters, ABC. (Photos courtesy of the Columbia Broadcasting System, National Broadcasting Company, and American Broadcasting Company.)

to a worldwide audience the flight of Apollo 11 and direct transmission of the pictures of mankind's first steps on the moon. Viewers saw black-and-white pictures originating from the moon for five hours, including two hours with the astronauts on the moon's surface. Some 125 million Americans saw the climactic nighttime broadcast, and a satellite network carried the pictures to an eventual audience estimated at 500 million. Truly a "See It Now" triumph of immediacy, the pictures from the moon gave all viewers a sense of participation in a great feat of exploration.

After Murrow left the CBS screen in 1958, Walter Cronkite became that network's leading personality. A United Press war correspondent, Cronkite joined CBS in 1950 and became the star of many of its documentaries, including "Eyewitness to History," "The Twentieth Century," and "CBS Reports." He took over the major CBS news program from Douglas Edwards and transformed it into a 30-minute dinnertime show in the fall of 1963, with Eric Sevareid as commentator. Mike Wallace, Dan Rather, Morley Safer, and Harry Reasoner made the documentary "60 Minutes" a "top ten" show. Rather succeeded Cronkite on the evening news show in 1981. Other leading CBS correspondents included Roger Mudd, Hughes Rudd, Charles Collingwood, Daniel Schorr, Charles Kuralt, Bernard and Marvin Kalb, Lesley Stahl, Bob Schieffer, Ed Bradley, Sharon Lovejoy, Phil Jones, Heywood Hale Broun, Bruce Morton, and Susan Peterson. Mudd and the two Kalbs joined NBC in 1980.

NBC's top stars were two seasoned newspapermen, Chet Huntley and David Brinkley, whose mixture of news and comments between 1956 and 1970 made them a top-ranking television team. When Huntley retired in 1970, John Chancellor emerged as the chief NBC newscaster. Frank McGee, Barbara Walters, Tom Brokaw, and Jane Pauley were hosts of the morning show in turn. Morgan Beatty and Merrill Mueller had major newscasts. Other NBC correspondents included Joseph C. Harsch, Irving R. Levine, and Elie Abel in Europe; Pauline Frederick at the UN; Hugh Downs, Ray Scherer, Tom Pettit, Aline Saarinen, Sander Vanocur, Edwin Newman, Herbert Kaplow, Marilyn Berger, Judy Woodruff, Don Oliver, Bob Jamieson, David Burrington, John Hart, and Garrick Utley. "NBC White Paper" was the network's major documentary, along with "First Tuesday" and "Weekend."

With fewer resources, ABC kept pace with such commentators and news anchorpersons as John Daly, Frank Reynolds, Howard K. Smith, and Harry Reasoner, who came from CBS in 1970. Barbara Walters came from NBC in 1976. Leading correspondents were Edward P. Morgan, William H. Lawrence, John Scali, Robert Clark, Peter Jennings, Peter Clapper, Nancy Dickerson, Ann Compton, Tom Jarriel, Sam Donaldson, Ted Koppel, Sylvia Chase from CBS, and Catherine Mackin from NBC. Marlene Sanders produced the "ABC Closeups" documentaries with Smith as the main narrator. Reasoner and Walters did "ABC News Reports" and special interviews until Reasoner returned to CBS. The

Jane Pauley, who rose to national prominence as cohost of NBC's "Today" program. (Photo courtesy of National Broadcasting Company.)

network scored with such programs as "The Soviet Woman" and "Women's Health: A Question of Survival."

Westinghouse's Group W (11 television and radio stations headed by KDKA, Pittsburgh; WBZ, Boston; and WJZ, Baltimore) had its own news organization with Jim Snyder as national news director. Mutual radio had Bob Moore as news director.

News by satellite became television's most sensational achievement of the 1960s. The successful launching of AT&T's Telstar on July 10, 1962, permitted the first live transmissions between the United States and Europe. These were "staged" shows of a few minutes' duration while the signals could be bounced off the satellite, but they thrilled TV audiences. RCA's Relay carried pictures of events surrounding the Kennedy assassination to 23 nations. Howard Hughes' efforts to launch a satellite that would achieve a fully synchronous orbit (an orbit and speed that keep the craft directly over one point on earth) met success with Syncom III in 1964. Four such satellites, equally spaced around the world, could provide television coverage to all inhabited portions of the planet. The Communications Satellite Corporation, formed by Congress in 1962 to unify the U.S. effort, put Early Bird into synchronous orbit in 1965, then followed with the (International Telecommunications Satellite Organization's) Intelsat II series in 1966 and 1967 and the larger Intelsat III series in 1968 and 1969. After the Intelsat IV satellites followed between 1971 and 1973, no fewer than 150 ground facilities located in 80 countries were connected to a greatly expanded television facility whose social and political potential remained to be realized. Impact was great, however; the 1978 World Cup soccer matches were seen by 1 billion people, a new alltime audience total. Intelsat grew increasingly independent of the United States Comsat enterprise and launched its own Intelsat V series beginning in 1980. With message capacity doubled for each orbiting satellite, there was promise of decreased costs and increased transmissions, including news and pictures.

TELEVISION AND ENTERTAINMENT

The period from the end of World War II to the present has been one of turmoil and indeed revolution in the world of visual entertainment. Television's sudden emergence as a major home entertainment medium affected all other media, but particularly radio and motion pictures. In the years after 1948 the aerial became a fixture atop almost every roof; inside the living room the TV screen grew from 7 inches in width to 12, to 17, to 21, and in some cases to 24 inches. During the first years of television's popularity, at least, the presence of such free entertainment had a profound effect on American social habits. Some families planned their day's activities so that they could be at home for favorite programs; that gastronomical phenomenon, the TV dinner, was marketed to be eaten by families sitting in partially darkened rooms with eyes focused on the screen. Gradually, audiences became more selective, but the average set still remained on for more than six hours each day.

Having captured a very large portion of the entertainment-seeking audience, television found many serious problems. Program directors discovered that, operating as they did many hours a day, the television stations devoured good program material faster than it could be created.

The writing and producing talent drawn into the television industry simply could not conceive enough fresh material of broad general appeal to fill the stations' program time.

As a result, the mass of television programming offered to the public was uneven in quality. Much of it was trite, inane, and repetitious. The critics denounced it vehemently, with good reason. Yet every week, at least during the winter months, a selective viewer could find many hours of literate, provocative, informative, and frequently very entertaining programs. Some of the best were the "spectaculars" or "specials" originated by Sylvester (Pat) Weaver for NBC to break the monotony of regularly scheduled series. The cost of these lengthy and star-studded productions also could be spread to several sponsors.

Television programming suffered from two major difficulties: 1) the tendency of many program directors and sponsors to underestimate the intelligence of the audience and 2) a severe case of overexposure—too many hours of program time in relation to the amount of good-quality program material, even when old Hollywood movies were added to the fare.

New program ideas quickly attracted imitators. The public was subjected to cycles of entertainment, a number of programs similar in nature. For two or three seasons in the late 1950s, quiz programs were extremely popular; these gave away fantastic amounts of money to contestants who made the correct replies to many kinds of questions. But the public began to grow weary of these giveaways, and when revelations of unethical assistance to some contestants were made, most of the quiz programs disappeared from the air. Western programs, a modification of the Western movie or "horse opera" that long was a standard item in the motion picture industry, came into vogue. Soon the obvious tales of the Old West were exhausted, and producers took to exploring many ramifications of life, transferred to a Western setting. In some cases they took classic fiction plots and reworked them as Westerns. At the peak of the Western craze, so many of these "oaters" (as the industry called such horse pictures) were being shot around the overcrowded Hollywood outdoor locations that the casts of competing shows had to wait in line for turns to perform their heroics before the camera.

Milton Berle was television's first great star, going on the air for NBC in 1948. During the medium's first decade, the top audience ratings went to variety shows and comedies. Holding steady places for several years each were Berle, Groucho Marx, Ed Sullivan, and Arthur Godfrey. "I Love Lucy," starring Lucille Ball, held its first-place rating for five years. Then, in 1958, came the Westerns, led by "Gunsmoke," and in 1959 half the top ten shows were action-filled, bullet-punctuated tales. "Wagon Train" took top honors for four years, then gave way to "Bonanza." A public outcry against violence contributed to a decline of the Westerns in the late 1960s and the rise to number one ratings of the "Smothers Brothers Comedy

Carroll O'Connor, as Archie Bunker, tackles an unfamiliar task in this scene from "All in the Family." In 1980 the program became "Archie Bunker's Place." (Photo courtesy of Columbia Broadcasting System and Tandem Productions.)

Mike Farrell, *left*, as Captain B. J. Hunnicutt, gets into the swing of off-duty life in the 4077th Mobile Army Surgical Hospital under the tutelage of Radar (Gary Burghoff), *center*, and Hawkeye (Alan Alda) in this scene from "M*A*S*H." (Photo courtesy of Columbia Broadcasting System and Twentieth Century-Fox Television.)

Hour" and "Laugh-In." Situation comedies such as "Gomer Pyle," "The Andy Griffith Show," and "Julia" ranked high. Perennials like Bob Hope, Dean Martin, and Lucille Ball kept their ratings.

The 1970s saw the demise of the Westerns ("Gunsmoke" in 1975) and the rise of family programs, led by "All in the Family" and "The Waltons." Shows featuring minorities also appeared, such as "Chico and the Man" (Mexican American) and "Sanford and Son" (black). "M*A*S*H" kept the Korean war years alive. The "Mary Tyler Moore Show" and its spinoffs were comedy successes, along with Carol Burnett's variety show. ABC finally got top rating with "Laverne & Shirley," "Happy Days," the 1976 Olympics, and a 1977 smash hit, "Roots," tracing black history for eight nights for a new top audience of 130 million. NBC recouped in 1980 with its "Shogun" mini-series while CBS scored with "Dallas" and "Lou Grant." ABC countered with its controversial "Masada" mini-series in 1981 examining the Jewish heritage in Israel.

But not all television entertainment was keyed to audience ratings. The educational program "Omnibus" was a rewarding contribution of the 1950s; so was "Playhouse 90." There were such artistic productions as "Peter Pan" and "Victoria Regina." Leonard Bernstein and the New York Philharmonic orchestra played for appreciative television audiences. Walt Disney's "Wonderful World of Color" even made the top ten lists of the 1960s. Such shows, combined with the news and documentary programs, gave television some claim to a role more socially useful than the casual entertainment role identified by critics as a "vast wasteland."

CHANGES IN THE MOTION PICTURE

The motion picture preceded radio as an entertainment medium. The genius inventor Thomas A. Edison used some of George Eastman's earliest Kodak film in inventing the Kinetoscope in 1889, but Edison was more interested in his phonograph and let the motion picture project lag. One of his assistants projected the highly popular *The Great Train Robbery* for the Nickelodeon era viewers of 1903, the first motion picture to tell a story. The first great milestone in motion picture art was David Wark Griffith's *The Birth of a Nation,* completed during 1914 and 1915.

Early motion pictures had to depend on sight and occasional printed titles; the arrival of the sound motion picture in 1926 gave the industry its modern basis. The electronic sound recording and reproduction process, developed by Warner Brothers, was a by-product of telephone and radio technology. The first synchronized music was heard in *Don Juan* in 1926; the first dialogue, in *The Jazz Singer* in 1927. Technicolor was the next step forward in making motion pictures; the first three-color feature appeared in 1935. Cinerama, hailed as the most important development since the introduction of sound in 1926, ushered in the wide-screen vogue in 1952. Magnetic sound arrived with Cinemascope in 1953; magnetic strippings were used to put the sound on the same film with the pictures. The wide-screen development was exploited by the motion picture industry to help offset the inroads of television.

The changes in Hollywood's film output were equally radical. The theme for the major producers became "fewer and bigger pictures," many of them filmed in Europe because of tax considerations and a favorable labor market. The producers found their market for the routine Class B drawing room drama and adventure tale taken over by the televised half-hour show, which the home audience could watch free. So the major studios turned to producing pictures of epic proportions in color, shown on gigantic screens. Here was sweep and grandeur the TV screen could not match, qualities sufficiently alluring to draw the viewer away from a comfortable easy chair and into the theater.

A segment of the film industry went off in another, less desirable direction in pursuit of ways to draw the viewer from television. These filmmakers tried to achieve shock value with material that was too grotesque, socially daring, or close to obscenity for the home TV screen.

One result of the film industry's struggle for survival was a breakdown in the self-imposed censorship code by which the producers policed themselves. This had been adopted in reply to outcries by organized religious and social groups against a too-liberal treatment of sex in some films. For years, some producers grumbled that the code was unrealistic in many respects, but generally it was respected and obeyed. Then, in the late 1950s, certain producers intentionally violated its strictures. Sensing a more liberal attitude among the citizenry, and arguing that they were dealing with socially significant subjects that had been forbidden unwisely, these filmmakers plunged ahead. One of these breakthrough efforts was Otto Preminger's picture on the previously banned topic of narcotics, *The Man with the Golden Arm.*

During the 1960s, numerous films were released by European and Hollywood producers that would have been taboo a decade earlier. Some of these rightfully could be credited to a more adult and open attitude toward social problems and were sponsored by people willing to fight against censorship barriers they believed to be outdated and unreasonable. Certain legal decisions hitting at film censorship practices in some states, such as that permitting the showing of the controversial British film, *Lady Chatterley's Lover,* broke down the barriers even further. These developments created a more friendly atmosphere for such films as the British *A Taste of Honey,* the American *The Graduate* and *Lolita,* and psychological studies such as the Swede Ingmar Bergman's *Through a Glass Darkly* and *Wild Strawberries.* Unfortunately they also opened the way for pictures that had no social purpose but that blatantly exploited the market for crime and sex films. The history of photography is related in Chapter 13, and detailed film developments may be found in Chapter 14.

Chapter 10

RADIO

A FLOURISHING MEDIUM

Radio's pervasive impact on American life is due primarily to its immediacy and flexibility. It is present almost everywhere: the mail carrier walks a route with a transistor fastened to the mail bag, the crowd on the beach listens to a singing group, the carpenter on a roof nails shingles in time to a rock beat. There are an estimated 456 million radio sets in the United States.

Most radio programs consist of recorded music, usually the pop-rock variety, interspersed with news, sports, commercials, and relatively little dramatic or intellectual content. Although radio offers generally undistinguished fare, it obviously has broad popular appeal. While cynics describe much radio programming as that of an on-the-air jukebox with commercials, in fact radio not only provides mass entertainment but serves a vital function as a swift disseminator of information. Industry leaders anticipate better programming during the 1980s than in recent years; they say this will result in part from the expansion of radio transmission by satellite, which is expected to enlarge network operations.

As a commercial industry, radio flourishes. Through trial and error it has developed a new personality following a crisis that arose when the emergence of television destroyed its original elaborate structure of general audience entertainment. For several years in the 1950s and early 1960s, radio floundered under the shock of television's visual competition. Then industry leaders began to realize that radio has several advantages over television in the competition for listeners. Chief among these is mobility, brought about by development of the small transistor radio. One can either listen to a program attentively, or have the music playing as background with almost a subliminal effect. Millions of people drive with their car radios turned on. Radio stations outnumber television stations more than eight to one, providing a broad choice of programs to hear around the clock. Hardly a square mile exists in the United States—this applies to most other countries, too—where the sound of radio cannot be heard.

Like television, radio operates under strict government control and scrutiny. Each station has a license from the Federal Communications Commission (FCC) to broadcast on a specified band with designated power, at certain authorized hours. If the government did not allocate the wavelengths in this manner, the broadcast spectrum would become a chaotic jumble of sound as station signals overlapped and the strong stations overpowered the weak.

In 1981 the FCC relaxed some of its requirements. It eliminated 1) its guidelines requiring that a certain percentage of programming be devoted to nonentertainment; 2) formal requirements concerning how a station documents how it is addressing community issues; 3) its stipulation that no more than 18 minutes per hour be devoted to commercials; and 4) its requirement that detailed program logs be maintained for FCC and public inspection. Nevertheless, when it seeks a renewal of its license every three years, a station still must demonstrate that it is operating in the public interest, convenience, and necessity. The industry, however, is seeking further lessening of the complex FCC regulations.

Radio stations range from extremely strong, clear-channel, 50,000-watt transmitters whose signals can be heard for hundreds of miles to low-powered noncommercial stations with a range of only a few miles. While many radio stations operate under joint ownership with television stations, hundreds of small ones are unaffiliated with television or other media. In metropolitan areas, competition among radio stations for audiences has created a jungle. Approximately 60 stations broadcast in the New York metropolitan market, for example; Chicago has about 50. Some of these stations earn generous profits for their owners while others struggle along on a shoestring, continually hunting a new format with which to boost their ratings.

The Growth of AM Radio

Radio transmissions are of two types, amplitude modulation (AM) and frequency modulation (FM). AM transmitters send their signals high into the air, while FM consists of "line of sight" (horizon) broadcasting. AM came into existence first; until after World War II, almost all commercial stations were AM outlets.

President Carter once recalled to a group of broadcasters his boyhood days on a farm in Georgia that had no electricity, and how the family gathered outdoors at night to hear a radio hooked up to the battery of his father's automobile. The music, drama, comedy, and political talk they listened to opened the world to them, as it did to millions of other persons when mass listening to radio began to develop after World War I.

From a fascinating novelty in the early 1920s, radio grew swiftly into an essential element in family life. At first, listeners used earphones and brought in programs by meticulously moving a "cat-whisker" wire across a crystal. Many sets were homemade; equipment in the broadcasting stations was almost as amateurish. On certain nights, local stations would remain silent so listeners could tune in distant stations. Call letters of stations east of the Mississippi River were designated to start with the letter W, those west of the Mississippi with a K. Two pioneer exceptions were KDKA and KYW in Chicago. When the loudspeaker was developed, radio's place in the living room was assured.

Families were transported in their imagination to far-off places by clever use of sound effects. As the Lone Ranger and Tonto rode off in pursuit of bandits, the hoofbeats of their horses echoed from the loudspeaker, made by studio technicians drumming a half-dozen toilet plungers on pebbles. When Sergeant Preston of the Royal Canadian Mounties stalked killers through the snow with his dog King at his side, listeners thought they heard King's heavy breathing; what they actually heard was an actor panting into a megaphone close to the microphone.

As network programming expanded, listeners developed habits similar to those exhibited by television audiences today. They planned their activities so they would be home for the weekly broadcasts of their favorite shows. They set aside time every day to listen to the observations of the commentators and the emotional sufferings of the soap opera casts. Although radio performers at work were only disembodied voices to the listeners, their physical features became nationally known through newspaper and magazine publicity, and public appearances.

The first glimmerings of radio's future disc jockeys came during the 1930s, when a few stations offered "Make Believe Ballroom" programs. During those shows an announcer played records and pretended to be broadcasting from a ballroom, simulating the live performances of orchestras broadcasting from hotels and nightclubs that were a staple of local and network radio programming. Expanded from terse telegraphic reports, play-by-play descriptions of baseball games in distant cities were simulated by imaginative studio announcers, including a young Midwestern sportscaster named Ronald Reagan.

The Growth of FM Radio

When FM broadcasting began to develop, the industry treated it as a minor novelty. Few sets were equipped to receive FM signals. Those AM stations that also had FM licenses regarded them as a sideline of little consequence or potential. During the past dozen years, however, the poor relation has grown tremendously and has begun to overshadow its one-time big cousin. Although there are more AM stations on the air (4575) than there are FM stations (4350), surveys show that FM stations nationally claim a share of more than half the total radio listening audience. This share is growing.

AM stations have longer range and in most cases greater power than FM stations, but are subject to static interference. In some instances, government regulations require them to reduce their power or sign off at sundown to avoid conflict with other station signals, which carry farther at night. FM stations can be heard only for relatively small distances but are virtually static free and transmit music with greater fidelity in stereophonic sound. Investment in FM stations generally is smaller.

At first, FM stations played semiclassical or classical recordings without commercial interruptions. Stations with both AM and FM licenses often transmitted their AM programs on FM as well as in simulcasts, just to keep the FM signal on the air at virtually no cost.

Gradually, broadcasters and advertisers became aware that FM could be an effective commercial medium. New sets for homes and automobiles were built with both AM and FM bands. Hundreds of additional FM channels were authorized. Many FM stations took on much the same mixture of advertising and entertainment heard on AM stations. From the advertiser's point of view, FM is attractive because stations can target the content of their broadcasts to audience segments with special listening interests. While individual FM station audiences are usually smaller than those hearing AM programs, use of demographic studies enables the FM stations to shape their programs for specific age ranges and listening preferences. Thus an advertiser may choose a station that features progressive rock, to reach the young liberal audience with a message, or one that plays softer, easy-listening music, to appeal to an older, more conservative group with different purchasing desires. Because of their larger audiences, AM stations cannot specialize to the degree that FM stations can. Some still cater to a mixture of tastes, staying in the middle of the road musically.

Tangible evidence of FM's huge strides is found in the prices purchasers will pay for an FM station. By the early 1980s, FM outlets that once were money losers were being sold for as much as $12 million because buyers saw in them potentially strong profits. A few top-level AM stations sell for more than that. To capitalize on the trend, stations that operated AM and FM channels under the same call letters changed the FM letters to something entirely different and set up the FM channel as a separate advertising and programming entity. The anticipated development of AM stereo during the 1980s may offset the FM trend somewhat.

RADIO PROGRAM STYLES

Recorded music is the largest ingredient of contemporary rad disc jockey is the person who gives its presentation style and shape. Although some disc jockeys (DJs) develop an extensive knowledge of music and performers, many seem to possess only a glib tongue. The talking that the DJ does between records, however, helps to create a station's personality and bring it closer to its listeners. Many station managers urge their DJs to publicize local events and thus to develop an atmosphere of community involvement by the station.

A disc jockey's on-the-air job is to package several hours of record playing in a lively manner, so that it seems to the listener to have recognizable form. Usually the disc jockey's broadcast time is listed under the performer's name as, say, the Jim Nelson Show. Jim Nelson does not simply introduce the records and read the commercials. He gives traffic reports, announces the time and temperature, offers free tickets and gifts as promotional tie-ins with advertisers, and chats on the air with listeners who call in. Since his voice is the only tool with which to sell personality, Jim

A radio disc jockey on the air. The microphone, clock, control board, rack of tape cassettes, and records are his tools, along with a smooth flow of language. On the small screen in front of him is a radar weatherscope. (Courtesy of the South Bend *Tribune*.)

Nelson cultivates a tone that is easily recognizable—jovial, confidential, aggressive, or theatrical—whatever is effective.

The art of the DJ is specialized. The peppy "morning drive time" announcer has techniques to hold listeners' attention as they arise and drive to work; the noontime performer's style is more leisurely; then the late afternoon "drive time" announcer adopts a style for listeners who are driving home from work. DJs who broadcast in the lonely after-midnight hours develop rapport with their listeners by using a confidential, intimate tone. Automobile audiences are especially important to radio, because they are captive within the confines of their cars and are somewhat compelled to pay attention to the commercials. This is not true of listeners in other circumstances, who may turn their radios on to provide half-heard background companionship.

Radio stations exploit Americans' tendency to value numerical superiority by playing tunes that are ranked as the Top Forty of the current week. The ranking of records in descending order from the week's Number One favorite is done by trade publications such as *Billboard* and *Cash Box*, based on sales in stores. Indeed, in this age of specialization separate Top Forty lists are compiled for contemporary-rock, country-western, and soul single-record categories, and for albums of multiple selections.

Some stations follow the Top Forty lists so dogmatically that they will play only those songs. A few have reduced their play list even further, to the Top Thirty, having their DJs play the same few tunes again and again. Their theory is that when a record is a hot new favorite, listeners want to hear it repeatedly. Constant on-air exposure of a song that has just reached the lower rungs of the Top Forty ladder helps it to climb to a higher position. The program director of a station determines its play list, often with the guidance of an outside consultant. Some stations vary the Top Forty diet by interspersing "golden oldies" and "extras."

Radio and the recording industry are tied together in a relationship of convenience and mutual need. They could not survive in their present forms without each other. Radio depends upon the record manufacturers for a constant flow of new material to broadcast. The recording industry must have exposure of its products to promote their sale. Without radio play, new recordings would not come to the attention of potential purchasers. The relationship between radio and recording companies will be examined more closely in Chapter 11.

Program directors usually strive for a special "sound" that will make their stations distinctive. Often this means broadcasting music of a special type. A station may air only country-western, hard rock, or reggae and soul, hoping to build a loyal following from devotees of the genre. Or it may stress a blending of styles, such as folk rock, and emphasize the play of albums rather than single records. Extremes in specialization are found most often in urban FM stations. The easy-listening format of heavily stringed background music, sometimes called wallpaper or Pablum music, is heard more frequently on FM than AM. During the late 1970s disco music was widely played as a novelty, but its fast repetitive beat proved more popular for dancing than for radio listening. Only a handful of stations, mostly FM, play classical music. Religious programs, many of them syndicated, are frequent fare on smaller stations.

Automated radio has made large gains, as station managers try to reduce expenses by eliminating some of their on-the-air personnel. These stations broadcast packaged taped programs obtained from syndicates, hour after hour. The closely timed tapes contain music and commercials, along with the necessary voice introductions and bridges. They have spaces into which a staff engineer can slip local recorded commercials. By eliminating disc jockeys in this manner, a station keeps its costs down but loses the personal touch and becomes a broadcasting automaton.

As radio pours out rock-pop sounds and DJ chatter, it inevitably runs up against questions of censorship. Lyrics of contemporary records frequently allude to drugs and sex, at times in terms so frank that broadcasting them to a general audience may be questioned. Stations may refuse to air certain selections. Even so, parents occasionally express shock at what their children are hearing on radio. Some radio announcers, professional and amateur, go beyond conventional boundaries of good taste in emphasizing their points and demonstrating their right of free expression. Although the Communications Act of 1934 prohibits the Federal Communications Commission from censoring broadcast matter, the "dirty words" issue reached the United States Supreme Court under a special set of circumstances in the late 1970s. The court banned the use of seven specific words during daytime broadcasts, when children were most likely to be listening. Radio station managers have the responsibility for monitoring what their stations broadcast, and of dealing with public objections.

News Coverage

When an event of tremendous national or global significance occurs, such as a presidential assassination or a great natural disaster, news of it is delivered faster by radio than by any other medium. Radio's programming flexibility enables news bulletins to go on the air immediately. During a hurricane, tornado, or other continuing crisis, radio is invaluable in delivering information and instructions over a wide area. Announcements of school closings and highway advisories during snow and ice storms usually reach people first by radio.

Unfortunately, routine daily news reporting on radio frequently fails to achieve a similar high standard. Some of the larger AM stations are noted for the scope and excellence of their local news operations and national affairs reporting, but many AM and FM station managements regard news as a costly nuisance. Radio stations operating under joint ownership with television stations tend to have better-quality newscasts than those without TV ties. Staff-prepared news stories are broadcast on both outlets, and often TV news reporters do some radio broadcasts.

Hundreds of stations offer their listeners little more than rip-and-read news summaries that their announcers take from the press association machines. All stations have pronunciation guides that announcers are supposed to use, though some do not, and it is evident that they have not read the copy before going on the air. The press association summaries are headline coverage of national and world news. At many smaller stations, coverage of local news consists primarily of stories rewritten from the local newspaper or obtained from the police station, plus announcements of meetings or events submitted by community organizations. Local news reports are especially sparse on weekends.

In contrast, a few metropolitan stations use an all-news format, broadcasting news summaries, commentaries, and sports 24 hours a day. Close to them in style are the "talk" stations that broadcast to their listeners discussions, commentaries, and live phone-in conversations between announcers and audience.

There are wide differences between types of news broadcasts. Some announcers deliver the news in strident, excited tones, a fashion sometimes referred to as the "town crier syndrome." This occurs especially on rock and roll stations, whose managements believe that their young audiences are not interested in news at all. Newscasts designed for this audience emphasize soft items about life styles and rock stars, instead of heavier, hard news about world and national affairs.

Stations affiliated with one of the four traditional national radio networks in the United States—NBC, ABC, CBS and Mutual—or with one of the other networks that develop from time to time, offer brief hourly network news summaries. The networks supplement these with five-minute news commentaries and other examinations of news situations in more depth. Using these services and the audio "actualities" offered from the scene of the news by the Associated Press and United Press International, as well as other special radio services, an alert station with an able news director can keep its listeners well abreast of national and foreign news. Hundreds of stations, however, have no network affiliation.

News staffs are expensive to maintain; yet without enough reporters, a station cannot cover the police, municipal, school, and other beats fundamental to comprehensive newsgathering. As a result, many small stations tend to abandon all but the most cursory local news coverage to the television stations and newspapers.

While this is regrettable, it is also understandable. The financial resources of many radio stations, especially in small cities, are sparse because the revenue they generate from a limited market is not great. If they invested heavily to build a large, competent news department, the effort might wipe out the annual profits. So a small station may try to do the best it can afford to with a news director and possibly one assistant. The news director also may have other on-the-air responsibilities. The management of a lucrative station that gives little more than lip service to news coverage because it does not find such programming profitable could be considered more open to censure.

A continual turnover among news directors tends to weaken the quality of radio news. These directors move rapidly from job to job; this shuffling undercuts the consistency of news coverage. Just as they are becoming well acquainted with local names, politics, and community background, news directors often depart. They may step up the career ladder to a larger station; perhaps they leave because of disputes with station management; quite frequently they leave in frustration over budget restrictions. A recent survey by the Radio Television News Directors Association showed that the median tenure of radio news directors was less than two years. Forty-four percent held their jobs a year or less, while only 5 percent held the same position for more than ten years. According to the survey, the greatest turnover occurred in areas of 250,000 to 1 million population. For newcomers entering the radio field, this may be good because it creates frequent job openings, but the goal of reliable, enterprising news coverage suffers.

Closely linked to news on radio is sports. Sometimes the news director carries the title of sports director as well, or may also be a disc jockey. For example, a help-wanted advertisement published recently in a broadcasting trade journal read: "Small market adult contemporary AM needs morning drive announcer to jock and anchor news block." Play-by-play reports of baseball and football games attract large radio audiences.

Looking ahead through the 1980s, radio industry executives see an improved pattern of nationally oriented news coverage, at least among AM stations. Transmission of radio programs by satellite is growing rapidly, to the point that total conversion to satellite transmission by the radio networks is anticipated within a few years. Transmission by satellite to receiving dishes at or near affiliated stations gives the networks greater flexibility in special programming, including sports, over the use of traditional land lines, which are subject to interruptions and expensive to install in some places. This should enable the networks to deliver a richer diet of information. Because of their superiority in fidelity, FM stations are likely to remain primarily music oriented, while AM stations concentrate more on sports, news, and talk-show formats.

Through the networks, drama is making a limited comeback on radio. Though common on radio years ago, dramatic shows almost disappeared from the air until the CBS Mystery Theater was revived in the late 1970s and built a strong following. Younger audiences of this show and other dramas discovered how the use of sound can create moods and stimulate the imagination.

THE ECONOMICS OF RADIO

Radio stations have only one thing to sell, and that is an inventory of time, intangible and perishable. The majority of each hour a station is on the air is devoted to entertainment and information. The rest is cut into small segments and sold to advertisers as commercials. A station's financial success depends on the number of commercials it sells each day, and the prices it can charge for them, based on the size of its audience. When a station broadcasts a network program containing commercials, the network pays to the station an agreed-upon fee.

In the older days of radio, before television, sponsors commonly bought 15- or 30-minute portions of air time during which their commercials alone appeared. Today, stations fill the hours with brief spot commercials paid for by many different advertisers.

This practice of scheduling commercials at such frequent intervals influences the recording industry; it holds the length of its popular song releases to about three minutes. Between these brief segments of music the disc jockey can work in two or three commercials, keeping a staccato pace to the program and accommodating many advertisers. The heavy loading of AM programs with commercials has turned many irritated listeners to FM stations. However, some FM stations now follow the same practice of loading their air time with commercials.

A station's sales staff seeks to convince clients that radio is an effective medium on which to spend advertising dollars and that its station is the place to spend them. Having achieved this objective, the sales staff works with the advertiser to select the programs and times of day best suited for the clients' commercials. The station's rate card shows the price it charges for commercials at different hours, depending upon the size and type of audience it reaches at those times. Combinations of time slots and prices can be agreed upon. When a station has difficulty selling its available commercial minutes and its income is suffering, it may go "off the rate card" and make cut-rate deals giving advertisers special bargains, such as including one or several free commercials.

Sales representatives stress demographics, to show an advertiser the size and nature of the audience that can be reached. This information includes income, education, occupation, ethnic background, marital status, and buying behavior. Program and sales directors are especially anxious to reach the audience of young adults born after World War II. At the start of the 1980s their median age was 32; they were a group with ample income, young children, and strong purchasing desires.

A station cannot identify and count every listener in the way a newspaper can determine its audience by the number of copies sold each day and the addresses of its subscribers. Thus, radio depends upon surveys and polls, along with statistical research. The Arbitron rating service provides information to many stations. Researchers for large stations also make contact with a limited number of individuals, by telephone or mail, or in person, then project the results to cover the entire population of the station's listening area. The return addresses on cards and letters the listeners send to the station in response to a gift offering made by a disc jockey can be analyzed by researchers.

The primary advantage that radio offers to advertisers compared with television is lower cost, both for air time and for preparation of the commercials. Radio is more flexible, too, in time availability and the speed with which it can accommodate new advertising copy. Radio, however, lacks the visual appeal that helps television sell goods.

In one form of broadcasting, taxpayers rather than advertisers underwrite operating costs. This is National Public Radio (NPR). The Corporation for Public Broadcasting, which is funded by Congress, finances NPR; more than 200 noncommercial radio stations that use its service pay annual membership fees. Most of these are FM stations. They receive NPR programming that includes political news from Washington. NPR also distributes cultural, information, and classical music programs.

JOB OPPORTUNITIES IN RADIO

Success as a performer in radio depends heavily upon the kind of vocal personality the individual projects. If it is vibrant and distinctive, a voice the listener will remember, the beginning performer has a much better prospect of advancing to the large stations. A performer's physical appearance is of no importance except in occasional public appearances, but a lively, friendly personality usually is evident in a person's voice.

Voice quality, however, is not enough. Professional coaching can improve vocal technique and confidence, but it cannot create intelligence and a good command of English. Successful radio newscasters, talk-show hosts, and disc jockeys have quick minds and an ability to articulate their thoughts smoothly in ad lib situations.

The advice for a person beginning a career in radio is much the same as that for newspapers: start small. Most young people begin work at low-powered stations, then move to larger ones as they gain experience. Their first jobs on the air may be as fill-in DJs, perhaps part-time, during weekends and night hours. Often they do news work as well, reading the press association news summaries, and covering events. Not only must beginners acquire confidence and a sense of timing; they must learn production techniques and the fundamentals of radio engineering. At small stations, some announcers sell advertising during their off-air hours. Keeping the station log is another duty sometimes done by on-the-air personnel.

Announcers on small stations may function at times as station engineers. This task involves at least a rudimentary knowledge of electricity and knowing what meters to read and what switches to turn to keep the station on the air.

The ability to write radio news copy and advertising messages is important. As in television writing, the basic technique is to compose conversational English that rings true to the ear. Such writing avoids complex and inverted constructions, and uses simple, declarative sentences and broken phrases in the manner in which people normally talk. Also, it uses repetition more heavily than writing for print does, especially for commercials.

Job applications in radio normally include demonstration tapes. A prospective employer wishes to hear the vocal styles of applicants, in order to screen the candidates and select a few for personal interview. Samples of writing style may be requested as well.

The hiring of minority individuals and women by radio stations has increased substantially in recent years, both for on-the-air and behind-the-scenes jobs, and continues to increase. As their experience in radio grows, members of these groups are beginning to occupy management jobs. The FCC's equal opportunity provisions have stimulated the trend.

High among the career goals of radio personnel are the positions of program director, news director, and station manager. Salaries for these posts vary widely according to the size of the station and the experience of the individual. For example, a survey by the Radio Television News Directors Association in 1979 showed the median income of radio news directors in major markets to exceed $23,000; salaries have continued to rise with the rate of inflation. In urban areas, a news director for a major station earns well above the median. Big-city disc jockey stars have incomes of $100,000 or more, depending upon the agreements they have with station managements. A popular air personality attracts advertisers willing to pay higher rates in order to have their messages on the show, and the performer may earn extra fees from personal appearances. The classified advertising columns of *Broadcasting* magazine provide a guide to job opportunities and requirements in radio.

Chapter 11

RECORDING

MUSIC WITH A MESSAGE

The explosion of popular music into the public consciousness during the past quarter-century, particularly among persons under 30 years of age, has been insufficiently recognized as a means of mass communication. Although the electric guitar does not yet rank with the typewriter as a tool for distributing ideas, the records, cassettes, and live performances by musicians have had a strong impact on the thinking and social habits of younger generations. Popular music has been an effective channel for the antiwar movement of the late 1960s and early 1970s, the environmental crusade, the challenge to traditional institutions and government, the women's movement, and, more recently, the antinuclear campaign. Some people view this as seductive propaganda for a hedonistic attitude toward life that encourages the use of drugs and casual sexual relationships. Rock and roll became the music of disenchantment. Unorthodox ideas and uninhibited language that challenged codes of conventional social conduct, and had difficulty breaking into print, were transmitted to youthful listeners by the compelling rhythms and exotic sounds of rock and roll.

Making and marketing recordings is a large and volatile industry, far less structured than the print media, radio, and television. Approximately 1200 American companies produce more than 700 million records and tapes each year, according to figures supplied by the Recording Industry Association of America, Inc. (RIAA). Many of these companies are small, some handling only one performer or category of recordings. More than 95 percent of the recordings sold in the United States are made by the 55 companies belonging to RIAA. The industry's gross sales each year are around $4 billion, based on listed retail prices of records; net sales are difficult to ascertain because of price discounting and heavy returns of unsold records.

Success in the industry depends upon one's ability to exploit the quicksilver changes in public taste; indeed, to stimulate those changes through the production of new sounds and the promotion of fresh performing groups and individuals. The pursuit of novelty in sound and performance style is endless. Although half a dozen large companies dominate the industry and concentrate enormous promotion and sales efforts on their big-name stars, it is still possible for an unknown performer recorded by a minor studio to attain overnight fame with a record that catches the public fancy. The hope that lightning will strike in this manner keeps thousands of performers struggling along in obscure night spots, trying to assemble enough material and money to make a demonstration record that will convince a producer to offer them a contract.

This is a business for quick-witted individuals who can recognize trends, make deals, take risks for the "big buck"—those who know how to practice the art of "hype," the tricks of providing an exciting buildup for the performers they are selling. They must be able to sense which performers have the magical ability to stir audiences, while others of equal musical ability do not. An industry built on such an ephemeral base inevitably contains an element of chaos.

Popular music has long been a pleasurable element in the lives of most people. In the past, its songs dealt with love in the romantic sense, or were light novelty tunes. Few lyrics with messages were heard. That changed during the 1950s. Performers created the driving, compelling rock and roll rhythm. Almost simultaneously, electronic recording techniques built around the use of tape were developed to provide greater flexibility in making records. No longer is a studio recording session a simple act of capturing on tape or vinyl a group or an individual singer performing a piece of music before a microphone. Now a record is an intricate melding of several taped sound tracks into a master recording. The skill of the studio sound mixer, sometimes called an aural architect, is now as important as the ability of the performers. An increase in the use of high fidelity sound equipment in homes also has enlarged the recording market.

When a mood of dissatisfaction with orthodox standards of life developed among young people in the 1960s, heightened with protest against American involvement in the Vietnam War, the swiftly expanding recording industry provided a ready-made vehicle for the angry voices.

Rock and roll's first spectacular star was Elvis Presley, a young Tennessee truck driver who made his first amateur record in 1954, was heard on a Memphis radio station, and quickly became a national, even international phenomenon. Not only did he sing in the pulsing rock and roll style; he added sexual overtones by gyrating his hips in a manner many audiences found lascivious. In his first national television appearance, on the Ed Sullivan Show singing "Hound Dog," the cameras showed him only from the waist up to avoid offending viewers. He was called Elvis the Pelvis. Yet by the time he died, at 42 years of age, Presley had become a legendary figure, leaving an estate of $15 million derived from the sale of more than 500 million records. His death touched off mass mourning. His style did not change much during the two decades of his career, but the public grew to enjoy the sensuality of his performances.

Although rock and roll began in the United States, many of its most popular groups came from Great Britain. The exuberant Beatles made a spectacular American tour in 1964, followed by the more arrogant Rolling Stones, who proclaimed and practiced a life style involving drugs, violence, and blatant promiscuity. Other groups at the top of the rock scene during the late 1960s and 1970s bore such off-beat names as Jefferson Airplane, the Grateful Dead, Grand Funk Railroad, and Led Zeppelin. These and others like them created a fashion of long hair and ragged clothing. They flaunted a defiant manner to further their carefully calculated images as the Pied Pipers of the revolt against the establishment. During the 1970s public appearances by some groups grew more outlandish. One rock star, Alice Cooper, sought shock effect by having a guillotine and a severed "head" on stage. He dismembered baby dolls and tossed dead chickens into the audience. Such behavior apparently helped the sale of millions of dollars worth of tickets and records.

As counterpoint to these rock groups were quieter folk singers such as Joan Baez. Their songs of protest against war, big business, government conduct, traditional mores, and damage to the environment influenced young persons whose intellectual horizons were expanding during their formative years. Country-western music, which had always been popular on small-town radio stations in the West and South, had a surge of national popularity in the late 1970s. "Crossover" blends of rock, folk, and country emerged, while the sales appeal of more traditional popular ballad singers such as Frank Sinatra remained high.

The American public was jarred into realization of the impact rock and folk music had on its young listeners by what happened on a muddy farm near Bethel, New York, during a humid August weekend in 1969. Known as the Woodstock Music and Art Fair, this three-day marathon performance by rock and pop stars drew an amazing throng of 400,000 people who swarmed around the grounds in an unfettered demonstration of independence from their parents' social norms. The participants camped out in the fields, sang, drank, swam in the stream, used drugs, listened to the bands on the stage, and talked defiantly against the Vietnam War. Three persons died of drug overdoses and hundreds were treated for drug illnesses. The crowd itself was as much an event as the music it had come to hear. Woodstock became the historic symbol of the counterculture.

RECORDING AND RADIO

Producers of popular recordings have three principal ways to introduce their new numbers to the public—"play" on the radio, advertising in trade and youth-oriented publications, and live concerts by performing groups. The most important of these is radio. Without it, the mass marketing of discs and cassettes would collapse. Not only do record distributors provide copies of their new products to radio stations free of charge, but their promotion staff members try to encourage the stations to play them. If a new record is introduced on a major Top Forty station in a metropolitan market, listeners in search of something fresh will buy it in the stores. Industry trade magazines and tip sheets report that the record is "hot" in that city. By telephone calls and personal visits, promoters spread the word and cajole stations in other cities to add the song. If it catches on, sales flourish in those cities also, and onto the Top Forty charts it goes.

With commercial success of a record so dependent upon radio exposure, promoters sometimes resort to unethical tactics to obtain air play. The result has been the recurring payola scandals. In its simplest form, payola is under-the-counter payment of cash to a radio program director or disc jockey to play certain records frequently. Payola may take more subtle forms as well, such as free trips and other favors paid for by a record company. Another device is including the radio decision makers in profits on "backdoor sales," an industry racket. Stacks of new records are slipped out of the normal commercial distribution system and given to a radio executive or disc jockey; that individual sells them at a reduced price to a retail music store and pockets the proceeds. It should be emphasized, however, that most radio personnel reject such practices.

In the dizzy promotional milieu of the recording world, a valuable accolade for a single record or an album is to be certified "gold" by the Recording Industry Association of America (RIAA). This means that a record has sold 1 million units (copies), and an album has sold 500,000. To be declared "platinum," a single must sell 2 million units and an album 1 million. An album often has twelve or more songs on one long-playing disc. Recently, in a typical year, 193 albums and 61 singles won the golden laurel, while 102 albums and 10 singles were certified platinum. Yet competition is so intense and production costs so high that 75 percent of the records produced fail to earn a satisfactory profit for their creators.

THE CONCERT CIRCUIT

Groups and individual performers in the pop-rock world whose records have sold well enough from radio exposure to earn them a reputation frequently capitalize on this by doing live concert tours. These tours stimulate sales and build the performers' followings.

An intricate public appearance circuit has developed. Famous stars play the circuit of arenas in cities and on university campuses that seat 10,000 or more people. Performers with a growing reputation, but who are not yet at the top, are booked into smaller houses that seat 2,000 to 5,000. If the touring performer demonstrates drawing power at this level, a promoter may risk booking the act onto the arena circuit. Another way in which a group promotes itself is to perform as the opening act in a big-name show. Opening-act performances are watched closely by promoters. If the openers please the crowds—not an easy task, before a restless, often boisterous throng waiting impatiently for the main act—promoters may finance the act on a tour as a headliner on the small-house circuit.

A look backstage at a concert given by a famous rock group in a university arena seating 12,000 provides an insight into the live concert business.

The promoter of the concert takes the principal financial risk. If the house is full, he or she can make a generous profit. If the act fails to draw well, the promoter takes a financial beating. The five-member rock group booked into this arena has received a guarantee of $25,000 for its performance, plus a percentage of gross ticket sales. On this night the arena grosses $80,000, so the star group leaves town with payment in excess of $40,000. Grosses of more than $100,000 for a single performance in very large arenas were relatively common before the music industry suffered a severe slump in late 1979. One cause of the slump in record sales was the growth of home recording of new hits from radio broadcasts.

The basic rent the promoter has paid for the arena is $3,000, plus several thousand dollars more in a percentage of the gross and fees for cleanup, ticket selling, security, and other services. Also, the promoter has paid $5,000 to a specialty firm to set up the group's bulky sound and light equipment. Four semi-trailers were needed to haul this equipment, which represents an investment of more than $100,000. While the headline acts take in immense sums, they have heavy expenses for travel and equipment.

The setup for the night's performance started at 8 A.M. and has continued all day as carpenters, electricians, and sound technicians build the stage sets. Uninvolved with all of this, the star act flies into town aboard its private airplane in late afternoon. At the airport the group is met by the two chauffeured limousines specified in its contract to be available at all times. The performers stay at the best hotel in the city, and dine on the special menus their contract demands. Traveling pop-rock stars enjoy luxuries and wealth most of them hardly dared dream about as children, yet many complain about life on the road because of the physical drain they feel from their nightly high-decibel, high-energy shows.

Altogether, more than 50 persons are involved in staging the night's performance—the headline group and the opening act, managers, publicity people, and stage and setup crews. The majority of the crowd, as on most nights, range in age from 16 to 25, with many 14-year-olds and some audience members near 30 years old.

JOB OPPORTUNITIES IN RECORDING

Young people who wish to enter the popular music business for careers in management or writing have no clear path to follow. Some management personnel are drawn from the ranks of former performers; knowledge of electronics, sales, and marketing is more valuable than traditional training in mass communication processes. Most pop-rock songs performed by groups today are written by a member of the group or its entourage. One nontechnical, nonmusical type of job opportunity is in the promotion department of record producers and distributors, advertising new releases and performers and urging radio stations to play specific new recordings. Those individuals best suited for such work are extroverted, personable, and aggressive, with enthusiasm for and knowledge of contemporary music.

Chapter 12

TELEVISION

THE IMPACT OF TELEVISION

Robin Williams was an obscure comedian when he was cast as the zany spaceman Mork from the planet Ork in the ABC network situation comedy, "Mork and Mindy." The show was an instantaneous hit. Suddenly Williams was a celebrity, often surrounded by autograph seekers. His face appeared on magazine covers, and talk-show hosts competed to have him as a guest. Once in a French restaurant in New York, an obsequious waiter was bowing and fawning in the manner used for all guests when he realized suddenly who his customer was. "It's Mork!" he exclaimed, shattering the elegant ambience. The astounding power of television to create public awareness was apparent once again. For Williams, and for many others caught up in the phenomenon, a feeling of unreality hangs over their daily lives. Even those who work in television are not fully conscious of its impact.

Television is not content to cover athletic events. It dictates the hour at which they take place and when the game action will halt for commercials. The World Series, for generations an afternoon event, now is played on cold October nights, to the acute discomfort of players and crowds, so that networks may sell their commercials between innings at prime-time rates. National political conventions are staged and timed like theatrical performances to lure a TV audience. Protest demonstrations that would pass almost unnoticed gain national exposure when a television news crew arrives and photographs protestors shaking their fists at the camera. In the home, the program listings influence meal- and bedtimes. Parents may use the TV set as a babysitter, relieved that it keeps the children quiet, and too often unconcerned about the ideas and images they are absorbing. According to A. C. Nielsen statistics, the average American family watches television 6 hours and 36 minutes per day.

Although television has been a force in American life for more than 30 years, a large percentage of viewers have not yet developed a discriminating attitude toward it. In its finest hours—coverage of the assassination and funeral of President John F. Kennedy and the landing on the moon by astronaut Neil Armstrong, to cite two examples—television with its enthralling visual immediacy gives its audience a feeling of participation far more powerfully than any other medium. Each season, a limited number of dramatic programs such as Alex Haley's series, "Roots," and NBC's spectacular "Shogun," rise above the tightly packaged limits of commercial television, stirring viewers' emotions. Television's spokespersons cite a long list of distinguished accomplishments. But these are almost obscured in the daily TV grist. The monotonous succession of game shows, soap operas, reruns of old movies, inane situation comedies, and violent police shows, interrupted relentlessly by commercials, becomes an opiate for some adults, an escape from the reality of daily life while purporting to be reality. It is an artificial reality: in the television world, hardly anyone grows old, even the poor are well dressed, the private detective hero always finds a parking place, and the emotional impact of tragedy is blunted by the bouncy, cheerful toothpaste and laundry detergent commercials that follow it.

THE MONEY ROLLS IN

Television yields large profits for the three primary American networks, the American Broadcasting Company (ABC), the Columbia Broadcasting System (CBS), and the National Broadcasting Company (NBC), and the owners of most of the 764 commercial stations. Television stations are of two types: *VHF* (very high frequency), and the less-powerful *UHF* (ultra high frequency). In 1980 the FCC proposed technical changes that could add hundreds of low-powered, short-range television stations in both VHF and UHF bands. The money rolls in because advertisers have found that commercials on TV sell merchandise in such enormous quantities that they will pay very high prices for air time to broadcast those commercials. This is not surprising, since there is at least one television set, and often more, in 98 percent of American homes.

The Television Bureau of Advertising calculates that in 1979 advertisers spent $4.7 billion on network advertising. Huge additional amounts were spent for commercials placed directly with local stations. Proctor & Gamble alone spent $289.6 million on network advertising that year. General Foods spent $203.2 million.

The 1981 *Broadcasting Yearbook* quoted official figures from the FCC that total television industry revenues for 1979 were $10.6 billion and profits were $1.9 billion, a rate of earnings that makes executives in other industries envious. *Broadcasting* also reported that the average television station had a 25.85 percent profit margin in 1979.

When CBS televised the 1980 Super Bowl game between the Pittsburgh Steelers and the Los Angeles Rams, it paid $7.3 million to broadcast the show—$6 million for the right to show the game and $1.3 million in production costs. In return, it charged advertisers $476,000 for each minute of commercial time. The program lasted 5½ hours, including a 90-minute pregame show, the game itself, and locker room postgame show. Advertisers were willing to pay such enormous prices because the network claimed an average audience of 80 million viewers, peaking at 105 million. The game was on the air in all 50 states and in 15 foreign countries.

CBS covered the game with 16 cameras and had six instant-replay machines in operation; altogether, it used between $7 million and $10 million worth of equipment and a staff of more than 200. This is television at its most grandiose. If a few wry voices ask, "All this, just for a football game?" television leaders reply that the Super Bowl is not merely a game, it is "a great American spectacle"—a spectacle spawned by television.

A year later, when NBC telecast the Oakland Raiders' victory over the Philadelphia Eagles in the 1981 Super Bowl, the charge per minute for commercial time had risen to $550,000 and the program lasted six hours, including a two-hour pregame show. The audience was estimated at 104 million people.

Aided by an enormous, months-long promotion campaign, the installment of the CBS serial "Dallas" that revealed the identity of the person who shot the villain, J. R. Ewing, set the all-time TV audience record in November 1980. According to the A. C. Nielsen Co. survey, viewers in more than 41.4 million homes saw the episode. CBS charged $500,000 per minute for commercial time on the show and, according to industry estimates, earned a profit of $2 million for the hour.

The American television industry employs about 150,000 persons, a relatively small number in relation to the money involved in the medium. Their jobs run the gamut of executive, technical, on-the-air performance, and routine office work. At the top, the monetary rewards for star performers and executives are great, although their job tenure is far from certain. For example, early in 1980, Jane C. Pfeiffer was the highest-ranking woman in television, as chairperson of NBC. She was earning more than $400,000 a year in salary, bonus, and other benefits. Within a few months, however, she was forced to resign when the network's profits fell because of poor ratings. Top network news stars such as Dan Rather were reported to be earning more than $1 million a year.

HOW A TELEVISION STATION OPERATES

Unlike the printed media and the commercial motion picture industry, a television station gives its product away. Anyone possessing a television set may watch hour after hour of programs free of charge. The station, of course, must earn money to cover its high cost of operation and return a profit. It does so through the sale of commercial advertising time.

Examination of the operation of a successful TV station of medium size, affiliated with one of the three major networks, shows how American television functions. In most respects this station is typical of many in the United States, although it has a considerably larger news operation than many of its size.

The station is headed by a general manager. Reporting to the manager are four major department heads—chief engineer, program director, news director, and sales manager. The head of the production department reports to the program director. The promotion director is closely linked to the sales department but reports to the general manager.

Although it is on the air 18 hours a day, the station creates only about three or four hours of programming in its own studios, mostly local news. The rest is obtained from the network and from independent suppliers of filmed shows. To do this job, the station has a staff of 55 people, plus eight to ten part-time employees. Some of the latter are local college students who usually help with live show production. The station offers a full hour of local news, weather, and sports at the dinner hour preceding the evening network news program, and another 30 minutes of news in the late evening. During the week it presents other local background news and discussion programs. Fourteen people of varying degrees of experience comprise the news staff.

The necessary income with which to operate the station is obtained from three primary sources: the network, national spot commercials the station puts on the air during station breaks, and local and regional commercials. One widely held misconception is that an affiliate station pays the network for the national programs it puts on the air. The reality is just the reverse.

Each of the three major networks has approximately 200 affiliated stations. In addition, the federal government permits each network to own and operate seven stations of its own, five VHF and two UHF. They are known in the trade as O and Os. An affiliate contracts with a network for the exclusive right to broadcast in its coverage area all programs distributed by the network. It also has the right to refuse to broadcast any network program. Rejections occur when the station believes its audience will find a particular program objectionable, or when it prefers to use that block of air time to broadcast a program it originates on its own, or obtains from another source. In practice, most affiliates broadcast more than 90 percent of the network programming. When a network plans to present a controversial program, it transmits the show in advance to the affiliates on a closed circuit; the station executives then decide whether to use it. The network also provides advance summaries of all its scheduled programs, letting the affiliates know what to expect.

With certain exceptions, the network pays the station to air a network program; the price is based on the size of the station's market. In our example, the station's average compensation is approximately $700 per hour. The network pays the station 30 percent of its card rate. During an hour-long show, most of the commercials are put on the air by the network, which receives all the income from them. However, station break slots in which the local station inserts its own commercials, either national or local, are left open. The local station keeps all the revenue from these spots.

Thus it follows that the larger the number of affiliates carrying a show, the larger the network's audience and the greater the amount of money it can charge an advertiser that places a commercial on the show. Television advertising rates are based on the cost of reaching 1000 viewers. That is why there was great concern in the industry when in 1977 national ratings services revealed that both daytime and nighttime viewing had declined after almost two decades of an almost continuous rise. Changing demographic patterns of the viewing audience were among several factors cited as the possible reasons for the decline, which continued into the 1980s.

To supplement network and local programming, stations obtain programs from other sources as well, under varying financial arrangements. A common example of this is the syndicated show, such as the Mike Douglas afternoon interview program. The station purchases the show from a syndication firm for a flat, negotiated fee. All commercial time slots are open for local commercials. If the station's sales staff is effective, it fills those spots with high-paying sales messages. A variation of this is the barter program, of which the Lawrence Welk Show is an example. The station receives the program without charge, and the Welk organization does not provide any compensation. Half the spots in the hour-long program are sold nationally by the Welk organization. It keeps all this income, from which it covers the expense of preparing the show. The other half of the commercial slots are reserved for the local station's own commercials.

Still another variation is the network show provided to an affiliate without the usual compensation from the network. Enough local spots are left open during the program for the station to profit satisfactorily. The "Today" show and Sunday professional football broadcasts are examples of this arrangement. The audiences for these broadcasts are so large that, in these instances, a local station can afford the noncompensation arrangement.

Occasionally, a station will replace a network program in prime time with a nonnetwork program that it considers exceptionally important or more lucrative. This action often angers loyal audiences of the preempted program, so it is done infrequently. The Billy Graham evangelistic crusade, for example, will purchase consecutive evenings of prime time, for which it pays the station more than the $700 hourly network rate. This is a good financial arrangement for the station because it receives full income for the hour and at the same time appeals to the portion of the viewing population that finds the Graham message inspiring.

THE BATTLE OF THE NETWORKS

The three principal networks are in such a battle among themselves to attract viewers, and the advertising dollars they bring, that the weekly ratings report of their standing is a popular news story in the newspapers, but not on the network news programs.

For years CBS was the consistent overall winner, helped by a group of exceptionally successful comedy programs including "All in the Family," the "Carol Burnett Show," the "Mary Tyler Moore Show," and the "Bob Newhart Show." One by one these shows left the air, to collect additional income for their producers as syndicated reruns on independent stations. In the late 1970s, ABC, long the holder of third place, made a spectacular surge into the top spot. Its success was built around a group of youth-oriented comedies, more "sexual" and contemporary in tone than the other networks offered, such as "Happy Days," "Mork and Mindy" and "Three's Company." Innovative sports programs helped, too. ABC's success led some stations to move their affiliation to it, away from the other networks. Finding itself at the bottom, NBC hired Fred Silverman, the man credited with leading the ABC climb to the top, to revive its programming fortunes. In the early 1980s, CBS and ABC were running neck and neck; NBC had failed to close the gap and had discharged Silverman.

So massive is the potential network television audience during the prime-time evening hours that a show attracting only 10 million viewers may be considered a failure, and cancelled. Decisions by network executives on the survival of a show are made primarily upon its drawing power as reported by the ratings; its appeal to a youthful audience is especially vital. If a show's rating is low, advertisers will avoid it or pay a reduced fee for their commercials to appear in or adjacent to it. It is not a profit center, as the trade jargon goes, so it is dropped. A few programs are carried by each network in defiance of this practice because management believes they provide prestige or has faith that they eventually will grow in popular favor. In the minds of many, perhaps most, network executives, television functions primarily as a selling medium, and entertainment and news shows are judged less on their intrinsic values than on their ability to attract advertisers.

Entertainment on Television

With fanfare, every September the major networks put their fall lineup of prime-time entertainment shows on the air. Each new program is publicized as a sure winner, yet relatively few survive through the winter. Many vanish after the first 13-week programming cycle, some after only two or three episodes. Since the network executives know that this will happen, they are continually ordering replacement programs to be tossed into the breach.

Rarely do the networks produce the entertainment programs they show, although at one time they produced many. They agreed to halt the practice after Justice Department suits charged that they were operating a monopoly. This claim was based on the fact that when network executives decided what programs to show, they could choose only programs that the network owned, while eliminating the products of independent firms. Now the shows are created by independent production firms, which sell air rights to the networks.

After a network agrees to use a program idea proposed by one of the production firms, or commissions a firm to develop a program from an idea the network provides, the relationship between producer and network is close (Figure 12.1). The network supervises the stories used and has the final word on casting. Its censors must approve the scripts. Ownership of the shows, however, remains with the production firm. Among the largest entertainment film producers are MTM, Inc., Tandem/TAT (Norman Lear), Aaron Spelling, Four D, and motion picture companies including Twentieth Century-Fox, Paramount, Universal, and MGM.

The odds against any specific program being placed on a network schedule are enormous. In the process of program development, on which millions of dollars are spent every year, the network staffs study audience demographics, programming and advertising sales goals, and the programming desires of affiliated stations. They weigh proposed program ideas in this light. For example, in a recent season one network examined 2500 program ideas, studied scripts for 150 of them, and underwrote production of 37 pilot films. Out of this mass the network actually obtained nine new programs, most of which did not last beyond this first season. Occasionally, a network will show a pilot film it has made, but never developed into a series, as a single free-standing program.

Each network seeks in planning its prime-time schedule an overall effect, with a balance of programming in which situation comedies such as "M*A*S*H" and "Barney Miller," dramatic series such as "Lou Grant" and "Dallas," and police and private detective action shows such as "CHiPs," are principal ingredients.

The hour at which a program is shown, and the nature of the programs the rival networks put on the air against it, may be the deciding factor in its survival. Like generals maneuvering their battle forces, network program executives move the programs on their lists around from time slot to time slot. On the offensive, a programmer may place a promising new show at a time when the competition's offerings are weak, giving it favorable audience exposure. As a defensive act, a well-established program may be shifted into a slot opposite a popular show on another network, in the hope that it will siphon off some of the rival's rating. It is common practice to

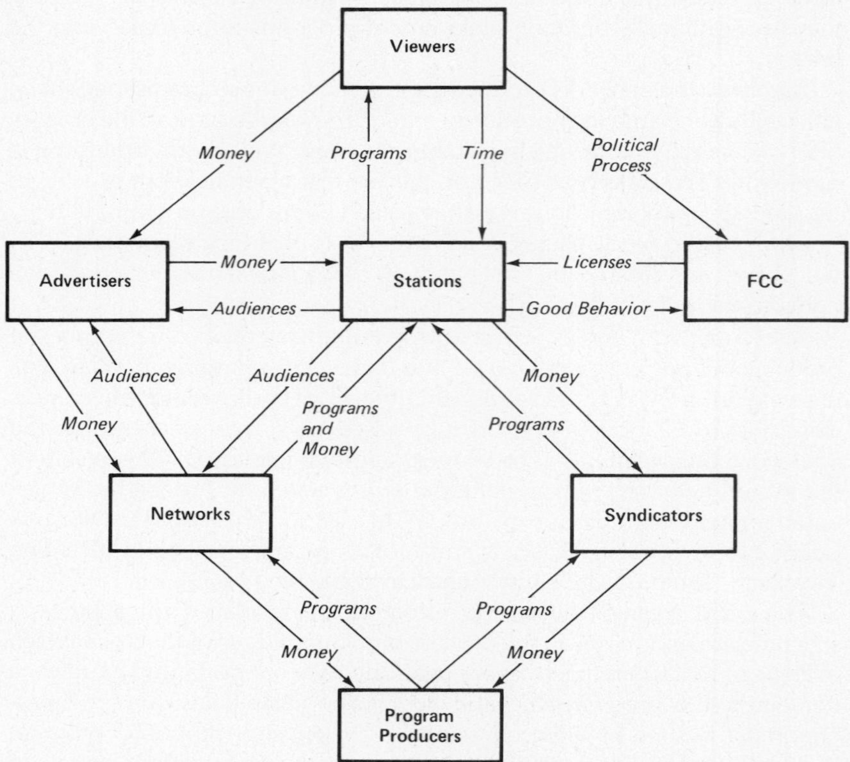

Figure 12.1 Organization of the television industry. *Source:* Reprinted by permission of the publisher, from *Television Economics* by Bruce M. Owen, Jack H. Beebe, and Willard G. Manning, Jr. (Lexington, Mass.: Lexington Books, D. C. Heath and Company, 1974).

have a new show follow an established hit, to pick up the lead-in audience, viewers who watched the previous show, then decided to take a look at the new show, rather than get up and turn the dial. Another device is to "hammock" a show, placing it between two hits. Concentrating a group of a network's best shows, especially comedies, on the same night of the week is often done; executives hope that the combined impact of their high ratings will enable the network to claim that it "owns" that particular night in the relentless network warfare. The ploys used in programming are myriad. If one of them raises the rating of a show in trouble or reduces the rating of a rival network's hit, the maneuver is hailed as a success even though some viewers are irked because their comfortable routines have been disturbed.

Those who conceive and produce programs watch constantly for "spinoff" possibilities—that is, taking a character from one situation show and building a new series of programs around that character. An example is "Benson," an ABC comedy. The minor role of Benson, the sardonic butler in the zany, sexy series "Soap," was played so effectively by Robert Guillaume that in the following season he was made the star of his own show, in which he was the major domo in the home of a bumbling but well-intentioned governor. The highly rated "Laverne and Shirley" was a spinoff from "Happy Days." TV series often are derived from popular movies, using the same characters and settings. The "M*A*S*H" series is an example.

Analysis of listings discloses that on a day-long basis the entertainment portions of television programming on most stations consist predominantly of game shows, soap operas, talk shows, old movies, and reruns of former network situation comedies. In some cases independent stations show old episodes of a series such as "Love Boat" while new episodes still are appearing on a network. Rarely do locally created entertainment programs get on the air.

The degree to which the networks are dependent upon a steady flow of prime-time programs from the production companies was evident in 1980, when a prolonged strike of actors forced NBC, CBS, and ABC to delay the opening of the fall prime-time season. The actors demanded and received a share of the steadily growing income that producers obtain from placing their programs on pay television, videocassettes, and videodiscs.

In a sense, the networks are victims of their own success. Executives know the kind of programming that sells. None of them cares to experiment daringly because if the innovative program fails to draw a mass audience, viewers and advertisers will turn to the rival network channels. The result is year after year of predictable formula programming in prime time. This has a ripple effect throughout television because much air time on independent stations is filled with reruns of programs that have finished their first-run life on the networks.

Once television and the motion picture industry were such rivals that the film studios would not allow their stars to appear on TV, even on talk shows. Then the studios realized how much money they could make by selling their backlog of old films to television. Now the two industries are closely tied financially and in the production of material. Much of what we see on TV is filmed on Hollywood sound stages. Movie producers make their films knowing that they will be aired on television in a couple of years, after being shown in theaters. Many films are made specifically for original showing on TV, using camera techniques suitable for the small screen and dramatic development carefully paced for the insertion of commercials. This has led to the mini-series. Instead of telling a story in one long piece, as a feature motion picture does, the producer packages the story into segments that can be shown on television on several successive nights, a technique reminiscent of the Saturday afternoon serials of the early movies.

Rating the TV Shows

When a network claims that 30 million viewers saw a show, it is obvious that the viewers have not been counted one by one. Television viewership is determined by monitoring the viewing habits of a small, scientifically selected sample, then extrapolating the percentage results into nationwide statistics. Although these projected statistics have built-in potential for error, television producers and sales people quote them as though they are completely accurate. The fact is that the viewing preferences of 1200 American families determine the national ratings for a show.

Two firms provide most of the ratings reports, the A. C. Nielsen Company and Arbitron. Arbitron specializes in monitoring local TV markets. Programs are dropped or renewed, executives keep or lose their jobs, and advertising revenues rise and fall, depending upon what the "Nielsens" and Arbitron ratings reveal. These reports give two kinds of data about a show, its *rating* and its *share*. The rating of a show is the percentage of all households having TV sets that viewed the particular program. Nielsen placed the number of television-owning households in 1981 at approximately 77.8 million. Thus, according to Nielsen calculations, a show with a rating of 20 was viewed in more than 15 million homes, a fact an advertiser is anxious to know. The share figure is based on the number of households having their sets turned on at a given time. The show with a rating of 20 has a 31 share; that is, 31 percent of the sets turned on at that time were tuned to it. The share figure measures a program's popularity against other shows on the air at the same time. Nielsen assumes that nationally, 10 percent of the viewers are watching independent stations, public television, or their own cassettes. The networks thus believe that, to be called successful, one of their shows must have at least a 30 share—one-third of the network viewers watching television at that time.

Nielsen obtains its information by placing small electronic boxes in 1200 homes chosen by sampling techniques, whose household members' identities are secret. Each box, wired to every TV set in the house, records details of each set's use—when it was turned on and to what channel. A computer-dialed telephone call from the Nielsen center in Florida to each of the homes in the sample automatically collects this information twice a day.

In order to ascertain the age and sex of viewers, and to learn how many household members are watching television, Nielsen runs a supplementary service in which 2400 participating household members complete weekly diaries for each quarter-hour of viewing.

Critics of television and its manner of measuring its own success emphasize that, huge as the viewership figures are, many people watch very little television. Les Brown of the New York *Times* contends that one-third of the households owning television sets in the United States account for two-thirds of the actual watching. Thus an enormous market remains to be tapped, if the industry can provide programs that will attract the other two-thirds.

NEWS ON TELEVISION

Television news programs have become a hot property. In earlier days they were regarded as something of a public service that the individual stations and networks felt obliged to perform. Now these programs are important sources of income. The individuals who "anchor" the news shows—that is, read news items and introduce stories taped or filmed by correspondents in the field—achieve an aura of stardom that in some instances is based more upon their talent as entertainers than as newspeople.

Television news has two advantages over newspapers: its ability to deliver stories visually from the scene of the action, making viewers feel as though they are at the scene themselves; and the ease with which viewers can receive the news. Reading a story in a newspaper requires much more concentration than watching one on television. A routine newscast on a local station or the networks simply sketches even the main stories of the day, devoting about one to two minutes to major stories and barely a sentence or two to secondary ones. Network executives concede quite readily that they provide little more than a headline service, and that for detailed information viewers must read newspapers. The other side of this coin is that many individuals do not wish to know more about the day's events than television provides.

Because of the impact of on-the-scene reports and the carefully nurtured air of believability that those anchoring the news seek to project, annual surveys by the Roper organization have found that a large percentage of those questioned regard TV news as more believable than newspapers. This disturbs newspaper editors and reporters. They argue that they provide their readers with more comprehensive stories on events than TV does, and protest that this is more important than the personality of an anchorperson. Such a reaction is not entirely fair. Many TV reporters are anxious to develop their stories more fully on the air, and are well prepared to do so, but cannot because of the rigid time restrictions of the medium. Consultants hired by station managements to increase the ratings of their news shows often require performers to engage in "happy talk" chit-chat among themselves and to use other devices that have little relationship to intrinsic news values. On-camera people may hold or lose their jobs on the basis of measured physiological response by sample audiences.

Rivalry among the networks in the news field is intense, especially in

A television reporter at a minority housing project is on camera for ABC-affiliate KSTP-TV in St. Paul, Minnesota. (Photo by Irene Clepper.)

their early evening half-hour newscasts. During the 1970s the "CBS Evening News With Walter Cronkite" held consistent supremacy in the ratings. A former press association correspondent who went into radio and then television, Cronkite projected an unflappable good-uncle image on the screen that gave an air of authenticity to whatever he read or said. His retirement from the daily program early in 1981 and replacement by Dan Rather, whose manner is more aggressive and hard-edged, changed the atmosphere of the CBS show to a degree. John Chancellor, long the chief anchorman on NBC, comes across as a literate, low-key personality, suggesting a slightly intellectual approach. After being a perennial last, ABC switched to a new format without a single anchorperson, instead using three anchorpersons stationed in Washington, Chicago, and London, and achieved substantial gains in the ratings.

Networks have only a half-hour for their evening news shows because local stations will not relinquish additional time, since they make more money with an hour-long or 90-minute-long local news program. ABC expanded its network news time by adding a 20-minute "Nightline" newscast at 11:30 P.M., Eastern time, starring Ted Koppel.

Supplementing their staccato-paced daily newscasts, the networks provide detailed background on occasional big stories through special half-hour-long and hour-long programs, and explore newsworthy situations in intermittent documentaries. CBS has had spectacular success with its "60 Minutes," an hour-long show in which veteran correspondents develop several stories each week in considerable depth, often through aggressive interviewing. Several years after it came on the air, "60 Minutes" achieved the remarkable feat for a news program of being the highest-ranked show in the weekly Nielsen ratings, outranking the most popular comedy and drama shows.

Behind the smooth delivery of each anchorperson is a large staff of writers and film editors. The executive producer of a network news show decides which taped reports from correspondents will be used. The writers prepare the "tell" stories, those brief summaries that the anchorperson reads, perhaps with drawings or other graphics on the screen to illustrate them, as well as the lead-ins with which the anchorperson introduces the taped field reports. A frequent charge against TV news is that producers tend to judge stories by the kind of footage available to illustrate them, rather than by their news merit.

Preparation and delivery of local news programs resembles the network method, on a smaller scale. Many local stations offer editorials delivered by a high-ranking station executive. A news department staff member on a small station may be reporter, film editor, and writer, and serve as the anchorperson as well.

Film for use on a local television news program is edited by the news editor and a photographer. (Courtesy of the South Bend *Tribune*.)

PUBLIC TELEVISION

Viewers who prefer more educational and cultural programs than commercial TV usually offers can find them on the approximately 270 nonprofit (noncommercial) public television stations operating in the United States. Their programs are presented without commercial interruptions.

These nonprofit stations obtain operating funds from several sources, including government grants, underwriting grants from large corporations trying to build a good public image, and public subscriptions. About $50 million a year is contributed by the public to the nonprofit stations. A federally funded organization, the Corporation for Public Broadcasting, established by Congress in 1967, provides money for production and distribution of programs through the Public Broadcasting Service (PBS).

Some of the programs seen on PBS are created in production centers at seven noncommercial stations or at the Children's Television Workshop. Numerous others are imported, often from Great Britain. Indeed, PBS is sometimes accused of being more concerned with depicting Victorian and Edwardian England than contemporary American life. This is because of the resounding success of the "Upstairs, Downstairs" series in particular and other English imports about those eras shown on "Masterpiece Theater," the best known of PBS adult programs.

Among the strengths of the public broadcasting system are its intelligent and stimulating programs for children, of which "Sesame Street" is the best known. Science programs such as "Nova" and Carl Sagan's "Cosmos" attract older children along with an adult audience. The MacNeil-Lehrer news report is applauded for in-depth examination of major news developments.

Despite the excellence of some of its programming and the audience PBS has developed, there are doubts that public television works as well as it should. A recent report by the second Carnegie Commission on the Future of Public Broadcasting recommended that the government spend large additional amounts to improve it. In an inflationary period when balanced federal budgets are a widely heralded political goal, such increases by Congress are at best uncertain.

The most frequent criticisms of public television are that its programs are dull at times, elitist in tone, and intended only for the well-educated upper middle-class; that it is not sufficiently innovative; and that a cumbersome management bureaucracy impedes its progress. A public opinion poll taken for the Public Broadcasting Service and made public in 1980 revealed that while PBS has broad public support in principle, its broadcasts draw a somewhat limited audience. Public television attracts only one-seventh of the median weekly viewing accorded to commercial TV.

The most frequent negative attitude stated in the poll was that public television spends too much air time on fund raising. Of greater potential importance was the second most frequent criticism, that public television could mean government control over what viewers watch, because of the federal subsidy it receives.

The Public Broadcasting Service's independence in programming was severely tested in 1980 when the Mobil Corporation, one of its major underwriters, publicly questioned the PBS decision to show the British program, "The Death of a Princess." The film dealt with the public executions of a Saudi Arabian princess and her commoner lover, for adultery. The Saudi Arabian government was so enraged when the film was shown in Great Britain that it temporarily expelled the British ambassador. Mobil at that time had a heavy financial interest in the Saudi Arabian oil industry, which supplies a large quantity of oil to the United States. Mobil ran an advertisement in major American newspapers asserting that showing the film here would not be in the national interest and urging PBS to reconsider its decision. The State Department and the Saudi government also asked that the show be cancelled. Despite the pressure, PBS showed "The Death of a Princess"; only seven of its 240 affiliates failed to carry the program.

According to the PBS survey, "Viewers perceive many valuable assets and only few drawbacks in public television's existence, yet their allegiance to PTV does not run deep. Despite the credit that public television receives for its cultural broadcasts and its service to children, less than a third of our respondents say that it would make a great deal of difference to them if there were no public television at all. Others might feel a sense of loss if PTV were to go out of business, but their responses indicate that their sense of loss would not be great."

In short, the American public regards public television as a welcome alternative, to which it turns for specific programs or when it is tired of commercial fare, but does not accept public television as a primary source of TV viewing.

TELEVISION BY CABLE

Television pictures ordinarily are received in the home by electrical impulses transmitted through the air. Since rugged terrain interferes with such transmission, in 1949 a method was developed to carry TV signals by cable into regions with poor reception. The first Community Antenna Television (CATV) systems were constructed in the hills of eastern Pennsylvania and Oregon. Only three to five channels were provided in early cable operations.

In the intervening three decades, technical improvements have revolutionized the TV-by-cable concept. Instead of being a fill-in service of limited capacity, cable TV has developed the means to deliver many programs and services into the home. So many possibilities are open that their full scope is not yet understood, let alone developed for general use.

By 1981 a single cable was capable of carrying up to 107 channels, as compared with previous successive maximums of 12, 36, and 54. From the point of view of available programming and operating economics, just how many available channels will be used by various cable systems is uncertain. Whatever the precise number is, cable TV viewers of the future will have an enormous choice of programs to watch. But unlike conventional over-the-air television, they must pay for the privilege.

Cable systems are expensive to install, especially in areas where the wires must be placed underground, so a cable system usually receives an exclusive franchise from local government to serve a specified area. Each household electing to receive cable service pays a monthly fee to the franchise holder, much as it pays to receive electricity or gas service. Large corporations with ample capital have moved heavily into ownership of cable TV systems, either by obtaining original franchises or by purchasing existing systems and enlarging them. They see an enticing prospect of large long-term profits.

Cable television's commercial success was assured in 1972 when, after a five-year dispute among broadcasters, cable operators, and copyright owners, the FCC for the first time permitted cable systems to operate with distant signals in the 100 largest markets. Various restrictions were imposed, however, and cable TV's development was slowed for several years by the lack of venture capital.

A surge in the attractiveness of cable TV to viewers, and in profit potential for operators, came with development of pay television. Programs such as sporting events and feature-length motion pictures unbroken by commercials are brought into the home by special cable channels. To receive these extra programs, the resident must pay an additional sum beyond the monthly basic cable charge. Subscription TV is also available in over-the-air form in some cities, by use of a scrambling device.

Conventional TV broadcasters and motion picture theater operators are opposed to pay cable TV, fearing harm to their businesses. The legal ground was cleared in 1977 when the Supreme Court refused to review a landmark decision by the United States Court of Appeals for the District of Columbia in *Federal Communications Commission v. Home Box Office*. The appeals court declared that there was no evidence that pay cable TV would adversely affect either the public interest or over-the-air television; that the FCC had no statutory authority to regulate pay cable TV; and that any restrictions violated the medium's First Amendment right of free speech. With this victory, pay cable TV had the go-ahead for expansion. Cable companies such as Home Box Office and Showtime offer the viewer an array of new movies, sports activities, and special events that conventional television does not provide.

Transmission of TV signals by satellite, bouncing them off a relay station 22,300 miles in space and back down to receiving dishes at individual stations across the country, is a fundamental ingredient in cable TV growth. Transmission cost is cut when a signal goes across country by satellite rather than by leased land lines. Flexibility is greater. New combinations of producing and receiving stations can be put together without following the traditional patterns of the three major networks. Ted Turner, an imaginative television entrepreneur in Atlanta, Georgia, challenged ABC, CBS, and NBC as suppliers of news in 1980 by initiating his Cable News Network. With its own newsgathering force, the Turner CNN beamed a news program 24 hours a day by satellite to cable systems that purchased the service. In order to fill all the cable channels that will be available, new types and sources of programs must be developed.

So far, cable television has not fully achieved the size of audience its most enthusiastic supporters anticipated (Figure 12.2). Technical de-

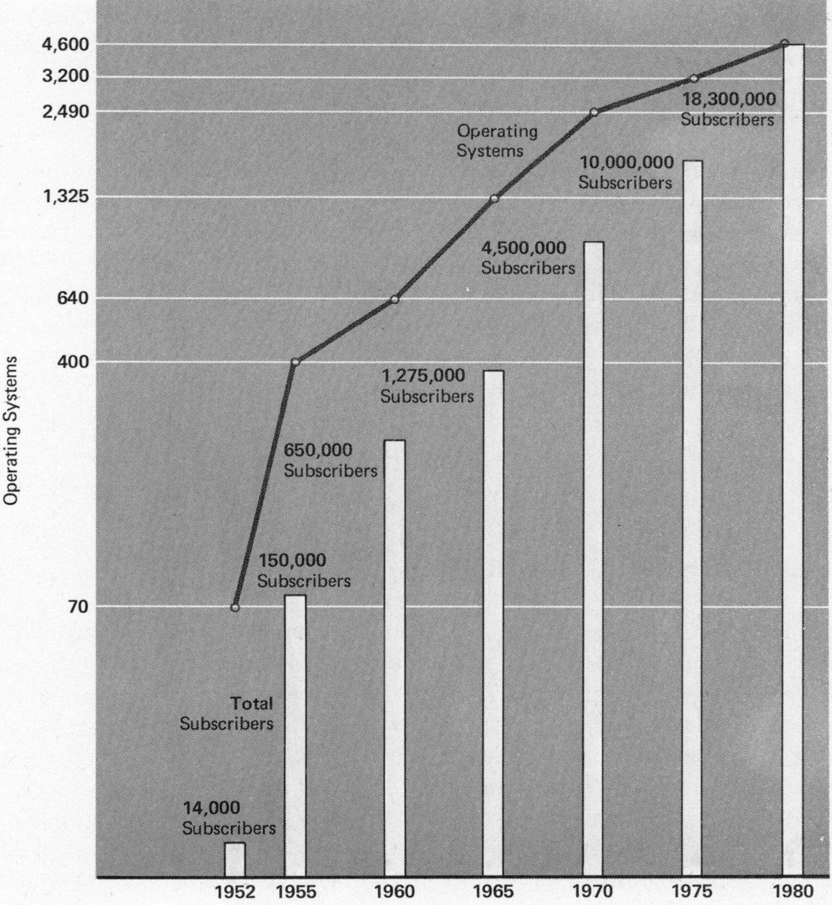

Figure 12.2 Growth of the cable TV industry in the United States as of January of each year. (*Sources:* Figures for 1952 to 1974: *Television Factbook,* services vol. no. 44 [1974–1975 ed.]. Figures for 1975: National Cable Television Association. Figures for 1978: *Television Factbook,* services vol. no. 47 [1977–1978 ed.]. Figures for 1980: Television Digest, Inc.)

velopments have come faster than the industry's ability to use them commercially and the audience's readiness to accept them. A question remains: How many viewers of free conventional television are ready to pay $8.50 a month, the national average, for basic cable service, plus another $10 or more a month for the supplemental services being offered? In the early 1980s more than 40 satellite services of various types were offered commercially. Viewers must be sold on the value of the additional programs offered to them.

As shown by Figure 12.2, in 1980 there were 4,600 operating cable systems serving approximately 18,300,000 subscribers, well over 20 percent of the potential cable TV homes. Home Box Office (HBO), largest of the supplemental cable services, reported that it had more than 4 million subscribers nationally. Thomas R. Wheeler, president of the National Cable Television Association, predicted that by the mid 1980s about 30 to 35 million homes would receive basic cable TV. He contended that the growth of cable TV would bring more viewers to their sets but would not steal viewers from conventional television, a view not shared by the latter.

Still in its infancy, but expected to grow, is the sale of advertising on cable TV, beyond the commercials already included in the conventional network TV programs carried on some cable channels. Since advertising rates at this stage of cable development are much lower than time charges on the over-the-air networks, they offer companies an attractive alternative. Still uncertain is the willingness of the viewing public to accept commercials on cable when they are paying substantial fees to receive the service.

GREAT CHANGES AHEAD

Even the most sagacious futurists are unsure what will happen in the video field during the 1980s, but all agree that great changes are occurring. The home television set of the 1970s was used mostly to receive over-the-air programs of the three networks and local independent stations. As commercial applications of the new electronic techniques develop, the set becomes a multipurpose video center.

Already, set owners enjoy the enticing fare offered by pay cable TV, growing more elaborate each year. They play video games on the set. With a videotape recorder, they record programs aired at times during which they are not able to watch, and view them later. They purchase or rent videocassettes of movies, including Hollywood classics; the market in pornographic film cassettes to be shown on the home screen is booming. Or they make videotapes with their own cameras and view them on the TV set. Ordinary home movies may be transferred to videotape. Just coming onto the market are videodiscs that look and operate like phonograph records, but play 30 minutes or more of uninterrupted color or black-and-white programs, with sound.

The legal right of the home-set owner to use a videotape recorder was challenged by Universal City Studios and Walt Disney Productions, which contended that their ownership rights in the commercial TV films they made were violated if the shows could be copied at home, free of charge. Specifically, they sued Sony Corporation to stop the manufacture, sale, and use of its Betamax videocassette recorder. A federal judge ruled in favor of Sony Corporation in 1979, stating that home use of recorders to tape programs broadcast by commercial television does not violate copyright laws. The ruling, however, did not apply to recording programs from pay television.

Most of the uses of television just mentioned are primarily for the entertainment of set owners. Equally fascinating, with an educational and informational potential still unrealized, is the development of a means of showing textual matter on the home screen. This is known as *teletext.* Originated by the British Broadcasting Corporation, teletext is the generic name for three systems of electronic information delivery—Ceefax, Oracle, and Viewdata (also known as Prestel). Teletext is electronic "print" that is readable with a maximum of 24 lines on a glass screen and is transmitted on the unused portion of the ordinary television signal. By use of a decoder they purchase, home TV owners select material for printing on the screen from about 800 pages that are being broadcast continually—news bulletins, sports results, stock market quotations, almost anything the broadcaster believes the audience might enjoy. This service costs the set owner nothing except purchase of the decoder.

Viewdata is a different system from Ceefax and Oracle. Home viewers pay for this service. The set is linked by telephone to the Viewdata computer, in which information of many varieties is stored. Set owners telephone the computer, asking that certain portions of text be shown on the home screen. They are billed automatically for the showing of the material they order. This system is also known as *videotex* (without the final *t*).

Will newspapers eventually be delivered in this form, instead of on newsprint? That is one possibility. Or might the operators of videotex offer so many of the special features of newspapers, such as classified advertising and theater listings, that many readers no longer would buy newspapers, obtaining their news summaries from TV news shows? Economic and legal questions must be answered. For example, newspapers are not under federal regulation (the First Amendment prevents it); but television is. If the newspaper delivers its product to the reader via the TV screen, rather than on newsprint, does the First Amendment protect the rights of the news organization or not?

Above all, still in doubt are the public's desires and the degree to which it is willing to pay for its video viewing. The cost of videotape recorders and players is relatively high, as are the tapes and discs, but may decline with mass production. Time is a factor as well. Will the availability of these additional programs and services induce the chronic viewer to spend even more time watching the screen and lure owners who turn on their sets only occasionally to do so more often? Those who are investing heavily in the new video technology are gambling that it will.

Other human factors remain to be tested: eyestrain from close scrutiny of type on the screen; the impatience of fast readers because pages are held on the screen at a rate slow enough for the average reader; the concentration required on the part of the viewer to read the text of a news story instead of having a newscaster deliver it in predigested form.

Two-way television is already a reality, in limited form. The QUBE home terminal system introduced by Warner Cable in Columbus, Ohio, allows a viewer to give an opinion or answer a question immediately to the originating studio when the broadcaster asks him or her to do so. Turning to various channels of the 30 offered by QUBE, the viewer may also order pay TV programs, participate in games, and watch local community-interest shows designed for specific audience interests.

These stimulating and imaginative uses of the home TV screen may have a shattering effect on the commercial television structure as we knew it in the 1970s. The three major networks may dwindle in significance from the dominant role they had during that decade. Some industry forecasters see ABC, CBS, and NBC becoming primarily purveyors of news and other information, while their traditional entertainment function is taken over increasingly by pay TV and by the smaller, specialized networks that are springing up, now that satellite transmission has eliminated the restrictions imposed by the old land-line wire system. Carried even further, as small-diameter dishes come on the market, the possibility exists for the delivery of programs by satellite from originating points directly into homes equipped with low-cost, rooftop receiving dishes. In 1981 the FCC took its first step on behalf of "space video" by accepting, for filing, an application to provide direct broadcast satellite (DBS) service from Satellite Television Corporation (STC), a subsidiary of Comsat, the Communications Satellite System. Other applications followed. DBS service, which could be operational by 1985 or 1986, would offer both pay TV and advertiser-supported free programs.

Determined to protect their enormous investments, the three major networks began developing subsidiary companies to provide programming for cable outlets. RCA's subsidiary, RCTV, for example, acquired first-run pay cable rights to BBC television programs in the United States.

In another development, the FCC in 1981 requested applications for the establishment of low-power television stations throughout the country. These mini-stations, with a radius of only about 25 miles, will be free to originate programming or to pick it up from another source. They may sell subscriptions or advertising and receive donations or tax money, but the

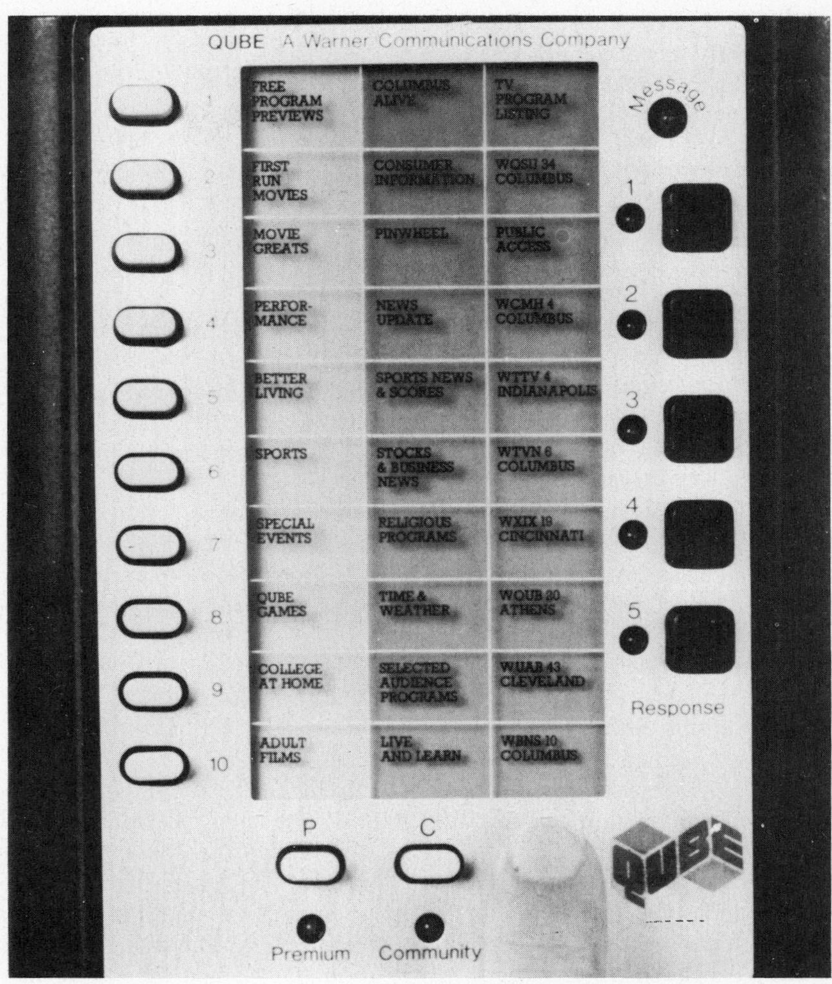

QUBE home terminal unit, introduced in Columbus, Ohio, in 1977, connects to the subscriber's television receiver and enables the viewer to select from 30 channels of programming. Subscribers also may play interactive games, take tests, instantly register their opinions, and participate at home in other television programs and events. Pay-TV programs may be selected on an individual basis and are automatically billed by a computer. The QUBE unit was developed by Warner Cable engineers in collaboration with Pioneer Electronic Corporation, of Tokyo, Japan, a major manufacturer of high-quality electronic products. (Photo courtesy of Warner Cable Corporation.)

stations will have secondary status and will not be permitted to interfere with full-service stations. This FCC move opened the door for even greater diversification in television.

JOB OPPORTUNITIES IN TELEVISION

Young people hoping for careers in television may find them in three areas: on-the-air performing in news and entertainment programs, production, and sales and business management.

Starting one's career at a small station is almost essential. Competition for jobs is intense, so most stations of medium and large size usually hire persons with experience. A beginner should not shun an opportunity to take what appears to be a menial job; getting a job on the "inside" is what counts. Numerous high-ranking executives of the networks started their careers in entry-level jobs.

In the news department, the first level in a small station is that of a beat or general assignment reporter. Beginners have a few on-the-air appearances with news stories. As they develop a screen personality and prove to be accurate and dependable, the news director may allow them to sit in as weekend or vacation relief anchorpersons on a local news show. The top job in news at a station is held by the news director, the person who makes the assignments and decides which stories will appear on the air. A study released by the Radio Television News Directors Association in 1980 revealed that women held the news director job at 30 TV stations; since 94 percent of all television news staffs now employ one or more women, the percentage of female news directors will rise with their growth in experience. Becoming a news director is a desirable career goal. When an applicant seeks a position on a larger station, the videotapes of on-the-air performances that he or she submits will play a critical part in the prospective employer's decision. A nationwide study by three University of Illinois researchers disclosed that broadcast newspeople change jobs more frequently than those in any other news occupation.

Jobs on news staffs of the networks go to people who have learned their trade at individual stations over a period of several years. Salaries of station TV news personnel are generally comparable to those paid by newspapers. Network salaries are high, as are those for top-level reporters on metropolitan stations, a few of whom receive more than $100,000 per year if they project that nebulous but vital star quality.

Another major job on a TV station staff is that of the program director, who handles programming policy and scheduling. This job requires detailed knowledge of network and syndicated program operations, as well as an understanding of tastes and interests among the audience the station serves. The upward route to this job usually is through the production or business staffs, rarely through the news department. The production department puts together locally produced shows and commercials, giving beginners an opportunity to work behind the cameras with cue cards, timing signals, and props, and also in the control booth. Directors and producers of individual programs usually rise to those positions along this path.

On the business side, novices eventually may become account executives selling commercial time. To do this well, the salesperson needs technical knowledge of TV operations, understanding of the station's audience characteristics, and skill to match up the time spots the station has to sell with the needs and budgets of potential advertisers. Another important factor is the salesperson's ability to present effectively to a potential client his or her station's advantages over competing media. The promotion manager's role is to publicize programs that the station will present and build a friendly public image for the station through community service endeavors.

At the top of the hierarchy is the station manager, who usually has had experience both on the air and in production. Managers of larger stations may earn in excess of $100,000 a year.

Chapter 13

PHOTOGRAPHIC COMMUNICATION

THE VISUAL DIMENSION

Photographic communication has emerged dramatically in recent decades as a key mode of mass communication—a visual dimension, capable of providing a wealth of description and detail not communicable through the written or spoken word.

The art of telling a story with photographs—both still and motion pictures—developed centuries later than the technique of telling it with words. Photographic equipment was relatively slow to become available, and those who worked with pictures needed time to develop the editorial methods of photographic narration. The rapid development of equipment in recent years and of our comprehension of how to use these sophisticated new tools, however, has made photojournalism a fundamental mode of mass communication.

Photojournalism for newspapers and magazines developed rapidly during the 1930s. Film, first used in the motion picture theater to provide entertainment, news, and documentaries for mass audiences, became in the 1950s and 1960s a dominant ingredient of televised news, public affairs, documentary, and advertising communication. Photojournalism thus has expanded in concept and function, and today is part of the larger field known as photographic communication.

To have full knowledge of the communication process, the student must understand the functions performed by pictures, how photography developed, and the essential techniques used by professional photographers and editors. This chapter discusses those topics, as well as the opportunities and working conditions for visual communicators.

Less than 150 years elapsed from the moment when the first photographic image was produced until a fascinated world watched astronauts Neil Armstrong and Edwin Aldrin transmit a live television picture from the surface of the moon. In that century and a half, the growth of photography as a medium of communication was spectacular. But in the decade following 1969 the image became even more important both in print media and on the screen. A new wave of picture agencies gave newspapers and magazines searching and revealing visual reporting and spectacular, compelling on-the-spot news coverage. Presidential elections hinged on the perceptions Americans gained from television screens—images rather than words. Millions of amateur photographers ranged worldwide, many with sophisticated equipment and subscriptions to *American Photographer, Popular Photography, Modern Photography,* or *Camera 35.*

HOW PHOTOGRAPHY DEVELOPED

Pioneering Photography

Joseph Nicéphone Nièpce, a retired French lithographer, began searching for a method to capture the photographic image in 1813. Three years later he is believed to have succeeded in producing a negative image, but he could only partially fix the image after exposure—that is, desensitize it to light. In 1826 he made a photograph on a pewter plate showing a view from his workroom window. He called this process Heliographie (sun drawing).

Photography took a significant step forward with creation of the Daguerreotype by another Frenchman, Louis Jacques Mandé Daguerre, in 1839. In this process an invisible (latent) image was developed by using mercury vapor. The exposure time was reduced from eight hours to 30 minutes, giving photography a practical application. The Daguerreotype process had three major limitations: 1) The image could be only the size of the plate in the camera; 2) the image was unique in itself and could be duplicated only by reshooting; and 3) the image was a *negative,* coated on a mirrored metallic surface, so a viewer could see it as a *positive* only if the mirror reflected a dark background.

Wet Plates

The third important approach to photography was the collodion wet plate process, developed in 1851 by Frederick Scott Archer, an English sculptor. The collodion process required the coating of a glass plate with a light-sensitive solution that had to be kept wet until exposed in the camera and processed in a darkroom. Very sharp paper prints could be made from a collodion negative. A photographer could use this process outdoors to record exposures of only ten seconds to a minute, a spectacular improvement in photographic speed. He was required, however, to work from a portable darkroom on location.

It was with this wet plate process, so clumsy by modern standards, that Mathew Brady produced his magnificent photographs of the Civil War. A successful portrait photographer, Brady asked President Lincoln for permission to document the conflict. He sent out 20 teams of photographers, led by Timothy O'Sullivan and Alexander Gardner, who followed the Union soldiers onto the battlefields and into their bivouacs. Brady's photographs have preserved for posterity a fascinating record of the war. For the first time, photography proved its value as a news medium.

Flexible Film and New Cameras

The next leap forward, opening the door for modern photography, came in 1889 when the Eastman Kodak Company, headed by George Eastman, introduced a transparent film on a flexible support. Creation of this film made the motion picture possible. It increased the picture-taking possibilities for still photographers, too; they could use smaller, less obtrusive cameras and no longer were burdened with heavy glass plates.

In 1912 the famous Speed Graphic press camera, which was to become the workhorse for news photographers for a half-century, was introduced. The small camera came into use in America in the 1920s. Ernst Leitz's Leica, a German camera using 35 mm film, was followed by another German make, the Rolleiflex, a larger 2¼ × 2¼ camera. Both remain popular in professional circles today, along with Japanese cameras.

The small camera freed the photographer from carrying bulky film or plate holders. It enabled him or her to operate less obtrusively, to take 36 pictures in rapid succession, and to use the fast lens to take pictures without flash in low-level lighting situations. The pictures thus were less formal, more candid, and honest. A German lawyer, Dr. Erich Salomon, who declared himself to be the first photojournalist, began using such a camera in 1928, photographing European nobility. Two other Europeans who influenced the development of photojournalism were Stefan Lorant, who edited German and English illustrateds, and Alfred Eisenstaedt, a West Prussian, who moved from the Berlin office of the Associated Press to become one of *Life* magazine's first photographers.

Color photography became a commercial reality when the Eastman Kodak Company announced development of its Kodachrome color film in 1935. In the same year the first motion picture in Technicolor, a high-fidelity color process, was presented on the American screen.

Two more fundamental breakthroughs in photographic equipment followed World War II. In 1947 Edwin H. Land introduced the Polaroid system for producing a positive black-and-white print 60 seconds after exposure. Soon this time was reduced to 10 seconds. Then in 1963 a

50-second Polaroid color print process opened new avenues for amateurs and professionals alike. The second of these breakthroughs came in the mid-1950s: the recording of moving pictures on *magnetic videotape*. This was an electronic approach; all the other advances in the photographic process had depended on chemistry.

By the early 1980s the photojournalist had fast zoom lenses that could go from wide angle to telephoto; motor drives that enabled the camera to shoot multiple frames per second; and the automatic exposure camera that allowed the user to set either shutter speed or aperture and then automatically adjust the other factor. Laser technology not only was permitting the Associated Press to transmit prized photographs almost instantly to waiting users around the world, but also was being used in reproduction to give great detail in shadows and highlights. And Polaroid had a "Time Zero" instantly producing color shots as they emerged from the camera.

Newspaper Photographs

From a mass communications viewpoint, taking good photographs in the 1860s was not enough: a way had to be found to reproduce them in newspapers and magazines. Woodcuts had been used in the Civil War period, but they were slow to produce, expensive, and not exact. A direct photographic method was needed.

This was achieved by two men working separately, each of whom developed a *halftone photoengraving* technique. Frederic Eugene Ives published a halftone engraving in his laboratory at Cornell University in June 1879, and Stephen Horgan published a photograph "direct from nature" in the New York *Daily Graphic* in March 1880. Several years passed, however, before such photographs came into frequent use in newspapers; by the mid-1890s halftone engravings were appearing in supplemental inserts of the New York newspapers, and in 1897 the New York *Tribune* was the first to publish a halftone in the regular pages of a high-speed press run.

During the early years of the twentieth century, pictures in newspapers generally were used singly, to illustrate important stories. The newspaper picture page, making use of special layouts and unusual picture shapes, was developed during World War I. A major new force in American journalism, the *picture tabloid,* came into being shortly after World War I. In these newspapers with their small page size and flashy makeup, designed to appeal to street sale readers, the photograph was given the dominant position, often overshadowing the text of the news stories. The tabloid front page usually consisted of a headline and a dramatically blown-up news photo.

The New York *Daily News* began publication in 1919, followed by Hearst's *Daily Mirror* and the *Evening Graphic*. Intense picture competition among these three New York tabloids led at times to the publication of photographs that violated many people's sense of good taste. The *Evening Graphic* illustrated major stories with faked composograph photos, and the *Daily News* shocked readers by printing a full-page photograph of the electrocution of Ruth Snyder, a murderess. Of these three original New York tabloids, only the *Daily News* survives, still sharply edited but less flamboyant and less a "picture" paper than in its earlier days.

During the 1920s, when the picture newspapers were flourishing, experiments were carried out in transmission of a photographic image by wire and by radio. The first American photos sent by wire were transmitted from Cleveland to New York in 1924. A decade of development passed before the Associated Press established its Wirephoto network on January 1, 1935. Distribution of news photos by wire enabled newspapers across the country to publish pictures from other cities only a few hours after they were taken.

The Picture Magazines

The expanded interest in all forms of photographic communication in the 1930s led Time Inc. to establish the weekly picture magazine *Life* in November 1936. *Life* was patterned after photographic publications developed in Germany and England. In 1937 the Cowles organization established *Look,* published every other week and more feature-oriented than *Life,* with less emphasis on news. *Look* ceased publication in 1971 and *Life* followed in 1972. (*Life* was revived, first through special issues and then as a monthly with 1.3 million circulation by 1980.)

Both *Look* and *Life* emphasized editorial research and investigation preceding assignment of photographers to all but spot news stories. Photographers were well briefed as to the significance of a story before arriving on the scene to begin interpreting it with their cameras. In that sense photographers on the two magazines controlled a mind-guided camera. In its early years *Life* was even more stringent in controlling its photographers, suggesting to them before they left the office exactly how key pictures should be made. This practice diminished during World War II, which provided swiftly changing stories that did not fit an editor's preconceived plan.

From the mid-1930s into the 1960s a small group of well-known magazine photographers contributed to the development of the photographic essay and interpretive picture story. Dorothea Lange's sensitive images of America's condition during the Great Depression stand as examples of still photography at its finest. So also do the pictures of Margaret Bourke-White and photographs by Gordon Parks, whose creative abilities transcended the photographic medium to include writing, musical composition, and Hollywood film. Henri Cartier-Bresson, a French photojournalist, defined the "decisive moment" during this period, and Robert Capa demonstrated how the still camera could record the reverberations of war. W. Eugene Smith and David Douglas Duncan were major

Margaret Bourke-White and Gordon Parks, whose creative photography has been among the nation's best. (Photo of Margaret Bourke-White courtesy of the estate of Margaret Bourke-White, © Time Inc.; photo of Gordon Parks by Alfred Eisenstaedt, Time-Life Picture Agency © Time Inc.)

contributors to *Life* during and after World War II. Smith's picture essays, including "Spanish Village," "Country Doctor," and "Nurse Midwife," stand as classics. David Duncan's word-and-picture reports of the Korean War have been matched only by his equally powerful Vietnam War magazine stories and photograph books.

The Picture Agencies

When the great photographic teams developed at *Life* and *Look* dissolved in the wake of the financial crises that forced the closing of the two magazines, there was a slump in photojournalism in America. Some of the photographers and editors migrated to the *National Geographic,* which became a center of photographic communication in the 1970s under the guidance of Robert E. Gilka as the director of staff photographers and freelance assignments. Its circulation approached 10 million in the early 1980s. Even more spectacular was the rise of the *Smithsonian* magazine. Founded in 1970 by the Smithsonian Society, in Washington, it had 1.8 million circulation a decade later. Edward K. Thompson came from *Life* to make *Smithsonian* a superb example of photographic communication. A highly sophisticated and expensive entry was *Geo,* founded in Germany and introduced in America in the early 1980s.

But none of these publications gave an outlet for the on-the-spot news photography that had made *Life* and *Look* so memorable, and which was still seen in *Paris-Match* and other European picture magazines. The press associations, the networks, and picture agencies such as Black Star were at work, but falling short of the tradition of the 1950s and 1960s.

Filling the gap in the 1970s and early 1980s were a group of new picture agencies; strongly European based, devoted both to photojournalism and to high-level action news photography. One was Contact, developed by Robert Pledge and including such photographers as Eddie Adams, David Hume Kennerly, Annie Leibovitz, and David Burnett. Another was Sipa, French-based and represented in the United States by international picture agencies such as Black Star and its director, Jocelyne Benzakin, with Charles Steiner and Maggie Steber as leading photographers. Gamma, a European leader directed in New York by Jennifer Coley, scored with Matthew Naythons' Guyana suicide story photos. Sygma, Paris-based, had Eliane Laffont in New York as director. All had crews of photographers available for assignments on contract with *Time, Newsweek,* and the revived *Life.* Their picture essays were marketed at high prices; Naythons' Guyana pictures earned $250,000 for Gamma.

Motion Pictures

Only two years after Eastman's development of flexible film, Thomas A. Edison developed the Kinetoscope in 1891, thereby laying the foundation for the motion picture. The Kinetoscope was a motion picture projector designed to show still pictures in rapid succession to produce the visual illusion of motion on a screen in a darkened room.

The Lumiere brothers presented the first public performance of a motion picture for pay in the Grand Cafe of Paris in 1895. Edison made jerky, primitive motion pictures of President William McKinley's inauguration in 1896, Admiral Dewey at Manila in 1898, and McKinley's speech in Buffalo, New York, shortly before his assassination in 1901. William Randolph Hearst personally took motion pictures of action in Cuba during the Spanish-American War. These early efforts showed the motion picture's potential as a recorder of history. Exhibition of commercial motion picture films began with regularity about 1900.

Edison's pioneer efforts at recording news events on film led within a few years to creation of the newsreel, a standard short item on virtually every motion picture theater program for half a century until the faster news coverage of television drove the last newsreel out of business during the 1960s. The first regular newsreel series is credited to the Pathé "Journal" of 1907. Among the familiar newsreel names in American theaters were Pathé, Fox Movietone News, Metrotone, and International Newsreel.

The documentary film, a more elaborate method of recording the lives and activities of real people, had its start in 1922. Hired by a New York fur company to film the life of an Eskimo family, Robert Flaherty overcame great technological difficulties in the Arctic climate to produce *Nanook of the North.* From this film developed the documentary tradition that has given filmmaking some of its finest products.

During the Depression years Pare Lorentz produced *The Plow That Broke the Plains* for the Farm Security Administration (FSA) in the same spirit of the FSA team of photo documentarians who, under the guidance of Roy E. Stryker, made more than 272,000 negatives and 150,000 prints of the United States and its dustbowls and migratory workers. Lorentz's 1937 film, *The River,* visualized the problems of erosion in the Mississippi River basin with more power than his previous documentary had.

A third form of factual storytelling on film, halfway between the newsreel and documentary, was the *March of Time,* a weekly news magazine of the screen. Started by Time Inc. in 1935, it played for 16 years. At its peak in the late 1930s and the early years of World War II, it was seen by audiences of nearly 20 million per week in more than 9000 American theaters. Louis de Rochemont, the producer, used real events and actors, skillfully blended, to present an interpretive account of an event in relation to its background.

When television became a commercial force in the late 1940s, the tools and techniques developed by the motion picture industry were adopted for presenting news on television. A motion picture camera was relatively small and portable, and film shot at news events could be shown on the television screen. Until remote telecasting became technically practical, visual presentation of on-the-spot news had to be done with motion picture film, but this medium has been largely replaced by videotape.

The television documentary became an established part of the networks' programming. Some outstanding examples have been CBS's "The Selling of the Pentagon" and its "Hunger in America," done in the tradition of Edward R. Murrow's earlier documentary, "Harvest of Shame"; NBC's documentary on chemical and biological warfare, "The Battle of Newburgh," shown on its "White Paper" series; and a religious documentary, "A Time for Burning," aired over many educational stations. CBS's "60 Minutes" and ABC's "20/20" reflect another documentary trend.

PRINCIPLES OF PHOTOGRAPHY

A photograph reproduced in a newspaper, magazine, or book is a two-dimensional representation of a subject that originally had four dimensions: length, width, depth, and existence, and perhaps movement through time. Moreover, the printed image in almost every instance differs in size from its original model. Frequently it is a black-and-white representation of a subject with many colorful hues. The photographic communicator must master the technique of condensing these dimensions and conditions into a space having only length and width.

Photography is capable of high-fidelity reproduction of very fine details and textures. A skillfully made photograph can communicate the essence of tactile experience. It can be controlled to represent a subject in various perspectives, determined by the photographer as he or she selects a particular lens and the camera-subject relationship for the picture. Black-and-white photographs provide the photographer almost unlimited control in representing the original subject in shades of gray and the extremes, black and white. Thus the photographer's technical skill and mental attitude influence the picture that is taken. Two persons photographing the same subject may produce widely dissimilar pictures.

Since photography relies upon a lens to form a clear, sharp image and a shutter to control the length of time during which light strikes the sensitive film, two additional visual qualities are unique in photographic communication. As the lens aperture is opened or closed to allow varying amounts of light to strike the film, a change occurs in the depth of field, that is, the area in front of and behind the subject that appears in sharp focus. The photographer may render only the subject sharp, with details in foreground and background blurred to reduce their importance. Or, by controlling the aperture size of the lens, an entire scene may be rendered in sharp focus, from the nearest to the farthest object shown.

By selecting a shutter speed for a picture, the photographer begins control over the fourth dimension, time. He or she may use a long exposure, in which case a moving subject might blur in the finished photograph, or a very short exposure time to "freeze" a moving subject at a precise instant. Having determined a shutter speed for the effect desired, the photographer must decide which moment to capture out of the millions available. The French photojournalist Henri Cartier-Bresson refers to this act as determining the *decisive moment.*

Still Pictures

Photographic communication for the printed page may be in the form of a single picture; or it may be a *series,* a *sequence,* or a *picture story.* The series of pictures can be distinguished from the sequence by noting that the series is generally photographed from more than one viewpoint and has been made over a relatively long period of time. The sequence is a group of pictures made from the same viewpoint and generally covering a very short period of time, such as a group of pictures on the sports page on a Sunday morning newspaper showing stages of a sensational touchdown run. Most picture magazines today present picture series rather than picture stories; the latter are the most complex form of photographic communication in the print media, requiring logical visual continuity built upon a well-researched idea. Excellent examples of the picture story include W. Eugene Smith's "Spanish Village" and David Duncan's "This Is War," both published in *Life* during the 1950s. In book form, Edward Steichen's *The Family of Man* has been widely acclaimed as a photo essay.

In attempting to re-create the essence of an event, photographic communicators feel the need to couple their pictures with some sort of "sound track." They use the written word in the form of captions, headlines, and overlines. When one looks at a picture and reads its word accompaniment, one's eye serves two sense functions. While it studies the image, it functions as a normal eye; when it begins reading words, the eye functions as an ear, picking up the sound track. This reading and seeing occur through time, thus further developing the fourth dimension in a two-dimensional photograph.

Wilson Hicks, for many years executive editor of *Life*, contributed in the introductory chapter of Smith Schuneman's *Photographic Communication* a definition of the photojournalistic form. In its simplest unit it is a blend of words plus one picture. Words add information the picture cannot give, and the picture contributes a dimension the words cannot. When the two have been blended, there emerges a greater meaning for the reader than could be received from either words or picture separately. Hicks suggests that this blend develops a communicative overtone.

The Movies

Although the characteristics of the still photograph apply to motion picture film and television magnetic tape, both of which are sequences of still pictures, there are important distinctions about the moving picture as a medium. Films and videotape reproduce natural movement and sound, two elements extremely difficult to communicate in still photography.

Moving picture communicators in addition have as their most important tool creative control over the fourth dimension, time. An audience viewing a message on film or tape is captive to the communicator in terms of pace, emphasis, and rhythm. A reader can spend as much or as little time as he or she chooses in studying a picture, and can do it whenever desired, returning later for another look. When one is a member of an audience in a motion picture theater or in front of a television screen, one does not have these options unless a home viewing device is being used.

The producer of film and videotape is concerned with the continuity, the sequence of images. He or she knows how to use the "establishment" shot at the beginning of a particular scene and medium shots and closeups to continue the action, adding variety and emphasis. During the shooting and editing of film or tape, photographer and editor concern themselves with such visual techniques as screen direction, cutaways, cover material, reverse angles, and sound effectiveness. Film may be shot as silent footage, with a narrator adding description later in a studio, or it may be shot with natural lip-sync (synchronized) sound. Electronic videotape recording is used in place of film for most stories and advertisements on television. The first moon pictures sent back by Armstrong and Aldrin were an example of live presentation of moving pictures produced electronically without film or tape.

FUNCTIONS OF PHOTOGRAPHERS AND EDITORS

Photographs are used, just as are words, to inform, persuade, and entertain users of the mass media. Their effectiveness depends upon how well they are taken by the photographer and how well they are assembled for presentation to the audience by the editor. Each medium has special problems of picture presentation that require special knowledge and experience. Television is not radio with a picture of the announcer added; there is an important visual dimension. The still photograph is not decoration as it was in the newspaper and magazine early in the twentieth century. The development of candid photography with its quick, intimate glimpses of subjects off guard has given photojournalists exciting new possibilities by permitting them to avoid the stilted aspect so common in older pictures with slower cameras.

Daily newspaper photographers perform one of the fundamental tasks in photojournalism. On a typical day they receive three or four assignments, usually to events fairly close to the office. They most likely will use a staff car, equipped with a two-way radio. The editor has written an assignment sheet describing the event and what is wanted, and perhaps has discussed the job in detail. On many newspapers, photographers use their own equipment, for which the publication pays a monthly depreciation allotment; on others, they use office-owned cameras.

Once at the scene, the photographer will make a number of pictures, gathering names and important caption material. Back at the office, the film will be processed, either personally or by a laboratory assistant, and finished prints delivered to the editor. On most assignments, only one of the pictures taken will be published; in fact, frequently none of the pictures will be printed because of space limitations or the development of later, bigger news stories.

A photographer on a general magazine staff works on more elaborate projects than does the daily newspaper staff member, often taking several weeks or even months to complete a single job. Assignments at times range far from home. The photographer is well briefed by researchers concerning the background of the story, and receives large research folios for "homework." On a major assignment the photographer will shoot from 1000 to 5000 images, sending them home in "takes" to the editors, who keep the photographer posted on how the work has turned out. After all this effort, 12 to 20 of the pictures most likely will appear in print.

Life had a staff of 15 photographers in 1970, as well as various contract and freelance contributors. These photographers as a group were shooting nearly 1,000 pictures per day—300,000 per year—for the magazine, which printed about 75 in each weekly issue. At *Look,* which had been published biweekly, about 150,000 photographs were shot each year by an eight-person staff.

Major television stations use eye-witness news crews, reporting live during news broadcasts from the scene of a major news event. In metropolitan areas the stations compete with helicopter coverage, with one standard assignment being the tracing of traffic snarls on the freeways. The local television station news photographer works in a manner similar to that of his or her daily newspaper colleague. The TV photographer has four to six assignments a day, usually travels in a radio-equipped staff car, and carries lightweight videotape camera equipment. The photographer takes notes ("spot sheets"), including the names of those appearing in various scenes. Camera operators may work alone, with a reporter, or with a full crew to handle lighting and sound. After their return to the station, the tape is edited and a script is written.

With so much more film and tape being shot than can be used either in print or on the air, the role of the editor is essential. The editors of tape, film, and still pictures have three functions: to procure the picture by assigning staff photographers, buying material from freelancers, and subscribing to syndicate services; to select the pictures to be used; and to present them in an effective manner. Once the raw material has been obtained, the editor makes a selection from the entire take submitted. In the print media, the editor must crop and scale the pictures to emphasize their most interesting aspects and to work them into a layout. In television, the editor is concerned with juxtaposition effects from scene to scene and with time considerations. The presentation each editor puts together

Student photographers at work in a large laboratory. (Courtesy of Henry W. Grady School of Journalism and Mass Communication, University of Georgia.)

represents a blending of pictures and words, a designing of space and time.

Beginning in the 1970s, photocommunication students increasingly turned to advertising illustration as both a challenging and potentially lucrative area. It offered many opportunities for freelance photographers in metropolitan areas with substantial numbers of advertising agencies and company headquarters. Visual communication conferences devoted program time to trends in advertising illustration and graphics.

JOB OPPORTUNITIES IN PHOTOGRAPHIC COMMUNICATION

Qualifications

Stimulating opportunities await young people who decide to enter the photographic aspect of mass communications. The work at times is exciting, and always interesting; each day brings new assignments that give the photographer room for creative expression and the use of professional techniques.

Anyone contemplating such a career should be healthy and possessed of physical stamina, because the work can be dangerous on assignments such as fires and riots; and the hours frequently are irregular. The photographer must carry equipment and guard it against loss or damage. Both physical and emotional exhaustion may affect a photographer involved in a long, difficult assignment.

Career photographic communicators also should have initiative, energy, and creative motivation. A degree of aggressiveness is necessary, but it should be tempered by thoughtfulness. Visual imagination is essential—the ability to see various interpretations of a subject in a given visual form. Photographers should have an interest in design and the knack of examining pictures for each one's special qualities. They must be curious about the world around them and have an ability to mix with people. Being able to sketch scenes and individuals roughly is an important asset, but by no means a requirement.

Photographic communicators should have a good general education. About one-fourth of their studies should be spent in learning how to relate general knowledge to the discipline of photo communication. Those who plan to work in the news and information function of the mass media should take courses in basic reporting, editing, law and history of the press, and graphic design and typography. In photography courses they must develop foundations in both the technical and visual dimensions of the medium. They should include courses in both still and motion photography, both black-and-white and color. Attention to the picture story, the documentary film, and advertising illustration is all-important. They should study the history of film and photography and also take courses in basic design.

Technical qualifications include an understanding of the photographic medium in terms of optics, lighting, color theory, and photographic processes, which include basic photochemistry and physics. With the growing importance of electronics in nearly all areas of photographic communication, an understanding of electronic theory is desirable.

Earnings

A college graduate with photographic skills will start on a daily newspaper at from $9,000 to $12,000 per year. An experienced newspaper photographer, with five years or more on the job, may earn from $15,000 to $30,000 annually in large cities. The starting salary for a college graduate photographer on a local television station will vary from $8,000 to $11,000; after five years the range is $12,000 to $20,000. A staff photographer for a general or specialized magazine can expect to earn $9,000 to $15,000 in early career years. The salary may rise rapidly, faster than in newspaper or television work. Top professionals on *National Geographic* earn as much as $50,000.

Some photographers prefer to freelance; that is, to work for themselves and sell their pictures to clients either directly or through picture agencies. The agencies take a commission of 25 to 35 percent of the selling price of the pictures. A freelancer also may work on contract, under which a magazine guarantees an agreed-upon earning in return for a commitment to be available to it on call. A freelancer usually begins as a staff photographer, then branches out after establishing a reputation and a group of clients. Freelance photographers can earn around $40,000 a year if very successful, although they start much lower in their early years. To be a successful freelancer, one must have good business sense and know how to market pictures as well as take them. The American Society of Magazine Photographers sets minimum rates for its members. The rate in effect in 1980 averaged $300 per day plus expenses.

Chapter 14

THE FILM

THE ROLE OF MOTION PICTURES

"It is imperative that we invent a new world language . . . that we invent a nonverbal international picture-language. . . . ," writes Stan VanDerBeek, painter and experimental filmmaker. As corollary activities, VanDerBeek proposes using present audiovisual devices in the service of such a language, developing new image-making instruments to find the best combination of machines for nonverbal interchange, and establishing prototype theaters called Movie-Dromes to house these presentations—described as "Movie Murals," "Ethos-Cinema," "Newsreel of Dreams," and "Image Libraries."

While VanDerBeek's method is radical, the principle underlying his approach is as old as the motion picture itself. Early in the history of film, its practitioners and advocates recognized that the motion picture was truly an international language. And, while the "image-flow" described by VanDerBeek is as yet imperfectly realized, the desire for "peace and harmony . . . the interlocking of good wills on an international exchange basis . . . the interchange of images and ideas . . ." is as old as tribal man. Although, on the surface, VanDerBeek's "A Proposal and Manifesto" is naive and idealistic, on a smaller, infinitely more conventional scale, the language of motion pictures is helping to bridge the gap among the people of different nations.

As motion picture critic Stanley Kauffmann observes, "Film is the only art besides music that is available to the whole world at once, exactly as it was first made." And film, like opera, can be enjoyed despite the viewer's ignorance of the language employed in the dialogue or narration. Kauffmann contends, "The point is not the spreading of information or amity, as in USIA or UNESCO films, useful though they may be. The point is emotional relationship and debt." To understand this observation, consider the Russian entertainment film *The Cranes Are Flying* (1957), a romantic drama of life and death, of love and loss, set in the years 1941 to 1945 and played by Russian actors against a Russian background. If one empathizes with the young lovers, sharing their anguish at war and separation and their desire for peace and reunion, the viewer has been drawn into an emotional relationship with the characters that makes it impossible to view all Russians as unfeeling puppets, solely committed in thought and deed to advancing the Communist state.

Although the advent of sound tended to nationalize film and reduce film's claim to being an international art as in the days of the silent movie, the current popularity of foreign films in America and the even more widespread distribution of American films in foreign markets demonstrate the primary role played by a film's visual elements, and the lesser importance of language as a communications device. In fact, when a motion picture is subtitled for distribution in a foreign market, the subtitles convey little more than one-third of the dialogue. Yet the meaning of the film is seldom, if ever, impaired, and its beauty is often enhanced.

The film *Years of Lightning, Day of Drums* (1964), made for the United States Information Agency (USIA), illustrates the lesser role played by verbal language in motion pictures, even in a nontheatrical film. Approximately 40 percent of the film uses neither dialogue nor narration. Designed as a tribute to John F. Kennedy and as a vehicle to bolster confidence that the work Kennedy had begun would continue after his death, the film presents the six facets of the New Frontier, interlacing such programs as the Alliance for Progress, Civil Rights, and the Peace Corps, with sequences depicting the funeral. These funeral sequences are largely wordless, with the sound track carrying natural sound: the heavy footsteps of the marchers, the more staccato hoofbeats of the horses, and the steady, muffled drumbeat. Yet no words are necessary during these sequences. Assembled from stock footage, *Years of Lightning, Day of Drums,* by sharing Kennedy's death with the foreign viewer, shares his political achievement and America's aspirations.

A note of warning: Film is probably the most powerful propaganda medium yet devised. As a consequence, its potential for aiding or injuring civilization is enormous. In addition to supplying a verbal message through dialogue, narration, or subtitles, the film provides an instantaneous, accompanying visual message—supplying the viewer with a picture to bulwark what has been learned through language. Thus the imagination need not conjure a mental image to accompany the words; the viewer leaves the theater complete with a concept and its substantiation. If a picture is worth 1,000 words, a picture together with three or four carefully chosen words is worth 10,000 words. Makers of television commercials know this; so does anyone who has ever thought carefully about this compelling and contemporary medium of communication.

In the past, American motion pictures have been associated with Hollywood. Persons desiring careers in the film industry saw and followed one road—and that road led to the golden West. But the situation has changed. There are many roads leading to important and satisfying work in films, and not all end in Hollywood, as this chapter will reveal.

THE ENTERTAINMENT FILM

Hollywood: 1945–1965

The late 1940s found "old" Hollywood at the peak of its prosperity. With World War II ended, the market for Hollywood films was huge worldwide. Television had not yet developed as a rival medium of mass entertainment. The major studios churned out a flow of movies, from low-budget B films to big-name epics, using the actors they kept under contract. They were assured of distribution for their products through the theaters they owned, under the block-booking system.

During 1949, more than 90 million tickets were sold weekly in American movie houses, compared with 21 million in 1968. In 1949 the major studios—among them Metro-Goldwyn-Mayer, Twentieth Century-Fox, Columbia Pictures, RKO, and Warner Brothers—released 411 new motion pictures. By the early 1960s their annual output had decreased to barely 200. Still administered by the people who established them, the major companies offered such entertainment films as the horror-thriller *The Beast With Five Fingers* (1946) and the slick romantic comedy *June Bride* (1948), along with provocative and candid films such as *The Best Years of Our Lives* (1946) and *Crossfire* (1947), to a receptive and apparently uncritical American audience.

Then, around 1950, two developments staggered the motion picture industry. Television rocketed into prominence; millions of families watched free TV shows at home instead of making one or two trips a week to the neighborhood movie house. The second blow to the old order came from the federal courts. Bowing to government pressure and a lawsuit charging them with restraint of trade, the major studios signed consent decrees in which they agreed to sell their chains of theaters and to end the practice of block booking. In doing so, they lost the automatic outlet for the pictures they made. Instead of arbitrarily booking their pictures—good, bad, or indifferent—into hundreds of theaters, the moviemakers were required to sell pictures on their merit, one by one. With their audiences shrinking because of TV, the theater operators did not want to show the shoddy "program" films being ground out. The result was a severe reduction in the number of pictures made, leading to the death of the contract player system, under which a studio paid a performer a salary and assigned him or her to whatever picture it desired.

Hunting for ways to save itself, Hollywood made drastic alterations in its films, both in appearance and in content. The great change in appearance came with the introduction of the wide screen, which has been called the most significant innovation in film technology since the advent of sound. Since the pictures on early TV sets were so small, the massive scope of the wide screen was intended to entice audiences away from their living rooms and into the theaters. Until the appearance of the first wide-screen motion picture, *The Robe* (a $5 million Cinemascope film produced and distributed by Twentieth Century-Fox in 1953), the standard screen shape had been a rectangle 20 feet wide and 15 feet high; this represents a ratio of 4 to 3, or 1.33 to 1—a proportion determined by the width of the film, and going back to Thomas Edison and the Kinetoscope. Cinemascope settled its wide-screen proportion at 2.55 to 1. Regardless of trade name, most new screens are at least twice as wide as they are high.

Initial critical reactions to the wide screen were mixed, with some filmmakers insisting that the new screen size signaled the end of the closeup and rendered established directorial and cutting techniques ineffective. In time, however, the advantages and possibilities of the wide screen became apparent to filmmakers, who have used its inclusiveness to achieve a naturalness and spontaneity, and its new dimensions to experiment with new kinds of visual compositions and new uses of the closeup.

In response to the wide screen and as a further effort to bring the American public back into the movie theaters, Hollywood began to produce longer and more expensive movies with casts of thousands and an abundance of well-known stars. Often, best-selling novels or successful dramas that called for copious action and spectacle provided the story for these productions—as in *The Ten Commandments* (1956), *Raintree County* (1957), *El Cid* (1961), and *Cleopatra* (1963).

As a further lure to their audience, the filmmakers lowered the censorship barriers of their self-imposed Production Code and made pictures about topics and situations they knew would not be shown on the home TV screen. In 1956, revisions in the code permitted depiction of drug addiction, kidnapping, prostitution, and abortion. Soon, movies portraying narcotics addiction, such as *Monkey on My Back* (1957) and *The Pusher* (1959), and films involving prostitution, such as *Butterfield 8* (1960) and *Girl of the Night* (1960), were released bearing the Motion Picture Seal of Approval. Although the new freedom of subject matter resulted in the creation of a few artistic successes, Hollywood quickly managed to create new clichés from the once-forbidden subject matter at its disposal.

At first, the Hollywood studios tried to shun television, hoping that it was merely a novelty. However, they soon changed course. Hollywood executives decided to do business with the new electronic medium, recognizing a potential for immense profits. Television needed a continuing supply of programs, and the studios had masses of material available: the old movies stored in their vaults. The studios sold rights to this backlog of films to the TV networks and individual stations for high prices—a windfall not anticipated when the movies were made. Between 1955 and 1958, Hollywood sold almost 9000 pre-1948 feature films to television, and by 1960 the major studios were vying with each other for sale of films produced after 1948. This bonanza for the studios began a relationship of interdependence between them and television that continues to grow.

Although Hollywood studios profited from old work in this manner and created a fresh source of income by renting out sound stages and equipment to TV companies shooting television series, the major studios' basic business of making movies continued to dwindle. Foreign films found increasing popularity in the United States and American experimental filmmakers gained attention, but the traditional Hollywood film, lavishly produced, lost much of its audience appeal. The audience itself was changing. It grew more sophisticated and was weary of shallow, innocuous fare. By 1965 box office receipts in the domestic market had fallen to barely half what they were in 1946. Even the appearance of stars such as Elizabeth Taylor, Doris Day, Cary Grant, Rock Hudson, Burt Lancaster, and Marlon Brando on the screen did not help. Stars alone did not draw large audiences. Three studios—RKO, Republic, and Monogram—stopped production entirely. Approximately 6000 movie houses closed their doors.

THE FOREIGN FILM

Italy

If Hollywood chose to ignore, by and large, the realities of the post-World War II world, that was not true of Italian filmmakers. Responding to the grim reality of war-torn, impoverished Italy, Roberto Rossellini directed *Open City* (1945)—the first important film shot in a style that was quickly dubbed by the critics as neorealism. Combining stock newsreel footage with his own film (shot chiefly on the streets of Rome and scratched to resemble newsreels), Rossellini depicted the hardships endured by Italians during the Nazi occupation and their courageous resistance. To heighten the authenticity gained by the use of actual locations and natural lighting, he employed only a handful of professional actors whom he encouraged to ad-lib, and chose ordinary Roman citizens as supporting players. Although none of these techniques in isolation was new, they had not been used so successfully together before; and *Open City* became, as the film historian Arthur Knight has said, "the key film in the entire neorealist Italian revival."

Equally as personal and visually intense, and equally as concerned with social realism, are two early films by Vittorio De Sica. In *Shoeshine* (1946), De Sica portrays the lives of a group of homeless Roman boys involved in the corrupt underworld of the Italian black market. *Bicycle Thief* (1947) treats the relationship between a father (played by a factory mechanic) and his son (played by a Roman newsboy) who together try to beat insurmountable odds occasioned by unemployment, poverty, and corruption.

In recent years, amid a rash of conventional and often sensationalist films, the work of two masterful directors has emerged. Described as "second generation realists," Federico Fellini (*La Dolce Vita,* 1960; *8½,* 1962; *Juliet of the Spirits,* 1965; *Satyricon,* 1970; *Amarcord,* 1974; *Fellini's Casanova,* 1976) and Michelangelo Antonioni (*L'Avventura,* 1959; *La Notte,* 1960; *The Red Desert,* 1964; *Blow-Up,* 1966; *The Passenger,* 1975; *Suffer or Die,* 1979) have little in common except a compulsion to use the surfaces, rituals, and hidden recesses of contemporary existence as theme and subject matter, and a proven ability to use improvisation as an effective cinematic technique.

France

During 1958 and 1959, the New Wave erupted on the French film scene, with Francois Truffaut's *Les Quatre Cents Coups* and Alain Resnais' *Hiroshima Mon Amour* winning awards at the 1959 Cannes Film Festival. Other films that heralded the New Wave were Claude Chabrol's *Le Beau Serge* (1958), Louis Malle's *Les Amants* (1958), and Jean-Luc Godard's *Breathless* (1959). Although heterogeneous and resistant of labels in the manner of all creative artists, these New Wave directors do share many cinematic ideals as well as an outlet for these ideals in the influential film journal *Cahiers du Cinema*. Truffaut, Godard, and Chabrol had been film critics in the early 1950s, and they continued to write about the cinema. Describing his own procedures, Truffaut has said:

> I start with a very imperfect script, in which there are certain elements that please and stimulate me. Characters that strike some chord of response in me. A theme that lets me "talk about" something I want to film. As I work I find I am eliminating all the scenes of story transition and explanation. So it can happen that when the film is done, it is completely different from what it was proposed to say in the first place. The shooting of the film is that sort of adventure.

In *Breathless,* Godard took his camera onto the Paris streets. Using a hand-held Arriflex and a three-page script outline by Truffaut, Godard allowed the camera to follow the actions and reactions of Michel (a small-time gangster, played by Jean-Paul Belmondo) and his American girl friend (played by Jean Seberg), depicting a life devoid of logic or purpose.

Although the New Wave dissipated itself (by 1964, Cannes was denigrating the very movement it had applauded five years earlier), these films and their directors made great and irrevocable contributions to cinema art. In particular, these lasting contributions are the imaginative and free camera work that characterizes New Wave films, the encouragement of a liberated acting style dependent on improvisation and self-portraiture rather than on self-conscious or stagey performance, the fanciful use of silent film techniques, the absence of conventional plotting and continuity, and a movement away from a cinema grounded in literature and drama to one that uses the strengths of the film medium to make its own powerful, highly cinematic statements.

Great Britain

Room at the Top (1958) was the first in a remarkable series of outspoken realistic British films to gain widespread critical attention. Soon, motion pictures such as *Saturday Night and Sunday Morning* (1960), *A Taste of Honey* (1961), *The Loneliness of the Long-Distance Runner* (1962), *A Kind of Loving* (1962), *Billy Liar* (1963), *Morgan* (1966), *The Leather Boys* (1963), and *This Sporting Life* (1962) had established the reputations of their directors—Karel Reisz, Tony Richardson, John Schlesinger, Sidney Furie, Lindsay Anderson—and the significance of the British feature film. Describing their work as "free cinema," these directors brought to the screen a penetrating social realism focused on the English working class, preparing the way for the Beatles (who themselves are featured in Richard Lester's *A Hard Day's Night,* 1964; and *Help!,* 1965) and the ascendancy of Liverpool over Pall Mall.

Other Countries

In Soviet Russia, film production is not only nationalized, but the work of individual studios such as Lenfilm, in Leningrad, and Mosfilm, in Moscow, is closely supervised by a specially designated state committee. Not unexpectedly, therefore, many Soviet feature films have either implicit or explicit social messages, as in the strongly chauvinistic *The Turbulent Years* (1960). But there are also films that focus on personal crises and solutions rather than on social problems. Among them are the previously mentioned *The Cranes Are Flying* (1957), *Clear Sky* (1961), *I'm Twenty* (1965), and such adaptations of literary classics as Sergei Youtkevich's *Othello* (1955) and Grigori Kozintsev's *Don Quixote* (1957) and *Hamlet* (1963).

In Sweden, recent filmmaking has been dominated by Ingmar Bergman, who uses film to explore such abstract and eternal problems as the meaning of life and death (*The Seventh Seal,* 1956), the nature of truth (*The Magician,* 1958), and our tragic inability to communicate (*The Silence,* 1963, and *Cries and Whispers,* 1972).

The Japanese film has become best known to American audiences through the work of Akira Kurosawa. Like Bergman, Kurosawa depicts elemental problems and passions using highly stylized, historical settings to underscore the timelessness of his themes. *Rashomon* (which won the Grand Prize at the Venice Film Festival in 1951) concerns the nature of truth, while *Throne of Blood* (1957), like *Macbeth* after which it is patterned, depicts the breaking down of morality through greed.

RECENT DEVELOPMENTS IN THE AMERICAN FILM

American Experimental Filmmakers

While Hollywood producers during the 1940s and 1950s persevered on a chosen course, determinedly oblivious to innovations in European filmmaking, a segment of the American moviegoing public was well aware of their importance. Excited by the new techniques and possibilities for film, dismayed at the impersonality and inanity of most Hollywood movies, and aware that film is as much an art form as the novel, dance, or painting, numerous young Americans turned to film to give shape to their feelings and ideas, as their predecessors (and many of their contemporaries) had chosen the more conventional vehicles of drama, fiction, poetry, painting, or sculpture.

Much of the credit for publicizing and organizing the work and aesthetic doctrines of America's experimental filmmakers goes to Jonas Mekas, himself a filmmaker, in addition to being editor of *Film Culture,* occasional film critic for the *Village Voice,* and organizer of the Film Makers' Cooperative and Distribution Center. In describing his own work and that of other independent filmmakers, Mekas has said:

> Our movies come from our hearts—our little movies, not the Hollywood movies. Our movies are like extensions of our own pulse, of our heartbeat, of our eyes, our fingertips; they are so personal, so unambitious in their movement, in their use of light, their imagery. We want to surround this earth with our film frames and warm it up—until it begins to move.

Of extreme importance to the experimental filmmakers is the unambitiousness and intensely personal nature of their films, as described by Mekas. In many instances, desire and budget dictate that the film be the result of one person who functions as producer, director, cameraperson, editor, and often distributor. The actors are often friends, and usually nonprofessionals. Most films are done on 16 mm. And, as in the New Wave films, there is an absence of chronological continuity and carefully plotted story lines, along with considerable use of improvisation and emphasis on spontaneous action and reaction rather than upon stagey performance.

As the New Wave is a convenient rubric that lumps together highly individualistic directors, so the New American Cinema Group—"a free organization of independent filmmakers dedicated to the support of the men and women giving their vision to the filmic art"—is a convenient label, embracing filmmakers with divergent purposes, talents, and methods. But, like the New Wave directors, the New American Cinema Group shares an outlet for its views, the magazine *Film Culture,* and evinces a common hatred and a common enthusiasm. As the French directors rebelled against film's prior dependency on literature and rejoiced in the cinema as an art form with its own aesthetic, so the New American Cinema rebels against all that is unimaginative, standardized, and hopelessly phony about Hollywood and celebrates, too, the film as an art form.

Among the more notable experimental filmmakers are Jonas Mekas (*The Brig; Diaries, Notes, and Sketches; Reminiscences of a Journey to Lithuania*), Stan VanDerBeek (*Mankinda, Skullduggery, Summit, Breathdeath*), Stan Brakage (*Dog Star Man, Window Water Baby Moving, Scenes from Under Childhood*), Bruce Conner (*A Movie, Cosmic Ray, Liberty Crown*), Kenneth Anger (*Scorpio Rising, Inauguration of the Pleasure Dome*), Gregory Markopoulos (*Twice a Man, Serenity, Ming Green*), Charles Boultenhouse (*Handwritten, Dionysius*), Shirley Clarke (*The Connection, Skyscraper, The Cool World*), and, of course, Andy Warhol and Paul Morrissey.

Parodying Hollywood's film factories with his own Factory, Hollywood's star system with his own superstars, Hollywood's trumped-up and ultimately phony retailing of sex and sex goddesses in *Screen Test,* and Hollywood's bad guys, good guys and Westerns in *Horse,* Warhol has been enormously and unabashedly prolific and successful. In all his films, whether in the early "documentaries" such as *Empire, Sleep,* and *Eat,* or in the later "feature" films, *Kitchen, The Chelsea Girls, My Hustler, Bike Boy,* and *Lonesome Cowboys,* Warhol's constant subject has been the film itself. Even as producer for Morrissey's films, notably the highly successful *Trash,* Warhol's personality and vision dominate. Using a variety of techniques, from a static camera focused on one object for more than eight hours, to cinéma vérité pushed to an extreme, to employing two screens and running two films simultaneously, Warhol has drawn attention through technique and subject matter to the film as product and substance, reveling in and revealing its particular properties as a physical entity.

The many purposes and styles of American experimental films range from social criticism using documentary techniques to embodiments of the subconscious through surrealism and myth to psychedelic experiments with light and color. At their best, the films of the avant garde are exciting, fresh, sensitive, and fully able to transmit their maker's vision. At their worst, they are very bad indeed—as bad as the worst products of any art form—as trivial and boring, for example, as the worst Hollywood movie.

Hollywood Today

Motion pictures made in Hollywood dominate the world market today, as always, but both the films and the industry that produces them are far different from what they were in the early 1960s. After floundering,

Hollywood has found a profitable new course. The box office gross in the domestic market, the United States and Canada, reached an alltime high in 1979, above $3 billion—this compared to only $1.2 billion in 1953. Rampant inflation, which has pushed the average ticket price above $3, was partially responsible for the new high, of course, but admissions were slightly on the rise, too. They exceeded 22 million in 1979. Examination of the list of all-time box-office champions shows that eight of the top ten were released during the 1970s, when inflation with its less-valued dollars produced higher figures in all forms of business.

Perhaps the most fundamental difference between old and new Hollywood is that with a few exceptions, notably the Walt Disney studio, moviemakers have stopped producing films intended for the traditional family audience. They concentrate instead on a youthful audience, primarily between the ages of 14 and 25. Research shows that 60 percent of moviegoers are in this age bracket. They like to "get out of the house," as one studio executive put it, while couples with small children and older adults tend to stay home at night and watch television. Only 12 percent of the movie audience is aged 40 or older. Since the target audience is now more liberal in its attitudes toward sex, profanity, and violence than the older age categories, and since the target audience is also more fascinated by fantasy, and more rebellious against the social and political establishment, film producers choose stories and ways of telling them that cater to its tastes.

The power structure of Hollywood has been altered radically. The generation of movie moguls—men such as Louis B. Mayer, Samuel Goldwyn, Harry Cohn, Adolf Zukor, the Warner brothers, and Darryl F. Zanuck—are gone, and so is the way in which they ran the industry. In their day, a major studio created a story, arranged financing for it, cast it with performers from its roster of contract players, and filmed the story on its back lot, which housed standard sets such as a Western cowtown or a Manhattan street. Then it booked the movie into the theaters it controlled. Its overhead was tremendous, especially the salaries of stars under contract.

Today, the majority of Hollywood's films are independent productions. This is the era of the package deal, in which the outside talent agent or producer has in a sense replaced the old-time studio czar. Independent companies avoid excessive overhead investment by having neither costly studios nor large production staffs.

Independent producers came to prominence during the 1950s as the once-awesome power of the big studios diminished. Some of the independent production companies were formed by the stars themselves—among them Burt Lancaster, Frank Sinatra, Kirk Douglas, and Bob Hope. One advantage for them was that, by incorporating, the stars could take part of their income from the films they made in the form of capital gains, rather than as straight salary from the studios, which would be subject to much higher personal income tax rates. Other independent companies were started by directors—William Wyler, Alfred Hitchcock, Elia Kazan, and Otto Preminger. Some independent company heads had been producers, such as Sam Spiegel and Arthur Hornblow. Still others had been writers, for instance, Richard Brooks, Joseph Mankiewicz, and Robert Rossen. In itself, the independent production company was not a new commodity in Hollywood. But the independent producer had never made any significant inroads in the Hollywood system until the 1950s. At that time, the major studios, having involved themselves in fewer productions, began increasingly to finance and then distribute films made by an independent production company. Gradually, therefore, the studios began to function like United Artists, which had been started in 1919 as a releasing company without studio facilities.

By accepting the lesser roles of financier, promoter, and distributor, even at times leasing their own facilities to the independent production companies, the major studios relinquished artistic control over the films they were underwriting. Control passed to the independent producer, creating a situation that allowed a film to have a style impressed upon it by those who created it, rather than by a studio boss who would oversee a dozen or more films simultaneously.

Although not all the motion pictures produced by the independent companies have been either artistic or commercial successes, many independent productions are of outstanding quality and have increased the prestige of the Hollywood movie both in the United States and abroad. Seven of the nine films that won Academy Awards for Best Motion Picture of the Year between 1954 and 1962 were produced by independents: *On the Waterfront* (1954), *Marty* (1955), *Around the World in Eighty Days* (1956), *The Bridge on the River Kwai* (1957), *The Apartment* (1960), *West Side Story* (1961), and *Lawrence of Arabia* (1962). Other successful independent productions were *The Diary of Anne Frank* (1959), *The Hustler* (1961), *Advise and Consent* (1962), *Guess Who's Coming to Dinner* (1967), *In the Heat of the Night* (1967), *The Graduate* (1967), *Bonnie and Clyde* (1967), *Easy Rider* (1969), and, more recently, *Rocky* (1977).

The trend of recent years has been toward spectacular pictures such as *Star Wars, Close Encounters of the Third Kind, The Godfather,* and *The Exorcist*, with many stars and big-budget effects. These films are designed to attract large crowds and run for weeks or months, especially in urban theaters. The economics of distribution are weighted by the distributors in such a way that a theater operator must keep showing the same films for many weeks in order to make money on it. Relatively few small pictures of modest income potential are being made: the "blockbuster" is the goal.

Themes of sexuality, space fantasy, horror, and disaster are the contemporary favorites of both filmmakers and audiences. Some films with these themes are drawing audiences unprecedented since the advent of

ALL-TIME BOX OFFICE CHAMPIONS

These ten motion pictures are the largest revenue producers in film history, based on film rentals in the United States and Canada market.

Star Wars (1977)	$175,849,013
Jaws (1975)	$133,429,000
Grease (1978)	$ 93,292,000
The Exorcist (1973)	$ 88,100,000
The Godfather (1972)	$ 86,275,000
Superman (1978)	$ 81,000,000
The Sound of Music (1965)	$ 79,000,000
The Sting (1973)	$ 78,889,000
Close Encounters of the Third Kind (1977)	$ 77,000,000
Gone With the Wind (1939)	$ 76,700,000

Source: Compiled by *Variety*, the show business publication, as of January 1, 1980.

television. Application of the ratings system has been liberalized with regard to nudity, obscene language, and violence; films that once would have been rated X are now rated R. This permits people under the age of 18, even small children, to attend if they are accompanied by their parents. Some theater owners do not enforce the rule. Because films with a G (general) rating often fare poorly at the box office, producers may include gratuitous profanity and violence in the films to require that they have a PG (parental guidance) rating. This is supposed to attract larger audiences; apparently it does, in some cases. Extensive criticism within the industry as well as outside was voiced in 1980 when *Cruising*, starring Al Pacino, received an R rating rather than an X rating. The film contained violent homosexual sadomasochistic activity, so extreme that some theaters refused to show the film. The trade paper *Variety* commented, "If this is an R, then the only X left is actual hardcore."

Hollywood filmmakers recognize that their movies are less a mass medium today than an elitist medium—that is, less a form of mass art than of high art. Persons who have attended college are more than twice as likely to see movies as those without a high school diploma. They are more willing to accept films as extreme as *Cruising* if they believe the films contain socially significant themes.

Anyone in Hollywood hoping to produce a popular movie is guided by a few economic rules of thumb. Production of the movie will be very expensive. According to Jack Valenti, president of the Motion Picture

Association of America, the average film cost nearly $8.5 million to make in 1980. To break even, this average movie must sell 10 to 12 million admissions. Because of other expenses, a film breaks even, or should, when the maker collects 2½ to 3 times its production costs.

Behind the performers, there is a costly phalanx of off-screen personnel: producers, directors, writers, camera operators, editors, stunt men and women, script consultants, script personnel, costumers, set designers, wardrobe assistants, prop men and women, lighting technicians, makeup artists, carpenters, actors' agents, painters, publicists, and the sales staff. One cause of the huge overhead is the high degree of unionization among motion picture personnel. Few industries are so highly structured; there are rigid restrictions on the duties each worker may perform and the kinds of physical properties he or she may touch.

As the movie industry has changed, the old picture palaces have been replaced by hundreds of new, small cluster theaters, in which different pictures are shown simultaneously in two or more relatively small auditoriums that one enters through a central lobby. Often these theaters are located in shopping centers.

A look at the history of the science fiction movie, *Alien,* a box office hit in 1979, reveals how the system functions. The story is about seven astronauts who encounter an awesome galactic horror in outer space—a fine vehicle for the use of fantasy, horror, and the spectacle of special effects. The script was submitted to Twentieth Century-Fox by an independent production company; it was also offered to other companies. Fox finally agreed to produce the movie on a participation basis. Under the agreement, the story writer-producer and the screenwriter, as well as other members of the independent company, were to share in the film's profits as well as receive salaries while the movie was being filmed.

Alien was filmed in England at the cost of nearly $10.8 million, higher than average but less than many other films. Included in the cost was a 15 percent fee collected by Twentieth Century-Fox for production overhead, that is, for expert assistance that the independent producer received from the larger company. Fox also distributed the movie: it handled promotion and advertising, booked the movie into theaters, and circulated the prints. For its distribution services, Fox received 30 percent of the rental fees taken in domestically and a somewhat higher percentage abroad. Rental fees amount to about 50 percent of the actual money moviegoers pay at the box office.

Making a film is merely part of the task. Selling it may cost more than filming it, as was the case with *Alien*. Twentieth Century-Fox spent $15 million on advertising, including more than $3 million on television commercials.

If the costs were high, so were the returns. The movie quickly became a hit. Released during 1979, it brought in $40 million in domestic rentals by the end of that year, continued to play during 1980, was sold to ABC television for $14 million for four network showings, and was expected to collect between $20 and $30 million from foreign showings. From gross rental receipts in 1979 alone, Twentieth Century-Fox collected more than $15 million in distribution fees under its percentage agreement with the independent production company.

Variations of the independent production system exist. Some independent companies handle their own distribution. They also do their own filming without ties to a major studio, frequently on location abroad. Others rent production facilities from a large studio. An independent company's success depends not only upon the popularity of the film that it produces, but also on the financial deals it can arrange. Although they do not see their names on the marquees, accountants and deal makers keep the wheels of Hollywood turning.

The ties between television and motion pictures will grow even stronger during the 1980s as pay TV develops and moviemakers design their films with an eye toward the home market. Four major companies—Columbia Pictures, MCA, Inc., Paramount Pictures, and Twentieth Century-Fox—in partnership with Getty Oil Company, announced plans for an all-movie pay TV network featuring their films. Since these films would not be made available to other satellite-fed pay networks until nine months later, and these four companies comprise half of Hollywood's eight major production firms, the impact on cable TV could be heavy. The plan evoked cries of restraint of trade, and an antitrust suit by the Justice Department.

To the dismay of theater owners, Twentieth Century-Fox also proposed offering videocassettes of its new films for sale to the public for home viewing within a month or two of a film's first release to theaters. Later, the film would be aired on pay TV, and finally on conventional network and syndicated TV broadcasts. This timing would let stay-at-home viewers who were willing to pay the price of a cassette see a new movie almost as soon as persons who went to the theaters. Since many of the former are nonmoviegoers at present, industry executives see a lucrative new market for their films, the proceeds of which they must share as a result of strikes by actors, writers, and directors. The new forms of film distribution that are emerging will affect the types of movies Hollywood makes in the next decade, because producers will shape their products to please the market.

The International Movie

Part of the life style that characterizes the new Hollywood involves the international movie. A step toward internationalization occurred in the 1950s. The independent producers, not being shackled to particular film studios, made movies in Europe and other foreign locations in order to profit from cheaper labor costs and national subsidies, to use authentic locales, and to please the movie stars themselves who, by establishing residence in a foreign country, could avoid paying United States income tax on money earned while working abroad.

At present, the change in tax laws and increase in foreign labor costs have reduced the advantages of filming in foreign locations. But the transporting of Hollywood actors, directors, camera operators, and all the assorted personnel connected with movie production continues, and this transatlantic and transpacific traffic has helped to return movie making to its international beginnings. The new mobility of contemporary moviemakers has been aided tremendously by certain technological developments. Lightweight cameras and sound recording equipment, as well as ministudios capable of being airlifted, are allowing movie producers to set up shooting where whim and geography dictate.

Further, the directors and writers, as well as the financial backing and distribution arrangements, have done their share to internationalize the industry. For example, *Blow-Up,* which won the 1967 Cannes Film Festival Golden Palm Award, was a British entry, with an Italian director (Antonioni), produced for MGM. *Taking Off,* which won the 1971 Cannes Jury Special Prize, was a United States entry directed by the Czech director Milos Forman. The 1966 Berlin Festival winner was a British entry, *Cul-de-Sac,* made by the Polish director Roman Polanski, who also directed *Rosemary's Baby.* The list could go on and on. Even such an American movie as *Bonnie and Clyde* was almost a French product. Its American writers, Robert Benton and David Newman, wrote the screenplay first for Francois Truffaut. When Truffaut rejected the script (he was then filming *Fahrenheit 451*), Benton and Newman approached Jean-Luc Godard, who was interested but ultimately decided against undertaking the project. It was only at this time that Warren Beatty began negotiations, finally buying the script for $75,000.

The many film festivals prevalent today are additional evidence of the internationalism of the film industry. Festivals in Cannes, Berlin, Venice, San Sebastian, New York, Moscow, Montreal, Cork, Chicago, and Mexico City have provided showcases for films from every nation and a meeting site and marketplace for actors, directors, writers, and producers.

FILM CRITICISM

As film's potential for personal and artistic expression was realized, and as its capability for being more than a cheap entertainment medium was understood, an accompanying aesthetic developed to explain and analyze the form and content of motion pictures. Vachel Lindsay's *The Art of the Moving Picture* (1915) and Rudolf Arnheim's *Film* (1933) are early examples of enlightened film criticism.

Good film criticism, like good literary criticism, serves two functions: 1) It explicates the work at hand, and 2) it elevates the public taste. The first function is the more obvious. As film techniques have become more complex, as film has probed deeper into human sensibility and experience, and as films have become identifiable as the work of individual directors who use personal symbols in the manner of contemporary poets and novelists, effective film criticism seeks to explain this heightened complexity by clarifying techniques, images, and relationships of time, place, and character.

The second purpose is perhaps best explained by Walt Whitman's often-quoted remark that great audiences make great poets. An audience knowledgeable about film history and techniques is in a position to recognize the second-rate, the false, the vacuous, the film that appears to be saying something but in reality says nothing, and the slick directorial tricks that attempt to hide the untrue. Great audiences make great poets (filmmakers) because they provide a need and a receiving ground for great poetry (films); they inspire the poet (filmmaker) to create a great film by providing a reason for being that transcends the individual's physical identity. Advances in film technology and subject matter have occurred and will continue to occur because film artist and film audience have become knowledgeable together.

At its best, good film criticism is informative, expanding the reader's knowledge by relating the film at hand to other works of a particular filmmaker, or to other films of similar or dissimilar genre; it respects the film and glories in its potential being realized; it bears the stamp of its creator's mind by possessing a distinctive style; it bridges epochs and nations by linking past with present achievement regardless of country of origin.

In all this, the film critic must be distinguished from the film reviewer, who serves a reportorial function. Whereas the film critic seeks to analyze and explain, the film reviewer seeks to ascertain the merits of a particular film with the intention of warning audiences against an inferior, boring, or morally degrading film, or touting those films with a high entertainment value. Gene Shalit has served this function in his frequent reviews on NBC's "Today" show. For the most part, movie reviewers write for the daily papers, previewing and describing films for their readers; they seldom go beyond the value of amusement as a criterion.

In contrast, film critics generally write for the magazines: *Film Quarterly, Cahiers du Cinema* (available in an English edition), *Film Culture, Sight and Sound, New Yorker,* and *Esquire.* Stanley Kauffmann in *New Republic* and Arthur Knight and Hollis Alpert in *Saturday Review* have written weekly pieces that combine previewing a film with deeper, more thoughtful, analysis. A few well-known American film critics are Andrew Sarris, Pauline Kael, Wilfrid Sheed, Jonas Mekas, Molly Haskell, and John Simon.

THE DOCUMENTARY FILM

In both England and America, the documentary film came of age in the 1930s through direct patronage by national governments, and matured, still under government auspices, during the troubled years of World War II.

Perhaps this is not surprising, as a documentary's purpose is always partially social—setting forth public and private crises and victories, showing us where humanity has been and what, inevitably, humanity will become unless proper action is taken.

In England, the earliest documentaries are associated with the Empire Market Board (EMB) Film Unit, headed by John Grierson. Grierson's first documentary, *Drifters* (1929), filmed on location on the North Sea, portrays the daily existence of the herring fishermen. When the EMB Film Unit was shifted to the General Post Office in 1933, Grierson and the film unit continued the production of quality documentaries, including *Weather Forecast* (1934), *Song of Ceylon* (1934), *Coal Face* (1935), *Night Mail* (1936), and *North Sea* (1938). "By the time the war broke out," Arthur Knight writes, "the British documentary movement—headed by men like Paul Rotha, Stuart Legg, Basil Wright, Harry Watt, Alberto Cavalcanti, Arthur Elton and Edgar Anstey—had achieved a worldwide reputation and inspired scores of directors outside England to attempt documentary movements in their own countries."

In America, the Depression and the New Deal gave rise to a remarkable series of documentaries produced under the auspices of the Farm Security Administration. As noted in Chapter 13, the most famed were two produced by Pare Lorentz: *The Plow That Broke the Plains* (1936) and *The River* (1937).

World War II gave impetus to increased documentary film production, ranging from training films for United States service personnel to informative films for a civilian population needing instruction in wartime procedures. As well, Hollywood directors such as John Huston, William Wyler, and John Ford began making films for the military. *San Pietro* (1944), *Memphis Belle* (1944), and *Battle of Midway* (1944) are memorable documentaries filmed on and around World War II's battlegrounds.

In England, the documentary filmmakers, now working under the aegis of the Ministry of Information, also turned their attention to wartime subjects, producing films such as *London Can Take It* (1940), depicting London during a Nazi air raid; *Target for Tonight* (1941), documenting an air force bombing mission; and *Desert Victory* (1942), an account of the North African campaign.

Basic to many recent documentaries is a problematic cinema technique known as *cinéma vérité*, spontaneous cinema, or direct cinema. Cinéma vérité applies to film that uses the camera to record reality in an unbiased and unmanipulated way. In presenting the essence of a situation, the director does not work from a preconceived shooting script, and, for all intents and purposes, does not direct—if by directing one means organizing and controlling what happens before the camera. By making use of the new lightweight cameras and recording equipment, the filmmaker goes into the field where he or she, and camera, act as witnesses and scribes. The intent is to provide either minimal or no interpretation and to retain the spontaneity and natural characteristics of the actual event.

In practice, documentary films exhibiting pure cinéma vérité are hard to find. Either consciously or unconsciously, most filmmakers impose an interpretation on their subject matter with in-camera editing, or editing after the film has been made. Others "edit" reality before any filming occurs by carefully selecting the persons and objects to be photographed and only then applying cinéma vérité filming techniques. For example, *Chronique d'un Eté,* by Jean Rouch and Edgar Morin, shows evidence of rather stringent preshooting editing, although the most effective parts of the film result from the characters behaving in ways that could not have been predicted beforehand.

In contrast, *Showman* and *The Beatles* provide good examples of pure cinéma vérité. Directed and produced by Albert and David Maysles, these films have been criticized for their superficiality. But, the Maysleses contend, their vow has been to avoid interfering wih the subject during filming; any superficiality, therefore, is inherent in the subject and is inevitably part of the truth that the film depicts.

Robert Drew, Richard Leacock, Donald Pennebaker, and Gregory Shuker have produced many outstanding documentary films under the label The Drew Associates. *On the Pole* depicts the ambitions, anguish, and ultimate failure of an Indianapolis race-car driver named Eddie Sachs. *Primary* concerns the Hubert Humphrey–John F. Kennedy primary contest in Wisconsin. *Crisis* depicts the Robert Kennedy–George Wallace fight over the token integration of the Alabama schools. *The Chair* is about an effort to prevent a young black from going to the electric chair. *Jane* is a portrait of Jane Fonda on the opening night of an unsuccessful play.

Other notable documentaries include Lionel Rogosin's *On the Bowery,* filmed on location in New York City, and Frederick Wiseman's controversial *Titicut Follies, High School,* and *Hospital.* Still others are Allan King's *Warrendale,* which concerns the treatment of emotionally disturbed children, and Frank Simon's *The Queen,* on a beauty contest for transvestites.

In recent years, television has provided a ready market for documentaries. A fine example of a television documentary, and one that also makes use of cinéma vérité techniques, is *Royal Family*, produced by a consortium of BBC and England's independent television companies and shown on American television. Richard Cawston served as producer-director, working with an eight-person crew throughout nearly a full year of shooting 43 hours of film. Cawston has attributed the success of this film to the royal family's willingness to talk without restraint, ad-libbing in front of the cameras, with the knowledge that Queen Elizabeth and Prince Philip had the right to veto any sections they found unacceptable in retrospect. "I decided it could be done only with some sense of humor and with a sort of cinéma vérité technique," Cawston has said. "Therefore, nothing was really rehearsed. We would discuss beforehand what would happen, and then simply shoot it. It worked out very well."

Contemporary documentaries made for American commercial television rarely have the political and social impact of earlier programs such as

CBS's *The Selling of the Pentagon* and NBC's *Pensions: The Broken Promise*. However, "60 Minutes" on CBS-TV, an hour show consisting of three or four shorter documentary-style sequences, has won top ratings, outdrawing popular entertainment shows, and has started a trend toward magazine-type "mini-documentary" shows, many of which are built around personalities and trivia. ABC-TV sought to match the success of "60 Minutes" with "20/20" and NBC-TV offered "Real People."

Arthur Knight has conjectured that, in the near future, regional filmmakers may be celebrating their regions through film as, traditionally, novelists, poets, and musicians have done. Certainly, the field for documentary production is wide open. Invariably, it seems, truth is stranger and more interesting than fiction. As a purveyor of facts and feelings, as a conveyor of an increasingly important photographic reality, and as a molder of public opinion, the documentary film is a powerful force in modern communications.

FILMS FOR INDUSTRY, GOVERNMENT, EDUCATION

This is a mushrooming industry in which an estimated 1200 firms are at work in the United States, producing films on a multiplicity of topics for showing to industrial and sales groups, schools and universities, government and community organizations, the armed forces, and professional and religious groups. These firms might be compared to the hundreds of small trade journals in the magazine field. Few of them are major organizations, but in the mass they form an influential channel for communicating information and ideas.

Nontheatrical filmmaking is heavily financed by American industry, which has found in this type of motion picture a highly effective means of presenting its purposes, methods, and achievements. Approximately 15,000 nontheatrical films are produced each year. Most are on 16 mm film, the standard size for projection by small and portable machines. A few of the more elaborate are made on 35 mm, some even for wide-screen projection. This total includes some 9,400 business and industrial pictures, 1,900 government films, 1,700 educational films, 250 for medical and health use, 300 for community organizations, and 150 religious films. Nearly $1.5 billion is being spent annually to produce these films and for other audiovisual aids, such as filmstrips, slides, and equipment.

The price of making and distributing a good company film averages $175,000, with some major productions exceeding $500,000. As many as 200 prints are made for some films to satisfy the demand. The average total audience for such a film is estimated to be 1.5 million. Many educational and instructional films are produced on far smaller budgets, some of them only a few thousand dollars, and are shown to more limited audiences.

Production of educational and informational films began with the development of the 16 mm portable projector in 1923. At present more than 750,000 projectors are in use in the United States, mostly in schools and businesses, but also in clubs, libraries, homes, and churches.

A large proportion of these nontheatrical films are available for use by organizations and private citizens free of charge. The cost is underwritten by business organizations as part of their institutional public relations budget; by federal, state, and local governments; by social or economic organizations that seek to present educational material in their particular fields; or by tax-supported institutions such as public libraries or adult education schools. There are 2,600 film libraries in the United States, distributing 16 mm films. *The H. W. Wilson Educational Film Guide* lists more than 20,000 films that can be borrowed.

JOB OPPORTUNITIES IN FILM

There are abundant opportunities for young persons in both theatrical and nontheatrical film areas today. Many of those entering the field begin their studies at the more than 800 colleges and universities that offer work in film (see Chapter 18). Beginning salaries compare favorably with those of other mass communications industries and professions, and almost limitless financial returns may be achieved by highly creative and productive individuals.

A *Saturday Review* article affirms that "the opportunities for young filmmakers have never been greater, not just in theatrical motion pictures, but also in the burgeoning industrial, educational, and commercial film fields." The article continues, "Writers with an ear for the dialogue of the contemporary life problem and an eye for the contemporary setting are in demand." Even the "much maligned producer function" is being reappraised and its important role reaffirmed. Undeniably, although at one time getting into film work was a hit-or-miss affair, the college student today may find a well-paved academic route into one of the many careers available in the thriving and multifaceted film industry.

Part Four

THE PERSUASIVE PROFESSIONS

Chapter 15

ADVERTISING

THE ROLE OF ADVERTISING

Advertising plays a unique and central role in the American economic system. Along with other forms of marketing communication, it helps to sell ideas, goods, and services. As a large part of the environment in which we live, advertising both reflects and affects our very life styles and thus plays a substantial social role. And, particularly since the advent of television, advertising figures prominently in our political decisions.

The American Marketing Association defines advertising as *any paid form of nonpersonal presentation and promotion of ideas, goods, or services by an identified sponsor.* Thus, advertising is distinguished from publicity in that the medium using publicity does not receive payment for its use, and the sponsor is not always identified. It should be noted that, in view of the presence of celebrities and other persons on the television screens in our living rooms today, much advertising is not nearly so nonpersonal as it was in the beginning years of American television, when this definition was formulated.

Advertising has become a workhorse that serves many communication needs of society, including needs other than goods and services. Business firms, labor unions, government agencies, and political leaders, among others, are successfully employing advertising to inform and persuade preselected audiences about major issues.

Americans live in an advertising environment. A Harvard study, for example, indicates that the average adult is potentially exposed to 500

Table 1 GROSS NATIONAL PRODUCT AND ADVERTISING DOLLAR VOLUME
U.S.—Projections, 1980 to 2000 (billions)

	1980	1985	1990	1995	2000
Gross National Product	$2,600.0	$4,000.0	$5,900.0	$8,800.0	$12,200.0
Advertising Volume*	$ 56.8	$ 92.5	$ 140.5	$ 211.0	$ 305.0

*Including miscellaneous
Source: Reprinted courtesy of *Advertising Age* 51:19 (April 30, 1980).

advertisements per day from television, radio, newspaper, and magazines. Add to that billboards, direct mail, such specialty items as book matches and ballpoint pens, and the packages in which most products are displayed so attractively, and the amount of advertising to which one is exposed is increased. Without advertising, most Americans would not be able to afford the cost of broadcast programs, newspapers, and magazines; even book matches, now distributed so freely, would bear a price.

Stanley E. Cohen, an authority on consumer-government relations as well as on advertising-government relations, wrote the following in the April 30, 1980, issue of *Advertising Age*:

> It is hardly strange that advertising has become a focus for so much attention. It comes uninvited into the home. Sometimes volunteering useful information, often probing into hidden feelings and yearnings. Sometimes subtle, sometimes harsh. Often useful. Occasionally brash and offensive. It brings championship football into the living room but breaks the spell as the action nears the climax. It provides TV programs which keep children occupied on rainy afternoons, but it encourages them to want a multitude of things, some of which don't especially appeal to their parents. It encourages contributions to a multitude of causes; pleads the diverse viewpoints of politicians, causes and special interests. It exercises a powerful, but undefined, influence on the life cycle of products and companies, ringing in the new, while silently marking the passage of the old.
>
> Name a problem and someone will almost surely find a way to link it to advertising, whether it is the wasteful use of energy, changing moral standards, bad eating habits, or the poor quality of TV programming. For advertising is a communications tool which influences our attitudes toward products, companies, lifestyles, and public issues. Advertising helps determine which styles are fashionable, which resorts are "in," what music we hear, which public figures are our next folk heroes.

It is estimated that advertisers in the United States now spend more than $57 billion each year, compared with $1.69 billion spent in 1935, according to census reports. As the nation's gross national product (GNP) has risen beyond $2.6 trillion, advertising expenditures have kept pace, ranging close to 2 percent of the GNP each year. Advertising, with its marketing aids of sales promotion, product design, point-of-purchase

Table 2 ADVERTISING DOLLAR VOLUME PROJECTIONS
By Media Category*—A Supposition, 1980 to 2000 (billions)

	1980	1985	1990	1995	2000
Newspapers	$15.9	$24.8	$35.5	$50.0	$74.2
Magazines	3.4	5.8	9.2	14.4	21.0
Television	12.4	22.8	38.7	64.3	98.9
Radio	3.8	6.0	8.9	13.0	17.8
Direct Mail	7.6	11.3	15.8	21.6	27.5
Business & Farm Publs.	1.9	2.8	3.9	5.4	7.0
Outdoor & Transit	.6	.8	1.0	1.2	1.3

*Excluding miscellaneous
Source: Reprinted courtesy of *Advertising Age* 51:19 (April 30, 1980).

displays, product publicity, and public relations, thus plays an obvious role in the growth of the nation's economy.

Table 1 shows how the amount of money spent on advertising in the United States is expected to increase from 1980 to 2000 in relation to the anticipated increase in gross national product. Table 2 shows how the expenditures are expected to be distributed among the media.

Because so many other factors contribute to our purchasing decisions, it is difficult to measure the effectiveness of any single advertising campaign, and it has not been possible to determine the overall impact of advertising on the marketplace. For decades, economists generally ignored advertising and its influence on the economy. Today, many maintain that advertising people have not proved their claims of advertising's value to society. Writing in the April 30, 1980, issue of *Advertising Age*, Dr. Richard H. Holton of the University of California at Berkeley, an authority on marketing and economic development, says that the proponents of advertising would like to have economists agree on at least four points:

> First, because of advertising, *the country's gross national product is greater and the standard of living is higher than they would otherwise be.* Advertising creates generic demand as well as demand for individual brands and thus assists in the marketing of more and better products. So advertising creates jobs, the argument runs, and provides us with a greater variety of products, while the quality of goods is improved over time in part because of advertising.
>
> A second argument put forth by advertisers is that *advertising plays a major role in informing the consumer so that more intelligent choices are made in the marketplace.* Thus advertising aids the competitive process.
>
> A third rationale for advertising is that *the firm's cost of production per unit of output is lower because advertising increases demand for the firm's output.* Thus substantial plant economics or economies of scale are achieved; fixed costs are spread over a larger number of units of output. So advertising leads to a more efficient use of resources in the economy.
>
> Finally, advertising's proponents ask economists to recognize that

> because of advertising, *new firms have an easier time entering the market than would be true if advertising were restricted or prohibited*. Advertising helps the new firm, or the firm with a new product, take on the giants in the industry and carve out a niche in the marketplace. Thus, advertising, again, is pro-competitive.

Since the 1950s, with better data on advertising, the refinement of analytical techniques, and the introduction of the computer, economists have seriously studied the economics of advertising. The results have been inconclusive, but Holton asserts that economists today are much more likely to have a balanced view of advertising than before these inquiries were undertaken.

HOW ADVERTISING DEVELOPED

Advertising is as old as civilization itself. In the ruins of ancient Egypt, explorers have found papyrus posters offering rewards for the return of runaway slaves. In the ruins of the Roman city of Pompeii, archaeologists have discovered political advertisements painted on walls along streets bearing such entreaties as, "Vote for Cicero, the friend of the people." However, until the advent of mass selling in the nineteenth century, advertising played only a minor role in the conducting of business. In early Greek and Roman days, signboards were placed above the doors of business establishments, and town criers proclaimed that merchants had certain wares for sale. These were merely means to attract customers to a shop, however; in contrast with modern advertising and sales techniques, the display of merchandise and personal selling were depended upon to make the sale.

After the invention of movable type accelerated printing in the mid-fifteenth century, handbills, posters, and then newspapers were used in increasing quantities to advertise products. Advertisements appeared in early American newspapers, but the volume did not grow to sizable proportions until trade began to flourish in the metropolitan centers in the early days of the republic. Almost all selling was local until about 1840, when the development of railroad transportation enabled industry to send its products to consumers who lived far from the manufacturing plants. National advertising resulted as business people used both magazines and newspapers to broaden their markets. The first advertising agency in the United States was organized by Volney B. Palmer circa 1840. His agency, and those that followed his, did not prepare copy but served primarily as publishers' representatives. By 1860 approximately 30 agencies were selling space for more than 4000 American publications. Since there were no public lists of these publications and no way of substantiating circulation claims, the agents could manipulate the buying and selling of space to substantial personal advantage.

In 1869, however, George P. Rowell began publishing *Rowell's American Newspaper Directory,* a rather complete list of newspapers, together with careful estimates of circulation. The same year F. Wayland Ayer and his father founded N. W. Ayer & Son, Inc., to buy space in the interest of clients rather than to sell it for newspapers, and the agency began its continuing directory of all periodicals in 1880. Soon other agencies were started along professional lines of providing planning and space buying services for their clients. There was an upsurge in the use of pictorial art in advertisements, and the nation began to be conscious of the first widely quoted slogans such as Ivory Soap's "$99^{44}/_{100}$ Per Cent Pure" and "It Floats," Eastman Kodak's "You Press the Button—We Do the Rest," and "Good Morning, Have You Used Pears' Soap?"

As newspaper and magazine circulations increased and new technological advances were made, at the turn of the century advertising developed new slogans, better copywriters and artists, and improved methods of analyzing products, media, and markets. Because much advertising was deceptive and grossly exaggerated, a strong movement to regulate advertising was begun in the 1910s. This involved both federal and state laws and control systems initiated by responsible advertising leaders. (The history of this movement is described later in this chapter.)

The advent of radio and a steady improvement in the techniques of advertising, such as copy-testing, the study of psychological appeals, and plans for integrated campaigns, characterized the 1920s. Advertising fought to hold its own during the depression years of the 1930s against both the near-paralysis of business and organized consumer objections to improper practices. During that decade, advertisers increasingly used research methods, such as readership studies and audience measurement.

During World War II, the War Advertising Council was established by advertising agencies, media, and advertisers as a voluntary contribution to the war effort. So successful was the council in promoting the sale of war bonds, donation of blood, rationing, and the like, it was continued as the Advertising Council, Inc., headquartered in New York. This private, nonprofit organization conducts about 25 major public service campaigns each year pertaining to such matters as health and safety, education, the environment, the disadvantaged, consumerism, the economy, and community and international projects.

During the past four decades Smokey the Bear has told Americans that forest fires cost them money as well as the loss of recreational facilities and the natural beauty of the country ("Smokey Says: Remember, Only You Can Prevent Forest Fires!"). More recent council campaigns have borne slogans such as: "Thanks to You It Works for All of Us: The United Way," "People Start Pollution; People Can Stop It!," "Take a Bite Out of Crime," "Red Cross Is Counting on You," and "Let's Save Energy Now!"

Major American advertisers provide volunteer coordinators. The agencies alternate in conducting the campaigns, and the media offer free time and space for the ads. Each year the media donate approximately $600 million in time and space in support of these campaigns. Urging Americans to participate in the 1980 census consumed almost $38 million in such donations. Through 1979, the media's dollar contribution totaled $9.1 billion.

The booming economy after World War II produced rapid growth in all areas of advertising. Staffs were enlarged, branch offices of agencies proliferated, and small agencies formed networks to provide reciprocal services for their clients across the country. Television—described by industry leaders as the most important development affecting advertising in the twentieth century—accelerated the trend toward larger agencies because it increased the complexities of advertising. Television arrived at a most opportune time, for advertisers were introducing hundreds of new products and consumers were eager to learn their merits. Advertisers turned increasingly to research to provide facts about their products and services and to discover the motivations of consumer markets.

During the 1960s and 1970s advertising was confronted with the staggering task of helping to move into the hands of consumers an unprecedented volume of manufactured goods. Periodic recessions made this task more difficult. More money was entrusted to advertising personnel, and their responsibilities mounted. Management demanded more efficient methods of measuring the effectiveness of advertising as distinguished from other marketing functions. Many large agencies went public—that is, converted their proprietorship to shares that were traded and priced on the stock market. In order to generate greater profits for principals and stockholders, some agencies diversified into side businesses, such as retail stores and product manufacturing.

The computer, long used for the common chores of accounting and billing, came into more sophisticated use, providing the breakouts and analyses necessary for sound manufacturing and marketing decisions. As information increased, the computer helped management, advertising, and marketing people understand the new world of product proliferation, market segmentation, automated distribution, population shifts, and the profit squeeze. National computer networks were established by large agencies using high-speed data transmission telephone lines and other communications facilities. The computer was used to analyze consumer surveys, to assist in media buying, to help in predicting the effectiveness of one media plan as opposed to another, to calculate television program cost efficiencies in relation to client objectives, and in numerous other ways.

Increasingly large amounts of money were allocated to marketing and advertising research. The emphasis on research resulted from high entry costs into markets, high costs of new product development, market failures, the rapidly changing marketing environment, changing life styles of consumers, and the urgency of having more information for decision-making. Companies found it necessary to involve specialized outside consulting groups as well as their own in-house groups to analyze the changing market. As a consequence, independent research groups increased threefold throughout the United States during the 1970s.

The attention paid to creativity, cleverness, and wit in the preparation of print and broadcast messages and campaigns led to a widely discussed "cult of creativity" in the industry, a trend that seems likely to continue. Humor, of course, is a prime ingredient of many successful advertisements. Examples of this include the television commercials of Clairol's Herbal Essence Shampoo, launched with an animation technique that included warm humor; Morris the 9-Lives Cat commercials; and those portraying the Keebler elves. Humor also is playing a larger role in slice-of-life commercials as consumers become more sophisticated and more critical of how they as consumers are portrayed in advertising. Recent humorous advertisements followed earlier highly entertaining creations by satirist Stan Freberg for Jeno's Pizza and Chun King products, and popular Braniff, Avis, Volkswagen, and Benson & Hedges advertisements. Many new agencies were established as the most creative advertising personnel went into business for themselves.

Some advertising people decried the extensive use of wit and humor, contending that it might be entertaining but that it does not always help to sell goods and services. Because of the business slowdown during the 1975 and 1980 recessions many commercials of a humorous, awareness, and image-building variety gave way to "hard-sell" advertisements. "Less emphasis on showmanship, more on sellmanship," is the way one observer put it. Creative research, entailing repeated testing and weeks, even months, of hard work, became even more important. Humor, however, remained a basic ingredient for many spot advertisements. For example, a Speidel watchband commercial shows the faces of a man and a woman rotating on watches. The man finally asks the woman what she is doing that night. "Oh, I'm flexible," she replies, and her watchband flexes once again. Three weeks of filming and four months of "rotoscoping" were required to produce the 30-second commercial, but product, demonstration, and interest all were present, and the commercial was deemed highly effective.

The number of animated commercials and those using celebrities also increased. Animated commercials, such as those for Levi Jeans and Herbal Essence Shampoo, helped brighten the array of customary spots. For many years, celebrities would not perform in or do "voice-overs" for commercials, but that has changed. Karl Malden for American Express, James Garner for Polaroid, and Lou Rawls for Budweiser are among the countless celebrities who now earn well over $100,000 for each of their contributions.

In comparison with the "product era" of the 1950s and the "image era" of the 1960s, positioning emerged as a primary characteristic of the 1970s.

In a media-oriented society, many companies found it necessary to "position" a product in the public's mind—a position taking into consideration not only the product's own strengths and weaknesses, but those of its competitors as well. Examples are Seven-Up's "Un-Cola" campaign, *Sports Illustrated's* "Third Newsweekly" program, a beer company's "First class is Michelob" assertion that it is the first American-made premium beer, and the positioning of Beck's beer against Löwenbrau with the advertising line, "You've tasted the German beer that's the most popular in America. Now taste the German beer that's the most popular in Germany."

At the insistence of the Federal Trade Commission, comparative advertising emerged as another weapon in the battle for sales. In 1965 advertising leader Fairfax Cone had summed up the industry's general sentiment on the practice when he said, "It's bad manners and I can't believe the public will stand for it." During the 1970s, however, both the public and the majority of advertising practitioners seemed to favor the technique. Some commercials named competitive products, others merely alluded to them. For example, a campaign for Scotti automobile mufflers explicitly scoffed at "the Midas touch," pointing out that Midas, Inc.'s famous lifetime replacement muffler guarantee did not include other parts of the exhaust system installed by the company, whereas under Scotti's guarantee customers could get off "Scot free." A Dictaphone commercial proclaimed, "Bad news for IBM." Seneca apple juice commercials showed a set of triplets, each with Hi-C, Hawaiian Punch, and Seneca apple juice; all three children love those products, the commercial stated, but only Seneca contained 100 percent fruit juice. Without naming its competitor, the Scope campaign referred to a competing "medicine breath" mouthwash, whereupon Listerine retaliated by proclaiming that its product lasted "two times longer than the leading sweet-tasting mouthwash." Comparative advertising also was widely practiced in print advertising.

Industry code review boards watched carefully over the technique, condoning comparisons considered significant to product performance, but banning disparagement, unqualified language, and dangling comparisons. Legitimate comparison was viewed as saying "ours is better than theirs" and disparagement as saying "theirs is worse than ours."

Advocacy advertising, in which corporations run paid ads that take sides on important issues, became increasingly popular. When the broadcast networks, because of their access policies, refused to carry commercials telling their side of the energy story, major oil companies inserted their messages in newspapers and magazines. Other corporations used print advertising to respond to what they considered unfair treatment in such network programs as "60 Minutes" and "20/20." In the historic case of *First National Bank of Boston* v. *Bellotti,* the Supreme Court in 1978 stated that the government may not limit the range of issues upon which a corporation may express itself. The Court, however, did not define the outer boundaries of such expression.

Other recent trends include a major increase in government advertising; a movement toward worldwide conglomerates, consortiums, and working alliances through which agencies cooperate or interact without actual partnership or cross-ownership; the acquisition of some agencies by those from other countries; and the merging or near-merging of the advertising and public relations functions of many companies and agencies.

Target marketing gained strength in the early 1980s. Carrying positioning a step further, companies and agencies sought specific demographic and psychographic information from the media in order to reach their markets as precisely and inexpensively as possible.

Undergoing tests for effectiveness was the idea of compressing commercials (electronically removing "blank spaces" between and within words so that, for example, a 36-second commercial would fit a 30-second spot). Early research indicated that time-compressed commercials could improve product recall by as much as 40 percent, but some critics remained skeptical.

Many problems confronted the industry. Foremost were those raised by the powerful consumer movement and the threat of increased government regulation (to be discussed later in this chapter). How to recruit able young persons so as to refresh and replenish the industry's more than $15 billion pool of advertising talent was another major problem. "Talent napping" was a continuing practice, and the agencies' annual turnover rate stood at 35 percent. Mounting areas of friction between clients and agencies contributed to the annual shifting of about 20 percent of all advertising accounts from one agency to another. These problems included poor communications, account conflicts, comparative advertising, and the feeling by some clients that agencies overcharged or were overpaid. Despite the problems in this mercurial, exciting business, however, few deserted it, and the level of earnings remained generally high.

CRITICISMS OF ADVERTISING

Because advertising is so much a part of our lives, criticisms are rampant. Some of the more common complaints and the replies that have been made to each of them are:

1. *Advertising persuades us to buy goods and services we cannot afford.* Persuasion is present, but never coercion; it is up to each of us to exercise self-control and sound judgment in our purchases.

2. *Advertising appeals primarily to our emotions, rather than to our intellect.* Since all of us are motivated by emotional drives, it is only natural that advertisers should make such appeals. Again, a cautious buyer will avoid obvious appeals to the emotions.

3. *Advertising is biased.* This, too, is natural; all persons put their best foot forward in whatever they say or do. Being aware of this bias, we can discount some of the superlatives used in advertising.

4. *Advertising involves conflicting competitive claims.* But advertising is "out in the open," never hidden as are some forms of propaganda, and we can decide for ourselves.

5. *Advertising is unduly repetitious.* This is because the public is essentially a passing parade, not a mass gathering; there are always new users whom the appeal has never reached. Slogans such as "It Floats" have sold goods successfully for generations.

6. *Much advertising is vulgar, obtrusive, irritating.* Actually, only a handful of advertisers employ poor taste in their appeals; their excesses damage the higher standards of many other advertisers. The very nature of radio and television, whose commercials cannot easily be turned off, accounts for much irritation; this complaint is seldom voiced in relation to printed advertising, which may be ignored.

Other criticisms are directed toward advertising by those who fear that their very lives are being manipulated by clever and unscrupulous Madison Avenue word wizards whose sole objective is to sell goods and ideas regardless of the social consequences. These critics are generally persons who resist classification among the masses to whom most advertising is directed. Their intense desire to think and act of their own volition in an increasingly monolithic world leads them to attack advertising—"mass" by its very nature—at every turn, with little thought of the inevitable consequences of a society in which advertising is unduly shackled.

Some opinion leaders consider advertising to be almost devoid of ethics. Frederic Wakeman's 1946 bestseller, *The Hucksters,* spawned a series of antiadvertising novels. Advertisers and the broadcast industry shared blame for the rigged quiz shows and the disc jockey payola scandals of the late 1950s, the latter emerging again as a problem in the 1970s. The image of the earnest young-man-about-Madison Avenue complete with gray flannel suit, attaché case, sincere smile, and lavish expense account was not one to inspire confidence. Set against the background of yesterday's patent medicine quackery, extravagant advertising, and the doctrine of *caveat emptor* (let the buyer beware) and today's allegations of misleading drug advertising, the bill of indictments is devastating.

Add to this the question of good taste in broadcasting—the jarring loudness of some commercials, the so-called insulting and obnoxious advertisements, the cramming of multiple commercials into segments of broadcast time, and the clutter and length of some TV program credit crawls—and it is perhaps understandable that some critics of advertising have grown so heated in their denunciations. "TV is a series of tasteless and endless interruptions," cried one critic. "The people are tired of being screamed at, assaulted, and insulted by commercials," exclaimed another.

Some years back, Morton J. Simon, Philadelphia lawyer and author, cited six principal reasons for unfavorable government and public attitudes toward advertising. Five of the reasons are still valid:

1. *Advertising is a horizontal industry.* It cuts across almost every business and service, so an attack on any industry almost always includes advertising.

2. *Advertising represents a lot of money.* It spends billions of dollars annually, and some persons view these funds as apparently untaxed and outside the grip of government (a complaint expressed by many Third World countries in their quest for a new world order of communications).

3. *Advertising lives in a glass house.* By its nature, it cannot hide its sins.

4. *The gray flannel suit image is pervasive.* Many consider that advertising people live lavishly and improperly on tax-deductible expense accounts (a view that led to President Carter's attack against the "three-martini lunch" as a tax-deductible business expense).

5. *Advertising is not constitutionally protected.* Some persons in government believe that advertising is somehow tainted by its commercial purpose and therefore is not protected by the First Amendment; its legal status has still not been made wholly clear.

Simon also pointed out that advertising has rarely lobbied; in recent years, however, advertising interests have felt compelled to maintain a Washington lobby to offset determined attacks by consumer groups.

REGULATION OF ADVERTISING

Business people and consumer groups alike agree that advertising should not be dishonest or misleading and that it should provide pertinent information for the public. At issue is the question of how much regulation is reasonable and necessary. Historically, federal and state laws and self-regulation by the industry have provided the control mechanisms, with laws serving in the primary role. The first legal restraint was a postal fraud law enacted more than 100 years ago, designed to ensure that persons ordering goods from mail-order catalogues received what the catalogues promised. During the progressive reform era after the turn of the century, business abuses, including the gross exaggerations and misleading claims of some advertisers, prompted a flurry of actions supported both by consumer groups and by various advertising organizations determined to elevate the ethics of the advertising business. They included the following:

1. Many states, beginning in 1911, enacted a model Truth in Advertising law proposed by *Printers' Ink,* a magazine formerly published for advertising people. State controls, however, were weak, so pioneer advertising leaders supported federal legislation to deal with interstate advertising.

2. Advertising organizations adopted codes of behavior, and some publications established guidelines for accepting or refusing advertising.

The *Good Housekeeping* Seal of Approval is a notable, more recent, example of evaluations of advertising by magazines.

3. The first Better Business Bureau was organized in 1913. Bureaus have since been established in major cities across the nation to promote ethical practices and to help consumers with problems.

4. The Audit Bureau of Circulations, a nonprofit organization making unbiased periodical audits and statements concerning a publication's circulation, was established in 1914.

5. Congress enacted the Federal Trade Commission Act of 1914, establishing the agency (FTC), which steadily increased the extent and nature of its regulation of advertising.

In 1931 the Supreme Court ruled that the FTC could restrict deceptive advertising only if it could show that such advertising injured competition. With the passage of the Wheeler-Lea Act in 1938, however, the FTC was given a clear-cut mandate to deal with advertisements that deceived consumers. In the 1950s the FTC—well before the Surgeon General's warning condemning cigarette smoking—challenged the use of cigarette advertising slogans that implied that smoking was harmless. In addition, the agency attacked "bait and switch" advertising, misleading discount offers, misleading use of the word "free," extravagant claims for indigestion products and headache remedies, and other such practices.

The first serious attempt at self-regulation of advertising occurred in 1952, when the National Association of Broadcasters (NAB), through the operation of its Code Authority and accompanied by threats from the Federal Communications Agency that it would take action if self-regulation failed, established extensive sets of advertising and program standard guidelines for radio and television stations. The NAB code's professional staff began clearing commercials prior to their airing, and the networks, operating independently, began reviewing commercials for truth, taste, and fairness to children. It was a major undertaking; each year NBC, for example, processes about 16,000 commercials.

Another wave of consumerism occurred during the 1960s, led by the Ralph Nader organization and other activist groups. Regulatory agencies were accused of operating more in favor of the industries they were supposed to supervise than for the public. An American Bar Association task force, established at the request of President Nixon, urged that the FTC "get tough" or be abolished. As a consequence of these demands, the agency vastly enlarged its operations. Among other actions, the FTC began to require factual substantiation of advertising as well as factual disclosures in future ads and, in some cases, corrective statements to offset previous misstatements. In the belief that consumers would benefit if advertisers argued with each other in their ads, the FTC vigorously urged comparative advertising. The agency asked the FCC to require the airing of countercommercials, particularly regarding those addressed to children, so that consumer groups could reply to advertising claims. The FCC declined to do so, however, contending that such action would amount to "a tortured or distorted application of fairness doctrine principles." Even broader powers were extended to the FTC through the Moss-Magnuson Act of 1975.

By the 1960s more than 20 federal agencies, including the Internal Revenue Service and the Securities & Exchange Commission, had taken steps to regulate advertising. More than 12 states had begun to tax advertising. In 1966 Congress passed the Fair Packaging and Labeling Act, covering food, drug, and cosmetics packages. A Department of Commerce program to reduce the proliferation of package sizes followed. In 1968 came the Truth in Lending Act requiring disclosure of the annual interest rate on revolving charge accounts. It was still permissible to use the phrase "Easy Credit" in an ad, but if specific language such as "$1.00 down and $1.00 a week" was introduced, the annual interest rate had to be stated. Congress banned the broadcasting of cigarette commercials in 1971.

In that same year, the advertising industry sought to forestall further legal action with a two-tiered system of self-regulation. A permanent professional staff working within the structure of the Council of Better Business Bureaus began receiving complaints from the public and from business, and to do its own monitoring. In addition, a National Advertising Review Board was created. Fifty persons, including ten public members with no advertising connections, were designated to consider complaints in five-member panels throughout the country. The board considers about 400 complaints each year. Although no penalties are imposed, findings are published. Legal complications have arisen, however, including lawsuits in Colorado and Louisiana that have chilled the enthusiasm of many volunteers and caused insurance companies to withdraw liability protection for advertisers. Nevertheless, the industry continues to support the review system.

The direct mail industry in 1971 began cooperating with postal authorities in a plan enabling recipients of direct mail advertising to have their names removed from mailing lists. Guidelines of ethical business practice in the industry were established in 1978.

In numerous governmental hearings, industry leaders strongly defended the social and economic values of advertising. They warned that imposing broad restrictions on all advertising because of the misleading or deceptive content of some would destroy the integrity of the marketing process and the need to foster public confidence in the free enterprise system—which some people saw as the real target of the most militant consumer advocates. The House of Representatives blunted the consumer drive in 1978 when it defeated a bill to establish an Agency for Consumer Representation.

Responding further to business complaints of too much government interference, in 1980 Congress passed legislation subjecting FTC regulations to two-house congressional veto and limiting the agency's public participation funding. The FTC's children's advertising inquiry was allowed to proceed, but any new rule would have to be published in full in advance and such inquiries would have to be based on charges of false and deceptive, rather than simply unfair, advertising. Because the broadcast industry had instituted reforms that the FCC incorporated into a policy statement, broadcasters continued to resist any further FTC restrictions involving children's advertising on television.

The FTC's wings also were clipped in a Supreme Court decision in 1976 overturning a Virginia ban against prescription-drug advertising and flatly asserting First Amendment protection for "commercial speech." "Speech is not stripped of First Amendment protection merely because it appears in the form of a paid advertisement," wrote Justice Harry Blackmun. However, in the landmark decision, *Virginia State Board of Pharmacy* v. *Virginia Citizens Consumer Council,* the Court pointed out that commercial speech is different from other types of expression and may be regulated under certain circumstances.

THE SIZE OF THE ADVERTISING FIELD

In the United States

More than 400,000 persons are employed in all phases of advertising in this country. This estimate by industry spokespersons includes those who create or sell advertising for an advertiser, medium, or service, but not the thousands behind the scenes such as printers, sign painters, and clerical workers. Manufacturing and service concerns employ the largest number of advertising workers. Next in order are the mass media, including radio, television, magazines, outdoor, direct mail, and transportation advertising departments. Following them are retail establishments, advertising agencies, wholesalers, and miscellaneous specialty companies.

In addition, it has been estimated that approximately 1 million persons fill jobs related to advertising. They include paper salespeople, representatives of media, advertising printing, and typography companies, and others. Of the approximately 20,000 newcomers attracted into the advertising business each year, about 1,500 are hired by the advertising agencies directly from college, although this number diminishes considerably during periods of economic recession.

Approximately 8,000 advertising agencies employed more than 82,000 people in 1977, according to census figures. The American Association of Advertising Agencies (4As) has about 500 members. They place approximately 75 percent of all agency-placed advertising in the United States. The agencies are usually small businesses; only 80 (1 percent) of the agencies in business in 1977 had gross incomes of $50 million or more and only 48 grossed $10 million or more. *Fortune* magazine reported in 1979 that 15 agencies each had reached the $500 million billing level. The three largest—Young & Rubicam, J. Walter Thompson, and McCann-

Erickson—reportedly were approaching $1.5 billion in billings. Although profits are not often published, industry observers indicated that at least 7 of the 15 top agencies earned more than $10 million each during the 1978–1979 fiscal year. It is significant to note that, although the dollar volume of business has increased, because of the more efficient use of personnel the number of employees per agency has in fact decreased. Not long ago, an average of four employees handled $1 million in billings, but the figure today stands closer to one.

International Advertising

United States advertisers, agencies, and advertising personnel have been engaged in international advertising for decades. Today our participation is steadily and dramatically increasing. Standards of living in Europe, the Far East, Latin America, and other heretofore untapped marketing areas are constantly improving. Literacy rates have been rising, and the growth of both print and broadcast media in many countries has provided a larger audience for advertising. American wares are in great demand. We are exporting billions of dollars worth of products each year. These join the flow of goods produced by overseas plants in which Americans have invested well over $50 billion.

As a consequence, giant corporations such as IBM World Trade, Exxon, Coca-Cola Export, General Motors, and Monsanto, long in the international field, are being joined by countless other companies seeking their share of the world market. IBM now conducts business in more than 120 countries and receives more than one-half of its corporate gross income from sources outside the United States. The IBM payroll in 1979 supported approximately 147,000 employees engaged in non-United States operations. Almost all non-U.S. employees are nationals of the countries in which they work.

In 1979 the top ten United States agencies engaged in advertising in other countries grossed $932 million in income through their non-U.S. operations. Of this total, McCann-Erickson, the J. Walter Thompson Company, and SSC&B grossed almost one-half. The Thompson company pioneered in global agency operations, opening its first overseas office in London in 1889. Today it has more than 5600 employees at work in 60 offices in 25 countries. McCann-Erickson staffs its more than 70 full-service offices mostly with nationals of the 47 countries in which they are located. The firm is a subsidiary of Interpublic, Inc. The other agency leaders in gross income earned in other countries in 1979 are Ogilvy & Mather International, Young & Rubicam, Ted Bates & Co., D'Arcy-MacManus & Masius, BBDO International, Leo Burnett Co., and Campbell-Ewald. In all, there are 15 truly international United States agencies, as compared with only three or four a decade ago.

The smaller domestic agencies operate overseas in four ways: through subsidiaries, of which they own part or all of the stock; through exclusive affiliations; through account affiliations with overseas agencies that may also work with other American agencies; and through export media, such as *Reader's Digest International* and *Vision*. The fourth method is often used along with any of the other three.

As noted in Chapter 23, many other countries, most notably Japan and those in Europe, have developed large advertising agencies, for the most part modeling their operations after those in the United States. Some of these agencies have developed branches in the United States designed to garner accounts from their own nationals who have invaded the U.S. market. A few are merging with agencies in this country; for example, Univas, a French agency, purchased New York-based Kelly, Nason, Inc., in 1978.

WHAT ADVERTISING PEOPLE DO

Advertising people disseminate messages through purchased space (print) or time (television and radio), or through expenditures in other media, in order to identify, inform, and/or persuade. How some of these people accomplish this objective can be described by examining briefly the roles they play in agencies, in advertising departments of the mass media, in retail store and company advertising departments, and in the planning of a national advertising campaign.

Advertising Agencies

An agency first studies its client's product or service to learn the advantages and disadvantages of the product itself in relation to its competition. It then analyzes the present and potential market for which the product or service is intended. Taken into consideration next are the distribution and sales plans of the client, which are studied with a view toward determining the best selection of media. A definite plan is then formulated and presented to the client.

Once the plan is approved, the agency staff writes, designs, and illustrates the proposed advertisements or prepares the broadcast commercials; contracts for space or time with the media; produces the advertisements and sends them to the media with instructions; checks and verifies the use of the ads; pays for the services rendered and bills the client; cooperates in such merchandising efforts as point-of-purchase displays; and seeks to measure results.

Who are the persons who perform these services? The answer varies, since advertising agencies range in size from small operations to full-service agencies employing 1000 persons or more. The executive heads of an agency usually are people who have proved they can achieve results for clients through print, broadcasting, and other media and who are capable of procuring new business for the agency. These executives may be organized into a plans board, giving general direction to such departments as research, planning, media, copy, art and layout, television production, print production, traffic, merchandising, checking, and accounting.

The key persons in servicing an account—that is, in providing a liaison between the agency and the client—are the account executives. These executives must have a general knowledge of all phases of advertising, merchandising, and general business practices, as well as the ability to be creative in solving a client's special advertising problems and in planning campaigns. Account executives call on the agency's various departments for assistance and correlate their efforts in behalf of clients.

Copy and art chiefs are responsible for the actual creation of advertisements. Copywriters are salespeople, inventors, interpreters, and perhaps artists, but always competent writers. Art directors are salespeople, inventors, interpreters, perhaps writers and sometimes producers, but also are visually oriented persons who usually can draw. They see to it that all the visual elements come together at every phase of the work from rough layouts to finished ads. They supervise every aspect from the graphic approach to selection of type. For television, they begin by making a storyboard, the series of pictures representing the video portion of the commercial. Often they help choose the film techniques, music and other sounds, and models.

From the moment an ad is designed and written to the time it actually appears in magazines and newspapers or on billboards, it is in the hands of the print production people. They are up-to-date on typography, printing, photoengraving, electrotyping, and allied crafts and processes. They know what is practical for reproduction and help to guide the creative departments in planning their work. They buy graphic arts services and materials and see assignments through to completion.

Because so many agency functions, including copy, art, production, and media, are involved in the same assignment—that of producing a single ad or commercial or an entire campaign—it is vital to keep everyone working smoothly and on schedule. Planning the flow and timing of all the work is the function of traffic control. Whether the project is large or small, traffic sees that all do their parts on time in order to meet deadlines and publishers' closing dates.

The marketing research department gathers the facts that make it possible to solve sales problems. Research findings provide vital intelligence for the agency. Facts—for instance, about what type of people use a product and why—may help to provide creative people with the central idea for an advertising approach. Or media people may plan an entire advertising campaign based on research about the way consumers read certain magazines or which television programs they watch. Most agencies depend upon their clients for the majority of their marketing information.

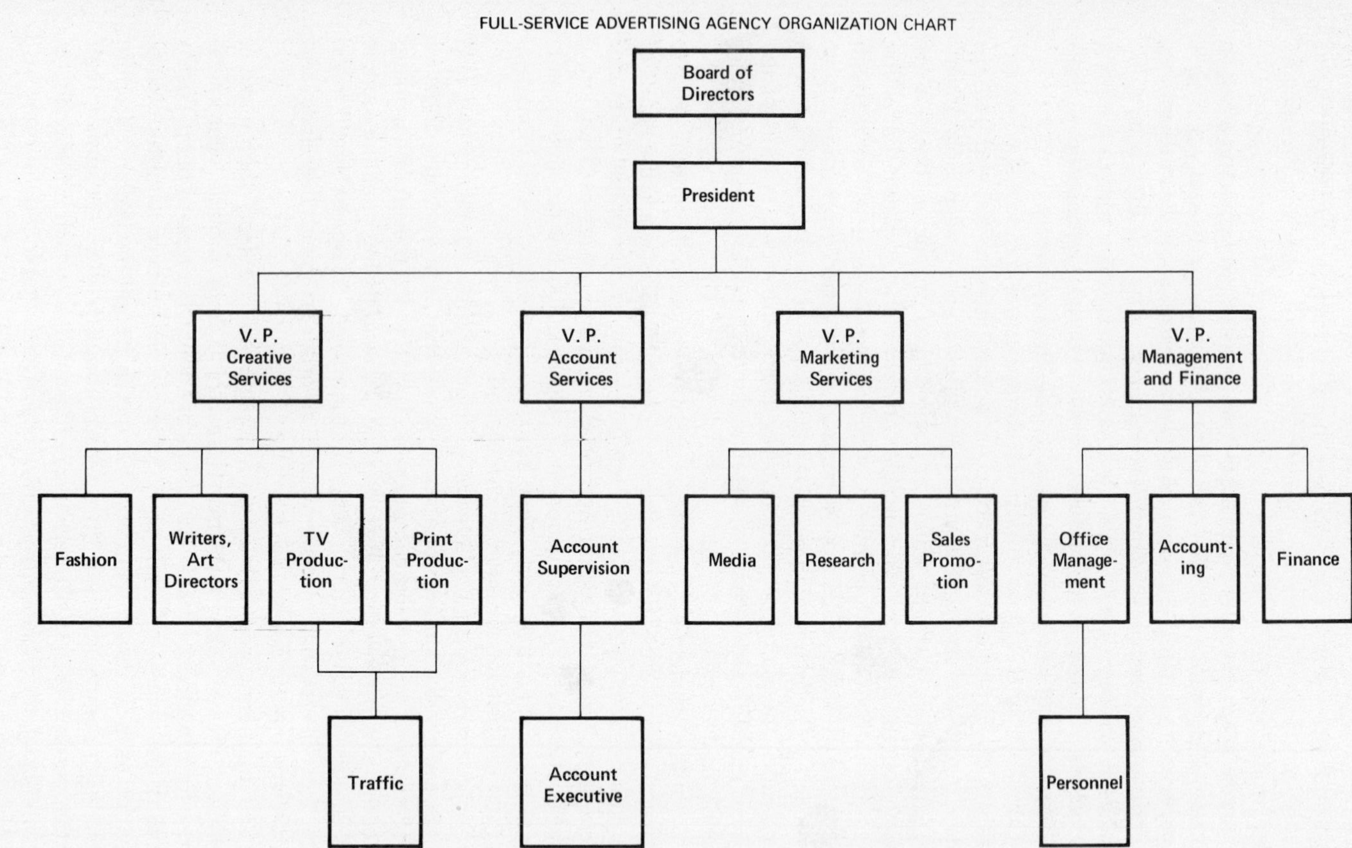

Figure 15.1 Full-service advertising agency organization chart.

Media people select and buy print space for ads and air time for commercials. They get many of the facts and figures from the research department. They must know the tones and attitudes of magazines, the psychological environments of TV shows, and the editorial tone of any given newspaper. From daily and weekly newspapers, national magazines, business magazines, radio and television stations, outdoor posters, and direct-mail lists they choose the most effective combinations for each advertisement and product. And they must be able to stay within a budget.

Agencies also have people who handle such matters as sales promotion, merchandising, public relations, fashion, home economics, and personnel. Then too, like other firms, agencies need comptrollers, secretaries, general office workers, bookkeepers, and billing clerks. (Figure 15.1 shows a typical organization chart.)

Most of an agency's compensation comes in the form of commissions received from the media in which the advertisements appear. This usually is 15 percent of the medium's national rate; if the advertising space or time costs $1000, the agency collects that amount from the client and pays the medium $850. These commissions account for 75 to 80 percent of the agency's gross income. In addition, the agency bills the client for actual costs incurred in preparing the advertisements, such as for typography, photostats, filmed commercials, artwork, and any special services, plus a service charge—usually 17.65 percent. For example, if these costs amounted to $1000, the agency would bill the client $1000 plus 17.65 percent, or a total of $1176.50. After all expenses have been met, the agency usually winds up with a 2 to 3 percent net profit on its gross income each year. Verification that the advertisements have been used by the media is accomplished by the national Advertising Checking Bureau.

Advertising Departments of Mass Media

All the media employ space or time sales personnel and almost all engage national sales representatives to obtain advertising for them. Let us consider several actual newspaper and radio operations.

One newspaper publishes both morning and evening newspapers with a combined circulation of 38,000. The combined retail advertising staff consists of six sales representatives and a retail manager. Advertisements handled by the department comprise 70 percent of the newspaper's total advertising volume, the remainder being in classified and national.

Each salesperson handles between 75 and 100 accounts, ranging from department stores to small shops. Unlike the practice on large newspapers, these salespeople are not assigned to specific territories. After calling on their business firms that have accounts with them, they prepare semicomprehensive layouts using artwork from one of several advertising layout service books. The layouts are then sent to the offset composing room.

Proofs are delivered to any retailer placing an ad that contains 15 or more inches of space.

These salespeople work from 8:30 A.M. to 6 P.M. five days a week. Each salesperson is required to produce at least one "speculative" layout each week. They are paid a base salary plus commission, and annual incomes range from $10,000 to $12,000. Commissions are paid when the amount of space sold at the same time the previous year is exceeded, and in connection with the 15 or so special editions (such as "back-to-school") printed each year, as well as color ads and departmental sales contests.

In contrast, 32 salespersons are employed by a nearby morning, evening, and Sunday newspaper selling more than 350,000 copies primarily in a 15-county metropolitan area. Each must serve accounts only in a specified district. If the ad is too elaborate for the salesperson to prepare, the newspaper's art department lends assistance. After the typed copy and artwork are arranged on the dummy ad, it is printed on a proof sheet exactly as it is to appear in the newspaper. The salesperson checks the ad and may send it to the customer for signed approval before it is printed. These salespeople work in air-conditioned, carpeted offices with easy access to a covered parking lot. They earn commissions above their base salary if they produce more sales than their monthly quotas.

A nearby 1000-watt medium-market AM station employs four salespeople. Among them is the commercial manager who doubles as station manager but spends most of her time calling on accounts. One salesperson also announces occasional play-by-play sports broadcasts. The station owner handles all national accounts as well as a dozen local ones. People on the sales staff earn $10,000 to $12,000 annually in commissions. The commercial manager receives a salary, plus 15 percent of the collections on her own accounts and a graduated percentage of the sales volume of the entire staff.

A copywriter prepares the commercials and the station announcers tape them. The spots are played over the telephone for client approval before being aired. The traffic manager then schedules them on cartridge tapes ("carts"). Many of the commercials also are aired on the station's 5200-watt FM station.

All advertising personnel provide fresh, up-to-date information about the markets that their newspaper, magazine, or station covers and about the "pulling power" of the medium itself. These facts are provided regularly by their own research and promotion departments or by national trade associations or bureaus.

Most magazines deal directly with national advertisers or indirectly through national representatives. As is true with the other media, copywriters, artists, and production, promotion, and merchandising personnel supplement the sales force. And there is a similar ladder of promotion to executive positions.

Retail Store Advertising

Retail firms employ more than 80,000 persons in their advertising departments. These range from one-person staffs to those employing dozens of persons. In a large store the advertising manager works closely with sales promotion and marketing specialists. In one large Chicago department store, the staff consists of a copy chief, production manager, and proofreader; an art director and assistant art director, together with six layout artists, five "finish" artists, and two apprentices; and five copywriters, people with a high degree of creativeness who specialize in women's and children's apparel, men's apparel and accessories, and home furnishings. In addition, two copywriters are assigned to the basement store and the suburban store. Other journalistic personnel may be found in the public relations and publicity office and in the radio-television division preparing special product demonstrations. Mary Wells Lawrence, a talented copywriter and founder of her own successful agency, started at the retail copy department level.

Those charged with planning a store's advertising must be familiar with all aspects of the market, consumer behavior and attitudes, and such factors as product images and characteristics. The steps normally taken in planning a campaign include these: 1) setting a sales goal or budget, based to a large extent on sales the preceding year; 2) deciding how much advertising is needed; 3) determining which products or services to promote and when; and 4) preparing a day-to-day schedule. Store displays and other merchandising efforts are coordinated. The volume of sales produced during each advertising period is carefully monitored to determine the probable success of the advertising and to help in future planning.

Industrial and Trade Advertising

The public is well aware of consumer goods advertising. We see and hear advertisements almost every moment of the waking day, and often advertising jingles course through our minds even as we sleep. Not so with industrial and trade advertisements, for they are not addressed to the general public. *Industrial* advertising is employed by producers of industrial goods, such as steel, machinery, lubricants, packaging, and office equipment, in order to sell these products to other industries. *Trade* advertising is employed by the producers and distributors of branded and nonbranded consumer goods in order to reach the retailers and wholesalers of consumer goods. They, in turn, sell these goods to their own customers.

The industrial or trade advertising department may employ only one person, the advertising manager, or may employ as many as 400 or more persons. The typical department, however, employs about six. These are likely to include the advertising manager, a secretary, a writer, perhaps an artist, and one or two persons engaged in marketing research, media evaluation, or production work.

The department handles inquiries and prepares catalogues and technical data sheets, direct mail, exhibits, and sales promotion materials such as slide films, movies, and props for sales meetings. It may engage in market research, but most departments obtain market data without charge through business paper research services.

Almost all industrial and trade advertising departments employ outside agencies to handle trade advertisements. More than half the advertising placed in business publications comes from general agencies. Others identify themselves as industrial advertising agencies, although most of them also handle consumer goods advertising. They specialize in industrial, technical, scientific, commercial, and merchandising products and services. A few agencies confine themselves to such fields as financial or pharmaceutical advertising.

The industrial agency is most likely to emphasize the services of account executives who work directly with the client, write copy, and make media-buying analyses and decisions on their own. There is a minimum of creative direction by an overall planning board. Between 20 and 50 percent, or more, of industrial agency income is derived from fees rather than media commissions. This is because commissions are limited, generally amounting to only $150, often even $25 or $50, per insertion. And an agency may be called upon to prepare between 50 and 100 different advertisements each year per $100,000 in annual space expenditures. With costs for research, layout, merchandising, and public relations running high and commissions low, the charging of supplemental fees for these services is a necessity.

National Campaigns

Selecting appropriate media for a particular advertising campaign demands great business acumen and reliance on research studies. If an advertiser decides to use magazines as his vehicle, for example, the class or group, such as women's interest magazines, must be chosen, and then the specific publication, such as *McCall's*, must be chosen. The size of the advertisement and the frequency of publication also must be determined. Similar choices must be made for all the media to be employed.

Rarely has so much depended upon the success of a national marketing, advertising, and promotional campaign as that which heralded the introduction of the all-new, front-wheel-drive, fuel-efficient "K" cars of the Chrysler Corporation in 1980. The company had just suffered its most dismal year economically and psychologically, marked by near-bankruptcy and the need for federal loan guarantees, coupled with a national recession and resulting poor sales. In addition, the company, and others, had been portrayed as builders of "gas guzzlers," products out of step with a market that demanded fuel economy. The success of the "K" car and the success of the corporation were inseparable.

Advertising strategy thus focused upon a "prelaunch" effort designed to create awareness and interest in the cars and also to establish Chrysler's credentials as a marketer of economical, front-wheel-drive products, and upon the designated "launch period" devoted to fixing the divisional names, Dodge Aries and Plymouth Reliant, in the public mind and to accomplish the distinctive marketing objectives assigned to each division.

Television and Sunday newspaper supplements were selected for the preannouncement campaign. Commercials 30 seconds long were run throughout the five-day mini-series, "Shogun," which reached about one-third of all television households and more than 50 percent of the viewing audience. This was followed by the insertion of eight-page, four-column advertisements in *Parade, Sunday, Family Weekly,* and other supplements carried in more than 500 newspapers reaching about 70 percent of all American households. Research disclosed that public awareness of the "K" cars rose from 23 percent to 40 percent during the one-week period.

The two divisions then announced their specific lines of three models each. Strategy called for positioning the Plymouth Reliant as a product with a broad national appeal—a family automobile designed to meet the needs of most new-car buying households as either a primary or secondary car. The Dodge Aries was positioned at the other end of the spectrum as exciting, youthful, and fun to drive—a stylish performance car, as contrasted to a sensible family automobile. The positioning objectives were followed in the creative and media executions for the product lines, with the Reliant featured as a four-door sedan and the Aries as a high-styled two-door vehicle.

Media were selected to correspond with the overall image objectives of each division. The Reliant's commercials were placed on a television schedule making heavy use of news-oriented programs such as "60 Minutes" and "20/20," reflecting the sensible car image. The Aries, on the other hand, was positioned in programming oriented to action-adventure and sophisticated comedies, such as "M*A*S*H," "The Dukes of Hazzard," "Vega$," and "The Tonight Show." The same separation was carried over into the magazine medium. The Reliant appeared in such magazines as *TV Guide, Reader's Digest, Fortune, Scientific American,* and *Money,* while the Aries made use of *Car & Driver, Motor Trend, Road & Track,* and *Hot Rod.*

Image building was reinforced with Chrysler President Lee Iacocca's proclaiming on TV commercials that "Yankee ingenuity" had produced cars with room for "six Americans" designed to "challenge the imports"—"the American way to beat the pump"—and with red, white, and blue as the colors in the advertisements and in materials provided to dealers.

Numerous promotions characterized the public relations aspect of the campaign. In one, the "K" cars were exhibited in front of K-Mart stores throughout the nation in connection with a public drawing that gave away some of the new models.

Few advertising and promotional budgets are this extensive. The procedure, however, is the same in each: the judicious expenditure of an allotted sum in a carefully coordinated campaign involving research, marketing, advertising, and public relations, and using every medium necessary to accomplish the specific objective.

JOB OPPORTUNITIES IN ADVERTISING

Men and women with a wide variety of interests and talents qualify for careers in advertising. As the American Association of Advertising Agencies puts it:

> Whether your career interests lie in marketing or management, design or decimals, psychology or public service, fashion or finance, computers or copywriting, people or products, ideas or imagery, the medium or the message, personnel or photography, communications or commerce, sales or show business, math or music, graphics or global markets, packaging or printing, research or retail promotion, television . . . or you name it . . . the multifaceted world of advertising offers opportunities to get involved in all these areas—and more.

The advertising world is made up of people who have creative, analytical, selling, or management abilities. Successful advertising people are said to be constructive, adaptable, and eternally curious. They must be constructively optimistic because they are called on to originate ideas and to initiate action—to visualize in full operation something that has not yet been started. They must be adaptable because of the infinitely varied problems and the different types of persons they meet almost daily. And they must have an unceasing interest in people and things and the operation of business in general and the industry in particular. They must keep abreast of developments in advertising and remain keen and interested students in many fields throughout their careers.

Imagination, foresight in sensing trends, the ability to reason analytically, a sense of humor, and a sense of form are characteristics of advertising people that are frequently cited. Also emphasized is a broad general education in the liberal arts, obtained either in conjunction with the offerings of schools of communication or commerce or entirely in the humanities, social sciences, or sciences. Generally, professional preparation in advertising opens doors most quickly.

Young persons with talent and ability rise rapidly in the advertising field.

More than one-fifth of the agencies that belong to the American Association of Advertising Agencies (4As) are run by executives who were less than 40 years of age when they stepped up to the chief executive's chair.

Women play important roles in nearly every phase of advertising. Industry reports indicate that about 50 percent of all agency employees are women, and almost one-third of the total are professionals. About one-half of the trainees brought into agencies from university campuses are female. Many women graduates go to work immediately as copywriters for agencies and for department stores and other companies. A number of women sell space and time for the media, with most newspapers employing virtually all women for desk jobs in their classified advertising departments.

A number of national advertising campaigns have been masterminded by women functioning as account executives. The advertising directors of some of the largest department stores are female, and women have also achieved success as media buyers for agencies. More and more women are being made vice presidents of agencies, and a number of very successful women now head firms of their own.

Although surveys indicate that men still hold most of the key positions in the jingle-composing field, a half-dozen or more women have established formidable reputations there. For example, the music production company headed by Susan Hamilton handled "The Burlington Look" and Dr. Pepper's "Most original soft drink." Anne Bryant composed such memorable jingles as Mountain Dew's "Hello, sunshine" and "Reach for the sun," and "Don't say beer, say bull" for Schlitz. Ginny Redington, in the $100,000 per year income bracket, scored with McDonald's "You, you're the one."

Minorities are gaining increased footholds in advertising and allied industries. One survey revealed that minorities accounted for about 7 percent of professional positions and about 20 percent of nonprofessional jobs in the 4As agencies. The board of directors of the 4As, stating that "it is vital to seek out, recognize, and employ the best talents available wherever they may be found," has supported a successful summer internship program for minority professional candidates as well as basic courses for creative people and government-connected programs for nonprofessionals.

Numerous career opportunities are also available in other advertising and related areas, cited as follows with their annual estimated volume of business: *direct marketing,* which evolved from direct mail, $82 billion (outranked only by television and newspapers); *outdoor* (billboards), $500 million; *business papers,* $1.5 billion; *specialty,* $2.4 billion; *sales promotion,* $40 billion; *trade shows,* $4 billion; *premium and incentive,* $7.5 billion; and *point-of-purchase,* $4 billion.

Rewards, both financial and psychological, come quickly for those who are imaginative and quick-thinking, can work under pressure, and have a bent for solving problems. About one-half of the people in a typical agency, for example, are professionals or executives. The sharing of ownership and profits with these key employees is practiced more often in advertising agencies than in most businesses.

Salaries

Because of inflation as well as increased business, salaries of those employed by advertising agencies have increased considerably in recent years. A survey by Rubel & Humphrey, Inc., a management consultant firm headquartered in Northfield, Illinois, revealed that salaries paid to agency employees increased 16.4 percent from 1975 to 1978. During this period smaller agencies increased salaries substantially more than the inflation rate, while larger agencies lagged behind. Basically, however, the salary level of agencies in metropolitan areas such as New York, Chicago, Los Angeles, Detroit, and Boston is about 10 to 15 percent higher than the level of agencies in smaller cities. In both metropolitan and nonmetropolitan areas, respectively, salaries vary little from one section of the country to the other. One fact, however, is evident: The higher the gross billings by an agency, the greater the salary scale.

As their skills and experience increase, advertising specialists generally find that they possess knowledge for which there is great demand. In moving from one agency to another, often taking accounts with them, they naturally move into higher pay brackets. A somewhat similar promotion situation is true in media and company advertising departments. The top advertising executives of newspapers, magazines, other media, and client companies generally earn about two-thirds of what their counterparts with the agencies receive. Other factors, however, such as security and fringe benefits, often more than make up for the lower salaries.

In the general magazine field, advertising directors earn from $15,000 to $60,000, depending mostly on circulation. Business paper advertising managers earn from $15,000 to $40,000. Advertising managers for newspapers are paid about the same. Commercial managers for radio and television stations earn from $10,000 to $35,000.

Beginning salaries in both print and broadcast media and in company advertising departments for college graduates average $9,500, whereas those possessing master's degrees are paid average starting salaries in excess of $11,000. Once they have proved their worth, qualified advertising people generally move upward rapidly.

AVERAGE AGENCY SALARIES, 1978

(in thousands of dollars)

The survey by Rubel & Humphrey shows the average salaries paid in 1978 by all-size agencies combined. These figures do not include bonus or stock option plans, which are a part of most compensation programs.

Work Function	High	Low	Average
ADMINISTRATIVE			
Chief executive officer	$107.5	$46.7	$69.7
Chief financial officer	57.1	25.2	39.3
Chief accounting officer	28.4	13.9	19.5
CONTACT			
Account supervisor/group head	57.3	23.1	35.3
Account executive	36.1	12.4	22.7
Copy/contact account executive	31.0	13.4	20.4
Public relations director	35.5	18.8	26.4
Public relations account executive	25.5	12.3	17.4
CREATIVE			
Creative director	64.2	27.5	41.5
Executive art director	43.8	21.7	31.4
Art director	32.0	12.8	21.4
Layout artist, senior	21.7	11.1	16.0
Layout artist, junior	15.0	8.1	11.0
Copy chief/copy supervisor	41.8	19.1	28.3
Copywriter, senior	31.0	14.4	20.9
Copywriter, junior	17.8	9.3	12.8
BROADCAST			
Production manager/producer	32.6	15.4	22.6
Associate producer	22.6	10.7	15.3
Business manager	20.3	11.5	14.7
MEDIA AND RESEARCH			
Media director	39.3	18.3	26.5
Media supervisor	25.5	12.0	18.4
Media buyer—space/time	18.1	9.0	12.7
Research director	41.6	20.4	29.3
Research analyst	20.0	11.0	15.0
PRINT PRODUCTION AND TRAFFIC			
Production manager	26.9	13.2	19.1
Production assistant	17.3	9.1	12.0
Traffic manager	16.2	8.6	12.0

Source: Courtesy of Rubel & Humphrey, Inc.

Chapter 16

PUBLIC RELATIONS

A NEW FIELD

Public relations is one of the newest and fastest growing fields in communications. It is estimated that as many as 100,000 persons are employed in various kinds of public relations jobs, some at high levels of management. More are being attracted every year from the mass media of communications and from among graduates of journalism schools. As our society becomes more complex—and the need for effective relationships between our numerous institutions and the individuals they serve becomes more essential—the field of public relations is likely to continue its steady growth.

The term *public relations* means many different things to different people. It has been used, and abused, to include a wide range of activities from legitimate attempts at persuasive communication to the bribery efforts of unscrupulous lobbyists. In its best and narrowest sense, public relations is *the planned and organized effort of a company or institution to establish mutually beneficial relationships with its various publics.* Publics, in turn, may be defined as the various groups of people who are affected by—or who can affect—the operations of a particular firm or institution. Each public is bound together by a common interest vis-à-vis the organization.

Thus, for a manufacturing corporation, such publics would include employees, stockholders, citizens of the community in which it is located, dealers who handle its products, and the ultimate purchasers or users of its products. Similarly, for a nonprofit hospital, these publics may include its professional staff, its employees, its patients and their families, the citizens in the community in which it is located, and its financial supporters.

Although many persons tend to consider public relations and publicity as synonymous terms, it should be obvious that more than effective communication is required to initiate and execute a sound public relations program. Effective public relations programming begins with the establishment of fair and equitable policies by management. The essence of these policies must be explained to those who work for the organization or who represent it, and to the interested publics, in varying forms of communication. In short, communication must explain the policies and actions of management, but the policies and actions must support the words. Finally, the responses of these publics to what the organization says and does must be reflected back to management so that—with recommendations—appropriate adjustments may be made in policies and operations.

Public relations has been defined by *PR News,* a weekly newsletter in the field, as "the management function which evaluates public attitudes, identifies the policies and procedures of an individual or an organization with the public interest, and plans and executes a program of action to earn public understanding and acceptance." In recent years, managements have tended to look toward their public relations executives for a continuing analysis of social, economic, and political trends that may have an impact on the operations of the business or institution so that future problems may be avoided or alleviated. In this capacity, the public relations people may be required to evaluate developments in such areas as consumer activism, the environmental protection movement, and government responses to minority problems.

James F. Fox, a New York public relations consultant and a past national president of the Public Relations Society of America, says that the public relations executive in business also must "lay claim to the title of company futurist, mastering the calculus of long-range forecasting: economic indicators, technological assessment, social indicators, political trend analysis." He adds: "We must be prepared to alert management to the early-warning signs of social change and advise how to cope with them."

In such areas, public relations practice—at its best—affords genuine opportunities for meaningful service to society. As this function develops more fully, the value of public relations people to management and the social significance of the public relations function will offer even greater opportunities to those who wish to follow a public relations career.

The student who desires a successful career in corporate public relations (the largest area of public relations practice) or who desires to be a member of a public relations agency serving business clients should be committed to the private enterprise system. But, beyond this, the proper exercise of the public relations function in corporate management offers opportunities for improving the profit system and making it work more effectively to serve society. Thus, careers in corporate public relations may provide compensations for idealistic persons beyond the relatively good salaries and fringe benefits.

In other areas of public relations work—for nonprofit organizations (health and welfare groups, educational institutions, etc.) and for government—similar personal, psychological compensations also will be experienced among those public relations practitioners who are dedicated to social service.

HISTORY AND DEVELOPMENT

The roots of public relations go far back into history. Caesar's *Commentaries,* the four Gospels of the New Testament, and *The Federalist* are examples of persuasive communications long before the public relations concept was crystalized. In times nearer our own, we have had the nineteenth-century press agents who achieved a less than respectable reputation for persuading—or duping—the masses. But if contemporary practice is the offspring of nineteenth-century press agentry, the child is quite unlike its parent.

The modern public relations concept was born shortly after the turn of the century when Ivy Ledbetter Lee, a newspaperman who had covered business news, conceived the idea of setting up a Business News Bureau to disseminate information to the press on behalf of business corporations. It was Lee's belief that much of the public's antipathy toward business at that time—an antipathy stirred up and exploited by the muckrakers—resulted from the fact that most businesses operated in complete secrecy and most business people would not discuss their policies or operations with the public. Lee offered to provide a service that would enable business people to address the public. His idea proved attractive. Among Lee's early clients were the Pennsylvania Railroad (then one of America's greatest corporations, known as the "standard railroad of the world"), the anthracite coal mine operators who were involved in labor strife, and later, John D. Rockefeller, Jr.

A second dimension was added to the public relations concept during World War I, when the Committee on Public Information was established by the federal government under George Creel. The committee conducted a massive and successful publicity campaign to mobilize the American public behind the war effort. The values of such massive communications efforts were impressed upon those who worked with Creel, and some of them became pioneers in the establishment of public relations agencies designed to conduct similar campaigns for private clients. They included Edward L. Bernays, who subsequently became the author of a classic but unfortunately named book on public relations, *The Engineering of Consent,* and Carl Byoir, who established what became one of the largest and most successful public relations agencies in the world, Carl Byoir and Associates.

Bernays is credited with adding another dimension to the public relations concept: the counseling function. He theorized aptly that if the public relations practitioner has the responsibility for explaining management's policies and actions to the public, then the public relations specialist also should have a voice in advising management on the formulation of its policies and the development of programs affecting the public. Although some managements still have not recognized this aspect of public relations practice, in many of America's largest corporations today the public relations executive is a vice-president who participates in boardroom discussions and has strong influence on the development of management policy.

Still another dimension was added to the public relations concept in the 1930s with the development of modern public opinion and marketing survey techniques by George Gallup, Elmo Roper, Claude Robinson, and others. This development provided a tool by which public relations counselors and executives could evaluate public attitudes quantitatively. Thus, instead of simply relying upon their own estimates of public opinion, they could achieve some degree of objective measurement. Public opinion measuring techniques still are far from perfect and their results subject to error, but they have become more reliable as the result of refinements over the years. Public attitude surveys have become a standard tool of public relations practitioners.

Another refinement in public relations practice in recent years, as has been mentioned earlier, is the idea that the public relations executive should be the monitor of social, economic, and political trends that may

Public relations people help to arrange press conferences and meetings like this one, in which insurance executives are briefed on developments affecting them in the federal government. (Courtesy of Insurance Information Institute, New York.)

affect the business or institution he or she represents. Thus, contemporary public relations, when practiced at the optimal level, involves three general responsibilities:

1. Continuing analysis of the social, economic, political, and human environment in which the business or institution operates in order to anticipate developments and provide a basis for advice to management;
2. Counseling management on the development of policies and operations to develop sound relationships with the various pertinent publics; and
3. Communicating essential information about managerial policies and practices, products, and services to the concerned publics.

In short, the public relations function, effectively implemented, helps correlate the private interests of management with the overriding public interest to facilitate the growth and development of the particular institution. No public relations program can expect to succeed if the private interests of the business or the institution run counter to the public interest. Only where the private and the public interests are effectively correlated can an organization expect to have a healthy environment in which to operate. As an adviser and an expert communicator, both to management and to its publics, the public relations executive helps to bring about this correlation.

PUBLIC RELATIONS AND THE MASS MEDIA

Public relations at its best has a unique relationship with the mass media. The communicative function of public relations practice has become an inextricable part of the mass communications network in the United States. It is not too extreme to state that, without the contributions of tens of thousands of public relations communicators, our media would not be nearly as accurate or as well rounded in content as they are.

Consider, for example, that no newspaper—not even the New York *Times* or the *Wall Street Journal*—nor any magazine, wire service, or broadcasting station or network can afford to support a staff large enough to have experts in every field of human endeavor. Even the largest media rely upon the public relations persons representing companies and institutions to provide the expertise, background, and the explanations and translations from the language of the experts to the language of the lay person that enable journalists to write about complex and arcane subjects with understanding. The smaller papers and the smaller news staffs of the broadcast media are even more dependent on public relations people for this kind of help. In one sense, then, public relations practitioners provide a necessary link between the media and many specialized areas of activity in our society, a link that the media usually could not afford to provide for themselves.

Inasmuch as public relations people also are responsible for presenting their companies and institutions in the best possible posture, the question may arise as to whether this situation leads to abuse of the channels of public communication. The answer is that, although admittedly it is possible for public relations people occasionally to take advantage of the media, over the long range it is imperative that public relations communicators establish their integrity with the media people. Public relations people cannot risk ending their usefulness by duping journalists. Most journalists recognize this fact, and over a period of time come to know which public relations people can be trusted. Thus, mutually honest and beneficial relationships can be developed.

Although public relations people are dependent to a considerable extent on the mass media in their communications activities, public relations communications are not limited to the mass media. Public relations staffs and counselors develop many specialized (or controlled) forms of communication, such as printed booklets or periodicals; exhibits; and motion pictures, slide films, and other audiovisual presentations aimed at specific publics. In this area also, public relations communicators are influenced not only by their innate sense of honesty but also by the knowledge that their long-range effectiveness must be built on a reputation for integrity.

JOB OPPORTUNITIES IN PUBLIC RELATIONS

Although many firms and some other types of institutions established their public relations departments many years ago (notably the American Telephone and Telegraph Company, which early recognized the importance of good public relations for a regulated monopoly), the major expansion in public relations has occurred since World War II. The initial thrust of this expansion occurred in business and industry, but it was followed by an expansion of organized public relations programs in many other kinds of institutions: public school systems and universities, hospitals, nonprofit health and welfare organizations, government agencies, business and professional associations, and even the military. Although federal law prohibits the employment of public relations people by United States government agencies, essentially the same function is carried out by "information officers." The army, navy, and air force all have designated public information officers who have been especially trained in military public relations policy at service schools or who have been sent for the same purpose to universities with good public relations programs, such as those whose public relations sequences have been accredited by the Accrediting Council on Education in Journalism and Mass Communications.

The largest subgroup of practitioners is engaged in public relations on behalf of business corporations. In 1980, Jack O'Dwyer, publisher of

O'Dwyer's Newsletter in New York City, surveyed 2375 large companies and 300 large trade associations. The results, published in *O'Dwyer's 1980 Directory of Corporate Communications,* disclosed that 80 percent of the companies had departments bearing such titles as public relations, corporate communications, communications, advertising and public relations, public affairs, corporate relations, public information, and external relations.

About one-third of the companies retained external public relations counseling firms; some relied on both internal and external public relations people.

Many thousands of public relations practitioners are employed in the 4,000 national trade and professional associations, as well as in some of the 40,000 state, regional, and local associations of the same type. Although many associations have small public relations departments with relatively few people, some have extensive staffs with budgets of several million dollars.

Most public relations people are full-time employees of the institutions they represent. But, since the end of World War II there has been a mushrooming growth of public relations counseling firms. Like an advertising agency, a public relations counseling firm may serve a number of clients on a fee-plus-expenses basis. Such counseling firms range in size from those with only one practitioner and a secretary to a complex organization such as Hill and Knowlton or Carl Byoir and Associates, with up to 700 or 800 employees and a variety of departments.

The public relations counseling firm often is in a position to offer a more objective point of view about a company's or an institution's problems than the internal public relations department. The counseling firm also is in a position to provide extra staff to supplement the internal staff in periods of intensified activity or to provide experts in certain fields that may not be represented on the internal staff. Scott M. Cutlip and Allen H. Center, in the 1978 edition of the textbook, *Effective Public Relations,* estimated that there are more than 1700 public relations counseling firms in the United States. But the 1980 edition of O'Dwyer's directory lists only 1010, presumably the largest or better known.

In large counseling organizations, separate departments may specialize in newspaper publicity, placing clients on television talk shows, developing and placing magazine articles, producing audiovisual presentations, developing special programs intended for educators and educational institutions, and so on. A similar pattern prevails in respect to in-house public relations staffs. Some smaller business firms and institutions may have only a two-person public relations department. Others, such as General Motors and the U.S. Steel Corporation, may have scores or hundreds of people in numerous subdepartments specializing in different areas of public relations or in differing communications techniques.

When one analyzes the overall situation it becomes clear that, broadly speaking, there are two types of public relations people: *generalists* and *specialists*. The generalists, a definite minority, are usually at the executive or managerial level. They are responsible for analyzing problem situations, developing programs to resolve these situations, participating in management-level discussions of policy, and supervising the implementation of programs. The specialists, much greater in number, are the experts in various techniques of communication and in the specialized areas of public relations practice. These men and women work under the direction of the generalists. The specialists write news releases, speeches, and booklets; answer inquiries from the press; arrange press conferences and special events; develop audiovisual presentations and educational materials; and so on. Most public relations careers start at the specialist level—for example, in publicity writing or magazine editing. After the individual gains experience and shows promise of generalist potential, he or she moves to a higher level.

Overall, the growth of public relations jobs since World War II has been spectacular. Prospects for well-trained and competent public relations people continue to be promising. As more and more companies and institutions compete for public understanding and support, as more and more managements recognize the values of—and the utter necessity for—effective public relations efforts, the demand for competent practitioners will continue. A study in 1980 by the "Future Committee" at the University of Missouri, Columbia, predicted that public relations will be the fastest-growing management function in American business during the 1980s. As a matter of fact, today there are more top-level public relations opportunities than there are experienced and competent persons to fill them.

Typical Public Relations Careers

Consider a male university journalism or communications graduate who goes to work for a public utility, such as the telephone company, after preparing himself for publishing, broadcasting, public relations, or advertising work. He joins the staff of one of the AT&T operating companies, perhaps as a member of the three-person magazine staff. His next assignment is in the company news bureau, preparing stories for the hometown newspapers in cities where the company operates—stories about personnel changes and promotions in the local telephone office, about the retirements of employees, about additional services or improvements in long-distance dialing, and so on. He is working at the "tool" level, using his journalistic skills. He is not making policy, although he attends staff meetings of the public relations department at which policy is discussed. He is being indoctrinated in company policy and procedures, and he is beginning to understand the total nature of the company operation.

Next the graduate may be sent to the community relations section, where he is more of an "idea" man. He consults with the local office manager in a town where customer attitude survey studies have shown dissatisfaction with service or misunderstanding of billing procedures and rates. They decide that they need better employee communication and arrange group meetings; they check to see if local managers are making effective use of company films that can be shown to civic groups; they plan an institutional advertising series in the local newspaper that will explain the company's costs and needs for revenue if the town is to have the best possible telephone service; and they plan other measures by which the firm can show responsiveness to community attitudes.

Next the young communicator returns to employee relations work, perhaps as editor of a magazine or as an information specialist who develops manuals and programs for the use of supervisory management. He attends employee meetings as a consultant, and suggests ways in which employees may become more interested in the company's financial problems. He may help run orientation sessions for higher supervisory personnel in which the public relations objectives of the company are explained. Why should a local manager spend time working with the local newspaper editor? How should he go about becoming a news source? Why should the manager belong to the Rotary or Kiwanis Club? The employee relations specialist tries to relate the total public relations program to the personal interests of employees.

There are other assignments. If he has had advertising experience, the public relations man may be placed in charge of institutional advertising. If he has had training in sampling procedures and statistical methods, he may take charge of a customer attitude survey and its interpretation. Or he may head the audiovisual section and handle films, slides, and pictures. He may return to the news bureau as director in charge of the major company stories. He may edit the company's annual report for a time and do shareholder relations work. He may become a policy adviser, preparing speeches for the company president, writing a manual explaining the public relations policies of the company, or working with various executives on long-range planning. He may in time become assistant director of the department. And finally he may become vice-president in charge of public relations, a member of the company's management group. Or, he may move on to the central public relations staff of the parent company, American Telephone and Telegraph. Or, he will remain in a median-level assignment, rounding out a comfortable and satisfying career as a telephone company officer who serves the community and other employees in a specialized staff role demanding technical journalistic skills and policymaking ability.

Another example might be a young female journalism graduate who is not certain whether she wishes to do newspaper work, but who has acquired an understanding of journalistic routines through her classes and summer work on a newspaper. She is more interested in magazine writing

A "highway booby trap" survey is conducted as part of a public service project sponsored by the Insurance Information Institute. Public relations people are involved in many projects of this nature. (Courtesy of Insurance Information Institute, New York.)

and layout and begins as assistant editor of a company employee magazine. One year later she becomes editor. Later she marries and decides to relinquish full-time employment but still work professionally. She finds that the local hospital needs someone to edit its staff bulletin, handle the printing of occasional brochures and reports, and represent the hospital with the local media when newsworthy events take place. She is able to advise the hospital administrator on both printing matters and news policy and develops interesting stories of value both to the hospital and to readers.

A third example might be a five-year veteran of metropolitan newspaper work who is offered a position with a major automotive company. She starts in information work, moves on to employee relations, and becomes assistant director for a major branch plant. Three years later she is transferred to Detroit, where she becomes assistant manager in the company's public relations department. She decides she would prefer to enter a public relations counseling firm, and becomes an account executive for one specializing in automotive clients. At age 40 she is a vice-president of the firm and receives as high a salary as a major executive of a large metropolitan daily. In a counseling firm she is freer to carry out her own plans and ideas than in a company staff. But she also needs to be more daring, for she has less personal security.

These are only three examples of an infinite variety of career possibilities in public relations. It is hardly necessary to point out that the highest salaries are earned by the generalists who reach the executive level and who are capable of analyzing problems, advising on policy, planning programs, and administering large staffs and budgets.

Qualifications

There was a time when most public relations people were hired away from the communications media. Many of the top-level executives in public relations today began their careers as journalists. Their progress and development as public relations people was the result of on-the-job training, usually on a trial-and-error basis. That they succeeded is a tribute to their intelligence, their adaptability, and their willingness to keep learning throughout their careers. This generation is now retiring. Although many employers still look to the media for public relations recruits, more and more employers are looking to young college graduates to fill beginning jobs in public relations departments.

Formal education for public relations practice dates from 1923, when Edward L. Bernays taught the first course in public relations at New York University. Since 1945, there has been a substantial proliferation of public relations courses and programs at both the undergraduate and the graduate levels. Dr. Ray Eldon Hiebert of the University of Maryland made a study of public relations education under a grant from the Foundation for Public Relations Research and Education in 1970. He found that, in all, 303 institutions provided some education in public relations. By 1975, according to another foundation-sponsored survey by Dr. Albert Walker of Northern Illinois University, this figure had grown to 320. Of the 144 institutions that responded to Dr. Walker's survey, nearly one-half offered an undergraduate sequence or a major program in public relations, and about 18 percent offered graduate sequences or major fields of concentration in public relations. Twenty-five undergraduate programs in public relations had been accredited by the Accrediting Council on Education in Journalism and Mass Communications, the official accrediting agency, by 1980.

Along with the graduates of public relations programs, many other graduates of journalism and communications schools, as well as those from liberal arts programs, are being employed in beginning public relations jobs—provided they have the vital ability to write and speak well. One of the few things that experienced public relations practitioners agree upon is that the primary qualification for anyone wishing to succeed in the field is the ability to articulate: to write clearly and with facility, and to express oneself well orally. No one can hope to succeed in public relations without the ability to use words effectively. Words are the basic tool of the public relations practitioner. To be successful, he or she must have an intimate understanding of language.

In addition, there is need for the ability to empathize with other people, to anticipate and understand their points of view. In the managerial structure, the public relations executive bears the responsibility for estimating how a particular policy or action on the part of management will be greeted by the public or publics affected. More than intuitive ability is necessary here. Whatever inherent abilities public relations practitioners may have in this area of human understanding should be supplemented by background education in the social sciences, particularly sociology and psychology, so that their estimates of human reactions will be more than mere guesses. Of course, in many situations, when the magnitude of the problem justifies such research, public relations practitioners will supplement their own interpretation of the situation, however well-equipped they may be to make an assessment, with formal surveys of public opinion and attitudes.

Salaries

In 1979 a survey by the *PR Reporter,* a weekly newsletter, showed that the typical public relations practitioner who had reached the executive level earned $31,000 annually. This median salary figure is misleading, however, inasmuch as salaries for these practitioners ranged from $10,400 to $350,000. This part of the survey dealt with public relations vice-presidents or department directors, or the equivalent, in consumer product companies, conglomerates and other industrials, utilities, banks and insurance companies, trade and professional associations, nonprofit organizations, and hospitals.

For the presidents or owners and principals of public relations counseling firms, the survey found the median salary to be $41,000, with a salary range of $18,000 to $350,000. Counseling firms tend to pay higher salaries than do other employers of public relations practitioners. One must take into account, however, that counseling firms offer less stability in employment and that frequently the fringe benefits for people in the counseling business are less extensive than in corporations.

Obviously, the new college graduate will not begin a public relations job at these salary levels. In 1980, the graduate was more likely to be offered between $12,000 and $16,000, depending upon the locale and the type of job. Salaries are likely to be higher in large cities such as New York, Washington, Chicago, and Los Angeles, and lower in smaller cities. A job with a profit-making corporation, an industry association, or a counseling firm is likely to pay a higher salary than a job with a nonprofit educational institution, a government agency, a hospital, or a charitable institution. Nevertheless, the kind of rounded experience that one gains in some of these lower-paying jobs can be valuable later.

PROFESSIONALISM IN PUBLIC RELATIONS

Among public relations practitioners there are considerable differences of opinion as to whether public relations is simply a craft or a developing profession. Certainly, at its present level, public relations does not qualify as a profession in the same sense that medicine and the law are considered to be professions. Public relations does not have prescribed standards of educational preparation, a mandatory internship, or barriers to admission into the field.

On the other hand, many persons in the field believe that the practice can become a profession and are working toward that end. Much of this effort has been conducted through the Public Relations Society of America (PRSA), which has more than 9000 members. To become an accredited member of the society, a person must have at least five years of experience in public relations practice or teaching, must have two sponsors who will testify as to integrity and ability, and must pass written and oral examinations. The PRSA accreditation program, instituted in 1965, has been a major step toward professionalizing the field. To be an associate member of PRSA, one need have only one year's experience in the field. For students who have just earned their college degrees and who have been members of the Public Relations Student Society of America, there is a preassociate form of membership in PRSA. The student organization, sponsored by PRSA, has chapters in more than 70 colleges and universities.

Additionally, both PRSA and the public relations division of the Association for Education in Journalism have worked to improve and standardize the curricula for programs of public relations studies at the bachelor's and master's levels. The society has developed a code of professional standards for the practice of public relations. Although parts of the code are phrased in general terms, such as requiring public relations practitioners to adhere to generally accepted standards of accuracy, truth, and good taste, other clauses and interpretive supplements deal with specifics. For example, a PRSA member cannot represent conflicting or competing interests without the express consent of both parties, nor can the member reveal the confidences of present or former clients or employers.

The Foundation for Public Relations Research and Education, which was established in 1956 with the support of the society but is now independent, seeks to advance professionalism through grants for research studies, publications, and sponsorship of a quarterly, the *Public Relations Review*. Under a grant from the foundation, Morton J. Simon, a lawyer who specializes in the law as it affects public relations and advertising, has published a book, *Public Relations Law*. It correlates for the reference of the public relations practitioner all aspects of the general laws, as well as regulations of the Securities and Exchange Commission and other government agencies, that affect the conduct of public relations practice. It is an example of the growing body of specialized knowledge pertaining to public relations practice.

Another organization for public relations practitioners is the International Association of Business Communicators, which by 1981 had 5000 members. IABC describes itself as "a professional organization for writers, editors, audio-visual specialists, managers, and other business and organizational communicators."

Thus, although public relations still suffers some stigma as a result of the occasional misuse of the term, it has come a long way from the time when the public relations practitioner was scorned by colleagues in journalism as a "publicity hound" or a "flack." Nevertheless, public relations still has a long way to go before it achieves the distinction of becoming a genuine profession. Today, at the very least, it is an essential link in the nation's mass communications network.

While public relations practice originated in the United States, it has spread to many other countries that encourage a free-enterprise economy. The art, or profession, is well developed in the Western European countries, and it is growing rapidly in Latin America, Africa, the Near East, and the Far East.

The International Public Relations Association (IPRA), an individual membership society for public relations professionals with international interests, was organized in 1955. IPRA now has more than 700 members in about 50 nations. Every third year it sponsors a World Congress of Public Relations, which attracts 60,000 or more practitioners.

This worldwide interest in the developing public relations profession is an encouraging sign for the future. The burgeoning of public relations, especially in countries where people may speak freely, is an encouraging indication of a bright future for all who excel in the practice.

Part Five

RESEARCH AND EDUCATION

Chapter 17

MASS COMMUNICATIONS RESEARCH

THE NEED FOR RESEARCH

The enormous growth of the various forms of mass communication in the twentieth century has resulted in an increasing need for better knowledge of the processes and effects of mass communication. The complex mass media system has produced a need for research not only among practicing communicators, but also among policymakers, consumers, and various social groups. Many of the problems and criticisms to be discussed in Part Six, for example, have led to research questions. Consequently, a core of specially trained research persons has risen to search for and supply this knowledge.

Much of the mass communications research conducted today attempts to answer the questions of broadcasters, advertising specialists, and other communicators. The magazine or newspaper editor, for example, needs to know things such as: How many persons read my publication? (Typically, each copy has several readers so the total audience may be something quite different from the total circulation.) What kinds of persons read my publication? (The New York *Times,* for example, is intended for a different audience from that of the *Daily News;* the audience of *True Story* is almost completely different from that of *Boys' Life*.) How am I doing as an editor? Am I printing the kinds of things my audience wants to read about? Are my stories easy to read or hard to read? How can I improve the content of my publication? How can I improve the presentation of this content in terms of layout and typography?

There was a time when an editor could know many of these things by personal contact with the people in the community or area. By informal means, through experience, the editor developed a rough idea of the composition of the audience and how well the publication was liked. This unsystematic, informal, intuitive method no longer is adequate for the modern communicator for several reasons:

1. *The increasing number of communications media.* In the present-day community, the average person has access to many media—local and out-of-town newspapers, a number of television and radio stations, cable, and hundreds of magazines, books, and films.

2. *Increasing competition among the media for the attention of the public.* Since no individual has enough time to read or listen to all the media, or even to pay attention to all the output of just one medium, this means a small fraction of the available output will be selected, and the rest ignored. This leads to intense competition among the different media to capture as much of the public's time and attention as possible—obviously, the newspaper or magazine or station that succeeds in satisfying the needs of the public, and whose messages are interesting and easy to absorb, will get a good share of public attention. Those that do not succeed in doing this will eventually fall by the wayside.

3. *The increasing number of people in the audience.* An editor or broadcaster reaches from several thousand to several million readers, viewers, or listeners, and the tendency is constantly toward reaching larger audiences. No communicator can possibly have personal contact with everyone in the audience and knowledge of all their varying needs, likes, dislikes, and opinions.

4. *The changing tastes of the public.* People are becoming better educated and more sophisticated; they travel more, know more about the rest of the world, and are constantly developing broader interests through exposure to more communications from outside their immediate environment. Any communicator's audience is in a state of continuous turnover and interest change. Decisions cannot be based on what was known to be true ten years or five years or even one year ago.

These are all good reasons why the effective communicator—whether advertising copywriter, editor, or broadcaster—can no longer rely on hunches and intuition alone to capture and hold the attention of the public. As Harry Henry says in *Motivation Research:* "There are examples, of course, of 'hunch-merchants' who hit on successful ideas with enormous success, and finish up as classic case histories. But no case histories are written up of the 99 equally self-confident but not so lucky venturers whose only spell of glory is in a brief trip to the bankruptcy courts."

In the face of all these changing requirements, then, just how do modern mass communicators get the precise information they need to make their media successful? They turn to communications research, a specialty that has grown up in the past three decades, to help answer some of the questions they do not have the time or training to answer for themselves. The communications researcher is just one member of the team of writers, editors, artists, advertising persons, and others working together to help a medium do its job, which is to transmit information, opinion, and entertainment to a mass public. Or the researcher may be a scholar in a university setting whose main objective is that of adding to our general knowledge of the communication process.

Modern communicators also face criticism and questions about their role in society. For example, do TV commercials in children's programs mislead or take advantage of young viewers? Is there any relationship between television programming and violent behavior? Do news media distort the news? Such questions often lead to research that is as important as that of describing the changing tastes of the public. Thus, although the media need research telling them how to compete with one another and how to serve their audiences, they also need answers to broader questions about their role in modern society. Much research of this type is being conducted in schools of journalism and mass communications.

WHAT IS COMMUNICATIONS RESEARCH?

A broad definition of research is simply "careful investigation," or a diligent inquiry into any subject. This broad term would include almost any kind of study—the literary scholar who reads all of Shakespeare's works, the biographer who finds out all he can about a famous woman, or the historian who compiles a history of American newspapers.

Mass communications research, however, has taken on a somewhat more specialized meaning. First of all, it is usually (though not always) considered *behavioral* research—the study of human beings (rather than inanimate or nonhuman objects). It is a branch of the behavioral sciences, which include psychology, sociology, and anthropology.

Thus we see that it is also *interdisciplinary* research; that is, it borrows the tools and knowledge of various other fields of study that will help in the understanding of mass communications problems. It does not confine itself to any particular point of view, theory, or subject matter. It may borrow from linguistics, general semantics, philosophy, economics, or any other discipline that might help communications effectiveness.

It is *scientific* research, since it uses scientific methodology in solving communications problems. As in any science, its intent is to explain, predict, and control. In achieving this end, its methods must be objective (as opposed to subjective) and systematic (as opposed to unsystematic). Although most mass communications research is done on specific problems, the goal—as in any scientific field—is to formulate general principles and theories that can bring about more effective communication. Being scientific, it is, of course, also *quantitative* research. Random sampling methods, the laws of probability, and mathematical statistical techniques all help to make more precise and meaningful the findings from any particular investigation.

It is generally *primary* research rather than secondary. That is, the mass communications researcher customarily gathers new and original information rather than relying on printed source material. This is not always the case, however, since one may, for example, have to consult year-by-year statistical figures gathered in the past by other researchers, in order to spot a trend over a period of time.

Of course, the subject matter of communications research is communication. More specifically, it is concerned with mass communication, the communication behavior of large numbers of people, particularly those who make up the audiences for the different media. Other groups may be studied, too, of course—newspaper reporters, news sources, magazine editors, or public relations specialists, for example. In order to understand the behavior of groups, however, it is usually necessary first to understand individual behavior.

To summarize the definition of mass communications research: It is the scientific study of the mass communication behavior of human beings, usually in current situations requiring the gathering of primary quantitative information. It also includes the study of the communicators, their media, and the content of their message.

This is not the only definition that might be legitimately applied. It leaves out other kinds of important research being done in the field of journalism and mass communications (historical, literary, biographical, legal, economic, international aspects), which are discussed in Chapter 18 on mass communications education; editorial research of the "fact-checking" variety; and the creative synthesizing of ideas and research findings. It also includes some topics that might be claimed by other disciplines. It is, however, a reasonably comprehensive definition of the specialized type of mass communications research that has grown up in recent decades.

AREAS OF COMMUNICATIONS RESEARCH

The volume of communications research has grown in recent years as an increasing number of scholars have been attracted to the subject. Two trends have accompanied that growth. The breadth of communications research has grown as scholars with varying interests have delved into different areas—those of political communication, consumer interests, and media economics, for example. And the depth of communications research has increased as scholars taking different avenues have tended to specialize within one area or another. Consequently, communications research could be divided in a number of ways. One approach is to categorize research within the four aspects of the communication process described in Chapter 1: the communicator, the message, the channel, and the audience. Extensive research has been done in each area.

Communicator Research

One way to improve communication is to find out what kinds of people are best suited for the role of communicator and what factors affect communicator performance. We need to know the essential characteristics of good reporters, editors, and advertising people, among others, so that the proper training may be offered to future professionals. Even the most professional communicator, however, may be unaware of some of the factors affecting performance. In one study it was found that stories resulting from assignments by editors were more accurate than those originated by the reporter or stemming from coverage of general meetings. Another study disclosed that news personnel with "supportive images" (more establishment-oriented than others) reported so-called good news more accurately than bad news, whereas those with critical images of society did a more accurate job on bad news. Communicators increasingly are using sophisticated tools such as the computer to analyze complex problems. How will journalists adjust to the new demands placed upon them in the era of cable? How are reporters performing with the new technologies? These are questions for communicator research studies.

Message Research

The effects of different forms of the same message may be compared through variations in style, length, degree of difficulty, and the like, with attention paid to comprehensibility, interest, and attention value. We often vary our personal conversations as to complexity and word usage in terms of some determination of the sophistication of the intended receiver. With scientific content analysis we can easily determine the relative degree of difficulty of any message, and we can make inferences about the intent of the communicator as well.

Channel Research

The channel through which a message is transmitted is closely related to the effectiveness of the message. This is due in part to the differing characteristics of the various media, which perform the functions of informing, interpreting, entertaining, and selling differently from one another. By their character, content, style, and geographic coverage, media, to a great extent, are able to select their desired audiences. Advertisers are especially interested in determining which media can best deliver their messages and in knowing something about the people who comprise the potential audience of a medium. In face-to-face communication, we often use facial expressions—a smile, for example—to much greater advantage than a flow of pleasant words.

Audience Research

The majority of communications research ultimately is concerned with mass media audiences. Communicators need to know the behavior, interests, tastes, attitudes, and opinions of the people whom they seek to reach. Advertisers must know the number and description of people in a medium's audience so that they may reach the right kind of person for their products. For example, a baby food manufacturer may want to learn which of two magazines with equal circulations has the greater number of young parents. Publishers and editors require audience information so that they may select editorial content that fits their readers' needs. The reading interests of young newspaper readers are quite different from those of older readers. More recently, researchers have gone beyond simply describing the audiences of mass media. In some studies, researchers are seeking to determine the motivations for media use; in others, the goal is to determine the gratifications people derive from using the media. Still other scholars are focusing on children of different ages, trying to learn how children understand what they see and hear on television. Specialists in political communication are examining how people use the media to follow candidates and their campaigns. One type of research focuses on the relationship between the media's inventories of campaign issues and the personal lists of readers and viewers.

The overall goal is to find out how mass communications affects audiences, just as we individuals need to know how our words affect other individuals with whom we communicate. The object of mass communications is to affect human behavior and attitudes. The object of communications research is to find out how and to what degree human behavior and attitudes are affected by mass communications.

COMMUNICATIONS RESEARCH METHODS

Communications research uses the same basic research methods as other branches of the behavioral sciences. Depending upon the needs of the researcher, any of the following methods may be applied to practically any problem.

In *survey research* the scientific sample is studied to gather demographic information or sociological facts as well as psychological information—opinions and attitudes. As opposed to the status survey, which produces an inventory of facts, survey research gathers both factual information and the opinions of subjects. Thus, the researcher is able to talk about the relationships among variables—for example, the relationship between educational level and media usage, or between sex and opinion in regard to a particular political candidate.

A similar method, but one in which independent and dependent variables are related and hypotheses tested, is the *field study.* In a third method, the *field experiment,* the independent variable is introduced by the researcher in an environment in which considerable control of extraneous variables is possible; the field study is ex post facto. In both the field study and field experiment an attempt is made to establish causal relationships between independent and dependent variables. The most closely controlled method of study of causal relationships is the *laboratory experiment,* in which all except the independent variable to be studied are eliminated.

The survey is frequently used to determine relationships between demographics and mass communication behavior, as in determining the relationships of sex and age to television program viewing. An example of a field study is a case in which it is hypothesized that the grade performance of school children has a stronger and more consistent relationship to the extent of usage and comprehension of mass communications than do other variables in the school and home environment. In a field experiment, one might designate two groups or communities that are similar in relevant characteristics and introduce variables, such as two forms of advertising of the same new product, to determine which form of advertising is more conducive to the purchase of the new product. Both the field study and the field experiment are difficult to control because variables other than those studied may affect the measured or dependent variable without the researcher's being able to know what really happened.

The laboratory experiment provides the best opportunity for control of variables since the researcher can be nearly certain that the causal variable introduced actually brings about the measured effect. For example, using two equivalent or matched groups, the researcher might present a message in oral form to one group and in written form to the other. If a standard test then demonstrates that comprehension was consistently higher for the oral message group than for the written message group, one could be reasonably certain that the oral message was more easily understood by people such as those in the two groups.

EXAMPLES OF COMMUNICATIONS RESEARCH

Research is used by every kind of communicator—newspaper and magazine editors and writers, television and radio personnel, advertising and public relations experts, government information specialists, book publishers, and film producers. Some research has immediate utility in that it can be applied by changing the content or layout. In a sense this can be called *feedback* research, since it is one way in which members of the audience may inform the editor or broadcaster what they like or dislike. In readership studies, subscribers indicate what they prefer to read; in graphics research, readers disclose what types of displays they find most attractive; in advertising research, readers indicate which ads are most effective; in public opinion research, the public relates how it feels about a medium; and in content analysis, the communicator learns how much print space or broadcast time is being devoted to various kinds of stories. Other research, such as that dealing with the processes and effects of mass communication, also provides important information for communicators. While it may have less immediate application, it is of great concern to policymakers, critics, social groups, and other consumers.

Readership Studies

Sometimes called reader traffic studies, these tell the editor how many and what kinds of people have read each item in a publication. For example, story A had 40 percent readership whereas story B had 10 percent, picture A had 37 percent readership whereas picture B had 12 percent. Such information, gathered by trained personnel in personal interviews with representative samples of readers, provides a check on editorial judgment. It is useful to the editor in following trends of audience interest, in evaluating effects of typographical makeup and display of stories on readership, in deciding which of several syndicated features should be retained or dropped, and so on. Effectiveness of various types of advertising also can be studied.

Similar research is conducted on television and radio programs. The various rating services determine how many sets were tuned in to each of a number of programs, how many people were listening to each set, and what kinds of people they were. One TV-radio research service gets its information from an electronic device permanently attached to the television or radio sets of a sample of households. Another rating service makes personal telephone calls to homes while programs are on the air. Another method is to have viewers and listeners keep diaries in which they record their media viewing and listening habits.

Graphics Research

Typography, layout, and makeup fall within the area called graphics by the print media. By experimentation with different methods of presentation, the researcher can tell the editor what the most effective means of presentation of a given item is. A book publisher or magazine or newspaper editor may choose to test audience preference for one kind of typeface as compared with another; the use of one large illustration instead of several smaller pictures; or the effectiveness of a news item published in an area two columns wide and 5 inches deep, as contrasted to the same item set in one column 10 inches deep. Much research has been done on the legibility of typefaces and aesthetic preferences for them.

Advertising people, too, are strongly interested in graphics research. Which ad gets across the most information—an ad with a big picture and a little text, or a little picture and a lot of text? Such research may be accomplished by split runs in the publication, so that the alternatives are presented to two different samples of readers whose reactions then can be compared after a readership survey, or by experimentation with a relatively small group of persons before publication of the ad.

Graphics research has its parallel in the broadcasting media. Research can tell whether 3 minutes of commercial time are most effective at the beginning of a program, at the end, or spread through it. Or it can tell whether, on a radio newscast, a summary of headlines at the start of the program will increase interest in the news items that follow.

Advertising Research

The various media and almost all advertising agencies conduct advertising research to help them in their job of persuading people to buy. *Market* research has been carried on since the start of the century and was the forerunner of other public opinion research. It includes consumer surveys on potential markets for new products, dealer studies, customer attitude surveys, and studies of effectiveness of brand names and package designs. Media use by advertisers is determined in part by market research results, and various media seek to point out their usefulness by undertaking market research studies for particular advertisers' products. *Copy* research includes analysis of advertisement readership studies, pretesting of advertisements, evaluation of printed advertisement campaign effectiveness, and graphics. In broadcasting, commercials and programs may be tried out on small samples of listeners by means of response-recording devices. The same is true of films.

Public Opinion Research

All communicators are interested in knowing the state of public opinion about themselves or their medium. Publishers want to know how the public feels about their newspapers, magazines, or books. Broadcasters and film producers are equally sensitive to public approval. Public relations and advertising specialists want to know if they have succeeded in creating a favorable image for their companies or products in the public mind. Surveys of attitudes held by specific customer groups, and by the public in general, give them some answers.

Communicators are interested in public opinion from an additional viewpoint—that is, public attitudes toward social and economic issues, government officials and their policies, and important events. The familiar national polls conducted by George Gallup, Louis Harris, Elmo Roper, and others offer a check on prevailing opinion. And since public opinion is news in itself, the polls are sold to many newspapers; in addition, some newspapers conduct their own polls and report the outcomes as news stories. Large companies subscribe to opinion survey services as a part of their public relations programs. Government also uses public opinion research—the United States International Communication Agency has a survey research division whose sole function is to measure public opinion toward the United States in other countries and the effects of our various foreign information programs, including the Voice of America. Politicians are constantly using public opinion surveys to gauge campaign progress and important issues.

Content Analysis

Much can be learned about a publication merely by studying its content. (This falls somewhat outside the definition of behavioral research.) Content analysis provides a clue to an editor's or writer's intentions and to the kind of audience a publication or broadcast attracts. Combined with readership studies, it gives clues to what people want to read about. This form of research can be especially valuable when more precise kinds of research are inappropriate or unavailable. For example, a content analysis of German wartime broadcasts gave the Allies useful clues to the enemy's war strategy. An analysis of Soviet cold war propaganda helped the United States government in the formulation of its own propaganda, since it revealed the themes that were currently being stressed and enabled us to combat them.

Processes and Effects Research

What are the effects of mass communication? For many years this question directed the work of scholars interested in mass media processes. The model of communication outlined in Chapter 1 provides the elements, with arrows indicating that the major flow is from communicator to message to audience. More recently, researchers have noted that the model is theoretical: TV viewers and newspaper readers are not just passive agents reacting to what they see and read. As explained in Chapter 2, research scholars have sought to determine what people seek in the media, what happens when they use the media, and what they get out of them. The more complex perspectives recognize that people have varying interests, biases, and needs that they "take with them" to the media. At the same time, other researchers have chosen to work with families, groups, and communities rather than with individuals. The following are a few examples of current trends in mass communication research.

1. *Community media systems.* One vein of research has focused on the role of the mass media in communities. Editors, broadcasters, and other communicators act as "gate-keepers," deciding what information community residents will receive about various issues. Are there differences in the types of information conveyed by communicators in small as contrasted to large communities? One study suggests that editors in smaller, more homogeneous communities tend to avoid controversial issues and concentrate on more positive, socially supportive information. Editors in larger communities, which have organized interest groups and more mechanisms for handling disputes, distribute more conflict information and are more likely to stress opinion leadership.

2. *Information diffusion.* People are provided with an abundance of information by the mass media, and technologies developing with the cable systems are accelerating this "information explosion." In coping with this barrage, people must be selective. They learn things from the mass media, but not necessarily the same things, nor the same amount. For example, those who use more of the print media—newspapers, magazines, and books—tend to be more knowledgeable than those who rely mainly on radio and television for their information.

3. *Media socialization.* Adults do not suddenly appear with full-blown reading, viewing, and listening habits. They acquire these habits through many years and under the influence of many factors. One approach to understanding the development of communication behavior is called socialization research. Scholars try to specify the social origins and processes by which people learn and maintain reading and viewing habits. In a sense they are turning around the question of effects and asking what leads to use of the mass media. Researchers taking this perspective have found varying TV viewing patterns among children from different family environments. In families in which children are encouraged to explore new ideas and to express them openly, children spend far less time with TV and pay more attention to news and public affairs programs when they do watch. By contrast, in families placing greater emphasis on obedience and social harmony, children spend the most time with TV of any group and their interest is concentrated on entertainment rather than on news and public affairs programs.

4. *Children and television.* Parents, broadcasters, government regulators, and others have been concerned with violence shown on television. This has led to a large number of studies trying to determine whether there is any relationship between watching TV violence and real acts of violence. Do children use the violent characters shown on TV as models for their own behavior? How do children understand the violence they view on the TV screen? These are among the questions researchers are asking. Obviously small children have more limited capacities than adults for understanding the world around them. For example, do children under the age of seven have difficulty relating the different parts of a plot sequence? This has implications for their TV viewing, since they may be

unable to connect the punishment accorded a TV murderer with the criminal act or the motive.

5. *Agenda-setting function.* For years, researchers have been interested in the relationship between media use and attitude change. More recently, studies have focused on information and the new cognitions acquired from the media. An example of this trend is the notion of an agenda-setting function of the press, which was explored in Chapter 2. The view is that the media often may not be successful in telling people what to think, but they have considerable success in telling people what to think about. Studies here, for example, look at the relationship between the agenda of political campaign issues set by the media and the personal agendas of the audience.

6. *Motives, uses, and gratifications.* As noted in Chapter 2, researchers are delving into the motives people have for using the mass media, and are trying to identify the uses and gratifications associated with newspaper reading, TV viewing, cable use, and the like. In one study, readers relied on the newspaper for help in deciding how to vote in a nonpartisan election. In another study, people who had switched to a four-day work week started watching TV programs that had direct application to activities planned for expanded weekends. Other researchers, particularly those for cable systems, are examining the different things people seek in the media—specific information, a chance to relax, favorite programs, and so on.

The preceding examples demonstrate the range of communications research today. Each area has implications for communicators. For example, editors may want to rethink their coverage of political candidates if their readers' issue agendas are not closely linked with a newspaper's campaign coverage. Media consumers also need to understand how communication works, and much of the research discussed helps to provide that information.

One of the most satisfying aspects of communications research is in doing original, imaginative thinking and investigation. Creative researchers try to think of different ways to do a particular communications job and then test the alternatives to see which is the most effective. They critically analyze the long-standing traditions and accepted practices of the media and then test these tricks of the trade to see if they are really the most effective ways to communicate. They devise new and original research techniques and methods to solve particular problems. They keep abreast of developments in related disciplines such as psychology and sociology, applying the findings and theories from those fields to communications problems. Creative communications researchers also make valuable contributions to theory and practice in those related disciplines. They both borrow from and contribute to other areas of knowledge.

A glance through a few issues of journals such as the *Journalism Quarterly,* the *Journal of Communication,* and *Public Opinion Quarterly* will reveal some of the directions that mass communications research now takes. Although some of the questions or problems explored do not differ greatly from those explored 30 years ago, the emphasis now is on the use of more scientific methods of studying those questions. Earlier expressions of subjective opinion by communications experts are being subjected to scientific scrutiny and the "folklore" of the media are being tested.

JOB OPPORTUNITIES IN COMMUNICATIONS RESEARCH

Research is being conducted in every kind of communications and business enterprise today. All the media are engaged in research to some degree: newspapers, magazines, radio, television, cable, publishing houses, film producers. So are the supporting agencies: press associations, advertising agencies, public relations films, specialized commercial research firms. Further, manufacturers of consumer and industrial products, retail and wholesale business firms, the federal government, and colleges and universities are engaged in communications research.

Surveys have revealed that four of every five United States companies have a department (one person or more) engaged in market research, which almost always includes some form of communications or opinion research in its activities. Even among the smaller firms—those with sales under $5 million annually—three of every five have a research department. Advertising agencies are the most avid users of research; more than 90 percent of all advertising agencies in the United States have a research department. And the large publishing and broadcasting organizations employ researchers.

Naturally, the larger the firm, the more likely it is to have a research department. However, both the larger and the smaller firms frequently turn to commercial research firms, whose sole business it is to conduct research for outside clients. Most medium-sized and large cities in the country today have at least one commercial research firm, and the number of such firms is increasing yearly. Many of these firms serve clients on a national basis, and a few conduct research in foreign countries. Some of the largest are the Opinion Research Corporation of Princeton, New Jersey; International Research Associates and Alfred Politz Research of New York City; A. C. Nielsen Company in Chicago; and Field Research, on the West Coast.

Advertising agencies tend to have larger research staffs than other kinds of businesses; the largest agencies employ an average of 50 persons in their research departments. Large publishing and broadcasting firms average four research employees, but a few have departments more the size of those in the agencies.

How high is the salary for a worker in communications research? Because of the extensive amount of advanced training and specialized knowledge required, researchers are well paid compared with other mass communications personnel. A person who has a master's degree and who has specialized in research may expect a starting salary of $12,000 to $15,000 per year. The more advanced student in communications research—who has completed most or all of the training necessary for a doctoral degree—may initially command $15,000 to $20,000 per year. These figures vary, of course, with location and size of the firm. With experience, communications research specialists may rise in salary to $50,000 or higher. Research analysts exceed the $12,000 level.

Opportunities for advancement in mass communications research are good because of the expansion taking place in the field. Not only can research be a rewarding and satisfying vocation in itself, but it also serves as a stepping-stone to other kinds of work, both in the creative and business aspects of communications. One example is Dr. Frank Stanton, who started in research and became head of the Columbia Broadcasting System. Two others are A. Edward Miller, who became publisher of *McCall's*, and Marion Harper, Jr., who became head of McCann-Erickson advertising agency.

Another excellent opportunity for researchers exists in schools of journalism and mass communications. More and more universities are adding communications researchers to their staffs, both to do research and to teach and train students in the skills involved. In addition, such schools often contract to do research for the media or for civic and government agencies. A doctoral degree is usually considered a requirement for such a faculty position.

TRAINING FOR RESEARCH POSITIONS

Until just after World War II, most scientifically trained researchers on mass communications problems came from psychology and sociology. The importance of research as a specialty has since led some of the nation's leading schools of journalism and mass communications to set up graduate programs in quantitative scientific research methods.

In some of these schools, mass communications research is offered as just one of several communications fields graduate students may elect in their courses of study; in others, the entire graduate program is devoted to courses in behavioral research theory and methodology, with a minimum of emphasis on the communications aspect. In almost all, however, the research specialization requires a sampling of appropriate courses drawn from several different disciplines and heavy emphasis on statistics and scientific method courses.

A typical graduate program calls for a major in mass communications with a minor in psychology, sociology, or statistics. Various other departments—anthropology, philosophy, economics, political science, speech communication, marketing, to name a few—may also figure in the program to a lesser extent, depending on the individual interests of the student. Some individuals prefer to major in social psychology or sociology and minor in mass communications.

It is considered desirable—though not necessary—for graduate students in communications research to have professional experience in one or more of the mass media. The first wave of communications research Ph.D.s—those receiving degrees in the 1950s—almost without exception had practical journalism experience as newspaper reporters and editors, radio news personnel, and so on. The value of a practical journalism background lies in the greater awareness of crucial communications problems, a better knowledge of the questionable assumptions of the trade, and a more critical perspective based on an understanding of journalistic processes and folkways.

It should be emphasized, however, that prior journalistic experience is not a requirement, but merely helpful for the person interested in mass communications research. He or she can acquire knowledge of the media and of journalistic techniques in journalism courses and in postdegree professional work. It should be noted, too, that the only distinction between the graduate program of a mass communications researcher and that of the less specialized behavioral scientist is the former's preoccupation with mass communications as the subject matter of the research; in practice, the student may engage in almost any kind of social research.

Chapter 18

EDUCATION FOR MASS COMMUNICATIONS

THE ROLE OF EDUCATION

Informing and enlightening the public is a difficult task. Few can succeed as practitioners in mass communications without mastering the principles and practices of broad areas of knowledge that comprise the basic ingredients of a college education. Society has become so complex, its specialties so numerous, and its varying relationships so involved that only a person with a sure intelligence and a comprehension of many facets of human activity can understand the meaning of events. Without understanding, any attempt at reporting or interpreting is not only superficial but actually dangerous to the security of a democratic nation.

It is true that the exceptional individual can acquire a broad education without entering the portals of an institution of higher learning. A number of persons with limited academic backgrounds are exerting genuine leadership in the mass media offices of the country today. But for most of us the only certain path to acquiring knowledge about our world lies in formal courses of instruction in the social sciences, the natural sciences, and the humanities. Here we discover the precise methodology of the researcher and the scientist and the skills of the writer or artist; we have guided access to the accumulated wisdom of the ages; we learn what people have considered to be the good, the true, and the beautiful; and we study the behavior of human beings, both as individuals and in their relationships with others.

Acquiring such a basic education has special importance to future communicators. For one thing, they are exposed to areas of thought and criticism that give them opportunities to become cultured persons of discrimination and taste in their own right. From these experiences they should be able to acquire a sound working knowledge of society and a sensitivity to its many problems that will enable them to exercise the type of forthright citizenship so essential in our democracy. If their exposure to the processes of education has been productive, they will be enabled, in the words of Cardinal John Henry Newman, "to see things as they are, to go right to the point, to disentangle a skein of thought, to detect what is sophistical, and to discard what is irrelevant."

Education, however, assumes an even greater importance to future communicators: almost every bit of knowledge and every insight that they acquire in college, from a study of the love life of the oyster to Thorstein Veblen's views on "conspicuous consumption," eventually seem to become grist for the mill as they report and interpret the kaleidoscopic nature of life in the most practical of working assignments.

CHANNELS OF EDUCATION FOR MASS COMMUNICATIONS

Students desiring to equip themselves for careers in mass communications may follow several avenues toward reaching their goal. The most common method is to enroll in a school or department of journalism or communications offering a four-year program leading to a degree in journalism. Approximately 300 colleges and universities in the United States provide such courses of study. Some of these institutions have provided separate administrative units (colleges, schools, divisions) for their journalism or communications instruction. The majority have located the school or department of journalism or communications within the liberal arts college. In either case, students typically take no more than 25 to 30 percent of their course work in journalism or communications; the remainder is spread throughout the social sciences, humanities, and natural sciences, as well as physical education or military fields, in accordance with the university's requirements for both breadth and depth of study in the various areas of learning. In effect, students elect a major specialization in professional studies that give them instruction in basic communication skills and in social science-oriented courses that relate journalism and communications to society. They do this just as other students elect a major concentration in geology, physics, political science, or English—and they are no more specialized in one subject than are these others.

Many practitioners in mass communications are college graduates who have pursued noncommunications majors in liberal arts institutions. Some employers among the mass media seek out such students, in the belief that their background in general liberal arts study best equips them for full development within their organizations. It seems more reasonable, however, that students who acquire both professional and general liberal arts education while enrolled in schools and departments of journalism, television-radio, speech, or communications will be better prepared for professional work and will be employed more readily. This fact has been corroborated by numerous surveys.

Journalism educators know about this increasing reliance by newspapers upon their graduates through the operations of their placement offices. The placement service is one of the most important functions of a mass communications school as far as the prospective graduate is concerned. Employers rely on the schools to recommend applicants for both beginning and advanced positions and make calls directly to the school rather than to the college's general placement service. A large journalism or communications school will receive several hundred requests each year from newspapers, press associations, television and radio stations, magazines, advertising agencies, major industrial companies seeking advertising and public relations personnel, and others wishing to employ graduates with communications skills.

Many students are introduced to the mass communications field through study at the more than 500 four-year institutions in the United States that offer some journalism courses but not a full major. High schools and junior colleges provide the beginning courses for thousands of other students. Some work on the campus newspaper, yearbook, and television or radio staffs, or find part-time employment with a local newspaper or broadcast station while still in school. Many eventually find jobs in communications and related fields.

Students desiring careers in advertising and communications management frequently find the courses of study they want under the professional and liberal arts listings of schools and departments of journalism, speech, radio-television, and communications. Much of the background they need is offered through schools of business. In many universities a cooperative arrangement exists so that, regardless of the type of degree sought, such students obtain their specialized courses in both business and communications areas. The business major must become familiar with the peculiar problems and structure of the branch of the communications industry he or she proposes to enter; the communications major must learn the principles of sound business practice.

With the tremendous expansion of industry since World War II, public relations has risen to prominence as a career sought by thousands. Most schools and departments of journalism offer one or two orientation courses in combination with preparation in basic journalistic training; they, and those schools with more fully developed curricula, suggest programs emphasizing electives in economics, psychology, sociology, and other social sciences, and in business areas. Few schools of business offer separate courses in public relations, although they incorporate course units emphasizing the theory and overall knowledge of public relations essential to successful management. Journalism school courses seek to offer the student both this background and the instruction necessary for becoming an actual practitioner in public relations.

In the broadcast area, students desiring careers in performance and production usually concentrate on courses in speech and radio-television. Those desiring to become radio and television newscasters and writers combine journalism, speech, and radio-television courses. Those headed for sales, promotion, public relations, and management positions may choose to major in business with allied instruction in journalism and radio-television. Those entering educational broadcasting frequently obtain teaching certificates while also acquiring a background in radio-television and speech. Television production and performance students will most likely take as much work in theater and dramatic literature as possible. The possible variations in these emphases are almost endless, depending upon the students' objectives. Common to all these career paths, however, is a strong background in the liberal arts. The interlocking nature of broadcast instruction is a factor in the recent development of schools or colleges of communications, linking speech, radio-television, film, advertising, public relations, and journalism.

Courses in the film are offered by more than 800 radio and television, speech communication, journalism, theater arts, and education schools and departments. They range from a single film appreciation course in some institutions to multiple courses in production, history, and aesthetics leading to a film major in others. Among institutions emphasizing study in the film are the University of Southern California, the University of California at Berkeley, Boston University, Indiana University, Columbia University, New York University, Northwestern University, Michigan State University, the University of Kansas, the University of Texas at Austin, and San Francisco State University.

Combination programs have been developed at many universities in order to enable the student interested in a career as a communications specialist in such areas as agriculture, home economics, medicine, or science to obtain basic proficiency through courses made available in two or more departments, schools, or colleges.

Students often supplement classroom and laboratory instruction with part-time jobs on campus and with nearby commercial media and by accepting internships, normally ten-week to three-month summer stints, with media, government agencies, business firms, and institutions. Upon obtaining permanent employment, they often are placed in training programs.

In an effort to identify talent at institutions with no journalism programs, the Newspaper Fund, Inc., of Dow Jones and Company, has awarded more than $500,000 in intern scholarships to 1140 students since 1960. Approximately 520 students, mainly enrolled in journalism schools and departments, have received grants totaling more than $300,000 to participate in the Fund's newspaper editing program.

HOW COMMUNICATIONS EDUCATION DEVELOPED

Journalism, a comparative fledgling among university disciplines, gained its foothold in college curricula early in this century. Formal education for journalism was inevitable in the face of the steadily increasing complexities of the twentieth century, which demanded better-trained personnel on American newspaper staffs. General Robert E. Lee first proposed a special college education for printer-editors. That was in 1869, when the general was president of Washington College, now Washington and Lee University, in Virginia. Little came of his proposal. Other early attention was given to printing instruction, such as that beginning at Kansas State College in 1873.

In 1904 the first four-year curriculum for journalism students was organized at the University of Illinois, and journalism instruction began the same year at the University of Wisconsin. Four years later the first separate school of journalism was founded at the University of Missouri by an experienced journalist, Dean Walter Williams. In 1912 the Columbia University School of Journalism, endowed with $2 million from Joseph Pulitzer, opened its doors. By that year more than 30 colleges and universities were offering courses in journalism.

The first courses were largely vocational in nature as pioneer teachers in the field endeavored to prepare college students for careers on newspapers, then the primary medium of mass communication. During the 1920s, however, emphasis on technique lessened and curricula began to reflect an increasing interest in the social, ethical, and cultural aspects of journalism. Dr. Willard G. Bleyer, director of the University of Wisconsin School of Journalism until his death in 1935, is credited with leading the movement away from a preoccupation with technique. Also influential was exposure to methods of teaching the social sciences that journalism instructors were receiving in graduate programs. Courses in the history and the ethics of journalism became popular, and they were followed by studies of the newspaper as a social institution, of the interpretation of current affairs, and of public opinion.

These courses, together with those dealing with foreign news channels and legal aspects of the press, heightened respect for journalism as a discipline among other college teachers. At the same time, graduates from journalism departments were earning a grudging acceptance from curmudgeons of the editorial offices who, as Horace Greeley put it, learned their journalism through eating ink and sleeping on the exchanges. Teachers began to offer courses to prepare students for careers in newspaper management, advertising, photography, and other such specialized fields. While recognizing the importance of the humanities and the natural sciences in the total educational program of their students, teachers came to achieve the closest working relatonships with the social sciences.

As both the breadth and depth of subject matter in journalism increased, master's degrees were offered. In 1935 the Pulitzer School at Columbia restricted its year's course to those holding a bachelor's degree, and the Medill School of Northwestern University established a five-year plan for professional training in 1938. Graduate study for journalism majors developed at a rapid pace after World War II, as the schools themselves and some of the media units began to urge advanced study in both journalism and the social sciences. Many of those who obtained master's degrees entered journalism teaching, but increasing numbers spent five years of study in preparation for professional careers.

At the doctoral level, most graduate schools that recognized journalism instruction followed the lead of the University of Wisconsin in providing a minor or a double minor in journalism for candidates who generally majored in fields such as history or political science. The University of Missouri, however, awarded the first degree of Doctor of Philosophy in journalism in 1934, and by the 1940s other programs were under way. Some were based on strong supporting emphasis on the social sciences; others related the study of mass communications to psychology and sociology as a behavioral science. In 1980 the Ph.D. degree in mass communications was offered at 18 universities. Some Ph.D. recipients entered the communications industry or other research areas, but most became faculty members.

The growth of the philosophy that journalism and communications schools should develop research scholars capable of critical analysis of the media and their social environment coincided with the rise of television and the increased importance of departments of speech communication and radio-television in providing preparation for broadcast careers. New, integrated instructional units emerged, a few merely for administrative convenience, but most devoted to the serious study of communication as the common denominator linking several academic areas of study. For example, Michigan State University brought its speech communication, journalism, advertising, and broadcast instruction together into a College of Communication Arts, with a research unit at its center. The University of Texas at Austin similarly combined its speech communication, radio-television-film, journalism, and advertising programs into a School of Communication. Today, "Communication" or "Communications" is a part of the name of instructional units at many institutions.

ORGANIZING FOR HIGHER STANDARDS

Because of their diversity of interests, mass communications educators find teaching and research inspiration and assistance through membership in a number of regional, national, and international organizations. They include the Association for Education in Journalism, Speech Communication Association, International Communication Association, Broadcast Education Association, American Academy of Advertising, Popular Culture Association, and a number of others.

The Association for Education in Journalism (AEJ), founded in 1912, is the so-called umbrella organization for many scholars in fields of study such as mass communication and society, theory and methodology, law, media history, international communication, photojournalism, graphics, newspapers, magazines, advertising, public relations, and radio-television. AEJ publishes *Journalism Quarterly, Journalism Educator, Journalism Monographs,* and *Journalism Abstracts.* It has two administrator organizations as coordinate members. They are the American Association of Schools and Departments of Journalism (AASDJ), comprised of schools with programs of study accredited by the Accrediting Council on Education in Journalism and Mass Communications (ACEJMC), and the American Society of Journalism School Administrators (ASJSA), to which both administrators of schools with ACEJMC-accredited curricula and those that have not sought or have not obtained such accreditation belong. AEJ headquarters are located at the University of South Carolina at Columbia.

All three groups—AEJ, AASDJ, and ASJSA—have representatives on ACEJMC, together with three public members and representatives of 19 industry and professional organizations: the American Society of Newspaper Editors, American Newspaper Publishers Association, Southern Newspaper Publishers Association, National Newspaper Association, and Inland Daily Press Association (the five groups that helped establish the council in 1939); and the National Association of Broadcasters, American Society of Magazine Editors, Public Relations Society of America, Newspaper Advertising and Marketing Executives, International Association of Business Communicators, National Conference of Editorial Writers, National Press Photographers Association, Radio Television News Directors Association, Associated Press Managing Editors Association, California Newspaper Publishers Association, Associated Press Broadcasters Association, Broadcast Education Association, Women in Communications, Inc., and the Society of Professional Journalists, Sigma Delta Chi.

Through its accrediting committee the council evaluates programs of instruction in American universities, visiting schools on invitation approximately every six years. Currently accredited are programs in news-editorial, advertising, broadcast news, radio-television general (telecommunications), public relations, magazine, photojournalism, publishing, and technical, agricultural, and home economics journalism. The council evaluated only those programs leading to the first professional degree, whether bachelor's or master's, until 1978, after which both professional undergraduate and graduate programs in the same schools were examined, and unit accreditation was extended to those with at least 51 percent of their students enrolled in accredited offerings.

The Speech Communication Association, founded in 1914, consists of teachers and administrators at all educational levels, speech scientists and clinicians, media specialists, theater artists and craftsmen, communication consultants, students, and industry representatives. Primary publications are *The Quarterly Journal of Speech, Communication Monographs,* and *The Speech Teacher,* as well as a newsletter, annual directory, bibliographic annual, and convention abstracts. Its divisions are forensics, instructional development, interpersonal and small group interaction, interpretation, mass communication, public address, rhetorical and communication theory, speech sciences, and theater. Administrators of speech communication departments are organized as the Association for Communication Administrators.

The International Communication Association, formed about 30 years ago, brings together academicians, other professionals, and students whose interest is focused on human communication. Publications are *The Journal of Communication, Human Communication Research,* and a newsletter. Its divisions are information systems and interpersonal, mass, organizational, intercultural, political, instructional, and health communication.

The recently organized Council of Communication Societies brings together leaders of the ICA, SCA, American Business Communication Association, American Forensic Association, American Medical Writers Association, American Translators Association, Industrial Communication Council, Society for Technical Communication, and Society of Federal Linguists. The council publishes a news digest and a communication calendar.

A COMMUNICATIONS EDUCATION NEVER ENDS

It is a truism, of course, to point out that a college diploma, or its equivalent in individual attainment, is only the beginning of a lifetime of education. This fact holds great validity for those who embark on careers in mass communications. Every aspect of human experience and emotion can become their concern; the world changes and so must their ability to understand and interpret those changes.

People who want to develop to their fullest potential in the field of mass communications cannot neglect their reading, both fiction and nonfiction, and the selective viewing of films, televised documentaries, and the like. Just as a physician peruses periodicals to keep abreast of advances of knowledge in medicine, so must the communicator read journals in communications and allied fields. These include research journals such as *Journalism Quarterly, Public Opinion Quarterly,* and the *Journal of Communication;* trade journals such as *Editor & Publisher, Broadcasting,* and *Advertising Age;* and general interest professional journals such as *Nieman Reports, Quill,* and *Columbia Journalism Review*.

Maintaining active membership in organizations that seek to improve their crafts also is the mark of the professional communicator. Highly stimulating to many communicators are the conferences and literature of the groups previously listed as supporting journalism accreditation, as well as state and local associations and the wire services.

Many media people return to college for regular courses as well as for continuing education activities such as institutes, workshops, and forums. Dow Jones and Company's Newspaper Fund, Inc., has sent more than 7000 high school and junior college journalism teachers back to college for special summer training in advising school newspapers and teaching journalism. Several hundred newspaper persons have been selected by the Nieman Foundation for a year's study at Harvard University. The American Press Institute provides seminars regularly at Reston, Virginia. The Southern Newspaper Publishers Association sponsors both public affairs and newspaper skills seminars. These are only a few examples of numerous such activities available to mass media personnel.

MASS MEDIA TEACHING IN THE SECONDARY SCHOOL

There are more potential openings for teachers of journalism in the secondary schools of the United States than in any other field for which journalism training provides preparation. The best estimates are that approximately 45,000 senior and junior high school publications—newspapers, magazines, and yearbooks—are issued regularly. More than 1 million students work on these publications, which cost collectively around $55 million per year. About 175,000 students are enrolled each year in journalism courses offered at approximately 5,000 high schools. Many others learn the principles of radio and television production in classes and activity clubs.

A phenomenon of the last decade or so has been the establishment of thousands of high school courses designed to acquaint students with the operations of the mass media and to consider the effects of mass communications on their lives. These courses, offered through language arts, speech, journalism, and other departments, have been one of the principal causes of the steady growth in mass communications enrollments in colleges and universities.

Secondary school journalism can be traced to the founding of the first known high school paper, the *Literary Journal,* in 1829 at the Boston Latin

Grammar School. It was not until 1912, however, that the first known class in high school journalism was started in Salina, Kansas. Secondary school journalism matured during the 1930s and 1940s as school boards, superintendents, and principals noted its educational value.

Those who have taught high school journalism over the years speak with genuine enthusiasm about the satisfaction they have derived from teaching journalism classes and advising school publications. For one thing, they enjoy having many of their school's brightest students on their publications staffs; frequently the highest ranking group of students in the English placement tests is assigned to the teacher producing the school paper. These imaginative and creative youngsters are stimulated by actually writing for print. Many of them go on to other fields of study at the universities, but some become the prize students of journalism or communications schools and eventually take their places in professional work. The school paper and the annual are major activities at the high school level; this gives their advisers additional prestige as teachers. They also are brought into close contact with school administrators, and quite a number of able journalism teachers have thus moved into administrative work.

Several organizations issue publications and guidebooks for teachers and students and conduct critical services providing professional evaluation and ratings of school media. They include the National Scholastic Press Association at the University of Minnesota, Columbia Scholastic Press Association at Columbia University, and the Catholic School Press Association at Marquette University. They publish, respectively, *Scholastic Editor, School Press Review,* and *Catholic School Editor.* Also providing services are the Future Journalists of America, at the University of Oklahoma, and the Student Press Service and Student Press Law Center, both in Washington, D.C. Quill and Scroll, the international honor society for high school journalists, with headquarters at the State University of Iowa, publishes a magazine bearing the society's name.

There are also regional associations, such as the Southern Interscholastic Press Association, with headquarters at the University of South Carolina, and the Mid-America Association for Secondary Journalism, at the University of Missouri, as well as state associations. The teachers themselves also are organized as the Journalism Education Association, affiliated with NSPA, which publishes *Communication: Journalism Education Today,* and the Columbia Scholastic Press Advisers Association, (CSPAA), which publishes the *CSPAA Bulletin*.

A recent study disclosed that about 30 percent of the states have no specific journalism certification requirements, about 30 percent grant journalism certification for completing fewer than 15 semester hours of college journalism course work, and about 40 percent require the equivalent of a minor in journalism.

Some prospective teachers major in journalism and minor in an area such as English or the social sciences, meanwhile acquiring sufficient hours in education courses to qualify for certificates. Others major in education and take first and second minors in journalism and some other field. Still others major in English or language arts and take as many journalism courses as they can work into a four-year program. All realize that they most likely will be teaching only one or two courses in journalism, with the balance of their instructional assignments in another subject. During the recent declining market for teachers, those with the greatest preparation in journalism were more likely to be employed.

TEACHING JOURNALISM IN THE COMMUNITY COLLEGE

Hundreds of opportunities for teaching journalism are available in community colleges throughout the United States, which are growing steadily in enrollment and importance as the population increases.

Fifty-nine percent of the 936 community colleges that responded to a survey conducted by Dr. Frank Deaver of the University of Alabama offer some courses in journalism. Most often these courses include introduction to mass communications, beginning newswriting and reporting, news editing, and photography. Two-thirds of the courses serve as laboratories for student publications—newspaper, magazine, or yearbook. In most of these two-year colleges the journalism program is designed to encourage these student publications and to give basic preparation for students planning to major in journalism or communications at four-year colleges and universities. A number of community college educators state that their primary purpose is to acquaint students with the mass media and to teach them to become discerning news and opinion consumers so that they will be better able to carry out their responsibilities as citizens. In some community colleges, enough advanced instruction is available to prepare graduates to take jobs with the media.

Two-year college educators are organized as the Community College Journalism Association, an affiliate of the Association for Education in Journalism. The Newspaper Fund worked with the educators to develop their organization through two institutes at the University of Texas at Austin during the late 1960s. In California, more than 60 two-year and city colleges belong to the Journalism Association of Community Colleges. The typical degree of the two-year college educators is the M.A., earned by 75 percent. Many serve as advisers to student publications or as college publicity directors.

THE FOUR-YEAR COLLEGE AND UNIVERSITY LEVEL

Journalism and communications faculty members at the university or college level are engaged in three major activities: teaching, research, and service. Most of them have one or more specialties in the journalistic techniques, acquired through their own professional experience with the mass media: reporting, news editing, magazine writing, radio and television news, typography and graphic arts processes, advertising, public relations, news photography, film, critical writing, broadcast programming and production, and editorial writing are among these technique fields. Teachers usually start at this techniques level, but they are well advised to be equipped for teaching and research in one or more of the scholarly fields of interest. They should be interested, too, in performing services for the mass media with which the school or department is in close contact and in spending long hours offering advice and counsel to students who turn to them for guidance and stimulation.

Those who aspire to the top ranks of university or college teaching in journalism and mass communications usually seek M.A. degrees in the field. They then undertake study toward the Ph.D. degree in a college or university that offers either a major or a minor in the subject and that has a journalism and communications faculty of graduate school caliber. Some prefer to minor in journalism or communications and to do their major doctoral work in political science, history, psychology, sociology, economics, speech, American studies, or another related field; others enter universities that award Ph.D. degrees in journalism or in communications. In either case, there is a blending of study and research in journalism or communications with study and research in the social sciences, behavioral sciences, or the humanities.

Not all college journalism or communications faculty members need to undertake doctoral work; some with sound professional experience and specialized abilities in fields such as graphic arts, news photography, weekly journalism, or radio and television writing, production, and programming find their services amply rewarded at the M.A. level. There have been shortages of qualified teachers in the advertising and broadcast media fields, particularly.

Opportunities for scholarly teaching, research, and publication in the mass communications field are almost unlimited. Many aspects of the history of communications remain to be explored, despite the fact that this area traditionally has been a favorite one for professors. The literary aspects of journalism constitute another little-plowed field. Important studies of the relationships between the press and society, and of the conflicts between press and government, await future scholars. Only a start has been made on penetrating studies of the economics of the mass media. Advertising offers wide opportunities for advanced study and research projects of both basic and applied character. As explained in Chapter 17, the fields of mass communications theory and research, of public opinion and propaganda, and of other studies allied to the behavioral sciences have barely been opened by scholars. Particularly, there is a need for interpretive analysis of scientific findings and quantitative data by those who can relate what the researchers have found to the everyday problems of the mass media. The processes of international communications and the study of foreign journalism have become more important in recent years also, with few faculty members qualified to do advanced teaching and research in the field.

Offering assistance to the publications adviser at the junior college and college level are the Associated Collegiate Press (ACP), companion organization of the National Scholastic Press Association (NSPA), and the National Council of College Publications Advisers. The ACP and NSPA issue guidebooks and other publications for college publications staffs and maintain critical services for newspapers, annuals, and magazines.

Salaries for communications teachers in colleges and universities run somewhat above the average for other disciplines, because of the competitive bidding from the mass media for the services of those who are preparing for teaching careers. University and college salaries have improved substantially in recent years, and those who reach professorial status may look forward to nine-month salaries running from $20,000 to $30,000 or more per year. There also are opportunities for additional income from summer teaching, summer refresher work in the media, consultantships to advertising agencies and other groups, research projects, book publication, and other writing.

Part Six

CRITICISMS AND CHALLENGES

Chapter 19

THE GOVERNMENT, THE MEDIA, AND THE PUBLIC

GOVERNMENT AND PRESS: A CREDIBILITY DUEL

The mass media during the era of Vietnam and Watergate came under the most severe attacks from the public and the federal government since the days of the Revolution and the Civil War, when patriots eliminated the newspapers they did not like by destroying the printing offices where they were published. The public, frustrated and bewildered by rapidly changing social and technological conditions, an unpopular war, and the emotional bombardment caused by near-total and near-instant mass communication, tended to blame the mass media for many of their problems. The federal government, always an adversary because of the constitutional role of the press in a democratic society, capitalized on the growing feeling of disenchantment with the media and engaged in a credibility duel characterized by both direct and indirect assaults.

It was a situation ripe for demagogues. A cult of disbelief had grown steadily since the days of Senator Joseph McCarthy's treason charges and the Republican party's 1952 election slogan of "Communism, Corruption, and Korea." A credibility gap between president and public developed for John F. Kennedy, and widened dramatically for Lyndon Johnson and Richard Nixon.

But another credibility gap, between the media and the public, emerged. There was much bad news that people did not want to believe, much reality that they did not want to have exist: the Bay of Pigs, the Berlin Wall, the assassination of a president, the Vietnam War, racial riots in big cities, college campus riots, the assassinations of Robert Kennedy and the Rev. Martin Luther King, Jr., the collapse of victory hopes in Vietnam, the secret bombing of Cambodia, the My Lai massacre, Kent State, sexual permissiveness and obscenity out in the open, and an inflation-depression. Blaming the source of the bad news—the press—became popular.

Some people did not believe the president; some did not believe the press; some believed neither. And both the president and the press encouraged people not to believe the other. In late 1972 Richard Nixon appeared to have the upper hand. Reelected with 61 percent of the vote, the president stood triumphant. But the ever-widening political conspiracy known as Watergate had already begun its course. At first dismissed by the White House as "a third-rate burglary," it developed into a major constitutional crisis. When it was over, 61 individuals and 19 corporations had been charged with violations of federal laws; 18 members of Nixon's administration had pleaded guilty or been convicted, including two cabinet members and four of his closest Oval Office associates; and the president had resigned in disgrace, joining his vice-president, who had resigned a year earlier rather than face bribe-taking charges.

The credibility of the media had been substantially restored, along with that of the government and its Congress and courts. "A President has been deposed, but the Republic endures," wrote one editor. Obviously, however, the long duel between press and government had been costly to both institutions. As the 1980s began, the cult of disbelief was still strong. It is important to understand how the governmental process could have been so brazenly subverted, and to appreciate why some media leaders took desperate gambles to expose the conspiracy known as Watergate.

VIOLENCE AND WAR

Violence and war occur all over the world. But no country welcomes the use of violence in its own social situations and neighborhoods, and nothing is more frustrating to a nation than an unsuccessful, costly war. Americans in the decade of 1965 to 1975 were subjected to violence at home and a stalemated war abroad; both widened the public credibility gap.

Vietnam, Cambodia, and Laos

Few Americans knew where these countries were when the first U.S. military advisers arrived in Saigon in 1955. Step by step, America descended into what David Halberstam, then of the New York *Times,* aptly called a quagmire, which was to swallow up one president and help destroy another.

By 1963 the most perceptive members of the United States press corps in Saigon were challenging the assumptions of the American intervention,

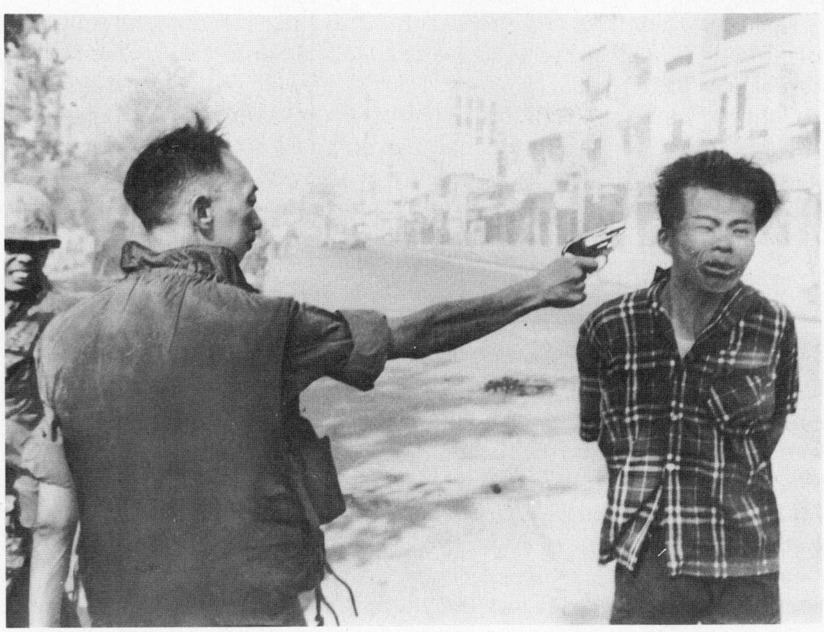

Saigon's chief of police executes a Vietcong prisoner on a Saigon street while the city was under martial law during the Tet offensive in 1968. Edward T. Adams, an Associated Press photographer, won a Pulitzer Prize for the picture. (Photo by permission of Wide World.)

but they were prophets without honor in their own country. The assassination of strong-man Ngo Dinh Diem opened the door to U.S. domination of South Vietnamese affairs; the "advisers" had grown to 16,300 in number at the time of President Kennedy's death. Lyndon Johnson responded to the Gulf of Tonkin incident by instituting bombing of North Vietnam and sending 180,000 more troops during 1965. The number rose to more than one-half million, but no victory was forthcoming. Instead, the Vietcong humiliated the United States command with its Tet offensive of early 1968, which reached the gates of the American embassy.

Public confidence in the war leadership collapsed. President Johnson, before he retired from public life, instituted peace talks in Paris that were to drag on for five years. Antiwar sentiment surged through the American youth and spread more widely. President Nixon's plan for "Vietnamization" of the war also included its widening into Cambodia in 1970. By the end of 1971, more than half the U.S. military force had been withdrawn, but there were 50,000 U.S. personnel dead. The country was divided in its attitude toward the war, which eventually would end in total victory for those the United States had opposed.

The press, which had to report these events and analyze American policy and strategy, heavily supported the war until 1968. Then many more voices were raised for peace. Television, which had for the first time brought the battles and the brutalities of war into the family living room, was not thanked for its effort. Americans did not want to hear about or see search-and-destroy missions, burnings of villages, results of the My Lai massacre, and saturation bombings. The majority wanted Nixon's "peace with honor," and the tragedy continued to unfold.

City Riots and the Kerner Report

Television was caught up in another credibility gap during the 1960s. It has been considered by many observers to be a primary cause of the so-called revolution of rising expectations among America's disadvantaged peoples. Both the programs and the commercials aired on television held out a better way of life for minority groups without changing the reality. Unfulfilled expectations built up angry frustrations that erupted into the ghetto riots of Los Angeles, Newark, Detroit, and other cities. America's affluence, of course, was also reflected in movies, radio, newspapers, and other media; undoubtedly, too, there were other factors contributing to the social unrest. But television, the medium most often viewed by minority groups, had made an impact that could not be denied. Before big-city riots, television had covered the suppression of civil discontent in the South, principally at Little Rock; Selma, Alabama; and Oxford, Mississippi. A new level of awareness and indignation had spread throughout the rest of the country.

Many public officials criticized television for its thorough coverage of the disturbances and threatened the network news services with new investigations. Critics maintained that black leaders Rap Brown and Stokely Carmichael had no real followings until television and radio broadcast their platforms almost daily. It was alleged that the mere arrival of a TV camera crew on the scene of a demonstration often set off crowd action that had not occurred before. Moreover, public opinion polls disclosed a widespread feeling that the news media incite the violence they report merely by being present during riots and reporting on them.

The National Advisory Commission on Civil Disorders, with Governor Otto Kerner of Illinois as chairman, criticized the news media, including television, for incidents in which it felt bad judgment had been displayed and material treated in a sensationalistic manner. But on the whole, the commission found, the media had tried hard to present a balanced factual account of the riots in Newark and Detroit in 1967. Errors in many cases were attributed to false police reports.

The Kerner Commission, however, indicted the mass media for failing to communicate to their predominantly white audience "a sense of the degradation, misery, and hopelessness of living in the ghetto" as well as "a sense of Negro culture, thought, or history," thus feeding black alienation and intensifying white prejudices. With few black reporters and fewer race experts, the report charged, the media had not seriously reported the problems of the black community. Pointing out that fear and apprehension of racial unrest and violence are deeply rooted in American society, coloring and intensifying reactions to news of racial trouble and threats of racial conflict, the commission asserted that those who report and disseminate news must be conscious of the background of anxieties and apprehension against which their stories are projected.

The news media admitted that they had not properly prepared the American people for an understanding of social unrest. Through television documentaries, radio and TV "talk" programs and interviews, in-depth newspaper and magazine articles, and the like, the media explored the issues and sought solutions. Efforts were intensified to recruit black and other minority reporters. But public support of the black movement dwindled.

Student Demonstrations and Chicago, 1968

As student unrest spread across the nation with disruptions at the University of California at Berkeley, Columbia University, and Kent State, coverage of the disorders by the mass media was criticized both by proponents of "law and order" and by the protesters themselves. A large segment of the public, greatly disturbed by what it saw and read, complained that television was being used by the demonstrators for purposes of propaganda against the war and the conventional social fabric. Furthermore, it was alleged, news coverage of the occupancy and burning of buildings and especially of counteraction by both civil and campus authorities provoked similar disturbances on other campuses.

On the other hand, student militants and their supporters complained that the mass media, which were part of the establishment they hated, failed to focus on the root problems of the disorders and thus to help the public understand the issues involved. They saw scant evidence that the media were bringing before the public such matters as the universities' tie-ins with the military, their heavy involvement in real estate and other extraneous enterprises, the role of ROTC on campus, the vesting of control of some institutions in boards composed of such remote groups as wealthy business people and lawyers, and the alleged depersonalization of campus life.

Student militants had observed the unprecedented media attention given to the problem of black employment and representation of blacks on the screen as a result of the civil rights protest movement and the later riots. Many now sought to direct nationwide attention to what they considered the ills of society as reflected in the universities. A hard core of militants obviously sought to tear down the entire structure, whereas most students merely desired changes in some patterns of national life. When the antiwar and protest movements coalesced in the campaign of Senator Eugene McCarthy for the Democratic presidential nomination, many of these students went to Chicago as delegates and workers for McCarthy. The militants also went, seeking to tear apart the political fabric by provoking street rioting. This they accomplished. Altogether, it was a tension-filled four days without precedent, as one TV network described them, "either in the history of American politics or in the experience of American journalism."

The National Commission on the Causes and Prevention of Violence asked Chicago attorney Daniel Walker to study the convention disturbances. Walker's staff took statements from 1410 eye-witnesses and participants and had access to more than 2000 interviews conducted by the FBI. The report described both provocation and retaliation. The provocation "took the form of obscene epithets, of rocks, sticks, bathroom tiles, and even human feces hurled at police by demonstrators," some planned, some spontaneous, and some provoked by police action. The retaliation was "unrestrained and indiscriminate police violence on many occasions, particularly at night," with reporters and photographers singled out for assault, and their equipment deliberately damaged. The final report of the commission in December 1969 said the Chicago police used "excessive force not only against the provocateurs but also against the peaceful demonstrators and passive bystanders. Their conduct, while it won the support of the majority, polarized substantial and previously neutral segments of the population against the authorities and in favor of the demonstrators."

Although the Walker Report disclosed that no fewer than 70 broadcast and print reporters and camera operators suffered injuries at the hands of the police, scant attention was paid to this fact by an uneasy public. In the words of TV news executive William Small, the public, rather than accept reality, will prefer "to kill a messenger." (Small wrote a book with that phrase as its title.) CBS anchorman Walter Cronkite, angered when he and the TV audience saw floor guards slug CBS correspondent Dan Rather to the floor, later found himself virtually apologizing to Chicago Mayor Richard J. Daley. CBS correspondent Eric Sevareid found the public's reaction obvious:

> Over the years the pressure of public resentment against screaming militants, foul-mouthed demonstrators, arsonists, and looters had built up in the national boiler. With Chicago it exploded. The feelings that millions of people released were formed long before Chicago. Enough was enough: the police *must* be right. Therefore, the reporting *must* be wrong.

THE GOVERNMENT ATTACKS

It was in this setting of a frustrating war, big-city riots, student demonstrations, radical militancy, and sex-drugs-pornography permissiveness that Richard Nixon became president. Beaten narrowly in 1960, apparently out of politics after losing the California governorship in 1962 and telling the press "you won't have Dick Nixon to kick around any more," he had rebounded into the political vacuum caused by the Goldwater debacle of 1964, Lyndon Johnson's retirement, and the assassinations of John and Robert Kennedy.

Hubert Humphrey, his campaign left in shambles by the Chicago convention, which alienated both conservative-minded voters and the antiwar intellectuals, ran a hard race but failed because he lost all the southern and border states except Texas. Nixon received 43.16 percent of the popular vote; Humphrey, 42.73; and Wallace, 13.63. The Democrats won both houses of Congress; indeed, Nixon was to become the first American president never to carry at least one house with him.

Richard Nixon's personality remains to be fully dissected, but he was clearly a loner, instinctively distrustful of others, a hard-nosed politician who nursed resentments into hatreds and insisted upon taking revenge. Feeling intense political isolation as a minority president and determined to win reelection in 1972, Nixon assumed that he had to attack his enemies, especially the media. He would coalesce his conservative support by continuing the Vietnam War until peace could be won "with honor," by blunting the black movement through the issue of unpopular school busing, and by taking roundhouse swings at those he hated—political radicals, student militants, Eastern establishment intellectuals, and influential large daily newspapers such as the New York *Times* and Washington *Post,* which he regarded as "soft" on social and political issues.

The president asked his top aides 21 times in one month in 1969 (mid-September to mid-October) to counter what he regarded as unfavorable media coverage, according to an internal White House memo made public in 1973 by a Republican member of the Senate Watergate committee, Lowell Weicker. The memo, written by presidential aide Jeb Stuart Magruder, argued that a "shotgunning" approach was not the best way "to get the media." Magruder recommended harassment of unfriendly news organizations by the Internal Revenue Service and the antitrust division of the Justice Department.

Attached to Magruder's memo was a log of Nixon's 21 requests to his aides to register complaints or "take appropriate action" against the media. The president's ire had been raised by "biased TV coverage of the administration over the summer," and the memos covered CBS, NBC, and ABC. One singled out Dan Rather, CBS White House correspondent. Among other targets were political columnist Jack Anderson, and *Time, Life,* and *Newsweek.* Nixon's associates proved responsive to his antimedia mood.

The Agnew Criticisms

The spark for a steadily growing conflagration of public debates, pressures against the media, and proposed and actual regulatory action by numerous agencies of government was touched off by Vice-President Spiro

Agnew in November 1969. In two speeches, he declared that the networks and newspapers with multiple media holdings exercised such powerful influence over public opinion that they should vigorously endeavor to be impartial and fair in reporting and commenting on national affairs. Specifically, Agnew criticized network managements for employing commentators with a preponderant Eastern establishment bias and for failing to provide a "wall of separation" between news and comment. A similar liberal bias, he inferred, affected the policies of the Washington *Post* and its other media holdings, and those of the New York *Times*. Because Agnew referred to the dependence of broadcast stations on government licensing, although disclaiming any thought of censorship, some observers saw in his remarks an implied threat to the freedom of broadcasters to report and comment freely on public affairs.

Never before had a high federal official made such direct attacks on those reporting and commenting on the news. A research study by Dennis T. Lowry comparing random samples of newscast items reporting administration activities for one-week periods in 1969 and 1970 bore out the contention that the criticisms generated by Agnew had significantly affected the newscasts in the direction of "safe" handling.

The Pentagon Papers

When the New York *Times* began in June 1971 to publish a series of news articles summarizing the contents of a 47-volume study of the origins of the Vietnam War, the "Pentagon Papers case" erupted. The study had been ordered by Defense Secretary McNamara, as a "History of the U.S. Decision-Making Process on Vietnam Policy" and had been made by a group from the RAND Corporation.

The study was historical and revealed no military secrets or strategy, but it was highly explosive in terms of political and diplomatic interest. As a Supreme Court justice put it, the Pentagon Papers were also highly embarrassing (to Kennedy, Johnson, and Nixon administrations alike).

Executives of the *Times* decided that it was in the national interest to report the documentary evidence that had come to their hands, even though it was stamped "top secret," as was the widespread custom in the government. A team of *Times* staff members led by managing editor Abe Rosenthal and reporter Neil Sheehan labored for three months to prepare the series.

When the first story appeared, Attorney General John Mitchell asked the *Times* to stop the series. The newspaper refused, and the Nixon administration went to court to seek a prior restraint order forbidding further publication. The government obtained a temporary restraining order but was refused a permanent one. It engaged in a second duel in the courts with the Washington *Post* and met increasing resistance from the Boston *Globe* and other newspapers dismayed that prior restraint had been invoked.

The case finally reached the Supreme Court, which by a five to four order continued the temporary prior restraint order, a shocking setback to the free press concept. The newspaper lawyers then avoided a historic showdown on the absolute nature of the constitutional ban on prior restraint, and argued only that the government could not prove any involvement of national security in the banned publication. To this, the Supreme Court agreed, six to three. Its members disagreed widely, however, on the ethics of the newspapers in printing documents stamped "secret" and on the nature of the prior restraint concept.

Subsequent alterations in the composition of the court, including the death of free press champion Justice Hugo Black, made it appear likely that the court would rule in a future case that it would be possible for the government to show justification for the imposition of prior restraint, even though the court said, "Any system of prior restraints of expression comes to this court bearing a heavy presumption against its constitutional validity." It was hoped that, as with the John Peter Zenger case, the Pentagon Papers case would not be repeated; that is, no president would again seek to impose a prior restraint upon the press, as had been done in 1971 for the first time in the history of the nation. The political sensitivities of the case made the Nixon administration pause in seeking criminal indictments against any newspaper editors or reporters involved in the Pentagon Papers disclosures, although it moved against Daniel Ellsberg, accused of taking the secret papers from the files.

Why did Nixon and his staff pursue this issue so relentlessly? Because the New York *Times* and Washington *Post* were involved; because Ellsberg represented the liberal intellectual element; because the majesty of the executive branch of the government and the presidency had been challenged on an issue they called "national security." And because, as FBI director William Ruckelshaus testified in May 1973, Nixon had instituted a wiretapping search to plug what he termed "security leaks" to the press as early as May 1969. Between then and February 1971, the FBI had wiretapped the telephones of four reporters and 13 government employees, mostly members of the National Security Council (this episode involved Secretary of State Henry Kissinger). One of the wiretaps recorded Ellsberg's voice.

When the FBI finally balked in 1971, the tapes were delivered to White House aide John Ehrlichman. Nixon then set up his own special investigative group, the infamous White House "plumbers," who were to implicate the CIA in their efforts. One of their jobs was to "get Ellsberg," and in July 1971 the White House unit obtained CIA "logistical support" in planning a September break-in at the office of Ellsberg's Los Angeles psychiatrist.

All this proof of White House subversion of the FBI and CIA came to light in May 1973 at the Los Angeles trial of Ellsberg and Anthony J. Russo for the Pentagon Papers theft. The CIA director admitted the facts in a memorandum to the U.S. district court, and Judge W. Matthew Byrne dismissed the case against Ellsberg and Russo, citing government misconduct. Nixon's zeal thus ensured Ellsberg's escape from prosecution. In July 1974, four members of the White House staff (Ehrlichman, Charles Colson, Egil Krogh, and Gordon Liddy) and two ex-CIA men were to be convicted on conspiracy charges or for the actual break-in.

CBS and "The Selling of the Pentagon"

Of the networks, the Columbia Broadcasting System especially drew the hatred of the Nixon staff. Dan Rather, White House correspondent, dueled with the president throughout the entire Watergate period and endured Nixon's sarcasm. Daniel Schorr and Marvin Kalb were harassed by White House-inspired investigations. Kalb was one of those who were wiretapped. (So was columnist Joseph Kraft; and joining these newsmen on the celebrated White House "enemies list" were columnist Mary McGrory and the managing editor of the conservative Los Angeles *Times*, Ed Guthman.)

It was not surprising, then, that CBS and its then president, Frank Stanton, should be involved in a major freedom of the press case in 1971. The program was "The Selling of the Pentagon," which had aroused anger both in the White House and in the Congress. At issue was Congress' right to legislative inquiry versus broadcasters' rights under freedom of the press. The case was sidelined in July 1971 when the House of Representatives returned to committee a proposed contempt citation against CBS and Stanton.

The citation was recommended by the House Commerce Committee when the network refused to supply all its "out-takes," or unused pieces of film and tape, used in the production of the controversial documentary. The award-winning investigative report contended that the Department of Defense was spending millions of dollars promoting both its activities and political points of view and that, moveover, it had stopped none of its promotions despite a presidential directive to do so. Critics, including Vice-President Spiro Agnew and high-ranking members of Congress, charged that CBS News edited some answers selectively and out of sequence. Other allegations of error and distortion were made.

In reply to a subpoena, Stanton testified before the House Special Subcommittee on Investigations, but declined to produce the out-takes of the program—those edited from the finished product. Pointing to the "chilling effect" not only of the subpoena but of the investigation itself, Stanton stated: "If newsmen are told that their notes, films, and tapes will be subject to compulsory process so that the government can determine whether the news has been satisfactorily edited, the scope, nature, and vigor of their newsgathering and reporting activities will inevitably be curtailed." On the contrary, contended Committee Chairman Harley Staggers, "Fraud and deception in the presentation of purportedly bona fide news events," he said, "is no more protected by the First Amendment than is the presentation of fraud and deception in the context of commercial advertising or quiz programs."

Dan Rather, who succeeded Walter Cronkite to become anchorman in 1981 of "The Evening News With Dan Rather" on CBS. As the network's White House correspondent, Rather engaged in verbal duels with President Nixon throughout the Watergate period. He also achieved prominence on the CBS "60 Minutes" program. (Photo courtesy of Columbia Broadcasting System.)

The House, by a vote of 226 to 181, declined to cite Stanton and the network for contempt. The dean of the Congress, Emanuel Celler, chairman of the Judiciary Committee, reflected the sense of the majority: "The First Amendment," he said, "towers over these proceedings like a colossus and no *esprit de corps* and no tenderness of one member for another should force us to topple over this monument to our liberties; that is, the First Amendment. . . . There may be no distinction between the right of a press reporter and a broadcaster. Otherwise, the stream of news may be dried up."

Nixon's Effective Use of Television

There was a positive side to Richard Nixon's involvement with the media. In the wake of his disastrous television debate with John F. Kennedy in 1960, he assiduously studied the medium. He loosened up, learned to joke about himself in televised interviews, and whenever possible utilized staged situations (convention press conferences with selected members asking questions, political speeches before controlled small audiences, person-to-person interviews) rather than rough-and-tumble news conferences with the pros.

Most effectively of all, he used television in live news-making situations in which no journalists were interposed between him and his audience. His visits to the Soviet Union were a television success. And his imagination-catching trip to mainland China was a triumph.

Such was Nixon's style. He did not like the regular White House press conferences. Instead, he relied upon prime-time requests for direct talks to the television audience. During their first 1½ years in office, according to one careful count, Eisenhower had made three such requests, Kennedy four, and Johnson seven. Nixon made 14 his first 18 months, and his final talk from the Oval Office the night he resigned the presidency was his thirty-seventh.

Nixon's use of television in the 1972 campaign was faultless. He selected controlled audiences for backdrops, avoided confrontations with his Democratic opponent, and capitalized on his foreign affairs leadership. The luckless George McGovern, plagued with controversies over his running mate and supported only by a loose confederation of political minorities—women's rights advocates, big-city intellectual liberals, blacks, young people—caught the media criticism while the Nixon campaign rolled on toward a nearly clean sweep of electoral votes.

WATERGATE AND THE MEDIA

If the president and his Oval Office advisers had been able to see ahead, they would not have become involved in Watergate. But they had assumed since 1969 that they would be fighting for their political lives in 1972 as minority party leaders against a strong Democratic party candidate—a Kennedy, a Muskie, a Humphrey. And they had put in motion a plan that could not be halted when McGovern appeared on the scene.

That plan involved the harassment of the media, the creation of an enemies list, the raising of a $60 million fund for the Committee to Reelect the President that often involved illegal pressure upon corporations, the creation of a "dirty tricks" group that sabotaged Democratic presidential candidates (notably Edmund Muskie), and the use of the IRS, FBI, and CIA to discourage political opponents and check on possibly vulnerable Democrats (notably Edward Kennedy).

It also had involved the creation of the White House plumbers group, whose talents were used against Ellsberg in 1971 and who now were to bring the Nixon administration to disaster. It was June 17, 1972; the target was the offices of the Democratic National Committee in the Watergate building complex, including that of Chairman Lawrence O'Brien; the apparent goals were to find interesting materials and to "bug" the O'Brien office in the hope of developing compromising tapes that could be used against the Democrats if they mounted a strong campaign threatening Nixon's reelection.

Disaster struck. The five men on the job bungled it; a watchman called the police; within two or three days the trail was leading from the plumbers back to their White House sponsors. The Washington *Post* assigned two youthful reporters, Carl Bernstein and Bob Woodward, to follow that trail. More experienced men might have faltered, but instinctively executives of the *Post* and its still obscure team of reporters sensed that an incredible story was in the making.

What the Tapes Finally Revealed

The twists and turns of the Watergate story can best be understood by first knowing the ending. What became referred to as "the smoking gun"—positive proof of President Nixon's participation in the Watergate conspiracy and consequent criminal obstruction of justice—did not publicly emerge until 780 days after the break-in. Four days later, Nixon was on his way to exile in San Clemente.

The president's entire defense had been built around his claim that he had not known about the Watergate problems until March 21, 1973, when his counsel, John Dean, told him there was "a cancer on the Presidency." Many dents were made in this defense, and Nixon's impeachment had been voted by the House Judiciary Committee, but the smoking gun was missing until the story's end.

It was the tape of June 23, 1972, conversations in the Oval Office. Why Nixon had taped his private conversations, and why the tapes survived to bring down his administration, remain topics for speculation. From the time a presidential aide revealed their existence in July 1973, a tense struggle developed over them. An incredibly detailed presidential daily diary, recording minute-by-minute his conversations, had readily been made available to investigators and the media. It proved to be the key to the tapes. There were three conversations listed for June 23 between the president and H. R. Haldeman, his chief of staff.

After losing a Supreme Court decision on custody of the tapes, Nixon had no recourse but to release the June 23 tape on August 5, 1974. As the impartial and authoritative research publication *Congressional Quarterly* summarized the event in its 1040-page detailed documentary review, *Watergate: Chronology of a Crisis,* "Nixon acknowledged in an accompanying statement that he had withheld the contents of the tapes from his staff and his attorneys despite the fact that they contradicted his previous declarations of non-involvement and lack of knowledge of the Watergate coverup." Six days after the break-in, the tape related, Nixon and Haldeman had developed and put into operation a plan to have top CIA officials tell the FBI to stay out of investigations of the Watergate break-in for national security reasons. Thus the employees of the Nixon reelection committee and White House staff members involved might escape detection.

(By permission of Paul Conrad, Los Angeles *Times.*)

There were other tapes, made public either late in the investigation or at the later trial of the coverup participants in 1974, which proved the depths of the Watergate conspiracy and Nixon's involvement. Some tapes revealed the attitude of the Nixon administration toward the media. The Washington *Post* obtained this censored portion of the September 15, 1972, tape from the House Judiciary Committee:

President The main, main thing is the *Post* is going to have damnable, damnable problems out of this one. They have a television station—
Dean That's right, they do.
President And they're going to have to get it renewed.
Haldeman They have a radio station, too.
President Does that come up too? The point is, when does it come up?
Dean I don't know. The practice of non-licensees filing on top of licensees has certainly got more . . .
President That's right.
Dean . . . more active in the, this area.
President And it's going to be goddamn active here.

Three months later, four application challenges had been filed against two Florida television stations owned by the *Post* interests by a number of Nixon friends and supporters. As Kenneth Clawson, White House communications officer, put it to the Los Angeles *Times* later: "I separate out TV from the print media when it comes to criticism. Newspapers are privately owned, but we all have a piece of TV's ass and we're entitled to do something—although I'm not sure exactly what—if it offends us."

Coverups by the White House

Government investigators of the caliber of Archibald Cox and Leon Jaworski, Watergate special prosecutors, and John Doar, Judiciary Committee counsel, were long aware of many of the events concealed in the tapes held by Nixon. Federal Judge John J. Sirica similarly suspected the wide ramifications of the conspiracy and helped to pry out the truth. Those media reporters who became deeply involved in the Watergate story also knew how it was going to end—if proof could be obtained.

It was therefore almost unbearably frustrating to those individuals, and to members of the public who held the same views, to be confronted with two years of false statements by the president, his White House staff, and those who came to his support gratuitously. When the Washington *Post* was awarded the Pulitzer Prize gold medal for meritorious public service in May 1973, the paper, predictably, was attacked by Vice-President Agnew. But it also was castigated by Democratic Senator William Proxmire for "the McCarthyistic destruction of President Nixon that is now going on with increasing vehemence daily in the press." Proxmire said Nixon "is being tried, sentenced, and executed by rumor and allegation" because the press was quoting John Dean as saying Nixon was involved in the Watergate coverup. He was joined in this gratuitous attack on the *Post* and other newspapers by Democratic Senator Mike Mansfield and Republican

Senator Hugh Scott, the two floor leaders. Both denounced "rumor and innuendo."

How the Media Fared with the Watergate Story

The Washington *Post* had led in Watergate coverage from the beginning. Its reporting team, Carl Bernstein and Bob Woodward, was backed by publisher Katharine Graham, executive editor Benjamin Bradlee, managing editor Howard Simons, and District of Columbia editor Barry Sussman (it started as a local police story). The *Post* was first to uncover the CIA connection; first to link the break-in culprits with White House sponsors; first on August 1, 1972, to print the proof that a $25,000 check donated to the Committee to Re-Elect the President had ended up in the Watergate conspirators' defense fund (Haldeman had informed Nixon about this slipup on June 23). On October 10, the *Post* broke its major story, identifying the Watergate affair as one of massive political spying and sabotage. It followed with two more October stories linking Dwight Chapin and H. R. Haldeman wih the operation.

But few were following in the *Post*'s footsteps. Press critic Ben Bagdikian calculated that of 433 Washington-based reporters who could in theory have been assigned to the Watergate story when it broke in the fall of election year 1972, only 15 actually were. Of some 500 political columns written by Washington pundits between June and Election Day, fewer than two dozen concerned Watergate.

Media critic Edwin Diamond found that during the seven-week preelection period beginning September 14, CBS devoted almost twice as much evening air time to Watergate as its competitors (CBS, 71 minutes; NBC, 42; ABC, 41). More than one-third of NBC coverage came on two nights, reporting the indictment of the Watergate break-in team September 15 and the *Post*'s October 10 sabotage story. Half of the NBC and ABC stories were less than a minute in length; CBS dealt so routinely with a major political story only five times. John Chancellor of NBC took honors in reporting the October 10 sabotage story fully; CBS ended its efforts with two special reports on Watergate the week preceding Nixon's reelection. George McGovern protested the general lack of interest in vain. Because of media inattention, the Gallup Poll found in October 1972 that only 52 percent of Americans recognized the word *Watergate*.

The Watergate break-in trial began in Judge Sirica's court in January, and attention increased with guilty pleas and convictions. A bombshell exploded in March when James W. McCord wrote Sirica a letter saying he and the other six arrested men were only agents for higher authorities. The Los Angeles *Times* contributed its first major newsbreak, linking John Dean and Jeb Magruder to the break-in; the *Post* followed with the names of John Mitchell and Charles Colson (all four eventually pleaded guilty or were convicted of conspiracy).

Watergate was now the consuming news story. Seven out of ten Americans listened on April 30, 1973, as President Nixon announced the resignations of Haldeman, Ehrlichman, Dean, and Attorney General Kleindienst; 41 percent gave him a positive rating, 36 percent, a negative rating. Gallup now found 83 percent had heard of Watergate, but more than half thought it was "just politics." The Senate Watergate Committee with Sam J. Ervin, Jr., as chairman began televised hearings on May 17; soon "Senator Sam" became a household character. Magruder and Dean made confessions and major charges against the White House in June testimony. At first the public split evenly (38 to 37 percent) on whether to believe Nixon or Dean; by April 1974, it found Dean more believable (46 to 29 percent).

Vice-President Agnew's resignation on October 10 after pleading no contest to a charge of income tax evasion, based on a court-submitted record of extensive bribe-taking, shocked the country. Attorney General Elliot Richardson accepted plea bargaining because the Watergate crisis pointed to the need for a new vice-president—Gerald Ford. The Washington *Star*, a rock-ribbed Republican paper, took honors on the Agnew exposé.

The crisis over the tapes now began to consume the Nixon administration. Judge Sirica's demand for their surrender had been upheld by the court of appeals; Nixon countered with a plan to submit transcripts only. Special prosecutor Archibald Cox was summarily fired when he objected, and Elliot Richardson and William Ruckelshaus resigned from the Justice Department in what became known as the "Saturday night massacre." A spontaneous wave of protest swept the country; Nixon hastily appointed a new special prosecutor and handed over the requested tapes. But some of them were missing and one had the famed 18½-minute gap blamed on secretary Rose Mary Woods' "stretch" for the telephone (Sirica found it was a deliberate erasure).

The ultraconservative *National Review* and the Detroit *News* ran November editorials calling for Nixon's resignation in the wake of the Saturday night massacre and the tapes scandal. They were joined by Time Inc., whose magazines had three times endorsed Nixon for president; by the Denver *Post*, and by the New York *Times*.

Public opinion, as reflected in the Gallup and Harris Polls, also began to shift. Everybody had now heard about Watergate; the number who believed Nixon's story that he had no knowledge of the break-in or coverup had dwindled to 15 percent. Harris found in December for the first time that more Americans thought Nixon should resign than wanted him to stay (47 to 42 percent).

The indictments for the Watergate coverup conspiracy came on March 1, 1974. The grand jury gave Judge Sirica a sealed envelope about Richard Nixon; on June 5, his longtime supporter, the Los Angeles *Times*, revealed that the president had been named an unindicted coconspirator

The Weather

Today—Rain, high in the low to mid 80s, low in the mid to upper 60s. Chance of rain is 60 per cent today, 40 per cent tonight. Saturday — Cloudy, high around 80. Yesterday's temp. range, 77-68. Details, Page D19.

The Washington Post

Index — 112 Pages, 4 Sections

Amusements	D 1	Metro	D13
Classified	C14	Obituaries	D19
Comics	D20	Outdoors	C 8
Editorials	A30	Sports	C 1
Fed. Diary	D21	Style	D 1
Financial	C 9	TV-Radio	D 8

97th Year No. 247 FRIDAY, AUGUST 9, 1974 Phone (202) 223-6000 15c

Nixon Resigns

The climax of the credibility duel waged between the White House and the press. Huge newspaper headlines of this nature heralded President Nixon's resignation throughout the nation and the world. (Reproduced by permission of the Washington *Post*, copyright © 1974 by the Washington *Post*.)

with Haldeman, Ehrlichman, Mitchell, and others. Some of their defense attorneys had been intimating the same. (The trial ended with four convictions on January 1, 1975.)

The story now came to a rapid end. Nixon released a massive mound of tape transcripts on April 29. The Chicago *Tribune* flew advance copies supplied them by the White House home in an airplane; had its editorial board read them; published them in full; and editorially announced, "We are appalled." The *Tribune* then called on Nixon to resign or be impeached.

The House Judiciary Committee opened its impeachment hearings on May 9, under chairman Peter Rodino and with the guidance of counsel John Doar. On July 24, it began its televised debate on the impeachment articles; that day the Supreme Court in an eight to zero decision read by Chief Justice Burger ordered the president to relinquish all tapes requested by the special prosecutor, including the fatal June 23, 1972, recording.

The Judiciary Committee hearings were conducted at the highest levels of democratic processes and did much to reassure the huge television audience that honesty and decency could still prevail. All 38 members had their say. There were 21 Democrats (three of them from southern conservative ranks) and 17 Republicans. Six of the Republicans joined the Democrats to seal Nixon's doom. On July 27, the committee voted 27 to 11 to impeach the president for obstruction of justice; it followed with two more articles charging abuse of presidential powers and contempt of Congress. Its report was still before the House when the President resigned on August 9, 1974, but became a permanent record.

The editorial words of the Los Angeles *Times* on August 7, written in the wake of reading the June 23, 1972, transcript, offer a fit closing:

> No one can read those conversations between Richard Nixon and H. R. Haldeman without anger—anger at these men whose arrogance let them, with such apparent ease, abuse trust, pervert the system of government and breach the law in a voracious bid for more power. . . .
>
> Mr. Nixon has brought dishonor to the Presidency—dishonor and disgrace. He has broken his oath of office. By his own admission, he has

> committed felonious crimes. He is not fit to remain the President. . . .
> We ourselves especially feel the betrayal of Mr. Nixon. This newspaper has supported him in his candidacy through a political career that we have more often cheered than criticized. As recently as 1972 we had supported his bid for reelection.

Too few newspapers were as forthright and candid as this conservative leader of American journalism in enlightening their readers.

What of the reporter heroes? Bernstein and Woodward became wealthy by writing the best seller, *All the President's Men,* and a movie was made of it starring Robert Redford. Dan Rather made less money with his book *The Palace Guard,* left the White House, and became a CBS commentator and anchorman.

What of the public's thanks to the press? Generally the press came out ahead. It could thank the House Judiciary Committee for so handling its hearings that public belief in the charges against Nixon—and in the media which had reported those charges—had been greatly enhanced. The polls showed in August 1974 that only 33 percent of Americans thought Nixon should be granted immunity (as he was the next month by President Ford), while 58 percent said he should stand trial. But in June 1974, in answer to a question asking opinion about the amount of space and time devoted to Watergate, 53 percent said "too much," as against 30 percent "about right" and only 13 percent "too little." The messenger was still only sometimes appreciated.

PUBLIC CREDIBILITY OF THE MEDIA

While many Americans in the last two decades viewed the mass media as "too liberal," despite their predominantly conservative ownerships, liberals and young activists saw the media as unresponsive, obtuse, and largely irredeemable as instruments for illuminating the root issues of social unrest. As a result, they turned to underground newspapers, discovered ways in which to use the media for their own ends, and increasingly sought government intervention with which to gain access.

Many intellectuals viewed the mass media with disdain for catering to mass tastes. Public officials generally resented the press' role of "watch-dog" for the public's interests. Specialists in most fields complained that reporting of their activities often was oversimplified or erroneously stated. Many persons felt that the media conspired with other elements of the establishment in withholding the truth of events. And many newspeople themselves dissented through publication of at least 20 critical journalism reviews. In addition, the media were caught in the public mood of distrust for almost all institutions, including business corporations, the church, educational institutions, and government.

A number of groups and individuals took up Vice-President Agnew's assault against what was considered to be biased and often inaccurate reporting of national issues and events, primarily by the Washington press corps, the New York *Times,* the Washington *Post, Newsweek, Time,* CBS, NBC, and, to a lesser extent, ABC.

Among them were two "nonpartisan, nonprofit" organizations, Accuracy in Media, Inc. (AIM) and the American Institute for Political Communication (AIPC). AIM investigated complaints of serious error in news reporting, such as those alleged in the CBS documentary, "The Selling of the Pentagon"; statements on defense spending made by NBC newsman David Brinkley; and New York *Times* articles about the Vietnam War. The American Institute for Political Communication began a series of studies in 1971 which, it reported, revealed "a significant degree of bias" in television news coverage of the 1972 Democratic presidential primary ("pro-McGovern") and the Vietnam War ("anti-Nixon").

In addition to numerous magazine articles and newspaper columns, a spate of books appeared with similar contentions of media pollution. They included Edith Efron's *The News Twisters;* Arnold Beichman's *Nine Lies About America;* and James Keogh's *President Nixon and the Press.*

In reaction to the criticism, the networks commissioned extensive studies of their own news practices and specifically examined the programs that were the subjects of the Efron and AIPC charges. Independent scholars in each instance questioned the methodology and the objectivity of those studies.

George Gallup, Jr., president of the Gallup Poll, reported in 1980 that, although survey findings clearly showed that a great deal of good will exists toward the press upon which it can build in the years ahead, Americans were leaning heavily, two to one, toward the view that present curbs on the press are "not strict enough" rather than "too strict." Said Gallup: "Tougher restrictions are favored by those who feel that newspapers sometimes publish information that is not in the best interests of the nation and should be kept confidential; distort and exaggerate the news in the interest of making headlines and selling newspapers; and rush to print without first making sure all facts are correct." He added that the proportion of Americans who said their newspapers were accurate in the treatment of news events about which they personally knew had dropped to 34 percent, a full 23 points since 1958.

The Gallup survey conflicted with findings of a Louis Harris poll in late 1980. Whereas Gallup found that 51 percent of the public said it had a "great deal" or "quite a lot" of confidence in newspapers, the Harris poll revealed that only 19 percent of Americans express high confidence in the press, a drop of nine points since 1979 and well below the 30 percent rating in 1973, when Watergate disclosures were widely carried in the print media.

High public confidence in television news, Harris reported, dropped to 29 percent in 1980 from 37 percent in 1979 and 41 percent during Watergate.

A survey conducted by the Public Agenda Foundation and funded by the John and Mary Markle Foundation disclosed in 1980 that the majority of Americans support laws requiring fairness in newspaper coverage of controversial stories or political races—laws similar to those already governing the broadcast media's handling of those matters.

Media leaders could take only scant comfort in the Harris findings that high public confidence in the profession of law had dropped from 24 percent in 1973 to only 13 percent in 1980, with several other occupations and institutions receiving even lower credence. As a consequence, efforts were intensified to encourage members of the media to maintain the highest principles of journalism and also, through a series of First Amendment congresses throughout the nation, to raise the level of consciousness of the American public regarding their basic freedoms.

Presidential Endorsements

The support given by newspapers on their editorial pages to presidential candidates has been another source for charges of political bias. Figures compiled by *Editor & Publisher* magazine explain why. Historically, the majority of daily newspapers giving support to a presidential candiate has been on the side of the Republican party.

In 1980 President Jimmy Carter was endorsed by newspapers with 21.5 percent of the polled circulation, compared with 48.6 percent endorsing the Republican challenger, Ronald Reagan, and 4.4 percent supporting independent candidate John Anderson. In this "campaign of frustration" newspapers with 25.5 percent of the polled circulation were uncommitted or unresponsive. Reagan's support was the lowest recorded in the poll for a Republican except in 1964.

In 1976 President Gerald Ford was endorsed by newspapers with 62.2 percent of the polled circulation. Jimmy Carter's 22.8 percent was the best for a Democrat since 1940 except during 1964. Newspapers with 15 percent of the polled circulation were uncommitted or unresponsive. But President Richard Nixon had the endorsement of 753 daily newspapers in his one-sided reelection victory in 1972, whereas only 56 supported Senator George McGovern, *Editor & Publisher* reported. In terms of the percentage of the polled circulation, Nixon had 77.4 percent to McGovern's 7.7 percent, with the remainder making no endorsement. This was Nixon's highest support in three presidential races. McGovern's meager total (representing 3 million circulation) was the lowest recorded for a major candidate since the trade journal began its studies in 1936.

In 1960 Vice-President Nixon was supported by newspapers with 70.9 percent of the polled circulation in his unsuccessful race against John F. Kennedy, who had 15.8 percent. A dramatic reversal occurred in 1964. President Lyndon B. Johnson, who succeeded to the White House after Kennedy's assassination, faced a right-wing conservative Republican,

Barry Goldwater. Johnson had the support of dailies representing 61.5 percent of the polled circulation; Goldwater, 21.5 percent. The trend swung back to the Republican side four years later, when Nixon faced Vice-President Hubert Humphrey, the Democratic nominee. Nixon had the support of newspapers representing 69.9 percent of polled circulation; Humphrey, 15 percent. Twelve papers supported George C. Wallace, the conservative third-party candidate.

The Journalist as Government Agent

The public's faith in the journalist as an independent gatherer and interpreter of the news, free from any connection with government, was diminished in 1977 with revelations that many American news personnel, in the decades after World War II, had served as salaried intelligence operatives for the Central Intelligence Agency (CIA) while also performing their duties as reporters.

Watergate reporter Carl Bernstein, after an extensive inquiry, said more than 400 American journalists had secretly carried out assignments for the CIA. The New York *Times* stated that between 30 and 100 journalists were paid for such work.

The *Times* reported that more than 50 news organizations, owned or subsidized by the CIA, had spread pro-American views as well as propaganda and lies in ways that often made Americans and foreigners the victims of misinformation. In addition, the *Times* reported, at least 12 full-time CIA officers had worked abroad as reporters or noneditorial employees of American-owned news organizations, in some cases having been hired by the news organizations whose credentials they carried.

Executives of the networks, newspapers, magazines, and wire services cited by Bernstein generally denied the charges affecting their organizations, on the basis of their own knowledge or of extensive investigations. Some reporters freely acknowledged that they had exchanged information with the CIA, maintaining that, during the era of the Cold War with the communist world, cooperation between journalists and the CIA represented both good citizenship and good craftsmanship.

CIA officials, who saw nothing untoward in such relationships, said the agency had cut back sharply on the use of reporters since 1973, primarily as a result of pressure from the media, but Bernstein insisted that some journalist-operatives were still posted abroad.

A House Intelligence subcommittee conducted hearings on the matter in 1978. The chairman, Representative Les Aspin, said that the hearings were intended to give the committee an idea of what kinds of relations with the press intelligence officers consider useful and what kinds of relations the media consider harmful or unethical. A chief concern expressed was the extent to which misinformation planted abroad finds its way back into the American press.

The issue remained alive in 1980, when Admiral Stanfield Turner, director of the CIA, told the American Society of Newspaper Editors in convention that in three separate instances since 1977 he had personally approved the use of journalists for secret intelligence operations. Replying to sharp criticism by editors, Turner said that the journalists had not in fact been utilized as operatives, but he insisted on reserving the right to employ them in future emergencies.

A similar threat to the integrity of the newsgathering process had occurred during the Vietnam War era when law enforcement agents masqueraded as reporters and camera operators in order to obtain information, primarily about dissident groups. The Twentieth Century Fund Task Force on the Government and the Press reported in 1972 that Army agents both in the United States and in Vietnam, as well as intelligence units of local police agencies, had posed as reporters. The FBI reportedly did not permit its agents to pose as news personnel, but placed journalists on the payroll when they initiated the move.

Fred P. Graham, in a background paper prepared for the Task Force, pointed out that government may need stratagems to determine the intentions of some militant organizations and prevent or anticipate acts of violence such as bombings. "The penetration of such groups by undercover agents is nothing new," Graham said, "but the use of newsmen as agents is relatively new—and hazardous. By making journalists suspect, the practice threatens to cut off the flow of information needed to enable the public to make sensible judgments about dissident groups. Conversely, a free press that can be trusted to report on dissident groups fairly may well defuse extreme militancy. The press is a safety valve for dissent that protects both the public interest and the right of legitimate social criticism."

COPYRIGHT LAW AND THE MEDIA

On January 1, 1978, a comprehensive copyright revision law, described by Congressional leaders as "the greatest advance in copyright legislation in our nation's history," went into effect.

For more than two decades Congress had endeavored to revise the amended copyright law of 1909, which rapidly became outdated by advances in technology. The development of modern photocopying machines, cable television, and the computer had raised serious and complex problems primarily affecting authors, performers, book and magazine publishers and distributors, libraries, educational institutions, cable television broadcasters, and motion picture and other audiovisual program suppliers.

Copyright is the exclusive right to reproduce, publish, and sell the matter and form of a literary, musical, or artistic work. Designed to encourage the creation and dissemination of original works to the public, copyright was originally established by statute in England in 1556. Prior to that time, the only protection that existed was under common law. The United States had recognized common law copyright, which protected works before publication. The new law, however, established a single system of copyright protection for all copyrightable works, whether published or unpublished.

The law extended copyright protection from the former maximum of 56 years to the life of the author plus 50 years. For works made for hire and copyrighted by others, as well as anonymous material, the new term is 75 years from publication or 100 years from creation, whichever is shorter.

The measure provides for the payment, under a system of compulsory licensing, of certain royalties for the secondary transmission of copyrighted works on cable television systems. The fees are based on the amount of distant nonnetwork programming carried and on subscriber receipts. The assessments are paid to the Register of Copyrights for later distribution to the copyright owners by a newly established copyright royalty tribunal.

The law permits archives and libraries, such as Vanderbilt University's TV news archives, to copy news programs for lending to researchers. The borrowers are restricted from using copies for profit or politics. An American TV and Radio Archives was established in the Library of Congress for collecting, cataloguing, and lending broadcast news and entertainment programs.

Noncommercial transmissions by public broadcasters of published musical and graphic works are subject to a compulsory license, thus eliminating the paperwork and legal costs of negotiation for the rights to such broadcast material. Public broadcasters are urged to negotiate their own royalty rates.

One section of the law recognizes the principle of "fair use" as a limitation on the exclusive rights of copyright owners. Within certain prescribed limits, copies may be made for purposes such as criticism, comment, news reporting, teaching (including multiple copies for classroom use), scholarship, or research. Libraries are permitted to make single copies of copyrighted works, also under stringent limitations. It quickly became apparent that the photocopying machines of the 1980s would disgorge increasing sheaves of materials for educational and research purposes.

The new law retains the provisions added to the former law in 1972 that accord protection against the unauthorized duplication of sound recordings. Compulsory licensing is provided for the recording of music.

The law removes the former exemption for performances of copyrighted music by jukeboxes. It substitutes a system of compulsory licensing based upon the payment by jukebox operators of an annual royalty fee to the Register of Copyrights for distribution to copyright owners.

Copyright secures only the property right in the manner and content of expression. Facts and ideas recited, or systems and processes described, are made freely available to the public. Although news itself is in the public domain and uncopyrightable, news accounts per se—that is, their particular literary arrangement—may be copyrighted, especially when they bear the mark of individual enterprise and literary style. "The Evening News With Dan Rather," for example, is copyrighted. Feature stories, editorials, columns, series of articles, cartoons, maps, photographs, and the like may be copyrighted. Newspapers usually copyright entire editions, by issue or weekly or monthly, in order to protect their advertising from piracy, although the copyright of an advertisement created solely by the advertiser may be retained by that person or company.

For infringement of copyright, courts may award statutory damages ranging from $250 to $10,000. In addition to or instead of a fine, conviction for criminal infringement carries a sentence of up to one year in prison.

Copies of the statute are available free of charge from the Copyright Office, Library of Congress, Washington, D.C. 20559.

Chapter 20

THE MEDIA'S LEGAL ENVIRONMENT

LAWS AFFECTING THE MEDIA

In the relationships of the press to society, through governing bodies and the courts, eight types of laws affecting the media may be listed. They are, in summary form:

1. *Common law,* written and reinforced by court decisions through the centuries;
2. *Constitutional law,* both federal and state, including the crucial First Amendment to the United States Constitution;
3. *Statutory law*—that passed by legislative bodies;
4. *Criminal law,* which concerns the press largely in the areas of treason, criminal libel, publication of lottery information, and fraudulent advertising;
5. *Civil law,* dealing with such matters as libel, invasion of privacy, and unfair competition;
6. *Equity*—seeking relief from the courts, such as the government's suit in the Pentagon Papers case;
7. *Administrative law,* as enacted by such agencies as the Federal Communications Commission and the Federal Trade Commission;
8. *Moral law,* which has no distinct position in our modern legal system, but which imposes a greater restriction on the press than any purely legal restraint. Conversely, it functions as a tremendous force that can overturn legal restraints and bring greater freedom for the press.

In this chapter, relationships between the media and the courts will be examined, tracing to the present the historic press freedoms first discussed in Chapter 3, involving the right to print, the right to criticize, and the right to report. A discussion of moral law will introduce Chapter 21, in which the media's social responsibilities are discussed.

THE FIRST AMENDMENT BATTLEFRONT

Freedom to print without prior restraint has been a basic tenet of Anglo-American civilization since 1694. It was written into the First Amendment to the United States Constitution as a part of the Bill of Rights. The high watermark for this concept was reached in 1931 when the Supreme Court, by invalidating a state law, applied the press guarantees of the First Amendment to the states in the case of *Near* v. *Minnesota.* But as supportive of the freedom to print as that decision was, it did not establish an absolute prohibition of prior restraint. The Pentagon Papers case of 1971 marked a diminishment in support of the philosophy of the freedom to print, and gave warning that the battlefront for even such an elementary freedom remained an active one.

Freedom to criticize is necessary to the realization of the proposition that the media are "the censors of their governors." A colonial jury's verdict in the John Peter Zenger trial of 1735 first challenged the theory of seditious libel, which had made it an automatic crime to criticize those in authority and thereby imperil their capacity to govern. But it was 1800 before Anglo-American law recognized the right to criticize public officials. The high watermark in the press-government duel was reached in the Watergate drama of 1974, but since then court decisions have whittled down this freedom.

The press has always had only a tenuous right to the freedom to report, first won when Parliament was opened to reporters in 1771 in England. What good is the freedom to print and to criticize, asked journalists, without access to news and information vital to the functioning of a democratic society? The frontier of freedom in this area was reached with passage by the United States Congress of the Freedom of Information Act in 1966 and its strengthening in 1974. But in the ebb and flow of the First Amendment battlefront, once again a reaction set in. The 1980s are thus certain to be years of challenge and struggle for writers, editors, broadcasters, and photographers who want to bring their words and images to the public.

THE RIGHT TO PRINT

During the 1981 celebrations of the fiftieth anniversary of the Supreme Court decision in *Near* v. *Minnesota,* it was generally recognized that this was the bedrock case for all constitutional defenses of First Amendment rights. In giving his five to four majority decision, Chief Justice Charles Evans Hughes had quoted from Blackstone on prior restraint and postpublication punishment:

> The liberty of the press is indeed essential to the nature of a free state; but this consists in laying no *previous* restraints upon publications, and not in freedom from censure for criminal matter when published. Every freeman has an undoubted right to lay what sentiments he pleases before the public; to forbid this is to destroy the freedom of the press; but if he publishes what is improper, mischievous, or illegal, he must take the consequences of his own temerity.

Hughes continued with a dictum, or observation, that weakened the case for absolute protection against prior restraint:

> The objection has also been made that the principle as to immunity from previous restraint is stated too broadly, if every such restraint is deemed to be prohibited. That is undoubtedly true; the protection even as to previous restraint is not absolutely unlimited. But the limitation has been recognized only in exceptional cases.

The chief justice defined some such cases: military secrets, overthrow of the government, and obscenity. But he excluded publication of censure of public officers and charges of official misconduct.

It was under this latter exclusion that the Supreme Court ruled six to three in favor of the New York *Times* in the Pentagon Papers case in 1971 (see Chapter 19). The court's earlier five to four vote to continue a temporary restraining order stopping publication of the Pentagon Papers series strongly indicated that it would not support a plea for application of the principle of absolute protection against prior restraint, so the newspaper attorneys argued successfully that the articles did not affect national security. But the court's *per curiam* decision did include these quotations from its decisions in previous cases:

> Any system of prior restraints of expression comes to this court bearing a heavy presumption against its constitutional validity.
>
> The Government thus carries a heavy burden of showing justification for the enforcement of such a restraint.

The Progressive Case

When press and government clashed over prior restraint in 1979, the Justice Department relied upon the Atomic Energy Act to obtain a U.S. district court's preliminary injunction prohibiting *The Progressive* magazine from publishing an article that supposedly contained secret information vital to the construction of a hydrogen bomb. Publication would result in "direct, immediate and irreparable" injury to national security, the government stated, by allowing nations not having the bomb to more easily construct one. The government relied upon the Atomic Energy Act's secrecy provisions being considered one of Chief Justice Hughes' "exceptional cases."

But the matter did not reach the Supreme Court, or even an appeals court verdict. First, it was discovered that documents containing "restricted data" similar to that in the *Progressive* article had been mistakenly declassified and been placed on open library shelves in Los Alamos. Then a computer programmer wrote an 18-page letter to a United States senator, using only library materials available to him, paralleling the *Progressive* article in content. He had sent the letter to several newspapers and magazines; one published it. The Justice Department immediately withdrew its suit, after six months of a previous restraint injunction, and *The Progressive* ran its article.

The Reporters Committee for Freedom of the Press stated: "But one thing remains clear; nothing was settled by *The Progressive* case, including the constitutionality of the Atomic Energy Act. The same type of complex and mostly secret court case could occur again the next time a publication has nuclear-related information that the government does not want published."

THE RIGHT TO CRITICIZE

Never had the press and a powerful political figure been so fiercely locked in struggle as in 1974, when the print and broadcast media persisted in pressing the Watergate inquiry until the courts and Congress forced President Nixon to make disclosures that brought about his resignation. The media were in danger, until the struggle had been won, for two reasons: the president had substantial support and the greater power of office, and many citizens thought it unwise to risk the political instability that might result from the forced resignation of a president. As we discussed in Chapter 19, the president's power evaporated, and the transition of office from Richard Nixon to Gerald Ford was a tranquil event.

Psychologically, the Watergate drama strengthened the historic press role of "censors of their governors." But perhaps in reaction to this demonstration of power on the part of the press, and more certainly as the result of the changing composition of Supreme Court membership toward a more conservative stance, constitutional cases involving the right to criticize public officials began to go against the media. The media thereby found themselves more restricted in their ability to comment and more vulnerable to suits for libel and slander.

Libel and Slander

One constant challenge confronting the communications media is to avoid libeling or slandering individuals or easily identifiable groups. Laws designed to protect persons from unfair and damaging attacks create well-defined limits as to what may be broadcast or printed without risking legal action and possibly heavy financial losses.

Defamation is communication that exposes people to hatred, ridicule, or contempt; lowers them in the esteem of their fellows; causes them to be shunned; or injures them in their business or calling. Its categories are *libel,* mainly printed or written material; and *slander,* mainly spoken words. Because a person may be injured as greatly in a radio or television broadcast as in a printed publication, the courts have come to treat broadcast defamation as libel.

Some defamation is considered privileged, such as statements made on the official record during court trials and public meetings of government bodies. For example, council member Jones may call council member Smith "a liar and a thief" during an official session, and the allegation may be safely broadcast or published because it is privileged by law. However, if Jones should make such a statement about Smith in the corridor after the meeting adjourns, the newspaper or broadcast station that reports it would risk a libel or slander suit from Smith unless it could prove that the charge was true.

The principal defenses against libel actions involving the press are provable truth, the privilege of reporting fairly and truly an official proceeding, the right of fair comment, consent, and the United States Supreme Court ruling in *New York Times* v. *Sullivan* that state libel laws must yield to the First Amendment freedom of the press guarantees.

Historically, the libel and slander laws have protected individuals or small groups of easily identified persons, but not large, amorphous groups. There is pressure now to enlarge protection to cover broader groups, such as ethnic minorities, but the difficulty in writing such laws has discouraged their adoption.

Criticism of Public Figures

A landmark case in broadening the media's right to comment was the Supreme Court ruling in *New York Times* v. *Sullivan* in 1964. The court held that a public official cannot recover damages for a defamatory falsehood relating to his or her official conduct without proving that the statement was made with actual malice. This and related rulings have broadened the interpretation of "public official" to include relatively minor public employees and even "public figures" such as former officeholders and prominent personalities.

The Supreme Court in *Rosenbloom* v. *Metromedia* extended the Sullivan ruling in 1971 to include a private person involved in an event of public interest. However, in *Gertz* v. *Welch,* in 1974, the court seemed to reverse its position. In a five to four decision, the court held that a "private person," regardless of involvement in a public event, might recover such actual damages as could be proved for injury or harm resulting from publication of a defamatory falsehood, without proof of actual malice by the libeler, but with proof of negligence as determined by a state standard.

The Colorado Supreme Court became the first state high court to accept the ruling, in 1975. Using the "reckless disregard" standard, the judges reviewed seven articles published in the Colorado Springs *Sun* and awarded an antique dealer actual and punitive damages for allegations that he had purchased stolen merchandise.

In *Firestone* v. *Time Inc.*, the Supreme Court ruled in 1976 that the wife of Russell Firestone III, scion of a prominent industrial family, was not a "public figure," even though she was a well-known citizen of Palm Beach, Florida, society and held press conferences during her celebrated divorce trial. She was awarded $100,000 in a libel suit against *Time* magazine for incorrectly reporting that her husband had been granted a divorce from her on grounds of extreme cruelty and adultery.

The decision unnerved news media executives and lawyers, occurring as it did during a period when more than 500 libel suits were being filed each year and juries seemed willing to compensate plaintiffs for their injuries with large settlements. With expenses ranging up to $100,000 or more per case, even when won, fears mounted that the threat of such high costs would make the news media more timid in their pursuit of news. These fears were somewhat allayed by the decision by Mrs. Firestone in 1978 to drop the case rather than go through a second trial, ordered by the Supreme Court to determine *Time*'s degree of negligence, (in order for her to collect the $100,000). Media lawyers expressed hope that the proving of negligence would be a difficult matter in such cases.

Another blow fell in 1979, when the Supreme Court ruled that engaging in criminal activity did not automatically make one a public figure, even for purposes of comment on issues related to the conviction. Since journalists had long operated under a "calculated risk" theory that a criminal cannot be libeled, this was a decision narrowing further the definition of a public figure that had been expanded in *Sullivan*.

The case *Wolston* v. *Reader's Digest Association, Inc.*, arose when a book author mistakenly identified Ilya Wolston as a Soviet espionage agent, when in reality Wolston had only been found guilty of criminal contempt for failure to appear before a grand jury in a case that had resulted in his aunt and uncle pleading guilty to espionage. A U.S. district court ruled that the author made an honest error when Wolston sued for libel, asserting that, since Wolston was a public figure as a convicted criminal, he had to prove actual malice. Therefore, the court granted a defense motion for summary judgment in behalf of the book publisher.

When the case reached the Supreme Court, Justice William Rehnquist wrote the reversal decision. He further limited the *Gertz* definition of a public figure, saying it included only those who voluntarily participated in public controversies over which the public itself was divided. Professor Paul Jess, of the University of Kansas, analyzing *Wolston* and other cases of 1979, said that Justice Rehnquist's language seemed to have sounded the death knell for newsworthiness as a defense in libel actions.

Things were made even more difficult for media libel lawyers when

Chief Justice Warren Burger commented in his decision of 1979, in the case of *Hutchinson* v. *Proxmire*: "We are constrained to express some doubt about the so-called 'rule' [of summary judgment on First Amendment grounds in libel cases]. The proof of 'actual malice' calls a defendant's state of mind into question . . . and does not readily lend itself to summary judgment." The District of Columbia Court of Appeals cited this Burger viewpoint in 1980 when it ordered columnist Ralph de Toledano to stand trial on libel charges brought against him by consumer activist Ralph Nader, rejecting de Toledano's argument that Nader was a public figure upon whom he had commented reasonably and that, therefore, there should be summary judgment. The Supreme Court refused to review the appeals court order, seemingly strengthening its opposition to the summary judgment pathway to libel defenses for the media. *Hutchinson* v. *Proxmire* also included a ruling that there was no immunity for those printing Senator Proxmire's press releases and newsletters. This, the court said, was an unwarranted extension of legislative immunity.

Another new rule for libel cases emerged from the decision in *Herbert* v. *Lando,* in 1979. This permits pretrial inquiry into the journalist's state of mind, as a means of establishing the presence of actual malice in a libel action. Colonel Anthony Herbert, a Vietnam War veteran, sued CBS and producer Barry Lando of the "60 Minutes" program for falsely and maliciously depicting him as a liar (Herbert had agreed that he was a public figure). His attorneys asked for the right to explore the states of mind of CBS newspeople at the time they were making editorial decisions. A United States court of appeals held that requiring reporters to divulge their thoughts and to reveal the content of their discussions with colleagues would "strike to the heart of the vital human component of the editorial process." The Supreme Court, in a six to three decision, reversed the appeals court decision, saying such inquiries were valid and necessary if the plaintiff was to be able to prove actual malice. Disturbing as the prospect of inquiry into a journalist's state of mind might be, there was merit to the contention that it was necessary in cases involving the need for proof of actual malice.

All told, the media entered the 1980s in a cautious manner, particularly when they were involved with comment on public persons. The expansion of latitude promised in the *Sullivan* case seemed largely evaporated by the prevailing judicial frame of mind exhibited by the Supreme Court.

THE RIGHT TO REPORT

While the narrowing of constitutional defenses in libel suits, particularly in reporting that involved public figures, became a problem for the media of the early 1980s, erosion of the right to report was even more extensive.

Supreme Court decisions of the 1970s adversely affected the media in four areas: 1) requiring reporters to reveal their sources in certain situations or face fines and imprisonment; 2) allowing police raids of newsrooms; 3) allowing law enforcement agencies access to telephone records of news organizations; 4) closing pretrial hearings and in some cases courtroom trials. These decisions, along with the erosion of the Freedom of Information Act that was gaining strength as the 1970s ended, affected not only the rights of newspeople, but of the public's right to know.

The Freedom of Information Crusade

Throughout American history, there has been conflict among the three branches of government—legislative, executive, and judicial. The acceptance of the principle of judicial review, making the Supreme Court the final authority on the constitutionality of legislative and executive actions, gave that branch relative freedom from conflict and attack. In the Watergate struggle, for example, President Nixon bowed to an eight to zero decision by the Court, which overruled his assertion of executive authority to suppress the Watergate tapes, and he relinquished the tapes. But the dueling between Congress and the White House over the principle of "executive privilege" continues unabated. The privilege of reporters to use public records and documents is involved in this infighting.

The Pentagon Papers case produced widespread realization that democratic principles are incompatible with the present sweep of executive privilege and its corollary, the executive practice of classification and withholding information from both the people and Congress. The knowledge that the government had classified the entire history of a foreign policy era, during which secret debate decided not only how but whether to conduct a war, resulted in the most concerted attack ever launched by the press and Congress on the classification system.

New Republic magazine reported that, since World War II, bureaucrats wielding classified labels had consigned 20 million documents to the government's "subterranean empire of buried information." Most of these documents had been classified under the authority of President Eisenhower's 1953 Executive Order 10501, which ruled that official secrecy would be limited to defense matters, under three categories: top secret, secret, and confidential. President Kennedy set up guidelines for declassification in 1961, but very little declassification actually took place.

After 11 years of wrestling with the problem of the people's right to know the facts of government, Congress passed the Freedom of Information (FOI) Act in 1966. The law states basically that any person may go to court to gain access to public records, and the burden of proof that secrecy is necessary is upon the government.

In 1972 the House of Representatives and the Supreme Court began separate inquiries into the effectiveness of the FOI Act. Samuel J. Archibald, of the University of Missouri Freedom of Information Center, was commissioned to plot the trend of court interpretation of the act by studying significant cases. His analysis concluded that court judgments have leaned toward the people's right to know. The courts, however, generally have protected "investigatory files compiled for law enforcement purposes," and they have been wary of second-guessing executive decisions about matters that are kept secret "in the interest of national defense and foreign policy."

Declaring that his action was intended to challenge the government's security system, in 1972 syndicated columnist Jack Anderson released secret and sensitive documents that revealed that Dr. Henry Kissinger, the president's adviser on foreign policy, had directed administration spokespersons to support Pakistan against India in the war between those two countries. The fact that the anti-India policy had not been revealed even to Congress provoked further outcries against White House secrecy.

President Nixon established a new system for classification and declassification in 1972. Among other things, the system reduced the number of authorized "top secret" classifiers and made declassification, except for particularly sensitive information, automatic after six to ten years (amended to six years). Media response was mixed. Noting that the Pentagon Papers would have been ineligible for release under the time period, one newspaper editorialized, "If the Congress is to have a voice in war and nuclear testing, it must have quicker access."

Congress moved to strengthen the Freedom of Information Act in 1974, by enacting its amendments into law over President Gerald Ford's veto. Ford argued that the amendments were "unconstitutional and unworkable" and a threat to legitimate military and intelligence secrets. The amendments, which went into effect in February 1975, narrowed the scope of exemption that protected certain categories of government files from public disclosure, such as secrets that affect the national security. Congress also required agencies to answer information requests within ten days of receipt, broadened avenues of appeal and court authority to declassify disputed documents, and established penalty guidelines for wrongful withholding of documents.

Since passage of the law, agencies such as the FBI and CIA have provided copies of thousands of documents about individuals, companies, events such as the Kennedy assassinations, surveillance of known or presumed radical groups, and even, under court order, items such as the transcripts of background briefings and official conversations conducted by former Secretary of State Henry Kissinger. Private citizens were able to obtain copies of FBI files about themselves compiled through extraordinary surveillance during the Vietnam War and years of national unrest. Activist organizations likewise could clarify their status in government records. And reporters and writers could request and receive documents essential to their work. There were costs to pay for the searches, and delays in responses, as well as refusals based on security claims by the agency involved. But the system seemed to be working, until 1978.

By then the CIA was complaining that foreign agents were using the FOI Act to attempt to gain information, while the FBI maintained that organized crime was attempting to discover FBI information sources. The Federal Trade Commission and business-related cabinet departments said that the FOI procedure was being used, not by the general public, but by law firms and commercial competitors attempting to gain trade secrets and business advantages.

These arguments helped to build support in Congress for amendments to the FOI Act. The 1980 session passed a bill exempting most consumer information from being disclosed by the Federal Trade Commission. Pending for the 1981 session were bills giving substantial or total exemption from the FOI Act to the CIA and the FBI, two of the principal targets of the reform activists of the 1960s and 1970s. Also in the process of being exempted from FOI provisions were the Nuclear Regulatory Commission's nuclear power plant information archives, offshore power plant information, and foreign trade information. This backpedaling seemed to be in response to a more conservative trend in American politics and a sharp decline in public interest in "exposure" movements after the emotional events of the Watergate era.

An encouraging sign in the battle for the right to know was the enactment by Congress of a Government in the Sunshine Law that took effect in 1977. This law requires more than 50 federal boards and agencies with two or more members to conduct most meetings in the open. The law allows closed meetings for certain specified reasons but requires that the reasons for any closed meetings be certified by the chief legal officer of the agency. In 1978 the House decided to open its debates to daily live broadcast coverage. The body voted, however, to control the broadcast feed itself rather than let a network pool produce it. Passage of "open meetings" laws in individual states had begun during the 1950s, and by 1975 virtually all of the states had some form of open meetings law as well as laws guaranteeing the opening of public records to reporters needing access to them.

But despite such evidences of progress, Washington correspondents say they are fighting a losing battle against administrative orders that forbid federal employees from talking to reporters and that employ other devices to keep an executive department's actions secret unless the administrator deems it desirable to make them public. In this battle, as in others involving the right to report, the reporter's best weapon is the power of the press, which is in turn based upon the pressure of public opinion. Reporters who are determined to find out the facts can usually prevail over reluctant public officials.

Reporters' Confidentiality

In 1972 the Supreme Court, by a five to four vote, decided that news reporters have no special immunity under the First Amendment not to respond to grand jury subpoenas and provide information in criminal investigations, even at the risk of "drying up" their sources.

One broadcast and two newspaper reporters, in separate appeals, urged the court to make it clear that the First Amendment guarantee of a free flow of information gives reporters at least some degree of immunity to government subpoena powers. The appeals from contempt citations were made by Paul M. Branzburg, a Louisville *Courier-Journal* reporter who had investigated the use of illegal drugs; and by Earl Caldwell, New York *Times* reporter, and Paul Pappas, newsman employed by television station WTEV, New Bedford, Massachusetts, both of whom had investigated Black Panther Party activities.

Justice Byron R. White, writing the decision with the support of four Nixon administration appointees to the Court, stated: "The Constitution does not, as it never has, exempt the newsman from performing the citizen's normal duty of appearing and furnishing information relevant to the grand jury's task."

Justice Potter Stewart, in an opinion in which he was joined by Justices William J. Brennan and Thurgood Marshall, said that the decision "invites state and federal authorities to undermine the historic independence of the press by attempting to annex the journalistic profession as an investigative arm of government." He added: "The full flow of information to the public protected by the free press guarantee would be severely curtailed if no protection whatever were afforded to the process by which news is assembled and disseminated . . . for without freedom to acquire information the right to publish would be impermissibly compromised."

In his dissent, Justice William O. Douglas wrote: "If [a reporter] can be summoned to testify in secret before a grand jury, his source will dry up and the attempted exposure, the effort to enlighten the public, will be ended. If what the court sanctions today becomes settled law, then the reporter's main function in American society will be to pass on to the public the press releases which the various departments of government issue."

The justices, however, did leave open some avenues for relief to the media:

1. They acknowledged, for the first time, that the process of newsgathering qualifies for some First Amendment protection. According to Justice White, the First Amendment might come into play to protect a reporter if he or she could show "a bad faith attempt by a prosecutor to harass a reporter and disrupt his relationship with his news sources" (a fact not in evidence in the three cases before the Court). Justice White declared that if a reporter does not believe a grand jury investigation is being conducted in good faith, the reporter could seek relief from the courts. That eventuality might occur, he said, if the reporter is called upon to give information "bearing only a remote and tenuous relationship to the subject of the investigation" or if the reporter has "some other reason to believe that his testimony implicates confidential source relationships without a legitimate need for law enforcement."

2. The Court left the door open for Congress to enact legislation binding on *federal* courts and grand juries.

3. The Court declared that state legislatures could enact "shield" laws preventing reporters from being forced to reveal sources of information to *state* courts and grand juries.

4. The Court conceded itself "powerless" to bar state courts from construing state constitutions so as to recognize a reporter's privilege of some type.

"Shield" laws were enacted in a number of states. Many journalists, however, declined to support campaigns to persuade Congress and the states to pass protective legislation, on grounds that the First Amendment guarantee of press freedom would be endangered by such action.

In recent years, numerous reporters and editors have been jailed on contempt of court charges for failing to reveal sources of information. One celebrated case was that of William Farr, a Los Angeles reporter who, during the mid-1970s, served 46 days in jail for protecting his sources for a story about the Charles Manson murder trial. Another case was that of Myron Farber, New Jersey correspondent for the New York *Times,* who spent 40 days in jail in 1978 and paid, along with the *Times,* $285,000 in fines. He had refused to relinquish to a judge documents subpoenaed by the defense in a murder case against a physician. When the doctor was acquitted, Farber was released from jail. The New Jersey legislature then weakened the New Jersey shield law to conform to the state supreme court's decision in the Farber case, only to see that court reverse itself in 1980 and uphold the shield principle.

In June 1980 the voters of California approved, by a 73 percent majority, a state constitutional amendment that included the exact language of that state's reporter's shield law. Thus a statutory protection became a constitutional one in California. Farr could breathe a sigh of relief, for his case had never been adjudicated.

Countless subpoenas also have been issued in both criminal and civil cases in which the protection of sources was not involved. In some cases newspeople have testified or given depositions; in others the media have provided clippings and tearsheets; and in still others the subpoena has been successfully refused, denied, or withdrawn.

Searches and Seizures

When police raided the offices of the student-run *Stanford Daily* in 1971 seeking photographs of a campus sit-in, the incident set off a series of events culminating in the signing of legislation by President Jimmy Carter in October 1980 that banned similar police raids on newsrooms. The legislative action was necessary because the Supreme Court's decision of 1978 in *Zurcher* v. *Stanford Daily* had declared that the First Amendment provides the press no special protection from police searches.

There had been two reactions to this court decision. Police in various parts of the country carried out at least 27 similar raids in two years, armed only with search warrants, instead of subpoenas that required advance warning of their action. But the other reaction was a welcome rebellion in Congress against increasingly conservative decisions by the Supreme Court that negated basic individual rights as well as First Amendment rights. The result was the passage, virtually without opposition, of the Privacy Protection Act in 1980, sponsored by the Carter administration and leading members of Congress.

The bill requires federal, state, and local authorities either to request voluntary compliance or to use subpoenas—with advance notice and the opportunity for a court hearing—instead of search warrants when they seek reporters' notes, films, or tapes as evidence. It also covers authors, scholars, and others engaged in First Amendment activities. Searches are allowed only in very limited situations. The bill also calls for the attorney general's guidelines to limit the use of search warrants against nonsuspect third parties who are not covered by the First Amendment.

Presumably the Supreme Court would note this reaction by Congress and the president in its future deliberations involving First Amendment rights. As President Carter commented when signing the bill, "The Supreme Court's 1978 decision in *Zurcher* v. *Stanford Daily* raised the concern that law enforcement authorities could conduct unannounced searches of reporters' notes and files. Such a practice could have a chilling effect on the ability of reporters to develop sources and pursue stories. Ever since the court's decision, my administration has been working with Congress to prevent this result by enacting legislation."

But in the case of *Reporters Committee for Freedom of the Press* v. *AT&T,* the Carter administration's Justice Department sided against the media in their effort to prohibit secret seizure of their telephone call records by law enforcement agencies. The case began with the disclosure in 1973 that various Nixon administration agencies had secretly subpoenaed both office and home telephone call records of columnist Jack Anderson and the bureau chiefs of the New York *Times,* St. Louis *Post-Dispatch,* and Knight-Ridder. The Reporters Committee for Freedom of the Press asked AT&T to agree not to permit such seizures without advance warning to the news persons involved so that they could seek relief within the courts. AT&T refused. The Reporters Committee went to court, seeking First Amendment rights. But it lost in the United States district court and court of appeals trials, at which the Justice Department declared that, "the First Amendment does not permit reporters to withhold information about their news sources . . . in the course of a legitimate criminal investigation." In 1979 the Supreme Court refused to hear the case, leaving unanswered the question of how reporters could protect themselves against highly dubious seizures and searches such as those made by the Nixon administration merely to find out who was leaking news—a noncriminal offense.

The Carter administration executed a change of direction in September 1980 when it reprimanded the Justice Department's criminal division for the secret seizure of the telephone records of the New York *Times*' Atlanta bureau. Once again, apparently, the seizure was part of an effort to trace the leak of information from within the Justice Department.

Reporters in the Courtroom

A Nebraska murder trial in 1976 brought about a press-bar confrontation when the trial judge entered an order restraining the news media from reporting the existence of any confession or admission made by the defendant until the trial jury had been impaneled. The order followed the guidelines developed after the Supreme Court had in 1966 overturned the murder conviction of Dr. Sam Sheppard in Ohio because he had been subjected to massive pretrial publicity. In the Supreme Court decision in *Nebraska Press Association* v. *Stuart,* Chief Justice Burger held that the press was entitled to report all evidence presented in an *open* preliminary hearing, including confessions and admissions. By that time the Nebraska trial had ended. It was noted that Burger's decision made it plain that the ruling did not prevent future "gag" orders, and that it did not cover the issue of First Amendment rights when pretrial hearings were closed.

Media people's fears were justified when in 1979 the Supreme Court ruled in *Gannett* v. *DePasquale* that members of the public have no constitutional rights under the Sixth and Fourteenth amendments to attend criminal trials. But apparently not all members of the court realized the implications of the decision, which once again struck at a long-cherished individual right. Within a few months various justices were implying that the ruling had been misinterpreted by judges who were busy closing courtrooms to public and press. Within one year there were 160 successful closings of courts—126 pretrial proceedings and 34 trial proceedings.

The situation was clarified, to the satisfaction of First Amendment advocates, in July 1980 when Chief Justice Burger read a seven to one decision in *Richmond Newspapers* v. *Commonwealth of Virginia* declaring that the public has a constitutional right to attend criminal trials even when defendants want to exclude them. The decision overturned a Virginia judge's closing of a murder trial in 1978. Burger cited First Amendment rights in his decision, but, as usual, warned that "the constitutional right to attend criminal trials is not absolute." The decision left pretrial hearings still subject to closing, a matter the Richmond papers elected to pursue.

Justice John Paul Stevens called the decision a "watershed" case, saying: "Until today the court has accorded absolute protection to the dissemination of ideas, but never before has it squarely held that the acquisition of newsworthy matter is entitled to any constitutional protection whatsoever." And so, at least in one justice's mind, the right to report is a constitutional right.

Cameras in the Courtroom

The United States Supreme Court ruled unanimously in 1981 that states have the right to allow television, radio, and photographic coverage of criminal trials, even if the defendant objects. Although the decision did not guarantee news media a right to insist on such coverage, it clarified the fact that any state is now free to allow cameras and microphones into courtrooms as long as the defendant's right to a fair trial is protected.

The decision bolstered the movement to permit still and television cameras in trial and appellate courts, which had spread to many states. Among them was Florida, where the courts had allowed their use in the courtroom during the conviction of two former police officers who said that television coverage of their burglary trials in Miami Beach deprived them of their constitutional rights to a fair and orderly proceeding. It was their appeal that produced the Supreme Court decision.

In 1965 the Supreme Court had overturned the swindling conviction of Billie Sol Estes in Texas after large, movie-type cameras and bright lights were used to televise his trial. But the Court indicated then that television coverage might be approved if unobtrusive equipment were used. In its latest decision the Court declared that the Estes ruling had not meant that TV and photographers must be banned forever under all circumstances. Regarding the Florida trials, the Court said, "The defendants have offered no evidence that any participant in this case was affected by the presence of cameras."

The decision left unchanged the ban against the use of cameras in federal courts. This restriction stems from a vote by the American Bar Association (ABA) in 1937, reinforced in 1979 when the ABA voted down a resolution to amend its long-standing Canon 35 (renumbered 3A7). Because Chief Justice Warren Burger has long opposed the use of cameras in federal courtrooms, it was apparent that his view of states' rights in this matter was responsible for his vote in the Florida case.

THE MEDIA AND THE INDIVIDUAL

Free Press, Fair Trial

The reporting of arrests and trials, especially in crimes of a sensationalist nature, came under attack from the American Bar Association and certain civil rights groups during the 1960s. This development coincided with an increasing concern by the U.S. Supreme Court about the rights of defendants. Editors were accused by their critics of "trying the case in the newspapers" and printing or airing material prejudicial to the defendant.

In 1968 the ABA house of delegates adopted guidelines prepared by a special committee to restrict the reporting of crime news. The guidelines are known as the Reardon report, named for the committee chairman, Associate Judge Paul C. Reardon of the Supreme Judicial Court of Massachusetts. Newspaper people protested that the attorneys had overstepped their role and were trying to sabotage freedom of the press. Eventually a press-bar committee, set up through the American Society of Newspaper Editors, resolved much of the conflict. Under court and ABA pressures, the newspapers grew more cautious with regard to what they printed about a crime and the suspects before the matter reached trial. Broadcast newspeople took similar precautions. In addition, the police now became reluctant to disclose the facts of a crime to reporters—information ordinarily given freely in the past.

For many years, courts have forbidden the reporting of trials by print photographers, television camera operators, and radio newspeople operating tape recorders. In order to improve public awareness of legal procedures, however, courts in 26 states by 1980 had begun permitting TV and still-photo coverage of trials.

In nontrial settings, numerous state legislatures have authorized television coverage, the House of Representatives has opened its doors to radio and television under controlled conditions, and network officials have urged the Supreme Court to follow suit.

The Right of Privacy

Closely allied to libel and slander is the question of which is more important, the privacy of the individual or the privilege of the press. The right of privacy, perhaps the most cherished right of all, is guaranteed, but more and more it is coming into conflict in the courts with the First Amendment right to report news freely.

As previously discussed, public figures such as politicians, entertainers, and athletes give up their right to privacy in return for being public figures. But how much right to privacy does a person who is not a public figure have when that right conflicts with the rights of the press? Privacy rights have been obtained through a series of judicial rulings in this century.

An individual's privacy may be violated if that person is depicted in a "false light," an action that is similar to but separate from libel law, and if private facts about private persons are publicly disclosed. In a case pertaining to the latter, in 1975 the Supreme Court struck down a Georgia law that made it a misdeameanor to print or broadcast the name of a rape victim. Following a court hearing for six youths accused of raping a 17-year-old girl who subsequently died, presumably from rape-related trauma, Atlanta station WSB-TV used the girl's name in a newscast. Claiming serious disruption of the family's privacy, the girl's father filed suit. The Georgia courts upheld the suit as a matter of law, and the TV station appealed.

Although the Supreme Court ruled in favor of the Cox Broadcasting Corporation, it would not go so far as to make truth an absolute defense in invasion of privacy cases. The court held that "once true information is disclosed in public court documents open to public inspection, the press cannot be sanctioned for publishing it." The court then dampened the ruling somewhat by stating that it was confining its judgment to "the narrower interface between press and privacy" involved in printing the name of a rape victim rather than "the broader question whether truthful publications may ever be subjected to civil or criminal liability."

Despite the ruling, Georgia editors and broadcast news directors were quick to point out that they would continue to exercise great care in deciding whether it was necessary to report the names of rape victims.

Media lawyers hope that eventually the Court will permit the publication of any and all information about individuals unless clear and convincing proof can be shown that such information is false and that the communicator either knew it was false or acted in "reckless disregard" of the facts—the test laid out in the *New York Times* v. *Sullivan* case.

The Privacy Act of 1974 stipulated types of information about individuals that could not be disclosed by federal agencies and provided means whereby persons could determine the nature of information about themselves in official files. A Privacy Protection Study Commission, created by the act, undertook a two-year study of the application of the law and submitted a 654-page report to President Carter in 1977. The report listed five "competing social values" that must be taken into account in protecting personal privacy: the First Amendment, freedom of information, law enforcement interests, the cost of privacy protection, and federal-state relations.

The commission recommended that no action be taken that would affect the ability of the press to request or obtain information. The commission did suggest, however, that medical records be kept strictly confidential and that it be considered a crime to seek such information through misrepresentation or deception.

Further restrictions on the newsgathering function of the media were imposed when the federal Law Enforcement Assistance Administration (LEAA) decreed in 1975 that, effective December 31, 1977, if a state or community wanted federal money for collecting, storing, or disseminating criminal history records, policies would have to be enacted to limit the release of such information. That meant that the only information available to the public and the media would be police station "blotter" lists that are organized chronologically. The only way to obtain noncurrent records would be to have available the name of the person and the date of the arrest or court record.

The restrictions brought strong protests from media organizations and, in 1976, the LEAA decided to leave the matter up to individual states. Some states have adopted restrictive or modified policies; others have liberal dissemination plans, usually because an open record or "sunshine" law covers criminal history or arrest records; and some, with no plan, must follow the LEAA revised policies calling for open release of conviction data and restricted release of nonconviction information.

ACCESS TO THE MEDIA

The role of the mass media in influencing important public policy decisions, in maintaining or changing the status quo of our society, and in providing outlets for all types of views is enormous. So great is the impact of the media today that it has become common, though it is ungrammatical, to use the plural word "media" in the singular ("The media does this"). Gaining access to such a powerful force is the goal of innumerable business firms, ethnic organizations, labor leaders, consumers, government officials, and other special interest groups. All realize that much can be gained or lost through what is printed or broadcast in the nation's communications media.

Because of the theory that "the airwaves belong to the people," special interest groups have met with greater success in obtaining access to radio and over-the-air and cable television than to the print media.

Newspapers

In 1969 Jerome A. Barron, a law professor at George Washington University, proposed a new concept of the First Amendment in relation to newspapers. Pointing out that in the *New York Times* v. *Sullivan* case the Supreme Court had created a new relative freedom from libel for newspapers by the way it had interpreted the First Amendment, Barron said that similar techniques could be used to fashion a right of access to the press for the public:

> If this approach does not work, then a carefully worded right of access statute which would aim at achieving a meaningful expression of divergent opinions should be attempted. The point is that we must realize that private restraints on free expression have become so powerful that the belief that there is a free marketplace where ideas will naturally compete is as hopelessly outmoded as the theory of perfect competition has generally become in most other spheres of modern life.

In 1974 the Florida Supreme Court, in *Miami Herald Co.* v. *Pat L. Tornillo,* upheld a state law requiring that newspapers give "right of reply" space to political candidates criticized by newspapers. The U.S. Supreme Court, however, unanimously overturned the decision, its opinion reading in part as follows:

> The Florida statute fails to clear the barriers of the First Amendment because of its intrusion into the function of editors. A newspaper is more than a passive receptacle or conduit for news, comment, and advertising. The choice of material . . . the treatment of public issues and public officials—whether fair or unfair—constitutes the exercise of editorial control or judgment. It has yet to be demonstrated how government regulation of this process can be exercised consistent with First Amendment guarantees of a free press as they have evolved to this time.

Newspaper editors long have sought to obtain replies from possibly maligned individuals, companies, and institutions both before and after the printing of controversial stories. Letters to the editor columns traditionally have been open to all readers. A number of newspapers have solicited articles from the public to run in the columns opposite their main editorial pages.

Recognizing the pressures for greater access to their publications, however, many newspapers more recently have employed persons called ombudsmen, or have assigned certain staff members, to consider complaints; have endeavored to establish local and state press councils and given support to the recently established National News Council; and have hired reporters and editors from minority groups who bring with them the special attitudes of their communities. But the editors insist that the final decision as to what is printed must be theirs alone. Others call attention to the fact that today's technology permits persons with only limited capital to start their own newspapers.

About the only infringement upon publishers' prerogatives in recent years has been the federal requirement that in classified advertising male and female notices may no longer be kept separate.

Broadcasting

By contrast, broadcasters have had to contend with a multiplicity of efforts to gain access and influence what is aired: the fairness doctrine; threats by minority groups and others to take over their licenses; the necessity every three years (broadcasters want to extend this period to five years) to prove that they have ascertained community interests and have been operating for the public good; bans on cigarette, postal service, and armed forces advertising; "countercommercials," the airing of viewpoints replying to commercial spots; attacks on television documentaries; demands by citizen groups to provide special programming; network antitrust suits; efforts to reduce televised violence and children's advertising and to maintain good taste in programming; the control of prime-time program segments; access to cable channels; the staging of demonstrations and other "pseudo-events" to gain news attention ("Just do your thing; the press eats it up. Media is free. *Make news,*" proclaimed Yippie Abbie Hoffman). It is small wonder that the broadcaster is harried, but that is the price that must be paid for the prestige, pride in community involvement, and substantial profits that are attained in the broadcast world.

During the last decade, minority groups have applied consistent pressure to station managements in efforts to achieve more programming of special interest to them, to have minorities presented favorably in existing programs, and to have greater ethnic representation on station staffs. These groups obtain agreements from individual stations and they also seek policy changes from the FCC and Congress, in part because of commission and federal court encouragement over the years and in part from an increasing awareness that broadcasters and the government often respond to pressure. Action before the FCC consists principally of participation in license renewal procedures, either as petitioners to deny or as parties to agreements that head off litigation. Many such groups form local coalitions in dealing with broadcasters.

Other special interest groups, such as Accuracy in Media (AIM), join in suits against both the networks and individual media in efforts to promote their causes if voluntary action to alter programming practices cannot be obtained. A discussion of the threats action groups make to the economic security of broadcasters is provided in Chapter 22.

Cable television and public broadcasting are the avenues most open to individuals and special interest groups. More than 20 percent of the cable systems originate some local programming and they welcome community participation.

The Fairness Doctrine

For many of the nation's broadcasters, one specific legal requirement—the "fairness doctrine"—has had the effect of discouraging coverage of many important social issues. Since 1949, broadcasters have been obligated to offer reasonable opportunity for opposing sides to respond to the coverage of controversial public issues. This statutory requirement to be fair was based on two legal philosophies not relevant to print media: 1) the airwaves are public property; and 2) broadcasters are licensed to operate in the "public interest, convenience, and necessity." Public interest is served, Congress and the FCC have ruled, if the airwaves are made accessible to many differing viewpoints.

Most broadcasting leaders took issue with the fairness doctrine, charging that it abridged the principles of freedom of speech and press traditionally applied to electronic media by forcing the presentation of various sides of an issue, even when the views may be unfounded, untrue, or hard to identify in a local community. Even more annoying to broadcasters was the "personal attack" clause of the fairness doctrine. This clause stated that if an individual is attacked in an editorial or program, a script or tape of the attack had to be sent to the individual, with an offer of a reasonable opportunity to reply. Furthermore, if the licensee endorsed or opposed legal candidates for office in an editorial statement, the same notice and offer of time had to be made within 24 hours after the program was aired.

The industry considered the clause unconstitutional, a violation of freedom of the press. Its effect would be to curtail meaningful discussion of issues because of the expense involved in offering time for reply and because the licensee would avoid controversial issues if uncertain about the freedom to comment.

The Supreme Court did not agree with the broadcasters; in 1969 it held the personal attack rules constitutional, noting that "it is the right of the viewers and listeners, not the right of the broadcasters, which is paramount" in such instances. If broadcasters were not willing to present representative community views on controversial issues, Justice Byron White of the court wrote, the granting or renewal of a license might be challenged. To make this threat of a license loss, he continued, "is consistent with the ends and purposes of those constitutional provisions forbidding the abridgement of freedom of speech and freedom of the press." In law circles, this became known as the "Red Lion" decision *(Red Lion Broadcasting Co.* v. *Federal Communications Commission).*

The FCC has been confronted with fairness questions covering a wide spectrum of material ranging from news and public affairs programs to commercials and political broadcasts. Its rulings have raised serious questions about the criteria for fairness. What is reasonable balance in the presentation of opposing views? How does a government agency determine whether a viewpoint is favorable, unfavorable, or neutral? In what amount of time, at what hour, and to what audience should an opposing viewpoint be presented? And the larger question: Should the government be involved in such matters at all? If so, how extensively?

Broadcasters have continued to oppose the doctrine as inhibiting the free flow of ideas, and measures have been introduced in Congress to eliminate the requirement. Many who now favor the doctrine have expressed the viewpoint that, once an abundance of electronic channels permits the airing of many viewpoints on controversial issues, the requirement should be eliminated.

Chapter 21

THE MEDIA'S SOCIAL RESPONSIBILITY

THE MORAL LAW

Of all the laws that the mass media and their supporting industries, advertising and public relations, must obey, the moral law is the strongest. Public opinion produced the First Amendment, and public opinion can take it away. As pointed out in Chapter 20, not only does moral law impose a greater restriction on the media than any purely legal restraint, it also functions as a force that can overturn legal restrictions and bring greater freedom for the press. A monumental example is the manner in which public opinion slowly overturned laws against the right to print and the right to criticize in the fifteenth through eighteenth centuries. A more familiar, specific example is the John Peter Zenger case in 1735, when an aroused public prevented the government from punishing an editor for criticizing it.

Moral law has grown principally out of religion and may be found embodied in the precepts of all major religions. In Christianity, for example, it is found in the Old and New Testaments, most notably in the Ten Commandments and the teachings of Jesus Christ; in the Muslim world, moral law is set forth in the Koran of the Islamic religion.

Examine in Figure 21.1 the five concentric circles, each succeeding one placed within the other, much like the bull's-eye used in target practice. These may be termed the "circles of control affecting the mass media" (or, for that matter, most other human activities).

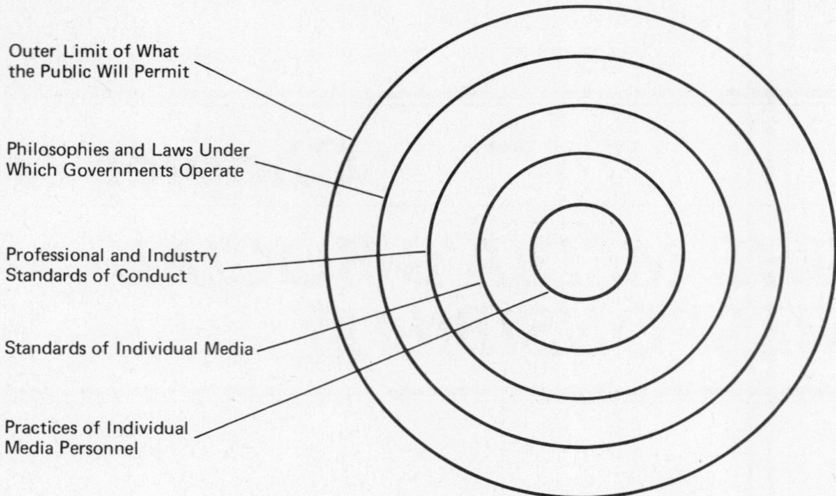

Figure 21.1 Circles of control of the mass media.

1. The innermost circle represents the professional standards and ethical practices of *individuals*—publishers, reporters, editors, station and network owners, news directors and film and videotape editors—the "gate-keepers" of what we read, see and hear. In all that they do, these people must keep in mind the other four circles of control that surround them.

2. The second innermost circle represents the standards of practice and the codes of ethics established by the *individual media*. All the mass media—newspapers, magazines, broadcast stations, and so forth—operate under certain guidelines, whether these guidelines consist of written codes or simply unwritten assumptions, lore, and traditions. The persons who work for these media—those in the innermost circle—must subscribe to the standards and practices of organizations for which they work, or look elsewhere for their employment.

3. The third circle, moving outward, consists of *professional and industrywide* standards of conduct as embodied in the statements of sound practice affecting radio, television, film, newspapers, magazines, and books, and the codes of ethics of groups such as the American Society of Newspaper Editors, the National Association of Broadcasters, and the Society of Professional Journalists, Sigma Delta Chi. Broadcast standards are enforced, only in part, however, by the Federal Communications Commission; print codes are entirely voluntary. Professionalism and peer pressure are the major forces leading to compliance by individual media and those working for them. There are other pressures, of course, economic considerations being among the strongest. Stories that an editor or news director regards as socially responsible and significant may strike some readers or listeners as obscene, or certain advertisers as harmful to their business. They try to strike back economically by cancelling their subscriptions, withdrawing their advertising, or, in the case of perceived lapses in good taste by broadcasters, filing a complaint with the FCC. Theoretically, such protests should not influence news decisions and most of the time, on better newspapers and broadcast stations, they do not directly. But the pressure exists.

4. The fourth circle represents the *basic press philosophies and laws of individual governments.* In Chapter 3 we discussed the four theories of the press: authoritarianism, Soviet Communist, libertarianism, and social responsibility. Under the concept of social responsibility, so strongly insisted upon by today's press critics, it is the obligation of all owners and managers of the press to be socially responsible, to ensure that all public issues are presented fairly and fully so that the people may form their own opinions about the issues. Should the media fail to do so, its proponents insist, it may be necessary for some other agency of the public to enforce this concept. The threat of such action by the public—which would draw us dangerously back toward authoritarian control of the press—illustrates how important it is that the three innermost circles of control function as they should.

5. The fifth circle represents the *limits that people will tolerate regarding all types of human activity.* No individual or organization can pass beyond that outer limit without reprisal; history shows that even the most powerful governments eventually fall (as did that of ancient Rome) if they exceed the outer limit of what the people will permit. And those in the three inner circles also fall if they disregard that outer limit circumscribing their conduct.

These circles of social and legal control are not fixed, immutably, for all time. They shift from century to century, from generation to generation. For example, in the Western world the relative social permissiveness of the Chaucerian and Shakespearian eras may be contrasted to the puritanical restraints and Victorianism of the nineteenth century and they, in turn, may be contrasted with the accelerating permissiveness of the twentieth century.

The outer limits vary, as do the inner circles. Governments rise and fall, greatly affecting human rights, including the freedom of the press. Governments in India and Spain are among recent examples. Codes of conduct stiffen, then relax, then stiffen again. The standards of the individual media respond to changing social mores as do the decisions of our media gate-keepers concerning what will be printed, filmed, or broadcast.

In 1947 the report of the Commission on Freedom of the Press, whose chairman was the late Robert Maynard Hutchins, then chancellor of the

University of Chicago, set forth twentieth-century America's requirements of the mass media. Although denounced by much of the media because no news person was a member of the commission, these requirements reflect the code of ethics enacted in the 1920s by the American Society of Newspaper Editors and they have been incorporated in all codes of ethics subsequently established by media organizations. The press, the commission declared, should provide the following in a democratic society:

1. A truthful, comprehensive, and intelligent account of the day's events in a context which gives them meaning.

2. A forum for the exchange of comment and criticism.

3. The projection of a representative picture of the constituent groups in the society.

4. The presentation and clarification of the goals and values of the society.

5. Full access to the day's intelligence.

The news media, of course, may choose not to attempt to fulfill all of these obligations, but, as we have noted, they may do so only at their own peril—and ours. In this chapter we shall point out the manner in which the media are responding to such social issues as the portrayal of violence, sex, and obscenity, and the standards of good taste and conduct—whether the media are moving toward the outer limit of what American society will permit without further recourse to law or whether, although the First Amendment permits irresponsibility as well as responsibility, they are following the dictates of moral law. And we shall delineate the numerous ways in which the media, voluntarily, are constantly seeking self-improvement.

VIOLENCE

Effects of Televised Violence

A dispute over the effects of viewing acts of violence on television by the American public, particularly by children, other young people, and the emotionally disturbed, has raged for a number of years. The late Senator Estes Kefauver held hearings on the subject as far back as 1954, and testimony was heard again in the Senate in 1961. As the rate of violent crime in America grew, a greater number of critics pointed to television as one of the possible causes. The assassinations of Senator Robert Kennedy and the Rev. Martin Luther King, Jr., and the attempted assassination of Governor George Wallace of Alabama, combined with civil disturbances and riots at universities, all focused attention on the violent behavior of Americans, forcing them to ask what kind of people they are.

In 1972, the 12-member Scientific Committee on Television and Social Behavior, appointed by U.S. Surgeon General Jesse L. Steinfeld, completed a two-year, $1 million study to determine whether there is a causal relationship between television programs that depict violence and aggressive behavior by children. Summarizing its five volumes of research encompassing 23 projects, the committee reported that the study "does not warrant the conclusion that televised violence has a uniformly adverse effect nor the conclusion that it has an adverse effect on the majority of children." However, continued the report, "the evidence does indicate that televised violence may lead to increased aggressive behavior in certain subgroups of children, who might constitute a small portion or a substantial portion of the total population of young television viewers." The difficulty of finding evidence, the group reported, "suggests that the effect is small compared with many other possible causes, such as parental attitudes or knowledge of and experience with the real violence in our society." In addition, "the sheer amount of television violence may be unimportant compared with such subtle matters as what the medium says about it: Is it approved or disapproved, committed by sympathetic or unsympathetic characters, shown to be effective or not, punished or unpunished?"

Despite the qualified nature of the report, Surgeon General Steinfeld later told the Senate Subcommittee on Communications that, in his opinion, the causal relationship between televised violence and antisocial behavior was sufficient to warrant "appropriate and immediate remedial action"—on the part of the networks and stations, however, and not through government intervention.

Public concern over televised violence intensified with news reports that a young woman was fatally set on fire with kerosene in a lonely Boston neighborhood soon after a similar scene had been depicted on television. Concern turned into outrage when three adolescents (two girls and a boy) raped a 9-year-old girl with a bottle in San Francisco only three days after, the attackers admitted to police, they had seen the made-for-television movie, *Born Innocent*. In the movie a 15-year-old girl was portrayed as being raped with the handle of a plumbing device in the shower room of a mental hospital by four other girls. On behalf of the real-life victim, suit was brought against NBC and the Chronicle Publishing Company, owner of the local television station. It alleged negligence and intentional wrongful conduct in presenting a program that eventually led to the physical and mental harm inflicted on the girl.

Charging that television had become "a school of violence and a college for crime," the California Medical Association filed a friend-of-the-court brief urging that NBC and the station be held accountable for the assault. The brief also pointed out that several months previously, "based on the overwhelming scientific and medical evidence," the American Medical Association had declared television violence to be "an environmental health risk."

After viewing the film and hearing arguments, Superior Court Judge John A. Ertola threw the case out of court. He ruled that the First

Amendment gives broadcasters an absolute immunity from civil liability for personal injuries arising out of their programming.

An even more celebrated case occurred in Miami, Florida, where Ronald Zamora, 15 years old, in the state's first televised criminal trial, had been given a life term in prison for murdering his 83-year-old neighbor. A year later the youth and his parents sought $25 million from ABC, CBS, and NBC, claiming that TV programming "showed the impressionable teenager . . . how to kill." Zamora, the suit maintained, was a victim of "involuntary subliminal television intoxication" caused by viewing shows such as "Kojak" and "Police Woman."

United States District Judge William Hoeveler dismissed the suit on First Amendment grounds. He declared that otherwise he would have to "find in law a new duty, a new cause for action" and that it would be impossible to enforce any rule seeking to protect certain viewers. "Obviously there's a large segment of our population that wishes to see that violence," the judge said. "Presumably they have a right to watch it."

At about the same time, the Chicago *Sun-Times* interviewed scores of psychologists and sociologists at universities and other research centers and reported general agreement that watching violence on television and movie screens indeed makes some children more violent. Even the minority of dissenters, the newspaper said, agreed that it is now the majority view that make-believe violence breeds real violence.

The newspaper reported the results of a study of 875 boys and girls in a semirural New York community over a 10-year period beginning in 1960, when they were third-graders. The study was made by Leonard D. Eron, editor of the *Journal of Abnormal Psychology* and chairman of the psychology department at the Chicago Circle campus of the University of Illinois.

Eron concluded that one of the best predictors of how aggressive a boy will be at age 19 is the violence of the television programs he prefers at age 8. "If you take those kids who were nonaggressive at age 8 but preferred and watched violent TV, at age 19 they were significantly more aggressive than children who were aggressive at age 8 but watched nonviolent TV," Eron stated, "which indicates it's the TV violence causing the aggression, rather than the other way around."

For girls, however, the study found that "viewing television violence may lead to lessened aggression," possibly because television may provide girls a vicarious outlet for aggression not socially acceptable in females or because women depicted on television are usually victims or passive observers of aggression.

Drs. Jerome L. Singer and Dorothy G. Singer, codirectors of the Yale University Family Television Research and Consultation Center, found in studying a group of 3-year-olds from middle-class homes that most of them watch television four or five hours a day during winter, with an average of three hours a day for the total year. Some of the children in the sample watched as much as 50 hours a week. These psychologists reported evidence that viewing violent action stimulated aggressive behavior by the children.

Researchers at the Annenberg School of Communications at the University of Pennsylvania have found that persons who watch a great amount of television show greater fear and mistrust than those viewers who watch less. In answer to questions about their chances of encountering violence in real life, the former tend to express attitudes "more characteristic of the television world than of the real world." They tend to see themselves as potential victims, not aggressors. They believe there are more policemen than there really are and that "most people just look out for themselves, take advantage of others, and cannot be trusted."

In response to complaints, the networks insisted that program producers reduce the senseless mayhem on Saturday cartoon shows and also decrease depictions of violence on other programs, in accordance with the industry's broadcast standards. Several constructive juvenile programs were created. In 1975 the networks began devoting the first hour of prime time (8 to 9 P.M. on the East and West coasts, an hour earlier in the Central time zone) to programs considered suitable for family viewing. Warnings that parental viewing guidance should be exercised were flashed across the screen preceding some programs shown after that hour.

Nevertheless, the annual "violence profiles" for all network programming, produced by Annenberg's Dean George Gerbner, showed that, after a decline in 1977, the level of violence on all three television networks rose to near-record levels in the fall of 1978, with Saturday morning cartoons accounting for most of the increase.

Complaints against televised violence were strongly registered with Congress, the FCC, stations, networks, and advertisers by the Parent-Teachers Association, Action for Children's Television, the American Medical Association, and numerous religious and activist groups, including, more recently, the so-called Moral Majority. Many companies set their own standards for programs on which they would place advertising. Concern was expressed that some of the violence was being replaced by the excessive use of sexual innuendoes and other controversial subjects.

The Parent-Teachers Association summarized six possible hazards that may exist when children watch too much television of the wrong kind:

1. Aggression in young people is contributed to by television violence.

2. Some children and youth imitate violence seen on television.

3. Television distorts children's understanding of how to solve real-life problems.

4. Young people and adults become immune and desensitized to real-life violence.

5. Youth and adults who regularly view television violence can develop paranoia and become fearful of real life.

6. The quality of life is diminished for both adults and children who are exposed constantly to television versions of murder, arson, assault, and other forms of violence to persons and property.

Violence in Newspapers

Because of the nature of the medium, the reporting of violent crimes in American newspapers has drawn less criticism than its display in television and films. However, through the years many readers have objected to sensationalistic treatment of murders, rapes, and other such crimes, often in the form of detailed front-page stories and photographs published under large headlines. Some people have felt that newspapers glorified violent activities, in effect making heroes of criminals. Objections have also been expressed against mayhem in the comic strips (although comic books were more severely criticized on this account) and against the reporting in some papers of almost every minor crime that occurs in the community. Newspaper accounts of violent actions, however, have a minimal impact compared with that which is televised and shown in movie houses.

The report of the Commission on Freedom of the Press decried sensationalism. The commission commented:

> To attract the maximum audience, the press emphasizes the exceptional rather than the representative, the sensational rather than the significant. Many activities of the utmost social consequence lie below the surface of what are conventionally regarded as reportable incidents: more power machinery; fewer men tending machines; more hours of leisure; more schooling per child; decrease of intolerance; successful negotiation of labor contracts; increase of participation in music through the schools; increase in the sale of books of biography and history.
>
> In most news media such matters are crowded out by stories of night-club murders, race riots, strike violence, and quarrels among public officials. The Commission does not object to the reporting of these incidents but to the preoccupation of the press with them. The press is preoccupied with them to such an extent that the citizen is not supplied with the information and discussion he needs to discharge his responsibilities to the community.

The press, however, has matured since those days; newspapers depending upon sensationalism for their circulation have, for the most part, been replaced by those such as the Washington *Post* and the Louisville *Courier-Journal,* which subordinate crime news of this sort to stories treating criminal activities in a sociological manner. One reason is that, since the advent of radio and television, single-copy street sales constitute only a minor part of most newspapers' circulation; most copies are delivered to homes. For such sales, so-called screaming headlines and breathtaking accounts of crime are no longer necessary. Another reason is that most readers today, more educated than in the past, want their news in a different form. And the better newspapers are inquiring into the causes of conflict and violence, presenting in-depth background stories to throw more light on social problems.

Much of the nation's press, however, played up the 1977 arrest of David Berkowitz, suspected of killing six persons in New York City, in what critics called "a highly irresponsible manner" reminiscent of coverage of the noted Hall-Mills, Charles Lindbergh, and Sam Sheppard cases of earlier eras. Although some network and news magazine coverage was criticized, the charges, including those of exploitation and sensationalism, centered on the New York *Daily News* and on the New York *Post,* the latter owned by Australian publisher Rupert Murdoch, noted for sensationalism.

The "Son of Sam" case, as it was termed, raised such thorny questions as: 1) the degree to which constitutional guarantees of press freedom imply unstated responsibilities; 2) the difference between reporting and exploiting the news; 3) the propriety of reporters' becoming part of the story they are covering; 4) the conflict between the public's right to know and the defendant's right to a fair trial; 5) the question of reporters' violating the law to obtain information; and 6) the ethics of the media's paying for information.

During the early 1980s the New York *Post,* seeking to lure readers from its rivals, the *Daily News* and the New York *Times,* assumed an increasingly sensationalistic tone. "MOB STONES AMBULANCE AS MAN DIES," read the headline covering half the front page of one issue of the tabloid. At the height of a transit strike, a 3-inch-high headline proclaimed, "CHAOS." Many stories carried such violence-sex themes as, "JFK's blazing trysts with beauty who worked as a spy for Hitler" and "Nude bathers look on in horror as 2 die in air crash." Such stories were designed for the huge street sales necessary to keep the paper alive since major retail advertisers were giving the paper only 6.3 percent of the total advertising in New York's major dailies, against 38 percent for the *Daily News* and 55.7 percent for the *Times.*

Meanwhile, on the advice of consultants and reader surveys, the *Daily News* sought to halt a seven-year circulation decline by abandoning much of its sensationalism and also seeking middle- and upper-class commuters and the sophisticated business and financial community with a new afternoon paper, *Daily News Tonight.* The *Daily News,* overtaken by the *Wall Street Journal* as the paper with the nation's largest circulation, was joining the nationwide newspaper trend, caused partly by television, toward more investigative and life-style journalistic fare and fewer fast-breaking, perishable stories. Its *Tonight* venture failed, however.

Terrorism and the Media

The substantial increase in terrorism throughout the world during the last decade poses another problem for the mass media: How can they report the news but avoid disseminating terroristic propaganda? A solution to this dilemma is yet to be found.

A prime example is the exceptionally heavy television and print coverage that followed the Iranians' takeover of the U.S. Embassy in Tehran. Did the media contribute unduly to the wave of anti-Iranian hysteria that swept the United States? Were they "used" by those holding the hostages, who were determined to focus American and worldwide attention on the crimes that they claimed had been perpetrated by the former Shah with the support of the United States government? One State Department official called the whole affair a "tele-crisis." However, media spokespersons pointed out that the holding of the hostages was news that had to be reported and that print and broadcast reporters provided almost the only informational link between Iran and the United States during that period.

Serious problems involving the media arose when Hanafi Muslims took control of the B'nai B'rith building in Washington, D.C., in 1977. News reports of a basket being lifted by rope to the fifth floor, where some people had evaded being taken hostage, were monitored by the Muslims and those hiding were discovered. Another reporter referred to Khaalis, the leader, as a Black Muslim. Khaalis, whose family had been murdered by Black Muslims, became enraged and threatened to kill the hostages in retaliation; he was pacified only when the reporter apologized. Another broadcaster reported that what appeared to be "boxes of ammunition" were being taken to the building in preparation for an assault. Fortunately, the terrorists did not hear this report, especially since the boxes contained food for the hostages.

Because publicity for a cause almost always is the reason for terrorism, the media inevitably are drawn into such crises beyond their task of disseminating news. When a bomb goes off in a public place, at least one terrorist group invariably contacts a newspaper or broadcast station to claim responsibility. Sometimes, because lives are at stake, the media have no choice but to air grievances. Witness the front-page publication of reams of political material from the Symbionese Liberation Army after Patricia Hearst was kidnapped. Or consider the live broadcast in Indianapolis of the obscene verbal tirade by another kidnapper who had wired a shotgun to the head of his victim and demanded television time.

Since government censorship is precluded by the First Amendment, some observers have called for voluntary news blackouts during such crises. "That's not serving the public's interest at all," CBS reporter Walter Cronkite has replied. "All that does is lead to rumor, speculation, to doubt that the press is telling the whole story under any circumstances. . . ." And Harold Kaufman, a professor of law and psychiatry at Georgetown University, says that he is persuaded that coverage of such events is helpful. "It allows whoever these people are to have some method of ventilating their anger and frustration, and making known their grievances," Kaufman said. "The more coverage is given, the more likely they are to see themselves as part of, rather than outside of, the system."

Self-regulation appears to be the only answer. Most major media, which have always cooperated with legal authorities in voluntarily withholding salient information about crimes, have prepared guidelines for their reporters. Americans have always demanded, and have a right to expect, thorough news coverage of all major happenings; in view of the competitive nature of the media, whether newspeople are able to walk the tight line between reporting and abetting terroristic activities remains to be seen.

OBSCENITY

Pornography in books, magazines, and films became big business during the 1960s and 1970s as sexual mores changed and a new permissiveness in regard to individual conduct permeated American society. At the same time, serious works of art increasingly dealt with so-called adult themes and explicit sexual acts of every nature. The right to read and view what one desired conflicted with the opinions of those who felt that society had the innate right to proscribe such activities.

Obscenity usually is defined in terms of whether the materials are lewd, lascivious, prurient, licentious, or indecent. After more than two decades, however, the U.S. Supreme Court has been unable to draw firm legal lines as to what is obscene and what is not. Virtually each of the nine justices has had his own definition ("I know it when I see it," declared Justice Potter Stewart), and until 1973 a majority could not agree on any one definition. Yet the Court maintained that certain materials are not protected by the First Amendment and that the government may suppress those materials. Recognizing the importance of safeguarding constitutional freedom, the Court in each decision has attempted to limit severely the kinds of materials that can be suppressed as obscene. The problem has remained, however, that fundamental First Amendment values have been encroached upon, and are in constant jeopardy, because all the Court definitions are, as three justices wrote in 1973, "so elusive that they fail to distinguish clearly between protected and unprotected speech."

In *Roth* v. *United States* (1957), the Supreme Court ruled that the standard for judging obscenity is "whether, to the average person, applying contemporary community standards, the dominant theme of the material, taken as a whole, appeals to the prurient interest." The Court ruled that obscenity is not within the area of constitutionally protected expression, declaring that "All ideas having even the slightest redeeming social importance . . . have the full protection of the [constitutional] guaranties . . . but implicit in the history of the First Amendment is the rejection of obscenity as utterly without redeeming social importance."

To limit suppression of materials, the Court also declared: "Sex and obscenity are not synonymous . . . the portrayal of sex . . . is not itself sufficient reason to deny material the constitutional protection of speech and press. Sex, a great and mysterious force in human life, has indisputably been a subject of absorbing interest to mankind through the ages; it is one of the vital problems of human interest and public concern."

In *Memoirs* v. *Massachusetts* (1966), involving the celebrated eighteenth-century novel, *Fanny Hill,* the Court set forth a new definition of "obscene" wherein three elements must coalesce: "(1) that the dominant theme of the material taken as a whole appeals to a prurient interest in sex; (2) the material is patently offensive because it affronts contemporary standards relating to the description or representation of sexual matters; (3) the material is utterly without redeeming social value." The court stressed that material must be "utterly"—unqualifiedly—worthless.

In *Miller* v. *California* (1973), however, the Court, in a five to four vote, revised its definition to "(1) whether the average person, applying contemporary community standards, would find that the work taken as a whole appeals to the prurient interest; (2) whether the work depicts or describes in a patently offensive way, sexual conduct specifically defined by the applicable state law; (3) whether the work taken as a whole lacks serious literary, artistic, political, or scientific value."

The new *Miller* decision differed from the previous *Memoirs* test in three significant areas: First, community standards, as opposed to national standards, are to be used. The Court did not, however, specify what area it meant as "community." Second, the "utterly without redeeming social value" test became "lacks serious literary, artistic, political, or scientific value." This omits religious, entertainment, and educational genres and leaves more materials open to attack. Third, each state must specifically define the types of sexual conduct prohibited. Chief Justice Burger gave as an example: "(a) patently offensive representations or descriptions of masturbation, excretory functions, and lewd exhibition of the genitals; (b) patently offensive representations or descriptions of ultimate sexual acts, normal or perverted, actual or simulated."

In *Jenkins* v. *Georgia* (1974), the Court, ruling that the film *Carnal Knowledge* was not obscene, declared that "community standards" may be those of the state but do not necessarily have to be representative of any specific geographical boundary; they may be the jury's "understanding of the community from which they come as to contemporary community standards." On the other hand, the Court declared that juries do not have "unbridled discretion in determining what is 'patently offensive'" and may therefore be overruled on appeal (as here the decisions of the local and supreme courts of Georgia were reversed). The Court said that nudity alone is not obscene and prohibitions apply only to "public portrayal of hardcore sexual conduct for its own sake."

As a result of this and another decision in 1974, the legislatures of almost every state set about revising their own obscenity laws. They did so in the light of the sexual revolution of the last 20 years or so and the controversial report in 1970 of the distinguished Commission on Obscenity and Pornography, established by Congress. Concerning the effects of pornography, the commission declared:

> The conclusion is that, for America, the relationship between the availability of erotica and changes in sex-crime rates neither proves nor disproves the possibility that availability of erotica leads to crime, but the massive overall increases in sex crimes that have been alleged do not seem to have occurred. . . . In sum, empirical research designed to clarify the question has found no evidence to date that exposure to explicit sexual materials is a factor in the causation of sex crime or sex delinquency.

In contrast to its recommendations affecting adults, the commission did recommend "legislative regulations upon the sale of sexual materials to young persons who do not have the consent of their parents." The commission was of the opinion, however, that only pictorial material should be legally withheld from children.

Several other obscenity cases have attracted attention during the last two decades as the federal government and individual prosecutors have taken different approaches in an effort to secure convictions.

It was on the grounds of the manner in which he advertised three publications—with "the leer of the sensualist"—that in 1966 the Supreme Court upheld the conviction of publisher Ralph Ginzburg for mailing obscenity. The publications were the magazine, *EROS*; *Liaison*, a biweekly newsletter; and *The Housewife's Handbook of Selective Promiscuity*. Ginzburg served eight months of a three-year sentence.

In 1976, rather than trying Al Goldstein and his copublisher of two magazines, *Smut* and *Screw*, in New York City, where they are published, the government brought suit in Wichita, Kansas, one of a number of cities to which the magazines were mailed and in which a more conservative jury presumably could be found. The two were convicted on 11 counts of using the mails to distribute obscene material, and on one count of conspiracy. The original conviction was thrown out because the prosecutor raised improper issues in his summation. The retrial was held in Kansas City, Kansas, where the jury was hung, nine to three, in favor of acquittal, and the case was later dismissed.

Actor Harry Reems earned $100 in Miami for one day's work in the movie, *Deep Throat*, but suit was brought against him and his codefendants in Memphis, which he had never visited. His conviction on federal obscenity and conspiracy charges was overturned on the grounds that he had performed in the film before the *Miller* decision in 1973 and had been improperly tried by the standards of that case. The government decided not to retry him.

Larry Flynt published *Hustler* magazine in Columbus, Ohio, but was convicted by a Cincinnati, Ohio, jury, on a misdemeanor charge of pandering and a felony charge of "engaging in organized crime." He was sentenced to 25 years in prison and fined $11,000 (and subsequently crippled by an assailant's gunfire during another obscenity trial in Lawrenceville, Georgia). Because *Hustler*'s content openly exceeded the limits set by competing sex-oriented magazines, many civil libertarians found it difficult to oppose the decision. A survey of the editors of men's and women's magazines disclosed, however, that more than three out of four considered the conviction a threat to their magazine's First Amendment rights.

Today "peepshow" movies, pornographic books, and magazines with explicit sexual content may be found in most American cities. The courts, however, have upheld community zoning laws that provide either for dispersal of these establishments or their location in so-called "erogenous zones," as may be found in large cities, and that also require that no such sexual materials may be viewed by passersby. As Charles Rembar wrote in an *Atlantic* magazine article in 1977, "Don't pluck my sleeve as I am passing by, stop poking your finger on my chest; freedom includes freedom from your assailing my senses . . . on theater marquees or posters, in storefront windows or newsstand displays. . . ." Protecting the privacy of consenting adults, seeking to prevent the exploitation of children in hardcore magazines and films, and restricting the dissemination of erotic material to children all seem to have the support of most Americans, including the staunchest First Amendment supporters.

SEX AND GOOD TASTE

Television

Not only violence, but also nudity, explicitly portrayed seductions, innuendos, and obscene language—and more—have become common in the mass media and American society during recent years, pleasing some but offending others. The result is what sociologist and columnist Max Lerner has described as a sort of "Babylonian society," where almost anything goes.

Whereas magazines and books are directed to select audiences, mostly adult, and the audiences viewing motion pictures and plays in theaters may largely be controlled, television enters practically every home and, of course, is viewed by young and old alike. Accordingly, the television industry has developed its own Television Code of Good Practice and seeks, with only mixed success, to follow its tenets. Adhering to the code, on a voluntary basis, has been the primary responsibility of individual stations and networks.

The department of broadcast standards of each network seeks to ensure that nothing is broadcast that exceeds generally accepted standards of public taste as represented by their huge national audiences. During a

Performer Liza Minelli, in a scene from an NBC television special. Although her "bumps and grinds" were suggestive, they were adjudged appropriate for the production and were not cut. (Photo courtesy of National Broadcasting Company.)

typical season, editors of each network make judgments on more than 2000 program outlines and scripts. They look at a variety of potential problems, including language, treatment of crime, use of narcotics, religious sensitivities, attitudes toward gambling and drunkenness, depiction of physical handicaps, the image of minorities, treatment of animals, and theatrical motion pictures and how they adapt to television. By far the most sensitive subjects are sex and violence.

In an effort to retain mass audiences while presumably downplaying violence, television producers during the late 1970s began to load situation comedies and dramas with scripts of an increasingly salacious nature, using themes such as pornography and sadomasochism, as well as suggestive dialogue. In so doing they seemed to be following the radically changed life styles of young people and many older persons as revealed by nationwide surveys of people's sexual habits such as those conducted by *Cosmopolitan* magazine. ABC's "Soap," "Three's Company," "Charlie's Angels," and several game shows led the way.

Surveys have shown that sexual subject matter is acceptable to most viewers when it is presented with good taste and at times when children ordinarily are not watching. One survey found that people worry most about sexual themes that seem to impinge on the welfare of their children or their own concepts of normal family life. Some of the most strongly held opinions concerned child exploitation and homosexuality. Four out of five respondents, however, wanted to retain sex-related material on TV but at times when children were not watching, and with parents assuming responsibility. Few favored censorship, either by government or advertisers, although both were the objects of pressure from various organizations.

With only a few exceptions, such as an edited version of the movie, *Midnight Cowboy*, commercial television has never shown X-rated movies. However, the popularity of hardcore films such as *Deep Throat* and softcore films such as *Emmanuelle*, increased substantially with advent of videocassettes, which could be shown in the privacy of one's home. In addition, some cable television stations showed so-called "blue movies" late at night, usually after midnight, and cable operations in a few metropolitan areas, notably New York City, provide facilities, as formerly required by the FCC, for any person or group seeking access, and a few of the programs have bordered on public indecency. Even so, with its puritanical heritage, the United States has never witnessed such programming as is viewed in some other countries; for example, more than 150 private stations in Italy have presented hundreds of X-rated movies, striptease shows, nude exercise and sex-advice programs, and nude ballets.

Given the fact that television in the United States is constantly trying to please most of the people much of the time, without giving them more than they want, the medium has shown remarkable growth in intellectual freedom in recent years. Much of the maturation has gone virtually unnoticed because television has endeavored to keep pace with the reality of the nation's social growth. Twenty-five years ago subjects such as homosexuality, abortion, venereal disease, illegitimacy, and adultery were unheard of in television drama. Today they are the focus of many intelligent and sensitive dramatic programs.

"Those of us in network television particularly do not wish to see a slowdown in the legitimate expansion of programming boundaries," said

Herminio Traviesas, former vice-president in charge of broadcast standards for NBC-TV. "For while we do hear from our more conservative viewers, we also hear from the more liberal elements of our audience and, lest we forget, from the progressive people in the creative community. In a sense we are like Indians with our ears to the tube instead of to the ground. We are among the first to hear and witness new calls for greater freedom of expression. At the same time we are hearing complaints that television is going too far, too fast."

Radio

"Profanity, obscenity, smut, and vulgarity" are forbidden under the National Association of Broadcasters Radio Code, to which most radio operators subscribe. The Federal Communications Commission maintains a watchful ear for such aberrations from good programming and calls station managements to account at license renewal time if matters of sex and good taste have been violated.

During recent years, as controversial "call-in" shows have multiplied, a few stations encouraged late-night listeners openly to discuss their sex lives. This became known as "topless radio." Society's new permissive attitudes caused many listeners to accept such programs with equanimity; others were shocked. The industry in general and the FCC in particular, however, criticized instances of extreme verbal candor to such an extent that the practice has largely been abandoned. One station, WGLD-FM, Oak Park, Illinois, was fined $2000 for broadcasting a call-in show on oral sex. The use of a device that delays the broadcast of telephoned observations for seven seconds, giving announcers time to delete offending remarks made by callers, has been a major help with call-in shows.

Station WBAI-FM, New York, was reprimanded by the FCC in 1978 for broadcasting George Carlin's "seven dirty words" comedy routine. The Supreme Court ruled that broadcasters do not have a constitutional right to air obscene words that apply to sex and excretion.

Highly suggestive sexual lyrics on records ("Take Your Time, Do It Right," "Do That to Me One More Time," "Can't Get Enough") have long been a part of rock music. Adults and some youths, however, have strongly protested the airing of the most explicit of these songs, some of which refer to the use of drugs.

The FCC, although it has no jurisdiction over the recording industry, warned broadcast stations that they would be held accountable for knowing the content of songs played on the air. Because of the ambiguity of certain references and the changing nature of youthful jargon, the monitoring of records to be played proved to be no easy task. The broadcasters sought to fix the blame on the recording industry, which in turn declared its innocence. The airing of antidrug records and commercials only partially alleviated the problem.

Films

For many years, criticism of commercial motion pictures focused on the artificial world they created. The vision of life presented in Hollywood films was far from everyday reality. It had excitement, glamour, romance, and comedy, but rarely paid attention to the perplexing problems of life. The filmmakers were selling noncontroversial entertainment featuring stars who had been made bigger than life by publicity. The major Hollywood studios, which dominated the market, had developed a successful formula and rarely deviated from it. Before television, they had no important rivals in presenting visual entertainment.

A factor that limited realism on the screen was the highly restrictive censorship code, conceived and enforced by the producers' association as a result of scandals that besmirched some silent film stars in the 1920s. Pressure from the Catholic Legion of Decency and other such groups strengthened enforcement of the code.

The taboos were so extreme that a husband and wife could not be shown together in the same bed. Mention of narcotics was forbidden. Criminals could not emerge as victors, although Hollywood made millions of dollars with gangster pictures full of violence by having the criminal lose at the last moment. A frequently heard claim that movies were intended for the mentality of a 12-year-old had much evidence to support it.

Shortly after World War II, the attitude in Hollywood began to change. The postwar world wanted more realism. Television's rapidly developing lure was keeping potential moviegoers at home. Filmmakers realized that they needed to alter their approach. More daring producers started making films that dealt with narcotics and contained suggestive sex scenes. They placed their products in theaters without the supposedly essential code seal of approval and drew large audiences.

Eventually enforcement of the code broke down completely. The growing permissiveness of American society emboldened the filmmakers; the increasingly frank films they released in turn contributed to the trend. Several U.S. Supreme Court decisions greatly broadening the interpretation of what was permissible under the obscenity laws speeded up the process. So did the success of films imported to this country, especially from Sweden. Although they were shown mostly in metropolitan "art" theaters, their impact on American filmmaking was intense.

The second half of the 1960s saw swift acceleration of boldness on the screen. Nude scenes became commonplace. Sexual situations that had been only hinted at a few years earlier were shown explicitly. An imported Swedish film, *I Am Curious (Yellow),* broke a barrier by showing actual scenes of sexual intercourse. Actors casually used language in films that was taboo in polite conversation a decade earlier. Films dealt openly with themes such as homosexuality. Greater liberality in these fields brought no reduction in the amount of violence shown, which was a major source of complaint by Europeans against American films. The complaints against motion pictures thus were reversed: Instead of being accused of sugar-coated blandness, they were charged with undue frankness. But with all its boldness, was American filmmaking being realistic? Many critics said no. They contended that, although sex and violence obviously existed, film producers were putting too much stress on them in order to cash in on shock value at the box office, and still were not coming to grips with the broader social problems of the country. They accused Hollywood of forcing permissiveness upon its audience, often to the embarrassment of theater patrons.

Anxious to preserve their profits from this new freedom and to prevent any government censorship moves, the Motion Picture Association of America adopted a new rating plan. Starting in 1968, each new Hollywood film was released bearing a code letter. This was to inform potential viewers what kind of picture to expect. The letter ratings are: G—for general audiences; PG—for adults and mature young people (parents should decide if their children should attend); R—restricted, those under 17 must be accompanied by a parent or adult guardian; X—those under 17 not admitted.

Jack Valenti, president of the Motion Picture Association of America, has attempted to explain what determines each individual rating:

• G: *General audiences.* All ages admitted. This is a film which contains nothing in theme, language, nudity and sex, or violence that would be offensive to parents whose younger children view the film. . . . No words with sexual connotation are present in G-rated films. The violence is at minimum. Nudity and sex scenes are not present.

• PG: *Parental guidance suggested;* some material may not be suitable for pre-teenagers. . . . There may be profanity in these films but certain words with strong sexual meanings will vault a PG rating into the R category. There may be violence but it is not deemed excessive. Cumulative man-to-man violence or on-the-screen dismemberment may take a film into the R category. There is no explicit sex on the screen although there may be some indication of sensuality. Fleeting nudity may appear in PG-rated films, but anything beyond that point puts the film into R.

• R: *Restricted,* under 17's require accompanying parent or guardian. . . . This is an adult film in some of its aspects and treatment of language, violence or nudity and sex. . . . The language may be rough, the violence may be hard, and while explicit intercourse is not found in R-rated films, nudity and lovemaking may be depicted.

• X: *No one under 17 admitted*. . . . This is patently an adult film and no children are allowed to attend. It should be noted, however, that X does not necessarily mean obscene or pornographic. Serious films by lauded and skilled filmmakers may be rated X.

By using the code, the filmmakers placed the responsibility of censorship upon the audience, rather than upon themselves. They also discovered a profitable solution to competition from commercial television, which because of its home audience was more cautious in selection of material than theater operators were. As it turned out, relatively few G-rated and X-rated movies were produced. Audiences seemed to consider G-rated films "too tame." X-rated movies encountered two problems: the rating substantially reduced the number of moviegoers who could buy tickets and many newspapers refused to print advertisements for these films.

Undoubtedly the revolution in American films had made the films better related to the realities of life, more experimental and stimulating, and more influential in shaping the country's social patterns, especially among people under 30 years of age. Independent producers now were better able to get their films, often uncommercial by the old standards, before the public. This became especially true with the new markets afforded by satellite networks, cable television, and videocassettes and videodiscs.

EMPLOYMENT OF MINORITIES AND WOMEN

As is true in most American industries and professions, the news media are controlled by white males. Leaders of many minority and women's groups contend that, as a consequence, the public gets a distorted or incomplete view of American life. Women professionals have found through surveys that, for comparable jobs, men and women are not paid equally. Both women and minority group members point out that, although many more lower-level jobs have been made available to them in the past decade than had been previously, relatively few management positions have opened up.

After the Kerner Commission expressed the view, following the shocking city riots of 1968, that inadequate coverage of the black community was partly to blame for the riots (see Chapter 19), both print and broadcast media set out to improve the situation.

Since then the number of minority journalists on newspapers has grown from about 400 to approximately 2300, although in 1981 about 19 of every 20 professional journalists were white, and 99 of every 100 executives were white. Five percent of the nation's 47,300 newsroom professionals are members of minority groups, but more than half of all daily newspapers employ no minority journalists at all. In 1980 there was only one black editor of a major daily: Robert Maynard of the Oakland *Tribune/East Bay Today*. He was named publisher as well in 1981.

Industry and journalism education leaders have worked together in seeking to recruit minority journalists-to-be, and establishing internships and workshops for them. A "2000 goal" has been set by the American Society of Newspaper Editors and the Association for Education in Journalism. Their aim: to achieve, by the year 2000, minority newsroom representation proportionate to that of the country as a whole.

Both racial minorities and women have been aided by federal equal opportunity regulations regarding hiring, promotion, and pay. Class action suits have been partially responsible for improved conditions for women

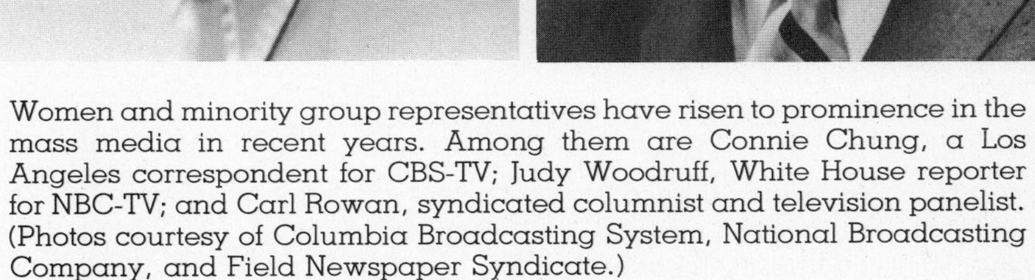

Women and minority group representatives have risen to prominence in the mass media in recent years. Among them are Connie Chung, a Los Angeles correspondent for CBS-TV; Judy Woodruff, White House reporter for NBC-TV; and Carl Rowan, syndicated columnist and television panelist. (Photos courtesy of Columbia Broadcasting System, National Broadcasting Company, and Field Newspaper Syndicate.)

employees at some newspapers and magazines, such as the New York *Times* and *Newsweek*.

At the heart of the issue is power—the ability, through the employment of more women and minorities in top-management positions, to ensure a relatively even-handed and fair portrayal in the media of all social groups. Nancy Hicks, a former New York *Times* reporter who has been working closely with editors and publishers through the Institute for Journalism Education, sums up the viewpoint of many blacks: "The story so far has been, lamentably, [the portrayal of] minorities [as] less intelligent and more violent than whites, less hard-working and more inclined to take handouts than whites, less serious and a lot keener about drugs than whites, less able but on the whole better basketball players than whites." In her opinion newspapers have made vast improvements in their portrayal of minorities but completely fair treatment will come only with the opening up of top management positions.

Women journalists express similar sentiments. In recent years women have made dramatic inroads into the working force of newspaper newsrooms, but a recent survey revealed that women hold only 6.5 percent of the directing editorships of newspapers in the United States. Kay Mills, the only woman out of eight people who write editorials at the Los Angeles *Times,* says, "I can point to many editorials that I know simply would not be in the *Times* if I were not there—either because the men are not in the network to hear of the issues emerging, or don't think they rank with cosmic world affairs when they do hear of them."

With the possible exception of magazines, the problem seems to be endemic to all the mass media. In radio and television, for example, the FCC reported in 1980 that, of the approximately 169,000 employes in the industry, 31.7 percent were women and 14.7 percent were members of minority groups. Among the top levels constituting 80 percent of all the jobs, however, only 21 percent of the upper four job categories were held by women and only 11.7 percent by minorities.

Charging that some broadcast stations either refuse to comply with equal employment regulations of the FCC or falsify their reports, in 1980 a coalition of religious groups, women's groups, and civil rights groups undertook a several years' study of the hiring and promotion practices for women and minorities at every radio and television station in the country. The initial funding of the study was made through a $100,000 grant from the Office of Communications of the United Church of Christ, a longtime activist organization.

EFFORTS TO IMPROVE THE MASS MEDIA

It is generally agreed upon that government can play only a minor role in efforts to improve the mass media, if they are to remain free. This means that efforts at improvement must come from within the media themselves or be generated by groups outside the media that represent the general public. In this section we shall note the heavy emphasis placed by media organizations upon the development of codes of ethics, particularly during the 1970s. Then we shall take a closer look at these innumerable organizations, including foundations and the National News Council, through which the media seek to meet the challenges raised by society.

Codes of Ethics

Standards of professional conduct have emerged after the harsh public distrust of all institutions—including the news media—that buffeted the nation during the Watergate era and that still widely persists.

Sensing the public mood, the Associated Press Managing Editors Association (APME), even before Watergate, began to examine influences on the probity of the press. The report of the APME professional standards committee in 1972 was the first salvo in what turned out to be a barrage of attention to the problem of media ethics.

The APME sent Carol Sutton of the Louisville *Courier-Journal* to report on the extent of gratuities received by the press during three fashion events in New York and Montreal. Two weeks later she returned with a new canvas suitcase full of what her newspaper colleagues termed "loot" and "goodies"—assorted cosmetics, jewelry, tote bags and other objects—along with a report of countless other gratuities offered at these events. She returned all the gifts she could and gave others to charity, in line with the Louisville newspapers' long-standing policy against the acceptance of gifts by staff members.

The Detroit *News* discovered that during one year alone at least $56,000 worth of free gifts and services were offered to its staff members. *New York* magazine reported on the receipt by media news staff members of free tickets to events at Madison Square Garden and the influence of public relations people with the New York *Times*.

The model for modern codes of ethics is the Canons of Journalism, established in 1922 by the American Society of Newspaper Editors. Accuracy, fair play and responsibility are its hallmarks.

The Society of Professional Journalists, Sigma Delta Chi (SPJ, SDX) adopted the ASNE code as its own in 1926. Then, in 1973, SPJ, SDX broke new ground with the introduction of a new code of ethics. Two years later, APME and the National Conference of Editorial Writers adopted codes of their own. Other organizations either did likewise or closely examined standards they had previously established. In addition, more than 80 percent of the large newspapers spelled out rules of conduct for their staffs.

The foreword to the code of fair publishing practices adopted in 1955 by the Catholic Press Association points out that: "Like all promises, the code can be as effective as the will and determination of the members of the association make it. . . . But if it is not reaffirmed by practice and conduct it can become only an empty statement, a pledge ignored and a promise forgotten and broken. . . ." Moral law, it added, undergirds all such codes.

The code of the National Press Photographers Association affirms, in part, that: "It is the individual responsibility of every photojournalist at all times to strive for pictures that report truthfully, honestly, and objectively." The code ends with the statement: "No code of ethics can prejudge every situation; thus common sense and good judgment are required in applying ethical principles."

The code adopted in 1966 by the Radio Television News Directors Association is regarded as much more stringent than the radio and television codes of the National Association of Broadcasters, which have been criticized as containing "weak, ambiguous, evasive and permissive language."

A study of journalists' opinions about gratuities, conducted by Keith P. Sanders and Won H. Chang of the University of Missouri School of Journalism, revealed "a strong regard for individual professionalism, a general distaste for freebies, a rejection of freebies as essential, and a general support for the SPJ, SDX code of ethics."

The respondents rated highest the statement: "A professional journalist, secure in himself and his understanding of his public trust, will report honestly not because of a code, but because of what he is and believes."

The APME's professional standards committee studied approximately 50 separate ethics codes adopted by individual newspapers. "None of the [survey] respondents expressed any negative thoughts about the wisdom of codes of ethics, either written or unwritten," the committee reported. "Most believe they are necessary to set a tone of behavior for all staffers while understanding that not every situation be specifically addressed in a code."

Journalists and journalism educators have mixed feelings about codes of ethics. Most media people seem to maintain that codes are useful as standards against which to measure their own value systems; others, steeped in the individualistic tradition, take a cavalier attitude toward codes, supporting conscience and principle but disdaining formalized strictures. A study of the ethical views of more than 200 Chicago area journalists, conducted by Dr. David Gordon of the University of Miami, revealed strong support for ethical behavior, with a slight plurality in favor of enforced codes. More than one-fifth of the respondents, however, said that ethical principles do not play a very large role in their professional lives. As might be expected, the journalists supported most strongly the statements that "freedom of the press is to be guarded as a vital right of mankind" and that "every journalist should be concerned with truthfulness, accuracy, and decency in his reporting."

Those who attack codes of ethics maintain, among other things, that the codes often contain internal contradictions, are poorly written, unwisely tend toward consensus thinking on the part of practitioners, and are largely products of management or organizations dominated by "management types," which, as Dr. Richard A. Schwarzlose of Northwestern University states it, "tend to focus on things reporters cannot do (as a protection for corporate and product credibility), rather than on ways of uplifting the reporters' self-image. . . ."

It is evident that, because of substantial public concern, communication ethics will be a hotly debated subject during the 1980s and schools of journalism and mass communications increasingly will seek better ways of sensitizing their students to the ethical decisions they must face as practitioners.

Organizations

Almost every mass communicator in the country either is a member of one or more journalism and mass communications associations or is represented by the organization for which he or she works. Generally, the managers fulfill institutional membership responsibilities and staff communicators belong to craft organizations. Thousands are active in local associations. The purposes of almost every organization are to interchange ideas for the advancement of professional ideals and to work collectively for the solution of common problems.

One group is composed of the various trade associations. For newspapers there are the American Newspaper Publishers Association, representing the dailies; the National Newspaper Association, for weeklies and small dailies; the National Newspaper Publishers Association, serving the black press; and other groups, including the International Circulation Managers' Association, International Newspaper Advertising and Marketing Executives, and Suburban Newspapers of America, Inc. There are also strong regional associations—Inland Daily Press Association, Southern Newspaper Publishers Association, New England Daily Newspaper Association, Western Newspaper Foundation, Northwest Daily Press Association—and state associations (usually emphasizing the concerns of weeklies). All issue publications of one sort or another, the most notable being ANPA's *presstime*.

The trade associations for other media include the National Association of Broadcasters, Magazine Publishers Association, Association of American Publishers, Motion Picture Association of America, American Business Press, Inc., American Association of Advertising Agencies, and American Advertising Federation.

Each trade association speaks for its industry in affairs of general interest to the members. The staffs represent the industries when necessary at congressional hearings and before other government organizations. The associations develop promotional materials for their media and operate central offices that act as clearinghouses for information about the industries. The daily newspapers organized a Bureau of Advertising that promotes their media; the Magazine Advertising Bureau, Radio Advertising Bureau, and Television Information Bureau do the same in their fields. The National Association of Broadcasters, Motion Picture Association of America, and American Association of Advertising Agencies have developed codes of conduct. Although they are primarily concerned with business matters, many of the associations sponsor discussions aimed at improving their media and encourage individual activities to raise the standards of members.

There are also groups of editors and writers. Most prominent is the American Society of Newspaper Editors (ASNE), limited primarily to editors, editorial page editors, and managing editors of dailies of 50,000 or more circulation. ASNE's convention proceedings are reproduced in book form in the *Problems of Journalism* series. The monthly ASNE *Bulletin* analyzes problems confronting editors and the press.

The National Conference of Editorial Writers meets annually in sessions providing small-group critiques of editorial pages. It publishes a quarterly, the *Masthead,* and has a code of principles "to stimulate the conscience and the quality of the American editorial page." The Associated Press Managing Editors Association (APME) continually studies the AP news report, each year publishes the *APME Red Book* reporting on committee findings and convention sessions, and has drawn up a code of ethics. The International Society of Weekly Newspaper Editors meets annually, publishes the quarterly *Grassroots Editor,* and presents a Golden Quill award for outstanding work in the weekly field.

The Radio Television News Directors Association has sought to elevate standards through adoption of a code of principles and has been instrumental in advancing the position of news and public affairs broadcasting in the industry. Among magazine people, the International Association of Business Communicators sets standards of performance and holds annual sessions for persons most of whom edit company publications. The American Society of Magazine Editors serves the broader field. The Public Relations Society of America requires practitioners to pass examinations before they may be certified as accredited members of the organization. All of these groups issue magazines for their members.

The American Academy of Advertising brings together educators and practitioners in annual meetings and publishes the *Journal of Advertising.* The Business and Professional Advertising Association is also active in this field.

The Newspaper Guild has done much to improve the standards of the newspaper business through the raising of salaries and has attempted to carry out programs of self-improvement. Its publication is the *Guild Reporter.* Membership is limited primarily to workers in larger daily newspapers and the press associations. Its role as a trade union is discussed in greater detail in Chapter 5.

There are other groups: the Society of Professional Journalists, Sigma Delta Chi (previously discussed) and Women in Communications, Inc., both more than 70 years old and both operating chapters for working journalists as well as on campuses; Pi Delta Epsilon, honorary collegiate journalism fraternity; Kappa Tau Alpha, journalism scholastic society; AAF/ADS, professional advertising society; Pi Alpha Mu, professional fraternity for men and women in the publishing, advertising, and journalistic management fields; Di Gamma Kappa and Alpha Epsilon Rho, professional broadcasting organizations; and the Public Relations Student Society of America. Most of them issue publications, the *Quill* of the Society of Professional Journalists being the best known.

A half-dozen or more centers, institutes, and action groups have been established in recent years. These groups are providing legal and other aid for investigative journalists (Reporters Committee for Freedom of the Press, and Center for Investigative Reporting), encouraging print and broadcast media to improve their accuracy (Accuracy in Media, Inc.), advancing the cause of female journalists and teachers (Women's Institute for Freedom of the Press), helping high school pupils and teachers in press freedom causes (Student Press Law Center), bolstering press freedom throughout the world (World Press Freedom Committee), and providing a mechanism for the airing of complaints against major media organizations (National News Council, to be discussed later in this chapter).

The Nieman Fellows, consisting of reporters and editors who have been given a year of study at Harvard University under the Nieman Foundation program, issue a quarterly, *Nieman Reports.* The *Columbia Journalism Review,* published by the Columbia University Graduate School of Journalism, offers a quarterly analysis and criticism of media performance. Media practices are examined by one dozen or more publications produced by critical reporters and editors, often with the support of journalism educators. A few metropolitan radio and television stations have instituted programs designed to criticize press coverage, and some metropolitan underground newspapers do likewise. A number of university journalism schools and departments publish periodicals containing media appraisal, among them being the *Montana Journalism Review,* of the University of Montana School of Journalism, and the *Iowa Journalist,* of the University of Iowa School of Journalism. Other roles of journalism educators and the cooperation extended to them by the mass communications industries are discussed in Chapter 18. Articles in *TV Guide* assess industry practices, and other magazines frequently print articles dealing with the media. The Gannett Company, Inc., issues *Gannetteer,* a monthly magazine.

In a broad-based program designed to increase the number of highly competent journalists, since 1965 the Ford Foundation has granted millions of dollars for postgraduate journalism education. The projects include an urban journalism program through the Northwestern University Medill School of Journalism, expansion of the Nieman program bringing young newspeople to Harvard University for a year's study, further development of the Graduate School of Journalism at Columbia University, a public affairs reporting program in cooperation with the American Political Science Association, a variety of study and seminar programs for journalists of the South in cooperation with the Southern Regional Education Board and the Southern Newspaper Publishers Association Foundation, and a Nieman-like program of study for experienced journalists at the Yale University Law School. Since 1973 the National Endowment for the Humanities has supported mid-career study for journalists at Stanford University and the University of Michigan.

The Newspaper Fund, supported by Dow Jones and Company (publisher of the *Wall Street Journal, Barron's* financial weekly, the Dow Jones News Services, and Ottaway Newspapers, a wholly-owned subsidiary that publishes newspapers in 22 cities) has spent more than $4.7 million since 1958 in attracting talented young people to newsroom careers. The Fund's program revolves around six major areas: providing a clearinghouse for career information, summer study on college campuses for high school and junior college journalism teachers, summer intern programs with training courses and scholarships for college students and minority graduate students, recognition to high school teachers for outstanding performances, programs for minority high school students, and an editor-in-residence program to bring working newspeople to college campuses in cooperation with the American Society of Newspaper Editors.

With the financial aid of the Don R. Mellett Fund of the Newspaper Guild, community press councils were established during the late 1960s in several states including California, Oregon, Illinois, and Colorado. The councils, composed of both public and media representatives, were intended to provide a forum for public criticism of the media and to enable editors and managers to respond. The idea, however, met with only limited success. Today the strongest councils are a state organization in Minnesota and a regional organization in New England.

Backed by eight foundations, the National News Council (NNC), with headquarters in New York City, was established in 1973 to serve the public interest in preserving freedom of information and advancing accurate and fair reporting of news. Similar organizations have long been active in Europe, the oldest being the British Press Council.

The council consists of 18 public and media members and a panel of six advisers who attend meetings and participate in case discussions but do not vote. The chairman is Norman A. Isaacs, an activist journalist and former news executive of the Louisville *Courier-Journal.* A four-member paid staff is headed by Executive Director William B. Arthur, former editor of *Look* magazine, and Associate Director A. H. Raskin, former assistant editorial page editor of the New York *Times.*

The NNC examines and reports on complaints from individuals or organizations concerning the accuracy and fairness of news reporting by the national print and broadcast organizations, and by local news organizations if the matter in question is of national significance as news or for journalism. The council does not accept complaints about editorial expression or personal opinion unless the facts are in dispute. It does not regulate or impose penalties; its only strength is the force of public opinion. In addition, the council conducts studies and reports on issues involving the freedom of the press. Fellowships and internships also are offered.

Initial media reaction to the council's establishment was mixed. Agreeing to cooperate were the AP, UPI, CBS, PBS, *Time, Newsweek, Wall Street Journal,* and *Christian Science Monitor.* The New York Times News Service declined to do so, and many media organizations took no position. Proponents maintained that the council would enhance media credibility and deal with public complaints before they could translate themselves into a push for governmental controls detrimental to freedoms provided by the First Amendment. Opponents argued that the media already were criticized sufficiently by readers, viewers, and professional groups and that such a council might be a forerunner of government control.

During its first seven years of operation the NNC agreed to consider 186 complaints of the many more submitted. Of these, 98 were found to be unwarranted, 48 were upheld in whole or in part, 35 were dismissed or resolved, and two were withdrawn. (The total includes seven complaints involving two separate decisions and one involving three separate decisions.) The networks drew the most complaints, with newspapers second.

Two examples may be cited. After NBC-TV aired a five-part nightly news series on the oil industry, Exxon Corporation and Shell Oil Company complained that portions of the news reports about them were seriously distorted; after investigation, the council agreed. In another instance, the NNC upheld a complaint by Accuracy in Media against columnist Jack Anderson concerning statements made by five students about their treatment at a training school for foreign police.

The council's actions are reported regularly in the *Columbia Journalism Review* but only sporadically or incompletely by the commercial media. NBC-TV News, for example, reported the Shell Oil Company complaint findings in only two sentences on the network's evening news broadcast.

Although the council is supported financially by 40 media and media foundations, five other nonmedia foundations, 16 corporations and corporation foundations, and three individuals, Chairman Isaacs is saddened by the fact that the council has been ignored by most elements of the media and steadfastly opposed by many others. "Although many news people have protested that the council could unfairly be used as a censor, its record and that of the British Press Council have proved such predictions groundless," Isaacs stated. "The record is that the press councils have resolutely defended freedom of opinion, and the more robust the better. . . ."

Chapter 22

WHO OWNS THE MEDIA?

PRODUCTS OF FREE ENTERPRISE

The mass media in the United States are part of the free enterprise system, operated to earn a profit. With the exception of noncommercial television and radio stations, they are expected to provide a return on the investment their owners have made in them. Even most of the noncommercial stations get into the money scramble because they must find financial grants and underwriting gifts to keep them on the air. So the demands of the marketplace influence and often determine the decisions of those who distribute the printed and spoken word: which books to publish, what type of films to produce, what kind of programs to televise, what size each day's newspaper should be.

In this respect, the American concept differs from that of many parts of the world. The federal government neither finances nor operates any of the media in this country, although it assists some noncommercial stations with subsidies. Nor do the political parties underwrite daily newspapers to enunciate their point of view. An American broadcasting station or publication survives only if it provides a product its audience likes and manages its finances prudently.

Contrast this to the practice in Europe, for example, where it is commonplace for the television and radio networks to be owned by the government. In many countries, especially Communist-governed ones, newspapers are published by the government, with the censorship and manipulation of news such control implies.

Because the United States is so vast and its population so diverse,

American media have historically and proudly lacked uniformity, both in content and ownership. Newspapers born as the frontier moved westward were the products of individual enterprise, reflecting the views of the editor-proprietor. So were the magazines. Book publishing for decades was largely controlled by individuals, families, or partnerships. When commercial radio came into being, stations were established by a potpourri of owners anxious to play with the new toy, among them newspaper executives, automobile dealers, manufacturers, and amateur engineers who could scrape together enough money for the primitive equipment needed. Licenses for television, when that medium's turn came, were obtained in many instances by companies already involved in radio. Thus the American media truly consisted of many thousands of voices, often highly individualistic.

Frequently these individual proprietors were more concerned with exercising influence in their communities than with drawing the last dollar of profit from their operations. Since they answered only to themselves or to small groups of private stockholders, they were free to function in that way.

In the print media especially, this multiplicity of ownership has been drastically reduced, many believe dangerously so. The media are caught in the rush to conglomerate corporate ownership that has characterized American business during the last two decades. Among daily newspapers, control is held more and more tightly in the grip of a relatively few large national corporations. Financial control of two-thirds of American daily newspapers no long rests in the home communities in which they are published. It is held by corporate headquarters of the newspaper groups which gobbled up independent newspapers with a voracious appetite during the 1970s and continued to do so during the early 1980s.

The headlong growth of group ownership followed another controversial development, the predominance of "one-newspaper cities." This resulted from the death through economic attrition of second and sometimes third newspapers in a city. Critics fear that, in a city with one daily newspaper, the publication will print only the news and opinion it wants its readers to see, leaving out or deemphasizing stories that might embarrass the publisher and his or her friends, or run contrary to the paper's political position. On the other side, there are frequent instances in which a monopoly publisher, sensitive to the charge, has made extra effort to provide the city with more extensive, deeper news coverage than was previously available in a competitive situation.

Closely connected is the charge that advertisers dictate a newspaper's coverage, or at least exercise veto power over certain kinds of stories that might damage their trade. Numerous episodes exist to document this complaint, in which stories went unreported because an advertiser requested that they be dropped. Yet many newspapers consistently reject such pressures, rebuffing all attempts to have stories suppressed.

Publication of columns called "Action Line" or some similar name, in which the newspaper acts as its readers' problem-solving agent, often causes it to print facts that show its advertisers in a poor light. The completeness of a newspaper's coverage of controversial issues and sensitive stories depends largely upon the moral courage and journalistic integrity of those who run it.

So many newspapers have ceased publication in competitive markets, especially in the metropolitan field, that fewer than 5 percent of daily newspaper cities and weekly newspaper towns have competing newspaper ownerships. Nevertheless, the total number of daily newspapers has remained stable for more than a decade, because new newspapers have begun publication, especially in areas of fast population growth around the fringes of metropolitan centers. Usually these newspapers are without competition in their cities of publication but face heavy inroads in circulation and advertising from nearby large-city papers. Indeed, far more competition exists in "one-newspaper towns" than the statistics indicate. Small-city dailies extend their coverage into the weekly towns with local news correspondents and advertising solicitors. In turn, the larger daily newspapers invade the small-daily cities with news bureaus and regional news pages designed for those cities. It is a matter of intense pride for a small-city newspaper staff not to be beaten by the "intruder" on a story in its own backyard.

The term "media voices" is a better description of the amount of competitive news delivery available to residents of a city than the traditional criterion, the number of daily newspapers. Media voices are those of all separate ownerships of media seen, heard, and read in a community, including those from outside sources.

Concurrent with the reduction to one daily newspaper in many cities is the rise of local news coverage by television and radio stations. Newscasts by these electronic media and coverage by "outside" newspapers supplement the news delivered by the local paper, so that in practice the inhabitants of virtually every city in the country have more than one source for their local news. While the presence of two daily newspapers in a city gives readers the benefit of rival coverage effort, a substantial argument exists on the other side. One strong newspaper in a city, if the publisher and editor are conscientious persons sensitive to their responsibilities, often can provide better news coverage and community service than two weaker ones. Also, a financially strong paper may be more willing to attack entrenched and harmful interests in a city because it can absorb the financial retaliation aimed at it.

The chief immediate reason for the disappearance of newspapers is the constantly rising cost of production. The wages of those who write, edit, and print the newspapers; taxes; the cost of newsprint and gasoline for the delivery trucks—these and many other expenses have risen precipitously. This has forced publishers to raise the sale prices of their newspapers and their advertising rates attempting to keep the newspapers profitable. In cases where a newspaper's hold on its readers and advertisers is not strong, or where its area of distribution loses population at the same time that radio, television, and competitive newspapers cut into its circulation and advertising revenue, the salvage effort fails and the paper must cease publication. This has been especially true among some papers in Northeastern metropolitan areas, whose inner cities have become depressed areas.

The Newspaper Preservation Act was passed by Congress in 1970 after lively controversy within the newspaper industry. This act created exemptions in the antitrust law, so that a struggling newspaper might join forces with a healthy publication in the same city. The newspapers were allowed not only to operate joint production facilities but to combine business departments and have joint advertising and circulation rates. Their editorial departments remained separate. An argument for the measure is that it would preserve a second newspaper voice in the city. Publishers who testified against it, especially those from aggressive suburban newspapers, asserted that it would increase the trend toward monopoly.

THE NEWSPAPER GROUP PHENOMENON

The rush toward combined ownership of American newspapers gathered momentum during the 1970s. By the start of the 1980s, two-thirds of the approximately 1750 daily newspapers were controlled by groups, as previously stated, rather than by the families or the privately held stock companies that predominated earlier. The percentage grows each year. A group is usually defined as two or more dailies in different markets under common ownership.

The trend reached the stage in which large chains were buying out small ones, thus increasing their holdings at a wholesale rate. Thirteen groups had aggregate weekday circulation of more than one million copies each. These organizations published more than 40 percent of the newspaper copies sold daily in the United States and more than one-half of those sold on Sunday.

The largest of the groups in number of properties owned is the Gannett Company. In 1980 it owned 82 daily newspapers, 21 weekly newspapers, seven television stations, 14 radio stations, a magazine, a film production company, the Lou Harris polling organization, and an extensive billboard business. Its stated goal is ownership of at least 100 dailies. Most of its newspapers are in medium-sized or small cities. The Knight-Ridder group of 34 daily newspapers includes several major metropolitan publications. These two groups are approximately even in total daily circulation, each with about 3.5 million. Other large groups include Newhouse, Scripps-Howard, Thomson, Dow Jones, Hearst, Cox, Chicago *Tribune,* Harte-Hanks, and the New York *Times.*

Why do owners of independent newspapers succumb to the lures of group corporations and surrender ownership that in some cases has been in their families for more than a century? The answer lies in a bedeviling economic headache for them, caused by the federal income tax and inheritance tax laws, compounded by inflation. The individual publisher who heads a family-owned newspaper, and who perhaps owns a majority of the stock, faces the distressing fact that upon death the inheritance taxes will be so high that any heirs may be forced to sell their stock in order to pay them. Because of the income tax laws, the family members cannot afford to receive high dividends from the paper's comfortable earnings. The family newspaper plant is growing obsolete and needs new electronic and press equipment in order for it to remain profitable. Yet inflation makes the price of that equipment extremely high, and the cost of borrowing money for it at soaring interest rates frightens the publisher.

Along comes a group publishing corporation whose stock is publicly owned. By using part of its profits to purchase additional newspapers, the corporation reduces the federal income taxes it otherwise would be required to pay. It has additional tax advantages and financial resources not available to the individual owner and never faces an inheritance tax problem. Thus it can offer the perplexed individual owner an extremely lucrative price for the newspaper; the publisher and other family stock owners may receive large cash payments which, after payment of capital gains tax, they may place in tax-free municipal securities. The publisher and heirs in turn are made financially secure instead of facing the likelihood of a forced sale of the paper for inheritance taxes. So the publisher sells to the highest bidder, after running up the price as far as possible. Competition among purchasers is intense. When the family owners recently put up for sale one small Midwestern city daily, 14 companies sought to buy it.

As a result of these circumstances, the prices at which newspapers are being sold approach the astronomical. Newspapers with less than 10,000 circulation bring prices of $5 million and $6 million. The venerable Hartford, Connecticut, *Courant,* with circulation of 215,000 mornings and 285,000 Sunday, was purchased by the Times Mirror Company at the end of the 1970s for $105.6 million. In 1980 Times Mirror paid $95 million for the Denver *Post,* which had been under independent ownership since 1892.

Some efforts were being made in Congress during the early 1980s to alleviate the tax problems of small, family-owned businesses, but progress was slow.

One aspect of this buying splurge that has attracted federal investigators of monopoly business practices is the manner in which the Newspaper Preservation Act is used to the advantage of large group owners. When passed, this measure applied to joint publishing situations in 20 cities. By the start of the 1980s, group owners had acquired partnership status in 16 of these situations, and thus the antitrust exemptions there. Proponents of legislation to curb monopoly practices regard this as perversion of the act's intent.

A primary difference between contemporary newspaper groups and the newspaper chains of an earlier era, of which the Hearst newspapers under the personal direction of William Randolph Hearst were an example, is the local editorial autonomy generally practiced today. In Hearst's heyday, his newspapers from coast to coast looked almost alike with the same screaming headlines, heavy typography, and crowded front pages. They took the same editorial positions on national issues and played up Hearst's personal campaigns, such as antivivisection.

Group managements today as a rule permit each newspaper to have an individual appearance and personality and to set its own editorial policy. Thus newspapers under the same ownership may be liberal or conservative, Democratic or Republican, and support different candidates for national public office.

CROSS-MEDIA OWNERSHIP

Just as worrisome to critics as the trend toward group ownership of newspapers is the growth of cross-media ownership by giant corporations. When we trace the financial lines, we find intricate interlocking patterns of media ownership. Conglomerates own combinations of daily newspapers, weekly newspapers, television and radio stations, magazines, book publishing houses, cable television networks, and film production subsidiaries, all of which report ultimately to sets of corporate officers far removed from their sites of operation. In a number of cities the daily newspaper, a television station, and an AM and FM radio station are under a single ownership.

To cite one example, the Times Mirror Company of Los Angeles publishes seven large daily newspapers in California, Texas, Connecticut, Colorado, and New York; operates seven television stations around the country; and owns the *Sporting News* weekly, the New American Library paperback book publishers, and *Golf* and *Ski* magazines. Through other subsidiaries it publishes medical books, art books, and road maps; operates cable television systems in 13 states serving nearly 500,000 customers; and produces programs for its cable companies. Among other operations, it manufactures newsprint and other paper products with holdings of more than 250,000 acres of timberland and owns a 25 percent share of Tejon Ranch Company, a huge oil, cattle, and farming firm.

A check of financial statements shows, among other cross-media ownerships, that CBS, Inc. not only owns the Columbia Broadcasting System but Holt, Rinehart and Winston book publishers; the magazines *Mechanix Illustrated, Woman's Day, Family Weekly,* and *Field and Stream*; Fawcett and Popular Library paperback book publishers; and subsidiaries that manufacture Steinway pianos and Erector and Tinkertoy construction sets for children. CBS also once owned the New York Yankees baseball team. The rival RCA Corporation, formerly Radio Corporation of America, in addition to operating the NBC network owns Random House, Inc, the book publishing company that in turn controls Alfred A. Knopf and Modern Library; RCA Records; the Hertz Corporation

PROPERTIES OWNED BY TIME INC.

The extent to which conglomerates have amassed cross-media ownership is shown by the structure of Time Inc. This company was established in 1922 with the founding of *Time* magazine. As the 1980s began, company holdings included:

Magazines: *Time*, with four international editions; *Sports Illustrated*, *Fortune*, *People Weekly*, *Money*, *Discover*, and *Life*, which was changed from a weekly to a monthly.

Books: Little, Brown & Co., general publishers; Time-Life Books, sold primarily by mail; Book-of-the-Month Club, Inc.

Newspapers: Washington *Evening Star*, Pioneer Press, Inc., publishers of 18 weekly newspapers serving the Chicago suburbs. The *Star* ceased publication in 1981.

Television: Station WOTV, Grand Rapids, Michigan; Time-Life Broadcasting International.

Cable television: Home Box Office, Inc., a pay-cable program network that distributes motion pictures, coverage of sporting events, and other features nationwide; American Television and Communications Corporation, which serves cable TV subscribers in 32 states; and Manhattan Cable Television, operating in the southern portion of Manhattan.

Motion pictures: Time-Life Films, Inc., producer of television films and videocassettes.

Recordings: Time-Life Records, which produces and markets records, primarily by mail order.

Along with these media operations, Time Inc. manufactures paper and cardboard products, fine art reproductions, furniture, graphic arts equipment, printing inks, and wrapping tape. It also engages in land development and industrial contracting and sells marketing information about supermarket product movement.

car rental firm; and Banquet frozen foods. Nine of the ten paperback houses that publish 90 percent of the paperback books in the United States are owned by conglomerates.

Excessive concentration of power over what Americans read, see, and hear is a specter that frightens many observers of the mass media. Traditionalists who feel a mystique about the media, and sense an aura of personal relationship between them and the public, are disturbed to see publications and stations bought and sold coldly like factories or truck lines, based on the balance sheets of accountants.

Leaders of the group ownership movement depict it in benign terms. They assert that it brings greater efficiency to the publications and stations taken over, through application of skillful management techniques, infusion of fresh capital, and use of bulk purchasing power. Group operation frequently increases a newspaper's profits. So far, those who watch the trend with distrust have failed to produce evidence that any conglomerate attempts to present a unified point of view through the cross-media voices it controls or uses them in unison to promote a political or social cause. Yet they sense potential danger. They fear what might happen in the future, in different political and economic circumstances.

The more immediate concern is that individual media units owned by a large corporation may be forced to reduce their public service and lower their editorial and programming standards in order to attain the profits the corporate headquarters demands. Corporate officers who set these goals are in turn under pressure from stockholders; the management team of a publicly held company must produce satisfactory profits or face replacement. The fear sometimes expressed that stockholders may try to influence the editorial policies of the media units their company owns seems to have little foundation. Stock ownership is so widely diffused as to make such pressure difficult to organize. Profit, not editorial influence, is the usual corporate goal.

The extremely high prices at which broadcasting stations, newspapers, and other publication companies are sold, and the rising operating costs, increasingly squeeze out small entrepreneurs from media ownership, including a growing number of weekly newspapers.

LIMITS ON BROADCAST OWNERSHIP

Using the licensing authority of the Federal Communications Commission (FCC), the government prevents excessive ownership of radio and television stations by corporations. This licensing authority exists because the number of broadcasting channels technically available form a limited national resource, unlike newspapers and magazines, for example, which can be started by anyone able to raise the capital. Those who propose government restrictions on newspaper ownership as a way to halt the headlong expansion of newspaper groups find themselves up against the strictures of the First Amendment.

Under FCC rules, a single company may own or control only seven AM radio stations, seven FM stations, and seven television stations; only five of the television stations may be the more powerful VHF outlets. A single firm is forbidden to own two of the same type stations—two AM outlets, for example—in the same area.

The FCC also enforces a one-to-a-market rule, whose goal is to prevent a company from owning more than one type of medium in a market. The rule states that a newspaper cannot own and operate a television or radio station serving its home community, nor can a radio station own a television station in the same market. Yet in many cities we see radio and television stations under the same ownership; indeed, numerous cases exist in which the local newspaper owns both a local radio station and a local television station, seemingly in contradiction to the FCC rule. These multiple-media combinations are legally permissible because they were "grandfathered"; that is, they were exempted from the FCC restrictions because they were in existence when the rules were imposed. If a grandfathered combination is sold in the future, the new rules will apply, requiring a separation of ownership.

License Renewal Threats

Radio and television stations must periodically satisfy the federal government that they are using the electromagnetic spectrum assigned to them in a manner that meets federal standards. FCC policy specifies that when a station comes up for renewal of its license, which occurs every three years, it must demonstrate that its programming "has been substantially attuned to the needs and interests of the community it serves." The industry has campaigned to have the renewal period extended to five years.

A period of uncertainty about FCC policy on license renewals occurred in the early 1970s, after the commission denied renewal of the license of station WHDH-TV, Boston, and awarded it to a competing applicant in 1969. The Boston decision encouraged the filing of competing applications against a number of major licenses, without success. Under current practice, a station that performs responsibly can anticipate license renewal but must provide evidence at each renewal time that it is doing so.

MINORITY GROUP REPRESENTATION AND OWNERSHIP

Blacks, Hispanics, and other minority groups have brought strong pressures to bear against the media in recent years. They seek a larger, more favorable role on the air, both in the number of minority performers and the elimination of false, stereotyped images of minority individuals.

Progress has been made. For example, a large increase is evident in the number of black performers in television commercials. However, on a more significant level, serious examinations of problems facing minorities have been shown more frequently on television recently—problems arising from history, economic injustices, and contemporary social attitudes. Among these presentations are "Roots," which made a tremendous impact on the American consciousness; "Holocaust," "I Remember Harlem," "Playing for Time," and "The Women's Room." Such productions provide an excellent showcase for actors from minority groups to display their talents. Some stereotyping still exists, but gradually it is being reduced through a sharpened awareness on the part of those who control television programming. Organized groups that focus attention on these evidences of stereotyping also help to promote more balanced programming.

Stations must demonstrate their efforts toward equal treatment of the races and sexes as part of their license renewal applications.

Efforts by minorities to assume ownership of television and radio stations have advanced more slowly, in part because of the heavy financial requirements. According to *Broadcasting* magazine, the number of minority-owned commerical broadcasting stations rose from approximately 62 in January 1978 to about 134 at the start of the 1980s. This represents only 1.5 percent of the nation's commercial outlets.

Private and governmental efforts are being made to improve the situation. The Carter administration undertook a program to promote minority ownership, one aspect of which was to have the Small Business Administration make loans to broadcasters. The National Association of Broadcasters created a nonprofit Minority Broadcast Investment Fund, whose goal was to raise $45 million in contributions to be used for direct loans and loan guarantees to minority owners. The National Radio Broadcasters Association has a program for its members to help minority workers learn station-operating techniques. A National Black Network was created in radio with the goal of its members owning a full complement of 14 AM and FM stations, along with the possible purchase of cable television franchises.

Chapter 23

INTERNATIONAL MEDIA AND ORGANIZATION ROLES

A BROADENING FIELD

For many years the term "Afghanistanism" was applied to editorial writing that avoided important local topics and instead focused on such seemingly inconsequential and faraway happenings as the overthrow of an Afghan leader, a poor rice crop in the Philippines, or tribal feuding in Somalia. But that ostrich-like posture no longer is tenable—if it ever was. The revolution in Iran and the Soviet invasion of Afghanistan, coupled with the energy crisis, inflation, and the spectre of world hunger, demonstrated anew to the American public what many observers have long realized—that there is scarcely a development anywhere that does not impinge upon our well being.

As a consequence, the maintenance of an open flow of communication has become a necessity, both for the United States and for all other countries. John E. Reinhardt, former director of the U.S. International Communication Agency, puts it this way:

> There are, of course, many elements that will determine our shared future on this planet. The one which is common to them all, however, is communications in its many forms—the sharing of ideas and emotions, the web of society. Only through an open communications system can we begin to hope for a stable world order. The alternative is national tribalism, economic protectionism, and social isolation—each of which feeds on ignorance of our common needs and of the prospects for meeting them.

In this chapter we shall discuss the roles that the mass media and the major organizations concerned with mass communications are playing in world society and some of the vexing problems that have arisen. These topics include the beginnings of international mass communication, national media systems, the explosion in telecommunications and other technology, the flow of international news and cultural information, international and national government and private sector organizations, advertising and public relations, the growth of communications research and education, and the demands of the Third World nations, which comprise two-thirds of humankind, that a New World Order of Communications be effected. Future mass communicators should be acquainted with these developments and be prepared to cope with them in their lives and careers. The days of Afghanistanism have ended.

HISTORICAL BACKGROUND

Origins

International mass communications may be identified as any communication transmitted by the mass media across national boundary lines. In the ancient world, most communication was oral, augmented by signals, ceremonies, coins, and forms of architecture, and later by signs identifying places of business (the forerunner of our advertising today). The earliest writing was done on stones, on walls of caves, or on primitive materials such as bamboo strips. Conquerors, traders, and missionaries gradually spread their own language and writing to other parts of the world. Books were first produced laboriously by hand.

International communication was accelerated by Gutenberg's invention of movable type and the introduction of the printing press. News sheets, or *corantos,* relating the most wondrous of happenings, were carried from country to country by travelers. Important financial families such as the Fuggers and Rothschilds in Europe hired couriers to bring them news of political events. Newspapers and magazines soon were printed and distributed by means of horseback and sailing ship, and later by means of steamship and train. When the telegraph, oceanic cable, radio, and improved newspaper presses appeared, international mass communication became an important element in modern world society.

The Global News Cartel

In 1835 Charles Havas, a Frenchman, began collecting European news for French newspapers. A few years later, Paul Julius Reuter, a German, began using homing pigeons to beat the Rothschilds' couriers. Telegraph lines linked continental countries but could not traverse the Skagerrak and the English Channel. Realizing that copper wire would revolutionize and standardize the newsgathering process, Reuter took his pigeons to London in 1851 and began gathering news for about a dozen newspapers in the British Isles. He then persuaded the British government to let him use government cables that were beginning to link the empire's outposts. Such an arrangement was mutually profitable: Reuter got his news, and his partner, the government, got favorable treatment in the news.

Finding that his service could not compete in world newsgathering with Reuter's use of the cables, Havas persuaded Reuter and Dr. Bernhard Wolff, who founded a German agency in 1849, that the world should be divided into three parts for the purposes of newsgathering. Havas covered the French empire, southwestern Europe, South America, and parts of Africa; Reuter covered the British empire, North America, Mediterranean countries, and most of Asia; Wolff covered the rest of Europe and Russia. Each agreed to exchange news with the others.

In the United States, the New York Associated Press had been organized in 1848 as forerunner of the modern AP. Since the British government wished to avoid offending its former colony, the cartel decided to admit the AP, and the agreement was formalized in 1887. Nevertheless, the AP was confined to the United States until early in the twentieth century when it was permitted to gather news in Canada and Mexico and, near the end of World War I, in Central and South America. So it was that, from 1858 to World War I, news was never quite free of the taint of government propaganda. Kent Cooper, longtime general manager of the AP, expressed the opinion that the news cartel, by monopolizing the distribution of international news and by coloring that news in nationalistic hues to suit clients in each of the countries served, had been in part responsible for the war.

Dissatisfied with the cartel's method of newsgathering and reporting, major newspapers in the United States and other countries increased their number of foreign correspondents. Radiotelegraphy, a cheap alternative carrier, challenged the monopoly of the cables. The high-speed Hoe rotary press enabled newspaper circulations to rise, and many afternoon papers, with multiple split-second editions for street sales, developed. By 1909 the United States had three press agencies. The AP was reorganized in 1900; E. W. Scripps established the United Press Association in 1907; and William Randolph Hearst's International News Service was formed two years later. The news cartel was finally broken by 1920, when through a friendship between a UP executive and the owners of *La Prensa* in Buenos Aires, the UP obtained contracts with a number of Latin American newspapers. At about the same time, several English provincial newspapers organized the British United Press and began exchanging news items with the UP. National news agencies such as Stefani in Italy, Fabra in Spain, and the Press Association and Exchange Telegraph in England also developed early, followed by Japan's Kyodo, the Federal Republic of Germany's Deutsche Press-Agentur (DPA), and Yugoslavia's Tanjug.

The Associated Press broke away completely from the cartel in 1934. The Havas agency ceased its operations in 1940, and British newspaper proprietors took over the Reuters agency in 1941. Stefani was succeeded a year later by the Agenzia Nazionale Stampa Associata, modeled after the AP and the new Reuters. An independent Agence France-Presse was organized in postwar France. The only major surviving government-controlled news agencies were Spain's EFE and the Russian agency, TASS, joined later by China's Hsinhua.

Today, four news agencies collect and distribute most of the world's news: AP, UPI, Reuters, and Agence France-Presse. Each has offices in all major news centers, employing hundreds of full-time and part-time correspondents, as described in Chapter 6. They are joined to a lesser extent in worldwide competition by TASS. All serve both print and broadcast media, as well as national and regional press agencies, in Arabic, English, French, German, Portuguese, Spanish, and other languages as necessary.

Most national and regional agencies exchange news with these services. The latter include Inter Press Service, formed by journalists in 1964 to provide news services supporting political and social reform in Latin America but now also functioning in Africa, Asia, and Europe; the Caribbean News Agency, founded in 1975 with United Nations aid and now serving 17 English-speaking countries; and the Middle East News Agency. The Pool of News Agencies of Non-Aligned Countries was established in 1975 under the aegis of Tanjug, the Yugoslav news agency; it is supported by about 50 countries. Approximately 35 nations, however, still have no agency of their own.

FOREIGN CORRESPONDENTS

Two London newspapers, the *Times* and *Morning Chronicle*, established foreign correspondence from the European continent in the 1820s and by 1850 had extended coverage to Asia and the United States. They thus pioneered the concept of individual newspaper enterprise to complement news agency services. William Howard Russell of the *Times* gained early fame by covering the Crimean War in 1854, and by reporting from Moscow, India, and the American Civil War.

James Gordon Bennett reported Queen Victoria's coronation for his New York *Herald* in 1838. Horace Greeley's New York *Tribune* boasted Charles A. Dana, Margaret Fuller, and Bayard Taylor as early European correspondents; Taylor was with Commodore Perry in Tokyo Bay in 1853. George W. Smalley opened the *Tribune*'s London bureau before 1870.

Major foreign news services, syndicated to other dailies, expanded rapidly in the 1920s, led by those of the New York *Times* and *Herald Tribune* and the Chicago *Daily News* and *Tribune*. Famous names were those of Walter Duranty, *Times* correspondent in the Soviet Union during the 1920s and 1930s; Paul Scott Mowrer and Edgar Ansel Mowrer of the Chicago *Daily News;* and Dorothy Thompson of the New York *Post* and *Herald Tribune.* The New York *Times* and Chicago *Tribune* services survived past 1980, joined in the 1960s by the syndicate sponsored by the Washington *Post* and Los Angeles *Times.*

Despite increasing involvement by the United States in foreign affairs and the increasing interdependency of the nations of the world, American mass media participation in reporting world news declined. Studies by Ralph E. Kliesch for the Overseas Press Club revealed a 28 percent drop in the number of full-time persons employed abroad by the American media during the years 1969 to 1975. A 1979 United States State Department study showed a leveling off at the low point in 1975. Of the total number of 676 employed, 429 were U.S. citizens, 8 percent of whom were women. These figures included all American mass media: news agencies, networks, newspapers, and magazines.

During the late 1970s, the AP employed 81 U.S. citizens abroad, and UPI employed 67. Other leading full-time staffs abroad numbered 35 members for *Time,* 31 members for the New York *Times,* 22 members for *Newsweek,* and approximately 15 members each for NBC, CBS, and ABC. In London, 27 U.S. media organizations maintained bureaus, including 11 major dailies and newspaper groups, 11 news and business magazines, and the news agencies and networks. Newspapers not previously mentioned were the *Wall Street Journal, Christian Science Monitor,* Baltimore *Sun,* and the Hearst, Scripps-Howard, Block, and Knight-Ridder groups. On the bright side, Knight-Ridder announced in 1979 that it would send eight correspondents abroad to live for the next two years in six countries, in addition to sending American staff members regularly on specific overseas assignments. The Chicago *Tribune,* with six overseas bureaus, sent 100 U.S. staff members to 70 countries during a three-year period, and the Gannett group was averaging four foreign bylines a week by U.S. staff. The high costs of maintaining resident correspondents led to this shift in policy, editors said.

American overseas coverage was admittedly inadequate, at all levels. The 27 U.S. bureaus in London could be compared to those in New York: 29 from Great Britain, 35 from the Federal Republic of Germany, 26 from Japan, and 22 from France. Altogether, 73 countries were maintaining media coverage in New York and 54 in Washington.

NATIONAL MEDIA SYSTEMS

As may be expected, the mass media are most highly developed in the industrialized parts of the world, such as the United States, Japan, and the European countries. These countries have moved well beyond the simple oral forms that still characterize much of the public communication in the poorest nations, especially in Africa and Asia. Most societies, however, contain elements of both media and oral public communication. In national *media* systems, professional communicators provide information, interpretation, and entertainment to mass audiences via the media. In national *oral* systems, information is conveyed by word of mouth directly to families and to worship and work groups by hierarchal leaders rather than by professional communicators.

Sociologist Daniel Lerner speaks of Type A and Type B systems. In Type A systems, information is provided by the mass media to largely urban groups that are mostly literate and are governed by elected officials. In Type B systems, information is transmitted orally to largely rural residents who are mostly illiterate and are governed by nonelected leaders. Transitional societies, including most of the Third World countries, employ both media and oral systems and are characterized by greater degrees of literacy and urbanization than are Type B societies.

In all countries the mass media help create and maintain a sense of nationhood, perform developmental tasks such as improving education and building political stability, distribute information for the formation of public opinion, provide a forum for public discussion, offer cultural information and entertainment, and, in nations where such activity is permitted, serve as a watchdog on government and prevent abuses of all kinds. Many of the poorer Third World nations, however, seek to use the media primarily for purposes of economic and social development and to maintain the governments in power.

Strengthening their communications facilities has been a primary aim of the almost 100 new nations—nearly all former colonies, almost all poor—that have been established during the last 30 years. Many have yet to meet the minimum standard established by the United Nations Educational, Scientific and Cultural Organization (UNESCO) of ten copies of daily newspapers, five radio receivers, and two cinema seats for every 100 persons. Because radio can reach scattered and largely illiterate populations least expensively of any medium, often by loudspeakers, the greatest progress toward reaching the UNESCO goals has been achieved in this field. Even so, in countries such as India, which has 72 different languages, the problem of establishing a national broadcasting system is almost insurmountable, and the use of other media is similarly obstructed.

TELECOMMUNICATIONS

A Communications Explosion

So rapidly is world telecommunications expanding that its growth may best be described not as a revolution but as an explosion. Telecommunications, as defined by international convention, is "any transmission, emission, or reception of signs, signals, writing, images, and sounds or intelligence of any nature by wire, radio, optical, or other electromagnetic systems." Thus it includes, among other means, the telegraph, telephone, telex, facsimile and data transfer between computers, and radio and television broadcasting.

Telecommunications takes place through the air, through land and oceanic cables, and, most dramatically, via satellite. It is used mostly for business and personal messages. Although almost 80 percent of the approximately 400 million telephones have been installed in only ten countries, the telephone links all nations. It is estimated that more than 440 billion calls are made each year. The latest transatlantic cable can carry 4000 calls simultaneously, and the use of fiber optics and laser beams will increase that number tremendously. There are more than 10,000 satellite circuits transmitting far more messages than cable. Through the marriage of the computer and cable television, the telephone itself has become a mass medium.

Computers capable of performing one billion operations a second are linking all parts of the world with a flow of electronic data that can be stored, processed, analyzed, and retransmitted in oral and visual forms. Data processing, in a field known as informatics (after the French word, *informatique*), is rapidly transforming industrial, scientific, commercial, and government operations. It is estimated that about one-half of the workers in the United States are now engaged in some form of information processing.

Satellites

Approximately 35 communications satellite systems of national, regional, or broader scope are functioning or under construction. Intelsat, started in 1965 and now operated by a consortium of more than 100 countries, has satellites in orbit over the Atlantic, Indian, and Pacific oceans. It serves nationally owned earth stations in about 90 countries. The Communications Satellite Corporation, a private, profit-making company, was established in 1962 by Congress to own and operate the American segment of this system.

The other global system, Intersputnik, was created in 1971 by an agreement among the Soviet Union, the countries of Eastern Europe, Cuba, and Mongolia. Available for use by all countries, it was developed from the Soviet Union's elliptical orbit system, consisting of satellites orbiting the earth every 12 hours, with a high arc over the northern hemisphere, and 40 earth stations. Simultaneous global diffusion of messages emanating from Intelsat and Intersputnik can be achieved by linking national and regional terrestrial networks.

Many countries have their own domestic and regional satellite systems, such as the United States' RCA and Comstar operations, and numerous others are planned. Additional satellite systems serve marine, aeronautical, and military purposes. Because it costs no more to transmit a message 10,000 miles than it does to transmit one 300 miles, the satellite systems rapidly are replacing, as well as supplementing, terrestrial operations.

Radio

Anywhere in the world a person with a shortwave or mediumwave radio may tune in voices in a multiplicity of languages, as well as music and Morse code signals, projected by powerful transmitters in many countries. Where boundaries are not far distant, regular mediumwave broadcasts from other countries may be heard.

International radio broadcasting is that which is intended, either exclusively or in part, for audiences outside the frontiers of the country from which the broadcast originates. Potential audiences are vast. With the development of portable transistor radios, many of which are capable of receiving the programs of international broadcasters, it is estimated that more than one billion sets are in use. The British Broadcasting Corporation (BBC) estimates that about 75 million adults listen to its programs at least once a week. The United States' Voice of America reaches a comparable audience, well over one-half of which is in the Soviet Union.

In 1922 Germany began daily propaganda news broadcasts to other countries in Morse code. During the mid-1920s, the Soviet Union became the first country to produce foreign language broadcasts in several languages, and Great Britain and other countries soon followed. During the early 1930s, several commercial stations in Europe, such as Radio Paris and Radio Luxembourg, began broadcasting on longwave or mediumwave in several languages.

In the United States, companies such as General Electric, NBC, and CBS built and operated shortwave transmitters, mostly relaying domestic programs but also transmitting some in foreign languages. Pearl Harbor convinced the United States government that it could not rely solely on commercial broadcasters for an international service, so the Voice of America was created in 1942 as a part of the Department of State. By 1946 it was broadcasting in 24 languages. During the Cold War the American effort was increased with the establishment in Munich, Germany, of Radio Free Europe and Radio Liberation (now Radio Liberty), both financed by the Central Intelligence Agency. Radio Free Europe broadcasts in Bulgarian, Czech and Slovak, Hungarian, Polish, and Romanian. Radio Liberty sends its broadcasts to the USSR in Russian and 15 other languages. The stations are now financed by the U.S. government and managed by the Board for International Broadcasting. They are not, however, part of the Voice of America.

Today the countries engaged in the most international broadcasting, ranked in order of number of programming hours each week, are the

Soviet Union, United States (broadcasting in 39 languages), People's Republic of China, German Federal Republic, United Kingdom, North Korea, Egypt, and Albania. In addition, many privately owned stations seek international audiences for religious, commercial, and clandestine purposes, the latter often seeking to provoke revolutions. Most of the stations intend their broadcasts for particular portions of the world.

Why do so many countries broadcast internationally? The answer takes many forms: promoting national interest, promoting national prestige, keeping in touch with nationals abroad, promoting understanding between nations, disseminating news with accuracy and objectivity, spreading a particular creed or doctrine, attempting to influence the internal affairs of another country, fostering the national culture including the teaching of the national language, and reserving a place in the broadcasting spectrum against a future need.

Allocations on the overly crowded spectrum are made by the International Telecommunication Union. The claims of the many new developing countries for increased allocations are now being considered in the aftermath of the World Administrative Radio Conference which convened in Geneva in 1979. With an estimated 4600 shortwave stations in the world, audibility is a genuine problem, so some leading broadcasters send taped material to relay stations that boost their output, or they transmit programs to them directly by shortwave or by satellite. Holding and increasing their audiences is a constant problem; therefore, in recent years many stations, including Radio Moscow, have improved the quality and style of their programming. Jamming of broadcasts from other countries is frequently attempted; the Soviet Union greatly increased its jamming of American broadcasts in the early 1980s.

World competition for listeners is expected to become more intense when direct radio reception from satellites becomes a reality. The number of receivers in use, particularly in the Third World, is expected to increase, and tuning has been made easier on sets with digital frequency displays.

Television

During the last decade or so, television has spread to all countries except a few in Africa and Asia. UNESCO estimates that there are 117 sets for every 1000 inhabitants of the world, about 366 million receivers in all. Television's impact ranges from heavy use in the developed nations to reception mostly by elite urban groups in poorer countries. The ratio of receivers to persons is estimated at one to two in North America, one to four in Europe, one to 12 in Latin America, one to 40 in the Arab states and Asia, and one to 500 in Africa. United States citizens possess about one-half of the world's sets. Usage is also high in Japan, the United Kingdom, the Federal Republic of Germany, France, Italy, and Canada, in that order.

The United States exports far more television programs than any other country. More than 150 American companies produce and export TV programs, with the nine companies comprising the Motion Picture Export Association accounting for about 80 percent of total sales abroad. America's competitive position has been enhanced by the rapid growth of color TV, the trend toward commercialization of TV operations in other countries, the sales of satellite telecasts of special events such as championship boxing matches, and the growing use of educational programs produced in the United States. The United Kingdom, France, and the Federal Republic of Germany also export much programming. In Mexico, where the "novella," patterned after American soap operas, is highly popular, many programs are sold to other Latin American countries. Nations in the Middle East obtain most of their programs from Lebanon and Egypt. Programs produced in communist countries are broadcast mainly in other such nations.

A cultural imbalance, however, is evident. According to a survey by Tapio Varis, a Finnish researcher, less than 2 percent of commercial and noncommercial programming viewed in the United States and China is received from foreign sources; in the Soviet Union, 5 percent; in France, 9 percent; and in Japan, 10 percent. By contrast, countries such as Chile, Mexico, Uruguay, Saudi Arabia, Italy, Australia, and Zambia import more than 50 percent of the programs viewed by their citizens—Saudi Arabia, in fact, imports 100 percent. Feature films, series and serials, and entertainment shows comprise the majority of these programs. British productions such as "Civilisation," "Upstairs, Downstairs," and "Search for the Nile" have been well received in the United States. Conversely, most of the imported programs viewed in Great Britain, such as the program that caught British fancy, "Dallas," are obtained from the United States.

American investors own stock in stations throughout the world. Most are minority holdings, representing from 10 to 20 percent of total investment. The largest investors have been the three networks and Time-Life Broadcasting International.

Film

The number of persons viewing motion pictures in cinema houses around the world generally coincides conversely with the availability of television. In almost all of the industrialized nations, movie attendance has declined considerably during the last decade or more. For example, admissions in Japan dropped dramatically from 373 million in 1965 to 165 million in 1977. On the other hand, movie attendance in India rose 23 percent from 1966 to 1975, and in the Soviet Union during a recent ten-year period the number of cinema houses increased 50 percent and the number of admissions 30 percent.

Of the estimated 3000 feature-length films produced worldwide each year, India makes the most. According to the *International Film Guide*

1979, that country produced 557 films in 1977, followed by Japan with 337, the United States with 225 to 250 (exact figure not provided), France with 222, Italy with 165, and the Soviet Union with 141. About one-half of the world's full-length entertainment films are made in 11 Asian countries and about one-third in Europe and the USSR. It is interesting to note that, although American movies are viewed almost everywhere, the United States is far from being the leader in film production. Language and cultural differences, including the expense of dubbing voices, are major problems in international distribution. Thousands of documentary, educational, and training films on the international market are produced each year for educational and industry use, primarily on television. Increasingly, feature films are being made expressly for sale to television and videocassette outlets.

The availability of small, relatively inexpensive still and 8 mm movie cameras, combined with increased jet age tourism, has made photography extremely popular, especially in the industrialized nations. The world production of photographic film, for example, increased about 30 percent from 1965 to 1976.

THE PRINT MEDIA

Illiteracy is widespread throughout the world—it is estimated that only about one of every four persons 15 years of age or older can read and write at a minimal level. Although there are more than 3500 identified languages, perhaps no more than 500 languages and dialects exist in written form. UNESCO estimates that more than two-thirds of printed materials are produced in English, Russian, Spanish, German, and French. In view of these facts, it is clearly evident that mass communication takes place far more widely by electronic means than by newspapers, magazines, and books. Nevertheless, the print media remain the primary base for enhancing and preserving world civilization.

Books

A post-World War II revolution in book production and distribution techniques, with emphasis on the paperback, has characterized the world book publishing industry. Between 1955 and 1976, world book production more than doubled in number of titles published annually, and tripled in number of copies printed. It is estimated that more than 590,000 titles and about eight billion copies per year are now marketed. Books were the first mass medium exported in large numbers when European publishers opened up markets and, later, subsidiaries in former colonies. Educational and scientific materials comprise substantial markets. The more limited book publishing in the Third World is overwhelmingly of an educational nature.

In many countries, publishing is primarily a private enterprise, although governments of almost all nations have their own printing departments and some subsidize private operations. In communist nations, publishing is part of the planned public economy.

United States publishing firms export more than $300 million in books each year, nearly one-half of these to one country, Canada. Almost one-half of the encyclopedia revenues of American publishers are accounted for through international sales. Mass-market paperback publishers sell about 10 percent of their books in other countries. Since there is only a limited market for English-language editions, many publishers rely on translated versions as well as copublishing arrangements with their own subsidiaries or independent foreign houses.

Reader's Digest has a healthy foreign book market. Time-Life books, translated into as many as 26 languages, are widely sold through offices in Amsterdam, London, Paris, and Mexico City. These offices handle copublishing or consortium printing arrangements in which expensive four-color printing is done at one time, with the texts in various languages added separately.

An alternative to publishing or exporting overseas has been the leasing of foreign rights to American books, subject to provisions of the Universal Copyright Convention.

Magazines

The magazines of leading countries circulate widely. *Reader's Digest,* for example, distributes about 11.5 million copies abroad—25 national editions printed in 13 languages. *Time* magazine sells about 5 million copies abroad. Other top news magazines are *L'Express* of France, *Der Spiegel* of the Federal Republic of Germany, and *Asiaweek*, circulating throughout that part of the world. News magazines with strong economic emphases include *The Economist* of London, one of the world's great quality periodicals, and the *Far Eastern Economic Review* for Asia. The best picture magazine in the world is *Paris-Match* of France.

Estimates of the number of magazines published worldwide vary widely. The International Federation of the Periodical Press reported in 1975 that there were approximately 410,000 periodical titles in existence. However, the *UNESCO Statistical Handbook* that same year reported only 123,000 in existence. The number of scientific and technical periodicals alone has been reported at 100,000.

Newspapers

There are approximately 8000 daily newspapers in the world and far more weeklies and semiweeklies. One estimate sets worldwide circulation of dailies in excess of 400 million copies. Sweden and Japan have the highest circulations of dailies, nearly 600 for every 1000 inhabitants. Since mass media usage correlates highly with economic development and the level of education, more than one-half of the world's dailies are published in the industrialized nations. Some large cities in the developing countries have high-quality newspapers, but beyond those urban areas the quality of content and appearance falls off sharply, largely because of illiteracy, the multiplicity of vernacular languages, low per capita income, and lack of distribution facilities.

As in the United States, the growth of chains and conglomerates characterizes much of the world's press. Except where resisted by unions, such as in England and Paris, modern printing techniques increasingly are being employed by newspapers in many countries. Newspapers in many less-developed countries, however, are printed with nearly worn-out equipment on antiquated flat-bed presses. Most of the world's daily newspapers are privately owned, but direct and indirect government controls are evident in many countries.

Because of its mass nature, much of the world's press is sensationalist and somewhat superficial in its treatment of the news. With the exception of a few countries including the United States, where the *Wall Street Journal* now enjoys the greatest daily circulation of any newspaper, dailies with the largest circulations almost always are those that emphasize entertainment value. Most countries, however, with the exception of a few in Africa and Asia, do have at least one high-quality daily newspaper that deals primarily with social and political ideas and issues and reflects the best practices of journalism. John C. Merrill and Harold A. Fisher, in their 1980 book, *The World's Great Dailies,* provide profiles of 50 newspapers that they consider, by reputation and the consensus of serious observers, to be the world's finest. To a considerable degree, the editors of these dailies read each other's newspapers and, with the serious magazines of their countries, help maintain a dialogue among themselves and their readers about important national and world issues.

An around-the-world traveler examining copies of these dailies might pick up *The Times* in Great Britain, *Le Monde* in France, *Corriere della Sera* in Italy, *Al Ahram* in Egypt, *Pravda* in the Soviet Union, *Rand Daily Mail* in South Africa, *The Statesman* in India, *The Age* in Australia, *The Straits Times* in Singapore, *Renmin Ribao* in the People's Republic of China, *Asahi Shimbun* in Japan, *Estado de S. Paulo* in Brazil, and the Los Angeles *Times* in the United States. The tourist might not be able to read all of these papers, but, since English-language newspapers are published almost everywhere, the tourist could keep up with news developments of major importance reasonably well. In addition to these national English-language newspapers, the traveler most likely would read newspapers such as the *International Herald Tribune*, circulated widely from Paris and, in the Orient, the recently established *Asian Wall Street Journal.*

ORGANIZATIONS

The United Nations

International communication has been a major concern of the United Nations since its founding in 1946. In that year the UN issued a Declaration on Freedom of Information, which stated that "all states should proclaim policies under which the free flow of information within countries and across frontiers will be protected. The right to seek and transmit information should be insured in order to enable the public to ascertain facts and appraise events. . . ." Because of conflicting legal and ideological positions, a convention as to how this principle would be invoked has never been worked out.

In 1948 the UN General Assembly issued a Universal Declaration of Human Rights, which, although not legally binding, carries great moral and psychological weight with UN members. Article 19 of the document proclaims that: "Everyone has the right to freedom of opinion and expression; this right includes freedom to hold opinions . . . and to seek, receive, and impart information and ideas through any media and regardless of frontiers." Article 2 extends the document's affirmation of basic human rights to every individual "without distinction of any kind" including the "limitation of sovereignty." Resolution 110 (II), passed in 1947, condemns all forms of conflict-inciting propaganda, and Article 4 of the International Convention on Elimination of Racial Discrimination, passed in 1963, condemns all forms of racist propaganda. The issue of human rights was reaffirmed in 1966 with the International Covenant on Civil and Political Rights and by the Helsinki agreements of 1975.

With the launching of the first space satellites, the UN became involved in questions relating to outer space, and in 1959 the Committee on the Peaceful Uses of Outer Space (COPUOS) was established. A declaration in 1963 was followed by passage of the Outer Space Treaty in 1967. It declared that outer space was to remain the "province of all mankind" to which all nations shall have equal access, that its uses should be nonmilitary but contributing to international peace and security. Two years later, with 102 nations in favor and the United States opposed, the UN called upon its committee to "elaborate principles governing the use by States of artificial earth satellites for direct television broadcasting with a view toward concluding an international agreement or agreements." Although the sending of satellite signals directly into homes is unlikely in the near future, almost all nations fear the loss of national sovereignty and control by such an action. On the other hand, the United States considers that the unrestricted exchange of information is vital for the full development of all countries. The problems of the relationship between sending and receiving states, including consent and participation, program content, and unlawful and inadmissible broadcasts, are yet to be resolved. The gathering, storage, processing, and dissemination of data obtained by earth-sensing satellites comprise yet another problem to be solved by the UN.

UNESCO. The involvement of the United Nations Educational, Scientific, and Cultural Organization (UNESCO) with mass communications was mandated in Article 1 of its constitution, which states that the organization shall "collaborate in the work of advancing the mutual knowledge and understanding of peoples, through all means of mass communication, and to that end recommend such international agreements as may be necessary to promote the free flow of ideas by word or image." UNESCO is composed of official delegations of all the nations, which convene biennially. Between these general conferences, UNESCO's work is carried out by its Secretariat, based in Paris. Its activities include research, field projects, meetings of experts, regional conferences, and seminars. Among its actions was a declaration in 1972 calling for the principle of prior consent to be applied to broadcasts from satellites. In recent years UNESCO has become the primary forum for Third World communication complaints, which will be reviewed later in this chapter.

International Telecommunication Union. This UN agency traces its history back to an 1865 European conference establishing rules for transmission of telegraph messages across national boundaries. The telegraphic union thus formed was followed in 1906 by the establishment of a radio-telegraphic union. The two merged in 1932 to form the International Telecommunication Union (ITU), which became a UN agency in 1947. Its primary function is engineering—to govern frequency allocation and coordinate procedures for the world's electromagnetic spectrum. In recent years the ITU has become highly politicized as new nations have sought space on the crowded spectrum and older countries have sought largely to preserve the "first-come, first-served" principle that has given them priority. World Administrative Radio Conferences, conducted every 20 years, are supplemented by special conferences dealing with satellites and other matters.

National Government Organizations

The governments of virtually every country have one or more departments involved in international communications. Almost all oversee broadcast operations, and many exercise direct and indirect control over the print media including fields such as news and editorial content, the acquisition of newsprint and equipment, the collection and dissemination of news by foreign correspondents in their countries, the news agencies that receive and transmit information, and their international information and propaganda activities.

In the United States, the U.S. International Communication Agency (USICA), (formerly known as the United States Information Agency), administers a wide variety of information, educational, and cultural exchange programs around the world. The agency reports to the president and receives policy guidance from the secretary of state.

USICA employs approximately 8600 persons, of whom about 4200 are non-Americans serving abroad. About one-half of the USICA's 3400 employees in the United States are engaged in the broadcasting operations of the Voice of America. Many of the others provide supporting services for 600 Foreign Service information and cultural affairs officers working overseas alongside colleagues from the Department of State and other United States agencies at more than 200 embassies, consulates, and other missions in 125 countries. Among other activities, USICA operates regional libraries, plans exhibits and tours of performing groups, produces radio and television programs and research reports, and provides opportunities for foreign residents to learn English.

The Office of International Communication Policy of the Department of State performs various functions such as preparing the United States position for World Administrative Radio Conferences. As do the Soviet Union's KGB and the intelligence agencies of other countries, the Central Intelligence Agency (CIA) engages in numerous clandestine communications activities abroad on behalf of American interests.

Nongovernment Organizations

Hundreds of private mass communications organizations operate throughout the world. A few of them will be noted here.

Fédération Internationale des Éditeurs de Journaux. The International Federation of Newspaper Publishers (FIEJ) founded in 1948, links more than 25 national publishers' organizations on five continents in the free world to promote their interests in such fields as management, marketing, news-editorial, and freedom of information.

The International Press Institute. Founded in 1950, the IPI is an association of editors, publishers, broadcast executives, and associates in 63 nations dedicated primarily to promoting press freedom, fostering research, and training Third World journalists. The IPI continuously protests the imprisonment and murder of outspoken journalists.

The Inter American Press Association. The IAPA, organized in 1942, among other activities monitors press situations in all Western hemisphere countries, protests restrictive measures, sends special missions to problem countries, and promotes the exchange of journalists for educational purposes.

The Inter-American Association of Broadcasters. The IAAB provides representation and technical and educational help for broadcast stations and associations in South and North America.

The International Federation of Journalists. Through 28 national unions in 24 countries, the federation seeks to raise professional standards, defend press freedom, and help news media in developing nations.

The International Organization of Journalists. This Marxist organization, headquartered in Czechoslovakia and linked to groups in 109 countries, promotes various journalistic activities.

The World Press Freedom Committee. Activated in the United States in 1976, the WPFC links 32 national and international media organizations in monitoring perceived challenges to world press freedom and in providing training programs, equipment, and consultants for Third World countries.

THE THIRD WORLD COMMUNICATIONS CONTROVERSY

Not only is the majority of the world's news transmitted by Western news agencies, but the Western powers also are the most advanced in the use of telecommunications channels, including satellites. The nonaligned and some other nations view this dominance of communications channels as a vestige of colonialism that must be shaken off if they are to develop culturally, politically, and economically. They believe that their goal of a New World Economic Order cannot be realized without a corresponding New World Communications Order. Their principal demands, as detailed in a document written by Mustapha Masmoudi, a Tunisian government official, include the following:

- Establishing independence and equity in access to global communication resources in order that their own views, values, and developmental efforts might be reported more fully.
- Substantial help from the West to speed their own communication development.
- Support of the Pool of News Agencies of Non-Aligned Countries, established in 1975 under the aegis of Tanjug, the Yugoslav news agency, and supported by 50 countries.
- Legitimizing the right of governments to limit access to news sources and the right to censor or restrict the flow of information across national borders.
- The adoption by UNESCO of resolutions proclaiming the right of governments to become involved in the licensing of journalists in order to "protect" them, and in the adoption of an international code of ethics and an international right of reply.

• Establishment of a supranational tribunal by UNESCO to monitor media behavior throughout the world.

The Third World complaints gained the full attention of the Western nations in 1976, when the Soviet Union's draft copy of a declaration proposed for adoption by UNESCO stipulated the "use" of the mass news media for certain purposes and made independent journalists subject to control by governments. Alarmed, Western governments and the independent news media mounted a strong defense that won a two-year delay, based mainly on promises of increased aid to Third World news media. A 16-person International Commission for the Study of Communication Problems was created under the chairmanship of Sean MacBride of Ireland, recipient of both the Lenin and Nobel Peace Prizes.

By making further pledges to help Third World countries develop their news agencies and media, and by skillful maneuvering, Western leaders again warded off the state control threat at the 1978 UNESCO conference. A declaration was adopted that dropped the phrase, "free and balanced flow of information," the antithesis of a free flow, and called for "a new equilibrium and greater repricocity"—a balancing of news reports between the developed and developing countries and among the developing nations. The declaration also noted "the aspirations of the developing countries for the establishment of a new, more just, and more effective world information and communication order."

At the conference the U.S. government pledged $25 million in free transponder time on Intelsat for public service use in four areas of the developing world, and Nordic countries promised to spend $4 million on Third World projects. USICA Director John Reinhardt also announced plans to send communications educators to help establish six regional training centers for journalists. American news leaders said that their organizations would send senior correspondents and editors, on rotating three-month assignments, to demonstrate professional skills at the centers.

Through the World Press Freedom Committee, American news organizations already had raised more than $500,000 toward an initial goal of $1 million and were engaged in spending almost $300,000, mainly for training programs on three continents, soliciting donations of used equipment, and sending consultants abroad from a pool of 900 volunteer consultants. Plans were made to seek funding for substantial technology transfer through the United Nations Development Program (UNDP), the International Telecommunication Union (ITU), and the World Bank.

Although Third World activists wish to focus communication development on UNESCO, the UN General Assembly voted in late 1979 to examine the implications of a new information and communications order and discuss the matter at future sessions.

When the MacBride Commission released its final report in 1980, the World Press Freedom Committee noted the following positive aspects of the report, from its traditional democratic-capitalist point of view:

• Censorship in all forms is condemned.

• The right of access applies to private as well as public sources of information.

• Journalists should have no special protection; they will be protected when the rights of all citizens are guaranteed.

• Licensing of journalists is rejected because it would require stipulation by some authority as to who is eligible and on what basis.

• Employment of journalists by intelligence agencies of any country is condemned.

Negative aspects from the Western point of view:

• A proposed International Center for Study and Planning of Information and Communications, to be established within UNESCO, conceivably could become a training ground for those challenging the Western concept of privately owned news businesses operating with traditional Western news values.

• News media (including "transnationals"—the international news agencies) would be pressured, or required, to promote government-set social, cultural, economic, and political goals.

• Private ownership of news media and communication facilities is questioned.

Because of the moderate tone of the MacBride Commission's report, UNESCO Director-General Amadou Mahtar M'Bow of Senegal—who has favored Third World aims while trying to avoid a blowup with the West—declined to present the report for formal adoption at UNESCO's twenty-first conference in Belgrade, Yugoslavia, in 1980. Instead M'Bow asked the delegates simply to consider it.

After several weeks of wrangling, delegates adopted a resolution calling for the free flow of information; expressing the need to safeguard freedom of opinion, expression, and information; supporting the widest and most democratic access possible to the functioning of the mass media; and repudiating censorship and licensing.

No concrete steps were taken toward the establishment of a New World Communications Order; however, the delegates agreed to underwrite a three-year study of what would be included in such a document. In addition, they authorized funding for a series of ten regional conferences on topics (mainly objectionable to the West) such as the protection of journalists, a definition of journalistic standards, international right of reply and rectification, responsibility in communications, and the advertising content and management of the media. The delegates decided that UNESCO itself should direct a program intended to help Third World media modernize their facilities and train people to use such equipment, a project previously conducted mainly by Western donor countries and private organizations.

All sides of the controversy registered some gains and some losses in these decisions, and the stage was set for continued maneuvering at forthcoming UNESCO conferences.

THE PERSUASIVE ARTS

Advertising

World trade expands constantly, and with the growth of multinational companies has come the growth of multinational advertising agencies to serve multinational clients. As trade barriers have fallen, manufacturing distribution and advertising agency practices have become international activities in which the old concept of home as distinct from overseas markets is increasingly irrelevant. Coca-Cola, Toyota automobiles, Gillette products, and Tide—these and hundreds of other products are sold throughout the world; Gillette, for example, spends more than $100 million in advertising each year in 170 countries.

The earlier American dominance of world advertising has been diminished by increasingly more sophisticated practice in many other countries. Edward Ney of Young & Rubicam International states: "Today great advertising can and does happen everywhere in the world. The U.S. no longer has a monopoly, no longer has to dispatch its advertising missionaries abroad and spread the faith because they've got religion over there; and, like the traditional converts, these once benighted natives are frequently more dedicated practitioners than those born to the faith."

During the last decade huge multinational advertising conglomerates took shape as a number of major American advertising agencies joined forces with companies in Europe and elsewhere. The J. W. Thompson Co. and McCann-Erickson had been methodically building their empires since the 1920s and 1930s, and other companies also had massive operations abroad. In 1969, the Chicago-based Leo Burnett Co. startled the advertising world with the acquisition of the major agency parts of the London Press Exchange, then the second largest London-based agency. Throughout the 1970s similar conglomerates took shape involving companies in many nations. At the same time other American advertising agencies continued to expand their international operations, as discussed in Chapter 15. The Japanese agency, Dentsu Inc., tops all others in the world with gross billings well in excess of $2 billion annually, although only about 3 percent come from outside its domestic market. Despite the agency-engulfing mergers that are taking place, many observers believe that medium-sized agencies still will be a strong force in most countries.

Multinational business firms operate subsidiaries in a number of countries, which often have vastly differing political, cultural, economic, and legal environments. Some companies centralize their marketing and advertising operations, while others assign much decision-making to their foreign managers. The environmental variables are so numerous and often so subtle—in areas such as eating patterns and customs, social class structure, income levels, and legal restraint—that creative sales and promotion strategy, to a considerable extent, must be custom-tailored for each country. With regard to the European market, S. Watson Dunn has concluded that, "the best approach is to preserve some covert multinationalism in the campaign but to add a deft touch that is distinctively French or British or Italian."

As in the United States and Canada, the consumer movement has gained momentum in recent years in most industrialized nations. Legislation to regulate and control advertising has been proposed or passed in Australia, Canada, Finland, Germany, Japan, Norway, the United Kingdom, the United States, and other countries. Cigarette and children's advertising, along with that considered dishonest, have been primary concerns. Statutes vary from country to country. Some countries, such as the United Kingdom and Ireland, rely on self-discipline by business itself. Most companies subscribe to the International Chamber of Commerce code of advertising practice. The International Advertising Association, composed of about 2500 individual members and more than 300 international companies and other groups, states that, in order to gain acceptance for self-regulation, its members should eliminate abuses in the marketplace and act as the champion of the public's interests in quality and performance of goods and services.

No Western advertising agencies are permitted to operate in the Soviet bloc countries. In the Third World nations, advertising is less developed but international agencies operate extensively. Some Third World countries seek to establish guidelines regarding advertising content and the values and attitudes it fosters, which are often perceived as contrary to national cultural values. Some of these nations also tax advertising, or plan to do so, in order to provide funding for national media development.

Public Relations

The concept of public relations arose in the United States at the beginning of the twentieth century. Since World War II public relations has spread throughout the nontotalitarian world. Wherever business and international institutions go in the free world, public relations practice should—and almost always does—accompany them. The leading international public relations agencies are American: Hill and Knowlton, Burson-Marsteller, and Carl Byoir. American managers provide the continuing, overall strategy, but—because every country's customs and values are different, and substantial variations often exist even within countries—its application must be carried out primarily by public relations employees and outside consultants native to each country.

Companies everywhere are confronted with essentially the same public relations problems as those in the United States, including relationships with local and national governments, consumer groups, the financial community, and employees. For a company operating outside its own borders, these problems often are aggravated by, among other things, the differences in languages, longer chains of command, evident and subtle differences in customs, and the varying levels of media and public relations development.

Everywhere, public relations functions both independently and in concert with marketing and advertising objectives. In addition, governments themselves must conduct public relations programs, utilizing their own nationals sent abroad, or through native consultants.

Public relations associations have been organized in about 50 countries. In Great Britain more than 2500 practitioners belong to the British Institute of Public Relations. Because the German language has no close equivalent, practitioners in Germany have formed an association known as the Deutsche Public Relations Gesellschaft. In Japan, where more than 1000 consultants practice, the Public Relations Society of Japan has been formed. Three regional associations have been organized: the European Center of Public Relations (CERP), the Pan Pacific Public Relations Federation (PPPRF), and the Inter-American Federation of Public Relations (FIARP).

As noted in Chapter 16, the International Public Relations Association has members in approximately 60 countries. Its objectives are to provide a means whereby its members may exchange information and ideas, improve skills and ethical standards, and work toward a better understanding among the peoples of the world.

RESEARCH

Cooperative research among nations is a strong component of mass communications research throughout the world. This is *true* international communications research, as exemplified by the study of the flow of news among nations and the determination of the international uses and effects of the transmission of information and cultural programs via satellite. Much more international communications research, however, is comparative in nature; for example, researchers may analyze media systems within individual countries and regions and then compare their findings with analyses of systems in other countries and regions that have been made by themselves or by researchers interested in only one country. In another category, researchers endeavor, for example, to determine the effects, within a particular country, of communication received from outside its borders; or they may analyze the nature and operations of the communicators who send messages to other countries.

International communications scholars employ all of the methodologies for gaining scientific information used by researchers in other fields. Their research may be quantitative in nature, employing such methodologies as content analysis, surveys, polling, and experimental techniques, or they may be qualititative studies, such as those of a descriptive, historical, and legal nature. These researchers are joined in international communications studies by scholars in other fields such as sociology, anthropology, economics, geography, and linguistics.

In the United States some international communications research began in the 1920s, when concern developed over matters such as World War I propaganda, the intermedia competition between newspapers and radio, and the impact of the rapidly growing mass media upon society. The real boom began during the period in which the United Nations was founded: after World War II, when the United States sought, in the words of B. L. Smith, "to develop an art and science of international and crosscultural communication and opinion, in the hope of reducing international confusion and irritation." International communications research slowly developed from its parent disciplines into a field of its own which, although still in its infancy, is exercised predominantly through the universities, independent research centers often supported by foundations, government agencies, and business corporations intent on developing foreign markets.

In recent years much study has focused on the dissemination of innovation—how new technological and cultural inventions and ideas have been accepted in various countries—and in rural, family planning, and development communications in Third World countries. Research under way at centers throughout the world seeks answers to all sorts of communications problems plaguing the developing world. Among these centers are the East-West Communication Institute at Honolulu, the Asian Mass Communication Research and Information Centre at Singapore, and the Centre for Mass Communication Research in Leicester, England. Other regions in the Third World are seeking to develop their own research centers. For three decades UNESCO has developed research worldwide. During the 1950s the organization was mainly preoccupied with compiling information about the mass media and news agencies, but since the early 1960s it has turned much of its attention to development communication and, at present, to planning related to the entire communications technological explosion.

EDUCATION

Closely related to research has been the widespread development of training and professional education centers throughout the world. Much of this development took place during the 1950s and 1960s, when, under the Fulbright (later Fulbright-Hays) and Smith-Mundt programs, American mass communications educators went abroad at the rate of more than one dozen per year to help establish schools of journalism and strengthen others that had already begun. They took with them the concept that a liberal education, as provided by a university or other institution, in combination with professional instruction, would best serve a country's longterm communications needs.

Because the inculcation of professional standards and principles in a country's journalists is perhaps the greatest guarantee of a free press, the established centers of journalism education, both national and regional, are now playing an increasingly important role in the full development of the media in Third World countries and elsewhere. Of note are the professional education programs in the universities of Mexico, Peru, Brazil and Argentina, as well as at the University of the West Indies; at Cairo University; in Kenya, Nigeria, and Ghana; and in India, Taiwan, Hong Kong, the Philippines, Malaysia, and Thailand.

During a typical academic year mass communications educators from American universities will study or lecture in countries such as Egypt, Indonesia, Mexico, Britain, Japan, Jamaica, India, Brazil, Portugal, Columbia, Liberia, Nigeria, Australia, and Singapore. At the same time, Fulbright lecturers and researchers come to the United States from Peru, Bulgaria, Japan, the Federal Republic of Germany, France, Norway, Argentina, Britain, South Korea, and elsewhere. Approximately 400 international graduate students from 73 countries studied mass communications in 58 schools and departments of journalism in the United States during the 1978–1979 academic year. To varying degrees, the exchange of educators and students is taking place among numerous other countries.

Seminars, institutes, and other educational programs throughout the world are supported each year by organizations such as the International Press Institute, World Press Freedom Committee, Inter American Press Association, the Ford Foundation, the Thomson Foundation, the Friedrich Naumann Stiftung (Foundation), Konrad Adenauer Stiftung, the UN Fund for Population Activities, UNESCO, and the International Development Research Centre. The press associations and print and broadcast media and organizations sponsor training programs annually.

Under the operating philosophy that Third World journalists may best be educated and trained in their own environs, governmental and private sector efforts are now being concentrated on the development of regional centers of professional and technical education, a movement coinciding with the growth of regional news agencies. Classes taught by native instructors who have studied in other countries and who write and use textbooks indigenous to each region's language and culture are in great demand.

Meanwhile, international communications instruction in American universities is advancing slowly, impeded by increasing student enrollments that are straining resources needed for all areas of instruction. Instruction is further constrained by accrediting requirements that state that communications instruction must occupy no more than approximately 25 percent of a student's total course of study.

JOB OPPORTUNITIES IN INTERNATIONAL COMMUNICATIONS

Students interested in international communications work will most likely find their first opportunities when, as beginning reporters and editors, they cover assignments involving international matters and, as gate-keepers, edit international news stories. As magazine and freelance writers, they may be assigned to stories with an international flavor. Those assuming advertising and public relations duties with business corporations will need to work their way into the international departments of those companies. The tourism and development divisions of state government may afford an entry point. United States Civil Service examinations are the beginning requirement for those seeking federal government positions that may lead to international communications work. Military service often provides yet another opportunity.

For those who seek foreign assignments with newspapers, magazines, broadcast networks, and wire services, the road to those assignments most likely will be long, with service first in the United States to acquire experience and establish a personnel record recommending the applicant for overseas service. The same is true for advertising and public relations people who wish to work abroad. Equally long will be the road for those desiring university teaching and research professorships or work with independent research organizations that will lead to travel and study in other countries. Foreign service work with innumerable federal agencies, such as the United States International Communication Agency (USICA), also often requires a substantial period of government or mass media service in this country before foreign assignments are received. In terms of adventure and salary, however, the rewards for those who "do their homework," preparing themselves adequately through experience and individual study, are ample.

Most of the USICA's foreign service information officers begin their careers via the Career Candidate Program. Applicants take a written examination offered each December at many locations in this country and abroad. The examination tests general knowledge, English expression, and aptitude for information, cultural, economic, political, administrative, and consular work. To qualify for the USICA, candidates must receive passing grades in all areas and show particular strength in their knowledge of American culture, history, government, and society and current affairs. Other evaluations follow this examination. After orientation and training in Washington, D.C., including geographic area studies and language instruction as appropriate, a career candidate is assigned to a USICA post overseas for approximately one year. This training assignment is followed by a tour of duty in positions such as assistant cultural affairs officer, assistant information officer, program assistant, and occasionally public affairs officer at a branch of a USICA post in a large country such as India or Brazil. Permanent tenure may then be awarded in the form of a presidential commission. A foreign service information officer usually spends about two-thirds of his or her career overseas. Inquiries about various USICA positions should be made to the agency at 1776 Pennsylvania Avenue, N.W., Washington, D.C. 20547.

An assignment as a foreign correspondent for a newspaper, news magazine, network, or wire service has been the dream of many young journalists. As previously noted, however, such assignments are limited. Keith Fuller, general manager of the Associated Press, said in 1979 that only 81 of the AP's more than 500 correspondents abroad were Americans. Since it costs so much to maintain a correspondent overseas, assignments often go to unmarried persons who require less outlay. Sometimes they are employed by a media news bureau abroad. One encouraging trend among major American newspapers is to send staff members on specific overseas assignments, lasting perhaps several months, which is less costly than assigning living quarters abroad. This gives more persons an opportunity to do reporting overseas.

Because an extensive knowledge of national history, customs, laws, and language is highly desirable, advertising and public relations personnel often are natives of the countries or regions in which they work. For example, Richard C. Christian, president of Burson-Marsteller, has observed that a new breed of marketing executive is emerging in Europe who is "multinational in attitude and multilingual and young."

Students interested in international communications careers of any type are advised to direct their programs of study toward obtaining substantive knowledge in international aspects of the social sciences, humanities, business, law, or other areas closely related to their individual talents and preferences. The choices are so numerous that career objectives should be narrowed quickly. For orientation, course work in international communications is highly desirable. Graduate study undoubtedly would be an asset.

The same necessity for early career decisions also applies to languages. Students should learn to speak and read one foreign language as well as they can. They may depend upon later intensive study or living experience in another country for the language mastery that will be necessary.

BIBLIOGRAPHY

This is a selected, annotated bibliography of books dealing with mass communications and journalism. It is organized to correspond with the six principal parts and 23 chapters of this book.

It is the authors' aim to introduce readers to some of the basic books that, if they have the time and interest to explore them, will take them beyond the necessarily limited syntheses of an introductory survey of mass communications. A student reader who has the interest and opportunity to elect further studies in the field will encounter many of these books again in advanced courses; if the student goes no further, this bibliography will provide a personal reading list for more detailed examination of various facets of the field. It is in no sense an all-inclusive bibliography; for that purpose the reader is referred to Eleanor Blum's *Basic Books in the Mass Media* (Urbana: University of Illinois Press, 1980). Its 1179 annotated entries cover general communications, newspapers, broadcasting, film, magazines, advertising, and public relations. For more depth, particularly in historical areas and biographies, see the 3147 entries in Warren C. Price's *The Literature of Journalism: An Annotated Bibliography* (Minneapolis: University of Minnesota Press, 1959) and the 2172 entries in a 10-year supplement to it compiled by Price and Calder M. Pickett, *An Annotated Journalism Bibliography* (1970).

Two valuable reference-research guides are *The Aspen Handbook on the Media*, whose 1977–79 edition was edited by William L. Rivers, Wallace Thompson, and Michael J. Nyhan (New York: Praeger, 1977), and *The Mass Media: Aspen Guide to Communication Industry Trends*, edited by Christopher H. Sterling and Timothy R. Haight (1978). *Mass Media Booknotes,* edited since 1969 by Christopher H. Sterling and published monthly by the Department of Radio-Television-Film, Temple University, offers extensive reports on books in all areas. See also the research journals listed below. A general source book is the annual Directory issue of *Journalism Educator,* published by the Association for Education in Journalism for the American Society of Journalism School Administrators.

This bibliography also lists the principal journals and trade publications with which students of mass communications should be familiar, and in a few instances makes references to articles in them. In cases where books have gone through revised editions, the date given is for the most recent revision. In subsequent listings of a book, place and date of publication are not repeated.

PERIODICALS, ANNUAL PUBLICATIONS, AND DIRECTORIES

General Research Journals

Journalism Quarterly Published by the Association for Education in Journalism, devoted to research articles in journalism and mass communications. Contains extensive book reviews and bibliographies of articles in American and foreign journals.

Public Opinion Quarterly Emphasizes political and psychological phases of communication. Book reviews and summaries of public opinion polls. Published by the American Association for Public Opinion Research.

Gazette International journal, published quarterly in Amsterdam, devoted to research in mass communications. Book reviews and bibliographies.

Journal of Communication Research quarterly focusing on methodology; material in speech and interpersonal communication areas; book reviews. Published by the International Communication Association.

Communication Research International quarterly focusing on research methodology. Published by Sage Publications.

Public Opinion Bimonthly journal; articles, reports on public opinion polls. Published by the American Enterprise Institute.

AV Communication Review Reports on research activities and findings in the communication area. Published quarterly by the Association for Educational Communications and Technology.

Quarterly Journal of Speech Research articles, book reviews. Published by the Speech Communication Association.

Journal of Popular Culture Quarterly publication with wide interests in field; articles, book reviews. Published by Bowling Green State University in cooperation with the Popular Culture Association.

Journalism History Research quarterly; articles, notes, book reviews for mass communications history. Published by the California State University Northridge Foundation with the support of the American Association of Schools and Departments of Journalism.

Mass Comm Review Quarterly publication of the Mass Communications and Society Division of the Association for Education in Journalism; articles.

Journal of Typographic Research Research quarterly of the graphic arts area, published by the Cleveland Museum of Modern Art.

Journalism Monographs Published serially by the Association for Education in Journalism, beginning in 1966, for research findings falling between article and book lengths; approximately quarterly.

General Professional Journals

Professional journals with general interest articles on press problems: *Nieman Reports* (Nieman Foundation); *Columbia Journalism Review* (Columbia University Graduate School of Journalism); *Quill* (Society of Professional Journalists, Sigma Delta Chi); PRO/COM (Women in Communications, Inc.); *Journalism Educator* (American Society of Journalism School Administrators); *Communication: Journalism Education Today* (Journalism Education Association); *Community College Journalist* (Community College Journalism Association); *Washington Journalism Review* (Washington Communication Corporation); *News Media and the Law* (Reporters Committee for Freedom of the Press); *Media Report to Women* (Women's Institute for Freedom of the Press).

International Journals

Sources for those interested in international communications and media include the following general publications.

International and European publications *UNESCO Courier; Gazette; IPI Report* (International Press Institute); *The Media Reporter* (research quarterly, Britain); *World Press Review* (Stanley Foundation, U.S.A.); *FIEJ Bulletin* (International Federation of Newspaper Publishers); *IFJ Information* (International Federation of Journalists); *Democratic Journalist* (International Organization of Journalists); *Intermedia* (International Institute of Communications); *WACC Journal* (World Association for Christian Communications); *IAPA News* (Inter American Press Association); *Canadian Journal of Communication; Communication Research Trends* (Centre for the Study of Communication and Culture, London).

Asia *East-West Perspectives* (East-West Center, Hawaii); *Media Asia* and *AMCB Bulletin* (Asian Mass Communication Research and Information Centre, Singapore); *Asian Messenger* (Chinese University of Hong Kong); *Indian Press; The Communicator* (Indian Institute of Mass Communication).

Broadcasting *EBU Review* (European Broadcasting Union); *Telecommunication Journal* (International Telecommunication Union); *OIRT Information* (International Broadcasting and Television Organization); *Combroad* (Commonwealth Broadcasting Conference); *ABU Newsletter* (Asian Broadcasting Union).

Directories *World Communications* (UNESCO, 1975); *Ulrich's International Periodicals Directory* (New York: Bowker); *Editor & Publisher International Year Book* (daily newspapers), and the British-published *Benn's Press Directory* and *Willing's Press Guide; Television Factbook* (*TV Digest,* U.S.A) and *World Radio-TV Handbook* (Denmark); *Japanese Press* (Japan Newspaper Publishers and Editors Association).

Newspapers

Research journals *Newspaper Research Journal* (Newspaper Division, Association for Education in Journalism); *News Research Report* series (News Research Center, American Newspaper Publishers Association).

Professional journals *presstime* (American Newspaper Publishers Association); *ASNE Bulletin* (American Society of Newspaper Editors); *Masthead* (National Conference of Editorial Writers); *News Photographer* (National Press Photographers Association).

Trade journals *Editor & Publisher,* whose focus is on the daily newspaper and general industry problems, but which reports on advertising, marketing, and public relations areas; *Publishers' Auxiliary* (National Newspaper Association), primarily covering weeklies and small dailies; *Guild Reporter* (Newspaper Guild); *Circulation Management; Inland Printer,* for the printing industry.

Annual publications *APME Red Book,* containing the record of the annual meeting and the reports of the continuing studies committee of the Associated Press Managing Editors Association; *Problems of Journalism,* covering the annual meeting of the American Society of Newspaper Editors; *News Research for Better Newspapers,* a compilation of materials published by the ANPA News Research Center.

Directories *Editor & Publisher International Year Book,* source for statistics and information about dailies; N. W. Ayer and Son, *Directory of Newspapers and Periodicals,* covering all newspapers and magazines.

Television, Radio, Cable, and Film

Research journals *Journal of Broadcasting* (Broadcast Education Association); *Television Quarterly* (National Academy of Television Arts and Sciences); *Public Telecommunications Review* (National Association of Educational Broadcasters); *American Film* (American Film Institute). Articles, book reviews, notes.

Professional journals *RTNDA Communicator* (Radio Television

News Directors Association); *Film Critic* (American Federation of Film Societies); *Film Quarterly Communication Arts,* for photography, television; *TV Communications*, for cable television; *Access* (National Citizens Committee on Broadcasting); *Telecommunications; Comsat Magazine; Satellite Communications; Channels of Communications.*

Trade journals *Broadcasting,* the voice of that industry; *Television/Radio Age; The Dial,* for public television; *Variety,* voice of the entertainment world; *Billboard.*

Directories *Broadcasting Yearbook,* source for statistics about radio and television; *Television Factbook; Broadcasting Cable Sourcebook.*

Magazines and Book Publishing

Professional and trade journals *Folio,* for the magazine area; *Publishers Weekly,* for the book publishing industry, whose focus is primarily on general trade and children's books; *The Retail Bookseller; Bookbinding and Book Production; Author and Journalist, Writer,* and *Writer's Digest,* for freelance magazine writers.

Directories *Literary Market Place,* for book publishing; *Directory of Newspapers and Periodicals* (N. W. Ayer and Son), for magazine statistics and information; *Writer's Market* and *Writer's Year Book,* guides for magazine article writers; *House Magazine Directory* (Gebbie Press).

Advertising and Public Relations

Research journals *Journal of Marketing* (American Marketing Association), articles and book reviews; *Journal of Marketing Research* (Advertising Research Foundation); *Journal of Advertising* (American Academy of Advertising); *Public Relations Review* (Foundation for Public Relations Research and Education), annual bibliography.

Professional journals *Public Relations Journal* (Public Relations Society of America); *PR News,* newsletter; *Journal of Organizational Communication* (International Association of Business Communicators). *IABC News,* newsletter.

Trade journals *Advertising Age,* the major organ of the advertising industry; *Advertising Agency; Advertising Requirements; Sponsor,* for buyers of broadcast advertising; *Industrial Marketing; Sales Management; Direct Marketing.*

Directories Standard Rate and Data Service, *Consumer Markets; Editor & Publisher Market Guide; Broadcasting Marketbook.*

PART ONE: THE ROLE OF MASS COMMUNICATIONS

William L. Rivers, Wilbur Schramm, and Clifford G. Christians, *Responsibility in Mass Communication* (New York: Harper & Row, 1980), is the best treatment of communications ethics. It discusses the role of the mass communicator in developing the political, social, and economic fabrics of a democratic society, and the development of modern mass communications. In a similar vein are Lee Thayer, editor, *Ethics, Morality and the Media* (New York: Hastings House, 1980); John C. Merrill, *The Imperative of Freedom* (New York: Hastings House, 1974); John L. Hulteng, *The Messenger's Motives: Ethical Theory in the Mass Media* (Englewood Cliffs, N.J.: Prentice-Hall, 1976); Lee Brown, *The Reluctant Reformation* (New York: David McKay, 1974); and Bruce Swain, *Reporters' Ethics* (Ames: Iowa State University Press, 1978).

An excellent introduction to the study of the communication process and to research in mass communication is found in Wilbur Schramm's *Men, Messages, and Media: A Look at Human Communication* (New York: Harper & Row, 1973), a readable survey of communication theory, mass communication audiences, effects, and social controls. John C. Merrill and Ralph L. Lowenstein have contributed their prize-winning *Media, Messages, and Men: New Perspectives in Communication* (New York: Longman, 1979), analyzing the changing role of the mass media, the communicators and their audiences, and media concepts and ethics. Elie Abel has edited essays by 12 leading scholars and journalists in *What's News: The Media in American Society* (San Francisco: Institute for Contemporary Studies, 1981). All three are in paperback.

Communication effects are analyzed in W. Phillips Davison, James Boylan and Frederick T. C. Yu, *Mass Media Systems and Effects* (New York: Praeger, 1976); *The Process and Effects of Mass Communication,* edited by Wilbur Schramm and Donald F. Roberts (Urbana: University of Illinois Press, 1971); and Joseph T. Klapper, *The Effects of Mass Communication* (New York: Free Press, 1960). A review of 25 years of literature on television audience effects is provided in George Comstock, Steven Chaffee, Natan Katzman, Maxwell McCombs, and Donald Roberts, *Television and Human Behavior* (New York: Columbia University Press, 1978).

Several books of readings deal with the role of mass communications in society. Listed in order according to the increasing complexity of their materials, they are *Interpretations of Journalism,* edited by Frank Luther Mott and Ralph D. Casey (New York: Crofts, 1937), a historical collection of utterances about the press over 300 years; *Enduring Issues in Mass Communication,* edited by Everette Dennis, Arnold Ismach and Donald Gillmor (St. Paul: West Publishing, 1978), a study of media impact, roles and reforms; *Communications in Modern Society,* edited by Wilbur Schramm (Urbana: University of Illinois Press, 1948), 15 essays on communications problems and research trends; *Mass Communications,* edited by Wilbur Schramm (Urbana: University of Illinois Press, 1960), selected readings on mass communications "through the windows of the social sciences"; and *Reader in Public Opinion and Communication,* edited by Bernard Berelson and Morris Janowitz (New York: Free Press, 1966), dealing with public opinion theory, media content, audiences, and effects.

The complex and specialized area of communications theory may be approached through a readable survey of contemporary theory by Melvin L. DeFleur and Sandra Ball-Rokeach, *Theories of Mass Communication* (New York: McKay, 1975), or in Dennis K. Davis and Stanley J. Baran, *Mass Communication in Everyday Life: A Perspective on Theory and Effects* (Belmont, Calif.: Wadsworth, 1980); Everette E. Dennis, *The Media Society, Evidence About Mass Communication in America* (Dubuque, Iowa: Brown, 1978); Charles R. Wright, *Mass Communication, a Sociological Perspective* (New York: Random House, 1975); and Dennis McQuail, *Towards a Sociology of Mass Communication* (London: Collier-Macmillan, 1969).

An overview is provided in Ernest G. Borman, *Communication Theory* (New York: Holt, Rinehart and Winston, 1980). Reed H. Blake and Edwin O. Haroldsen give brief explanations of basic concepts of communication in *A Taxonomy of Concepts in Communication* (New York: Hastings House, 1975). C. David Mortensen edited *Basic Readings in Communication Theory* (New York: Harper & Row, 1973). Provocative discussions are found in Marshall McLuhan's *Understanding Media: The Extensions of Man* (New York: McGraw-Hill, 1964); his earlier *The Gutenberg Galaxy: The Making of Typographic Man* (Toronto: University of Toronto Press, 1962); and *The Medium Is the Massage* (New York: Bantam Books, 1967).

A 1000-page reference volume for the serious scholar of communication theory is *Handbook of Communication* (Chicago: Rand McNally, 1973), edited by Ithiel de Sola Pool and Wilbur Schramm. Among collections of scholarly articles on mass communications research are three of the annual reviews published by Sage Publications of Beverly Hills, California: *Current Perspectives in Mass Communication Research,* edited by F. Gerald Kline and Phillip J. Tichenor (1972); *New Models for Mass Communication Research,* edited by Peter Clarke (1973); and *The Uses of Mass Communications: Current Perspectives on Gratification Research,* edited by Jay G. Blumler and Elihu Katz (1974). W. Phillips Davison and Frederick T. C. Yu edited *Mass Communication Research: Major Issues and Future Directions* (New York: Praeger, 1974). Among other books in the theory area are William Stephenson, *The Play Theory of Mass Communication* (Chicago: University of Chicago Press, 1967); Alex S. Edelstein, *The Uses of Communication in Decision Making* (New York: Praeger, 1974); and the classic *The Measurement of Meaning* by Charles E. Osgood, George Suci, and Percy Tannenbaum (Urbana: University of Illinois Press, 1957).

The effects of the mass media on the social fabric are discussed in various articles in *Mass Culture: The Popular Arts in America,* edited by Bernard Rosenberg and David M. White (New York: Free Press, 1957). There are sections on the mass literature, motion pictures, radio, and television. An updated version by the same authors is *Mass Culture Revisited* (Princeton, N.J.: Van Nostrand Reinhold, 1971).

Among the leading books on public opinion are Bernard C. Hennessy, *Public Opinion* (Scituate, Mass.: Duxbury Press, 1975), a text in its third edition; Alan D. Monroe, *Public Opinion in America* (New York: Harper & Row, 1975), emphasizing the political process; V. O. Key, Jr., *Public Opinion and American Democracy* (New York: Knopf, 1961); Dan Nimmo, *Political Communication and Public Opinion in America* (Santa Monica, Calif.: Goodyear Publishing, 1978); Erwin P. Bettinghaus, *Persuasive Communication* (New York: Holt, Rinehart and Winston, 1973); and Curtis D. MacDougall, *Understanding Public Opinion: A Guide for Newspapermen and Newspaper Readers* (Dubuque, Iowa: Brown, 1966). The role of the media in controversial policy decisions is analyzed in Phillip J. Tichenor, George A. Donohue, and Clarice N. Olien, *Community Conflict and the Press* (Beverly Hills, Calif.: Sage, 1980).

The impact of public opinion and the mass media upon politics is analyzed by Walter Lippmann in his classic *Public Opinion* (New York: Harcourt, Brace, 1922); by Douglass Cater in *The Fourth Branch of Government* (Boston: Houghton Mifflin, 1959), a study of the key role of the Washington press corps; by Bernard C. Cohen in *The Press and Foreign Policy* (Princeton, N.J.: Princeton University Press, 1963), a study of Washington diplomatic reporting; by James Reston in another study of press influence on foreign policy, *The Artillery of the Press* (New York: Harper & Row, 1967); by Elmer Cornwell, Jr. in *Presidential Leadership of Public Opinion* (Bloomington: Indiana University Press, 1965); and by William L. Rivers in *The Opinionmakers* (Boston: Beacon, 1965), a study of leading Washington journalists, and *The Adversaries* (Boston: Beacon, 1970), a study of press manipulation by public officials.

A research-oriented contribution to the subject was made in the 1975 Sage Publications review of communication research edited by Steven H. Chaffee, *Political Communication: Issues and Strategies for Research.* Others are Bernard Rubin, *Media, Politics, and Democracy* (New York: Oxford, 1977); Donald L. Shaw and Maxwell E. McCombs, editors, *The Emergence of American Political Issues* (St. Paul: West, 1977), studies of the agenda-setting function; Sidney Kraus and Dennis Davis, *The Effects of Mass Communication on Political Behavior* (State College: Penn State Press, 1976); L. John Martin, editor, *Role of the Mass Media in American Politics,* a special issue of the *Annals* of the American Academy of Political and Social Science (September, 1976); and Thomas E. Patterson and Robert D. McClure, *The Unseeing Eye* (New York: Putnam, 1976), television's role in elections.

PART TWO: THE PRINT MEDIA

While it is primarily a history of the print media, the most widely ranging of the journalism histories is Edwin and Michael Emery, *The Press and America: An Interpretative History of the Mass Media* (Englewood Cliffs,

N.J.: Prentice-Hall, 1978). It correlates the narrative of journalism history with social, political, and economic trends and is especially comprehensive in its treatment of twentieth-century journalism—newspapers, magazines, radio and television, press associations, and the relationship of the mass media to government and society.

Frank Luther Mott's *American Journalism: A History, 1690–1960* (New York: Macmillan, 1962) is designed for both classroom and reference shelf, contains much rich detail in its comprehensive treatment of newspapers, but puts little emphasis on other media. Alfred McClung Lee's *The Daily Newspaper in America* (New York: Macmillan, 1937) offers a sociological approach and much valuable data in its topical treatment of subjects such as newsprint, printing presses, labor, ownership and management, news, advertising, and circulation. Willard G. Bleyer's *Main Currents in the History of American Journalism* (Boston: Houghton Mifflin, 1927) remains an excellent account of American journalism until the early twentieth century, with emphasis on leading editors.

Kenneth Stewart and John Tebbel, in *Makers of Modern Journalism* (New York: Prentice-Hall, 1952), sketch early American journalism history and concentrate on twentieth-century journalism personalities. Tebbel, in his *Compact History of the American Newspaper* (New York: Hawthorn, 1969) and his *The Media in America* (New York: Crowell, 1975), does the reverse, sketching twentieth-century journalism in only the broadest terms. Sidney Kobre adds details in his sociologically based *Development of American Journalism* (Dubuque, Iowa: Brown, 1969). Robert A. Rutland wrote a brief popularized account in *The Newsmongers* (New York: Dial, 1973), as did George N. Gordon in *The Communications Revolution* (New York: Hastings House, 1977).

The role of women in American journalism history is explored by Marion Marzolf in *Up From the Footnote: A History of Women Journalists* (New York: Hastings House, 1977), a good synthesis. A research guide is Maurine Beasley and Sheila Silver Gibbons, *Women in Media: A Documentary Source Book* (Washington, D.C.: Women's Institute for Freedom of the Press, 1977).

Reproductions of full front pages of newspapers on an extensive, planned scale are found in Edwin Emery's *The Story of America as Reported by Its Newspapers 1690–1965* (New York: Simon and Schuster, 1965), and in *America's Front Page News 1690–1970,* edited by Michael C. Emery, R. Smith Schuneman, and Edwin Emery (New York: Doubleday, 1970). A collection of the best magazine articles about leading American newspaper editors and publishers of all periods is found in *Highlights in the History of the American Press,* edited by Edwin H. Ford and Edwin Emery (Minneapolis: University of Minnesota Press, 1954).

The best historical accounts of specific print media areas are found in the following:

Press associations Victor Rosewater, *History of Cooperative News-*

Gathering in the United States (New York: Appleton, 1930); Robert W. Desmond, *The Information Process: World News Reporting to the 20th Century* (Iowa City: University of Iowa Press, 1978), and Volume 2, *Windows on the World 1900–1920* (1981), of a projected five-volume series.

Magazines Frank Luther Mott's monumental *A History of American Magazines,* in five volumes (Vol. 1, New York: Appleton, 1930; Vols. 2–5, Cambridge, Mass.: Harvard University Press, 1938–68); James Playsted Wood, *Magazines in the United States* (New York: Ronald, 1956); Theodore Peterson, *Magazines in the Twentieth Century* (Urbana: University of Illinois Press, 1964); John Tebbel, *The American Magazine: A Compact History* (New York: Hawthorn, 1969).

Book publishing Hellmut Lehmann-Haupt and others, *The Book in America: History of the Making and Selling of Books in the United States* (New York: Bowker, 1951); Frank A. Mumby, *Publishing and Bookselling: A History from the Earliest Times to the Present* (London: Jonathan Cape, 1956); Douglas C. McMurtie, *The Book: The Story of Printing and Bookmaking* (New York: Oxford University Press, 1943).

Graphics Isaiah Thomas, *The History of Printing in America* (Albany, N.Y.: Joel Munsell, 1810 and 1874), is the earliest journalism history account; Daniel B. Updyke's two-volume *Printing Types: Their History, Forms and Use* (Cambridge, Mass.: Harvard University Press, 1937) is the standard work; S. H. Steinberg, *Five Hundred Years of Printing* (Baltimore: Penguin, 1974), is a briefer survey.

Additional references, by chapter topic, follow.

Chapter 3: Historic Press Freedoms

Companion books trace the story of American press freedom: Leonard W. Levy, *Freedom of the Press from Zenger to Jefferson,* and Harold L. Nelson, *Freedom of the Press from Hamilton to the Warren Court* (Indianapolis: Bobbs-Merrill, 1966). They are excellent surveys.

Lucy M. Salmon's *The Newspaper and Authority* (New York: Oxford University Press, 1923), is an extensive historical survey of restrictions placed on newspapers. Important periods of the history of press freedom struggles are covered in Fred S. Siebert, *Freedom of the Press in England, 1472–1776* (Urbana: University of Illinois Press, 1952); Leonard W. Levy, *Legacy of Suppression: Freedom of Speech and Press in Early American History* (Cambridge, Mass.: Harvard University Press, 1960); Clyde A. Duniway, *The Development of Freedom of the Press in Massachusetts* (New York: Longmans, Green, 1906); John C. Miller, *Crisis in Freedom: The Alien and Sedition Acts* (Boston: Little, Brown, 1951); Frank Luther Mott, *Jefferson and the Press* (Baton Rouge: Louisiana State University Press, 1943); and Zechariah Chafee, Jr., *Free Speech in the United States* (Cambridge, Mass.: Harvard University Press, 1941), a study emphasizing the effects of modern wartime conditions. James E. Pollard, *The Presidents and the Press* (New York: Macmillan, 1947), covers presidential press relations from Washington to Truman, and is supplemented by *The Presidents and the Press: Truman to Johnson* (Washington: Public Affairs Press, 1964).

Excellent discussions by newspaper editors of problems in protecting freedom of information and access to news are found in James Russell Wiggins, *Freedom or Secrecy* (New York: Oxford University Press, 1964), and Herbert Brucker, *Freedom of Information* (New York: Macmillan, 1949). More detailed studies are Harold L. Cross, *The People's Right to Know* (New York: Columbia University Press, 1953), and Zechariah Chafee, Jr.'s two-volume *Government and Mass Communications* (Chicago: University of Chicago Press, 1947).

Philosophical problems of press freedom are analyzed by the Commission on Freedom of the Press in *A Free and Responsible Press,* by William E. Hocking in *Freedom of the Press: A Framework of Principle* (Chicago: University of Chicago Press, 1947), and by Fred S. Siebert, Theodore Peterson, and Wilbur Schramm in *Four Theories of the Press* (Urbana: University of Illinois Press, 1956). Among discussions of press freedom by journalists are Walter Lippmann, *Liberty and the News* (New York: Harcourt, Brace, 1920); Elmer Davis, *But We Were Born Free* (New York: Bobbs-Merrill, 1954); and Alan Barth, *The Loyalty of Free Men* (New York: Viking, 1951).

Chapter 4: Growth of the Print Media

The best historical discussion of the news function is Frank Luther Mott's *The News in America* (Cambridge, Mass.: Harvard University Press, 1952), a survey of the concepts, forms, and problems of news. Michael Schudson takes a sociological approach in his *Discovering the News* (New York: Basic Books, 1978). Jim A. Hart traces the history of the editorial, from 1500 to 1800, in *Views on the News* (Carbondale: Southern Illinois University Press, 1971), and Allan Nevins continues in the introductions for sections in his collection of editorials, *American Press Opinion: Washington to Coolidge* (New York: Heath, 1928).

Arthur M. Schlesinger, *Prelude to Independence: The Newspaper War on Britain, 1764–1776* (New York: Knopf, 1958), analyzes one period of major press influence. Nevins, *American Press Opinion,* has an excellent section on the partisan journalism of the 1790s. C. C. Regier, *The Era of the Muckrakers* (Chapel Hill: University of North Carolina Press, 1932), examines magazines during the Progressive era; Louis Filler, *Crusaders for American Liberalism* (New York: Harcourt, Brace, 1939), also discusses newspaper people. So does Jonathan Daniels in *They Will Be Heard: America's Crusading Newspaper Editors* (New York: McGraw-Hill, 1965), a 200-year survey. Writings of the muckrakers are edited by Arthur and Lila Weinberg in *The Muckrakers* (New York: Simon and Schuster, 1961).

The best anthologies are *Voices of the Past,* edited by Calder M. Pickett (Columbus, Ohio: Grid, 1977); *A Treasury of Great Reporting,* edited by Louis L. Snyder and Richard B. Morris (New York: Simon and Schuster, 1962); Bryce W. Rucker's *Twentieth Century Reporting at Its Best* (Ames: Iowa State University Press, 1964), and John Hohenberg's *The Pulitzer Prize Story* (New York: Columbia University Press, 1959).

Top-flight biographies of key figures in the development of the news function include Carl Van Doren, *Benjamin Franklin* (New York: Viking, 1938); Oliver Carlson, *The Man Who Made News: James Gordon Bennett* (New York: Duell, Sloan and Pearce, 1942); Francis Brown, *Raymond of the Times* (New York: Norton, 1951); Fayette Copeland, *Kendall of the Picayune* (Norman: University of Oklahoma Press, 1943); Candace Stone, *Dana and the Sun* (New York: Dodd, Mead, 1938); Raymond B. Nixon, *Henry W. Grady: Spokesman of the New South* (New York: Knopf, 1943); W. A. Swanberg, *Pulitzer* (New York: Scribner's, 1967); Julian Rammelkamp, *Pulitzer's Post-Dispatch 1878–1883* (Princeton, N.J.: Princeton University Press, 1966); George Juergens, *Joseph Pulitzer and the New York World 1883–1887* (Princeton, N.J.: Princeton University Press, 1966); Oliver Knight, *I Protest: Selected Disquisitions of E. W. Scripps* (Madison: University of Wisconsin Press, 1966), both a biography and a collection of Scripps' writings; W. A. Swanberg, *Citizen Hearst* (New York: Scribner's, 1961); John Tebbel, *The Life and Good Times of William Randolph Hearst* (New York: Dutton, 1952), Gerald W. Johnson, *An Honorable Titan: A Biographical Study of Adolph S. Ochs* (New York: Harper, 1946); Merlo J. Pusey, *Eugene Meyer* (New York: Knopf, 1974); James H. Markham, *Bovard of the Post-Dispatch* (Baton Rouge: Louisiana State University Press, 1954); Homer W. King, *Pulitzer's Prize Editor: A Biography of John A. Cockerill* (Durham, N.C.: Duke University Press, 1965); Mary E. Tomkins, *Ida M. Tarbell* (New York: Twayne, 1974); and Marion K. Sanders, *Dorothy Thompson* (Boston: Houghton Mifflin, 1973).

Leading biographies of opinion makers include John C. Miller, *Sam Adams: Pioneer in Propaganda* (Boston: Little, Brown, 1936); Mary A. Best, *Thomas Paine* (New York: Harcourt, Brace, 1927); Glyndon G. Van Deusen, *Horace Greeley: Nineteenth Century Crusader* (Philadelphia: University of Pennsylvania Press, 1953); George S. Merriam, *The Life and Times of Samuel Bowles* (New York: Century, 1885); Joseph F. Wall, *Henry Watterson* (New York: Oxford University Press, 1956); Joseph L. Morrison, *Josephus Daniels Says* (Chapel Hill: University of North Carolina Press, 1963); and Ronald Steel, *Walter Lippmann and the American Century* (Boston: Little, Brown, 1980). William Cullen Bryant and Edwin Lawrence Godkin are most easily read about in Allan Nevins, *The Evening Post: A Century of Journalism* (New York: Boni and Liveright, 1922). The McCormick and Patterson families and their Chicago *Tribune* and New York *Daily News* are analyzed by John Tebbel in *An American Dynasty* (New York: Doubleday, 1947).

The best autobiographies are Benjamin Franklin, *Autobiography* (New

York: Putnam, 1909); *The Autobiography of William Allen White* (New York: Macmillan, 1946); *The Autobiography of Lincoln Steffens* (New York: Harcourt, Brace, 1931); Horace Greeley, *Recollections of a Busy Life* (New York: Ford, 1868); Fremont Older, *My Own Story* (New York: Macmillan, 1926), the memoirs of a crusading San Francisco editor; Josephus Daniels, *Tar Heel Editor* (Chapel Hill: University of North Carolina Press, 1939), volume one of a five-volume series; and E. W. Howe, *Plain People* (New York: Dodd, Mead, 1929), the story of a Kansas editor and his readers; also told in Calder M. Pickett, *Ed Howe: Country Town Philosopher* (Lawrence: University Press of Kansas, 1969).

Excellent reminiscences of journalists include Melville E. Stone, *Fifty Years a Journalist* (New York: Doubleday, Page, 1921); Will Irwin, *The Making of a Reporter* (New York: Putnam, 1942); Webb Miller, *I Found No Peace* (New York: Simon and Schuster, 1936); and Vincent Sheean, *Personal History* (Boston: Houghton Mifflin, 1969 reissue). The best of a great writer's news work is found in William White's *By Line: Ernest Hemingway* (New York: Scribner's, 1967), and in the biography by Carlos Baker, *Ernest Hemingway* (New York: Scribner's, 1969). Lee G. Miller, *The Story of Ernie Pyle* (New York: Viking, 1950), is very readable. Ishbel Ross, *Ladies of the Press* (New York: Harper, 1936), and John Jakes, *Great Women Reporters* (New York: Putnam, 1969), tell the story of dozens of women journalists. Helen Thomas in *Dateline: White House* (New York: Macmillan, 1975) tells the story of one.

Among important histories of individual newspapers are William E. Ames, *A History of the National Intelligencer* (Chapel Hill: University of North Carolina Press, 1972); Frank M. O'Brien's *The Story of the Sun* (New York: Appleton, 1928), covering the New York *Sun* from 1833 to 1928; Gerald W. Johnson and others, *The Sun-papers of Baltimore, 1837–1937* (New York: Knopf, 1937); Meyer Berger, *The Story of the New York Times* (New York: Simon and Schuster, 1951); and a later study, Gay Talese, *The Kingdom and the Power* (New York: New American Library, 1969); Chalmers M. Roberts, *The Washington Post—The First Hundred Years* (Boston: Houghton Mifflin, 1977), heavy on recent years; Erwin D. Canham, *Commitment to Freedom: The Story of the Christian Science Monitor* (Boston: Houghton Mifflin, 1958); Will C. Conrad, Kathleen F. Wilson, and Dale Wilson, *The Milwaukee Journal: The First Eighty Years* (Madison: University of Wisconsin Press, 1964); Lloyd Wendt, *Chicago Tribune* (Chicago: Rand McNally, 1979); and Robert Gottlieb and Irene Wolt, *Thinking Big: The Story of the Los Angeles Times* (New York: Putnam, 1977).

Two basic historical studies of the black press are Frederick G. Detweiler, *The Negro Press in the United States* (Chicago: University of Chicago Press, 1922), and Vishnu V. Oak, *The Negro Press* (Yellow Springs, Ohio: Antioch Press, 1948). A comprehensive survey is *The Black Press, U.S.A.*, by Roland E. Wolseley (Ames: Iowa State University Press,

1971). *Perspective of the Black Press, 1974* (Kennebunkport, Maine: Mercer House, 1974) is an extensive anthology edited by Henry G. La Brie III.

Among the books on the alternative and protest press are a good survey by Everette E. Dennis and William L. Rivers, *Other Voices: The New Journalism in America* (San Francisco: Canfield, 1974); an anthology edited by Tom Wolfe, *The New Journalism* (New York: Harper & Row, 1973); *The Reporter as Artist* (New York: Hastings House, 1974), edited by Ronald Weber; and David Armstrong, *A Trumpet to Arms, The Alternative Press in America* (Los Angeles: Torcher, 1981).

Magazine editors and publishers are the subjects of books by Oswald Garrison Villard, *Fighting Years* (New York: Harcourt, Brace, 1939), the memoirs of the editor of the *Nation;* Peter Lyon, *Success Story: The Life and Times of S. S. McClure* (New York: Scribner's, 1963); S. S. McClure, *My Autobiography* (New York: Stokes, 1914); John Tebbel, *George Horace Lorimer and the Saturday Evening Post* (New York: Doubleday, 1949); George Britt, *Forty Years—Forty Millions: The Career of Frank A. Munsey* (New York: Farrar and Rinehart, 1935); James Thurber, *The Years with Ross* (Boston: Little, Brown, 1957), the story of editor Harold Ross and the *New Yorker;* Raymond Sokolov, *Wayward Reporter: The Life of A. J. Liebling* (New York: Harper & Row, 1980), longtime *New Yorker* writer; Brendan Gill, *Here at the New Yorker* (New York: Random House, 1975); Norman Cousins, *Present Tense* (New York: McGraw-Hill, 1967), by the *Saturday Review's* editor; W. A. Swanberg, *Luce and His Empire* (New York: Scribner's, 1972); and Robert T. Elson, *Time Inc.* (New York: Atheneum, 1968) and *The World of Time Inc.* (New York: Atheneum, 1973), a two-volume history covering 1923 to 1941 and 1941 to 1960.

The story of a famous book editor is told by A. Scott Berg in *Max Perkins, Editor of Genius* (New York: E. P. Dutton, 1978).

Two individual histories of press associations are Oliver Gramling, *AP: The Story of News* (New York: Farrar and Rinehart, 1940), and Joe Alex Morris, *Deadline Every Minute: The Story of the United Press* (New York: Doubleday, 1957).

Chapter 5: Newspapers

Textbooks on reporting and newswriting Curtis D. MacDougall, *Interpretative Reporting* (New York: Macmillan, 1977), a 50-year veteran; George A. Hough, 3rd, *Newswriting* (Boston: Houghton Mifflin, 1980); Everette E. Dennis and Arnold H. Ismach, *Reporting Processes and Practices* (Belmont, Calif.: Wadsworth, 1981); Brian Brooks, George Kennedy, Daryl Moen, and Don Ranly, *News Reporting and Writing* (New York: St. Martin's Press, 1980); Mitchell and Blair Charnley, *Reporting* (New York: Holt, Rinehart and Winston, 1979); Melvin Mencher, *News*

Reporting and Writing (Dubuque, Iowa; Brown, 1981); Michael Ryan and James W. Tankard, Jr., *Basic News Reporting* (Palo Alto, Calif.: Mayfield, 1977); William Metz, *Newswriting* (Englewood Cliffs, N.J.: Prentice-Hall, 1977); Fred Fedler, *Reporting for the Mass Media* (New York: Harcourt Brace Jovanovich, 1979); Ralph S. Izard, Hugh Culbertson, and Donald A. Lambert, *Fundamentals of News Reporting* (Dubuque, Iowa: Kendall/Hunt, 1977); Julian Harriss, Kelly Leiter, and Stanley Johnson, *The Complete Reporter* (New York: Macmillan, 1977); Judith L. Burken, *Introduction to Reporting* (Dubuque, Iowa: Brown, 1979); Maxwell McCombs, Donald L. Shaw, and David L. Grey, *Handbook of Reporting Methods* (Boston: Houghton Mifflin, 1976); Daniel R. Williamson, *Newsgathering* (New York: Hastings House, 1979); and Ken Metzler, *Newsgathering* (Englewood Cliffs, N.J.: Prentice-Hall, 1979).

Valuable adjuncts to the reporting texts are E. L. Callihan, *Grammar for Journalists* (Radnor, Pa.: Chilton, 1979); William Zinsser, *On Writing Well* (New York: Harper & Row, 1980); and R. Thomas Berner, *Language Skills for Journalists* (Boston: Houghton Mifflin, 1978).

Three books combine coverage of reporting, writing, and editing for print and broadcast media with mass media introductory material: Verne E. Edwards, Jr., *Journalism in a Free Society* (Dubuque, Iowa: Brown, 1970); William L. Rivers, *The Mass Media: Reporting, Writing, Editing* (New York: Harper & Row, 1975); and John Hohenberg, *The Professional Journalist* (New York: Holt, Rinehart and Winston, 1978.)

Special fields of reporting Clark Mollenhoff, *Investigative Reporting* (New York: Macmillan, 1980); Paul Williams, *Investigative Reporting* (Englewood Cliffs, N.J.: Prentice-Hall, 1978); Philip Meyer, *Precision Journalism* (Bloomington: Indiana University Press, 1979), a reporter's introduction to social science methods; Henry H. Schulte, *Reporting Public Affairs* (New York: Macmillan, 1981); George S. Hage, Everette E. Dennis, Arnold H. Ismach, and Stephen Hartgen, *New Strategies for Public Affairs Reporting: Investigation, Interpretation, Research* (Englewood Cliffs, N.J.: Prentice-Hall, 1976); Chilton R. Bush, *Newswriting and Reporting of Public Affairs* (Philadelphia: Chilton, 1971); Louis I. Gelfand and Harry E. Heath, Jr., *Modern Sports Writing* (Ames: Iowa State University Press, 1968); Claron Burnett, Richard Powers and John Ross, *Agricultural News Writing* (Dubuque, Iowa: Kendall/Hunt, 1973); Todd Hunt, *Reviewing for the Mass Media* (Radnor, Pa.: Chilton, 1972); John W. English, *Criticizing the Critics* (New York: Hastings House, 1979).

Editorial page and opinion writing Harry W. Stonecipher, *Editorial and Persuasive Writing* (New York: Hastings House, 1979); A. Gayle Waldrop, *Editor and Editorial Writer* (Dubuque, Iowa: Brown, 1967); Curtis D. MacDougall, *Principles of Editorial Writing* (Brown, 1973); John L. Hulteng, *The Opinion Function* (New York: Harper & Row, 1973).

News editing and copyreading Bruce Westley, *News Editing* (Boston: Houghton Mifflin, 1980); Martin L. Gibson, *Editing in the Electronic*

Era (Ames: Iowa State University Press, 1979); Alfred A. Crowell, *Creative News Editing* (Dubuque, Iowa: Brown, 1975); Floyd K. Baskette and Jack Z. Sissors, *The Art of Editing* (New York: Macmillan, 1977); Robert E. Garst and Theodore M. Bernstein, *Headlines and Deadlines* (New York: Columbia University Press, 1961), a New York *Times* classic.

Community journalism John Cameron Sim, *The Grass Roots Press: America's Community Newspapers* (Ames: Iowa State University Press, 1969); Morris Janowitz, *The Community Press in an Urban Setting* (New York: Free Press, 1967); Bruce M. Kennedy, *Community Journalism: How to Run a Country Weekly* (Ames: Iowa State University Press, 1974).

Graphics and production Edmund C. Arnold, *Modern Newspaper Design* (New York: Harper & Row, 1969); and *Ink on Paper 2* (New York: Harper & Row, 1972); and *Designing the Total Newspaper* (New York: Harper & Row, 1981). Arthur T. Turnbull and Russell N. Baird, *The Graphics of Communication: Typography, Layout and Design* (New York: Holt, Rinehart and Winston, 1980); Anthony Smith, *Goodbye Gutenberg—The Newspaper Revolution of the 1980s* (London: Oxford University Press, 1980); Mario R. Garcia, *Contemporary Newspaper Design* (Englewood Cliffs, N.J.: Prentice-Hall, 1981); Roy Paul Nelson, *Publication Design* (Dubuque, Iowa: Brown, 1972); Allen Hurlburt, *Publication Design* (New York: Van Nostrand Reinhold, 1976).

Advertising and management Frank W. Rucker and Herbert Lee Williams, *Newspaper Organization and Management* (Ames: Iowa State University Press, 1979); Leslie W. McClure and Paul C. Fulton, *Advertising in the Printed Media* (New York: Macmillan, 1964).

Chapter 6: Press Associations and Syndicates

There is no one book describing the press associations. Frank Luther Mott paints a picture of the Associated Press operation in a chapter of *The News in America.* Emery traces their history in *The Press and America* and Ault tells youthful readers how big stories are covered in *News Around the Clock* (New York: Dodd, Mead, 1960).

Oliver Gramling, *AP: The Story of News,* and Joe Alex Morris, *Deadline Every Minute: The Story of the United Press,* capture a good deal of the reportorial excitement of the press associations. Hugh Baillie, *High Tension* (New York: Harper & Row, 1959), is the readable autobiography of a former president of UP. *Kent Cooper and the Associated Press* (New York: Random House, 1959) is the second personal account by the most famous general manager of the AP; the first, *Barriers Down* (New York: Farrar and Rinehart, 1942), is Cooper's story of his effort to break up international news monopolies. Melville E. Stone, *Fifty Years a Journalist,* is the autobiography of the first AP general manager.

A UNESCO publication, *News Agencies: Their Structure and Operation* (New York: Columbia University Press, 1953), gives summary accounts of the AP, UP, and INS and analyzes other world news agencies. John C. Merrill, Carter R. Bryan, and Marvin Alisky, *The Foreign Press* (Baton Rouge: Louisiana State University Press, 1970), includes world news agencies in its overall picture. UNESCO's *World Communications: A 200-Country Survey of Press, Radio, Television, Films* (New York: UNESCO, 1975) is a reference work for international communications. (For further references, see bibliography for Chapter 23.)

The annual July *Syndicate Directory* issued by *Editor & Publisher* updates Elmo Scott Watson, *A History of Newspaper Syndicates, 1865–1935* (Chicago: Publishers' Auxiliary, 1936).

Chapter 7: Magazines

A factual supplement to the magazine field texts is Leonard Mogel's *The Magazine: Everything You Need to Know to Make It in the Magazine Business* (Englewood Cliffs, N.J.: Prentice-Hall, 1979).

An overview of the field is provided by Roland E. Wolseley's *Understanding Magazines* (Ames: Iowa State University Press, 1969), which treats editorial and business operations of consumer, business, and specialized publications. Wolseley's *The Changing Magazine* (New York: Hastings House, 1973) traces trends in readership and management. *Magazine Profiles* (Evanston, Ill.: Medill School of Journalism, 1974) presents studies by 12 graduate students of nearly 50 current magazines. John Tebbel's *The American Magazine: A Compact History* (New York: Hawthorn, 1969) emphasizes an industry-wide survey. Robert Root, *Modern Magazine Editing* (Dubuque, Iowa: Brown, 1966), gives a general introduction; Russell N. Baird and Arthur T. Turnbull, *Industrial and Business Journalism* (Philadelphia: Chilton, 1961), covers the business press area in detail. James L. C. Ford, *Magazines for Millions* (Carbondale, Ill.: Southern Illinois University Press, 1970), tells the story of specialized publications in fields such as business, religion, labor, and homemaking.

Views of specialized magazine work can be obtained from Ruori McLean, *Magazine Design* (London: Oxford University Press, 1969); Rowena Ferguson, *Editing the Small Magazine* (New York: Columbia University Press, 1958); DeWitt C. Reddick and Alfred A. Crowell, *Industrial Editing: Creative Communication Through Company Publications* (New York: Bender, 1962); William C. Halley, *Employee Publications* (Philadelphia: Chilton, 1959); and Julien Elfenbein, *Business Journalism* (New York: Harper & Row, 1960).

Textbooks on editing and writing include Betsy P. Graham, *Writing Magazine Articles With Style* (New York: Holt, Rinehart and Winston, 1980); William L. Rivers and Shelley Smolkin, *Freelancer and Staff Writer* (Belmont, Calif.: Wadsworth, 1980); J. W. Click and Russell N. Baird, *Magazine Editing and Production* (Dubuque, Iowa: Brown, 1974); and Roy Paul Nelson, *Articles and Features* (Boston: Houghton Mifflin, 1978).

Writing in Style, edited by Laura Longley Babb (Washington: Washington Post Co., 1975), is an excellent anthology of articles, mostly in the New Journalism motif, from the *Post*'s "Style" section.

Chapter 8: Book Publishing

Charles G. Madison's *Book Publishing in America* (New York: McGraw-Hill, 1967) is the definitive survey of the book publishing industry by a former editor and publisher. There are many useful insights into the art of publishing and the history of the major companies. A well-rounded picture of the trade or general side of the book publishing industry is given by a score of specialists in *What Happens in Book Publishing,* edited by Chandler B. Grannis (New York: Columbia University Press, 1967).

Some of the economic factors behind publishing house mergers and sales are presented in Benjamin M. Compaine, *The Book Industry in Transition: An Economic Analysis of Book Distribution and Marketing* (White Plains, N.Y.: Knowledge Industry Publications, 1978).

Sir Stanley Unwin, *The Truth About Publishing* (New York: Bowker, 1960), is highly readable. John P. Dessauer, *Book Publishing: What It Is, What It Does* (New York: Bowker, 1974), gives an excellent overview. William Jovanovich, *Now, Barabbas* (New York: Harper & Row, 1964) presents thoughtful essays on his field by a publishing executive.

Roger Smith, editor, *The American Reading Public: A Symposium* (New York: Bowker, 1964), is a particularly succinct and useful collection of authoritative essays by a number of publishing executives.

John Tebbel has now completed his four-volume *A History of Book Publishing in the United States* (New York: Bowker). The first three volumes appeared in 1972, 1975, and 1978. They cover the years 1630 to 1865, 1865 to 1919, and 1920 to 1940. The last appeared in 1981.

PART THREE: THE ELECTRONIC AND FILM MEDIA

Chapter 9: The Growth of Radio, Television, and Film

An eight-year editing project by Lawrence H. Lichty and Malachi C. Topping resulted in more than 700 pages of *American Broadcasting: A Sourcebook on the History of Radio and Television* (New York: Hastings House, 1975). Two one-volume distillations are Christopher H. Sterling and John M. Kittross, *Stay Tuned: A Concise History of American Broadcasting* (Belmont, Calif.: Wadsworth, 1978), and F. Leslie Smith, *Perspectives on Radio and Television* (New York: Harper & Row, 1979).

Other historical accounts include Erik Barnouw's three-volume history of American broadcasting, *A Tower in Babel, The Golden Web,* and *The Image Empire* (New York: Oxford University Press, 1966, 1968, 1970); Sydney W. Head, *Broadcasting in America* (Boston: Houghton Mifflin,

1978); Gleason L. Archer's classics, *History of Radio to 1926* (New York: American Historical Society, 1938) and *Big Business and Radio* (1939); and Llewellyn White's *The American Radio* (Chicago: University of Chicago Press, 1947). For technical history, see Orrin Dunlap, *Communications in Space* (New York: Harper & Row, 1970).

Biographies include Alexander Kendrick, *Prime Time: The Life of Edward R. Murrow* (Boston: Little, Brown, 1969); Roger Burlingame, *Don't Let Them Scare You: The Life and Times of Elmer Davis* (Philadelphia: Lippincott, 1961); Carl Dreher, *Sarnoff: An American Success* (New York: Quadrangle, 1977); and Irving E. Fang, *Those Radio Commentators!* (Ames: Iowa State University Press, 1977).

Autobiographies are William S. Paley, *As It Happened: A Memoir* (Garden City, N.Y.: Doubleday, 1979); Lowell Thomas, *Good Evening Everybody* (New York: Morrow, 1976); Dan Rather, *The Camera Never Blinks* (New York: Morrow, 1977); *Father of Radio: The Autobiography of Lee De Forest* (Chicago: Wilcox & Follett, 1950); and H. V. Kaltenborn, *Fifty Fabulous Years, 1900–1950: A Personal Review* (New York: Putnam's, 1950). Two collections of writings are *In Search of Light: The Broadcasts of Edward R. Murrow 1938–1961* (New York: Knopf, 1967) and *Looking Ahead: The Papers of David Sarnoff* (New York: McGraw-Hill, 1968).

Historical accounts of networks are found in Sterling Quinlan, *Inside ABC: American Broadcasting Company's Rise to Power* (New York: Hastings House, 1979), and for CBS in David Halberstam's *The Powers That Be* (New York: Knopf, 1979).

Relationships with government are analyzed in Walter B. Emery, *Broadcasting and Government* (East Lansing: Michigan State University Press, 1971); John E. Coons, editor, *Freedom and Responsibility in Broadcasting* (Evanston, Ill.: Northwestern University Press, 1963); Harvey J. Levin, *Broadcast Regulation and Joint Ownership of Media* (New York: New York University Press, 1960); and by Head and White. For sources, see Frank J. Kahn, *Documents of American Broadcasting* (Englewood Cliffs, N.J.: Prentice-Hall, 1978).

Leading historical surveys of motion pictures are Paul Rotha and Richard Griffith, *The Film Till Now* (London: Spring Books, 1967), a world cinema survey; and Richard Griffith and Arthur Mayer, *The Movies* (New York: Simon and Schuster, 1970), American film history. Alan Casty offered an account of world filmmaking in *Development of the Film: An Interpretive History* (New York: Harcourt Brace Jovanovich, 1973). Two other top accounts are Gerald Mast, *A Short History of the Movies* (New York: Bobbs-Merrill, 1971), and Arthur Knight, *The Liveliest Art* (New York: Macmillan, 1957).

The history of documentary films is told by Paul Rotha, Sinclair Road, and Richard Griffith in *Documentary Film* (London: Faber and Faber, 1966), and by A. William Bluem in *Documentary in American Television* (New York: Hastings House, 1965). Newsreels are covered in Raymond

Fielding's *The American Newsreel, 1911–1967* (Norman: University of Oklahoma Press, 1972).

Chapter 10: Radio

Introductory books for radio include Robert L. Hilliard, *Radio Broadcasting: An Introduction to the Sound Medium* (New York: Hastings House, 1974), and Giraud Chester, Garnet R. Garrison, and Edgar Willis, *Television and Radio* (New York: Appleton-Century-Crofts, 1971). Sydney W. Head's *Broadcasting in America* (Boston: Houghton Mifflin, 1978) is one historical survey (for others see listings for Chapter 9). A specialized history is J. Fred MacDonald, *Don't Touch That Dial! Radio Programming in American Life 1920–1960* (Chicago: Nelson Hall, 1979). Two books about radio's comedy programs are Jim Harmon, *The Great Radio Comedians* (New York: Doubleday, 1970), and Arthur Wertheim, *Radio Comedy* (New York: Oxford University Press, 1979).

Books dealing with radio news include John and Denise Bittner, *Radio Journalism* (Englewood Cliffs, N.J.: Prentice-Hall, 1977), including documentaries; F. Gifford, *Tape: A Radio News Handbook* (New York: Hastings House, 1977); G. Paul Smeyak, *Broadcast News Writing* (Columbus, Ohio: Grid, 1977); and Mitchell Stephens, *Broadcast News* (New York: Holt, Rinehart and Winston, 1980).

In radio management and production, two key books are Edd Routt, *The Business of Radio Broadcasting* (Blue Ridge Summit, Pa.: TAB Books, 1972), one of a series issued by that publisher, and Robert Oringel's *Audio Control Handbook* (New York: Hastings House, 1972), a guide to radio sound. Jonne Murphy offers *Handbook of Radio Advertising* (Radnor, Pa.: Chilton, 1980). An excellent book about announcing is Stuart W. Hyde, *Television and Radio Announcing* (Boston: Houghton Mifflin, 1979).

See the listings for Chapter 12 for books dealing with both radio and television.

Chapter 11: Recording

Celebrating the centennial of the phonograph with its third edition is Roland Gelatt's *The Fabulous Phonograph: 1877–1977* (New York: Macmillan, 1977). A popular history is C. A. Schicke, *Revolution in Sound: A Biography of the Recording Industry* (Boston: Little, Brown, 1974). Another is R. Serge Denisoff, *Solid Gold: The Popular Record Industry* (New York: Transaction Books, 1975).

Chapter 12: Television

Introductory books for television include John R. Bittner, *Professional Broadcasting: An Introduction* (Englewood Cliffs, N.J.: Prentice-Hall,

1981), which covers history, business practices, and advertising; Robert L. Hilliard, editor, *Understanding Television: An Introduction to Broadcasting* (New York: Hastings House, 1974); Giraud Chester, Garnet R. Garrison, and Edgar Willis, *Television and Radio* (Englewood Cliffs, N.J.: Prentice-Hall, 1978); and Horace Newcomb, *TV: The Most Popular Art* (Garden City, N.Y.: Doubleday Anchor, 1974), an analysis of popular TV programming.

Books that deal with television news are Irving E. Fang, *Television News, Radio News* (Minneapolis, Minn.: Rada Press, 1980); Edward Bliss, Jr. and John M. Patterson, *Writing News for Broadcast* (New York: Columbia University Press, 1978); Robert C. Siller, *Guide to Professional Radio and TV Newscasting* (Blue Ridge Summit, Pa.: TAB Books, 1972); Vernon Stone and Bruce Hinson, *Television Newsfilm Techniques* (New York: Hastings House, 1974); and Edd Routt, *Dimensions of Broadcast Editorializing* (Blue Ridge Summit, Pa.: TAB Books, 1974).

Books treating various types of writing are Martin Maloney and Paul Max Rubenstein, *Writing for the Media* (Englewood Cliffs, N.J.: Prentice-Hall, 1980); Edgar E. Willis, *Writing Television and Radio Programs* (New York: Holt, Rinehart and Winston, 1967); Robert L. Hilliard, *Writing for Television and Radio* (New York: Hastings House, 1976); and Norton S. Parker, *Audiovisual Script Writing* (New Brunswick, N.J.: Rutgers University Press, 1968).

Management and production Ward L. Quaal and James A. Brown, *Broadcast Management* (New York: Hastings House, 1976), a standard account of radio and TV station management; Susan Tyler Eastman, Sydney Head, and Lewis Klein, *Broadcast Programming* (Belmont, Calif.: Wadsworth, 1980); Stuart W. Hyde, *Television and Radio Announcing* (Boston: Houghton Mifflin, 1979), excellent in its field; Alan Wurtzel, *Television Production* (New York: McGraw-Hill, 1979); Gerald Millerson, *The Technique of Television Production* and *Effective TV Production* (New York: Hastings House, 1972, 1976); Michael Murray, *The Videotape Book: A Basic Guide* (New York: Taplinger, 1975); Arthur Englander and Paul Petzold, *Filming for Television* (New York: Hastings House, 1976); and Richard L. Williams, *Television Production: A Vocational Approach* (Salt Lake City: Vision, 1976). Two books on graphics are Walter Herdeg, *Film and TV Graphics* (New York: Hastings House, 1967), and Roy Laughton, *TV Graphics* (New York: Reinhold, 1966). A reference work for the technologies of film and television is *The Focal Encyclopedia of Film and Television: Techniques* (New York: Hastings House, 1969).

The advertising area is described in Elizabeth J. Heighton and Don R. Cunningham, *Advertising in the Broadcast Media* (Belmont, Calif.: Wadsworth, 1976); Charles A. Wainright, *Television Commercials* (New York: Hastings House, 1970); and Sherilyn K. Zeigler and Herbert H. Howard, *Broadcast Advertising: A Comprehensive Working Textbook* (Columbus, Ohio: Grid, 1978).

Methods of displaying textual information on a video display screen are described in *Videotext,* edited by Efrem Sigel (White Plains, N.Y.: Knowledge Industry Publications, 1980).

Chapter 13: Photographic Communication

History and development Beaumont Newhall, *The History of Photography from 1839 to the Present Day* (New York: Museum of Modern Art, 1964); Helmut and Alison Gernsheim, *History of Photography* (London: Oxford University Press, 1970); Peter Pollack, *Picture History of Photography* (New York: Abrams, 1969); Nathan Lyons, *Photographers on Photography* (Englewood Cliffs, N.J.: Prentice-Hall, 1966); R. Smith Schuneman, *Photographic Communication: Principles, Problems and Challenges of Photojournalism* (New York: Hastings House, 1972); A. William Bluem, *Documentary in American Television* (New York: Hastings House, 1965); Paul Rotha, Sinclair Road, and Richard Griffith, *Documentary Film* (London: Faber and Faber, 1966).

Techniques Harold Evans, *Pictures on a Page* (Belmont, Calif.: Wadsworth, 1979), by the editor of the *Sunday Times*, London: Kenneth Kobre, *Photojournalism: The Professionals' Approach* (Somerville, Mass.: Curtin and London, 1980); Andreas Feininger, *The Complete Photographer* (Englewood Cliffs, N.J.: Prentice-Hall, 1978); Phil Davis, *Photography* (Dubuque, Iowa: Brown, 1975); Robert B. Rhode and Floyd H. McCall, *Introduction to Photography* (New York: Macmillan, 1981); David H. Curl, *Photo-Communication* (New York: Macmillan, 1979); Philip C. Geraci, *Photojournalism* (Dubuque, Iowa: Kendall/Hunt, 1976); Clifton C. Edom, *Photojournalism* (Dubuque, Iowa: Brown, 1976); Arnold Rothstein, *Photojournalism: Pictures for Magazines and Newspapers* (New York: Amphoto, 1965); Wilson Hicks, *Words and Pictures* (New York: Harper, 1952); Roy Pinney, *Advertising Photography* (New York: Hastings House, 1962); and Robert L. Kerns, *Photojournalism: Photography with a Purpose* (Englewood Cliffs, N.J.: Prentice-Hall, 1980), with a focus on public relations.

Biographical James Horan, *Mathew Brady: Historian with a Camera* (New York: Crown, 1955), and *Timothy O'Sullivan: America's Forgotten Photographer* (New York: Crown, 1966); Judith Gutman, *Lewis W. Hine and the American Social Conscience* (New York: Walker, 1967); Richard Griffith, *The World of Robert Flaherty* (New York: Duell, Sloan and Pearce, 1953); Margaret Bourke-White, *Portrait of Myself* (New York: Simon and Schuster, 1963); David Douglas Duncan, *Yankee Nomad* (New York: Holt, Rinehart and Winston, 1966); Carl Mydans, *More Than Meets the Eye* (New York: Harper & Row, 1959); Gordon Parks, *A Choice of Weapons* (New York: Harper & Row, 1966); Edward Steichen, *A Life in Photography* (Garden City, N.Y.: Doubleday, 1963); Cornell Capa, *Robert Capa* (New York: Grossman, 1974); Dora Jane Hamblin, *That Was the Life* (New York: W. W. Norton, 1977).

Picture books Alfred Eisenstaedt, *Witness to Our Times* (New York:

Viking, 1966); David Douglas Duncan, *War Without Heroes* (New York: Harper & Row, 1970); John Szarkowski, *The Photographer's Eye* (New York: Museum of Modern Art, 1966); Leonard Freed, *Black in White America* (New York: Grossman, n.d.); Cornell Capa, editor, *The Concerned Photographer* (New York: Grossman, 1969), 200 photos of protest by six leading photographers; Charles Harbutt and Lee Jones, *America in Crisis* (New York: Holt, Rinehart and Winston, 1969); Associated Press, *The Instant It Happened* (New York: Associated Press, 1974), great news photos from the Civil War to Watergate. The University of Missouri Press began issuing an annual, *The Best of Photojournalism,* in 1975.

Chapter 14: The Film

Gerald Mast's *A Short History of the Movies* (New York: Bobbs-Merrill, 1976), offers detailed, highly readable descriptions and analyses, primarily of American and European films. To the major film histories, Rotha and Griffith's *The Film Till Now* and Griffith and Mayer's *The Movies,* may be added Arthur Knight, *The Liveliest Art* (New York: Hastings House, 1978), particularly good for the years 1895 to 1930; D. J. Wenden, *The Birth of the Movies* (New York: Dutton, 1975), covering 1895 to 1927; Alan Casty's *Development of the Film: An Interpretive History* (New York: Harcourt Brace Jovanovich, 1973); James Monaco, *How to Read a Film* (New York: Oxford University Press, 1977); Jack C. Ellis, *A History of Film* (Englewood Cliffs, N.J.: Prentice-Hall, 1978); John L. Fell, *A History of Films* (New York: Holt, Rinehart and Winston, 1979), designed for the survey course; and James Monaco, *American Film Now* (New York: Oxford University Press, 1979), films of the 1970s.

The best social history is Garth Jowett, *Film: The Democratic Art* (Boston: Little, Brown, 1976), updating Lewis Jacobs' *The Rise of the American Film* (1939). Another is Robert Sklar, *Movie-Made America* (New York: Random House, 1975).

The standard work on the history, principles, and technique of the documentary motion picture is Paul Rotha, Sinclair Road, and Richard Griffith, *The Documentary Film* (London: Faber and Faber, 1966). Others are Lewis Jacobs, *The Documentary Tradition* (New York: W. W. Norton, 1979); Alan Rosenthal, *The New Documentary in Action: A Casebook in Film Making* (Berkeley: University of California Press, 1971); Richard M. Barsam, *Nonfiction Film: A Critical History* (New York: Dutton, 1973); Richard D. MacCann, *The People's Films* (New York: Hastings House, 1973), a history of United States government documentaries; and Erik Barnouw, *Documentary: A History of the Non-Fiction Film* (London: Oxford University Press, 1974), a well-integrated analysis.

Among introductory texts are Thomas and Vivian Sobcheck, *An Introduction to Film* (Boston: Little, Brown, 1980), and Bernard F. Dick, *Anatomy of Film* (New York: St. Martin's Press, 1978). John L. Fell's *Film: An Introduction* (New York: Praeger, 1975) is designed for survey courses as is Roy P. Madsen's *The Impact of Film* (New York: Macmillan, 1973). Suitable for text use is Thomas W. Bohn and Richard L. Stromgren, *Light and Shadows: A History of Motion Pictures* (Port Washington, N.Y.: Alfred Publishing, 1975).

In the field of theory and criticism are Gerald Mast and Marshall Cohen, editors, *Film Theory and Criticism* (New York: Oxford University Press, 1979); J. Dudley Andrew, *The Major Film Theories* (New York: Oxford University Press, 1976); Garth Jowett and James M. Linton, *Movies as Mass Communication* (Beverly Hills, Calif.: Sage, 1980); and Pauline Kael, *Reeling* (Boston: Little, Brown, 1976), by the noted film critic.

Lewis Jacobs, *The Emergence of Film Art* (New York: Hopkinson and Blake, 1969), offers carefully selected essays to illustrate the evolution of the motion picture as an art from 1900 to the present. Roger Manvell, in *New Cinema in Europe* (New York: Dutton, 1966), gives brief descriptions of movements, filmmakers and films in postwar feature filmmaking in Europe. Gregory Battcock's *The New American Cinema* (New York: Dutton, 1967) is a stimulating collection of essays covering theory and practice of experimental filmmakers.

Film direction is examined by Eric Sherman in *Directing the Film* (Boston: Little, Brown, 1976), and by Louis Giannetti in *Understanding Movies* (Englewood Cliffs, N.J.: Prentice-Hall, 1976). Personalities from the silent film era are interviewed in Kevin Brownlow, *The Parade's Gone By* (New York: Knopf, 1968). Also of note is Andrew Sarris, *The American Cinema: Directors and Directions 1929–1968* (New York: Dutton, 1968).

PART FOUR: THE PERSUASIVE PROFESSIONS

Chapter 15: Advertising

The role of advertising in society is discussed in John W. Wright, editor, *The Commercial Connection: Advertising and the American Mass Media* (New York: Dell/Delta, 1979); in Kim B. Rotzoll, James E. Haefner, and Charles H. Sandage, editors, *Advertising in Contemporary Society* (Columbus, Ohio: Grid, 1976); and in John S. Wright and John Mertes, *Advertising's Role in Society* (St. Paul, Minn.: West, 1976).

Among histories, the standard account is Frank Presbrey, *The History and Development of Advertising* (New York: Doubleday, Doran, 1930). James Playsted Wood, *The Story of Advertising* (New York: Ronald, 1958), is very readable. E. S. Turner, *The Shocking History of Advertising* (New York: Dutton, 1953), is constructively critical.

Research areas are outlined in Alan D. Fletcher and Thomas A. Bowers, *Fundamentals of Advertising Research* (Columbus, Ohio: Grid, 1979), and in James Leigh and Claude R. Martin, Jr., editors, *Current Issues and Research in Advertising* (Ann Arbor: University of Michigan, 1978), a brief reader.

Among the general text and reference books on advertising are Charles

H. Sandage, Vernon Fryburger, and Kim Rotzoll, *Advertising Theory and Practice* (Homewood, Ill.: Irwin, 1979); Jack Engel, *Advertising: The Process and Practice* (New York: McGraw-Hill, 1980); S. Watson Dunn and Arnold Barban, *Advertising: Its Role in Modern Marketing* (New York: Holt, Rinehart and Winston, 1978); Edgar Crane, *Marketing Communications* (New York: Wiley, 1972); John S. Wright, Daniel S. Warner, and Willis L. Winter, Jr., *Advertising* (New York: McGraw-Hill, 1977); Philip Ward Burton and William Ryan, *Advertising Fundamentals* (Columbus, Ohio: Grid, 1980); Stanley Ulanoff, *Advertising in America* (New York: Hastings House, 1977), persuasion; Otto Kleppner, *Advertising Procedure* (Englewood Cliffs, N.J.: Prentice-Hall, 1979); Dorothy Cohen, *Advertising* (New York: Wiley, 1972); Barbara Davis Coe, *Advertising Practice* (Englewood Cliffs, N.J.: Prentice-Hall, 1972); and James E. Littlefield, *Readings in Advertising* (St. Paul: West, 1975).

Media is the topic of discussion in Donald Jugenheimer and Peter Turk, *Advertising Media* (Columbus, Ohio: Grid, 1980); in Arnold M. Barban, Donald W. Jugenheimer and Lee F. Young, *Advertising Media Sourcebook and Workbook* (Columbus, Ohio: Grid, 1975); in Jack Z. Sissors and E. Reynold Petray, *Advertising Media Planning* (Chicago: Crain, 1976); and in Anthony F. McGann and J. Thomas Russell, *Advertising Media* (Homewood, Ill.: Irwin, 1981).

Copywriting techniques are described by David L. Malickson and John W. Nason in *Advertising—How to Write the Kind That Works* (New York: Scribner's, 1977) and by Philip Ward Burton in *Advertising Copywriting* (Columbus, Ohio: Grid, 1979). Copy, design, and production are covered by A. Jerome Jewler in *Creative Strategy in Advertising* (Belmont, Calif.: Wadsworth, 1980). Two classic writers on copy were Aesop Glim (George Laflin Miller) in *Copy—The Core of Advertising* (New York: Dover, 1963) and *How Advertising Is Written—and Why* (1961); and Clyde Bedell, *How to Write Advertising That Sells* (New York: McGraw-Hill, 1952).

Graphics and design Arthur T. Turnbull and Russell N. Baird, *The Graphics of Communication: Typography, Layout, Design* (New York: Holt, Rinehart and Winston, 1980); Roy Paul Nelson, *The Design of Advertising* (Dubuque, Iowa: Brown, 1977); and Edmund C. Arnold, *Ink on Paper 2* (New York: Harper & Row, 1972).

Advertising agencies Roger Barton, *Advertising Agency Operations and Management* (New York: McGraw-Hill, 1955), is a practical guide. Martin Mayer, *Madison Avenue, U.S.A.* (New York: Harper, 1958), provides a good picture of advertising agencies; Ralph M. Hower, *The History of an Advertising Agency: N. W. Ayer & Son at Work, 1869–1939* (Cambridge, Mass.: Harvard University Press, 1939) is a documented history of one agency. David Ogilvy tells a fascinating story about work in an agency in *Confessions of an Advertising Man* (New York: Atheneum, 1963; Dell paperback, 1964). The story of the pioneering Albert Lasker is told by John Gunther in *Taken at the Flood* (New York: Harper & Row, 1960).

Chapter 16: Public Relations

An excellent book to read in exploring the public relations field is Scott M. Cutlip and Allen H. Center, *Effective Public Relations* (Englewood Cliffs, N.J.: Prentice-Hall, 1978).

Other general books include those by Doug Newsom and Alan Scott, *This Is PR: The Realities of Public Relations* (Belmont, Calif.: Wadsworth, 1981); Bertrand R. Canfield and Frazier Moore, *Public Relations: Principles, Cases, and Problems* (Homewood, Ill.: Irwin, 1973); Fraser P. Seitel, *The Practice of Public Relations* (New York: Charles E. Merrill, 1980); John E. Marston, *Modern Public Relations* (New York: McGraw-Hill, 1979); Raymond Simon, *Public Relations: Principles and Practices* (Columbus, Ohio: Grid, 1980); L. L. L. Golden, *Only by Public Consent* (New York: Hawthorn, 1968); Charles S. Steinberg, *The Creation of Consent, Public Relations in Practice* (New York: Hastings House, 1975); Roy L. Blumenthal, *The Practice of Public Relations* (New York: Macmillan, 1972); Allen H. Center, *Public Relations Practices, Case Studies* (Englewood Cliffs, N.J.: Prentice-Hall, 1975).

Groups of public relations professionals contributed chapters for *Public Relations Handbook,* edited by Philip Lesly (Englewood Cliffs, N.J.: Prentice-Hall, 1978), and *Handbook of Public Relations,* edited by Howard Stephenson (New York: McGraw-Hill, 1971). A leading counselor, John W. Hill, tells his story in *The Making of a Public Relations Man* (New York: McKay, 1963). New York's practitioners are described by Irwin Ross in *The Image Merchants* (Garden City, N.Y.: Doubleday, 1959). Edward L. Bernays, in *Public Relations* (Norman: University of Oklahoma Press, 1979), presents a case history type of discussion by a longtime practitioner. His memoirs are in *Biography of an Idea* (New York: Simon and Schuster, 1965). Ray E. Hiebert contributed the biography of another pioneer in his *Courtier to the Crowd: The Life Story of Ivy Lee* (Ames: Iowa State University Press, 1966). Alan R. Raucher traced early PR history in *Public Relations and Business 1900–1929* (Baltimore: The Johns Hopkins Press, 1968).

Writing techniques are analyzed in Doug Newsom and Tom Siegfried, *Writing in Public Relations Practice* (Belmont, Calif.: Wadsworth, 1981), and in David L. Lendt, editor, *The Publicity Process* (Ames: Iowa State University Press, 1975).

Among books on specialized subjects are Ray E. Hiebert and Carlton Spitzer, editors, *The Voice of Government* (New York: Wiley, 1968), with two dozen Washington information men discussing their work; Benjamin Fine, *Educational Publicity* (New York: Harper, 1951); Harold P. Levy, *Public Relations for Social Agencies* (New York: Harper & Row, 1956); and Sidney Kobre, *Successful Public Relations for Colleges and Universities* (New York: Hastings House, 1974).

Bibliographies are Scott M. Cutlip, *A Public Relations Bibliography* (Madison: University of Wisconsin Press, 1965), and its extension, Robert

L. Bishop, *Public Relations: A Comprehensive Bibliography* (Ann Arbor: University of Michigan Press, 1974).

PART FIVE: RESEARCH AND EDUCATION

Chapter 17: Mass Communications Research

A major effort to describe mass communications research was made in *Research Methods in Mass Communication,* edited by Guido H. Stempel III and Bruce H. Westley (Englewood Cliffs, N.J.: Prentice-Hall, 1981). It examines both social science and documentary research fields. Two research area studies are John D. Stevens and Hazel Dicken Garcia, *Communication History* (Beverly Hills, Calif.: Sage, 1980), and Klaus Krippendorff, *Content Analysis* (Beverly Hills, Calif.: Sage, 1980).

Books that introduce the reader to research methods are Paul M. Hirsch, Peter V. Miller, and F. Gerald Kline, *Strategies for Communication Research* (Beverly Hills, Calif.: Sage, 1977); Maxwell E. McCombs and Lee Becker, *Using Mass Communication Theory* (Englewood Cliffs, N.J.: Prentice-Hall, 1979); Werner Severin and James Tankard, Jr., *Communication Theories: Origins, Methods, Uses* (New York: Hastings House, 1979), media-oriented; Albert H. Cantril, editor, *Polling on the Issues* (Cabin John, Md.: Seven Locks Press, 1980), with 21 contributors; Frederick Williams, *Reasoning with Statistics: Simplified Examples in Communication and Education Research* (New York: Holt, Rinehart and Winston, 1978); David M. White and Seymour Levine, *Elementary Statistics for Journalists* (New York: Macmillan, 1954); Charles H. Backstrom and Gerald D. Hursh, *Survey Research* (Evanston, Ill.: Northwestern University Press, 1963); Richard W. Budd, Robert K. Thorp, and Lewis Donohew, *Content Analysts of Communication* (New York: Macmillan, 1967); and Julian Simon, *Basic Research Methods in Social Science* (New York: Random House, 1969).

Advertising research methods are outlined in Daniel Starch, *Measuring Advertising Readership and Results* (New York: McGraw-Hill, 1966); in Charles Ramond, *Advertising Research* (New York: Association of National Advertisers, 1976), summarizing knowledge; and in Alan D. Fletcher and Thomas J. Bowers, *Fundamentals of Advertising Research* (Columbus, Ohio: Grid, 1979).

Many of the references listed for Part One of this bibliography also are pertinent to this chapter, especially those dealing with effects, the communication process, and public opinion.

Chapter 18: Mass Communications Education

The early growth of journalism education is reviewed in Albert A. Sutton, *Education for Journalism in the United States from Its Beginning to 1940*

(Evanston, Ill.: Northwestern University Press, 1945). *The Training of Journalists* (Paris: UNESCO, 1958) is a worldwide survey on the training of personnel for the mass media, updated by *Mass Communication: Teaching and Studies at Universities,* edited by May Katzen (Paris: UNESCO, 1975).

William R. Lindley's monograph, *Journalism and Higher Education* (Stillwater, Okla.: Journalistic Services, 1976), traces the development of four major American journalism schools.

Books about career opportunities include Herbert Brucker, *Journalist: Eyewitness to History* (New York: Macmillan, 1962); Edward W. Barrett, editor, *Journalists in Action* (New York: Channel Press, 1963), stories of 63 Columbia University journalism graduates; Leonard E. Ryan and Bernard Ryan, Jr., *So You Want to Go into Journalism* (New York: Harper & Row, 1963); M. L. Stein, *Your Career in Journalism* (New York: Messner/Simon & Schuster, 1965); George Johnson, *Your Career in Advertising* (New York: Messner, 1966; Gregory Jackson, *Getting Into Broadcast Journalism* (New York: Hawthorn, 1974); John Tebbel, *Opportunities in Publishing Careers* (Louisville: Vocational Guidance Manuals, 1975), book publishing; Elmo I. Ellis, *Opportunities in Broadcasting* (Skokie, Ill.: National Textbook Co., 1981); and Roland E. Wolseley, *Careers in Religious Communications* (Scottdale, Pa.: Herald Press, 1977).

Available in paperback are Arville Schaleben's *Your Future in Journalism* and Edward L. Bernays' *Your Future in Public Relations* and *Your Future in Advertising* (New York: Popular Library, updated, regularly).

Career information is available from the office of the Executive Secretary, Association for Education in Journalism, College of Journalism, University of South Carolina, Columbia, S.C. 29208. *Education for a Journalism Career* is available from the Accrediting Council on Education in Journalism and Mass Communications, School of Journalism, University of Missouri, Columbia, Mo. 65201.

Other pamphlets that are available include *Your Future in Newspapers* (American Newspaper Publishers Association), *Broadcasting the News, Careers in Television,* and *Careers in Radio* (National Association of Broadcasters), *Magazines in the U.S.A.* (Magazine Publishers Association), *Careers in the Business Press* (American Business Press, Inc.), *Your Personal Guidebook PRSA* and *Occupational Guide to Public Relations* (Public Relations Society of America), and *Careers in Communications* (Women in Communications).

Quill & Scroll, University of Iowa, annually publishes *Careers in Journalism,* in magazine form. The Newspaper Fund, Inc., issues a *Journalism Career and Scholarship Guide* annually.

Catalogues describing the curricular offerings of individual schools and departments of journalism and mass communications are available upon request to the school or department concerned or to the registrar of the institution.

PART SIX: CRITICISMS AND CHALLENGES

An excellent basis for any discussion of the duties and the performance record of the mass media is the summary report of the Commission on Freedom of the Press, *A Free and Responsible Press* (Chicago: University of Chicago Press, 1947). The commission printed four studies already cited, Chafee's *Government and Mass Communications,* Hocking's *Freedom of the Press,* White's *The American Radio,* and Ruth Inglis' *Freedom of the Movies,* as well as *Peoples Speaking to Peoples,* by Llewellyn White and Robert D. Leigh (Chicago: University of Chicago Press, 1946), an analysis of international news channels.

An in-depth study of four major media institutions and their principal operating heads is found in David Halberstam, *The Powers That Be* (New York: Viking, 1978). The four institutions are CBS, Time Inc., the Washington *Post,* and the Los Angeles *Times,* with the New York *Times* hovering in the background. The reportorial process is examined in Gay Tuchman, *Making News* (New York: Free Press, 1978), and the editing process in Herbert Gans, *Deciding What's News: A Study of CBS Evening News, NBC Nightly News, Newsweek & Time* (New York: Pantheon, 1979). Tom Wicker is reflective in *On Press* (New York: Viking, 1978).

Criticisms of the mass media are summarized in John L. Hulteng's *The Messenger's Motives* (Englewood Cliffs, N.J.: Prentice-Hall, 1976), by analyzing 150 cases involving ethical problems. Criticism of press managers is the theme of Ben H. Bagdikian in *The Effete Conspiracy and Other Crimes by the Press* (New York: Harper & Row, 1972). Hillier Krieghbaum examines this topic in *Pressures on the Press* (New York: Crowell, 1972). Probing the media scene are John L. Hulteng, *The News Media: What Makes Them Tick?* (Englewood Cliffs, N.J.: Prentice-Hall, 1979); David Shaw, *Journalism Today* (New York: Harper's College Press, 1977), and John Hohenberg, *The News Media* (New York: Holt, Rinehart and Winston, 1978). Bryce W. Rucker presents a comprehensive survey of media dilemmas while updating Morris Ernst's 1946 study by the same title, *The First Freedom* (Carbondale: Southern Illinois University Press, 1968).

Two books edited by Warren K. Agee provide extensive criticisms of the media: *The Press and the Public Interest* (Washington: Public Affairs Press, 1968) contains the annual William Allen White Lectures delivered by 18 of America's leading reporters, editors, and publishers; in *Mass Media in a Free Society* (Lawrence: Regents' Press of Kansas, 1969) six media spokesmen discuss challenges and problems confronting newspapers, television, motion pictures, and magazines. Other criticisms of press performance are found in *The Press in Perspective,* edited by Ralph D. Casey (Baton Rouge: Louisiana State University Press, 1963), a series of 17 lectures by leading journalists at the University of Minnesota over 16 years.

Ben H. Bagdikian's *The Information Machines* (New York: Harper & Row, 1971) projects the impact of technological change on the media and offers a wealth of research data based on findings of RAND Corporation research teams.

Selected readings on both media issues and the mass communications industries and professions, paralleling the organization of this textbook, are presented in *Perspectives on Mass Communications,* edited by Warren K. Agee, Phillip H. Ault, and Edwin Emery (New York: Harper & Row, 1982). A comprehensive collection of articles focusing on major media issues and criticisms is found in Michael C. Emery and Ted Curtis Smythe, *Readings in Mass Communication: Concepts and Issues in the Mass Media* (Dubuque, Iowa: Brown, 1980). Other books of readings include Alan Wells, *Mass Media and Society* (Palo Alto, Calif.: Mayfield, 1979); Francis and Ludmila Voelker, *Mass Media: Forces in Our Society* (New York: Harcourt Brace Jovanovich, 1975); Alan Casty, *Mass Media and Mass Man* (New York: Holt, Rinehart and Winston, 1973); John D. Stevens and William E. Porter, *The Rest of the Elephant* (Englewood Cliffs, N.J.: Prentice-Hall, 1973); Leonard Sellers and William L. Rivers, *Mass Media Issues* (Englewood Cliffs, N.J.: Prentice-Hall, 1977); Robert Atwan, Barry Orton, and William Vesterman, *American Mass Media: Industries and Issues* (New York: Random House, 1978); and Glen O. Robinson, *Communication for Tomorrow: Policy Perspectives for the 1980s* (New York: Praeger, 1978), an Aspen-sponsored publication.

Among general introductory surveys are Charlene J. Brown, Trevor R. Brown, and William L. Rivers, *Communication: The Media and the People* (New York: Holt, Rinehart and Winston, 1978); Melvin L. DeFleur and Everette E. Dennis, *Understanding Mass Communication* (Boston: Houghton Mifflin, 1981); John R. Bittner, *Mass Communication: An Introduction* (Englewood Cliffs, N.J.: Prentice-Hall, 1980); Mary B. Cassata and Molegi K. Asante, *Mass Communication: Principles and Practices* (New York: Macmillan, 1979); William E. Francois, *Introduction to Mass Communications and Mass Media* (Columbus, Ohio: Grid, 1977); Steven H. Chaffee and Michael J. Petrick, *Using the Mass Media: Communication Problems in American Society* (New York: McGraw-Hill, 1975), built around major problem areas; Fredrick C. Whitney, *Mass Media and Mass Communications in Society* (Dubuque, Iowa: Brown, 1975); Don R. Pember, *Mass Media in America* (Palo Alto, Calif.: Science Research Associates, 1981); Ray Hiebert, Donald F. Ungurait, and Thomas W. Bohn, *Mass Media* (New York: Longman, 1979), research-oriented; Peter M. Sandman, David M. Rubin, and David B. Sachsman, *Media: An Introductory Analysis of American Mass Communications* (Englewood Cliffs, N.J.: Prentice-Hall, 1976); and Robert D. Murphy, *Mass Communication and Human Interaction* (Boston: Houghton Mifflin, 1977).

Print media Two studies of the status of the daily press are found in Ernest C. Hynds, *American Newspapers in the 1980s* (New York: Hastings

House, 1980), and John L. Hulteng and Roy Paul Nelson, *The Fourth Estate* (New York: Harper & Row, 1971). A. Kent MacDougall collected *Wall Street Journal* articles in *The Press: A Critical Look from the Inside* (New York: Dow Jones, 1972). Selections from the *Nieman Reports* make a comprehensive survey of news problems and trends in Louis Lyons, *Reporting the News* (Cambridge, Mass.: Harvard University Press, 1965). Hillier Krieghbaum discusses one problem in *Science and the Mass Media* (New York: New York University Press, 1967). Curtis D. MacDougall, *The Press and Its Problems* (Dubuque, Iowa: Brown, 1964), is a revision of his *Newsroom Problems and Policies.* Lucy M. Salmon's *The Newspaper and the Historian* (New York: Oxford University Press, 1923) is a classic historical study.

Among professionals' criticisms, Herbert Brucker's *Freedom of Information* is an enlightened defense and analysis of the newspaper press. By contrast, Carl E. Lindstrom uses for the title of his book *The Fading American Newspaper* (Garden City, N.Y.: Doubleday, 1960). A. J. Liebling brought together his satirical articles on press shortcomings, written for the *New Yorker,* in *The Press* (New York: Ballantine, 1964), and in *The Wayward Pressman* (New York: Doubleday, 1948), devoted mostly to New York papers. Silas Bent, *Ballyhoo* (New York: Liveright, 1927) is strongly critical of the newspaper press of its day, as are Upton Sinclair's *The Brass Check* (Pasadena, Calif.: Published by the author, 1920), and George Seldes' *Freedom of the Press* (Indianapolis: Bobbs-Merrill, 1935). Oswald Garrison Villard, *The Disappearing Daily* (New York: Knopf, 1944), and Morris L. Ernst, *The First Freedom* (New York: Macmillan, 1946), exhibit a critical concern over newspaper ownership concentration trends but are not statistically accurate.

Broadcasting and cable A comprehensive collection of readings is in Ted C. Smythe and George A. Mastroianni, *Issues in Broadcasting: Radio, Television, and Cable* (Palo Alto, Calif.: Mayfield, 1975).

The best of *TV Guide*'s articles of the 1970s are collected in Barry Cole's *Television Today* (New York: Oxford University Press, 1981). Two other substantial readers are David Manning White and Richard Averson, *Sight, Sound, and Society: Motion Pictures and Television in America* (Boston: Beacon, 1968), and Harry J. Skornia and Jack W. Kitson, *Problems and Controversies in Television and Radio* (Palo Alto, Calif.: Pacific Books, 1968). Leo Bogart objectively analyzes scores of research studies, seeking to determine the social impact of television, in *The Age of Television* (New York: Frederick Ungar, 1972).

Among effective criticisms of broadcasting are George Comstock, *Television in America* (Beverly Hills, Calif.: Sage, 1980); Frank Coppa, editor, *Screen & Society: The Impact of Television* (Chicago: Nelson Hall, 1979); Horace Newcomb, editor, *Television: The Critical View* (New York: Oxford University Press, 1979); Muriel Cantor, *Prime Time Television:*

Content and Control (Beverly Hills, Calif.: Sage, 1980); Ron Powers, *The Newscasters* (New York: St. Martin's, 1977); Edwin Diamond, *The Tin Kazoo: Television, Politics, and the News* (Cambridge, Mass.: MIT Press, 1975), and Edward Jay Epstein, *News from Nowhere: Television and the News* (New York: Random House, 1973), an evaluation of 1968 to 1969 network news. Critical appraisals by the Alfred I. DuPont-Columbia University Awards committee were begun with *Survey of Broadcast Journalism 1968–1969,* edited by Marvin Barrett (New York: Grosset & Dunlap, 1969). Seventh of the series was *The Eye of the Storm* (New York: Harper & Row, 1980).

Two collections of scholarly original essays appearing in 1981 were *The Entertainment Functions of Television,* edited by Percy H. Tannenbaum, and *Television and Social Behavior,* edited by Stephen Withey and Ronald P. Abeles (Hillsdale, N.J.: Lawrence Erlbaum Associates). Coming from the Aspen Institute Program on Communications and Society are *Understanding Television: Essays on Television as a Social and Cultural Force,* edited by Richard Adler (New York: Praeger, 1980); *The Future of Public Broadcasting,* edited by Douglass Cater (New York: Praeger, 1976); *Television as a Social Force* and *Television as a Cultural Force,* edited by Douglass Cater and Richard Adler (New York: Praeger, 1975, 1976); *Cable and Continuing Education,* edited by Richard Adler and Walter S. Baer (New York: Praeger, 1973); Richard M. Polsky, *Getting to Sesame Street: Origins of the Children's Television Workshop* (New York: Praeger, 1974); and *The Electronic Box Office: Humanities and Arts on the Cable,* edited by Richard Adler and Walter S. Baer (New York: Praeger, 1974).

Additional references, by chapter topic, follow.

Chapter 19: The Government, the Media, and the Public

A 1000-page study of the Watergate years of 1972 to 1974 objectively presented with detailed documentary support and many cross-references integrating various facets of the episode, forms the basis for analysis of that gigantic crisis of media and presidential credibility. The volume is *Watergate: Chronology of a Crisis* (Washington: Congressional Quarterly, 1975), edited by Mercer Cross and Elder Witt with a staff of 30 from that research organization and contributors.

Among the most useful books about Watergate are Carl Bernstein and Bob Woodward, *All the President's Men* (New York : Simon and Schuster, 1974); Jimmy Breslin, *How the Good Guys Finally Won* (New York: Viking, 1975); William E. Porter, *Assault on the Media* (Ann Arbor: University of Michigan Press, 1976); and the fifth Dupont-Columbia University survey of broadcast journalism, *Moments of Truth?* (New York: Crowell, 1975). Backgrounds for the government and political leaders involved in a decade of credibility crisis are provided in Dan Rather and

Gary Paul Gates, *The Palace Guard* (New York: Harper & Row, 1974), and David Halberstam, *The Best and the Brightest* (New York: Random House, 1972). Harrison Salisbury gives an insider's view of the New York *Times* during the Pentagon Papers and Watergate crises in *Without Fear or Favor* (New York: Times Books, 1980).

Television news crises are covered admirably in William Small, *To Kill a Messenger* (New York: Hastings House, 1970), covering the 1960s with its crises of war, violence, rioting, and political polarization. Small was then CBS Washington bureau chief. One of television's problems was the subject of Newton Minow, John Bartlow Martin, and Lee M. Mitchell in *Presidential Television* (New York: Basic Books, 1973). A first-hand criticism of network policy affecting CBS News appears in Fred W. Friendly, *Due to Circumstances Beyond Our Control . . .* (New York: Random House, 1967). The 1969 speeches of Vice-President Spiro T. Agnew attacking the fairness of television commentators and other media news are collected in Spiro T. Agnew, *Frankly Speaking* (Washington: Public Affairs Press, 1970). Even stronger attacks were made by Edith Efron in *The News Twisters* and *How CBS Tried to Kill a Book* (Los Angeles: Nash, 1971, 1972).

Two recent studies of political reporting are Michael B. Grossman and Martha J. Kumar, *Portraying the President* (Baltimore, Md.: Johns Hopkins University Press, 1981) and Stephen Hess, *The Washington Reporters* (Washington: Brookings Institution, 1981).

One of the best reports on the 1972 campaign press corps was Timothy Crouse, *The Boys on the Bus* (New York: Random House, 1973). Another aspect of political reporting is surveyed in 50 selections edited by Robert Blanchard for *Congress and the News Media* (New York: Hastings House, 1974). Two interesting studies of press performance during political campaigns are Nathan B. Blumberg's *One Party Press?* (Lincoln: University of Nebraska Press, 1954), a report on how 35 metropolitan dailies covered 1952 presidential campaign news, and Arthur E. Rowse's *Slanted News: A Case Study of the Nixon and Stevenson Fund Stories* (Boston: Beacon, 1957).

For details on studies of violence in riots, see Robert K. Baker and Sandra J. Ball, *Violence and the Media* (Washington: Government Printing Office, 1969), a staff report to the National Commission on the Causes and Prevention of Violence giving a historical treatment and a review of research. Two major citations in commission reports are *Report of the National Advisory Commission on Civil Disorders* (Kerner Report, 1968), Chapter 15, "The News Media and the Disorders," and *Rights in Conflict*, the Walker Report to the National Commission on the Causes and Prevention of Violence, 1968, pages 287–327, "The Police and the Press."

The *Aspen Notebook on Government and the Media*, edited by William

L. Rivers and Michael J. Nyhan (New York: Praeger, 1973), offers a spirited debate of government-media relations and regulatory issues.

Chapter 20: The Media's Legal Environment

Two extensive casebooks on press law are Donald M. Gillmor and Jerome A. Barron, *Mass Communication Law: Cases and Comment* (St. Paul: West, 1979), and Marc A. Franklin, *The First Amendment and the Fourth Estate* (Mineola, N.Y.: Foundation Press, 1981). Two major general accounts are Harold L. Nelson and Dwight L. Teeter, Jr., *Law of Mass Communications* (Mineola, N.Y.: Foundation Press, 1978), and William E. Francois, *Mass Media Law and Regulation* (Columbus, Ohio: Grid, 1978). Briefer accounts are Don R. Pember, *Mass Media Law* (Dubuque, Iowa: Brown, 1981), and Paul P. Ashley, *Say It Safely* (Seattle: University of Washington Press, 1976). Pember's is the most satisfactory general account.

Two specialized books are Maurice R. Cullen, Jr., *Mass Media and the First Amendment: An Introduction to the Issues, Problems, and Practices* (Dubuque, Iowa: Brown, 1981), and Douglas H. Ginsburg, *Regulation of Broadcasting: Law and Policy Towards Radio, Television, and Cable Communications* (St. Paul: West, 1979).

Supreme Court trends are traced in William A. Hachten's *The Supreme Court on Freedom of the Press* (Ames: Iowa State University Press, 1968) and later in Kenneth S. Devol's *Mass Media and the Supreme Court* (New York: Hastings House, 1976). J. Edward Gerald's *The Press and the Constitution* (Minneapolis: University of Minnesota Press, 1948) analyzes constitutional law cases involving press freedom from 1931 to 1947. David L. Grey reports on court coverage in *The Supreme Court and the News Media* (Evanston, Ill.: Northwestern University Press, 1968). Donald M. Gillmor analyzes a major conflict in *Free Press and Fair Trial* (Washington: Public Affairs Press, 1966).

Chapter 21: The Media's Social Responsibility

The issue of sex and violence in television programming is explored in Geoffrey Cowan, *See No Evil* (New York: Simon and Schuster, 1979). Muriel Cantor, in *Prime Time Television: Content and Control* (Beverly Hills, Calif.: Sage, 1980), concludes that varied forces, pressures, and prejudices determine the final form of a television show.

Violence and sensationalism There are two collections of articles on the issues. One, with reasoned but conservative views, is edited by Victor B. Cline, *Where Do You Draw the Line? An Exploration into Media Violence, Pornography, and Censorship* (Provo, Utah: Brigham Young University Press, 1974). The other is the research-based *Violence and the*

Mass Media (New York: Harper & Row, 1968), edited by Otto N. Larsen. Of historical importance are Helen M. Hughes, *News and the Human Interest Story* (Chicago: University of Chicago Press, 1940), a sociological study; and Simon M. Bessie, *Jazz Journalism: The Story of the Tabloid Newspapers* (New York: Dutton, 1938).

Research findings have been reported by George Gerbner, et al., annually, and summarized in *Violence Profile No. 8: Trends in Network Television Drama and Viewer Conceptions of Social Reality,1967–1976* (Philadelphia: Annenberg School of Communication, University of Pennsylvania, 1977).

Censorship Ruth Inglis, *Freedom of the Movies* (Chicago: University of Chicago Press, 1947), argued the case for self-regulation for the Commission on Freedom of the Press. In discussions of censorship trends, the film area is covered by Ira H. Carmen, *Movies, Censorship and the Law* (Ann Arbor: University of Michigan Press, 1966), and by Richard S. Randall, *Censorship of the Movies* (Madison: University of Wisconsin Press, 1968); books by Richard McKeon, Robert K. Merton, and Walter Gellhorn, *The Freedom to Read: Perspective and Program* (New York: Bowker, 1957); and radio and television by Sydney W. Head, *Broadcasting in America* (Boston: Houghton Mifflin, 1978), and Walter B. Emery, *Broadcasting and Government* (East Lansing: Michigan State University Press, 1971). Movie and television censorship is decried in Murray Schumach's *The Face on the Cutting Room Floor* (New York: Morrow, 1964).

Children and television Included in the extensive literature are Mariann Pezzella Winick and Charles Winick, *The Television Experience: What Children See* (Beverly Hills, Calif.: Sage, 1979); Ellen Wartella, editor, *Children Communicating* (Beverly Hills, Calif.: Sage, 1979); and Scott Ward, Daniel Wackman, and Ellen Wartella, *How Children Learn to Buy* (Beverly Hills, Calif.: Sage, 1977).

Audience *The Continuing Study of Newspaper Reading,* sponsored by the American Newspaper Publishers Association and the Advertising Research Foundation from 1939 to 1952 and covering readership studies of 142 newspapers, offers evidence of readership trends. The results were analyzed by Charles E. Swanson in "What They Read in 130 Daily Newspapers," *Journalism Quarterly* (Fall 1955). Gary A. Steiner, *The People Look at Television* (New York: Knopf, 1963), is a voluminous study of viewing habits and attitudes of the American people by sex, education, income, religion, and so on.

Media organizations There are two histories of media organizations, Edwin Emery's *History of the American Newspaper Publishers Association* (Minneapolis: University of Minnesota Press, 1950), and Alice Fox Pitts' *Read All About It—Fifty Years of the ASNE* (Reston, Va.: American Society of Newspaper Editors, 1974).

Chapter 22: Who Owns the Media?

The Mass Media: Aspen Institute Guide to Communication Industry Trends, by Christopher H. Sterling and Timothy R. Haight, is a primary source. For data and trends analysis, see Benjamin N. Compaine, editor, *Who Owns the Media? Concentration of Ownership in the Mass Communications Industry* (White Plains, N.Y.: Knowledge Industry Publications, 1979), and Compaine's *The Newspaper Industry in the 1980s* (White Plains, N.Y.: Knowledge Industry, 1980).

Jon G. Udell, *The Economics of the American Newspaper* (New York: Hastings House, 1978), was sponsored by the American Newspaper Publishers Association and contains articles contributed by newspaper business people. James N. Rosse, Bruce M. Owen, and David L. Grey wrote a brief data-filled study of one problem for an FCC hearing, published as *Economic Issues in the Joint Ownership of Newspaper and Television Media* (Stanford, Calif.: Stanford University Research Center in Economic Growth, 1970).

Bryce Rucker, *The First Freedom* (Carbondale: Southern Illinois University Press, 1968), has a wealth of statistics and analysis. Trends in concentration of newspaper ownership historically are reported in Chapter 24 of Emery and Emery, *The Press and America,* and by Raymond B. Nixon in *Gazette* (1968, No. 3).

Two excellent articles are Ben H. Bagdikian, "Newspaper Mergers—the Final Phase," *Columbia Journalism Review* (March/April, 1977) and Christopher H. Sterling, "Trends in Daily Newspaper and Broadcast Ownership, 1922–1970," *Journalism Quarterly* (Summer 1975).

Chapter 23: International Media and Organization Roles

Often used in international communication classes as a general text is Heinz-Dietrich Fischer and John C. Merrill, editors, *International and Intercultural Communication* (New York: Hastings House, 1976), with 45 articles by scholars in many countries. A UNESCO publication, *World Communications: A 200-Country Survey of Press, Radio, Television, Films* (New York: Unipub, 1975), is the basic reference work for international media study. Another international survey is John C. Merrill, Carter R. Bryan, and Marvin Alisky, *The Foreign Press* (Baton Rouge: Louisiana State University Press, 1970).

More detailed studies of the world's leading newspapers were made for John C. Merrill's *The Elite Press* (New York: Pitman, 1969) and its 1980 update by Merrill and Harold A. Fisher, *The World's Great Dailies: Profiles of 50 Newspapers* (New York: Hastings House, 1980). Anthony Smith's brief *The Newspaper: An International History* (London: Thames and Hudson, 1979) offers a worldwide account and 111 illustrations.

Some regional accounts include Kenneth E. Olson, *The History Makers* (Baton Rouge: Louisiana State University Press, 1966), a survey of European press history; James W. Markham, *Voices of the Red Giants* (Ames: Iowa State University Press, 1970), a study of the Soviet and Chinese mass media systems: Mark W. Hopkins, *Mass Media in the Soviet Union* (New York: Pegasus, 1970); John A. Lent, editor, *The Asian Newspapers' Reluctant Revolution* (Ames: Iowa State University Press, 1971); William A. Hachten, *Muffled Drums: The News Media in Africa* (Ames: Iowa State University Press, 1971); G. A. Cranfield, *The Press and Society: From Caxton to Northcliffe* (London: Longman, 1978), a British overview; Francis Williams, *Dangerous Estate: The Anatomy of Newspapers* (New York: Macmillan, 1958), a social study of the British press since 1702; Anthony Smith, compiler, *The British Press Since the War* (Totowa, N.J.: Rowman and Littlefield, 1974); and Wilfred H. Kesterton, *A History of Journalism in Canada* (Toronto: McClelland and Stewart, 1967).

Three books by Burton Paulu, all published by the University of Minnesota Press in Minneapolis, offer detailed studies of European broadcasting: *Radio and Television Broadcasting on the European Continent* (1967), *Radio and Television Broadcasting in Eastern Europe* (1974), and *Television and Radio in the United Kingdom* (1981). Asa Briggs has produced four volumes of his *History of Broadcasting in the United Kingdom* (New York: Oxford University Press, 1961–1979).

Other broadcast books: Walter B. Emery, *National and International Systems of Broadcasting* (East Lansing, Michigan State University Press, 1969); Wilson P. Dizard, *Television: A World View* (Syracuse, N.Y.: Syracuse University Press, 1966); John A. Lent, editor, *Broadcasting in Asia and the Pacific* (Philadelphia: Temple University Press, 1978), with many chapters by nationals of the countries described; and Elihu Katz and George Wedell, *Broadcasting in the Third World: Promise and Performance* (Cambridge, Mass.: Harvard University Press, 1978).

Among studies of international news flow and press associations, the scholarly synthesis is Robert W. Desmond's *The Information Process: World News Reporting to the Twentieth Century* (Iowa City: University of Iowa Press, 1978); a second volume, *Windows on the World 1900–1920* (1981), continues a five-volume project. John Hohenberg covered foreign correspondents in his *Foreign Correspondence—The Great Reporters and Their Times* (New York: Columbia University Press, 1964). UNESCO surveyed press associations in *News Agencies: Their Structure and Operation* (New York: Columbia University Press, 1953). Two press association histories are Graham Storey, *Reuters* (New York: Crown, 1951), and Theodore E. Kruglak, *The Two Faces of Tass* (Minneapolis: University of Minnesota Press, 1962) (see bibliography for Part Two, Chapter 6, for other press association citations). Francis Williams briefly analyzed news transmission in *Transmitting World News: A Study of Telecommunications and the Press* (New York: Arno, 1972).

The dominant name in international communications research and writing has been that of Wilbur Schramm, beginning with his *Mass Media and National Development* (Stanford, Calif.: Stanford University Press, 1964). Two conferences at the East-West Communication Institute in Hawaii produced two books: Daniel Lerner and Wilbur Schramm, editors, *Communication and Change in the Developing Countries* (Honolulu: East-West Center, 1967) and Schramm and Lerner, editors, *Communication and Change: The Last Ten Years—and the Next* (Honolulu: University of Hawaii Press, 1976.)

Other research studies: Lucian W. Pye, *Communications and Political Development* (Princeton, N.J.: Princeton University Press, 1963); E. Lloyd Sommerlad, *The Press in Developing Countries* (Sydney, Australia: Sydney University Press, 1966); Colin Cherry, *World Communications: Threat or Promise? A Socio-Technical Approach* (New York: Wiley, 1971); George Gerbner, editor, *Mass Media Policies in Changing Cultures* (New York: Wiley, 1977); Alan Wells, *Mass Communication: A World View* (Palo Alto, Calif.: National Press, 1974); Wilbur Schramm, *Big Media, Little Media: Tools and Technologies for Instruction* (Beverly Hills, Calif.: Sage, 1977); Peter Habermann and Guy de Fontgalland, editors, *Development Communication—Rhetoric and Reality* (Singapore: Asian Mass Communication Research and Information Centre, 1978); and Syed A. Rahim, et al., *Planning Methods, Models, and Organization: A Review Study for Communication Policy Making and Planning* (Honolulu: East-West Communication Institute, 1978).

Basic documents of UNESCO's International Commission for the Study of Communication Problems (the MacBride Commission) include "The New World Information Order," a document presented by Mustapha Masmoudi of Tunisia as a spokesman for the Third World, in July 1978; the Commission's "Interim Report on Communications Problems in Modern Society," published by UNESCO in September 1978; and the Commission's "Final Report" submitted in December 1979 and published as *Many Voices, One World* (Unipub, 1980).

The Third World campaign for a New World Information Order is analyzed by Rosemary Righter in *Whose News? Politics, the Press, and the Third World* (London: Times Books, 1978). Various viewpoints on free flow versus balanced flow are found in Philip C. Horton, editor, *The Third World and Press Freedom* (New York: Praeger, 1978). The International Press Institute in London published *UNESCO and the Third World Media: An Appraisal* in 1978. Sage Publications produced *International News: Freedom Under Attack,* edited by Dante B. Fascell, and containing four essays (Beverly Hills: Sage, 1979). The essays, also published separately by Sage, were *International Broadcasting: A New Dimension of Western Diplomacy,* by David M. Abshire; *Mass News Media and the Third World Challenge,* by Leonard R. Sussman; *International News and the American Media,* by Barry Rubin; and *Access Denied: The Politics of Press Censor-*

ship, by Sean Kelly. Television's impact is analyzed in Chin-Chuan Lee's *Media Imperialism Reconsidered* (Sage, 1980).

Criticisms of the American mass media abroad, giving substance to Third World arguments, were voiced by Herbert I. Schiller in *Mass Communications and American Empire* (Boston: Beacon Press, 1969) and in *Communication and Cultural Domination* (White Plains, N.Y.: International Arts and Sciences Press, 1976). William H. Read's *America's Mass Media Merchants* (Baltimore, Md.: Johns Hopkins University Press, 1977), focuses on press agencies, news magazines, the *Reader's Digest,* television, and the movies. Thomas H. Guback described *The International Film Industry: Western Europe and America Since 1945* (Bloomington: Indiana University Press, 1969). And Jeremy Tunstall wrote *The Media Are American: Anglo-American Media in the World* (New York: Columbia University Press, 1977).

INDEX

83 84 85 9 8 7 6 5 4 3